ENVIRONMENTAL LAW AND JUSTICE IN CONTEXT

This innovative collection of essays discusses the extent to which considerations of justice and fairness have permeated the legal debate on environmental protection. Written by a wide range of contributors who have approached the subject from fresh theoretical and practical perspectives, the essays examine how these permutations of justice have influenced policy choices relating to topics like climate change, protection of the stratospheric ozone layer, trade and the conduct of warfare. The significance of participatory rights as a medium for the realisation of environmental justice is given extended treatment, and the contributors also assess the congruence between environmental justice and structural issues, such as gender, class, state borders and, on a global scale, North–South relations. The book will inform and stimulate debate on an important-yet-neglected aspect of the environmental discourse, and is highly recommended for researchers and students of international and domestic law, political science and international relations.

JONAS EBBESSON is Professor of Environmental Law and Director of the Stockholm Environmental Law and Policy Centre, Stockholm University

PHOEBE OKOWA is Reader in Public International Law at Queen Mary, University of London

ENVIRONMENTAL LAW AND JUSTICE IN CONTEXT

Edited by

JONAS EBBESSON

and

PHOEBE OKOWA

CAMBRIDGE
UNIVERSITY PRESS

CAMBRIDGE UNIVERSITY PRESS
Cambridge, New York, Melbourne, Madrid, Cape Town, Singapore, São Paulo, Delhi

Cambridge University Press
The Edinburgh Building, Cambridge CB2 8RU, UK

Published in the United States of America by Cambridge University Press, New York

www.cambridge.org
Information on this title: www.cambridge.org/9780521879682

First published 2009

Printed in the United Kingdom at the University Press, Cambridge

A catalogue record for this publication is available from the British Library

Library of Congress Cataloging in Publication data
Environmental law and justice in context / edited by Jonas Ebbesson and Phoebe Okowa.
p.   cm.
Includes index.
ISBN 978-0-521-87968-2 (hardback)
1. Environmental law.   2. Environmental justice.   3. Environmental policy.   I. Ebbesson, Jonas.   II. Okowa,
Phoebe N.   III. Title.
K3585.E5793   2008
344.04′6 – dc22   2008035709

ISBN 978-0-521-87968-2 hardback

CONTENTS

CONTRIBUTORS

Jutta Brunnée is Professor of Law and holds the Metcalf Chair in Environmental Law in the Faculty of Law, University of Toronto, Canada. She is co-editor of the *Oxford Handbook of International Environmental Law*.

Hans Christian Bugge, dr. juris, is Professor of Environmental Law at the University of Oslo, Norway. Before becoming an academic lawyer he held senior positions in Norway's Ministry of the Environment.

Philippe Cullet, PhD, is Reader in Law at the School of Oriental and African Studies (SOAS) in London, UK. He is the author of *Differential Treatment in International Environmental Law* (2003).

Jan Darpö is Associate Professor of Environmental Law at Uppsala University, Sweden. His research focuses on enforcement and environmental law procedures. Between 2001 and 2004 he was an additional member of the Swedish Environmental Court of Appeal.

Qun Du, PhD (Peking University), LLM and BA (Wuhan University) is Professor of Environmental Law and Natural Resource Management at the School of Law and Research Institute of Environmental Law of Wuhan University, China.

Jonas Ebbesson is Professor of Environmental Law and Director of the Stockholm Environmental Law and Policy Centre at Stockholm University, Sweden. Since 2005 he has served as a member of the Aarhus Convention Compliance Committee.

Richard Falk is Milbank Professor of International Law Emeritus, Princeton University and, since 2002, Visiting Professor, Global Studies, University of California, Santa Barbara, USA. He is the author of numerous books, including *This Endangered Planet* (1972).

Malgosia Fitzmaurice is Professor of Public International Law at Queen Mary, University of London, UK. Her research includes international environmental law, water law, indigenous peoples law, and the law of treaties.

Ellen Hey is Professor of Public International Law at the Erasmus University Rotterdam, the Netherlands, and co-editor of the *Oxford Handbook of International Environmental Law* and the *Netherlands Yearbook of International Law*.

Patricia Kameri-Mbote is Associate Professor and Chair of the Department of Private Law, School of Law, University of Nairobi, Kenya. She is also the Africa Programme Director for the International Environmental Law Research Centre.

Bo Kjellén is Senior Research Fellow at the Stockholm Environment Institute, in Stockholm, Sweden. He chaired the negotiations for the Convention to Combat Desertification and was Chief Negotiator for Sweden on sustainable development and climate issues.

Ludwig Krämer is former Judge at Landgericht Kiel, and former official at the Environmental Department, European Commission. He teaches European environmental law in Bruges, Bremen and London. He is currently a consultant for the Derecho y Medio Ambiente Consultancy, Madrid, Spain.

Karin Mickelson is Associate Professor at the Faculty of Law, University of British Columbia, Canada. Her research focuses on the North–South dimension of international law, with an emphasis on international environmental law.

André Nollkaemper is Professor of Public International Law at the Faculty of Law, University of Amsterdam, the Netherlands.

Phoebe Okowa is Reader in Public International Law at the Department of Law, Queen Mary, University of London, UK.

Hanne Petersen is Professor of Law and on the board of directors of the Centre for Studies of Legal Cultures, starting at the University of Copenhagen, Denmark, in 2008.

Jona Razzaque is a Barrister and Reader in law at the University of the West of England (UWE), Bristol, UK. Her research interests include environmental governance and access to environmental justice.

Nicolas de Sadeleer is a Law Professor based in Brussels, Belgium. In 2004–5 he held the EU Marie Curie chair. His areas of research include international, EU and Belgian environmental law.

Priscilla Schwartz is Lecturer in Law at the University of Leicester, UK. Her research interests are in international environmental law, and economic and development law.

Dinah Shelton holds the Manatt/Ahn Chair of International Law at the George Washington University Law School, Washington DC, USA. She writes on human rights and environmental law, and serves on the Board of Editors of the *American Journal of International Law*.

Stephen Stec is Adjunct Professor at the Central European University, Associate Scholar at Leiden University Institute for East European Law and Russian Studies, and Head of the Environmental Law Programme at Regional Environmental Centre for Central and Eastern Europe, in Szentendre, Hungary.

William Twining is Quain Professor of Jurisprudence Emeritus at University College London, UK, and Visiting Professor of Law at the University of Miami, USA. His books include *The Great Juristic Bazaar, Globalisation and Legal Theory*, and *General Jurisprudence*.

PREFACE AND ACKNOWLEDGMENTS

This book is the culmination of a project which started in August 2005, when the board of the Stockholm Environmental Law and Policy Centre adopted, on its agenda, the plan for an international conference on environmental law and justice. The plans materialised, and the '2006 Stockholm Conference on Environmental Law and Justice' took place at Stockholm University on 6–9 September 2006. The project could not have been accomplished without the generous support of the Swedish Research Council (Vetenskapsrådet), the Bank of Sweden Tercentenary Foundation (Riksbankens Jubileumsfond), the Swedish Research Council for Environment, Agricultural Sciences and Spatial Planning (Formas), the Cassel Foundation (Casselstiftelsen), the Department of Law, Stockholm University, and Nordforsk through the Nordic Environmental Law Network (NELN). In addition, the Stockholm Consumer Cooperative Society (Stockholms Konsumentförening) supported the conference with Fair Trade coffee and sweets.

Almost all contributions are based on papers presented at the conference. We are grateful to all the contributors for their co-operation and patience. All were generous with their time. We are particularly grateful to William Twining for advice in carrying through the book project, and to Hanne Petersen, who, although not a conference participant, responded readily to our request to fill a significant gap in the book's content. In selecting the speakers for the conference, and thus the contributors to this book, we were supported by the other members of the conference organising committee, Jutta Brunnée, Ludwig Krämer and Richard Falk. The conference papers have been considerably rewritten, edited and updated so as to fit the book. The Law Department at Queen Mary, University of London and the Cassel Foundation at the Faculty of Law of Stockholm University have generously assisted with research expenses over the last twelve months.

A number of people assisted us either directly or indirectly in the work for this volume. We would like to thank Annette Löf, PhD student at Umeå University, for her enthusiastic administrative assistance in organising the 2006 conference, and Irfan Khan, LLM, and Mba Nmaju, PhD student, at Queen Mary, for assistance in editing the book. We would also like to record our thanks to Finola O'Sullivan of Cambridge University Press for steering the project through the production process.

Editing the book has been an exciting venture, and we hope it will spur further debate and research on this essential topic. We are grateful for all the support for the conference as well as for the book.

Jonas Ebbesson and *Phoebe Okowa*
Stockholm, Sweden and London, UK
September 2008

Introduction: dimensions of justice in environmental law

JONAS EBBESSON

1 Outline

Environmental laws and policies are predominantly *goal-oriented*. Standards, principles and procedures for the protection of the environment are often instrumental to achieve, say, the conservation of fragile ecosystems and endangered species, the preservation of fresh water and other natural resources, the restoration of contaminated soils as well as the stratospheric ozone layer, and the protection of human health. This goal-oriented feature is evident in national as well as international law. It is apparent also when legal approaches to managing environmental problems are compared with economic or market-based instruments, such as emission trading, environmental taxes and voluntary agreements and codes of conduct. National statutes and international treaties, standards, instruments and procedures are assessed with these underlying objectives in mind, and mainly analysed in terms of effectiveness and achievability of the set objectives. Even *sustainable development*, as an overarching societal objective with obvious environmental connotations, reflects this goal-oriented conception of environmental law and policy.

Yet, environmental law also involves priorities, conflicts and clashes of interests – and concerns for justice and fairness. In fact, any drafting, negotiation, adoption, application and enforcement of environmental laws – indeed comprehending environmental law in general – induces justice considerations: i.e. concerns for the distributive and corrective effects of laws and decisions pertaining to health, the environment and natural resources, as well as concerns for the opportunities of those potentially affected to participate in such law-making and decision-making in the first place. Although well-established concepts in environmental law, whether based on custom or statutes, appear neutral on their face, a closer study, or simply placing them in a *context*, may reveal disproportionate burdening or restricting effects for certain groups or categories when these concepts are applied. It may also show how certain interests or subjects are ignored or demeaned. Such concerns are indeed raised in local as well as global contexts, and they also include structural issues, such as gender, class, ethnicity and – on a global scale – North–South relations.

We see it in local situations when individuals and neighbourhoods contest the establishment of industrial plants, and when environmental associations protest against activities likely to harm sensitive ecosystems: whose interests prevail in conflict with the interests of others? We see it when neighbourhoods or communities complain that they are disproportionately affected by hazards to health, and even challenging environmental laws for being racist or sexist: how come allegedly neutral laws have such effects? We see it in global climate change negotiations: most states today agree that climate change should be abated, but how are the costs for cutting down CO_2 emissions to be discharged among the industrialised and non-industrialised regions? And which regions are worst affected by a failure to combat climate change? We see it when nuclear wastes are to be deposited: is it fair to pass on the burdens of radioactive wastes to future generations, while the present enjoys the benefits? Already this set of preliminary observations indicates the critical value of considering the distributive, corrective and procedural features of environmental law. Also, sustainable development as such implies such considerations.

Justice concerns trigger academics and activists alike, and in part for the very same reason: to critically appraise existing institutions and to guide for social change. Thus, as argued by John Rawls, principles of justice provide 'an Archimedean point for appraising existing institutions as well as the desires and aspirations they generate' and 'an independent standard for guiding the course of social change'.[1] Critical justice appraisals can reveal unjust distributive effects of legal concepts, institutions and principles with bearing on health and the environment. In so doing, critical appraisals also guide us and may spark off social change and reforms of national, international and transnational institutions.

These motives have been essential for the 'environmental justice' movement as well. This movement originated in the USA in the 1970s and 1980s,[2] and was largely driven by charges of 'environmental racism' in US developmental and environmental policies.[3] It showed not only the disproportionate burdens on certain groups entailed by hazardous activities and substances, but also highlighted the lack of real opportunities for participating in decision-making. The notion of environmental justice has spread to numerous countries and regions of the world,[4] and, while the (in)justice factors may be contextual and differ from one country to the other, it has taken the form of a critical voice, e.g. by revealing what is seen as unjust consequences of existing

---

[1] Cf. Rawls 1972, p. 520.

[2] Bullard 1998–9, p. 454, when describing the background of the US environmental justice movement, argues that the environmental justice framework 'attempts to uncover the underlying assumptions that may contribute to and produce unequal protection. This framework brings to the surface the ethical and political questions of "who gets what, why, and how much"'. Thus, it 'rests on an ethical analysis of strategies to eliminate unfair, unjust, and inequitable conditions and decisions. The framework seeks to prevent environmental threats before they occur.'

[3] Bullard 1998–9, pp. 460–8; and Lazarus 2000.

[4] Studies of environmental justice considerations in national laws are provided by Bosselmann and Richardson 1998. A brief account of this development is also given by Schrader-Frechette 2002, pp. 6–13.

social arrangements and norms.[5] For the same reasons, concerns for justice arise in the contexts of international environmental law as well.[6]

This book is also framed by the dual motive of critically appraising existing institutions and guiding for social change. Yet, the book also reflects another motive, namely, to better understand how certain legal regimes, concepts and legislation came into being. Some contributions show to what extent justice considerations influenced negotiations, jurisprudence and legal debate. Rather than providing for one common Archimedean point, however, the book reveals several such points, and several ways of understanding justice in environmental contexts. Yet, while their approaches to justice in environmental matters differ, most contributors nevertheless focus on the procedural, distributive and/or corrective elements of justice, and even stress the link between the procedural dimension and the distributive and corrective repercussions. Some contributions also discuss the theoretical foundations for justice considerations, whether based on social contract theories or on theories of entitlements or capabilities.[7]

The thesis framing this book is that justice considerations arise in just about any legal context involving health, the environment and the use of natural resources. It permeates the development and application as well as evaluation and analysis of environmental laws. In these contexts, justice is an aspiration in its own right, but it also matters for the legitimacy and effectiveness of the policies and laws intended to protect health and the environment. This, of course, does not prevent some contributors from questioning whether environmental justice is the best way to phrase the concerns for the environment,[8] or from suggesting a radical shift in the understanding of environmental justice.[9] The answer partly depends on how justice is measured and which interests, factors and subjects are taken into account.

Throughout this book environmental law and environmental matters are broadly understood so as to include not only the protection of the natural environment, but also concerns for health and for sustainable access to natural resources and ecosystem services. Rather than insisting on a strict demarcation between environmental and

---

[5] Cooper and Palmer 1995.   [6] E.g. Cooper and Palmer 1995, pp. 91–134; Cullet 2003; and Anand 2004.

[7] This distinction of theoretical bases for justice appraisals is in itself far from clear. For instance, in questioning Rawls' premises for the distribution of assets and purporting a theory of entitlement, Nozick 1974, pp. 149–50, argues that the holdings of a person are just if he (or she, one may add) is entitled to them by the principle of justice in acquisition and transfer, or by the principle of rectification of injustice. This is a very different notion of 'entitlement' from that proposed by Nussbaum 2006, pp. 69–92. For her, 'fundamental entitlements' refer to 'an account of minimum core social entitlements'. This, in turn, is based on a natural rights conception of human dignity, which she transposes to a list of 'central human capabilities' to be accomplished in order to achieve the threshold of social justice. While her outline is in part inspired by Rawls' contract theory, she also draws on the capacity approach of Sen. For him, freedom is the foundation for justice, and 'capability' is the substantive freedom of a person to achieve alternative lifestyles; see e.g. Sen 1999, pp. 54–86.

[8] See e.g. Twining in Chapter 4 of this volume.   [9] See Petersen in Chapter 5 of this volume.

social matters, this book shows that in some cases these matters overlap and link to each other.

The book is divided into six parts, each one with three to six chapters, titled:

Part I: The notion of justice in environmental law (Chapters 2–5)
Part II: Public participation and access to the judiciary (Chapters 6–11)
Part III: State sovereignty and state borders (Chapters 12–14)
Part IV: North–South concerns in global contexts (Chapters 15–17)
Part V: Access to natural resources (Chapters 18–20)
Part VI: Corporate activities and trade (Chapters 21–23)

Although each part deals with discrete issues, there is still considerable overlap between them. While some of the more general contributions deal with the notion of justice in the context of state sovereignty, global matters and North–South concerns, these issues are also covered by the more specific contributions in Parts III and IV. Gender issues are both dealt with in Part I, on the notion of justice in environmental law, and Part V, on access to natural resources. Participatory aspects of justice are considered in Part II, but are also touched upon in Parts III, V and VI. Justice in the context of access to natural resources is the theme of Part V, but it is also discussed in Part VI. Conceptual matters are not limited to Part I, but occur in all parts of the book. And so on. So the structure is only intended to guide the reader and show the diversity of relevant aspects and contexts, rather than denoting conceptually important divisions.

Together, the twenty-two contributions give a valuable picture of situations where justice considerations arise. Justice is not the only concern when assessing, analysing or debating environmental laws, but it provides highly important entries for appraising environmental laws; as an impetus for social change, and as a means for better comprehending the factors – often not made explicit – behind different legal developments.

2 The notion of justice in environmental law

The discourse on environmental justice may originate from the late 1970s and early 1980s, but the philosophy of justice has a far longer history in which the procedural, distributive and corrective aspects of law and policy are essential. As already mentioned, justice in environmental matters, and even the concept of environmental justice itself, embraces concerns for distributive, corrective and procedural justice. Other related concepts that occur in this volume are 'participative justice', 'criminal justice', 'retributive justice', 'restorative justice', 'social justice', 'cooperative justice' and 'cosmopolitan justice'. The given contexts will reveal their meaning, but generally speaking each of these concepts involve some element(s) of distributive, corrective or procedural justice as well.

Developing notions of justice includes making appropriate limitations of what to include in the analysis or debate. In the sphere of environmental law, justice is discussed and measured with different parameters and on different theoretical bases. Which burdens, which interests and which subjects should be included in such a theory and debate? Environmental law takes the forms of national, supranational (e.g. European Community), international and transnational laws, so the justice considerations discussed here reflect this broad arena. However, expanding the notion of environmental justice from domestic contexts across state borders, so as to include transboundary and even global concerns, may lead in different directions depending on whether the individual or the state (or the people) is taken as the starting point.[10] For instance, when appraising the global climate change negotiations from a justice perspective, one may take each state as the measure and thus compare the opportunities to participate in negotiations and how the burdens are discharged among the parties to the 1997 Kyoto Protocol to the 1992 UN Framework Convention on Climate Change (Kyoto Protocol)[11] and its successor. International law and its critics have tended to be state-centred and quite naturally take the state as the starting point. Alternatively, and probably more provocative, one can appraise the global regimes from a cosmopolitan point of view, thus assessing the procedural, distributive and corrective effects from the perspective of the individual. Only then can the distributive concerns *within* each state be part of the calculation of global justice.[12] Take the case of India, which is considered a developing country in international environmental negotiations, even though its middle class population amounts to the size of several Western European states put together. It can be questioned why the Indian middle class should get away with less stringent legal requirements for combating climate change than the European or American middle class, just because there is a huge poor Indian population which does not contribute much counted per capita. Should international law in this way endorse great or even increasing inequalities within countries?[13] If individuals were the units, the appraisal might look quite different.[14] There are some tendencies in international law, with respect to the use of shared natural resources, to take the situation of the individual, not only states, into account.[15] Yet, considering the position of individuals rather than states is even more relevant with respect to non-democratic countries, where the governments do not really represent the people(s) of a country.[16]

Justice concerns can be traced back in the history of international environmental law at least to the 1941 *Trail Smelter Arbitration*, which is regarded as the *locus*

---

[10] See e.g. Ebbesson in Chapter 14, and Hey in Chapter 18, of this volume.

[11] 1997 Kyoto Protocol to the United Nation Framework Convention on Climate Change, 37 *International Legal Materials* (ILM) (1998) 22.

[12] See Caney 2005, p. 747.

[13] See Du in Chapter 7 of this volume, where she describes how economic growth in China has led to increased environmental injustice.

[14] This issue is also discussed in Part IV on the North–South concerns in global contexts.

[15] See Hey in Chapter 18 of this volume.   [16] Cf. Caney 2005.

classicus in this field. The tribunal, mandated to resolve a dispute between the USA and Canada concerning air pollution, was not only concerned with the apportionment of rights and duties between the parties, but was also asked to 'reach a solution just to all parties concerned'.[17] While the *Trail Smelter* Award includes inter-state justice considerations, there is not much of explicit references to justice in the major global policy documents concerning the environment. Some efforts for expanding the geographical scope of justice considerations can indeed be found in the 1972 UN Declaration on the Human Environment (Stockholm Declaration)[18] as well as the 1992 UN Declaration on Environment and Development (Rio Declaration),[19] by the linkage between environmental degradation to poverty. The two declarations also highlight the different economic and social conditions for different states, and the Rio Declaration even sets out the principle of 'common but differentiated responsibilities'.[20] Still, there is no explicit reference to justice considerations, and neither declaration is as outspoken in this regard as the 2000 UN Millennium Declaration:

> Global challenges must be managed in a way that distributes the costs and burdens fairly in accordance with basic principles of equity and social justice. Those who suffer or who benefit least deserve help from those who benefit most.[21]

The language as well as the context, although not limited to environmental matters, reveal that the justice considerations should not be limited to or even concentrated on inter-state issues, but rather involve the concerns for all individuals in all international relations. While the approaches of the Millennium Declaration and the *Trail Smelter* Award differ, they reveal justice considerations that transcend state borders in international jurisprudence as well as international policy documents with a bearing on environmental matters.

In addition to possible geographical limitations and approaches to transcend state borders, justice considerations also involve temporal aspects.[22] As apparent in the context of climate change and international law, the concerns for future generations are frequently invoked. The interests of future generations are often either explicitly referred to in international treaties, national statutes or case-law, or can be somehow

---

[17] It was to this end that the tribunal concluded the principle 'that no State has the right to use or permit the use of its territory in such a manner as to cause injury by fumes in or to the territory of another or the properties or persons therein, when the case is of serious consequence and the injury is established by clear and convincing evidence'. 3 *United Nations Reports of International Arbitral Awards* 1905, at pp. 1908, 1963–6.

[18] United Nations Declaration on the Human Environment, UN Doc. A/CONF.48/14/Rev.1 (1972), 11 ILM (1972) 1416.

[19] United Nations Declaration on Environment and Development, UN Doc. A/CONF.151/26/Rev.1 (1992), 31 ILM (1992) 876.

[20] Rio Declaration, previous note, Principle 7.

[21] United Nations General Assembly, Resolution 55/2, United Nations Millennium Declaration (A/55/L.2, 18 September 2000), para. 6.

[22] Brown Weiss 1989.

implied by legislation, and it is not far-fetched to include future generations in climate justice considerations. Temporal considerations may also go back in time. An essential issue in the negotiations for cutting down CO_2 emissions is whether and how previous inputs should be taken into account. To what extent should a system of 'grand-fathering' be used, meaning that the industrialised countries should be allowed to stay at a higher average than developing countries, just because they are used to a certain level of welfare and comfort, and may have invested a lot in different greenhouse contributing activities.

Yet another controversial justice debate, related to environmental issues, concerns the kind of subjects to be included. Most theories of justice (drawing on Kantian thoughts) are limited to the concerns for human beings, but increasing attention is also given to justice for non-human species. How come we take for granted that animals do not deserve justice, but only, at best, charity?[23] And can justice be done to the environment as such?[24]

While most of these conceptual and principled issues are dealt with in this and/or other parts of the volume, common to the four contributors in Part I is the attention given to the geographical scope of justice deliberations.

Richard Falk (Chapter 2) sets the global stage by linking environmental justice concerns to what he sees as the second cycle of ecological urgency. Mapping out the global geopolitical landscape, not least the North–South tensions, he provides a macro perspective to urgent issues of environmental degradation and highlights the likely distributive consequences of adverse ecological changes and the foreseeable energy squeeze.

Of particular importance in this scenery is the scant attention given to the bearing of fairness or justice in either the diagnosis of the environmental challenge or its cure. Richard Falk criticises environmentalists for failing to pay sufficient attention to this justice perspective – a failure which tends to benefit the rich and powerful as well as those currently alive, and to accentuate the burdens and grievances of the poor, marginalised and unborn. He also argues that those who have raised environmental justice issues have been preoccupied with local sites and activist struggles, but not given sufficient attention to the global scale of environmental degradation and the earth's capacity to cope with ecological stresses. Yet, he continues,

> to ignore the extent to which the inequalities of life circumstances in the world are associated with avoiding the externalities of modern industrial life and warfare is not only unfair, but also tends to aggravate national and geopolitical tensions of a North/South character, as well as class and race/ethnic tensions within particular states.

---

[23] For an overview of the ethical discourse and a critical account of the environmental justice debate for failing to include 'ecological justice' considerations, see Bosselmann 2006. A useful presentation of the ethical discourse is also given by Nussbaum 2006, pp. 325–407.

[24] See Krämer in Chapter 10 of this volume.

He compares the current (second) cycle of ecological urgency with the first cycle, which he places between the 1972 UN Conference on the Human Environment in Stockholm, and the 1992 UN Conference on Environment and Development in Rio de Janeiro. In this second cycle he sees two major challenges, of great importance for any environmental justice deliberation in a global context. The first is climate change and the resulting energy squeeze, which challenges concerns for justice. While the rising price of oil may encourage investments in alternative energy technologies, it is also likely to result in higher energy costs for the poor and especially on those living near subsistence level. The second issue refers to the impact of 'asymmetric warfare' and militarism, i.e. the effects on the human environment from high-tech warfare which is directed at destroying infrastructure and affecting the civilian population.[25]

He concludes that the discourse on environmental justice needs to delve deeply into structural constraints on policy that arise from special interests of governments as well as the private sector. This, in turn, requires exploring policy proposals that call for fundamental shifts in life style, budgetary priorities and market regulations. Admitting that some such changes may appear utopian and politically unattainable, he nevertheless finds them essential in order to enhance environmental justice considerations in any response to the sense of ecological urgency he addresses.

Whereas Richard Falk's notion of justice centres around the distributive concerns in global policy contexts, Dinah Shelton (Chapter 3) reveals the numerous alternative, often contradictory, ways international justice is described in legal debate. She identifies three broad categories to which the discourse of international justice refers – morality, equity and law – and observes how concerns not only for distributive justice, but also for reparative and retributive justice, arise in each of these three categories.

She discerns the moral underpinning of justice in some contexts of international environmental law, but it is clear that the notions of justice as equity or law as such are more robust in the legal discourse on environmental matters. In both these meanings of justice, the distributive aspects are shown to be essential. While the general value of equity is largely accepted, she argues,

> debate exists on the appropriate principles to determine equitable allocation, e.g. whether decisions should be based on need, capacity, prior entitlement, 'just desserts,' the greatest good for the greatest number, or strict equality of treatment.

She demonstrates that the concerns for international distributive and corrective justice mainly arise in the North–South context. This was evident in the struggle of newly decolonised states in the 1960s and 1970s for a New International Economic Order and the push of developing states for an equitable allocation of resources and burdens. These concerns would also influence concepts and instruments in international

---

[25] On the issue of environmental justice and armed conflicts, see also Okowa in Chapter 12 of this volume.

environmental law, such as financial mechanisms, double standards, requirements of technology transfers and certain flexibility in the time required for compliance. It has also resulted in explicit statements about economic and social development as well as poverty eradication as overriding concerns in the context of global environmental agreements.

Dinah Shelton describes how the concerns for distributive justice are reflected in various substantive norms intended to accommodate the different situations of developed and developing countries. One such case is the principle of equitable utilisation, which applies to various kinds of shared resources, such as the seabed, fish stocks and watercourses. Another case is the principle of common but differentiated responsibilities, as set out in global environmental agreements on ozone layer depletion, climate change and desertification.[26] While both these principles refer to the substantive issues and the distributive outcomes, she also points at the procedural dimension of justice, e.g. through arrangements for international dispute settlements. Even the adherence to the rule of law in itself is generally taken as a construct for international justice. In all, she sees in justice in international environmental law the rational sharing of the burdens and costs of environment protection, discharged through the procedural and substantive adjustments of rights and duties. This is not limited to the distribution among the present populations, but also pertains to intergenerational equity, i.e. the emerging notion that humans have a special obligation as custodians or trustees of the planet *vis-à-vis* future generations to maintain the planet's integrity and ensure the survival of the human species. She concludes that international justice is not only a matter of morality and equity, but may also foster more effective actions and implementation of legal norms.

William Twining (Chapter 4) is less convinced about the merits of framing major concerns for the environment in the language of justice. He places the debate on environmental justice in a broader jurisprudential context: in light of general theories of law, the discourse on law and globalisation, and normative jurisprudence. While sceptical of the usefulness of the environmental justice language, he also shows that the canonical, predominantly Western, legal theories – not least in normative jurisprudence – fail to explain the post-Westphalian world or to grasp issues, facts and concerns that are essential for the environmental justice debate.

In doing so, he emphasises the lack of a global perspective in normative jurisprudence. First, it is largely bound to the nation-state, and fails to look beyond the confines of state borders in theories of justice. Therefore, it does not provide an adequate theoretical basis for justice considerations once the issues transcend narrow, territorially defined concerns – which is often the case in the context of environmental law.[27]

---

[26] See also the contributions by Mickelson in Chapter 15, Brunnée in Chapter 16, Kjellén in Chapter 17, and Bugge in Chapter 21 of this volume.

[27] See also Ebbesson in Chapter 14 of this volume.

He criticises John Rawls, whose work has probably been the most influential for any contemporary theory of justice:

> From a global perspective, it is bizarre to find a purportedly liberal theory of justice that rejects any principle of distribution, treats an out-dated conception of public international law as satisfactorily representing principles of justice in the global arena, and says almost nothing about radical poverty, the environment, increasing inequalities, American hegemony (and how it might be exercised), let alone about transnational justice or reparations or other issues that are now high on the global agenda.

Second, he argues, a genuinely cosmopolitan general jurisprudence cannot be limited to the conventional canon of juristic texts, based on the 'Country and Western tradition' of legal theorising and comparative law. Rather, it must be adjusted so as to include writings, ideas and controversies from non-Western traditions and viewpoints. It is indeed contradictory, that, while most Western legal theories (including theories of justice) take the (Western) nation-state as the starting point, these theories are often put forth with claims of universal validity. In the same vein, he cautions against conveying human rights notions, crucial to many theories of justice, as if they reflected universal values, without taking the plurality of beliefs into account. Although he suggests that human rights are best conceived as a language for expressing claims and arguments rather than as an abstract set of universal values, he also questions the usefulness of considering environmental issues exclusively from a human rights perspective.

As a way out of these anachronisms, William Twining presents new thoughts of general jurisprudence that are being developed by theorists, who build upon, but also distance themselves from, canonical Western jurists, e.g. by expanding beyond state borders and by challenging the anthropocentric focus of jurisprudence. In this context, he also points at the striking anthropocentricity in jurisprudence and normative theories of justice – even among philosophers, such as Peter Singer, who are outspoken advocates of animal liberation. While such an anthropocentric approach to theories of justice does not necessarily imply an indifference to environmental concerns or that 'ecocentric reasons' are invalid, William Twining questions whether a theory of environmental justice leaves sufficient scope for other values and whether the language of justice is the most appropriate way of expressing all major concerns for the environment.

Hanne Petersen (Chapter 5) agrees with William Twining as to the need to go beyond the 'Country and Western tradition' of legal theorising in search for a normative jurisprudence to deal with general questions about values and law. And this she does by challenging the limits of environmental law – as an instrument of modern states – for combining and taking care of the colliding traditional values of conservation of the environment and the values of securing modern, equality-oriented, distributive justice in gender relations. When considering the gendered aspects of environmental justice, she asks whether the practices of traditional feminine virtues around the world have led to the dominant understanding and perception of women as environmentally friendly and considerate. If so, traditional gendered virtues may support care for the environment from a modern perspective, but they may also block 'women's claim to a fair share of justice' in terms of modern equality and distribution.[28]

Yet, she finds it too narrow an understanding of justice, and too narrow a goal, to perceive gendered environmental justice as equal distribution of environmental risks between men and women. Rather, concerns for the environment should force us to find new ways of reconciling and balancing the values of gender justice and equality.

She emphasises the notion of virtue, as something to be practised by everyone, and argues that this has been much ignored in legal thinking in favour of welfare concerns to be secured by political and state actions. In order to go beyond the traditional jurisprudential tradition and highlight justice as a virtue, Hanne Petersen searches for inspirations and explanations in the Arctic cultures – for instance its myths and taboos – and in different cultural articulations, such as music and arts. How, then, could environmental justice as a virtue for women and men be conceptualised? Instead of focusing on the possible characteristics of women, Hanne Petersen considers whether a changed masculinity – a 'sustainable masculinity' – could guide towards a more gender-just environmental law.

After analysing stereotypical, and indeed depressing, descriptions of male lawyers – as constantly overworked 'trained working horses' with health problems,[29] a lack of feeling, and a sense that most things in life are 'mediocre' – she asks how one can expect any environmental passion from powerful and globally influential men in such situations. She does, however, observe some indications of change of Western masculine self-perception and lifestyle, into a more caring attitude, and argues that this may also come to change general societal norms as well as the law-maker's views on the relation between man and the environment. Hanne Petersen suggests that 'common but differential responsibilities' should be understood not only as a legal principle among states,[30] but also as a move towards a practice of environmental virtues to guide in relations among individuals. Environmental justice and environmental virtues, such as sustainability, she concludes, should not be thought of too legalistically. Rather than being caught in a 'traditional' dichotomy of national and international law, environmental justice should be expanded so as to encompass practices and norms as well as normative and virtuous behaviour in a broader spectrum of communities.

---

[28] See also Kameri-Mbote in Chapter 20 of this volume.

[29] For myself, as a Swedish lawyer, this should be even more depressing, since her quote on working horses refers to Swedish lawyers.

[30] This concept is also discussed in the contributions of Shelton in Chapter 3, Mickelson in Chapter 15, Brunnée in Chapter 16, Kjellén in Chapter 17, and Bugge in Chapter 21 of this volume.

Already the contributions to this first Part of the book reveal the range of issues – from the practical concerns of ecological urgency to the general conceptual concerns – embraced by notions of justice in environmental matters. There is more to come.

3 Public participation and access to the judiciary

Moving on to the more specific issue of public participation and access to the judiciary, the institutional settings and procedural arrangements are decisive for just decisions and distributions of burdens and benefits. The outcome of decision-making procedures, but also the trust in the procedure for reaching decisions, depend on who has the opportunity to be part of the decision-making process. Following John Rawls and others, just distribution is the result of due process, that is, of fair procedures and institutions that provide equal opportunities (rather than equality): justice as fairness. In this sense, the issue is not what *is* just, but rather how to *get* a fair decision. While concerned with the fundamental principles for justice rather than the detailed design of environmental decision-making, these thoughts are relevant also for the analyses of existing institutions and procedural opportunities in environmental contexts, at least in domestic settings.

Such opportunities, to take part in decision-making and access to the judiciary in environmental matters, link to human rights law.[31] Several international human rights instruments thus provide for a right to be part of political decision-making,[32] and for a fair trial, the latter meaning a right to equal access before courts or other independent and impartial tribunals.[33] Drawing in part on notions of human rights law, the 1992 Rio Declaration also stipulates that:

> Environmental issues are best handled with the *participation of all concerned citizens*, at the relevant level. At the national level, each individual shall have appropriate access to information concerning the environment that is held by public authorities, including information on hazardous materials and activities in their communities, and the opportunity to participate in decision-making

---

[31] Ebbesson 1997, pp. 69–75.

[32] E.g. 1948 Universal Declaration of Human Rights, UNGA Res. 217, UN Doc. A/810 (1948), Art. 19; 1966 International Covenant on Civil and Political Rights, 999 UNTS (1976) 171, Art. 25; 1969 American Convention on Human Rights, 9 ILM (1970) 673, Art. 23; 1981 African Charter on Human and Peoples' Rights, 21 ILM (1982) 59, Art. 13. There is no such provision in the 1950 European Convention for the Protection of Human Rights and Fundamental Freedoms, 213 UNTS 221, or related protocols. Instead, it obliges the parties to hold free elections and ensure free expression of opinion in the choice of the legislature. Participatory rights for indigenous peoples are set out in the 1989 ILO Convention Concerning Indigenous and Tribal Peoples in Independent Countries, 28 ILM (1989) 1382, Arts. 6 and 15.

[33] E.g. 1948 Universal Declaration of Human Rights, previous note, Art. 10; 1966 International Covenant on Civil and Political Rights, previous note, Art. 14; 1950 European Convention on Human Rights and Fundamental Freedoms, previous note, Art. 6; 1969 American Convention on Human Rights, previous note, Art. 8.

processes. States shall facilitate and encourage public awareness and participation by *making information widely available*. Effective *access to judicial and
administrative proceedings*, including *redress* and *remedy*, shall be provided.[34]

Principle 10 of the Rio Declaration has been instrumental for the international debate
on public participation in environmental matters,[35] and also for the 1998 UNECE
Convention on Access to Information, Public Participation in Decision-making and
Access to Justice in Environmental Matters (Aarhus Convention).[36] This is a unique
convention in setting out minimum standards on access to information, public participation and access to legal review procedures. As indicated by the title of the
Convention, 'access to justice' is essentially perceived as access to a fair review procedure, whereby decisions, acts and omissions by the public administration, but also by
private persons, should be challengeable before a court of law or another independent
and impartial body established by law. Thus, the rationale is not to set out what is
justice, but to provide means for getting just results (or for avoiding unjust results).
Even though the Aarhus Convention only applies to countries in the UNECE region,
it has had some influence on the political discussion and legal developments also in
other parts of the world, as noted by a number of contributions in this volume.

Part II of the book focuses on institutional arrangements for public participation
in environmental decision-making and for 'access to justice'. By covering different
regions of the world – South Asia, China, Eastern Europe and the EU – it shows that
participatory institutions and access to the judiciary matter for procedural justice,
not only in Western Europe and North America. With the Aarhus Convention and
a few other international regimes, public participation and access to justice issues
have become clearly international. This Part also considers the role of the European
Court of Justice in the EU as well as two existing international complaint procedures,
thereby indicating the international context. In all, the chapters also make it possible
to compare the legal developments in different regions and the achievements of
procedural justice in environmental matters.[37]

The importance, from a justice point of view, of adequate institutional arrangements
for public participation is evident in Jona Razzaque's (Chapter 6) study on the participatory rights of communities in South Asia. Her paper begins with a discussion of the
pivotal role of the Rio Declaration and the Aarhus Convention. Central to her argument is the idea that environmental justice can only be ensured through meaningful
involvement of communities. Her examination of the opportunities for communities

---

[34] Rio Declaration, note 19 above, Principle 10 (emphasis added).

[35] This is shown, for instance, by *Partnership for Principle 10*, a venue for governments, international organisations and civil society groups engaged in furthering the message of Principle 10 of the Rio Declaration;
see www.pp10.org (visited 1 November 2007).

[36] 1998 UNECE Convention on Access to Information, Public Participation in Decision-making and Access to
Justice in Environmental Matters, 38 ILM (1999) 515.

[37] See also Kameri-Mbote's contribution, in Chapter 20, discussing the participatory opportunities in East
Africa, and Schwartz' contribution, in Chapter 22, concerning West Africa.

in India, Pakistan and Bangladesh, to engage themselves in decision-making processes and to challenge erroneous acts and omissions by the public administration in court, is carried out with this in mind. She shows that there are possibilities in all the three countries for communities to access national courts through public interest litigation, but it remains complicated for them, as groups, to show sufficient special interest in bringing such actions.

While recent legislation in the field of environment protection mentions public participation, the exact nature of participation is decided by governmental agencies at their discretion. This gives the laws and policies on public participation a rather soft character, which makes it all the more important for the courts to decide on the possibilities for participation. An established way of community participation in this region is to bring a case to court with a claim of a violation of a constitutional right, e.g. the right to life, along with provisions or environmental regulations. One example of the influence of the courts in this field is the development by the Indian courts of the public trust doctrine, which makes it possible for members of the public to question ineffective management of natural resources.

India, Pakistan and Bangladesh have all approved multilateral environmental agreements which encourage community participation, although these are not developed to the same extent as the Aarhus Convention regime. Although the existing legislation fails to impose a burden on the authorities to collect or disseminate environmental information, there are today at least some provisions related to access to information in framework legislation of all three countries. Moreover, participatory provisions and practices are being developed in South Asia, and the courts have helped expanding communities' participation. There are also some signs that the governmental agencies are willing to work with communities, and thus to contribute to environmental justice through useful procedures. Even so, Jona Razzaque notes that access to public hearings is still restricted, and the lack of elaborate guidelines on good practice makes existing rules less effective. 'Excessive technical and bureaucratic procedures for public involvement along with financial costs make it hard for poor communities to participate effectively.' She concludes that the institutional arrangements as well as the legal backing remain insufficient to ensure adequate public participation and access to environmental decision-making for the communities concerned in this region.

Qun Du (Chapter 7) brings us further east and finds that environmental justice concerns have recently arisen in China as well. She scrutinises the opportunities for public participation, and argues that the government-dominated decision-making approach in public affairs, including environmental concerns, became a root-cause to unfairness and environmental injustice due to the exclusion of citizens' involvement and democracy. In the course of economic growth, the increasing gap between rich and poor, rural and urban, and the social impacts of economic reforms has revealed that social and environmental justice has not been achieved. Thus, top-down planning without local participation has added to degraded environmental quality for the majority, while a minority has been able to benefit from the expanding economy. As a result, she argues, the dominating governmental principle of 'efficiency in priority, fairness in balance' has been criticised for being one of the fundamental causes of social unfairness and environmental injustice.

While some reforms have been proposed with respect to citizens' access to information, public participation and freedom of expression, she argues that there has been very little attempt in the last decades to redress shortcomings in environmental decision-making. Environmental laws have given far more weight to the power of the public administration than to the opportunities for citizens and the general public.

Qun Du argues that the legal instruments initiated in the first years of the twenty-first century, which encourage public participation, are inclined towards distributive justice, by the socially fair allocation of opportunities for public participation in environmental governance. In the first phase, it was made by the introduction of environmental impact assessment procedures. This legislation has subsequently been changed so as to promote public participation, for instance, by enabling environmental organisations to actively participate. As a result, she observes a significant increase in public participation.

Grass-roots movements in 2002 triggered a second phase of pushing for public participation, in which more specific procedural rights were created, but also expanded to a broader scene of environmental decision-making. Despite these changes, Qun Du argues that the selection of representatives to the hearings has not been transparent, and they have been nominated mainly by public authorities rather than by interest-related communities or groups. As to corrective justice in environmental matters, she points at the malfunctioning of public participation in the supervision and review of the environmental administration, and at the lack of litigation rights and procedures for public interests in the judicial system.

Qun Du concludes that, despite the changes in the Chinese legal framework for public participation in environmental matters, numerous shortcomings remain. Thus, she argues, 'to overcome legislative obstacles and make the judiciary more responsive to corrective justice ought to be a high priority task in advocacy of environmental justice in China in the near future'. By showing how the failure to provide for procedural justice, e.g. through adequate participatory structures, has aggravated distributive inequalities, her study confirms the essential link between these two dimensions of justice in cases concerning natural resources and the environment.

Stephen Stec (Chapter 8) makes a similar observation, that procedural justice in environmental contexts is a prerequisite for distributive justice, when examining the role of the courts in the countries in Eastern Europe previously governed by 'scientific socialism'. Yet, he adds that adequate procedures are not enough: enabling citizens to make effective use of their procedural rights also requires capacity-building. This confirms the points made already in the early environmental justice movements in other parts of the world. In Eastern Europe, environmental conflicts have been at the root of legal disputes with an impact on the development of fundamental principles and of the rule of law as such. While it is difficult to lump these countries together, he sees a common feature in the fact that the environmental justice struggles often involve challenges to actions of those in power, who increase their wealth and status at the expense of others. Thus, environmental justice becomes a useful and potentially forceful concept for defining the relationship between those in power and the governed, to be applied to situations where the power elites govern in the absence of sufficient legal controls. In this way it also highlights the respect for the law in the first place as well as for overall notions of justice and equity.

Despite some influential cases for the promotion of the rule of law, the total number of court proceedings concerning environmental issues in these countries remains relatively small, largely due to non-litigious traditions in these societies in general. By a handful of cases in Romania, Kosovo, Russia, Bulgaria and Ukraine, Stephen Stec illustrates the difficulty of environmental interest organisations to successfully pursue their cause in court. He also highlights the distributive dimension of justice when natural resources are at stake, and argues that in quite a number of situations ethnic minorities have suffered disproportionate burdens of adverse environmental effects.

Stephen Stec also observes that in some cases social dialogue has been used, quite successfully, as an alternative way to preserve important areas. Yet, he argues that, to be effective as a means for challenging the power elites, such dialogues must have some legal backing, e.g. by international standards and the possibility of administrative responsibility. He also makes the observation that, despite the fact that environmental justice has proved to be elusive, court cases are nevertheless being brought in the hope of achieving a measure of it.

Jan Darpö (Chapter 9) develops the procedural aspects of justice by assessing the role of courts in environmental matters. He uses the Swedish Environmental Courts to illustrate important concerns for third party interests in environmental decision-making, including judicial processes. He starts by setting out criteria to be met by the court systems in order to ensure justice in cases of environmental decision-making. It is important, he argues, that the procedure allows a broad range of issues to be considered and invoked by the different parties, at an early stage in the proceedings. Moreover, all actors should be able to voice their concerns and to invoke relevant interests and arguments.

He begins with a description of Sweden's peculiar court system which has a distinct set of courts devoted to environmental matters, and then moves on to show the great diversity of environmental procedures, including the courts, in Europe. A state may comply with the European Convention on Human Rights in environmental matters as long as there is a court or other independent and impartial body of law somewhere in the line of appeal. Even so, Jan Darpö reveals the differences in the systems from a justice point of view, depending on the position of the courts. Some court systems are adversarial, while others, including the Swedish one, are inquisitorial in the sense that the decision-making body is responsible for ensuring full compliance with all legal requirements before issuing a permit. The use of experts who sit in courts also differs among the European states, and that is likely to influence the outcome of decision-making.

Of course, the issue of standing is highly important from a justice point of view. Different methods are employed in different states for defining the range of persons with sufficient interest, and it is obvious that the criteria for standing can effectively block access to courts. In addition, the scope of review undertaken by courts matters from a justice point of view. Is the role of the court limited to merely approving or annulling the decision in question or can it reconsider the decision in its entirety, including substituting its judgment for that of the inferior tribunal? Yet, another issue of revelance to the justice debate is whether decision-making is 'sliced' into different procedures and stages where different matters are considered separately. While there may be good technical arguments for such sectioning, serialised decision-making may drastically weaken the possibility for the public concerned to participate and challenge decisions in court.

Jan Darpö concludes by pointing out that, while the Aarhus Convention was greeted with enthusiasm by environmentalists, lawyers representing third party interests, environmental organisations and academics, the responses from the governments of the EU member states have been far less enthusiastic. He is also worried about the strong resistance from the industry to any proposal to increase the opportunities for environmental organisations to participate in judicial proceedings, and emphasises that access to justice requires a continuous discussion on these matters.

Whereas Jan Darpö considers the role of national courts for environmental justice, Ludwig Krämer (Chapter 10) searches for possible environmental justice considerations in the European Court of Justice, which is the final arbiter in legal cases involving European Community law.[38] In his analysis, he contrasts the European jurisprudence and debate against that of the USA, and submits that there is no perception in Europe of problems that link the social status of certain groups of the population to the concerns for environmental justice. In other words, the race/poverty arguments that have characterised the environmental justice debate in the USA have no distinct parallels in Europe. Rather, he continues, a European lawyer ignorant of the American debate would probably think of environmental justice as an attempt to do justice to the environment itself.[39]

In fact, little is known about the possible disproportionate effects of environmental laws in Europe. However, it is known that, while, for example, European legislation concerning sewage treatment or the quality of drinking water does not differentiate between different urban agglomerations according to income etc., these laws are not complied with throughout the twenty-seven member states. Moreover, European

---

[38] The jurisprudence of the European Court of Justice is also analysed by de Sadeleer in Chapter 23 of this volume.

[39] The specific issue of justice towards the environment itself is discussed by Nollkaemper in Chapter 13 of this volume.

environmental legislation cannot ensure that decisions on planning, zoning and the location of harmful industries are not influenced by the social and political interests of persons or groups which are better organised, represented and protected than those of minority groups. Still, he contends that there has been no corresponding complaints in Europe as in the USA and elsewhere about disproportionately affected minority groups. Nor is there any jurisprudence of the European Court of Justice concerning environmental law and discrimination against minority or low-income groups.

However, Ludwig Krämer observes, that, if environmental justice is given a slightly broader meaning, so as to generally concern precautionary approaches and participatory rights, the ruling of the European judiciary is more elaborate. It has, for instance, made clear that there is no special treatment of certain groups, such as farmers, in the application of environmental laws. The European Court of Justice has resisted attempts to allow vested interests groups to escape from respecting European Community law. It has also avoided making some groups, regions or member states disproportionately charged with environmental impairment.

The European Court of Justice has in multiple cases defended the protection of the natural environment, as far as possible, even against the interests of planning administrators, local interests or special uses. On the other hand, the European judiciary has not shown a particular sensitivity with regard to citizens' rights of access to information, public participation and access to justice in environmental matters. In particular, the European judiciary has remained conservative as regards standing before itself. Ludwig Krämer concludes by placing hope in the full implementation of the Aarhus Convention in the European Union, as that would constitute a big step towards environmental justice, as an adequate protection of the environment, by means of law.

But what if the parties fail to comply with international standards for access to information, public participation in decision-making or access to justice, or any other provisions of international environmental agreements? Unlike human rights instruments, only few of the environmental treaties provide for individual complaints procedures to international appeal bodies.

The Aarhus Convention is one such international environmental treaty in which members of the public have the right to make complaints to an independent and impartial committee at the international level. Another regime with comparable possibilities is the 1993 North American Agreement on Environmental Cooperation (NAAEC).[40] By comparing these two regimes, Malgosia Fitzmaurice (Chapter 11) devotes her contribution to the question whether international complaints procedures can promote justice in environmental matters. She focuses on the procedural arrangements for complaints by members of the public, including non-governmental organisations, and wonders whether the procedures also satisfy the participants' expectations of justifiable distributions of costs and benefits.

---

[40] 1993 North American Agreement on Environmental Cooperation, 32 ILM (1993) 1480.

In addition to setting out minimum standards for public participation in decision-making and access to justice,[41] the Aarhus Convention mandates the establishment of an international Compliance Committee. While some of the features of the Aarhus Convention Compliance Committee are similar to other existing compliance committees, it also has some distinct characteristics, which draw on the principles of the Convention itself and are well suited to promote legitimacy and justice in environmental decision-making. The main feature is of course the right of members of the public, including NGOs, to submit complaints about a state's compliance with the Convention. Moreover, the members of the Compliance Committee are independent and serve in their personal capacity. While the purpose of the Committee is to improve compliance rather than redress violations, Malgosia Fitzmaurice argues that the difference between the decisions of the Compliance Committee and the redress of human rights is very fine and sometimes difficult to distinguish. Yet, its findings have the character of dialogue with the parties, and the Committee provides a consultative process with the aim of facilitating compliance.

The international complaints procedure of the NAAEC Commission on Environmental Cooperation operates on a different rationale. It is entrusted with the task of investigating alleged breaches in the enforcement of environmental legislation in the three member states (Canada, Mexico and the USA). Unlike the Aarhus Convention Compliance Committee, NAAEC's governing body consists of cabinet members of each of the three states. The main tool for civil society participation – the Citizen Submission Procedure – is intended to deal with failures by the states to enforce their own national environmental laws, and not with non-compliance with international minimum standards. The final and only result of this procedure, if successful, is the publication of a factual record. Malgosia Fitzmaurice is critical of the NAAEC complaint system: it is lengthy and only few factual records have been publicly released. She also catalogues a number of features which are not particularly helpful in advancing the cause of environmental justice.

In assessing and comparing the two systems, she sees in the Aarhus Convention Compliance Committee a significant role in promoting environmental justice and even in contributing to the implementation of democratic governance. Her assessment of the NAAEC Commission is different. This institution is more politicised, due to its internal composition, and the value of the process has been undermined by the obstructive practices of the three states concerned. Thus, she concludes, it cannot be said to embody or further principles of environmental justice, despite its potential for doing so under different circumstances.

From all the different contributions in this part, it is clear that procedural and participatory institutions are no longer national issues only, if they ever were. Rather, the developments in different countries are influenced by international debate and

---

[41] The minimum requirements on access to justice in the Aarhus Convention are described by Darpö in Chapter 9 of this volume.

international law. The supranational structure of the EU and also the international complaint procedures show that there is at least some development of procedural justice above the purely domestic context.

This brings the book to Part III and the impact of state sovereignty and state borders on justice considerations in environmental matters.

4 State sovereignty and state borders

Despite the effects on state relations as a result of the forces of economic globalisation, state sovereignty, state borders and the distinction between international and national law still have significant impact on law and legal thinking. While these concepts are challenged by the notion of environmental justice, they simultaneously influence considerations of justice. As already mentioned, one such challenge is to decide on the appropriate unit – the state, the individual and/or other categories – for justice appraisals. Should international law at all be concerned with environmental justice, and should justice appraisals transcend state borders?

Even if we agree that justice considerations should not be defined by state borders, we also recognise the imperative of peoples' self-determination and self-rule. If international law were to set out in detail how states should choose between various social, economic and environmental issues, that would curb states' possibility to define their own preferences. The issue of balancing the concerns for transboundary or global justice – cosmopolitan justice – against self-determination is addressed in two contributions in this part of the book.

The first contribution in this Part, however, draws our attention to justice concerns in a very special case, namely, in armed conflicts. Phoebe Okowa (Chapter 12) observes that there is an apparent tension between state sovereignty and environmental protection in such conflicts, not least because some of the most significant damage to the environment, including unsustainable patterns of resource, has taken place in situations of war. She begins by cataloguing the devastating environmental effects of a number of recent conflicts including Vietnam, Iraq, the Democratic Republic of Congo and Kosovo. The responsibility for this, she argues, rests squarely with all the belligerents including the territorial state, especially in civil war situations. Given the involvement of governments in much of the war-related environmental damage, she argues that the presumption, that a government always acts in the best interests of its people, should be displaced, at least when natural resources within the territory are involved.

In general, environmental justice – whether in a procedural, distributive or corrective sense – has not been a feature of the enforceable content of the international law of armed conflict. Phoebe Okowa relates the lack of environmental justice in such contexts to the significant normative gaps in the content of the law of war, as it applies to the environment and natural resource protection generally. Rather, much of this law reflects the increased public sensitivity to the importance of human rights values.

While this is quite understandable, she finds it remarkable that considerations for the environment as such have continued to be an afterthought even when the opportunity arose to revise the 1949 Geneva Conventions on the law of wars. She also makes the point that, on the whole, this body of law remains state-centred in the face of over-whelming evidence that the bulk of conflicts are intra-state rather than inter-state in character. For instance, even the requirements, that the manufacture of weapons be accompanied by tests to show that they do not entail disproportionate damage when used in conflict, are limited to inter-state conflicts. Yet, as her powerful account of the devastating effects of the Congolese conflict illustrates, much environmental damage occurs in internal conflicts. While there may be good reasons, from a justice point of view, to distinguish between inter-state and domestic situations of war, this does not justify excluding such internal conflicts from the application of the laws of war.

In assessing the post-conflict corrective mechanisms for warfare, such as in peace settlements, Phoebe Okowa also shows that existing law is confined to the account-ability for human rights violations without any significant attention being paid to the restoration of the damaged environment. She notes that the existing legal regime on damage to the environment lacks internal coherence and only partially reflects con-cerns for environmental justice. Thus, she argues, the existing regimes for corrective justice, such as that which followed the 1991 Gulf War and the setting up of a United Nations Compensation Commission, are only selectively applied and do not result in any coherent development of legal principles that involve an overarching concern that protection of the environment should be a matter of the law of war. Her conclusion, not surprisingly, is pessimistic.

The other contributions in this Part on state sovereignty and state borders wrestle with the question of how, if at all, environmental justice affects states powers under international law with respect to natural resources and the environment within their respective territory. André Nollkaemper (Chapter 13) begins with the proposition that, despite the challenges to state sovereignty brought on by environmental justice considerations, states retain considerable freedom to use, enjoy and destroy their environment as they see fit. Provided that the law and policy of a state does not cause harm to any other state (or areas beyond national jurisdictions), he asks whether it is desirable to set out at the international level how a state, in its domestic system, should make choices between environmental, developmental, social and other values.

He analyses relevant international decisions by courts and other tribunals (e.g. *Trail Smelter, Corfu Channel, Gabçikovo Nagymaros Project, Pulp Mills on the River Uruguay* and the *Advisory Opinion on the Legality of the Threat or Use of Nuclear Weapons*) and concludes that, apart from treaty obligations, international law does not substantially limit states' power with regard to their own environment. Rather, international law is essentially limited to concerns with transboundary issues, while remaining quite 'agnostic' as to what states do to their own environment.

Enters environmental justice. Would the notion of environmental justice provide any guidance for interpretation or the further development of international law in these respects? To what extent is it relevant for the limitations of state sovereignty? The answer, André Nollkaemper argues, is determined by how 'environmental justice' is defined, and he makes the useful distinction between four different understandings of environmental justice, i.e. environmental justice as (a) justice towards the environment, (b) international distributive justice, (c) intergenerational justice, and (d) social justice. Environmental justice, he argues, could only qualify the scope of states' sovereign powers over their domestic environmental policies if construed as intergenerational or social justice. Even then, however, the qualifications would proceed at a highly abstract level. International law does not seem able to resolve in a substantive way the conflicts between social, economic and environmental claims within states. Such balances must be contextually determined.

Despite some scepticism, André Nollkaemper sees in environmental justice a potentially useful concept which overlaps with other concepts, such as sustainable development, equity and integration. By leading in the same direction as these concepts, it may underpin our thinking and perhaps our policies for integrating social, economic and environmental issues. Still, it would not provide any clear-cut answers with regard to the levels or forms of environment protection. While environmental justice may provide the contours for the exercise of state powers, international law would continue to confer on states the power to make detailed choices between developmental and environmental policies.

A slightly different view is reflected in my own (Jonas Ebbesson, Chapter 14) examination of possible pursuits for justice in transboundary environmental contexts. Relevant from a justice viewpoint is whether persons affected by nuisance or risks outside the state of the activity have the opportunity to engage themselves in decision-making in the state of the activity. This presents a profound challenge on how their interests and concerns ought to be integrated in the foreign decision-making. The other case of transboundary pursuit for justice that I consider refers to the transboundary subjectivity and corporate structure rather than bio-physical effects across state borders. The issue, then, is whether it is possible to make transnational corporations responsible for environmental wrongs outside the state of the activity/harm, for instance in the home country of the corporation. Transnational corporations may benefit from the lack of effective environmental laws, adequate environmental administrations and poor judicial institutions, so as to escape responsibility for harms caused to health and the environment. In such cases, precluding the locals, adversely affected by the corporate activity, from the possibility of bringing claims against the corporations outside the state of the activity/harm – for instance, in the corporation's home country – would in effect result in a denial of justice. On the other hand, when courts outside the state of the activity/harm are available to settle conflicts in environmental matters, caution in the choice of law is required in order to avoid a form of environmental imperialism, whereby one country or region imposes its laws onto another.

In discussing the transboundary aspects of justice, I also make the point that such considerations cannot be reduced to inter-state matters, but require a more cosmopolitan notion of justice. The procedural opportunities and distributive effects among the persons concerned on both sides of the borders must be taken into account in the institutional arrangements. State borders simply do not mark out who is concerned by the decision. Therefore, the fact that, in international law, state borders constitute the dominant, formal delimitations of a society, does not prevent taking individuals as the measure in justice deliberations, and in appraisals of international law. Moreover, some international regimes actually provide for transboundary participation in decision-making and transboundary access to justice. International law is less developed to cope with pursuits of justice in cases of transboundary corporations than in situations of transboundary effects to the environment.

In analysing the possible transboundary constellations between the harmful activity, the harm and the forum for settling or deciding the case, it is shown how different justice considerations occur in each one of them. From this discussion, I conclude by addressing what is needed to ensure or at least promote justice – largely procedural, but also distributive and corrective – when state borders are transcended.

The three contributions in this Part reveal the enduring influence of state sovereignty on legal thinking in environmental matters and show how sovereignty could be accommodated so as to better square with concerns for justice in environmental matters. Some of these findings matter for the coming discussion on global justice in Part IV.

5 North–South concerns in global contexts

The concerns for global justice are not limited to issues where the environmental problems as such are global in scope. Also, access to natural resources, more generally, triggers concerns for justice in a larger geographical context. Still, the concerns for global justice are most apparent in the international negotiations concerning depletion of the stratospheric ozone layer, climate change, and desertification, i.e. issues of a worldwide geographical scope. These three concerns are interrelated, and they have all resulted in multilateral regimes with some 170–190 states involved, and with more or less precisely defined obligations for the states concerned.

In these global contexts, distributive, corrective, procedural and environmental justice have quite different implications compared with the domestic contexts. Distributive justice may refer both to the inequitable impact on states and regions caused by the environmental problem at hand, and to the distribution of costs and measures for avoiding the predicted harms. Corrective justice need not refer exclusively to past wrongs, but also to who – which states, regions, individuals, companies etc. – should do what to avoid further decline. The procedural element of justice is evident in the ways the global agreements are negotiated and debated. To achieve legitimacy, but also procedural justice, it is essential that all states (and other relevant actors) are able to partake in the negotiations of international agreements, and in the shaping of international policy.

The three chapters in Part IV show that similar issues have arisen in the three global regimes. The negotiations of a global treaty to combat the depletion of the stratospheric ozone layer influenced the later negotiations concerning climate change, biodiversity and desertification, for instance by the development of the principle of common but differentiated responsibility. This principle, it is submitted, is one of the most apparent expressions of the concern for distributive justice in international environmental law (another being the principle of equitable sharing of water resources).[42]

Karin Mickelson (Chapter 15) analyses the debate surrounding the Montreal Protocol on Substances that Deplete the Ozone Layer (Montreal Protocol),[43] signed in 1987 and subsequently amended and adjusted several times. She focuses on the possible differences in the narratives of justice by the North and the South during these negotiations. With some 190 parties, the Montreal Protocol is the main legal instrument for defining states' obligations to combat the depletion of the stratospheric ozone layer. It is considered an international environmental 'success story'. Moreover, the concerns about fairness were inextricably linked to the debates surrounding the Protocol from the start. Thus, it provides a useful case for examining the concerns for justice in global contexts.

Various ozone depleting substances, such as CFCs, have been used in the North for a wide range of industrial processes and consumer goods, and in the negotiations the countries in the South realised that the proposed phase-out of these substances could have a major impact on their own domestic development. The acknowledgment of the different per capita contribution by the North and the South influenced the negotiations, and is reflected in two ways in the Montreal Protocol: first, by the differentiated obligations and, second, by the requirement that industrialised countries transfer financial resources to developing countries in order to secure compliance.

Karin Mickelson uses the documentation of the negotiations to analyse the arguments presented concerning the distribution of responsibilities for cutting down the production and use of ozone depleting substances. She observes how the arguments of justice and fairness were invoked on all sides from the beginning of the negotiations, and shows how these arguments became critical to the negotiation process. She also makes the point that, while there was a consensus regarding the importance of ensuring that the Montreal Protocol was fair to developing countries, there was no agreement on how to achieve this goal.

The new consensus that developed with the Montreal Protocol – that industrialised countries should assist developing countries by transfers of technology and financial additional costs – was to be reflected in the later treaty arrangements concerning climate change and biodiversity. Karin Mickelson concludes that the outcome of the ozone negotiations cannot be explained by the traditional notions of corrective or distributive justice only. Rather, she argues, the concept of environmental justice is

---

[42] The principle is also discussed by Bugge in Chapter 21 of this volume.
[43] 1987 Montreal Protocol on Substances that Deplete the Ozone Layer, 26 ILM (1987) 1550.

best suited to capture the stance taken by the South, as it reflects the idea that a broader and more inclusive vision of environment protection and sustainability is required, which also encompasses concerns for social justice and ecological integrity.

Her study shows that, while new dimensions and aspects of justice arise when the debate is expanded to the entire international community, the issues considered in domestic deliberations, such as concerns for social justice, are also relevant in the global context.

Although the complexity of the problems surrounding climate change is far greater than that of ozone layer depletion, there are some similar features. Thus, the average contribution per capita to the increasing concentration of greenhouse gases is greater in the North than in the South, and countries in the South are likely to be disproportionately affected by climate change. Moreover, Northern countries have a larger economic and technological capacity to mitigate greenhouse gas emissions as well as to adapt to its consequences. Yet, climate change involves costlier, more comprehensive adjustments, and – still – greater uncertainties as to causal links between the activities and the harms caused than in the case of ozone layer depletion.

Against this background, Jutta Brunnée (Chapter 16) sets out not only to identify possible signs that justice considerations have influenced the climate change negotiations, but also – like some of the other contributors – to address whether environmental justice can be global in the first place. She acknowledges the difficulty in agreeing on shared understandings and expectations in international society with its global diversity of views and perspectives, but she insists that shared expectations of justice have been emerging. Drawing on Lon Fuller's criteria for the 'inner morality' of law, she sees that, as diverse actors interact through law, 'opportunities do arise to deepen shared understandings, provided that all relevant actors can participate in the process and are able to do so in a meaningful fashion'. With this significant proviso (and not ignoring the influence of power) in the North–South context, she argues that there are possibilities to establish an inclusive international legal order in which procedural justice may provide for the emergence of substantive commitments in a genuinely normative community. Thus, one may add, procedural justice may result in some sense of substantive, distributive justice as well.

Having defended the idea of global climate justice as a meaningful concept, Jutta Brunnée turns to the question whether a globally shared conception of environmental justice has in fact emerged in international climate change law. To do so, she also starts off by analysing the principle of common but differentiated responsibility from a justice perspective. She stresses that it is not enough that this principle is contained in salient international instruments, such as the UN Framework Convention on Climate Change or the 1992 Rio Declaration. The question is whether it also represents a globally shared understanding of distributive justice in the face of climate change. There seems to be a broad consensus that states' responsibilities are differentiated, that their different capacities are relevant for this differentiation, and that the industrialised states should take the lead in combating climate change. But beyond that?

Jutta Brunnée points at several crucial and complex issues where the understandings seem to diverge, in particular between the industrialised and developing countries. She concludes that the principle of common but differentiated responsibilities represents a nucleus of a framework for global burden-sharing, but an internationally shared understanding of how and why mitigation and adaptation burdens should be allocated remains to solidify. Achieving any sense of environmental justice through law is a continuous effort; and, if justice is to be pursued through the climate change regime, the hard work of international law has only begun.

Bo Kjellén (Chapter 17) shares his experience in international environmental negotiations, and in particular his extensive participation as the chairperson of the negotiations leading to the 1994 UN Convention to Combat Desertification, Particularly in Africa (Desertification Convention).[44] These negotiations reflect a new diplomacy for sustainable development, which differs significantly from traditional diplomacy. While the new diplomatic efforts also concern real threats, there is not only one easily identified adversary on the other side of the table to be bullied. The environmental problems are real and often global in scope, and they require that multiple countries agree on common action to be taken in order to modify certain practices. What also characterises this scene and significantly frames the negotiations is the fact that, while the long-term threats are real though diffuse, in the short term very concrete and important economic and social interests are challenged, once we move from vision to the stage of actually taking the measures required to prevent the problem at stake.

As already pointed out with respect to ozone layer depletion and climate change, these negotiations involve diverse values and ethical considerations of different kinds. Therefore, concerns for justice and fairness are inherent in the practice of this new diplomacy. This has been evident also in the desertification negotiations, although the justice debate, as such, only had a limited impact on the proceedings.

Seen in the context of diplomacy for sustainable development, Bo Kjellén argues that it was inevitable in the desertification negotiations that the focus on justice at the UN level would centre on distribution. While the financial provisions in the Desertification Convention are certainly not satisfactory in terms of environmental justice, he points at several provisions which reveal the ambitious approach on issues of social and environmental justice that underlies the Convention. Comparing the Desertification Convention with the parallel regimes on ozone layer depletion, climate change and biodiversity, he argues that the broad approach to justice that permeates the treaty texts goes further in the Desertification Convention than in any of the other treaties.

In emphasising distributive justice, he also points at his experience as chairperson in creating a participatory structure of the negotiations, as reflected in the bottom-up approach, with active engagements of grass-root NGOs. Thus, he shows that there

---

[44] 1994 UN Convention to Combat Desertification in Those Countries Experiencing Serious Drought and/or Desertification, Particularly in Africa, 22 ILM (1994) 1328.

was also an element of procedural or 'participatory' justice in the negotiations. He concludes that the role of the Desertification Convention in the continuous struggle to combat poverty and improve global distributive justice remains unclear, not least in light of the difficulties in mobilising financial resources. On the other hand, it has been relatively successful from a 'participatory justice' point of view, by reaching out to local groups, including women's groups, and by achieving cooperation with NGOs. He contends that, in the continued quest for effective implementation, an increased concern for justice and fairness would definitely support the gradual strengthening of the Desertification Convention.

The global issues dealt with in this Part all involve distributive reflections with regard to access to natural resources. Agriculture, fish stocks and forests are adversely affected by ozone layer depletion as well as climate change. Moreover, both climate change and desertification have great impact on access to water and the possibility of operating activities in coastal areas.

6 Access to natural resources

Part V of this volume looks more closely at access to natural resources as an element of environmental justice. Two of the three contributions examine justice considerations in the context of access to water and genetically modified resources, whereas the third contribution examines the gendered aspects of environmental law and justice with particular focus on access to natural resources. Obviously, justice considerations arise also with regard to other kinds of natural resources, such as forests, fisheries and minerals,[45] both at the local and international level.

Ellen Hey (Chapter 18) explores how international law addresses water crises, and makes the point that international water law is moving from the inter-state paradigm towards a 'global water law'. This does not refer to the geographical coverage, but rather to some of the legal features. She sees in 'global water law' an increasing emphasis on the functional role of states, in fulfilling certain obligations and meeting prescribed standards, in order to protect the interests of individuals and groups in society. This differs from classical international water law, which underlines state sovereignty with the implied discretionary powers of each state to decide independently on water uses. While she is sympathetic to this change of focus in water law, she stresses that 'global water law' does not necessarily meet standards of fairness.

In tracing this change – and its influence on considerations of justice and fairness – she starts off from classical international water law, as reflected in customary principles on equitable and reasonable utilisation, and codified in the 1997 UN Convention on the Law of the Non-navigational Uses of International Watercourses (UN

---

[45] Justice issues in the context of mining and the exploration of minerals are looked at by Stec in Chapter 8, and by Schwartz in Chapter 22 of this volume.

Watercourses Convention).[46] This treaty concentrates on inter-state relations and on the discretionary role of states in determining what is fair with regard to the uses of a particular watercourse. Crucially, it does not provide for the participation of non-state actors.

She contrasts the approach of the UN Watercourses Convention with the regional 1992 UNECE Convention on the Protection and Use of Transboundary Watercourses and Lakes (Helsinki Convention) and, in particular, its 1999 Protocol on Water and Health.[47] This Protocol distances itself from classical inter-state paradigm, e.g. by imposing minimum standards on water management, by focusing on the interests of individuals and groups in society rather than states, and by stressing the importance of access to information, public participation and access to justice in water matters.[48] She finds a yet more comprehensive formulation of a right to water in the so-called General Comment 15, where the UN Committee on Economic, Social and Cultural Rights comments on the substantive issues arising in the implementation of the 1966 UN Covenant on Economic, Social and Cultural Rights.[49] In providing for a human right to water, General Comment 15 addresses fairness and, in particular, distributive justice concerns at national and international levels. By stressing the need for access to information, public participation and transparency at the national level, it provides for procedural fairness as well. She also observes that the World Bank safeguard policies, relevant in the context of water law, provide for consultation at the inter-state level, and for participation at the level of individuals and group within a state; thus addressing issues of procedural justice.

Ellen Hey concludes that, due to the diverse interrelationships in 'global water law', fairness can only be assessed through a multi-faceted approach, which takes the various interrelations involved into account. While 'global water law' is not necessarily fair, either in terms of distributive or in terms of procedural fairness, she suggests that it fares better than classical international water law in offering the weak a voice and in providing a promise of justice.

The complex structure of actors involved in the use, knowledge and exploitation of genetic resources is just as diverse as in water uses, and the development of the relevant legal frameworks necessitates different justice considerations. Philippe Cullet (Chapter 19) observes that, while legal incentives for the use of genetic resources have

---

[46] 1997 Convention on the Law of the Non-navigational Uses of International Watercourses (Watercourses Convention), 36 ILM (1997) 700.

[47] 1992 Convention on the Protection and Use of Transboundary Watercourses and International Lakes, 31 ILM (1992) 1312; and 1999 Protocol on Water and Health to the 1992 Convention on the Protection and Use of Transboundary Watercourses and International Lakes, 29 *Environmental Policy and Law* (1999) 200.

[48] The 1999 Protocol on Water and Health also establishes an international complaints procedure which draws on the Aarhus Convention, as described by Fitzmaurice in Chapter 11 of this volume.

[49] 1966 International Covenant on Economic, Social and Cultural Rights, 6 ILM (1967) 368; General Comment 15(2002), The Right to Water (Arts. 11 and 12 of the International Covenant on Economic, Social and Cultural Rights), UN Doc. E/C.12/2002/11, 20 January 2003.

rapidly developed, much less has been done with regard to the protection of rights and interests of the holder of these resources and the associated knowledge concerning their useful characteristics. The development of rules on access to genetic resources, the sharing of related benefits and the asymmetrical protection of knowledge raise questions of equity in the existing legal frameworks. He makes two initial points in this respect. First, the legal protection of knowledge and the compensation systems, for instance through benefit sharing, trigger concerns for distributive justice. Second, there are important international law dimensions in the existing and proposed frameworks for knowledge protection, either because these frameworks are adopted at the international level or because they concern transboundary transactions. From a justice point of view, it is therefore relevant to take into account the possibility of differential treatment of countries with different capacities to benefit from these frameworks.

Philippe Cullet highlights two factors that complicate the achievement of an equitable access regime. While international law is relatively clear as regards access to resources, it remains unclear concerning access to knowledge. Moreover, the existing access regime under the 1992 Biodiversity Convention gives countries of origin relatively strong rights to control transboundary movements, but does little for individuals and groups that are the actual holders of genetic resources and related knowledge.

He observes that, generally speaking, the notion of benefit sharing has been seen as an acceptable toll by developed as well as developing countries, but for different reasons. However, despite the wide acceptance of benefit sharing in principle, there is still little consensus regarding the specific benefits to be offered in individual cases. While he contends that on the whole benefit sharing seems to foster a weak form of distributive justice in favour of the provider – often developing – countries, as a mechanism for compensation benefit sharing can still be improved, for instance by adopting a binding regime at the international level.

The existing system for knowledge protection is highly imbalanced because it only rewards one particular type of knowledge, namely, that held by patent holders. It aggravates inequity by protecting certain forms of knowledge with exclusive or monopoly rights, while deeming all other forms to be part of the public domain that can be freely appropriated by anyone. Philippe Cullet makes the point that the failure of the existing system to ensure differential treatment among states and distributive justice among the concerned actors, necessitates the consideration also of new approaches, such as a system of open access. He concludes that, in order to create a more equitable legal regime, the protection of genetic resources and associated knowledge must be reconsidered more fundamentally. There are possible alternatives, like the open access framework, that may provide a more equitable outcome for the actors involved.

Although the laws on access to natural resources – be it water, genetic resources and associated knowledge, or any other resource – may be gender neutral on their face, they may still result in injustices in their application. In her study on the gendered aspects of environmental justice in East Africa, Patricia Kameri-Mbote (Chapter 20) observes that the laws on natural resources and the environment are largely gender neutral. Nevertheless, ownership control and access to these resources is indeed gendered. Constrained access to resources, lack of ownership rights and vesting of control of land and resources on men have implications for women's performance of their duties. Moreover, marginalisation, outlawing or demeaning women's ways of managing environmental resources impact on their work and also their political leverage. Therefore, it is somewhat paradoxical that the environmental movement, in considering environmental concerns, has failed to distinguish women's concern from more general human concerns. The state of the environment often impacts differently on men and women, due to societal structures; and the gendered social ordering of society mitigates human encounters with the environment. Therefore, environmental laws that fail to factor in the gender dynamic contribute to accentuating women's poverty and to increasing their workload where it depends on environmental resources. It also has the effect of making environmental laws less effective in actually protecting the environment.

Environmental management shapes decisions and actions on how resources are developed and it determines to whom they are provided. Yet women, who are most likely to be affected by such management, are not included often enough. Taking East Africa – Kenya, Uganda and Tanzania – as her case study, she observes how excluding women in environmental decision-making and property ownership contributes to environmental injustice. While environmental resources are often managed at the local level, where customary law determines ownership, access and control of resources, the dominance of older male members over property and lives of women and their juniors is the hallmark of African customary law. In many regions, parts of Africa included, women have the main responsibilities to safeguard the natural environment, but their participation in decision-making is limited and their knowledge and interests often excluded when environmental decisions or development plans are made.

Gender aspects of environmental law have become a global concern, as shown by international meetings where the need to upscale women's role as 'key allies' in sustainable environmental management has been accentuated.[50] This has also been acknowledged in international legal frameworks and policy documents. At the national level in East Africa, she observes that the particular role of women is not recognised in existing environmental laws. While some steps have been taken to increase the involvement of communities in resources management, these remain insufficient to ensure women's access to the resources or their participation in the management. Patricia Kameri-Mbote concludes by calling for the development of

---

[50] This is also observed by Petersen in Chapter 5 of this volume.

tools to mainstream gender into environmental management and for the growth of expertise in gender and environmental issues, and she provides several proposals to this end.

7 Corporate activities and trade

The last part of the book is devoted to environmental justice in different contexts of corporate activities and trade. While the three contributions have different focal points, they all – also – include a transboundary dimension. There are obvious reasons for this, taking into account not only the transboundary feature of trade and corporate activities, but also the dissemination of new legal concepts across state borders.

Hans Christian Bugge's (Chapter 21) analysis of the Polluter Pays Principle shows exactly this. The principle has achieved broad recognition in numerous national jurisdictions, but also in international and European Community law, as a legal principle for the allocation of costs related to polluting activities. Yet, it is also subject to doubts and criticism, and he contends that it raises issues of both distributive and corrective justice: the distribution of environmental quality between social groups, the allocation of benefits and costs between the polluter and the victims, between multiple polluters, between the polluter and society, between humans and non-humans, and between generations.

Hans Christian Bugge analyses the justice implications of three 'versions' of the Polluter Pays Principle. In the narrow version, the principle focuses on the allocation of the costs with the polluter, without achieving full cost internalisation. While generally seen as 'just' in this version, he reveals that the assessment is more complex, and that justice arguments could even be made against applying the Polluter Pays Principle in this manner, due to distributive consequences. Understood in a wider sense, the Polluter Pays Principle implies the internalisation of the social costs of pollution. This version, too, creates serious problems of distributive justice and fairness, for instance in the use of taxes or charges on the polluter. Conceiving the Polluter Pays Principle as a principle of liability and compensation for pollution damage means that the person who causes pollution is liable for damage and the costs of preventing damage. While 'just', 'normal' and 'natural' on its face, a closer look at its application again raises concerns from a justice point of view, in both the corrective and distributive senses.

Hans Christian Bugge shows that, when bringing the Polluter Pays Principle up to the level of international cost allocation between states, we are faced with many of the same dilemmas of fairness and justice as in the situation between private actors. Understood in the narrow sense described, it may stimulate a race to the bottom, which does not promote environmental justice in the sense of improving the environmental conditions for marginalised groups in poor countries. There are noticeable exceptions to the Polluter Pays Principle in international environmental law, e.g. in the contributions to the Multilateral Fund under the 1987 Montreal

Protocol, but also in the Global Environmental Facility, established in order to transfer funding and facilitate environment protection measures in developing countries. The wider version of the Polluter Pays Principle in transboundary contexts coincides with the principle of non-discrimination, as it implies internalising the costs also of the pollution damage caused to other countries. Understood as a principle for liability and compensation for transboundary damage, the Polluter Pays Principle is somehow reflected in the duty of states not to cause harm to other states, and, if that happens, to compensate for the harm. That seems like a 'just' rule, but it turns out to be difficult to apply, as can be seen in the case of climate change.

Although he finds the Polluter Pays Principle 'just' in each of the three forms discussed, Hans Christian Bugge concludes that exemptions and modifications are required in order to avoid unreasonable results from both a corrective and a distributive justice point of view.

Priscilla Schwartz (Chapter 22) takes us from the conceptual discussions to environmental justice hands-on, by exploring the control of transnational corporate activities from a developing country perspective. She uses the West African state of Sierra Leone as a case to assess whether the current legal and institutional structure for regulating corporate mining activities conforms with generally agreed concepts of justice, since 'nowhere does the concept of "justice" in environmental law find more immediate relevance than in Sierra Leone's mining industry'. Sierra Leone is a small country remarkably rich in mineral resources, but seriously affected by the long civil war between 1991 and 2002, a war largely funded and perpetuated by the country's mineral resources.

Transnational mining corporations operate in the form of foreign direct investors or as locally incorporated companies, subsidiaries or affiliates of companies based or operating in other countries. These corporations have very few links with the domestic economy. Rather, their activities are largely externally controlled, with outflows of wealth dominated by the export of raw materials or unprocessed minerals. The environmental impacts of the corporate activities go well beyond harm to the physical environment and include severe impact on the social and cultural well-being of the mining communities. Yet, no effective mechanism has existed to make these companies – or the government – responsible to ensure environmental protection or to invest in critical mineral-related social projects.

Priscilla Schwartz analyses the legal situation in Sierra Leone by considering distributive and participatory issues. She makes the point that, while applicable legislation and relevant agreements oblige the companies to minimise the adverse effects of mining, and also establish trust funds and impose criminal sanctions for the environmental wrongs of the companies, they still fail to provide remedies for the public concerned. Thus, there is no clear role for members of the public to participate in the decision-making and no right of recourse to the courts to claim compensation or enforcement of environmental obligations. Moreover, she argues, Sierra Leone's judiciary has had a dismal record in enforcing environmental law against mining companies as well as officials, and it has shown no attempt to fill the gaps in the substantive law by applying internationally recognised standards (as has happened, for instance, in South Asia).[51]

As to distributive justice considerations, the applicable acts in Sierra Leone do formalise certain benefit sharing and equity in the allocation of resources from mining, e.g. by requirements to set up compensation funds and various trust funds. Yet, the mechanisms for such distribution have not been well structured, which has prevented the even distribution of benefits in particular mining communities.

Moving beyond domestic law, Priscilla Schwartz also considers whether voluntary commitments undertaken by transnational corporations has had any impact on their corporate social responsibility. She questions to what extent international institutions and cooperative arrangements have influenced the mining activities in Sierra Leone, and discusses the possibilities of bringing claims against the corporations in their home countries rather than in Sierra Leone.[52]

Although mining companies are increasingly becoming aware of various environmental justice concerns, mainly due to pressure from NGOs and civil society, she concludes that environmental justice will remain elusive under the current institutional structure, 'no matter how compliant or motivated transnational enterprises become'.

So far, more attention has been given to environmental concerns in international trade law than in international investment law. Nicolas de Sadeleer (Chapter 23) shows how issues of fairness and access to natural resources arise in the context of international trade law.[53] He sees the doctrine on free trade, based on the premise that products should be able to circulate freely without hindrance from technical obstacles erected by states, as diametrically opposed to national or regional regulations in the areas of public health and environmental protection. While the need to open up markets directly conflicts with the need to promote legitimate environmental objectives, efforts to reconcile these two goals have been quite unsuccessful; and issues of environmental justice in these contexts have not yet gathered momentum. Hazardous products and wastes could nevertheless have significant effects on the environment of poor people and minorities; and given the lack of economic resources, education etc., populations of poor countries could more easily become vulnerable to these goods.

In comparing the developments and considerations in international trade law, under the World Trade Organization (WTO), with European Community trade law, he assesses the different relevant regimes on transboundary movements of hazardous wastes, chemicals and pesticides. He notes that, despite attempts, there is no ban on movements of hazardous wastes for final disposal in international law. While the worst forms of waste dumping on developing states seems to have ceased, there is

---

[51] See also Razzaque in Chapter 6 of this volume.   [52] See also Ebbesson in Chapter 14 of this volume.
[53] See also Cullet in Chapter 19 of this volume.

still an unresolved issue about the compatibility of a trade prohibition and WTO law. European Community law also prohibits qualitative restrictions and measures with such effects, but the European Court of Justice has pushed for the integration of local environmental considerations in the field of trade law. According to this court, environment and health protection constitutes a legitimate objective in the public interest capable of justifying restrictions of trade. Yet, Nicolas de Sadeleer also notes that there are some trade-related cases, which mirror the justice considerations rather imperfectly.

European law not only imposes limits on the member states to restrict the free movements of goods, it also imposes minimum standards for the protection of health and the environment that the member states are obliged to implement and comply with. When such legislation intends to result in total harmonisation, the question remains whether European Community law leaves some space for further national measures driven by justice considerations. While the leeway for such exceptions should not be exaggerated, he shows that it should be possible for a member state to invoke particular demographic, geographical or epidemiological circumstances to justify such extra measures with an impact on trade. Still, in general, trade restrictions must be justified by reasons of risks for health or the environment. Procedures for risk assessments and, more importantly, risk management decisions, have been developed, and such environmental management decisions have environmental justice implications, since they involve considerations of policy. In this context, he argues, nothing prevents the national legislator in the member states from placing greater emphasis on social groups at risk.

While each member state may also invoke the precautionary principle with the objective of thwarting the occurrence of uncertain risks, this must be done on the basis of scientific information. In these contexts, little attention has been given to environmental justice considerations. Nicolas de Sadeleer concludes that, when considering the nature of environmental trade-related measures, so far broader health and environmental factors, rather than justice considerations as a discrete concept, have had a key role in shaping these instrument. The European Union has indeed been active in international discussions on environmental issues with adverse impact on poor countries, and the European Court of Justice has been involved in some cases with a bearing on environmental justice.[54] Yet, he holds that these are exceptions, and his central finding is that the concept of environmental justice does not occupy the central stage in discussions about trade and the environment.

* * * * *

As this brief introduction reveals, the volume's twenty-two contributions confirm the thesis that justice considerations arise in just about any legal context involving health, the environment and natural resources, be it local, global or structural. The studies help clarifying essential issues in justice deliberations in the context of environmental

---

[54] See also Krämer in Chapter 10 of this volume.

law; not necessarily by telling what *is* just and fair, but rather by highlighting important factors and indicators of justice considerations. Although the approaches to justice are not identical, most contributors concerned with the theoretical basis for distributive and/or procedural justice draw on John Rawls' structural conception of justice rather than other theoretical bases, such as historical entitlements or capabilities.[55] This does not prevent some contributors from criticising his theory, in particular with regard to justice considerations in transboundary or global contexts, whether justice in these contexts should refer to individuals or states. Yet, Rawls' conception of justice and equal opportunity is useful when considering different forms of environmental decision-making, be it a local decision to permit a harmful activity or the use of a natural resource, or an international decision to adopt a global agreement on cutting down greenhouse gases.

The notion of equal opportunities provides a useful starting-point for justice deliberations and a critical input when appraising existing institutions and norms on environmental protection and access to natural resources in general. To be given a voice, or rather an opportunity to voice a concern that is taken into account, is essential from a justice perspective. Depending on the context, this opportunity may refer to marginalised groups of people, whether based on gender, ethnicity, colour or class; to poor communities, countries or regions; to future generations; and to non-human species. Inclusion matters for justice, and there can be no distributive justice without procedural/participatory justice. As revealed by this volume, however, core legal conceptions and institutions, such as state borders, but also structures of legal discourse, political power, and ignorance may block interests and issues from being sufficiently taken into account in environmental decision-making.

In different ways, the contributions also highlight the distributive effects and aspects of environmental law from a justice perspective. Thus, all analyses concerning global environmental arrangements (climate change, ozone layer depletion and desertification) point at the importance of distributive justice considerations in the different treaty negotiations. Distributive justice is also a core concern in some of the conceptual chapters as well as in the studies on state borders and sovereignty, corporate activities and access to natural resources.

Certain issues are covered only slightly by this volume, such as the connection between justice and human and animal rights in environmental contexts,[56] and several regions, environmental concerns and uses of natural resources remain to be further studied from a justice perspective. Yet, when put together, the contributions provide a robust line of thought with regard to procedural, distributive and corrective aspects of environmental law. They also confirm the value of critically appraising existing rules,

---

[55] For a reference to some of these conceptions, see note 7 above.

[56] See Bosselmann 2004, who criticises mainstream liberal justice conceptions for failing to include concerns for 'ecological justice'. Environmental justice in relation to non-human species is discussed e.g. in Cooper and Palmer 1995. See also Nussbaum 2006, pp. 325–407, arguing that non-human species should be part of justice considerations beyond 'compassion and humanity'.

principles, institutions and concepts of environmental law from a justice perspective, and the usefulness of such an approach to guide social change.

Bibliography

Anand, R., 2004. *International Environmental Justice: A North–South Dimension*. Aldershot: Ashgate.

Bosselmann, K., 2006. 'Ecological Justice and Law', in B. J. Richardson and S. Wood (eds.), *Environmental Law for Sustainability*. Oxford and Portland, OR: Hart Publishers, 129.

Bosselmann, K., and Richardson, B. J. (eds.), 1998. *Environmental Justice and Market Mechanisms: Key Challenges for Environmental Law and Policy*. The Hague, London and New York: Kluwer Law International.

Brown Weiss, E., 1989. *In Fairness to Future Generations: International Law, Patrimony and Intergenerational Equity*. Dobbs Ferry, NY: Transnational Publishers.

Bullard, R. D., 1998–9. 'Levelling the Playing Field through Environmental Justice', 23 *Vermont Law Review* 453.

Caney, S., 2005. 'Cosmopolitan Justice, Responsibility and Global Climate Change', 18 *Leiden Journal of International Law* 747.

Cooper, D. E., and Palmer, J. A. (eds.), 1995. *Just Environments: Intergenerational, International and Interspecies Issues*. London and New York: Routledge.

Cullet, Ph., 2003. *Differential Treatment in International Environmental Law*. Aldershot: Ashgate.

Ebbesson, J., 1997. 'The Notion of Public Participation in International Environmental Law', 8 *Yearbook of International Environmental Law* 51.

Lazarus, R. J., 2000. '"Environmental Racism! That's What It Is"', *University of Illinois Law Review* 255.

Nozick, R., 1974. *Anarchy, State and Utopia*. New York: Basic Book Publishers.

Nussbaum, M., 2006. *Frontiers of Justice: Disability, Nationality, Species Membership*. Cambridge, MA: Harvard University Press.

Rawls, J., 1972. *A Theory of Justice*. Oxford: Oxford University Press.

Sen, A., 1999. *Development as Freedom*. New York: Anchor Books.

Shrader-Frechette, K., 2002. *Environmental Justice: Creating Equality, Reclaiming Democracy*. New York: Oxford University Press.

PART I

The notion of justice in environmental law

The second cycle of ecological urgency: an environmental justice perspective

RICHARD FALK

1 Ecological urgency and environmental justice: two views

There has for several years existed a growing consensus among experts that a circumstance of ecological urgency on a global scale exists. What is new and potentially hopeful, is the rapidly increasing public acceptance of the reality of this urgency, at least with respect to climate change, and a resulting willingness of politicians across the political spectrum to put environmental protection high on their agenda. Encouraging as this is from the perspective of prospects for action, it could still produce a variety of regressive results if the impacts of policy adjustment fall heavily on the poor and vulnerable, and even more invisibly on future generations. It is crucial to bring environmental justice concerns in from the shadow lands of concern where they have long been consigned.

Without assessing the *substantive* character of ecological urgency on which there exists some divergence of opinion, Gus Speth and Peter Haas in their book *Global Environmental Governance* formulate a three-part conclusion that seems beyond controversy: (1) the conditions relating to the global environment are worsening; (2) current responses to address these conditions are grossly insufficient; and (3) major new initiatives are needed that address the root causes.[1]

The identification of root causes remains, although to a diminishing degree, somewhat contested, at least as far as selecting the primary explanation of this set of disturbing circumstances, and what to do about it. Among prominent participants in the recent phase of debate on environmental policy, Lester Brown continues to focus on anticipated population increases in the decades ahead putting an unacceptable strain on food supplies, although his latest prescriptions for policy are of a more comprehensive character;[2] Gus Speth emphasizes the continuing reliance on destructive technologies, especially with respect to energy; and Paul and Ann Ehrlich call attention to the wasteful burdens on the environment associated with consumerism (that is, consuming more than is related to a satisfying life defined in moderate terms).[3] Overall, the greatest convergence of concern about environmental conditions involves

---

[1] Speth and Haas 2006 at 139.   [2] Brown 2006.   [3] Ehrlich and Ehrlich 2004.

the adverse effects of climate changing trends, and the growing pressure to establish stringent controls on greenhouse gas emissions, especially of carbon dioxide. Two highly respected reports based on scrutiny of the evidence by leading scientists have gone a long way to resolve any fundamental sense of uncertainty about the acute threats to planetary well-being posed by anticipated levels of global warming over the course of the next several decades.[4]

Notable in all of these assessments is the scant attention given to the bearing of fairness or justice on either the diagnosis of the environmental challenge or its cure. The tendency of environmentalists is to focus on their sense of what is causing the problems, and offer prescriptions designed to mitigate or end the perceived threat. This inattention to the justice perspective tends to benefit the rich and powerful, as well as those currently alive, and to accentuate the burdens and grievances of the poor and marginal, and the unborn. To ignore the extent to which the inequalities of life circumstances in the world are associated with avoiding the externalities of modern industrial life and warfare is not only unfair, but tends to aggravate *national* and *geopolitical* tensions of a North/South character, as well as *class* and *race/ethnic* tensions within particular states. The relevance of these geopolitical tensions is particularly neglected in environmental policy-making circles, but it is evident from patterns of contemporary warfare, which is seldom focused upon battlefield encounters of opposing armies.[5] These tensions have their most pronounced effects on the vulnerable civilian members of a society, as well as perversely on some of the already most blighted and stressed regions in the world, especially sub-Saharan Africa. For instance, the destruction of the water purification system in Iraq during the first Gulf War or the destruction of an electric power plant in Gaza during an Israeli military offensive in the summer of 2006 resulted in environmental degradation that was especially harmful to the health and well-being of the already extremely poor and vulnerable Gazan population.

To be sure, rhetorical acknowledgments are frequently made that *humane* global governance is a precondition to gain the sort of international cooperation that is required if a sustainable environment is ever to be achieved.[6] Speth and Haas, for instance, conclude their book by invoking the following sentiment expressed in the Earth Charter: 'We must join together to bring forth a sustainable global society founded on respect for universal human rights, economic justice, and a culture of peace.'[7] To similar effect is the assertion by Robert Nadeau, in his important book

---

[4] *Climate Change 2007*; Stern 2007. For a less technical assessment see McKibbon 2007 at 44–5.
[5] Kaldor 1999; Shaw 2005.
[6] There is an alternative conception of *inhumane* global governance resting on coercive control of behaviour, and often associated with the establishment of a global empire under the control of the United States. In contrast, *humane* forms of global governance assume voluntary patterns of adjustment made explicit and formal by law-making treaties and given operational relevance by the development of institutional arrangements of various sorts. For elaboration see Falk 1995.
[7] Speth and Haas 2006 at 150.

The Environmental Endgame, that 'any realistic and pragmatic assessment of what will be required to resolve the crisis in the global environment clearly indicates that the gross inequalities between the lives of the haves and have-nots on this planet are not commensurate with the terms of human survival'.[8]

In this respect there are justice concerns expressed both expedientially, that is, to provide a realistic and pragmatic foundation for problem-solving, and ethically, to validate a dynamic of drastic adjustment. For instance, Nadeau insists that 'achieving the goal of a sustainable global environment will require that material flows in industrialized economies be reduced by 90%, or by a factor of ten'.[9] With adjustments of this magnitude, it is difficult to envision how social and ethical considerations can be brought to bear, or indeed how democratic procedures can be maintained. If the circumstances really do require such drastic adjustments, we may already be in the position anticipated decades ago by Garrett Hardin that only austere authoritarian politics can manage the challenge of transition to a sustainable environment, with considerations of justice pushed far into the background.[10] What is clear is that, to the extent that adjustments can be fashioned in an atmosphere of *choice* rather than *necessity*, the prospects for humane and democratic transition are improved. Of course, the boundaries between choice and necessity are blurred and contested, and even interrelated.

Whether we are already situated within the domain of necessity depends on how seriously the present situation is regarded from the perspective of environmental sustainability and the carrying capacity of the earth. The collective imagination of the peoples of the planet, and especially the governing elites, remains in a circumstance of deep denial with respect to the overall scale of the environmental challenge, although under growing pressure as the extent of the threat is validated by evidence and a more attuned public opinion. Nevertheless, the predominant mood remains one of denial and contradiction, increasingly acknowledging the problems and yet still unwilling to demand major changes in the policies that are responsible for the growing menace. This dangerous, multi-faceted condition of denial is accentuated by special interests, especially associated with overseas corporate operations and governmental complicity, by the hostility of neoliberal ideology to regulation, and by the geopolitical preoccupations and distractions on comparatively minor issues of immediacy that remain the characteristic focus of major state actors. The regressive leadership role of the United States early in the twenty-first century is nowhere more detrimental to the global public good than with respect to environmental policy. Without strong institutions of global governance, the quality of the world order remains, for better or worse, dependent on the outlook and priorities of those shaping the policies of leading sovereign states. The role of the United States as global leader has become

---

[8] Nadeau 2006 at 172.   [9] Nadeau 2006 at 177.
[10] For classic argument along these lines see Hardin 1968.

increasingly controversial since the collapse of the Soviet Union in 1991, particularly during the Bush presidency that commenced in 2001.[11]

It is important to couple the overall issue of denial with respect to the ecological condition of the planet with normative questions raised by the suffering specifically associated with environmental injustice.[12] At present, in most of the environmental literature the two concerns (protection and justice) are effectively *decoupled*. It is true that each orientation pays lip service to the other, but not in a policy relevant manner. That is, those alarmed principally about environmental unsustainability argue that to restore conditions of sustainability requires attention to poverty and a commitment to human rights for all persons, but the preoccupation is with 'fixes' of various kinds, especially in pricing for the market to include environmental costs and technologies that operate more benignly with respect to pollution and toxic wastes. The challenges of distributive justice relating to the environmental agenda are essentially ignored.[13]

Similarly, those who have tried to raise the environmental justice issue in the last decade or so have understandably focused on bringing their concerns about environmental injustice to the fore. This effort has necessarily been preoccupied with a variety of *local* sites of *activist* struggle where global and national capital has been deployed to build dams or nuclear power plants, or to dump toxic wastes, or to mine uranium, or to site polluting industries, or to neglect contaminated water and air. As a result, the bigger, global picture of environmental degradation and the earth's carrying capacity are bracketed, and are not being given the attention they require.[14]

What seems of great ethical and political importance at this time is to insist on the inclusion of environmental justice assessments and prescription in the wider dialogue on global environmental policy, and, at the same time, to encourage environmental analysts to bring environmental justice priorities as well as fairness to unborn generations into their scenarios for a future condition of environmental sustainability. Planning for a sustainable future is what Lester Brown dubs 'Plan B' to distinguish it from the prevailing 'Plan A', business as usual, but of course there are an almost unlimited number of potential candidates for Plan B, and the ones that I am advocating treat environmental justice goals as inseparable from environmental sustainability goals.[15]

There is a second disconnect that also is not accorded the attention it deserves by either of these two perspectives: that is, the growing energy squeeze, relating to

---

[11] Among the many critiques of US global leadership see Johnson 2006; Brzezinski 2004; for a more constructive assessment see Held 2004.

[12] Bullard 2005 at 281–2 summarizes the harmful impact on the poor and ethnically marginalized.

[13] See Nadeau 2006 on need to connect justice and ecological policy; a good example of the more typical tendency to approach the ecological challenge without regard to social issues is Brown 2006.

[14] For overview see Bullard 2005; also, see Broad and Cavanagh 1993.   [15] See Brown 2006 at ix–xii.

petroleum supplies and prices, as a world order dimension of the present setting.[16] James Howard Kunstler's challenging book is essentially about the deep dislocations likely to afflict America, but his assessments have global implications, as well as help explain the geopolitical struggles for the control of oil reserves in the Middle East. It is amusing to notice that the big oil companies are trying to get on this ecological bandwagon; BP proclaims in recent TV ads that its vaunted initials now stand for 'Beyond Petroleum'!! At this point, the immediate environmental justice effects are pronounced: higher energy costs impact most heavily on the poor, especially those living near subsistence levels, although in some instances the very poor cannot afford energy at any price, and are not therefore adversely affected by the recent rapid rise of fuel costs. From a strictly environmental perspective, the rising price of oil greatly encourages investment in alternative energy technologies, but it also diverts agricultural land into more profitable bioenergetic uses, foreshadowing food shortages, rising food prices, and famines that would again most certainly disproportionately harm the poor. So far, although I suspect not for long, neither of these two types of environmentalists has given sufficient attention to the emergent challenge of planning a transition to a post-petroleum world, and even Kunstler does not worry enough about the *global* side of this profound challenge to the affluent modern world associated with a seemingly fixed supply of oil in the face of dramatic expansions in demand from such fast growing giants as China and India.

The third disconnect involves war and militarism in the early part of this new century. What has been called 'asymmetric warfare' now dominates the global stage, and is currently exemplified by the long war in Iraq and the thirty-four-day Lebanon War initiated by Israel during the summer of 2006.[17] The high-tech side in twenty-first century wars relies on its formidable capabilities to destroy the infrastructure of the 'enemy' that is dispersed throughout the society. This form of warfare is directed primarily at the civilian population, especially in countries of the South, producing great suffering among the poorest sectors of such a society, largely as a result of environmental damage to water and food supplies, producing massive outbreaks of disease, shortages and in the end heavy civilian casualties, especially among the young and infirm. Also, the targeted areas are environmentally deteriorated by attacks in a number of ways that have not yet been reliably established, but include widespread use of depleted uranium armour and warheads that appears to induce radioactive illness, and have long-lasting health effects.

From these preliminary remarks, then, several conclusions emerge:

- The character of environmental justice should be understood in relation to distributive inequities associated with race and class, as well as with respect to the injustices visited on non-Western societies as a result of colonial and post-colonial

---

[16] The inevitability of a catastrophic future is starkly presented by Kunstler 2005.
[17] For a discussion of the Lebanon War see Falk and Bali 2006 at 34–41.

practices, and in relation to the persisting failure of present political actors to take responsibility for the life circumstances of future generations.

- To promote environmental justice it is necessary to take specific account of current and anticipated inequities in framing recommendations for environmental reform on all levels of social order, as well as in relation to the future.
- To ground the environmental justice dialogue about policy options, it is necessary to give attention to the energy squeeze as it affects the poor, the non-Western world, and future generations.
- Geopolitical circumstances need to be taken into account in assessing environmental injustice, including the grossly disproportionate current investment in extremely wasteful and dysfunctional military forms of security, especially by the United States. It is also necessary to take account of the civilian and environmental impacts of the most prominent modes of contemporary warfare: that is, asymmetric warfare in which high-tech air, land and sea power, along with missiles and artillery, are characteristically used against non-state adversaries armed with light weaponry, but relying on well-conceived tactics to inflict major physical and symbolic harm on powerful state actors or to mount resistance to a belligerent occupation that has been based on military superiority.

2 The first cycle of ecological urgency

The first cycle of ecological urgency can be located for convenience in the period between 1972, the date of the UN Stockholm Conference on the Human Environment and the publication of *The Limits to Growth* study of the Club of Rome, and the Earth Summit of 1992.[18] In this period, environmentalism took off as a grassroots movement, as a subject for serious academic study and controversy, and as a stimulus for transnational grassroots activism. It was an exciting period of rising public consciousness and mobilization, perhaps epitomized by the prominence of Greenpeace as an organizational presence and the founding of green political parties, especially in Europe. But it was also a time for retrenchment of powerful vested corporate and governmental interests, for Promethean reaffirmations of the capacity of technological innovations to overcome whatever harm could be attributed to the role of technology as the engine of human progress. The environmental movement was effectively accused of 'crying wolf', using 'scare tactics', and advocating policies of environmental protection that were insensitive to the developmental aspirations of the poor nationally and globally. Environmentalism was initially derided as a superfluous, hysterical movement of elitists in the affluent North who cared only about preserving their vacation wilderness haunts and their affection for exotic animals, and were oblivious to the dependence of the poorest of the poor on robust economic growth.

---

[18] See also Goldsmith *et al.* 1972; Commoner 1972; and my own effort, Falk 1972.

There were important elements of truth in this critique, mixed with a dogmatic and cynical neoliberal optimism that refused to be shaken by the facts. There is no doubt that this first cycle of awareness was initially insensitive to the three broad concerns of environmental justice depicted above. At the same time, as the Stockholm Conference illustrated, it was overly sensitive to geopolitical concerns, keeping the impact of war on the environment off its agenda because the United States did not want to deal with accusations that its modes of warfare in Vietnam were environmentally destructive, and additional influential states did not want to deal with environmental objections to the continuing testing of nuclear weapons. The official name of the 1972 Stockholm Conference was the Stockholm Conference on the Human Environment. It was a huge success in at least two respects: providing an arena for NGO activism as a counter to the immobility, formalism and geopolitics of the UN intergovernmental approach dominated by Westphalian canons of protocol; and as a learning experience for governments around the world about the dependence of their future prospects for sustainable development and eventual prosperity upon a more attentive and knowledgeable approach to environmental issues.

Stockholm was also a rude awakening to an impending North/South clash on global environmental policy. This encounter was more bitter than necessary due to the failure of the conference organizers to anticipate the objections of non-Western countries to several environmental challenges, which, if directly addressed, would appear to imperil the highest priority of the countries of the South, namely, rapid economic growth achieved in the face of existing circumstances that highlighted uneven development, accompanied by dramatic disparities in standards of living. For developing countries, recently freed from the shackles of colonialism, it seemed dangerously threatening to discuss, much less to constrain, future development by an expensive regime of regulation focused on polluting technologies. From the perspectives of the South, it seemed that the industrialized countries of the North had already reaped the economic benefits of these polluting technologies, making the curtailment of their availability at this point shut the gate on the South in relation to their delayed pursuit of developmental goals. Representatives from the South expressed their anger and anxiety in the form of a non-negotiable claim: that the countries of the South were entitled, without interference, to cause whatever pollution was necessary to go forward with programmes of rapid development. Part of the distress arose from the perception that environmentalism was emerging as a way to shackle the formerly colonized world in conditions of permanent backwardness and mass poverty while the colonial powers went about stabilizing their circumstances of affluence.

In the years following the conference, both sides of this Stockholm debate moderated their positions somewhat to enable a measure of forward progress. No major international initiative addressing environmental concerns was held after Stockholm that did not include the word 'development' in its title, amounting to a conceptual recognition that environmental protection needed at every step to be fully reconciled with developmental goals. In the 1992 Rio Earth Summit, for instance, the title of the meeting was 'The UN Summit on Environment and Development'. This was a way of signalling the Third World that their objections to Stockholm had been registered. The Rio approach was prefigured by the influential Brundtland Commission report that also recognized the importance of bringing concerns about environmental justice into the policy mix, offering the memorable emotional observation that poverty was the worst form of pollution.[19] The report proposed doing this in two major ways: by ensuring that development concerns were taken into full account when assessing environmental challenges and recommending policy responses. Rio adhered to these rhetorical guidelines but it was notable through its reformulation of the essence of the environmental threat as no longer being one of pollution. It was at Rio that global attention was for the first time seriously focused on the emergent dangers of climate change due to global warming, as well as the importance for the sake of development and future generations to take urgent steps to protect biodiversity. The Rio conference also exhibited three other crucial trends: first, the increasing influence of global civil society as evidenced by the participation of thousands of NGO representatives and delegations, as well as their greater impact on the media; and, secondly, through the visible participation of world business in the work and funding of the conference, seeking to convey the impression that a convergence of interests between market forces and environmental protection existed; and, thirdly, the stridently regressive leadership of the United States, as expressed by the notorious pre-conference assertion by then President George H. W. Bush who failed to attend but sent a disheartening message that 'the American way of life is not negotiable' that continues to resonate among critics of the US approach to global environmental concerns. American anti-environmentalism was carried to brash new heights by the second President Bush, including a very public and denunciatory rejection of the Kyoto Protocol. This is not a politically partisan point as neither political party has distinguished itself with respect to the environment, although overt hostility to the environmental agenda is more clearly associated with the Republican affinity with business interests and their ideological championship of autonomous markets minimally regulated. Given the general atmosphere in the United States ever since the end of the Cold War supportive of neoliberal capitalism, a Democratic president would not have been able to gain the level of support in the US Senate that would be needed to ratify even the minimalist treaty negotiated at Kyoto to restrict the emission of greenhouse gasses, and, until very recently, even an attempt would seem futile.

Environmental justice concerns surfaced by stages during this first cycle, and became more or less influential in a variety of international policy arenas, including the World Bank and the IMF.[20] There is no doubt that the Third World encounter with environmentalism had a dual character during this period. At first, as indicated,

---

[19] Report of the World Commission on Environment and Development. *Our Common Future*. New York: Oxford, especially at 1–23 and 118–46.
[20] Rich 1994.

the main response was an undifferentiated opposition to any kind of environmental checks on developmental priorities. But later on, especially at local levels where large development projects were being situated, successive waves of environmental activism swept through the Third World, and were often mixed with the protection of poor peoples' traditional habitats from environmental destruction.[21] Environmentalists in the South also struggled against corporate practices in their countries and opposed government arrangements that called for the dumping of toxic wastes from developed countries.

At the same time, there was beginning to be attention given in the North to environmental justice issues, especially a growing realization that the heaviest immediate burdens of environmental abuse were being experienced by the most vulnerable members of society and that the life prospects of future generations were being irresponsibly jeopardized and burdened for the sake of maximizing present prospects for economic growth.[22]

The first cycle of awareness did raise consciousness, and built some political momentum for making certain intergovernmental policy adjustments that were protective of the global environment (e.g. ozone layer) without imposing very heavy costs on market forces. Most governments in the South, as well as the North, came to appreciate the relevance of environmental concerns to their public policy goals, and created a new bureaucratic niche for environmental advisors. And social activists built on their effectiveness in raising environmental consciousness on a number of fronts. These civil society actors understood the necessity of maintaining as much public awareness as possible to offset environmentally detrimental activism associated particularly with amply funded and well-situated corporate and military pressure groups. Perhaps, the most ambitious civil society undertaking, and its most notable success, was to mount a worldwide campaign in opposition to the atmospheric testing of nuclear weapons, especially in the oceans. Greenpeace played a leading role, especially its imaginative symbolic resistance to French nuclear tests in the Pacific. The French government was so distressed by this campaign that it actually engaged in lethal sabotage against the Greenpeace vessel, *The Rainbow Warrior*, in 1985 while the ship was docked in the harbour at Auckland, New Zealand.[23] This unfortunate incident was by no means the last deaths associated with the struggle by citizens and civil society organizations to protect the people of the planet from environmental health hazards. The justice dimension of these encounters is obscure and contested with respect to global impact; there is no doubt that those living near nuclear test sites

[21] See Broad and Cavanagh 1993; Shiva 1992; Shiva 1995.

[22] Weiss 1989. On which see Mickelson, Chapter 15 in this volume.

[23] Gidley and Shears 1985. Also UNSCEAR, GAOR, 17, Session Suppl. No. 16 (A/5216) (1962), para. 7. See also the oral and written arguments of Australia and New Zealand in the *Nuclear Tests Cases* brought against France, *Nuclear Tests Cases* (1978) ICJ Pleadings, Volumes I and II; New Zealand Ministry of Foreign Affairs and Trade, *French Nuclear Testing in the South Pacific* (Wellington, 1996). For the French legal arguments see Comité Interministeriel pour l'information, *Livre Blanc sur les Experiments Nucleaires* (Paris, 1973).

are exposed to radiation hazards, but whether low-level radiation inflicts worldwide health hazards remains controversial.

The first cycle wound down for a series of reasons: a well-orchestrated backlash organized by business was promoted by the mainstream media and very influential with the public; some environmentally responsible policies were implemented, creating the misleading impression that governments were now sufficiently alert to environmental dangers to restore confidence in further industrial development; the doomsday predictions made by first cycle activists did not materialize in the form of worldwide famine, increasing urban pollution, and resource shortages.[24] The supposed 'population bomb' failed to explode. The carrying capacity of the earth seemed up to the challenge, and environmental optimists mounted a counter-attack.[25] Green political parties lost ground by not being able to address the spectrum of societal concerns in a credible manner, and by having their rhetoric and part of their proposal adopted by the mainstream. Other issues seemed more urgent to ethically sensitive civil society actors. There was growing concern about and opposition to the exploitative impacts of economic globalization, which were definitely widening the gaps between rich and poor within and among countries. There were also worries associated with American primacy in world politics after the end of the Cold War and the collapse of the Soviet Union. In the end, it is possible to conclude that, during this first cycle of ecological urgency, a robust environmental movement was generated, but that it lacked sufficient depth and perseverance to counter continuing and shifting patterns of environmental deterioration. Thus this first cycle came to a grinding halt without countering the most severe threats posed by the impact of human activities on the environment.

3 The second cycle of ecological urgency

In the first years of the twenty-first century, there were crucial shifts in the perception of ecological urgency as compared to the first cycle. Furthermore, public attention had diminished considerably, certainly at governmental levels, but also among the general public. There were some voices in the wilderness repeating environmental warnings, especially with respect to climate change causing global warming, polar melting, extreme weather, droughts and coastal flooding. And there were a variety of high-profile local issues (particular dams, power plants, nuclear facilities, toxic dumps) and specific events (tsunamis, extreme storms) that encouraged activism and media interest, but there were no high-profile comprehensive critiques of the sort that aroused widespread public interest of the sort that existed at the start of the first cycle.

---

[24] Meadows *et al.* 1972, which gave the world a mere decade to reverse course or experience the collapse of industrial civilization, and misleadingly claimed the authority of a large data set analyzed by a powerful computer program.

[25] Among those who were scornful of environmentalists who sounded alarms were Julian Simon. See Myers and Simon 1984; also Crichton 2004.

But this mood of complacency began to change in about 2003. There were renewals of an apocalyptic concern in popular culture such as the film 'The Day After Tomorrow' depicting the onset of a new ice age. At first, these ecological alarms were shrugged off as 'science fiction' or assimilated as entertainment. Rising energy prices and authoritative warnings about the human basis of climate change started to create a new political receptivity to the imposition of governmental restrictions on private sector behaviour. This mood has seemed to be most attuned to the need for urgent action within the framework of the European Union, which has only recently tendered a commitment to go beyond the Kyoto constraints on carbon emissions, and go even further if the other principal industrial powers will join with them.

Overall, attitudes of complacency have been difficult to displace, and have remained prevalent in the United States. In a sophisticated series of comprehensive reports prepared by the National Intelligence Council in Washington, DC, and closely related to CIA and other influential sectors of American society, environmental concerns were at the margins, while issues of environmental justice were either missing altogether, or were touched upon indirectly. For example, in the report 'Global Trends 2010', it was acknowledged, with elaboration, that more than three billion people will be living in what was described as 'water-stressed regions' in the South. In the 2004 'Mapping the Global Future: Report of the NIC's 2020 Project', environmental issues were modestly flagged as more likely to demand attention from policy-makers and pose what were called 'ethical dilemmas', but there was no consideration of whether or not environmental justice should be a policy goal. The report prepared by a large group of social scientists and policy analysts called attention to four world futures that they believed represented the most likely outcomes of present global trends. They were named 'Davos World', 'Pax Americana', 'A New Caliphate' and 'Cycle of Fear', to call to the mind of readers their principal characteristic. It seems remarkable that such an exercise failed to put forward a plausible fifth scenario ('Ecological Chaos') stressing issues of ecological urgency that are quite capable of fundamentally altering the political landscape in the next decade or so. It seems quite likely that rising anxiety about climate change has already had a sufficient impact on public consciousness so that think-tanks contemplating the future now could not overlook the potential central relevance of the environmental policy agenda, especially in the aftermath of highly respected and authoritative reports of a rather strong consensus within the scientific community.[26]

There is a rapidly emerging consciousness that the unresolved issues of environmental sustainability will produce severe adverse consequences if further ignored. The worst of the ecological problems, even at this point, may not be any longer remedied at acceptable costs. The widespread positive reaction to the grim message of the film 'An Inconvenient Truth', starring Al Gore and winning an Academy Award, is one

[26] See the reports cited at note 4 above.

expression of this rising curve of revived environmental concern within the popular culture. There are two clusters of environmental issues that are in the process of overcoming the period of ecological complacency that followed the first cycle of ecological urgency: climate change, including its multiple serious secondary effects on ocean levels, polar ice caps, extreme weather, desertification, petroleum supply squeeze and the desperate search for a viable post-petroleum energy policy. Both challenges are daunting in their complexity, and require massive adjustments in a relatively short period of time. It is difficult to suppose that such a process of adjustment will take place except in a top-down manner, and then only in an atmosphere of planetary emergency. If this were to happen, it would almost certainly be accompanied by a variety of stringent restrictions on general consumption, lifestyle and free choice that burdened ordinary people, especially the poor, far more than elites. Unless the call for environmental justice becomes part of the ethos of democratic societies, and is treated as an essential and inalienable human right of every person, patterns of unfairness will almost certainly be reproduced, and undoubtedly accentuated, as conditions of scarcity become so acute that harsh forms of rationing will need to be introduced.[27]

Comparing the second cycle to the first is instructive. In the first cycle, the stress was on the interaction between population, resources and pollution, making the collapse of modern industrial civilization appear as an almost inevitable outcome of a failure to make radical adjustments in modes of industrial production and in projected demographic trends.[28] There were concerns about resource depletion, including hydrocarbons, but more so in the vein of anticipated shifts to coal with its greater polluting impact. In the second cycle, the emphasis is more on restricting carbon emissions without further delays and hastening a transition to a post-petroleum economy, especially with respect to transport and living arrangements.[29] So far, the environmental warnings issued by scientists and through the impact of extreme weather events, as well as by the dramatic rise in the price of oil, have certainly registered rhetorically with the public or political leaders, but as yet without any serious tangible moves designed to minimize the environmental and human damage. And, to the extent that attentive citizens are growing increasingly concerned about these threats, they are not paying much discernible attention to the justice dimensions except possibly to take note of North/South implications. Of course, past international environmental negotiations have taken some account of the dynamics of uneven development, or else a consensus on policy and behaviour cannot be achieved. At Kyoto, this acknowledgment produced a graduated scale of differentiated obligations that recognized the developmental claims of the South. This approach was also critically invoked by the

---

[27] See Revkin 2007 at 1 and 6.   [28] For first cycle arguments see the books cited in notes 14 and 19 above.
[29] See Kunstler 2005 for a detailed presentation, although mainly preoccupied with the challenge as experienced in the United States.

United States and some other rich countries to bolster their insistence that the negotiated arrangements decided upon at Kyoto were unfair and unrealistic and did not
deserve their respect. No attention was given to the three other justice dimensions:
diminishing disproportionate burdens on the poor and marginal; protection of future
generations; diminishing the costs of militarism and war.

4 Conclusions

Addressing the second cycle of ecological urgency at this stage calls for careful thought
and societal action, including a consciousness-raising public discourse that incorporates an integral concern with rendering environmental justice. This discourse needs
to delve deeply into structural constraints on policy that arise from special interests
entrenched in government and the private sector, as well as explore the whole spectrum
of policy proposals that call for fundamental shifts in lifestyle, budgetary priorities
and market regulation. The following recommended steps intend to contribute to the
formation of such a discourse:

- Massive public education, including via the mechanisms of popular culture such as
  film, music and comic books, that conveys an understanding of both the dangers
  arising from global trends relating to the environment, and the importance of
  addressing these dangers in a manner sensitive to the claims of environmental
  justice.
- Unprecedented lifestyle adjustments on a societal scale in the high energy consuming
  countries of the world. John Lanchester writes provocatively that '[t]he remarkable
  thing is that most of the things we need to do to prevent climate change are
  clear in their outline. We need to insulate our houses, on a massive scale; find an
  effective form of taxing the output of carbon; spend a fortune on both building
  and researching renewable energy and DC power [high voltage energy transmission
  cables]; spend another fortune on nuclear power; double or treble our spending on
  public transportation; do everything to curb the growth of air travel; and investigate
  what we need to do to defend ourselves if the sea rises, or if food imports collapse.'[30]
- Governmental pressure to induce a more responsible treatment of the global environmental agenda by the mainstream media throughout the world. The emergence
  of so-called 'green hawks', retired military commanders, linking future national security concerns with environmental failure, is beginning to mainstream the importance
  of response in line with geopolitical priorities. The recognition that the countries
  with least capacity to cope with environmental harm are likely to be hardest hit, and
  susceptible to extremist politics is both leading to a rethinking of the cosmopolitan

[30] Lanchester 2007 at 3–9.

nature of nature security, but also insinuates environmental justice concerns, even if only with pragmatic motivations.[31]

- A UN world conference devoted to the second cycle of environmental urgency, with attention to environmental justice as an imperative for transition to environmental sustainability. One dimension of this attention is the degree to which the adverse impacts of climate change has had on low carbon-emitting regions, including upsetting delicate ethnic balances in poor and traditional African countries. There is a new appreciation in this regard that the terrible ordeal of Darfur in the last several years may be mostly attributable to droughts in the mid-1980s that disrupted relations between nomadic herders and crop-raising farmers. As Stephan Faris writes in an important article, '[t]o truly understand the crisis in Darfur – and it has been profoundly misunderstood' – you need to take account of this pattern of causation, which also raises the equity question as to whether the West should be deemed *responsible* for tragedies of the Darfur variety rather than to ponder its degree of philanthropic good will.[32]

- Demilitarization, especially by the United States, with a goal of 1 per cent of GNP as the ceiling for expenditures, adopting the Japanese approach that is written into their constitution. At this stage, the massive American over-investment in a military machine that is mostly unusable constitutes the worst misappropriation of resources in human history, and effectively precludes serious attention to the ecological agenda. At present, within the United States, and to a lesser extent within most states, the embeddedness of the military budget is not subject to political debate.

- Long-term mapping of environmental options and alternative futures by governments, international institutions, civil society actors and private sector actors.

- Appropriate emphasis by civil society actors, including religious institutions, on environmental justice alongside environmental sustainability.

- Inter-civilizational and intra-civilizational dialogues on environmental justice and the future.

This enumeration of steps to be taken is a mixture of feasible educative and consciousness-raising initiatives and rather utopian behavioural adjustments that currently seem both politically unattainable yet essential if serious responses are to be fashioned in the coming decade or so. It is this intermixing of perspectives that is the origin of the opening phase of the second cycle of ecological urgency. It is both an awakening to the urgency and a deflection of its radical implications. Such a phase is likely to give way in the years ahead to a more dedicated political programme of response. Mixing optimism and pessimism, the reality of ecological urgency is likely to be felt too directly in the near future to allow for the resurfacing of an ethos of complacency. Yet, whether the deepening of concern will also exhibit sensitivity to

---

[31] See Report of the Military Advisory Board of the CNA Corporation. *National Security and the Threat of Climate Change.* For a more popular discussion from a civilian perspective see Esterbrook 2007 at 52–64.
[32] Faris 2007 at 67–9.

considerations of environmental justice will depend on the dedicated and activist efforts of persons throughout the planet who regard the challenge as ethical as well as ecological.

Bibliography

Broad, R., and Cavanagh, J., 1993. *Plundering Paradise: The Struggle for the Environment in the Philippines*. Berkeley, CA: University of California Press.

Brown, L. R., 2006. *Plan B 2.0: Rescuing a Planet under Stress and a Civilization in Trouble*. New York: Norton.

Brzezinski, Z., 2004. *The Choice: Global Domination or Global Leadership*. New York: Basic Books.

Bullard, R. B., 2005. *Environmental Justice: Human Rights and the Politics of Pollution*. San Francisco: Sierra Club.

Commoner, B., 1972. *The Closing Circle: Confronting the Environmental Crisis*. London: Cape.

Climate Change 2007: The Physical Science Basis: Summary for Policymakers, Contribution of Working Group I to the Fourth Assessment Report of the Intergovernmental Panel on Climate Change, IPCC.

Crichton, M., 2004. *State of Fear: A Novel*. New York: HarperCollins.

Ehrlich, P., and Ehrlich, A., 2004. *One with Nineveh: Politics, Consumption and the Human Future*. Washington, DC: Island Press.

Esterbrook, G., 2007. 'Global Warming: Who Loses – Who Wins?'. *The Atlantic*.

Falk, R., 1972. *This Endangered Planet: Prospects and Proposals for Human Survival*. New York: Random House.

 1995. *On Humane Governance: Toward a New Global Politics*. Cambridge: Polity.

Falk, R., and Bali, A., 2006. 'International Law at the Vanishing Point', in R. Khalidi and N. Hovsepian (eds.), *The War on Lebanon: A Reader*. Northampton, MA: Olive Branch Press, 208.

Faris, S., 2007. 'The Real Roots of Darfur'. *The Atlantic*.

Gidley, I., and Shears, R., 1985. *The Rainbow Warrior Affair*. Sydney: Unwin.

Goldsmith *et al.*, 1972. *A Blueprint for Survival*. London: Tom Stacy.

Hardin, G., 1968. 'The Tragedy of the Commons'. *Science* 162:1243–8.

Held, D., 2004. *Global Covenant: The Social Democratic Alternative to the Washington Consensus*. Cambridge: Polity.

Johnson, C., 2006. *Nemesis: The Last Days of the American Republic*. New York: Metropolitan Books.

Kaldor, M., 1999. *New and Old Wars: Organized Violence in a Global Era*. Cambridge: Polity.

Kunstler, J. H., 2005. *The Long Emergency: Surviving the End of Oil, Climate Change, and Other Converging Catastrophes of the Twenty-First Century*. New York: Grove Press.

Lanchester, J., 2007. 'Hot Air'. *London Review of Books*.

McKibbon, B., 2007. 'Warning of Warming'. *New York Review of Books*.

Meadows *et al.*, 1972. *The Limits to Growth: A Report for the Club of Rome Project on the Predicament of Mankind*. New York: Universe.

Myers, N., and Simon, J., 1984. *Scarcity or Abundance? A Debate on the Environment*. New York: W. W. Norton.

Nadeau, R., 2006. *The Environmental Endgame: Mainstream Economics, Ecological Disaster, and Human Survival*. New Brunswick, NJ: Rutgers University Press.

Report of the Military Advisory Board of the CNA Corporation. 2007. *National Security and the Threat of Climate Change.*

Report of the World Commission on Environment and Development. 1987. *Our Common Future.* New York: Oxford University Press.

Revkin, A. C., 2007. 'Poorest Nations Will Bear the Brunt as World Warms'. *New York Times.*

Rich, B., 1994. *Mortgaging the Earth: The World Bank, Environmental Impoverishment, and the Crisis of Development.* Boston, MA: Beacon.

Shaw, M., 2005. *The New Western Way of War: Risk-Transfer War and Its Crisis in Iraq.* Cambridge: Polity.

Shiva, V., 1992. *Toward Hope: An Ecological Approach to the Future.* New Delhi: Indian National Trust for Art and Cultural Heritage.

　1995. *Captive Minds, Captive Lives: Essays on Ethical and Ecological Implications of Patents on Life.* Dehra Dim, India: Research Foundation for Science, Technology, and Natural Resource Policy.

Speth, J. J., and Haas, P. M., 2006. *Global Environmental Governance.* Washington, DC: Island Press.

Stern, N., 2007. *The Economics of Climate Change: The Stern Review.* Cambridge: Cambridge University Press.

Weiss, E. B., 1989. *In Fairness to Future Generations.* Dobbs Ferry, NY: Transnational.

Describing the elephant: international justice and environmental law

DINAH SHELTON[*]

1 Introduction

In a fable of Aesop, several blind men touch an elephant. Each one comes to a different conclusion about the type of animal it is. One feels the trunk and decides that the elephant is long and thin like a serpent. Another touches the leg and concludes that it is thick and round like a tree. The third strokes the side of the elephant and determines that it is related to the rhinoceros.

Like Aesop's elephant, the term 'international justice' had been described in many, often contradictory ways. One set of authors holds that the term signifies a fundamental source or rationale providing the moral underpinnings from which law emerges. Conversely, other writers posit that international justice is not a source of law, but the ultimate goal or objective to be achieved by legal norms. It has also been presented as an alternative to law, with a meaning akin to fairness or equity. Narrower usages center on (1) legal institutions and procedures for accountability and dispute settlement and (2) the substantive content of international norms regulating the use of state power over persons and resources. To some extent, the different invocations of international justice correspond to classic distinctions between reparative, retributive and distributive justice. Consolidated, the various meanings of international justice can be said to describe an international system of norms, institutions and procedures aimed at maximizing the well-being of present and future inhabitants of the planet. The primary modalities for achieving this goal include allocation and management of scarce resources, restraints on the exercise of power, and enforcement of the rule of law. Efforts to achieve this ideal just world are undertaken in the context of existing nation states, but the objective is not state-centric.[1]

[*] Acknowledgement: An earlier version of this chapter was part of a broader study on international justice prepared at the initiative and with the financial support of the JEHT Foundation, New York.
[1] Robert Keohane goes further, arguing that the evolution of a system of global justice requires the system's transformation from one based on states to one based on the primacy of world government and global citizenship: Keohane 1984. See also Skubik 1986 at 236–7 and 248–51.

Few legal writers who use the term 'international justice' define it. Lea Brilmayer, who does attempt a definition, views international justice as the objective of international law and as being composed of retributive, corrective and distributive justice.[2] Distributive justice is found in the primary aspirations of the international legal system – peace and prosperity, including a fair allocation of resources – while corrective and retributive justice seek to ensure that violators of international law are sanctioned in morally appropriate ways and wrongdoers compensate the victims for the wrongs that have been inflicted.

The following discussion attempts to build on Brilmayer's analysis by examining the various meanings of international justice in the context of environmental protection, primarily through a review of legal literature and references to international justice in treaties and other international texts. Based on these sources, international justice can be seen to comprise three broad categories: morality, equity and law. Different aspects of environmental justice arise under each of them, depending upon whether or not law extensively governs the matter. The principle of common but differentiated responsibilities, for example, is included under the heading of law because it is contained in environmental agreements, although the content and application of the principle may be a matter of equitable adjustment rather than precise legal formulation. Similarly, equitable utilization of shared resources is included as a substantive legal norm, because its content is increasingly detailed in legal instruments that enumerate and impose a set of factors to be balanced in achieving a just result. The proposed classification is by no means definitive.

2 Morality

For centuries, international legal scholars equated international justice with principles of natural law, the moral basis for the development of law.[3] National courts similarly saw positive law as derived from and conforming to 'larger considerations of the public good, of commercial liberality, and of international justice'.[4] In the first decades of the twentieth century, when many scholars and diplomats expressed enthusiasm for the codification of international law as a means to bring more detail and certainty to international obligations,[5] writers continued to evidence a conviction that all positive law emerges from and is inferior to international morality or natural law precepts of justice.[6] The existence of a common reservoir of universal principles

---

[2] Brilmayer 1996.

[3] See e.g. Blackstone 1783 (1978) at 66–67: Philimore 1871 at 20 *et seq.*

[4] *The Henry Eubank*, 11 F. Cas. 1166, 1170 (D. Mass. 1833 (No. 6376); see also *The Blackwall*, 77 US (10 Wall.) 1, 14, 2002 AMC 1808, 1815 (1869).

[5] See e.g. Nys 1911 at 871 and 886; Hershey 1912 at 51–3; Hudson 1928 at 339–50; H. Lauterpacht 1955.

[6] Nys 1911 at 874 (citing German author Karl Gottlob Guenther on the requirement for custom to conform to morality). For a response that 'the law of nature has played its part' and no longer has a role, see Oppenheim 1908 at 327–30. For a historical discussion of the view that natural law is anterior and superior to positive law, see Humphrey 1945.

governing 'civilized nations' and on which the positive law is based was generally accepted.

2.1 The Martens Clause and environmental harm in armed conflict

The view of international justice as a set of moral values which precedes, is superior to, and fills in gaps in the law, is reflected in the Martens Clause:

> Until a more complete code of the laws of war has been issued, the High Contracting Parties deem it expedient to declare that, in cases not included in the Regulations adopted by them, the inhabitants and the belligerents remain under the protection and the rule of the principles of the law of nations, as they result from the usages established among civilized peoples, from *the laws of humanity, and the dictates of the public conscience.*[7]

In the decades following adoption of the Martens Clause, the belief in such common moral values was increasingly challenged by the emergence of new political ideologies and by the actions of some states. In the aftermath of World War II, many saw an even greater need to articulate or reassert the existence of fundamental, higher norms of international justice. The existence of a superstructure or international public order within which law functions, a matter previously implicit among states with a common history and traditions, needed to be made explicit.[8] The increasingly accepted concept of *jus cogens* is one result.

During the past several decades, recourse to international justice as morality has sometimes been necessary or expedient during armed conflict, given gaps in positive law. For example, in 1991 the international community exhibited outrage at Iraq's deliberate attack on Kuwait's environment and natural resources during the invasion. The Security Council reacted with an unprecedented decision announcing that Iraq was liable for all environmental consequences and natural resource depletion resulting from its aggression against Kuwait.[9] The Security Council made no reference to positive law, which is relatively recent and still emerging on liability for environmental harm; its decision can be viewed instead as a matter of international retributive justice, or in part as an affirmation and application of the Martens Clause.

---

[7] Convention (No. IV) Respecting the Laws and Customs of War on Land, with annex of Regulations (The Hague, 18 October 1907), 36 Stat. 2277, TS No. 539, Preamble (emphasis added).

[8] See Silving 1961.

[9] See UN Security Council Resolution 687 (1991) of 8 April 1991, S/RES/687 (1991). The resolution affirmed that Iraq 'is liable under international law for any direct loss, damage – including environmental damage and the depletion of natural resources – . . . as a result of its unlawful invasion and occupation of Kuwait'. *Ibid.*, para. 16. This affirmation, and the establishment of the UN Compensation Commission to ensure reparation for the environmental harm caused by Iraq, are unprecedented in respect to environmental harm during armed conflict. See also the UN General Assembly Resolution on protection of the environment in times of armed conflict, A/RES/47/37 of 25 November 1992, which asserts that 'existing provisions of international law' prohibit wanton destruction of the environment not justified by military necessity. See also Okowa in Chapter 12 of this volume.

2.2 Humanitarian intervention

International justice as morality has been invoked *contra legem* as justification for humanitarian intervention. Some American scholars, in particular, argue that intervention may be illegal yet morally justified and therefore legitimate.[10] John Davenport has proposed the modalities of a new just war theory:

> Whether based on the respect required by common human dignity, or based on the universal charity required by the *imago dei* in all human beings, or on the moral presuppositions of legitimate popular sovereignty, then, just war theory must be part of a broader conception of natural justice that both limits what can be done to persons for the sake of any other end, and makes positive demands on us not to stand idly by the blood of our neighbor.[11]

The concept of illegal but justified intervention has led some to argue for a right of 'ecological intervention' in cases of environmental emergency.[12] Environmental treaties call for contingency planning, notification by the state that is the source of the harm to those states potentially affected, and cooperation in case of emergency,[13] but no conventional or customary law gives states a right to intervene on the territory of another state to prevent or mitigate environmental harm. Those who favor ecological intervention thus justify it on the basis of higher humanitarian values and point to the Chernobyl incident as one where intervention would have been justified. Similarly, in recent years, at least one state neighboring Indonesia has threatened to intervene if the Indonesian government fails to control the large fires that produce choking haze throughout the region and threaten the health of millions of persons.

In sum, international justice as morality suggests that there is a common moral core or set of values that are a source of positive law. This has practical importance because such values may be considered as peremptory and superior to positive law, in other words as a means to identify *jus cogens* norms.

3 Equity

A second meaning of international justice equates it with equity in the sense of fairness. In most national legal systems, equity has played a major part in determining the distribution of rights and responsibilities in conditions of scarcity and inequality.

---

[10] See e.g. the debates in 'Editorial Comments: NATO's Kosovo Intervention', 93 *American Journal of International Law* (AJIL) 824–63 (1999).

[11] Davenport 2005 at 766.

[12] Knight 2005; Keane 2004; Gaines 2006 (citing President Clinton's support for the US use of humanitarian intervention in this context).

[13] See, e.g. 1982 UN Convention on the Law of the Sea, 21 ILM (1982) 1261, Art. 199, 10 December 1982; Nordic Mutual Emergency Assistance Agreement in Connection with Radiation Accidents, 17 October 1963, 525 UNTS 75; and the Convention on Assistance in the Case of a Nuclear Accident or Radiological Emergency, Vienna, 26 September 1986, 25 ILM (1986) 1377.

The general value of equity is largely accepted in this context, but debate exists on the appropriate principles to determine equitable allocation, e.g. whether decisions should be based on need, capacity, prior entitlement, 'just deserts', the greatest good for the greatest number, or strict equality of treatment. As discussed further with reference to equitable utilization of shared resources, the various factors may point towards different allocations. In addition, a single factor, such as need, may be asserted by more than one actor or group of actors. Environmental justice may be invoked in this context to mean procedural equity through decision-making based on relevant criteria with the participation of those affected, aiming to produce outcomes that treat all affected groups fairly. Procedural fairness, guaranteed through measures on access to justice and due process or fair hearing, is more generally and properly considered as a matter of law, since it is often constitutionally-protected or based in human rights treaties and governed by detailed legal codes.

3.1 *Equity* contra legem

By affording individualized justice, e.g. mitigation of punishment in cases of coercion or accommodation for disabled persons, equity allows for exceptional adjustments or correctives to fulfill the underlying and overarching purpose for which the law was adopted. In international environmental law, some developing countries have argued for exemptions from legal norms or preferential treatment on the basis that international legal rules impose upon them a disproportionate environmental burden due to the export of pollution from wealthier countries, while they are unable to share in the benefits derived from activities producing the pollution. Trade preferences that accord differential and more favorable treatment to developing countries, as an exception to Article I of GATT, also reflect equitable adjustments to the law. In dispute settlement, Article 38(2) of the Statute of the International Court of Justice (ICJ) provides for equity to be applied as individualized justice (*contra legem*) if the parties so agree, but this option has never been utilized because states are apparently unwilling to confer such unlimited discretion on the court.

3.2 *Equity* praeter legem

Equity also may provide a basis for decision in the absence of law or when it is necessary to fill in gaps in existing norms, such as when new issues emerge that give rise to disputes. International tribunals have applied equity in this way, but usually on the basis that the equitable principle being invoked is a general principle of law. Thus, international courts have applied notions of equitable estoppel and similar doctrines; for example, in the case of *Diversion of the Waters of the Meuse*, where the Permanent Court of International Justice (PCIJ) held that it was inequitable for the applicant state to complain of a harmful act which the applicant itself had committed in the past.[14]

3.3 *Equity* infra legem

Finally, the law itself may identify equity as the rule of decision (equity *infra legem*) especially when different circumstances among subjects of the law necessitate differential treatment in order to achieve a just result.[15] In international environmental law, equity has been utilized most often *infra legem*, in an effort to fairly allocate and regulate scarce resources to ensure that the benefits of environmental resources, the costs associated with protecting them, and any degradation that occurs (that is, all the benefits and burdens) are fairly shared by all members of society. In this regard, equity is an application of the principles of distributive justice, which seek to reconcile competing social and economic policies in order to obtain the fair sharing of resources. It does this by incorporating equitable principles in legal instruments to mandate fair procedures and just results. An example is the reliance in watercourse agreements on equitable utilization of shared waters as a principle to allocate the resource among riparian states.

In the *Case Concerning the Continental Shelf (Tunisia/Libya)*, the International Court of Justice reflected the principle of equity *infra legem* in calling equity a *legal* concept to be applied. Notably, the parties themselves asked the Court to use equitable principles in deciding the case.[16] In other cases, the Court has variously referred to equitable principles, procedures, methods, and results or solutions without always clarifying these four aspects of equity and how they interrelate with legal norms. It is not always evident that the Court views equity as requiring a fair result. Yet, the Court has indicated that it 'will always have regard to equity *infra legem*, that is, that form of equity which constitutes a method of interpretation of the law in force, and is one of its attributes',[17] suggesting that it does give consideration to interpreting the law in a fair manner. The Court has also described 'the justice of which equity is an emanation' as 'justice according to the rule of law': constant and predictable. Even though it looks with particularity to the circumstances of a pending case, it also

---

[14] PCIJ Ser. A/B 70, p. 25.

[15] Akehurst 1976. See also Brunnée, Cullet and Mickelsen in, respectively, Chapters 16, 19 and 15 of this volume.

[16] In the *Tunisia/Libya Continental Shelf Case*, the special agreement asked the Court to decide how to delimit the continental shelf in the disputed area 'according to equitable principles, and the relevant circumstances which characterize the area, as well as the new accepted trends in the Third Conference on the Law of the Sea'. (1982) ICJ Reports 18 at 23.

[17] *Frontier Dispute (Burkina Faso* v. *Mali)*, (1986) ICJ Reports 554, 567. For the use of equity in maritime boundary cases, see also: *North Sea Continental Shelf Case (FRG* v. *Denmark/Netherlands)*, (1969) ICJ Reports 3; *Continental Shelf Case (Tunisia* v. *Libya)*, (1982) ICJ Reports 18; *Gulf of Maine Case (Canada* v. *US)*, (1984) ICJ Reports 246; *Continental Shelf Case (Libya/Malta)*, (1985) ICJ Reports 13.

invokes principles of more general application.[18] The Court aims for a degree of legal certainty in its choice and application of norms, but it must take into account the facts, the situations, and the specific interests or claims of the parties. Since equitable norms themselves provide no guidance in selecting among the various facts or factors that could weigh in the decision, an element of subjectivity is probably present in all cases.

3.4 Equity and distributive justice

International justice may represent an ethical imperative to engage in a just manner with communities, based on the notion of moral reciprocity in which all human beings are treated as equals. Relations that exist today between rich and poor countries may be seen as failing to promote equality and to narrow the gap between the haves and have-nots. If such relations are unjust, moral reciprocity may require extensive redistribution of wealth. Claims of the less advantaged, particularly for development aid, rest on principles of justice. Those in a position to respond to substantive claims must take account of the rationales provided by the principles of justice in weighing their response.[19] In trade relations, inequalities between developed and developing countries could alone be seen to require redistributive justice, but corrective justice may be a more appropriate model, to the extent that developing countries have been disadvantaged as a result of past injustices. 'Corrective justice . . . is a restorative form of justice, of putting into balance something that has come out of balance because of an injustice.' Redistributive justice, in contrast, 'involves the division of social goods which can be divided or allocated . . . socially, by custom, opinion, informal decisions, and formal allocative mechanisms.'[20]

Concerns for international distributive or corrective justice led newly independent, economically disadvantaged states to join in efforts to construct a 'New International Economic Order' which would reconstruct international economic arrangements to achieve equitable distributions of global wealth. In 1974, the Declaration on the Establishment of a New International Economic Order (NIEO) (UNGA Res. 3201) affirmed a determination to work urgently for the establishment of an international economic order based on equity, sovereign equality, interdependence, common interest and cooperation among all states. The Declaration recommended North–South technology transfers, and 'preferential . . . treatment for developing countries'. The NIEO became connected to the calls for recognition of global resources as the common heritage of mankind. Article 29 of the Charter of the Economic Rights and Duties of States, adopted by the UNGA in 1974, proclaimed the seabed and its resources the common heritage of mankind. Article 29 also asserted that benefits of exploitation should be shared equitably by all states, taking into account the particular interests and needs of developing countries.

---

[18] *Case Concerning the Continental Shelf (Libya/Malta)*, note 17 above, at para. 45.
[19] Nielsen 1992 at 28.   [20] Garcia 2003.

While the common heritage of mankind concept found its way into positive law in relation to the deep seabed and outer space, the New International Economic Order ultimately failed as a set of unilateral demands, albeit the 'right to development' emerged from the effort. The aim of realizing economic justice also resurfaced in altered form with the emergence of international environmental issues. Developing countries were able to press the issue of equitable allocation of resources and burden-sharing for several reasons. First, they hold the major part of the Earth's biological resources and need or want to use them for economic development. At the same time, developed states have an interest in the conservation and sustainable utilization of these resources, many of which are the source of desired products as well as a foundation of ecological processes (for example, tropical forests as carbon sinks). Secondly, developing countries could focus on fairness in pointing out the predominant responsibility of wealthier states for pollution. Thirdly, developing states could legitimately plead their inability to participate or comply in environmental protection agreements due to poverty and the need to develop.

Concern about the equitable distribution of the burdens of environmental protection has led to the creation of a series of financial mechanisms, exemptions, provisions for the transfer of technology, and flexibility in the time required for compliance with international obligations. Capacity-building through the provision of financial resources and the transfer of technology is widely included in global multilateral environmental agreements and often becomes a condition for compliance by developing countries. Explicitly stating that economic and social development and poverty eradication are the first and overriding priorities of developing country parties, the Convention on Biological Diversity (CBD) and the UN Framework Convention on Climate Change (UNFCCC) make the provision of financial resources and the transfer of technology from developed country parties a condition for the implementation of treaty obligations by developing country parties. Other conventions, such as the Convention to Combat Desertification in Those Countries Experiencing Serious Drought and/or Desertification, Particularly in Africa, express a concern for the special needs and circumstances of developing countries, particularly the least developed, in combating environmental degradation.[21]

3.5 Intergenerational equity

Intergenerational equity as a principle of international justice is based on the recognition of two key facts: (1) human life emerged from, and is dependent upon, the Earth's natural resource base, including its ecological processes, and is thus inseparable from environmental conditions; and (2) human beings have a unique capacity to alter the environment upon which life depends. From these facts emerges the notion that humans who are alive today have a special obligation as custodians or trustees

---

[21] Kjellén in Chapter 17 of this volume.

of the planet to maintain its integrity to ensure the survival of the human species. Those living have received a heritage from their forebears in which they have beneficial rights of use that are limited by the interests and needs of future generations. This limitation requires each generation to maintain the corpus of the trust and pass it on in no worse condition than it was received. Another way to consider the issue is to view current environmental goods, wealth, and technology as owing to the progress of prior generations. This debt cannot be discharged backward so it is projected forward and discharged in the present on behalf of the future.

The equitable concept of trust involves placing obligations on the trustees such as conserving and maintaining the trust resources. Since the trustees are also the present generation of beneficiaries, they are constrained in their use of resources. Meeting the obligation calls for minimizing or avoiding long-term and irreversible damage to the environment. Three implications emerge from the principle of intergenerational equity: first, that each generation is required to conserve the diversity of the natural and cultural resource base so that it does not unduly restrict the options available to future generations to satisfy their own values and needs. Secondly, the quality of ecological processes passed on should be comparable to that enjoyed by the present generation. Thirdly, the past and present cultural and natural heritage should be conserved so that future generations will have access to it. These rights and obligations derive from a notion of human society that extends beyond the totality of the current planetary population, giving it a temporal dimension.

It may be objected that there are no rights-holders present to correspond to the obligations imposed. Without identifiable individuals, can there be rights and duties? Edith Brown Weiss posits that the rights-holders are not individuals, who remain in the future, but generations, some of which are here and some of which are in the future. Generations hold these rights as groups in relation to other generations. Since the future individuals are indeterminate, a guardian or a representative of the group may enforce these rights.[22] In *Minors Oposa v. Secretary of the Department of Environment and Natural Resources*, the Philippine Supreme Court found that present generations have standing to represent future generations in large part because 'every generation has a responsibility to the next to preserve that rhythm and harmony for the full enjoyment of a balanced and healthful ecology'.[23]

4 Law

In a third construct, international justice can be taken to mean adherence to the rule of law generally, i.e. accepting that 'there is an international society within which every state accepts that the same basic principles of international norms are applicable to

---

[22] Brown Weiss 1989 at 95–7.
[23] *Minors Oposa v. Secretary of the Department of Environment and Natural Resources*, Philippine Supreme Court, reprinted in 33 ILM (1994) 168.

every other state and that they are all equal before the law and the international legal system. They can neither modify the rules by their own will nor ignore them . . . The concept of international justice denotes the existence of a common point of view between states for the maintenance of international peace and solving of international conflicts from different aspects of the law.'[24] This approach is not incompatible with, but instead may reinforce equity *infra legem*.

4.1 Procedural justice

Most of the early references to international justice concerned tribunals and procedures created to resolve inter-state disputes as an alternative to recourse to force. The predecessor to the present International Court of Justice was named the Permanent Court of International Justice probably to distinguish adjudication from arbitration. The distinction seems to have been clear to the drafters[25] who fixed the name of the Court in Article 14 of the Covenant of the League of Nations. According to Hudson, 'the name given in the Covenant . . . emphasizes the judicial nature of the new institution . . . ; in the minds of some persons the process of justice was to be distinguished from the process of arbitration.'[26]

The notion that inter-state mechanisms to settle disputes constitute international justice has not disappeared. What is unclear in most instances is whether international justice means the tribunal, the procedure, or the outcome. Some authors include the Permanent Court of Arbitration and mixed arbitral tribunals as mechanisms of international justice,[27] but references to international justice more often focus more on fair procedure or substantive outcome than on the tribunal itself.[28]

There has been a notable shift in recent years towards using international justice to mean only institutions and procedures of civil and criminal accountability. The Rome Statute of the International Criminal Court, in its preamble, maintains that the States Parties to the Statute are '[r]esolved to guarantee lasting respect for and the enforcement of international justice'.[29] In this sense, international justice is used in opposition to impunity[30] or sometimes to contrast international prosecutions from domestic criminal justice systems.[31] International institutions that afford access to victims of human rights violations, albeit against the responsible state rather

---

[24] Malekian 2005 at 678.   [25] Quoted in Hudson 1943.   [26] *Ibid.* at 96.

[27] See e.g. E. Lauterpacht 1991.   [28] Posner and de Figueiredo 2004.

[29] Statute of the International Criminal Court, 17 July 1998, 2187 UNTS 90, Preamble.

[30] See e.g. Dicker and Keppler 2004 (equating justice with prosecution); 'Brussels Principles against Impunity and for International Justice', 11–13 March 2003; Linton 2001; Beigbeder 2005; 'The UN Criminal Tribunals for Yugoslavia and Rwanda: International Justice or Show of Justice?', Hearing before the House Committee on International Relations, 107th Cong. 197–71 (2001).

[31] Rabkin 2005 ('international justice is, in some sense, more reliably available than national justice'). Carsten Stahn distinguishes domestic justice, international criminal justice, hybrid criminal justice, justice under transitional administration, and domestic transitional justice. See Stahn 2005.

than the individual perpetrator, also are referred to as mechanisms of international justice.[32]

Within the context of accountability, international justice is sometimes used to mean providing due process for the accused and/or the victims, based on international standards. Those working on this aspect of international justice focus on such principles of legality as the prohibition of *ex post facto* laws or appropriate application of the principle of *nullum crimen sine lege* to obtain jurisdiction over a person accused of committing an international crime. Others argue that the role provided for victims is central to the ongoing definitional process associated with international justice.[33]

4.2 Substantive norms

In contrast to the preceding procedural focus, another use of the term international justice refers to the substance of international law. Specific legal norms seen to promote this idea of justice generally fall within one of three categories: norms addressing the consequences of wrongful actions (state responsibility and liability); norms of humane treatment (human rights and humanitarian law); and norms allocating scarce resources. In substantive law, imposing equal obligations on subjects of law that are unequal in relevant ways is perceived as unjust if it exacerbates inequalities or imposes unfair burdens on those least able to bear the burdens. Legal systems, including the international legal system, therefore often seek to base the distribution of societal goods and burdens according to the principle of distributive justice, seeking substantive equality by treating like alike and unlike differently.

International law has attempted to allocate both shared resources and environmental burdens to achieve distributive justice. This equitable approach may call for accommodating pervasive inequalities of economic development or lack of capacity to tackle a given problem, by imposing differential obligations or providing preferential treatment. These unequal relationships seek to foster true equality, largely through favoring the least developed or most affected states.

Distributive justice as the basis for allocating limited resources plays a role in the rules governing the common heritage of mankind. Once resources have been identified as part of the patrimony of all humanity, because they fall outside the sovereignty of any state or group of states, it becomes essential to articulate principles for sharing the management and benefits from such resources and the rules to govern their use. Such rules may promote exploitation, as with deep seabed mineral resources, or may reject extractive operations in favor of conservation, as in Antarctica. The issue of fairness in the allocation of benefits has been a major issue in debates regarding the resources of the deep seabed, while much of the discussion about Antarctica has concerned procedural fairness and participation in decision-making. It may also be considered that the deep seabed regime is focused on intra-generational equity, while

---

[32] Cançado-Trindade 2004 at 310.   [33] Kuhner 2004.

the Antarctic designation as a nature reserve in Article 3 of the Madrid Protocol on Environmental Protection to the Antarctic Treaty gives priority to intergenerational equity.

Equitable utilization is a widely accepted principle applied in apportioning other shared resources, such as watercourses, fish stocks, and the continental shelf. It finds expression in Article 2 of the 1997 UN Convention on the Law of Non-Navigational Uses of International Watercourses, which calls on the parties to take all appropriate measures to ensure that international watercourses are used in a reasonable and equitable way.[34] The status of equitable utilization as a fundamental and just norm in the field of shared natural resources was affirmed by the ICJ in the *Case Concerning the Gabčíkovo–Nagymaros Project (Hungary/Slovakia)*.[35] In the *Fisheries Jurisdiction Cases (UK v. Iceland; FRG v. Iceland)*, the ICJ stressed the obligation of reasonable use and good faith negotiations aimed at an equitable result, taking into account the needs of conservation and the interests of all exploiters of the resource.[36] Thus, the notion of equitable utilization is one of distributive justice, attempting to make a 'reasonable' allocation or reach a fair result in distribution of a scarce resource, based on what are deemed to be relevant factors, such as need, prior use or entitlement, and other interests. On a substantive level, each party is held to have an equal right to use the resource, but since one party's use can impact the beneficial uses of others and not all uses can be satisfied, some limitations are necessary. The Watercourses Convention states that equitable and reasonable uses are to be 'consistent with adequate protection of the watercourse' (Article 5). The phrase suggests that uses that would substantially harm the watercourse could be inherently inequitable and indicates how positive rules may restrict the scope and application of equitable principles.

Notions of entitlement stemming from prior uses, strict equality, proportional use based on population, and priority accorded to certain uses all have been asserted at one time or another as a basis for determining what is an equitable allocation. In some instances, the parties agree in advance on certain divisions or priorities. The 1909 Boundary Waters Treaty between the United States and Canada relies upon equality of use for the generation of power (each country being entitled to use half of the waters along the boundary) and equitable sharing of water for irrigation. In contrast, the 1959 Nile Agreement between the Sudan and Egypt for Full Utilization of Nile Waters confirmed the 'established rights' of each party, without identifying them, while additional amounts were allocated on other equitable bases. While the Nile agreement seems to view established rights as guaranteed by law, most other instruments take the better view and include prior entitlements as one factor in determining equitable allocation.

---

[34] See Hey in Chapter 18 of this volume.
[35] *Case Concerning the Gabčíkovo–Nagymaros Project (Hungary/Slovakia)*, (1997) ICJ Reports 7.
[36] *Fisheries Jurisdiction Cases (United Kingdom v. Iceland; Federal Republic of Germany v. Iceland)*, (1974) ICJ Reports 3 and 175.

The idea of equitable utilization in the past had as a corollary that no use had inherent priority over any other. Today, there appears to be a move towards recognizing that some resource uses do have priority over others. In the use of freshwaters, for example, emphasis is being placed on the satisfaction of basic human needs, that is, the provision of safe drinking water and sanitation. The Watercourses Convention provides that, in the event of a conflict between the uses of an international watercourse, special regard is to be given to the requirements of vital human needs (Article 10), while the UN Committee on Economic, Social and Cultural Rights, in its General Comment 12 on the Right to Water, insists that priority be given to safe drinking water and sanitation, with a guaranteed minimum amount to be provided to every person. Thus, substantive human rights considerations take precedence over other factors in allocation.

Another application of international justice in legal norms is found in the principle of common but differentiated responsibilities.[37] Article 5(5) of the amended Montreal Protocol on Substances that Deplete the Ozone Layer (Montreal Protocol), for example, provides that developing countries' capacity to fulfill the obligations and implement the control measures specified in the Montreal Protocol will depend upon the effective implementation by developed nations of financial cooperation and transfer of technology as set out in the Protocol.[38] Similar statements are contained in Article 4(7) of the United Nations Framework Convention on Climate Change (UNFCCC)[39] and Article 20(4) of the Convention on Biological Diversity (CBD).

The 'common but differentiated responsibilities' principle provides a corrective justice basis for obliging the developed world to pay for past harms as well as present and future harms. According to this principle, even though the responsibility for protecting the environment is to be shared among all nations, countries should contribute differently to international environmental initiatives depending on their capabilities and responsibilities. Common but differentiated responsibility calls broadly for developed countries to take the lead in solving existing global environmental problems, in particular because of their contributions to the creation of these problems. Corrective justice justifies demanding that developed nations pay for any reductions or modifications the developing world has to make in the process of industrialization, because developed-world industrialization has unfairly circumscribed the ability of the developing world to pass off the negative externalities of development on the environment. Climate change, ozone layer depletion and biodiversity are issues today because we are nearing – or have already reached – an environmental cliff or tipping point. In each case, the global community finds itself at the tipping point because of the conduct of the developed world. It is precisely because of this conduct that the

---

[37] Drumbl 2002.

[38] 1987 Montreal Protocol on Substances that Deplete the Ozone Layer, 1522 UNTS 3, reprinted in 26 ILM (1987) 1550. See also Mickelson in Chapter 15 of this volume.

[39] 1992 United Nations Framework Convention on Climate Change (UNFCCC), reprinted in 31 ILM (1992) 849. See also Brunnée in Chapter 16 of this volume.

marginal environmental costs of developing-nation industrialization today are high. It is deemed unfair to allocate each state or each person an equal share of total permissible pollution in the present, given that some countries and persons have polluted so much in the past. The true social and environmental costs of developed-nation industrialization have never been accounted for, so the time has come to spread that unfairly obtained windfall.

Corrective justice thus has a place in substantiating the notion that developing nations are entitled to resources and technology from developed nations such that developed nations should have to internalize the environmental costs of ongoing and future developing-nation industrialization. In international law, this corrective justice model brushes against theories of formal equality, but justice in the present cannot ignore elements from the past.

A considerably broader formulation calls for adjustments on the basis of restitution. It suggests that developed nations are not 'entitled' to preserving the wealth they have accrued through industrial development as these 'entitlements' were obtained in a manner that does not justify their retention. If this last formulation passes from disentitling developed nations to retain their holdings to entitling developing nations to holdings of their own, this arguably sets the stage for the somewhat more aggressive notion of developmental justice. If 'entitlements' are perceived as transcending the area of environmental harms and extending into the externalities of the North's industrial development generally, including colonialism, mercantilism, and labor exploitation, then this could become a considerably more ambitious program.

Norms concerned with human rights and humanitarian law are sometimes generally referred to as norms of international justice. Specific legal claims, such as equality among all persons, are often cited as examples of international justice.[40] The Declaration on the 'Guidelines of the Recognition of New States in Eastern Europe and in the Soviet Union', adopted by the European Political Cooperation Ministerial Meeting of the European Union, made recognition subject to strong normative standards of international justice, in the sense of human rights.[41] The Guidelines include 'respect for the provisions of the Charter of the UN and the commitments subscribed to in the Final Act of Helsinki and in the Charter of Paris, especially with regard to the rule of law, democracy and human rights'.[42]

The modern recognition of 'the inherent dignity and of the equal and inalienable rights of all members of the human family [as] the foundation of freedom, justice and peace in the world' requires basing international law, public policy, and justice on 'normative individualism' (i.e. that 'all human beings are born free and equal in

---

[40] Elshtain 2003 at 168 (arguing that 'true international justice is defined as the equal claim of all persons, whatever their political location or condition' and 'equal regard is an ideal of international justice whose time has come').

[41] Declaration on the 'Guidelines on the Recognition of New States in Eastern Europe and in the Soviet Union' 16 December 1991, 31 ILM 1485 (1992).

[42] *Ibid.* at 1487.

dignity and rights'). Also, in international economic law, values and policies should be legitimized through individual consent, equal rights, and democratic procedures rather than only through utilitarian philosophies of maximizing individual and social 'utilities' on the basis of money and abstract notions of 'welfare' and 'economic efficiency'. In this view, 'justice' remains a never-ending regulatory task and 'cannot be related to any one value, be it equality or any other, but only to the complex value system of a man, a community, or mankind'.[43]

As the human rights paradigm of international justice develops, it is increasingly moving from an exclusive focus on the conduct of state agents to concern with the actions of legal and natural persons in the private sector. The UN Secretary-General's Global Compact, the ILO Tripartite Declaration of Principles concerning Multinational Enterprises, and the UN Sub-Commissions Norms on the Responsibilities of Transnational Corporations and Other Business Enterprises with Regard to Human Rights (2003) all reflect a growing trend of seeing human rights as comprehensively concerned with matters of international justice.

5 Conclusion: just process and/or just results

The assertion that international justice requires like cases to be treated alike while those that are not alike are handled in accordance with the differences requires determining which similarities and differences are relevant in which situations. To take an example from within national legal systems, income differences are generally accepted as a proper basis for allocating tax burdens but not for voting in national elections. Thus, while the general value of equity or fairness is largely accepted in the context of scarcity and inequality, debate centers on the appropriate principle on which to determine equitable allocation – whether decisions should be based on need, capacity, prior entitlement, 'just deserts', the greatest good for the greatest number, or strict equality of treatment. The various factors may point towards allocation in one direction or in many different directions. In addition, a single factor, such as need, may be asserted by more than one actor or group of actors. These latter problems have complicated international negotiations, for example, over access to, and equitable benefit sharing of, the use of genetic resources.[44] Some possible alternatives are the following.

Formal equality (for example, per capita distribution) is one method of allocating resources and burdens. As noted earlier, rules are generally deemed just if they apply to all without discrimination. Yet equal treatment may yield extreme outcomes when pre-existing economic or other inequalities exist in society. At the international level,

---

[43] Petersmann 2003 ('[C]ontrary to the suggestion by John Rawls to base international justice on equal freedoms of peoples, human rights offer a more appropriate constitutional basis for national as well as international justice'). As Petersmann puts it, '[t]he universal recognition of human rights requires basing "international justice" – contrary to the views of John Rawls – not only on freedom and equality of peoples, but also on equal human rights and multi-level constitutionalism'. *Ibid.* at 458.

[44] Cullet in Chapter 19 of this volume.

when allocations are based on formal equality, moreover, the issue of whether the appropriate apportioning unit is the state or the individual may arise, as in determining permissible emission levels. Requiring all states to implement environmental agreements in identical fashion would make many developing countries, or groups in those countries, worse off, at least in the short term. From the perspective of equity towards the most vulnerable or least well off, environmental protection should not result in further deterioration of their well-being. In order to address this problem, non-equal or differential obligations can and are being imposed as equitable means to foster substantive equality in the long term. The acceptance at Rio and henceforth of the principle of common but differentiated responsibilities seems to suggest a contraction of the use of formal equality as a means of allocation in environmental law.

Notions of *entitlement* uphold the existing distribution of goods if they were justly acquired according to the rules in force at the time of acquisition. Entitlement protection is contained in some environmental laws and agreements that 'grandfather' existing activities by exempting them from retrofitting to meet more exacting and newly enacted standards or allowing emissions to continue at pre-existing levels. Some international environmental agreements, such as the 1987 Sulphur Protocol to the Convention on Long-Range Transboundary Air Pollution, require equal reductions in pollution from historic baseline levels. This system rewards those who already have the goods and may not result in what is considered to be a fair distribution. An entitlement approach also may serve to deny essential goods to others.

Traditional international law largely reflects ideas that protect entitlement. All states, including those newly created, have equality of opportunity as sovereigns in principle but pre-existing natural endowment and activities make older states substantially stronger in wealth and power and developing states substantially stronger in natural (biological) resources. Since traditional international law entitles all states to an equal right to obtain or use common resources, from fish in the high seas to the geostationary orbit, technologically advanced states have the ability to, and may choose to, acquire the greatest part of the resources of the common area. Equality of rights, however, does not necessarily bring about equality of outcomes and the least favored may find themselves in a continually declining position.

Different *capacities* (from each according to her ability) may be the decisive factor chosen to achieve distributive justice, as expressed in environmental agreements that require the Organization for Economic Co-operation and Development (OECD) or other groupings of countries to finance poorer countries or transfer technology because they have the ability to do so. One problem that can arise is making the relevant determinations of ability to pay. States may argue that various factors make it fair for them to be grouped with the poorer countries. The Kyoto Protocol classifies Saudi Arabia and Singapore as 'developing', while Bulgaria is classified as developed, even though it is still an economy in transition state. Without objective criteria to determine the groupings, along with the flexibility to move states from one group to another, the problem will largely be a political one. Some treaties avoid this problem by incorporating notions of capacity generally, requiring each state party to take measures 'in accordance with its particular conditions and capabilities' or 'as far as possible and as appropriate'.[45]

Inequalities in the ability to access the benefits of natural resources and address environmental impacts are evident. While the reality of environmental interdependence imposes a need for inter-state cooperation, states are impacted differently by specific environmental conditions, have greater or lesser interest in or impact on a particular problem, and may lack the human or financial capacity to take actions deemed prudent or necessary by the international community. It is clear that the expenditures necessary to prevent or abate environmental hazards can be high in the short term. This factor often provokes in developing countries rational fears that participation in international environmental treaties may decelerate or limit industrial development. As a result of these types of considerations, the Food and Agricultural Organization's Code of Conduct for Responsible Fisheries[46] recognizes that the capacity of developing countries to implement the recommendations of the Code have to be taken into account because existing inequality with regard to resources and capacities influences the ability of such states to take action on specific environmental problems.

Different *needs* (to each according to her need) as a basis for equitable allocation are recognized in the Rio Declaration and reappear, for example, in the UNFCCC. In implementing the Convention, the parties are to be guided by 'the specific needs and special circumstances of developing country Parties, especially those that are particularly vulnerable to the adverse effects of climate change, and of those Parties, especially developing country Parties, that would have to bear a disproportionate or abnormal burden under the convention'.[47] The question of what would be 'disproportionate' is left open. Article 4(8) adds that all parties are to consider what actions, including funding, insurance, and transfer of technology, may be necessary to meet the specific needs of specially affected states. Determining need, like determining capacity, may require the development of objective criteria and the assessment of the situation over time of each state party.

Different *historical responsibility* or 'just deserts', that is, past and present contributions to environmental harm, is deemed by developing countries to be one of the most relevant factors in allocating burdens. The 1991 Beijing Declaration on Environment and Development stated the view of the developing world that 'the developed countries bear responsibility for the degradation of the global environment. Ever since the Industrial Revolution, the developed countries have over-exploited the world's natural

---

[45] Articles 6–11 of the Convention on Biological Diversity.
[46] FAO, *Code of Conduct for Responsible Fisheries*, Rome: FAO (31 October 1995).
[47] Article 3.2 of the UN Framework Convention on Climate Change.

resources through unsustainable patterns of production and consumption, causing damage to the global environment, to the detriment of the developing countries.' Fairness and a morally coherent response suggest that these states, which attained their current developed status through imposing non-internalized costs on the environment, take the major abatement actions, rather than demanding that everyone equally mitigate the externalities, including those not responsible for initially creating the problem. Equity, in this sense, is justified as a means of corrective justice, requiring remedial conduct to correct past wrongs.

Whichever approach is followed, a growing recognition of the interdependence of states and of problems that are insoluble through unilateral action, has led to acceptance of the moral principle of solidarity or partnership. Interdependence underscores the search for a just global society, which is a quest as old as human civilization. To many, a just society involves ensuring that the natural components of the environment continue to sustain life in all of its diversity and that the natural benefits that humans enjoy are fairly shared among all those present and to come. The moral dimension of equity is such that it is often deemed synonymous with justice and is an end in itself.

International justice in international environmental law thus would mean a rational sharing of the burdens and costs of environmental protection, discharged through the procedural and substantive adjustment of rights and duties. Justice in the sense of fairness also would mean warning states of imminent peril and cooperating to resolve problems that will impact the ecological processes or resources on which future well-being depends. While certain stated principles of environmental law seem to aim for such international justice, there has been an evident strong resistance to aiding the 'have-nots' on the part of some of those who 'have'. To the extent progress has been made in fairly allocating benefits and burdens in international environmental law, it may be considered the result of ecological interdependence and issue-linkages. Developed countries increasingly recognized that they *must* have the cooperation of developing states if the global environment is to be restored and maintained; they cannot do it on their own. Benefit and burden-sharing then becomes the just price demanded by the developing world for its cooperation.

Justice and equity are important and, with their emphasis on fairness, are more attractive to many than economic efficiency or open conflict as a means of deciding how to allocate and sustain limited commons resources. Without a cooperative and just solution to the issue of allocation, competitive utilization of the resource may continue until the resource is depleted. Equitable or differentiated obligations may induce participation in action among the competing states as well as among states that may not have any direct interest in a specific environmental issue. Developing countries have noted that ozone depletion, which is of greater concern to developed countries, has been addressed more rapidly and seriously than desertification or other issues of greater interest to the south. Such observations may be a disincentive to cooperation, notably, the 2002 GEF decision to fund desertification projects, which seems at least in part a response to criticisms heard before and during the World Summit on Sustainable Development that the limited mandate of the fund was unfair.

Equity also may be justified on the basis of self-interest. Developed countries gain from secure access to primary resources situated largely in developing countries. More generally, environmental protection is in everyone's interest, and the adjustment of legal obligations to achieve better protection is self-interested. An allocation of burdens that takes into account the more vulnerable position of developing states may benefit all through inducing their cooperation to improve global environmental conditions. Moreover, Scott Barrett's work has indicated that agreements perceived to be fair are not only likely to induce greater participation but are more likely to be self-enforcing and thus successful over the long term.[48]

In sum, international justice is not only a matter of morality and equity but may also foster more effective action on issues of common concern and more effective implementation of legal norms. Equity, as reflecting notions of fairness and legitimacy, may produce more or better compliance with environmental agreements. In practice, therefore, equitable differentiation probably has become the price to be paid to ensure universal participation in environmental agreements concerned with global problems. Yet, it should not be forgotten, as Thomas Franck has noted, that '[t]he law promotes distributive justice not merely to secure greater compliance, but primarily because most people think it is *right* to act justly'.[49]

Bibliography

Akehurst, M., 1976. 'Equity and General Principles of Law', 25 *International and Comparative Law Quarterly*.

Barret, S., 2003. *Environment and Statecraft: The Strategy of Environmental Treaty-Making*. Oxford University Press.

Beigbeder, Y., 2005. *International Justice Against Impunity*. Martinus Nijhoff Publishers.

Blackstone, W., 1783 (1978). *The Commentaries on the Laws of England*, Volume 4. (London) New York: Garland.

Brilmayer, L., 1996. 'International Justice and International Law', 98 *West Virginia Law Review* 611.

Brown Weiss, E., 1989. *In Fairness to Future Generations: International Law, Common Patrimony and Intergenerational Equity*. Dobbs Ferry, NY: Transnational Publishers.

Cançado-Trindade, A., 2004. 'The Merits of Coordination of International Courts of Human Rights', 2 *Journal of International Criminal Justice* 309.

Davenport, J. J., 2005. 'Just War Theory Requires a New Federation of Democratic Nations', 28 *Fordham International Law Journal* 763.

Dicker, R., and Keppler, E., 2004. 'Beyond The Hague: The Challenges of International Justice', *Human Rights Watch World Report 2004*.

Drumbl, M. A., 2002. 'Poverty, Wealth, and Obligation in International Environmental Law'. 76 *Tulane Law Review* 843.

---

[48] Barret 2003.   [49] Franck 1995 at 8.

Elshtain, J. B., 2003. *Just War Against Terror: The Burden of American Power In a Violent World.* Basic Books.

Franck, T., 1995. *Fairness in International Law and Institutions.* Oxford: Clarenden Press.

Gaines, S., 2006. 'Sustainable Development and National Security', 30 *William and Mary Environmental Law and Policy Review* 321.

Garcia, F., 2003. *Trade Inequality and Justice: Toward a Liberal Theory of Just Trade.* Transnational.

Hershey, A. S., 1912. 'History of International Law Since the Peace of Westphalia'. 6 *American Journal of International Law* 30.

Hudson, M. O., 1928. 'The Development of International Law Since the War', 22 *American Journal of International Law* 330.

    1943. *The Permanent Court of International Justice, 1920–1942.* New York: Bureau of International Research of Harvard University and Radcliffe College. Macmillan.

Humphrey, J. P., 1945. 'On the Foundations of International Law'. 39 *American Journal of International Law* 231.

Keane, D., 2004. 'The Environmental Causes and Consequences of Migration: A Search for the Meaning of Environmental Refugees'. 16 *Georgetown International Environmental Law Review* 209.

Keohane, R., 1984. *After Hegemony: Cooperation and Discord in the World Political Economy.* Princeton University Press.

Knight, A., 2005. 'Can the Security Council Protect Our Earth'. 80 *New York University Law Review* 1549.

Kuhner, T., 2004. 'The Status of Victims in the Enforcement of International Criminal Law'. 6 *Oregon Review of International Law* 95.

Lauterpacht, E., 1991. *Aspects of the Administration of International Justice.* Cambridge University Press.

Lauterpacht, H., 1955. 'Codification and Development of International Law'. 49 *American Journal of International Law* 16.

Linton, S., 2001. 'Cambodia, East Timor and Sierra Leone: Experiments in International Justice'. 12 *Criminal Law Forum* 185.

Malekian, F., 2005. 'Emasculating the Philosophy of International Criminal Justice in the Iraqi Special Tribunal'. 38 *Cornell International Law Journal* 638.

Nielsen, K., 1992. 'Global Justice, Capitalism and the Third World', in Attfield and Wilkins (eds.), *International Justice and the Third World.* Routledge. 28.

Nys, E., 1911. 'The Codification of International Law', 5 *American Journal of International Law* 871 and 886.

Oppenheim, L., 1908. 'The Science of International Law: Its Task and Method'. 2 *American Journal of International Law* 313.

Petersmann, E. U., 2003. 'Theories of Justice, Human Rights, and the Constitution of International Markets'. 37 *Loyola of Los Angeles Law Review* 407.

Philimore, R., 1871. *Commentaries upon International Law*, Volume 1. 2nd edn, Butterworths.

Posner, Eric A., and de Figueiredo, Miguel, 1004. 'Is the International Court of Justice Biased?'. University of Chicago Law and Economics, Olin Working Paper No. 234.

Rabkin, J., 2005. 'Global Criminal Justice: An Idea Whose Time Has Passed'. 38 *Cornell International Law Journal* 753.

Silving, H., 1961. 'In re Eichmann: A Dilemma of Law and Morality'. 55 *American Journal of International Law* 307.

Skubik, D. W., 1986. 'Two Models for a Rawlsian Theory of International Law and Justice'. 14 *Denver Journal of International Law and Policy* 231.

Stahn, C., 2005. 'Justice under Transitional Administration: Contours and Critique of a Paradigm'. 27 *Houston Journal of International Law* 311.

4

Law, justice and rights: some implications of a global perspective

WILLIAM TWINING

1 Jurisprudence

In academic life there is a widespread tendency for bodies of literature to talk past each other. This seems to be the case with much of the literature on environmental law, environmental justice, mainstream jurisprudence, and globalisation. This chapter suggests some chasms and some connections between them, and relates to the question: 'What are the implications of so-called "globalisation" for the institutionalised discipline of law and especially for jurisprudence, conceived as the theoretical or more general part of that discipline?'[1] I shall reflect on a number of themes, concepts, and distinctions that are broadly relevant to debating issues about environmental justice in today's world: including the nature of theorising about law; the discourses of globalisation; picturing law from a global perspective; normative jurisprudence, especially theories and discourses of justice and human rights.

I treat jurisprudence as the theoretical or more abstract part of law as a discipline.[2] Philosophy of law is the most abstract part of jurisprudence, which is also concerned with a wide range of theoretical issues that are not primarily philosophical. Jurisprudence can be conceived of as both a heritage and an activity. Western jurisprudence has a vast heritage of texts, questions, answers, and arguments. It can also be conceived of as an activity directed to posing, reposing, reflecting on, hypothesising answers to, and arguing about these questions.

In the Anglo-American tradition the heritage and the activity are sometimes classified into broadly defined, but overlapping, fields: Julius Stone categorised them as analytical jurisprudence, sociological (or functional) jurisprudence, and theories of human law and justice (censorial, critical, or ethical).[3] I prefer to talk rather more broadly of analytical, normative, empirical (or socio-legal), and critical jurisprudence. Such classifications serve a modest purpose provided that two points are born in mind:

---

[1] This presents in succint form themes that are developed at greater length in Twining, *General Jurisprudence* (2008). See also Twining (1997, 2000, 2003a, 2003b, 2003c, 2005b, 2005c). I am grateful to Andrew Halpin, Jonas Ebbesson, and John Tasioulas for helpful comments and suggestions.
[2] Twining (1997) at 110–14.   [3] Stone (1946) Ch. 1 (discussed in Twining (2003a)).

first, the boundaries between these activities are not precise and are often contested; and, secondly, most practical questions about law involve a combination of analytical, empirical, and normative elements. So any classification of these broad fields or activities should not be expected to bear much weight.[4]

If one stands back and surveys the vast heritage of Western legal theorising about law, one is reminded of two tendencies that are in tension. First, the Western heritage is vast. However, viewed from a global perspective, that same heritage can be criticised for being insular, parochial, quite narrowly focused, and even ethnocentric. Nearly all of it concentrates on the municipal law of sovereign states, mainly those in advanced industrial societies; it operates within and across only two of the world's major legal traditions, common law and civil law, with other major traditions marginalised or completely ignored. The 'Country and Western tradition' of legal theorising and comparative law is vulnerable to charges of parochialism and ethnocentrism.[5]

2 Globalisation and G-talk

Words like 'globalisation' and 'global' are used very loosely. Here, it is useful to distinguish between two primary uses. First, 'globalisation' is sometimes used to refer to certain recent tendencies in political economy – the domination of the world economy by a group of interrelated ideologies and practices, sometimes referred to as 'the Washington Consensus'. This usage is clearly illustrated by 'the anti-globalisation' movement, which has rather diffuse targets, including American hegemony, Western dominated international financial institutions, free market ideology, and capitalism in general. The issues are important, not least in respect of environmental matters, but this usage is too narrow in the present context. I shall use the term 'globalisation', following Anthony Giddens, in a much broader, less politically fraught sense, to refer to those processes that increase interaction and interdependence in respect of not only economy and trade, but also communications, science, technology, language, travel, migration, ecology, climate, disease, war and peace, security and so on.[6]

This second broader meaning can be quite useful, but it too is problematic. Terms such as global corporations, global law, global lawyers, global law firms, and global jurisprudence are indicative of a tendency to make exaggerated, misleading, meaningless, superficial, ethnocentric, or just plain false generalisations about processes and phenomena that are better discussed in less hyperbolic terms.[7] In particular, it is worth emphasising three points that are particularly pertinent to law.

(i) Lawyers need to be especially sensitive to boundaries, jurisdictions, and levels of ordering. Not only are national boundaries becoming more porous, but we are all

---

[4] Hart (1983) at 88–9.   [5] Twining (2000) at 184–9.

[6] Giddens (1990) at 64. See further Twining (2000) Ch. 1, at 4–10.

[7] Most global generalisations, even if true, refer to surface phenomena. In a sense, it may be true that Holiday Inns or CNN or British Airways circle the world, but these refer to surface phenomena that may conceal more than they reveal. This theme is developed in Twining (2008) Ch. 10, 'Surface Law'.

familiar with the idea of different levels of ordering – for example, the differences between general public international law (some of which is genuinely global), regional, state, sub-state, and so on. We are also familiar with the elusiveness of subsidiarity and margins of appreciation. But other complexities are often overlooked. For example, there is a tendency to move back and forth between the global and the local, not only leaving out intermediate levels but also implicitly accepting a picture of levels of law as being stacked in a single neat vertical hierarchy from outer space, through global, regional, and national down to the very local. But there are important legal patterns that are geographically more complex than that: for example, the Jewish and Islamic diasporas, the former European empires, the common law world, the British Commonwealth, NATO, OPEC, and other alliances, networks, religions, cartels, spheres of influence – all of these cut across simple vertical hierarchies and greatly complicate the picture of patterns of ordering and the diffusion of legal ideas.

(ii) Not all interaction between legal orders takes place at one level. Comparative law and studies of legal transplants have tended to focus on the relationship between different state legal systems and to neglect other aspects of interaction – cross-level diffusion, different forms of interlegality and, above all, legal and normative pluralism are now central concerns as the discipline of law becomes more cosmopolitan.[8]

(iii) Talk of 'levels' of relations and of ordering involves spatial metaphors that are not always appropriate in respect of law. There is a developing sub-field of law and geography and the idea of mapping law has its uses. Gordon Woodman has forcefully argued that state law is typically defined in terms of relatively determinate territory, but many laws and legal orders are not.[9] This is especially the case with personal and religious laws. Similar arguments apply to 'spheres of justice'.[10] The point is valid. However, if we conceive of law as a form of institutionalised social practice and if we are concerned with the law in action, then we are dealing with actual behaviour, which does take place at particular times in particular places. For example, if we agree that *shari'a* travels with every devout Muslim, a good map of Islamic diasporas can at least give a general indication of where Islamic law is likely to exist at a given time as an institutionalised social practice.[11] We need to guard against overusing spatial metaphors, but there is still scope for legal geography.[12]

Of course, there are genuinely global phenomena and issues that are or should be of concern to all humankind, such as climate change, nuclear proliferation, war and peace, radical poverty, and the exploration and exploitation of outer space. But even

---

[8] Twining (2000) at Ch. 6.   [9] Woodman (2003).   [10] Singer (1983).

[11] On Islamic law in England as a form of custom that has slowly influenced English municipal law, see Pearl and Menski (1998) especially Ch. 3.

[12] Blomley (1994), Economides (1996), Holder and Harrison (2003).

then there are still important questions about what are the most appropriate levels of policy and law for dealing with each issue.

3 A global perspective

If one is sensitive to different levels of relations and of ordering, then a global perspective can serve as much to emphasise diversity and complexity as to simplify. Thinking globally at least sets a *context* for focusing at other levels. A quick way in is to consider the limitations of a map of law that is confined to municipal legal systems, i.e. the domestic law of nation states. There are some obvious criticisms to be made:

(i) A map confined to national legal systems leaves out other levels of supranational, subnational and transnational levels of legal relations: public international law, European Commmunity law, Islamic law, Maori law, and *lex mercatoria* for example. (ii) It leaves out some of the major legal traditions in which law is not conceptually or politically tied to the idea of the state. For example, it leaves out Islamic law or confines it to countries in which Islamic law is formally recognised as a source of municipal law. But it is obvious that this distorts the extent, scope, and nature of *shari'a*. (iii) However, if we decide to include major religious and customary normative orderings, and perhaps other examples of non-state law, we run into major conceptual problems. First, we have to adopt a conception of law that includes at least some examples of 'non-state law'. That reopens the Pandora's box of the problem of the definition of law and all its attendant controversies.[13] Secondly, there is the problem of individuating legal orders. What counts as one legal order or system or unit for the purposes of mapping? How does one deal with vaguely constituted agglomerations of norms, which may be more like waves or clouds than billiard balls?[14] (iv) If one decouples the notion of law and state, one is confronted with another set of problems. If one moves away from the idea of one kind of institution having a legitimate claim to monopoly of authority and force, one has to accept the idea of legal and normative pluralism – i.e. the coexistence of more than one legal order in the same time-space context – and all the difficulties that entails.

4 Analytical and empirical jurisprudence: some brief comments

The topic of environmental justice *prima facie* falls within the province of normative jurisprudence. But, because most legal discourse, scholarship, and debate involve conceptual, factual, technical, and normative (i.e. ethical and evaluative) dimensions, it is useful to make some other general points about the implications of adopting a global perspective for legal theory and the discipline of law and for sub-fields, such as environmental law.

---

[13] Twining (2003b).   [14] *Ibid.*

(i) *Analytical jurisprudence.* Conceptual analysis is one important aspect of analytical jurisprudence.[15] Adopting a global perspective highlights the need for adequate analytical concepts that can transcend different legal cultures and traditions. Because traditional legal scholarship was mainly confined to domestic law and most analytical jurists have focused on the concepts of legal doctrine (e.g. legal rights, ownership, causation) and its presuppositions (rules, legal system, validity), the focus has been mainly on law talk rather than talk about law. The doctrinal concepts of a legal system (such as English law) or a legal culture (such as the common law) are mainly 'folk concepts' with limited transferability across legal cultures and traditions. Conceptual elucidation is just as important for socio-legal studies as it is for legal analysis and exposition. But concepts such as dispute, institution, process, function, impact, and even court have been relatively neglected. Precise well-developed analytical concepts are needed for making comparisons and generalisations about legal phenomena across legal systems, traditions, and cultures. Our stock of usable transferable concepts is limited, so is our bank of reliable comparative empirical data. So our capacity to make comparisons and generalisations across legal cultures and tradition is correspondingly limited.

(ii) *Empirical jurisprudence.* Most socio-legal and empirical studies of legal phenomena have been confined to a single society, even in regard to non-state law. Recently, comparative and transnational empirical legal studies have started to develop, but the field is still at a relatively primitive stage. From a global perspective, one of the most important topics in need of empirical research is what social scientists call the processes of diffusion – often referred to by lawyers as transplants or reception. I have argued elsewhere that legal writings about this subject have tended to be unempirical and have been unduly influenced by 'a naïve model of reception'.[16] This is an 'ideal type', which postulates a paradigm case with the following characteristic assumptions:

> [A] *bipolar* relationship between *two countries* involving a *direct one-way* transfer of *legal rules or institutions* through the agency of *governments* involving *formal enactment or adoption* at a particular moment of time (*a reception date*) *without major change*... [I]t is commonly assumed that the standard case involves *transfer from an advanced (parent) civil or common law system to a less developed one*, in order to bring about *technological change* ('to modernise') by *filling in gaps or replacing* prior local law.[17]

It is easy to show that none of these elements is necessary or even characteristic of actual processes of diffusion of law, which are much more diverse and complex than the 'naïve model' suggests. This is relevant in the present context because so many environmental problems involve cross-level interactions between different state and

---

[15] This argument is developed in Twining (2008), Ch. 2.   [16] Twining (2005b) and (2005c).   [17] *Ibid.*

non-state legal orders and the development of environmental law and justice involves diffusion of ideas developed at many different levels.

5 Adjusting the canon: filleting Hart, extending Bentham, realising Rawls

If one accepts the points about the importance of differentiating levels of ordering, about the significance of non-state law, and about legal pluralism, this raises some important questions about the relevance of twentieth-century canonical jurists to considering law and justice from a global perspective. For example, most of the leading Western jurists of the twentieth century have focused very largely on municipal state law, have had strong conceptions of sovereignty, and have assumed that legal systems and societies can be treated as discrete, largely self-contained units. They have either articulated or assumed that jurisprudence and the discipline of law is or should be concerned with only two kinds of law: the domestic municipal law of nation states and public international law, which was widely accepted as a secondary form of law, mainly concerned with relations between states ('the Westphalian Duo').

At first sight, this suggests that many of these canonical jurists have become outdated and irrelevant. However, a younger generation of theorists has begun to adjust the Western liberal tradition in ways that suggest that, with due modifications, some twentieth-century canonical jurists are of continuing relevance.

For example, Brian Tamanaha, stayed with Hart's two basic positivist premises – the separation thesis and the social sources thesis – but pared away all Hart's criteria of identification in order to construct a broadened conception of law that would include several forms of non-state and religious law, but which differentiated it from other social rules and institutions, such as those involved in the governance of hospitals, schools, and sports leagues.[18]

Thomas Pogge, a pupil of Rawls, has argued that Rawls' two principles of justice (somewhat modified) can be transferred directly to the international sphere, largely by challenging the idea of a society as a self-enclosed unit.[19] Pogge has been sharply critical of Rawls' attempts to limit his principles of justice to the domestic sphere.[20] Pogge has transformed what had increasingly come to be seen as a rather complacent and conservative theory of domestic justice into a quite radical theory as the basis for a sharp critique of the existing international order and its institutions. I shall return to Pogge in due course.

In a somewhat different way, Peter Singer has applied Benthamite utilitarianism to contemporary issues in international ethics, including environmental ethics.[21] Jeremy

---

[18] Tamanaha (2001), discussed in Twining (2003b).   [19] Pogge (1989), (2002), discussed below.

[20] Rawls (1971) at 378–82, developed in Rawls (1999b). Pogge's original criticism was directed to the treatment of transnational ethics in *A Theory of Justice*, but later he developed and extended his critique (especially, Pogge (2001) and (2002)).

[21] Especially Singer (1975/1990); cf. Singer (1972), (1993) and (2004).

Bentham prided himself in being 'a citizen of the world', he coined the term 'inter-national law', but has generally been interpreted as a theorist of strong sovereignty.[22] Bentham posed the question whether the sovereign's duty is to maximise the interests of his own people or of humankind as a whole?[23] Bentham did not really answer this question, but Peter Singer, who is widely considered to be the leading contemporary proponent of classical utilitarianism, has come out firmly in favour of the idea that national leaders owe a duty to humankind, even though this presents problems when democracy is largely confined to some nation states.[24]

Thus, already there are jurists who are reworking our heritage of legal thought to adjust to the changing global scene. In rather different ways, Patrick Glenn could be interpreted as reviving an earlier tradition of world history applied to law[25] and Boaventura de Sousa Santos could be viewed as a post-modern successor to Weber and Marx.[26]

6 Normative jurisprudence

Normative jurisprudence encompasses general questions about values and law. It deals with the relations between law, politics and morality, including debates between and among positivists and others about the relationship between law and morals, whether law is at its core a moral enterprise, and about political obligation and civil disobedi-ence. It includes questions about the existence, scope and status of natural, moral and non-legal rights; the relationship between needs, rights, interests, and entitlements; theories of justice; constitutionalism and democracy; and standards for guiding and evaluating legal institutions, rules, practices, and decisions. Normative jurisprudence now occupies a central place on the agenda of Anglo-American jurisprudence.

If one steps back and considers the Western heritage of normative jurisprudence from a global perspective, one can identify a number of tendencies that are relevant to discussing issues of environmental justice.

6.1 The collective ignorance of other traditions

As with other branches of jurisprudence, Western normative jurisprudence has been quite insular. Western jurisprudence has a long tradition of universalism in ethics.

---

[22] See generally Dinwiddy (2004). On Bentham's subtle analysis of sovereignty, see Hart (1982) Ch. IX.

[23] J. Bentham (1806–9) discussed in Twining (2003a) at 237–42.

[24] 'This book argues that as the nations of the world move closer together to tackle global issues like trade, climate change, justice, and poverty, our national leaders need to take a larger perspective than that of national self-interest.' Singer (2004) (preface to second edition). While a utilitarian, such as Singer, would argue for harmonising national and global interests, the scope of a locally elected leader's duty to humankind needs further development.

[25] Glenn (2004), discussed in Foster (2006).

[26] Santos (2002). The first edition, Santos (1995), is discussed in Twining (2000) Ch. 8.

Natural law, classical utilitarianism, Kantianism, and modern theories of human rights have all been universalist in tendency.[27] But nearly all such theories have been developed and debated with at most only tangential reference to and in almost complete ignorance of the religious and moral beliefs and traditions of the rest of humankind. When differing cultural values are discussed, even the agenda of issues has a stereotypically Western bias. How can one seriously claim to be an informed universalist if one is ethnocentrically unaware of the ideas and values of other belief systems and traditions?

As the discipline of law becomes more cosmopolitan it needs to be backed by a genuinely cosmopolitan general jurisprudence. To this end we need to adjust the conventional canon of juristic texts to include significant writings and salient ideas and controversies from other traditions or which represent other viewpoints. Until now this has been considered the province of specialists. The task is daunting, but not impossible. Despite criticisms of 'orientalism', there has been some excellent work by Western scholars on Islamic, Hindu, Bhuddist, and Chinese legal thought.[28] To a lesser extent, there are accessible writings by contemporary 'Southern' writers. As a modest first step I have considered the general approaches to human rights of four 'Southern' jurists: Francis Deng, Abdullahi An Na'im, Yash Ghai, and Upendra Baxi.[29] All four deserve to be better known, but this is a limited exercise as these particular ones were all trained in the common law, write in English, and belong to the immediate post-independence generation. There are many others, including not least Southern feminists, and prominent jurists whose work has not been translated into English.

6.2 Secularism and a world-wide religious revival

During the twentieth century Western normative jurisprudence has been dominated by three main types of ethical theory: utilitarianism, deontology (including Natural Law and Kantian theories of justice and human rights), and virtue ethics.[30] These have, of course, been subjected to persistent challenges from various forms of scepticism, relativism, subjectivism, post-modernism, and, lately, in a different way, communitarianism. Eco-centric theories of environmental ethics could also be interpreted to fall outside the mainstream.[31] Apart from Natural Law, nearly all of our stock of normative theories are explicitly or implicitly secular. Classical utilitarianism and consequentialism, Rawlsian justice, and most variants on these have their roots in post-Enlightenment rationalism. Human rights is sometimes presented as a form of secular liberation theology[32] or as an ethical theory for a Godless Age.[33]

---

[27] 'Universalism' is a highly ambiguous concept. Here it will suffice to use it to refer to claims that a given moral principle applies to all humans at all times and in all places.

[28] There are useful select bibliographies in Glenn (2004) and Huxley (2002).

[29] Twining (2006) and (2008), Ch. 13.   [30] Griffin (1996) Ch. VII.   [31] See below.

[32] Baxi (2006).   [33] E.g. Gearty (2006) and Klug (2000).

That we live in a secular age may be true of, say, most of the United Kingdom and of most, but not all, of Europe; but the rising visibility of religious minorities may soon change that perception here. It is not true of the United States. The reverse is true of the rest of the world, which is more appropriately characterised as going through a period of religious revival, some but not all of which is characterised by some quite aggressive and evangelical kinds of fundamentalism. This refers not only to the headline-catching spread of fundamentalism in Islam, but also to Christianity, as Philip Jenkins' important book *The Next Christendom* vividly portrays.[34] From this perspective, secular liberalism appears to be on the decline and is beginning to look 'distinctly dated'.[35]

From a global perspective, a central challenge to human rights is to provide a vision that is attractive not only to non-believers, but also to believers, be they Christians, Muslims, Hindus, or others. It needs to be shown to be compatible with their core religious beliefs, as Abdullahi an Na'im, and other committed Muslims, are trying to do.[36]

6.3 Belief Pluralism

A third tendency in Western normative jurisprudence has been that leading liberal thinkers have beaten a partial retreat into an odd kind of particularism.[37] Ronald Dworkin states that 'interpretive theories are by their nature addressed to a particular legal culture, generally the culture to which their authors belong'.[38] Similarly, John Rawls has stated that '[t]he aims of political philosophy depend on the society it addresses',[39] and went quite close to acknowledging that his project was to develop a criterion of justice that would appeal to reflective Americans.[40] Whereas in *A Theory of Justice* there is a consensus among its members about the appropriate moral basis for a well-ordered democratic society, *Political Liberalism* confronts the problem of belief pluralism.

In response to this new concern, Rawls insisted that 'justice as fairness is political, not metaphysical'.[41] It is a practical theory aimed at providing a moral foundation for political, social, and economic institutions in a modern constitutional democracy in which the members have diverse, incompatible views. It is not a metaphysical or epistemological theory dealing with universal moral conceptions; nor does it apply

---

[34] Jenkins (2002). Cf. Miztal and Sharpe (1992).   [35] Jenkins (2002) at 9.

[36] E.g. An Na'im (1990), Lindholm and Vogt (1993).

[37] MacIntyre (1985), Hampshire(1989).   [38] Dworkin (1986) at 102.

[39] See generally Rawls (1971), Rawls (1993), Rawls (1999b), and Rawls (1999a). Especially important in the present context are three papers: Rawls (1980) (see now Rawls (1993), Lecture III); Rawls (1985) (see also Rawls (1993), Lecture I, 'Fundamental Ideas'); and Rawls (1987) (reprinted in Rawls (1999a) Ch. 20).

[40] Rawls (1980) at 518–19.

[41] Rawls (1985) at 226. Cf. Joseph Raz on Rawls' 'epistemic abstinence' in Raz (1994) at 62.

to all societies.[42] It is a limited secular theory that can provide a basis for coexistence and cooperation in a diverse society independently of religious beliefs and ideologies. A key idea is that of an overlapping consensus: this does not refer to those doctrines that are common to the different belief systems in a given society, but rather to what free and equal citizens would accept as a freestanding political view of society as a fair system of cooperation.[43]

This aspect of political liberalism is clearly relevant when we think about the institutions and practices needed for coexistence and cooperation in a world characterised by a diversity of belief systems, traditions, and cultures. On most interpretations of 'globalisation', which emphasise interdependence, the decline of sovereignty, and the permeability of borders, only one such society exists: the world. A well-constructed and coherent political theory which provides a coherent moral basis for the design of structures and institutions that can ensure stable, orderly, and fair arrangements for coexistence and cooperation between its diverse members is badly needed. In light of the critical issues of radical poverty, environmental crises, and increasing inequalities, a theory that claims to deal with global justice is especially welcome.

6.4 Moving beyond domestic justice

In recent times, liberal democratic political and legal theories have tended either to be geographically indeterminate or to place some limits on their geographical claims. A great deal of recent Anglo-American normative jurisprudence has been relatively local in respect of provenance, audience, and even focus.[44] For example, most writings about the new communitarianism, critical race theory, and republicanism have been explicitly or implicitly or unself-consciously American or at least American-influenced.[45] Feminist jurisprudence has only recently begun to be genuinely transnational.[46]

---

[42] Rawls (1985). Justice as fairness is mainly concerned with individual liberty and distribution. Rawls deals only briefly with procedural justice, expletive justice (under the Rule of Law), and institutionally dependent concepts, such as 'access to justice'. So far as I know, he did not use the terms 'environmental justice' or 'transitional justice'. He treated questions about our duties to animals, endangered species, trees, and the environment as falling outside the scope of his theory of justice as fairness. See further below note 75.

[43] PLL at 40.

[44] Twining (2000) at 128–9. There are some important exceptions to the trend towards greater geographical particularity. The field of international ethics, exemplified by Peter Singer, Brian Barry, Onora O'Neill, Martha Nussbaum, Amartya Sen, and Thomas Pogge, addresses transnational issues from a global perspective. There have been lively debates about human rights and cultural relativism, and about universalism versus contextualism. The most politically influential ideas are probably still the ideological assumptions underlying the 'Washington Consensus' which links free market economics to the seductive catchphrase 'human rights, good governance, and democracy'. However, see now the Millennium Development Goals, which have been influenced by other, somewhat different strands of thought including the ideas of Amartya Sen (see Sen (1999)).

[45] Twining (2000) at 58–60. Critical legal scholars have quite recently turned their attention to comparative law, international law, and Latin America ('Lat-Crits') and issues of globalisation, but it is too early to assess the significance of these developments.

[46] E.g. Nussbaum (2000).

For many commentators, Rawls' *A Theory of Justice* has been the almost inevitable starting-point for any contemporary theory of justice. It was natural in the 1960s and 1970s to think of justice in terms of domestic justice within societies, conceived as clearly bounded units. As awareness of 'globalisation' developed and interest in 'international ethics' increased, it was hoped that Rawls would rethink the extension of his basic ideas to the international/transnational sphere and would develop a robust theory of global justice. Unfortunately, Rawls did not fulfil such hopes. His later works mark a retreat into a position that, from a global perspective, is a huge disappointment.[47]

From a global perspective, it is bizarre to find a purportedly liberal theory of justice that rejects any principle of distribution, treats an outdated conception of public international law as satisfactorily representing principles of justice in the global arena, and says almost nothing about radical poverty, the environment, increasing inequalities, and American hegemony (and how it might be exercised), let alone about transitional justice or reparations or other issues that are now high on the global agenda. What had promised to be a progressive critical theory ended up with a position that one of his pupils, Thomas Pogge, concluded amounted to 'arbitrary discrimination in favour of affluent societies and against the global poor'.[48]

Fortunately, Pogge has ably defended and refined Rawls' original theory and has substituted his own quite radical theory of international justice and human rights. Mainly by changing one of Rawls' key conceptions – the postulate that justice as fairness is only concerned with the internal ordering of societies conceived as self-contained units –, he has shown how much of Rawls' scheme can be converted from a parochial and quite conservative theory into one that could be of real value in providing a moral basis for a substantial critique and redesign of supranational and international institutions. Rawls' core ideas for a practical theory aimed at providing a criterion of justice for basic institutions can be applied to the global system with a few adjustments along the following lines: We live in an interdependent world, in which all are involved and from which 'we cannot just drop out'. There are no self-contained national societies in the modern world, nor are there likely to be. The only closed social system is humanity at large.[49] A theory of justice for any other kind of association, including the nation state, is dependent on background principles

---

[47] A sample of critical reviews includes Buchanan (2000) (this is part of a generally critical symposium on *The Law of Peoples*); Kuper (2000); Tasioulas (2002a); and Singer (2004) at 176–80. For a partial defence, see Tasioulas (2005).

[48] Pogge (2002) at 108.

[49] Pogge talks of 'the global system' (about which I have reservations); not much would be changed by substituting some looser term, such as humankind. He envisages an extension of the Rawlsian model of a hierarchy of associations acting as systems within systems, whereas the picture that I have suggested is a much more complex one of overlapping and cross-cutting semi-autonomous social spheres operating in a complex global context. However, we agree on the point that any theory of justice has to be set in a broad context which prescribes background rules and constraints for more localised spheres of justice.

or 'ground rules' formulated at the global level.[50] This is a world of widespread deprivations and disadvantages, many of which have been promoted by existing transnational institutions. One test of basic institutions is the benefits and burdens they engender. The position of the least advantaged is one important measure of just institutions. It is highly probable that improved global institutions would help to alleviate at least some of the existing deprivations and disadvantages of the worst off. Rawls' two principles (modified and extended to give more weight to social and economic needs) and some of his basic ideas – such as the veil of ignorance, search for an overlapping consensus, the individual as the ultimate unit of justice[51] – and the basic structure are more coherently applicable to 'the global system' than to artificially bounded societies or states, not least because 'all institutional matters, including the ideal extent of national sovereignty, are now systematically addressed within a single framework'.[52] On the basis of this neo-Rawlsian approach, Pogge concludes that 'our current global institutional scheme is unjust, and as advantaged participants in this order we share a collective responsibility for its injustice'.[53]

For present purposes, it is sufficient to make three points about the significance of Pogge's contribution: first, as a disciple of Rawls he has modified and refined the ideas in ways that many may agree represent an improvement on *A Theory of Justice*. Secondly, as an increasingly sharp critic of Rawls he has substituted a theory of international justice that is radically different from Rawls' own late effort, but which is nevertheless Rawlsian in spirit. Thirdly, by confronting in detail the facts of global poverty and some of the political practicalities it involves he has engaged with one of the major issues of our age from the point of view of a philosopher, who believes that abstract ideas are important in addressing practical problems. Whether or not one agrees with all of his arguments, the message is clear: if you are concerned about justice in relation to world poverty, read *World Poverty and Human Rights* rather than *The Law of Peoples*. In the present context, however, Pogge's approach has two limitations. First, it is highly focused on only one aspect of global justice, radical poverty, and he touches only incidentally on environmental issues. Pogge adopts a

---

[50] Rawls follows Kant (1795) in rejecting a centralised regime of world government on the ground that it would be either a global despotism or else an unstable and fragile empire torn by civil strife (Rawls (1993) at 54–5). This is a quite different point from the argument that the justice of any domestic political order needs to be set in a wider, transnational or global context, especially as societies become increasingly interdependent. Cf. Pogge (1989) at 255–6.

[51] Pogge (1989) Ch. 2, defends Rawls against charges of atomism, that is, of treating individuals as if they are socially and politically isolated and self-sufficient; but Rawls does treat the individual human being as the ultimate moral unit.

[52] *Ibid.* at 258.

[53] *Ibid.* at 277. Cf. *Ibid.* at 36: 'It is not easy to convince oneself that our global order, assessed from a Rawlsian perspective, is moderately just despite the widespread and extreme deprivations and disadvantages it engenders. Even if we limit our vision to our advanced Western society, it is hardly obvious that the basic institutions we participate in are just or nearly just. In any case, a somewhat unobvious but massive threat to the moral quality of our lives is the danger that we will have lived as advantaged participants in unjust institutions, collaborating in their perpetuation and benefiting from their injustice.'

thin interpretation of human rights for the specific purpose of arguing that present institutional arrangements contribute to poverty. Secondly, Pogge is constructing an argument that is intended to have a broad appeal that transcends a range of positions. He does not rely on arguments that we owe a positive duty to help the worst off, as Singer does, but restricts his argument to a negative duty not to maintain institutions that maintain or contribute to radical poverty.[54]

6.5 The salience of human rights discourse: the only show in town?

Some commentators claim that the language of human rights has become the dominant mode of moral discourse of the last fifty years, edging out moral tropes such as distributive justice, the common good, and solidarity.[55] Such claims to dominance and universality seem to me to be overstated. It is true that, after 'the collapse of communism', symbolised by the fall of the Berlin Wall, some former Marxist and socialist intellectuals adopted the discourse of human rights. It is also the case that enormous advances have been made in the development of an international regime of human rights law and that domestic bills of rights have also proliferated in the past twenty-five years.[56] Partly as a result, many other interested parties have jumped on the bandwagon. Indeed, one of Baxi's central themes is that human rights discourse has become commodified, professionalised by technocrats, and sometimes hijacked by powerful groups, so that it is in grave danger of losing touch with the experiences of suffering and the needs of those who should be the main beneficiaries – the poor and the oppressed.[57] More pragmatically, Yash Ghai has argued on the basis of his extensive experience of constitution-making in multi-ethnic societies, that human rights discourse provides a workable framework for negotiating claims between different interest groups, provided that the substance of the claims are not taken too literally.[58] In other words, human rights is best conceived as a language for expressing claims and arguments rather than as an abstract set of universal standards. Whether rights-based approaches to foreign assistance, development, and ecology are more than passing fashions is an open question. But claims that secular human rights can become a universal moral language are overstated and need to be treated with great

---

[54] As Singer has modified his pure utilitarianism in order to broaden the appeal of his argument, Pogge appears to have trimmed his philosophical views in order to persuade a broader political constituency. In reading contemporary writers like Pogge and Singer, it is often difficult to distinguish clearly between their philosophical positions and their more activist concern to persuade broader audiences about their conclusions. From a global perspective, if one accepts belief pluralism as a fact, I suggest that it is important to distinguish between constructing cogent philosophical arguments and advancing persuasive arguments that have a broad appeal and may contribute to workable political agreements among people with different ideologies and potentially conflicting interests. Both are worthy enterprises, but they should be recognised as separate.

[55] Baxi (2006) at 1 and Ch. 4. Cf. similar claims made by Conor Gearty (2006) and Henkin (1990).

[56] Gearty (2006) at 63–4.   [57] Baxi (2006). discussed in Twining 2006 at n. 2.

[58] E.g. Ghai (2000), discussed in Twining (2006).

caution. Let me give just two reasons: First, belief pluralism is a fact and human rights discourse just does not fit easily with the languages and ways of viewing things of the major religions and many other belief systems. For example, Abdullahi An Na'im, in his invaluable attempts to reconcile the values of liberal Islam and of the Universal Declaration of Human Rights, acknowledges that, while some, but not all, of the basic values are compatible, to be persuasive the discourse has to be translated into terms that fit the beliefs and ways of thinking of most Muslims.[59] Broadly speaking, the language of Islam is not the language of rights. There are also other belief systems that are more comfortable with the language of responsibility, or community, or civic virtue. Critics of the claim that human rights are Western values being imposed on Asian countries and cultures have rightly pointed out that the *origin* of human rights does not negate its *validity*, that there is no monolithic Asian culture, that there are many Asian supporters of human rights and civil liberties, and that the 'Asian Values' debate was largely stimulated by dictatorial leaders responding to outside criticism of repressive practices and in the process invoking the right to self-determination.[60] Such criticisms are no doubt justified, but the fact remains that the language of Confucianism and many other traditional cultures is different from the language of individual human rights.[61]

A second warning about the expansionist tendencies of human rights talk relates to the scope of human rights. One of the unresolved questions of human rights theory concerns the criteria for distinguishing between appropriate and inappropriate usages of human rights discourse.[62] In the present context, it is especially important to clarify the relationship between the discourses of justice, human rights and utility. It is worth remembering that Rawls developed his theory of justice as fairness to limit the scope of utilitarianism, not to reject all consequentialist arguments. Rawls also explicitly limited the scope of justice as fairness, allowing for other social values (such as efficiency and economic development)[63] and repeatedly disclaiming that his theory of justice was a comprehensive theory of human flourishing or the good life.[64] Furthermore, while acknowledging that humans owe some duties 'to animals and to the rest of nature', he explicitly excluded these from the province of his theory of justice.[65] It is also important to bear in mind the distinction between using consequentialist arguments instrumentally to work out the details of a deontological approach (as, for example, Aquinas and Finnis have done) and using rights- or justice-based arguments to trump consequentialist ones.[66]

---

[59] E.g. An Na'im (1990) and An Na'im and Deng (1990) and (1992). An Na'im's approach is discussed at length in Twining (2006). See also Lindholm and Vogt (1993).

[60] Sen (1997) at 40; Ghai (1993), (1995) and (1998b); and Castellino and Redondo (2006).

[61] This is acknowledged by Ghai (1998a).   [62] Griffin (2001), criticised in Tasioulas (2002b).

[63] E.g. Rawls (1971) at 9.   [64] E.g. Rawls (1993) at 11–15.

[65] E.g. Rawls (1971) at 17, 505ff, 512; and Rawls (1993) at 245.

[66] Pressure of space precludes doing justice here to the complex issues concerning claims for the relative merits of the language of rights, justice, and utility as rhetorical discourses.

In pluralist ethical theories, the spheres of human rights, justice, and consequentialism are not coextensive. To put the matter simply: climate change threatens to have catastrophic consequences for all humankind. The fact that most poorer individuals and communities are less well-equipped to deal with the consequences means that the impact will be distributed unjustly. That is an exacerbating, but secondary factor. Similarly, considering environmental issues exclusively from a human rights perspective can have a distorting effect. For human rights discourse tends to be binary: either one has a human right or one does not. Moreover, many human rights set minimum standards in an all-or-nothing way, often not allowing for differences of degree. In the same vein, I suggest that one of the key issues should be to what extent a theory of environmental justice leaves scope for other values and to what extent the language of justice is the most appropriate way of expressing all major concerns about the environment.

6.6 Universalism and cultural relativism

Accompanying the recognition of belief pluralism and the rise of evangelical human rights, there has been a resurgence of debates about relativism and universalism. There is a long tradition, especially in regard to human rights, of talking of a divide between universalism and cultural or other relativism.[67] But there is also a widespread tendency to treat such talk as involving a false dichotomy. Aristotle, and modern Aristotelians such as Gordley and Nussbaum, quite explicitly allow for differences between cultures; they merely insist on the universality of underlying principles. Another universalist, Alan Gewirth, argues that universalism can justify certain kinds of ethical particularism, in the sense that 'one ought to give preferential consideration to the interests of some persons against others, including not only oneself but also other persons with whom one has special relationships'.[68] Similarly, Joseph Raz, a committed universalist, sees 'the universal and the particular to be complementary rather than antagonistic', and argues that: 'At the heart of multiculturalism lies the recognition that universal values are realised in a variety of different ways in different cultures and that they are all worthy of respect.'[69] Indeed, among serious thinkers there seem to be very few strong universalists or extreme cultural relativists. And, of

---

[67] See generally Wilson (1997).

[68] Gewirth (1988). 'The ethical particularism with which I am concerned here, then, is confined to preferences for or partiality towards various *groups*, ranging from one's family and personal friends to larger pluralities of one's community, nation, and so forth.' *Ibid.* at 286. On utilitarianism and loyalty, see Twining (2000) at 66–7 and 131; on loyalty, see Fletcher (1993).

[69] Raz (1998) at 204 (citing earlier writings). Raz acknowledges that morality can change, but not radically, but only against an unchanging background of continuing moral principles that explain the change. 'Since . . . radical moral change is impossible, it follows that social relativism is untenable.' Raz (1999) at 180. An even stronger universalist might argue that it is not fundamental moral principles that change, but our understandings of them.

course, 'relativism' is a highly ambiguous concept.[70] There is a widespread view that polarising the debate merely serves to obscure a complex variety of issues that need to be differentiated.

6.7 Anthropocentric and ecocentric views in normative jurisprudence

A topic not much discussed in the mainstream jurisprudential literature, but prominent in the environmental literature, is the distinction between anthropocentric and ecocentric perspectives. For the sake of brevity, one can borrow a quite stark definition of these terms:

> An anthropocentric action is taken to be one in which the reason to act is the provision of a benefit to human beings. An ecocentric action is taken to be one in which the reason to act is the provision of a benefit to the environment.[71]

The extent to which the canonical jurists seem to be anthropocentric is quite striking. Utilitarianism focuses on the pains and pleasures of human beings, but Bentham famously extended the application of utility to all sentient beings.[72] Peter Singer followed him.[73] So utilitarianism seems to be committed to protect non-sentient nature only insofar as it bears on the pleasures and pains of sentient beings. Human rights discourse is anthropocentric on its face; ascribing rights to trees or plants or artefacts is generally acknowledged to be an extension, which many feel is analytically dubious. Rawls' justice as fairness is a virtue of social institutions, meaning human institutions. Dworkin's basic notion of 'equal concern and respect' relates to human beings only.[74] Similarly, concern for the interests of future generations is generally taken to mean future human beings. However, on closer examination, these jurists, while focusing on human rights and interests, do not necessarily exclude all eco-centric reasons. Rawls, for example, acknowledges that we have moral duties in respect of animals and nature, but he treats these as falling outside his theory of justice as fairness as a political conception, which only applies to those who have a moral personality.[75] Similarly, Peter Singer may have given a different impression in *Animal Liberation*, but, when he was accused of 'speciesism' in limiting his argument

---

[70] Haack (1998) Ch. 9.

[71] Donnelly and Bishop (2007) arguing that 'new' Natural Law, as exemplified by Finnis and George, is necessarily anthropocentric, because it does not purport to derive natural law principles from human nature, thereby avoiding criticism concerning the naturalistic fallacy. On the other hand, 'traditional Natural Law' can provide support for ecocentrism in that it can be based on the idea of human nature being but one part of the general natural environment.

[72] 'The question is not: can they *reason*? Nor, can they *talk*? but can they *feel*?' Bentham (1789/1970) at 283n.

[73] Singer (1990).

[74] See, however, the discussion of the Snail Darter case in Dworkin (1986) at 20–3.

[75] Rawls (1971) at 504–12, especially 512. Rawls (1993) at 20, 244ff. '[T]he status of the natural world and our proper relation to it is not a constitutional essential or a basic question of justice, as these questions have been specified [in Rawls' theory]. It is a matter in regard to which citizens can vote their non-political values and try to convince other citizens accordingly. The limits of public reason do not apply.' Rawls (1993) at

to sentient beings, he hotly denied the charge.[76] Singer argues that to restrict 'rights' to human rights and to restrict utility to sentient beings are not arbitrary boundaries, but such restrictions do not rule out the possibility of extending the circle of our moral concern to other aspects of nature on the basis of other moral principles. Singer has difficulty with the philosophical basis of a non-speciesist ethic, such as Rolston's 'respect for life'. Singer does not put forward an alternative basis. Instead, he extends the range of anthropocentric reasons for preserving the environment, by emphasising aesthetic, scientific, and recreational values of preserving natural ecosystems and argues that the environment should be preserved for future generations, not least to allow them to choose how to deal with it.[77] As I read him, Singer cares passionately about the environment; the main reasons he advances for valuing the environment are ultimately anthropocentric, but he leaves the door open for the evolution of a philosophically coherent ecocentric ethos, which in his view has yet to be achieved.

To sum up: it is undoubtedly the case that nearly all of the thinkers that I have discussed have an anthropocentric *focus*. However, it would be a mistake to infer from this that they are indifferent to environmental concerns or that they treat ecocentric reasons as invalid. Most do, however, seem to take the position that ecocentric reasons fall outside the scope of the mainstream discourses of utility, human rights, and justice as fairness.[78]

7 Conclusion

The French philosopher, Jacques Maritain, who played a significant role in the preparation of the Universal Declaration of Human Rights, relates a story of someone expressing amazement that proponents of opposed ideologies had reached agreement on a list of rights: 'Yes, they replied. We agree on these rights, *providing we are not asked why.*'[79] Maritain drew a sharp distinction between 'practical conclusion' and 'rational justification'.[80] He had a well-developed Thomist conception of dignity as part of his theory of Natural Law. But, to use a later distinction, he supported the use of the concept in the draft Declaration, but argued strongly for leaving the conception undefined.[81]

---

246. Rawls also enumerates a number of examples in which, because the treatment of animals and other aspects of nature bear on human interests, political values are involved. *Ibid.* at 245.

[76] Rolston (1999); Singer's response in the same volume is at 327–32. His position on environmental ethics is set out at greater length in Singer (1993) Ch. 10.

[77] See note 75 above.

[78] In earlier versions of this paper, there were sections on ecumenical arguments and *ius humanitatis*, but these have been cut for reasons of space.

[79] Maritain (1954) at 70.   [80] *Ibid.* Ch. IV.

[81] On dignity as a 'placeholder concept', see McCrudden (2008).

When Jacques Maritain drew a quite sharp distinction between philosophical argu-ments and pragmatic approaches to human rights, he was not saying that philosophy was unimportant. Rather, like Rawls and many twentieth-century philosophers, he emphasised that belief pluralism is a social fact that has implications both for philoso-phy and for the practical politics of coexistence and cooperation. Maritain's strategy in respect of rights suggests that we need coherent philosophies, ecumenical arguments, *and* a willingness to negotiate working agreements patiently, in detail, in a pragmatic fashion accepting the need to compromise.[82] Concepts like justice, utility, and rights all have a role to play in constructing such arguments and negotiations.

In concluding, six salient themes:

1. When using G-words, it is best to remember that nearly all processes of so-called 'globalisation' operate primarily at sub-global levels.
2. From a global perspective, if one adopts a reasonably broad conception of law, it is almost inevitable that the picture is one of great variety and complexity, involving multiple levels, non-state law, legal pluralism, cross-level diffusion, complex kinds of interlegality, and largely surface homogenisation and convergence. With due respect to Thomas Friedman, so far as law is concerned, the world is not yet flat.[83]
3. At first sight, many of our canonical jurists may seem out of place in a post-Westphalian world. However, a younger generation of jurists is developing new kinds of general jurisprudence, which builds on their predecessors as well as stab-bing them in the back: Tamanaha fillets Hart; Pogge transfers Rawlsian justice to the world stage more convincingly than Rawls; Singer modernises Bentham; and Santos post-modernises Weber and Marx.
4. Most post-Enlightenment moral theories in the West are avowedly secular. Human rights is sometimes conceived of as a critical secular theology or a theory of values for a Godless Age. But, from a global perspective, most of the world is going through a period of religious revival. Believers and non-believers alike need to be persuaded about global policies.
5. Most Western jurists have an anthropocentric *focus*. It does not follow that they are indifferent to environmental concerns nor that they treat ecocentric reasons as invalid. Most do, however, seem to take the position that ecocentric reasons fall outside the scope of the mainstream discourses of utility, human rights, and justice as fairness.
6. One of the challenges in approaching environmental issues is to what extent a theory of environmental justice leaves scope for other values and to what extent the language of justice is the most appropriate way of expressing all major concerns about the environment.

---

[82] On ecumenical arguments, see note 54 above.   [83] Friedman (2005).

Bibilography

An Na'im, A., 1990. *Toward an Islamic Reformation: Civil Liberties, Human Rights and International Law.* Syracuse, NY: Syracuse University Press.

(ed.), 1992. *Human Rights in Cross-Cultural Perspectives: Quest for Consensus.* Philadelphia: Pennsylvania University Press.

An Na'im, A., and Deng, F. (eds.) 1990. *Human Rights in Africa: Cross-Cultural Perspectives.* Washington, DC: Brookings Institution.

Baxi, U., 2006. *The Future of Human Rights.* 2nd edn, New Delhi: Oxford University Press.

Bentham, J., 1789/1970. *An Introduction to the Principles of Morals and Legislation.* ed. J. H. Burns and H. L. A. Hart. *Collected Works.* Oxford: Oxford University Press.

1806–9. *Principles of International Law, Works,* vol. 2. Bowring edition, 1837–43.

Blomley, N., 1994. *Law, Space and the Geographies of Power.* New York: Guilford Press.

Buchanan, A., 2000. 'Rawls's Law of Peoples: Rules for a Vanished Westphalian World'. 110 *Ethics* 697.

Castellino, J., and Redondo, E. D., 2006. *Minority Rights in Asia.* Oxford: Oxford University Press.

Commission on Global Governance, 1996. *Our Global Neighbourhood.* Oxford: Oxford University Press.

Dinwiddy, J., 2004. *Bentham: Selected Writings of John Dinwiddy.* W. Twining (ed.). Stanford: Stanford University Press.

Donnelly, B., and Bishop, P., 2007. 'Natural Law and Econcentrism'. 19 *Journal of Environmental Law* 89.

Dworkin, R., 1986. *Law's Empire.* London: Fontana.

Economides, K., 1996. 'Law and Geography: New Frontiers', in Philip Thomas (ed.), *Legal Frontiers.* Aldershot: Dartmouth.

Fletcher, G., 1993. *Loyalty.* New York: Oxford University Press.

Foster, N. (ed.) 2006. 'A Fresh Start for Comparative Legal Studies', Symposium on Patrick Glenn's *Legal Traditions of the World* (2nd edn), in 1 *Journal of Comparative Law* 100.

Friedman, T. L., 2005. *The World is Flat.* New York: Farrar, Straus and Giroux.

Gearty, C., 2006. *Can Human Rights Survive?* Cambridge: Cambridge University Press.

Gewirth, A., 1988. 'Ethical Universalism and Particularism'. 85 *Journal of Philosophy* 283.

Ghai, Y., 1993. 'Asian Perspectives on Human Rights'. 23 *Hong Kong Law Journal* 342.

1995. 'The Politics of Rights in Asia', in G. P. Wilson (ed.), *Frontiers of Legal Research.* Chichester: Chancery Law Publishing.

1998a. 'Rights, Duties and Responsibilities', in J. Caughelin, P. Lim, and B Mayer-Konig (eds.), *Asian Values: Encounter with Diversity.* London: Curzon Press, Ch. 2.

1998b. 'Human Rights and Asian Values'. 9 *Public Law Review* 168.

2000. 'Universalism and Relativism: Human Rights as a Framework for Negotiating Interethnic Claims'. 21 *Cardozo Law Review* 1095.

Giddens, A., 1990. *The Consequences of Modernity.* Stanford: Stanford University Press.

Glenn, P., 2004. *Legal Traditions of the World: Sustainable Diversity in Law.* 2nd edn, Oxford: Oxford University Press.

Griffin, J., 1996. *Value Judgement.* Oxford: Oxford University Press.

2001. 'Discrepancies Between the Best Philosophical Account of Human rights and the International Law of Human Rights'. Presidential Address, *Proceedings of the Aristotelian Society* 1.

Haack, S., 1998. *Manifesto of a Passionate Moderate*. Chicago: University of Chicago Press.

Hampshire, S., 1989. *Innocence and Experience*. London: Allen Lane.

Hart, H. L. A., 1982. *Essays on Bentham*. Oxford: Oxford University Press.

1983. 'Problems of the Philosophy of Law', in *Essays in Jurispudence and Philosophy*. Oxford: Oxford University Press.

Henkin, L., 1990. *The Age of Rights*. New York: Columbia University Press.

Holder, J., and Harrison, C. (eds.) 2003. *Law and Geography*. Oxford: Oxford University Press.

Huxley, A. (ed.), 2002. *Religion, Law and Tradition*. London: RoutledgeCurzon.

Jamieson, D. (ed.), 1999. *Singer and His Critics*. Oxford: Blackwell.

Jenkins, P., 2002. *The Next Christendom*. Oxford: Oxford University Press.

Kant. I., 1795/1970. *Perpetual Peace in Political Writings*. ed. H. Reiss, Cambridge: Cambridge University Press.

Klug, F., 2000. *Values for a Godless Age: The Story of the United Kingdom's New Bill of Rights*. London: Penguin Books.

Kuper, A., 2000. 'Rawlsian Global Justice: Beyond the Law of Peoples to a Cosmopolitan Law of Persons'. 28 *Political Theory* 640.

Lessig, L., 2002. *The Future of Ideas: The Fate of the Commons in a Connected World*. New York: Random House.

Lindholm, Tori, and Vogt, Kari (eds.), 1993. *Islamic Law Reform and Human Rights: Challenges and Rejoinders*. Copenhagen and Oslo: Nordic Human Rights Publications.

MacIntyre, A., 1985. *After Virtue*. 2nd edn, London: Duckworth.

Maritain, J., 1954. *Man and the State*. ed. Richard O'Sullivan, London: Hollis and Carter.

McCrudden, C., 2008. 'Human Dignity and Judicial Interpretation of Human Rights'. 20 *European Journal of International Law* 1.

Miztal, Bronislaw, and Sharpe, Anson (eds.), 1992. *Religion and Politics in Comparative Perspective: Revival of Religious Fundamentalism in East and West*. Westport, CT: Praeger.

Nussbaum, M., 2000. *Women and Human Development: The Capabilities Approach*. Cambridge: Cambridge University Press.

Pearl, David, and Menski, Werner, 1998. *Muslim Family Law*. 3rd edn, London: Sweet & Maxwell.

Pogge, T., 1989. *Realizing Rawls*. Ithaca: Cornell University Press.

2001. 'Rawls on International Justice'. 51 *Philosophical Quarterly* 246.

2002. *World Poverty and Human Rights*. Cambridge: Polity Press.

2005. 'Real World Justice'. 9 *Journal of Ethics* 29.

Rawls, J., 1971. *A Theory of Justice*. Cambridge, MA: Harvard University Press.

1980. 'Kantian Constructivism in Moral Theory' (reprinted in Rawls (1999a)).

1985. 'Justice as Fairness: Political, Not Metaphysical' (reprinted in Rawls (1999a) Ch. 18)

1987. 'The Idea of an Overlapping Consensus' (reprinted in Rawls (1999a) Ch. 20).

1993. *Political Liberalism*. New York: Columbia University Press.

1998. '*Commonwealth* Interview with John Rawls' (reprinted in Rawls (1999a) at 616).

1999a. *Collected Papers*, ed. S. Freeman. Cambridge, MA: Harvard University Press.

1999b. *The Law of Peoples*. Cambridge, MA: Harvard University Press.

Raz, J., 1994. *Ethics in the Public Domain.* Oxford: Clarendon Press.

    1998. 'Multiculturalism'. 11 *Ratio Juris* 193.

    1999. *Engaging Reason.* New York: Oxford University Press.

Rogers, B., 1999. 'Portrait: John Rawls', *Prospect*, Issue 42, June.

Rolston III, H., 1999, 'Respect for Life: Counting What Singer Finds of No Account', in Dale Jamieson (ed.), *Singer and His Critics.* Oxford: Blackwell, at 247–68.

Rorty, R., 1993. 'Human Rights, Rationality and Sentimentality', in Stephen Shute and Susan Hurley (eds.), *On Human Rights.* New York: Basic Books.

Sachs, J., 2005. *The End of Poverty.* London: Penguin.

Santos, Boaventura de Sousa, 1995. *Toward a New Common Sense.* London: Routledge.

    2002. *Toward a New Legal Common Sense: Law, Globalization and Emancipation.* 2nd edn, London: Butterworths Lexis Nexis.

Sen, Amartya, 1997. 'Human Rights and Asian Values: What Lee Kuan Yew and I Peng Don't Understand About Asia', *The New Republic*, 14 and 21 July, 33–40.

    1999. *Development as Freedom.* New York: Knopf.

Singer, P., 1972. 'Famine, Affluence and Morality'. 1 *Philosophy and Public Affairs* 229–43 (variously reprinted).

    1983. *The Expanding Circle.* Oxford: Oxford University Press.

    1990. *Animal Liberation.* 2nd edn, New York: Random House.

    1993. *Practical Ethics.* 2nd edn, Cambridge: Cambridge University Press.

    2004. *One World.* 2nd edn, New Haven: Yale University Press.

Stiglitz, J., 2002. *Globalization and Its Discontents.* London: Allen Lane.

Stone, J., 1946. *The Province and Function of Law.* Cambridge, MA: Harvard University Press.

Tamanaha, B., 2001. *A General Jurisprudence of Law and Society.* Oxford: Oxford University Press.

Tasioulas, J., 2002a. 'From Utopia to Kazanistan: John Rawls and the Law of Peoples'. 22 *Oxford Journal of Legal Studies* 367.

    2002b. 'Human Rights, Universality and the Values of Personhood: Retracing Griffin's Steps'. 10 *European Journal of Philosophy* 79.

    2005. 'Global Justice Without End'. 36 *Metaphilosophy* 3.

Twining, W., 1997. *Law in Context: Enlarging a Discipline.* Oxford: Oxford University Press.

    2000. *Globalisation and Legal Theory.* London: Butterworths.

    2003a. *The Great Juristic Bazaar.* Aldershot: Ashgate.

    2003b. 'A Post-Westphalian Conception of Law'. 37 *Law and Society Review* 199.

    2003c. 'The Province of Jurisprudence Re-examined', in Catherine Dauvergne (ed.), *Jurisprudence in an Interconnected Globe.* Aldershot: Ashgate, Ch. 2.

    2005a. 'Have Concepts, Will Travel: Analytical Jurisprudence in a Global Context'. 1 *International Journal of Law in Context* 5.

    2005b. 'General Jurisprudence', in M. Escamilla and M. Saavedra (eds.), *Law and Justice in Global Society.* Granada: University of Granada, World Congress of Philosophy of Law and Social Philosophy.

    2005c. 'Diffusion of Law: A Global Perspective'. 49 *Journal of Legal Pluralism* 1.

    2005d. 'Social Science and Diffusion of Law'. 32 *Journal of Law and Society* 203.

    2006. 'Human Rights: Southern Voices'. 11 *Review of Constitutional Studies* 203.

    2008. *General Jurisprudence: Understanding Law from a Global Perspective.* Cambridge: Cambridge University Press.

Wilson, R. A. (ed.), 1997. *Human Rights, Culture and Context*. London: Pluto Press.

Woodman, G., 2003. 'Why There Can Be No Map of Law', in Rajendra Pradhan (ed.), *Legal Pluralism and Unofficial Law in Social, Political, and Economic Development*, XIIIth International Congress of Commission on Folk Law and Legal Pluralism, Kathmandu, at 383–92.

2006. 'The Chthonic Legal Tradition – Or Everything That Is Not Something Else'. 1 *Journal of Comparative Law* 123.

5

Gender and environmental law and justice: thoughts on sustainable masculinities

HANNE PETERSEN

A society's symbols and images of nature express its collective consciousness. They appear in mythology, cosmology, science, religion, philosophy, language and art. Scientific, philosophical and literary texts are sources of the ideas and images used by controlling elites, while rituals, festivals, songs and myths provide clues to the consciousness of ordinary people.

Carolyn Merchant[1]

1 Gender and the development of a sense of justice: a Northern perspective

Carolyn Merchant's influential book *The Death of Nature. Women, Ecology and the Scientific Revolution,*[2] originally appeared in 1980. Two years later, another very influential book on gender, justice and care was published. Carol Gilligan's *In a Different Voice* started a discussion about the difference between a primarily male ethic of justice and a primarily female morality of care. The morality of care was understood to rest on the understanding of relationships primarily towards concrete persons with whom we have special and valuable relationships. Gilligan quoted Freud, who concluded that women 'show less sense of justice than men, that they are less ready to submit to the great exigencies of life, [and] that they are more often influenced in their judgements by feelings of affection or hostility'.[3] She also quoted Jean Piaget, who considered that the legal sense was essential to moral development, and who viewed that this sense 'is far less developed in little girls than in boys'.[4]

Merchant does not mention Gilligan in her later book from 1989 on *Ecological Revolutions: Nature, Gender, and Science in New England.* But the title of her book from 1995, *Earthcare. Women and the Environment,* indirectly seems to bear witness to the influence of the discussion on the 'ethics of care'. These parallel discourses on the relation between women and the environment, and on the female ethics of care have, perhaps indirectly, had as a consequence that relatively few writers seem to have dealt with issues concerning gender, *justice* and the environment. While, in the last decades, mainly *women* have dealt with issues concerning *gender*, this is slowly changing as

---

[1] Merchant 1989 p. 19.   [2] Merchant 1980.
[3] Gilligan 1982 p. 7. The quote from Freud is from a text from 1925.
[4] *Ibid.,* p. 10 (quote from Jean Piaget's book, *The Moral Judgment of the Child* from 1932).

the emerging field of masculinity studies demonstrates. Still, as Håkan Gustafsson notes, there remains a 'jurisprudential genderblindness', i.e. an ongoing indifference among male legal academics in dealing with gender problems as anything else but an acknowledgment of the relevance of equality issues.[5]

In Aristotelian thought, *justice* is considered a *virtue* amongst other virtues such as wisdom, courage and moderation. The tradition of Aristotelian ethics was a tradition in which morality was both realized through and manifest in outward forms.[6] Christianity added the virtues of faith, hope and love to the virtues, which were important for the Western world for many centuries.

Virtues have been considered gender-specific in the Christian world, as well as in many other religious and legal traditions and still are to a large extent. In many societies, women have been and still are expected to protect their sexual purity and virginity. In contemporary Egyptian Islamic society, shyness, modesty and humility are considered feminine virtues, which women have to perform in order to be able to play a role in public life.[7] Carol Gilligan wrote in 1982 that: 'The notion that virtue for women lies in self-sacrifice has complicated the course of women's development by pitting the moral issue of goodness against the adult questions of responsibility and choice. In addition, the ethic of self-sacrifice is directly in conflict with the concept of rights that has, in this past century, supported women's claim to a fair share of justice.'[8]

Perhaps the *practices* of traditional feminine virtues by many women around the world have led to results, which lie behind the dominant understanding and perception of women as environmentally friendly and considerate. It is, however, also a dominant perception that women bear the major burden of the consequences of environmental problems such as shortage of water, food and fuel. Thus it seems that virtuous practices such as environmentally friendly practices may hinder 'women's claim to a fair share of justice' where justice is understood not as a virtue, but from a distributive perspective. A paradox seems to emerge, where women's environmentally virtuous behaviour might lead to them being subject to modern forms of discrimination. I think this is a paradox, which modern environmental law has difficulty in handling. Modern environmental law generally does not value and acknowledge 'traditional' virtues as environmentally friendly behaviour, and it is most often gender neutral or gender blind.

Virtues came to be seen as obsolete, and old-fashioned in modern societies, where they were replaced by modern and increasingly gender neutralized *values* and ideals of liberty, equality and fraternity – values which have also strongly influenced the evaluation of relations between men and women. However, in scholarship and philosophy, discussions on classical virtues have been reappearing. Alasdair MacIntyre's book, *After Virtue*, has been especially significant in this respect.[9] Marja Heimonen, a

---

[5] Gustafsson 2006 pp. 3–26.   [6] Mahmood 2005 p. 25.   [7] *Ibid.*, pp. 6, 23.
[8] Gilligan 1982 p. 132.   [9] MacIntyre 1984.

Finnish researcher, musician and music educator, who has dealt with the interrelation between law and music, explores 'the role of music education in developing one of the fundamental virtues in society, the sense of justice'.[10] She argues that the exercise and possession of virtues is linked to participation in practices,[11] and that the sense of justice is connected to both moral group norms and individual behaviour. It is connected to emotions such as joy, anger and sadness – as is music.[12] The aim of (music) education is 'to achieve a more humane society, and the ethic of care and carefulness should thus also provide a guide for music educators'.[13] Thus, 'it should promote social justice worldwide by fostering understanding and tolerance in our global, multi-cultural world with its multitude of conflicting value systems'.[14] Heimonen here combines the ethics of care with social justice, and is concerned about how world citizens, who are sensitive not only to themselves but also to the needs and emotions of others living on the earth, could be nurtured in music education, and she emphasizes virtue ethics and the cultivation of sympathy and *phronesis* (i.e. practical wisdom) as an ethical guide. She argues that pupils could be encouraged to be more sensitive not only to music, but also to other people and to the world they live in.[15]

> Sensitivity and respectful listening to others is said to form an ethical basis for creating peace in the global world. Educating pupils to listen respectfully and sensitively to all kinds of music, letting the sounds touch them and release their feelings in supportive and caring surroundings could give music educators a unique opportunity to foster global understanding in pupils.[16]

Heimonen mentions that a majority of music-school pupils are girls.[17] She does not ignore the competitive aspects of the contemporary music world, but she underlines its ethical and global perspectives. Given that several events to fight global injustice over the last years have been organized by musicians and took place as huge concerts – as the Live 8 concerts in 2005, which aimed at putting pressure on world leaders to drop the debt of the world's poorest nations, increase and improve aid, and negotiate fairer trade rules in the interest of poorer countries – this seems a not completely unrealistic approach. Musicians were involved in similar attempts to raise awareness about global warming and climate change at the Live Earth concerts of 7 July 2007, a series of worldwide concerts that initiated a three-year campaign to combat climate change and advocate environmentally sustainable living. The concerts brought together more than 150 musical acts in eleven locations around the world and were broadcast to a mass global audience through radio, television and the Internet.

---

[10] Heimonen 2006a pp. 119–41. Cf. her doctoral dissertation, Heimonen 2002.
[11] Heimonen 2006a p. 128.   [12] *Ibid.*, p. 132.   [13] *Ibid.*, p. 133.   [14] Heimonen 2006b p. 88.
[15] *Ibid.*, p. 91.   [16] *Ibid.*, pp. 94–5.   [17] *Ibid.*, p. 52.

2 The limits of environmental law and justice

What is at stake here is the need for a multitude of normative approaches and instruments to deal with the complex interrelationship between gendered human beings and non-human nature. Environmental law being an instrument of the modern state has difficulty in combining and taking care of the seemingly colliding (traditional) values of conservation of the environment and the values of securing (modern equality-oriented, distributive) justice in gender relations. Gender relations are characterized by differences, which, from a modern perspective, are often – but not always rightly – understood as discriminatory inequalities. Traditional gendered virtues may support care for the environment also from a modern perspective, but may not secure modern equality and thus not justice in a distributive sense.

Rainer Wolf has written about the difficulties in using concepts of justice originating in the discourse from the eighteenth and nineteenth century, when dealing with what he calls 'ecological justice'.[18] This difficulty increases when ecological or environmental justice is linked to gendered justice. It is well known that both men and women belonging to the affluent parts of world society over-consume and over-pollute. Wolf questions whether it might be possible to develop a justice of nature, and writes of the difficulties in developing *a 'just' politics of self-restriction*. What would a just distribution of burdens look like? What would the principle of responsibility look like? Could we imagine gendered responsibilities for a just politics of self-restriction to be expressed in Western environmental law? I doubt it, and I think such discussions and norms would rather be expressed in other normative forms like guidelines, ethical rules, perhaps religious rules and local practices. It seems to me that we are at present developing a contemporary equivalent to the medieval system of sale of indulgences, where the West reaches the goals of self-restriction on emissions by buying quotas from less polluting countries with a surplus right to pollute. Westerners seem to be paying for a shorter period in the environmental purgatory. Perhaps we should also remember that the system of sales of indulgences in the Middle Ages contributed considerably to the weakening of Catholicism and canon law.

In the book, *Exploiting the Limits of Law: Swedish Feminism and the Challenge to Pessimism*, Margaret Davies writes that feminists and other critical theories do not need to choose between accepting and rejecting the established limits of law. 'Pragmatism can be combined with idealism, critique with utopianism, and pluralism with monism, even though scholarly habits of thought ordinarily lead us to avoid any position involving contradiction, real or apparent.'[19] Perhaps this is what I am to some extent trying to do here.

---

[18] Wolf 1991. See Petersen 1993 pp. 15–30, the title of which refers to a saying in Danish about throwing out the children with the bathwater.
[19] Davies 2007 p. 226.

William Twining mentions in his chapter in this volume that Westerners need more knowledge about legal cultures beyond our 'Country and Western tradition' of legal theorizing and comparative law, which he finds 'vulnerable to charges of parochialism and ethnocentrism'. We need to extend the canon, and we need to deal with normative jurisprudence, which deals with general questions about values and law. We also need to deal with our collective ignorance of other traditions, including our ignorance of non-secular legal cultures. He suggests that 'one of the key issues should be to what extent a theory of environmental justice leaves scope for other values and to what extent the language of justice is the most appropriate way of expressing all major concerns about the environment'.[20] Twining also quotes Patrick Glenn's discussion of 'Chthonic legal traditions'. With his move from a national legal theory to legal theories related to legal traditions in a global context, Glenn allows us to compare beyond the national field, and perhaps also to become inspired by how different traditions handle issues of gender, environment and justice.[21] Since my own experience is mainly from the Arctic, I will draw upon parts of the 'Chthonic legal traditions' below, presenting reflections on how other traditions deal with a plurality of norms, values and virtues.

3 Environmental practice as virtue?: Arctic and other inspirations

In secular societies with secular legal systems and cultures, not least in the Nordic societies, justice has long been considered of no or even negative importance in jurisprudence. It has been linked to natural law thinking, which has not had a high standing in Lutheran secularized, social democratic societies. In most of the twentieth century, positive law was considered the legal instrument to bring about welfare – which is not a virtue to be practised by everybody, but a result to be secured by political and state actions. However, in the 'peripheries' – such as at the music academies – and among the 'minorities' of the Nordic societies – such as the Saamis[22] and the Greenlanders – thoughts about virtue still play a role, also in the relation between humans and non-human nature. And, as shown by the late Henrik Zahle, 'care for justice' is again becoming a concern at the law faculties.[23]

One of the myths told in Greenland is known to all Inuit in the Arctic. It is called 'Nerrivik' – which means the meat dish, or the myth about the Sea Woman. It is normally understood as a tale about what happens, if Inuit hunters do not respect the taboos regulating their relations to animals.[24]

---

[20] See William Twining in Chapter 4 of this volume.
[21] Glenn 2007. This book was first published in 2000 and is now in its third edition, indicating the importance of the global perspective on law.
[22] See the dissertation by the Saami legal academic and singer-songwriter, Ànde Somby 1999.
[23] Zahle 2003; and Zahle 2005.   [24] Sonne 1990 pp. 1–34, gives a very detailed introduction to this myth.

NERRIVIK

A bird once wished to marry a woman. He got himself a fine sealskin coat, and, having weak eyes, made spectacles out of a walrus tusk, for he was greatly set upon looking as nice as possible. Then he set off, in the shape of a man, and, coming to a village, took a wife, and brought her home.

Now he began to go out catching fish, which he called seal, and brought home to his wife.

Once it happened that he lost his spectacles, and his wife, seeing his bad eyes, burst out weeping, because he was so ugly.

But her husband only laughed. 'Oho, so you saw my eyes? Hahaha!' And he put on his spectacles again.

Then her brothers, who longed for their sister, came out one day to visit her. And her husband being out hunting, they took her away with them. The husband was greatly distressed when he came home and found her gone, and, thinking someone must have carried her off, he set out in pursuit. He swung his wings with mighty force, and raised a violent storm, for he was a great wizard.

When the storm came up, the boat began to take in water, and the wind grew fiercer, as he doubled the beating of his wings. The waves rose white with foam, and the boat was near turning over. And, when those in the boat began to suspect that the woman was the cause of the storm, they took her up and cast her into the sea. She tried to grasp the side of the boat, but then her grandfather sprang up and cut off her hand.

And so she was drowned. But, at the bottom of the sea, she became Nerrivik, the ruler over all the creatures in the sea. *And, when men catch no seal, then the wizards go down to Nerrivik. Having but one hand, she cannot comb her hair, and this they do for her, and she, by way of thanks, sends seal and other creatures forth to men.*

That is the story of the ruler of the sea. And men call her Nerrivik because she gives them food.[25]

The myth is not only a story about virtuous behaviour and respect for taboos, but also about interdependence between and metamorphosis of humans and animals. It is a story about relations between humans and animals – as relations of both love and violent sacrifice of humans to nature for the purpose of both peaceful conditions and survival.[26] Sacrifice, from the Latin *sacri-ficare*, means to make holy. The woman in the story is 'married' to a bird – an animal with supernatural force – and forced to

---

[25] This version of the myth is a very short version taken from Knud Rasmussen's collections of myths and legends from Greenland. This specific myth is printed in the third volume which contains myths from the Cape York district and from Northern Greenland, printed in 1925. The translation is from Rasmussen 1921. Emphasis added.

[26] I have discussed this myth in a different context in Petersen 2005.

accept this difficult marriage through mutilation. The forces of nature are stronger than human force and are threatening human survival. Through the sacrifice of the woman it is possible to establish a proper and relatively peaceful and prosperous relationship with nature – mediated through shamanic interventions. And through the sacrifice she also becomes the ruler of the sea. In the contemporary versions of the myths it is understood as a need for respect for nature. If humans transgress taboos, or do not treat marine animals and their living conditions properly or pollute them, the Sea Mother will withhold her gifts, the animals, until practices have changed. Taboos are socio-psychic limitations to actions, which in this case also have ecological consequences. The Sea Mother both judges and sanctions those transgressing taboos.

The myth illustrates that a different world-view prevailed behind Inuit myths and customs than the world-view which dominates Western or Euro-Canadian societies and legal cultures. This difference is explained by the second Canadian aboriginal judge, Murray Sinclair, who argues that:

> The Aboriginal world view holds that human beings are the least powerful and least important element in creation. They cannot influence events, and are disrespectful if they try. Human interests are not to be placed above those of any other part of creation. Regarding the relative hierarchy and importance of beings in creation therefore, Aboriginal and Western traditions are diametrically opposed.

> Most Aboriginal societies value the interrelated principles of individual autonomy and freedom, so long as their exercise is consistent with the preservation of relationships and community harmony. Other values include respect for other human (and non-human) beings, reluctance to criticize and interfere with others, and avoidance of confrontation.[27]

As Sinclair writes, this element of the 'Chthonic legal tradition' has a very different view on relations between humans and non-human species than does the Christian-influenced Western legal tradition. This view on a non-hierarchical relation between humans and non-humans generally influences the normative view and understanding of 'the environment'. I am not claiming that the myth about Nerrivik – the sea as the big meat dish guarded by a woman – is describing a general practice strictly followed among Inuit in the Arctic today. But I think it gives us an example of other ways of dealing with environmental ethics and other ways of thinking about gender and environmental justice. In Inuit societies, it is traditionally men who hunt. Taboos are in practice gendered. Thus, if men – individually or collectively – do not act 'virtuously' towards other humans and non-humans during their hunting activities, this may interfere negatively to the point of threatening the survival of their communities. The same goes for women, whose transgressions of taboos may also threaten themselves and their communities.

---

[27] Sinclair 1994 pp. 23 and 25.

Very often, when we speak about justice and gender, we think in terms of modern values of equality and freedom, and justice issues often turn around topics of distribution and redistribution and to a certain extent also recognition. Maybe an increased concern about the environment may force us to rethink the value and the expressions and forms of both gender justice and equality in a globalized and planetarian context.[28] And maybe we need to think of new ways to reconcile and balance these values. Ways which may move beyond the dominant contemporary understandings of environmental law.

4 Reconsidering justice and/as virtuous behaviour?

As mentioned earlier, ecofeminist writing tended to portray women as especially close to nature – almost as indistinguishable from nature, and as guardians of nature, especially against modern white men who have been portrayed as particularly destructive towards nature.[29] Hopefully, we are now at a point in history where these stereotyped dichotomies may be overcome, and developed. Personally, I have tended to see parts of feminism as a continuation of the enlightenment project, and thus in a potential conflict with or at least challenged by ecological thinking.[30]

So what would environmental justice as a virtue mean for contemporary women and men in different parts of the world, if anything? Would it make sense anywhere? How would it affect our understanding of law and our legal conception? Would it mean that women should stop measuring our situation against that of the most over-consuming, over-earning white Western men – who have access to a considerable surplus of resources, which allows them to 'cash out the patriarchal dividend' as the foremost researcher of masculinity studies, Robert Connell, calls it.[31] Would it mean that some men would realize that they are cashing out this 'dividend', and that ecological crises may disproportionately affect women, since their work is often more closely related to nature, and since environmental destruction especially hits the poor, who are disproportionately female?[32] Would gendered environmental justice perhaps rather be about securing survival, contextual and cultural welfare, happiness and freedom for men and women, children and their surrounding non-human nature and about minimizing suffering due to environmental risks or hazards? Understanding gendered environmental justice as an equal distribution of environmental risks between men and women seems to me to be too narrow an understanding of justice, and too narrow a goal.

---

[28] Rochette 2005 pp. 223–4, also criticizes the reliance on the 'formal equality paradigm' amongst others because it leaves intact the 'masculinist institutions that have worked to exclude women and unsustainably exploit nature'.

[29] These views have been particularly criticized by Janet Biehl 1991. A similar critique of essentialism is given by Rochette 2005.

[30] Petersen 1997. See also Petersen 1996 pp. 125–42.   [31] See Gustafsson 2006 p. 14.

[32] This argument is put forward in an essay by Lisa Stenmark, 'An Ecology of Knowledge: Feminism, Ecology, and the Science and Religion Discourse', http://metanexus.net/magazine/ArticleDetail/tabid/68/id/2669/Default.aspx (visited 17 April 2007).

Working on this article has inspired me to think about the notion of 'sustainable masculinity'.[33] How might we understand such a concept? Could it transcend or/and expand the understanding of environmental law? Could it contribute to a contemporary development of practical virtues, which may serve as normative orientations for individual and collective behaviour? Could 'sustainable masculinity' also guide a more gender-just environmental law-making?

5 Thoughts on 'sustainable masculinity'

Could a renewed (male) focus upon *gender* issues in relation to *environmental* issues develop a discourse not only on 'environmental justice' but also on 'sustainable masculinities'? Attempts to deal with a concept such as 'sustainable masculinities' might underline that contemporary understandings of masculinity are not the only ones possible, and that one is born neither a man nor a woman, but becomes one – and that this process of becoming may change. In a website called 'Building Sustainable Masculinity: Building Peace', it is claimed that millions of men worldwide are embracing new male values. The website refers to Native American (Lakota) teachings which emphasize 'respect for women, the sacred bearers of life, and respect for mother earth; both provide life and sustenance.'[34] At a conference on 'Fostering Caring Masculinities' in October 2006, Victor Seidler used the term 'sustainable masculinities' and spoke of the rapidly changing relationship between masculinities and changing work cultures in a lecture on 'Masculinities and Work/Life Balance'.[35]

We are witnessing reflections upon and perhaps even changes to the hegemonic (Western) masculinity. Combining this with the existence of diverse masculinities on a global scale, we might expect this change to have implications not only for local gender relations, but also for relations between humans and nature on a more general scale in Western societies and in the world. This change may also have implications for Western law-making, which has for a long time had a traditional and patriarchal masculine lifestyle as its underlying norm and model.[36] One of the areas – apart from research – where we may find signs of such a changing – and perhaps sustainable – masculinity is in *art*. As Carolyn Merchant writes in the opening quote to this chapter, a society's symbols and images of nature express its collective consciousness. These images of nature appear amongst others in art.

The Swedish-Danish sculptor, Pontus Kjerrman, has produced a large number of figures combining humans and animals – mostly with human bodies and animal 'faces'. They are inspired by mythological figures and remind me of the many stories in Arctic myths about marriages between humans and different animals. Kjerrman's

---

[33] This term came up in my discussion with Håkan Gustafsson about topics related to this article.

[34] 'Building Sustainable Masculinity: Building Peace', www.pipcornall.com (visited 11 April 2007).

[35] Victor Seidler, 'Masculinities and Work/Life Balance', www.caringmasculinities.org (visited 11 April 2007).

[36] This was underlined more than twenty years ago by the late Norwegian Professor of Women's Law, Tove Stang Dahl, in her brilliant article, Dahl 1987.

male figures have horse-faces, and the female figures have cat-faces. These animal-like humans and human-like animals – some of whom have wings – are inspired by Egyptian gods with animal heads and human bodies, and are also related to the Greek centaurs and minotaurs. They bear witness to histories of long and close relations between humans and animals also in Western culture. They tend to capture the balance between nature and culture, which the artist is looking for.[37] Kjerrman has made a small sculpture called the 'Kafkat' (Kaf-cat) – a winged cat-woman – for a Danish association of legal policy. This sculpture is given annually to a person who has contributed to the promotion of a just society and politics. A number of his somewhat larger sculptures of 'horse-men' are placed in front of the Royal Veterinary and Agricultural High School of Denmark in Copenhagen. Kjerrman describes his relation to these inter-species beings as follows:

> The fabulous animals made their appearance in the world of my pictures at a time when, for some years, I had worked with naturalist sculptures treating of the relationship between man and woman, and man, woman and children. Many people regarded those sculptures as very grave and personal, whereas the fabulous animals gave me and the beholder the possibility of establishing a distance and a relaxed attitude to the sculptures. In that world, the man is a stubborn and hard-working horse who spends most of his time building a house out of what materials he happens to find, and cultivating his cabbage field. Since he cannot go very far away from his home, he is of a very melancholy disposition. The woman, a cat-person, is impulsive and capricious. She is provided with wings and loves moving (and changing her whereabouts). She catches sight of the horse-man when he is trying to pile up some shapeless stones in an attempt to build a house, and she falls in love with him. A child is born to them, and during the period when she is expecting the baby the cat-woman is very irritated because her freedom of movement is curtailed. Shortly after the birth of the baby, the cat-woman leaves the man and the child. The man's life reverts to the usual routine, yet, on account of the child, it is radically changed.[38]

I think Kjerrman's figures symbolize changes in relations both between humans and between humans and nature. In the interview he describes changing gender relations and a changing intergenerational relation. In all discussions on sustainability, the issue of intergenerational responsibility is central, due to the definition of sustainable development as one which 'meets the needs of the present without compromising the ability of future generations to meet their own needs'. What Kjerrman describes is that this intergenerational relation is changing. Woman has been considered closer to nature – not least because of her procreational power – and because of her relations to children. (Western) man is now – again – moving closer to nature due to his stronger

---

[37] Interview by Lisbeth Bonde, 'Portræt – Pontus Kjerrman', http://kunstonline.dk/profil/pontus_kjerrman. php4 (visited 11 April 2007).

[38] Pontus Kjerrmann homepage, from 'The Adventure', at www.kjerrman.dk/pontus/adventure.en.html (visited 11 April 2007).

Figure 5.1 Pontus Kjerrman: Armor and Psyche. Source: Hanne Petersen

relationship to the child, which he is expected to take more care of, and which changes his routines and rhythms. This change of masculine self-perception and masculine lifestyle, which is already taking place, could very well also be expected to change general societal norms as well as the law-maker's views on relations between humans and the environment. A change of lifestyle, self-perception and a practice of self-restriction may perhaps be due to interest not only in the survival of future generations, but also in the interest of survival and a better life for – some – contemporary men, amongst them lawyers and law-makers.

Writing from a Swedish horizon, Bo Wennström argues that the way to describe the stereotypical (Swedish) lawyer – based on readings of obituaries – is as a 'trained work horse': constantly hard working, accurate and with good legal knowledge. Lack of sleep, heart failure and other bad health as well as neglected families are almost considered something positive.[39] This is perhaps not only a description of the lawyer, but also of a modern masculinity, which is increasingly out of balance with a changing work and family life – but also with the surrounding environment.

This description of an unsustainable modern masculinity – not least in the legal profession – is also reflected in a book called *The Soul of Law: Understanding Lawyers and the Law*. The author, Benjamin Sells, an American lawyer and psychotherapist, describes some of the consequences for both law itself and for the legal professionals stemming from a lack of soul in both law and the profession. When he asks people to describe 'The Law' to him – the law as a person, that is – they most often describe 'the law' as an older man, gray-haired and distinguished looking. His clients tell him that the Law says it is misunderstood and overworked, sometimes even going so far as describing itself as 'alienated, isolated, anxious, depressed, besieged, and lonely'.[40]

Sells primarily describes the experience of the American practising lawyer, but, given the influential role of both the US and its legal profession on a global scale, this is perhaps not good news for people wishing well for the environment. 'Many lawyers complain of an amorphous lack of feeling, a sense of being anesthetized. Things are neither very good nor very bad, but just... mediocre.'[41] How can one expect environmental passion from powerful and globally influential men in such situations? Sells writes that (American) law students and lawyers are almost four times more likely than the general population to suffer from depression and anxiety. Clinical depression and substance abuse is twice the general prevalence rates for these disorders.[42] Sells claims that lawyers are being cut off from their sense of belonging to a broader community, and I guess this also includes being cut off from nature. He also writes that it is 'odd that the very mind-set that pays lip service to equality so adamantly demands its own unquestioned superiority'.[43]

Can one believe law and lawyers to be able to care for justice and the environment under such conditions? And how is it possible to develop a sustainable masculinity and sustainable practices for and by men as gendered beings? Victor Seidler writes that 'we need a framing of a sustainable masculinity that allows us to recognise that men also need to learn *how to care* for them selves. There has to be self-care and there has to be a way of framing self-care that is not simply seen as a form of egoistic self-indulgence or selfishness.'[44]

---

[39] Wennström 2002 pp. 45–54.

[40] Sells 1996 pp. 24–25. I would like to thank Ànde Somby for having given me this interesting but also somewhat dark book.

[41] *Ibid.*, p. 33.   [42] *Ibid.*, pp. 42 and 99.   [43] *Ibid.*, p. 106.

[44] Victor Seidler, 'Masculinities and Work/Life Balance', www.caringmasculinities.org (visited 11 April 2007).

Perhaps we have to look for traces of such a development in past reflections on the future. In the years 1985–2000, a group of environmentally concerned people – men and women – met on a yearly basis at the Ökoinstitut Südtirol/Alto Adige in Bozen, Austria, close to the border of Italy. Every year they held a dialogue and produced what are called the *Toblacher Thesen* about a more sustainable and environmentally balanced and just life, as we enter the 'solar age'. The continued motto for this group has been 'Slower, less, better and more beautiful' ('*Langsamer, weniger, besser, schöner*'). This slogan could perhaps be understood as a guideline for virtuous and sustainable self-restriction. It is directed towards many areas of life and has been an integrated part of the yearly *Thesen* which have dealt with the following topics: tourism, transportation, agriculture, construction, the 'eco-change' (*Ökologische Wende*), the eco-economy, energy, health, work, eco-welfare before growth, mobility, commerce and eco-innovation, beauty, and visions and experiences.[45] Every year, exactly twelve theses have been written on the topic of that year. In the theses from 1992 on health, the third thesis is the following:

> Civilizational diseases are spreading: Heart and circulatory diseases, cancer, diabetes, allergies, self immune diseases, rheumatism and Aids. Anxiety and depression is growing. Aggression, violence and brutalization are spreading. Unsocial behaviour, drugs, alcoholism, use of medicine and psychosomatic disturbances are answers to a lifestyle where 'always faster' and 'always more' is the supreme principle. The general immunological defence is disturbingly strained. As a new challenge humankind is confronted with Aids, a world wide epidemic, the dramatic social, economic and political consequences of which are completely underestimated.[46]

These theses about the health of individuals and society do not of course specifically concern men. But men need to reflect upon the sustainability of their lifestyle – as men – both in relation to health, work, transportation, energy consumption and all the other areas covered by the theses developed over fifteen years. As we all still live in a gender-divided world, the consequences of unsustainable lifestyles will be different according to time and space, class, race, religion and gender and other indicators. Women are bearing a lot of the burdens. Men are enjoying the privileges related to the 'patriarchal dividend,'[47] but also paying high prices for unsustainable lifestyles.

---

[45] www.toblacher-gespraeche.it; and Glauber 2006.

[46] My translation from German: 'Die Zivilisationskrankheiten breiten sich aus: Herz- Kreislauferkrankungen, Krebs, Diabetes, Allergien, Autoimmunerkrankungen, Rheuma und Aids. Ängste und Depressionen nehmen zu. Aggressivität, Gewalt und Verrohung greifen um sich. Unsoziales Verhalten, Drogen und Alkoholsucht, Medikamentenverbrauch und psychosomatische Störungen sind die Antworten auf einen Lebensstil, der "immer schneller", "immer mehr" zum obersten Prinzip hat. Die allgemeine immunologische Abwehrkraft ist besorgniserregend belastet. Als neue Herausforderung ist die Menschheit mit Aids konfrontiert, einer weltweiten Epidemie, deren dramatische soziale, ökonomische und politische Konsequenzen völlig unterschätzt werden.'

[47] A term used by Conell quoted in Gustafsson 2006.

Several authors in this volume discuss the principle of 'Common but Differentiated Responsibilities' (CBDR), as set out in the 1992 Rio Declaration on Environment and Development and included in various globally applicable treaties since then. This principle could perhaps also be understood as a move towards an ethical or just environmental practice – towards a practice of environmental virtues – which may spread not only to relations among states but perhaps may also serve as a guideline in relations among individuals and (privileged and unprivileged) groups and communities in world society, amongst others in businesses. The principles of Corporate Social Responsibilities (CSR) are directed towards the business communities, which have been addressed by the United Nations in order to take upon themselves duties and obligations towards local and global communities. In the discourse on CSR, it is argued that, being closely linked to the principles of sustainable development, such responsibility requires that enterprises make their decisions based not only on financial factors, such as profits and dividends, but also on the immediate and long-term social and environmental consequences of their activities.

The language of virtue differs from the language of rights in that it deals with responsibilities and obligations, practices and acts, which the virtuous person has to develop and to perform for him or her to be considered and to feel virtuous. Virtues belong to the realm of social and communal life, to the life of individuals as human beings, as eco-citizens perhaps, but not necessarily as citizens of states or inhabitants of cities. They deal with an incorporation of consciousness and values, which may to a modern mind seem oppressive and submissive. They may require a certain way of dressing, eating, speaking and behaving[48] as well as consuming and living. I am convinced that, in the twenty-first century, environmental justice and 'common but differentiated responsibilities' will be a matter not only for states but also for the many non-state agents and individuals, who will have to contribute to a change of mentality and change of practice. But of course not everybody will be convinced that the individualized approaches of 'sustainable masculinities' and the connected change of lifestyle are important.

Andrew Dobson, when writing about environmental justice and ecological citizenship, criticizes the three current approaches to climate change, including lifestyle changes, and argues that recent research in Sweden suggests that 'collectivist, social welfare societies are a better incubator of pro-environmental behaviour than individualist ones where welfare is looked on with suspicion'. He quotes another author, Sharon Witherspoon, who writes that a sense of community with others may be as important as concern over the biosphere in generating environmentalism.[49] It seems that not least smaller non-state groups, communities and societies – but also states – might be willing to take upon themselves greater responsibilities than others due to their adherence to environmentalist values and virtues.

---

[48] See Mahmood 2005 p. 4.   [49] Dobson 2007.

Such adherence to environmentalist values and virtues may produce practices which differ between women and men, between young and old, between professions and different types of jobs. Following values and practising virtues may allow for differentiated and contextualized practices which cannot be achieved through environmental law. We should perhaps not expect gendered just and sustainable virtues to be practised by men and women because of the influence from environmental law. The relationship between law, morality, practice and interpretations of different types of norm will therefore be important.

Thus we should not think too narrowly and legalistically about the concept of environmental justice or about emerging environmental virtues such as sustainability. Environmental justice should not only be related to 'traditional' national or international law, but be expanded to encompass also practices and norms, and normative and virtuous behaviour by broader communities, than national and international actors.[50] If 'environmental justice' is understood also as an environmental virtue, and if 'sustainable masculinities' are seen as other expressions of virtuous behaviour, we might have to look for the good examples on different community levels of environmentally and socially just, sustainable practices within or between generations, gender, rural and urban, northern and southern, rich and poor communities and states as well as in world society.[51] The practice of these virtues may differ according to context, and culture, as well as gender. Good environmental laws and principles are imitated around the world. It is to be hoped that sustainable masculine behaviour may also become developed and followed in this one world we live in.

Bibliography

Biehl, J., 1991. *Rethinking Ecofeminist Politics*. Boston: South End Press.

Dahl, T. S., 1987. 'Fra kvinners rett til kvinnerett'. 37 *Retfærd*.

Davies, M., 2007. 'Notes Towards an Optimistic Feminism: A Long View', in Gunnarsson, Svensson, and Davies, 2007.

Dobson, A., 2007. 'A Politics of Global Warming: The Social-Science Resource'. 29 March 2007, www.opendemocracy.net/globalization-climate_change_debate/politics_4486.jsp (visited 11 April 2007).

Gilligan, C., 1982. *In a Different Voice: Psychological Theory and Women's Development*. Cambridge, MA: Harvard Univrsity Press.

Glauber, H. (ed.) 2006. *Langsamer, weniger, besser, schöner. 15 Jahre Toblacher Gespräche: Bausteine für die Zukunft*. Oekom Verlag.

Glenn, P., 2007: *Legal Traditions of the World*. 3rd edn.

Gunnarsson, Å., Svensson, E.-M., and Davies, M. (eds.) 2007. *Exploiting the Limits of Law: Swedish Feminism and the Challenge to Pessimism*. Aldershot: Ashgate.

---

[50] See also Hey in Chapter 18 of this volume, where she focuses on the legitimacy and distributive justice aspects of global water law.

[51] I have dealt with the role of world society in an article in Petersen 2006.

Gustafsson, H., 2006. 'Cyklopens öga. En betraktelse av rättsvetenskapens könsblindhet' [Eye of the Cyclops: A Study on Jurisprudential Genderblindness]. 2/113 *Retfærd* 3.

Heimonen, M., 2002. *Music Education and Law: Regulation as an Instrument.* Helsinki: Sibelius Academy.

    2006a. 'Justifying the Right to Music Education'. 14/2 *Philosophy of Music Education Review* 119.

    2006b. *Music, Education, Public Life.* Helsinki: Sibelius Academy (unpublished).

MacIntyre, A., 1984: *After Virtue: A Study in Moral Theory.* Notre Dame, IN: University of Notre Dame Press.

Mahmood, S., 2005. *Politics of Piety: The Islamic Revival and the Feminist Subject.* Princeton: Princeton University Press.

Merchant, C., 1980. *The Death of Nature: Women, Ecology and the Scientific Revolution.* San Francisco: Harper & Row Publishers.

    1989. *Ecological Revolutions: Nature, Gender, and Science in New England.* Chapel Hill, NC, and London: University of North Carolina Press.

    1995. *Earthcare: Women and the Environment.* New York: Routledge.

Petersen, H., 1993. 'Bæredygtighed, børn og badevand. Feministiske og økologiske perspektiver på juridisk tænkning' [Sustainability, Children and Bathwater: Feminist and Ecological Perspectives on Legal Thinking]. 16/60 *Retfærd* 15.

    1996. 'Ecology, Women and Law: Erosion and Erotics', in H. Petersen (ed.), *Home-Knitted Law: Norms and Values in Gendered Rule Making.* Dartmouth.

    1997. 'Gender and Nature in Comparative Legal Cultures', in David Nelken (ed.), *Comparing Legal Cultures.* Dartmouth.

    2005. 'Greenland: Custom, Adaptation and Myth', in P. Ørebech, *et al.* (eds.), *The Role of Customary Law and Sustainable Development.* Cambridge: Cambridge University Press.

    (ed.), 2006. *Grønland i verdenssamfundet. Normer og praksis i udvikling og forandring* [Greenland in World Society: Norms and Practices in Development and Change]. Nuuk: Atuagkat/ Ilisimatusarfik.

Rasmussen, K., 1921. *Eskimo Folk-tales* (collected by K. Rasmussen and translated by W. Worster). Copenhagen and Christiania: Gyldendal.

Rochette, A., 2005. 'Transcending the Conquest of Nature and Women: A Feminist Perspective on International Environmental Law', in Doris Buss and Ambreena Manji (eds.), *International Law: Modern Feminist Approaches.* Oxford and Portland, OR: Hart Publishing.

Sells, B., 1996. *The Soul of Law: Understanding Lawyers and the Law.* Rockport, MA, Shaftesbury (Dorset) and Brisbane: Element.

Sinclair, M., 1994. 'Aboriginal Peoples and Euro-Canadians: Two World Views', in J. Hylton (ed.), *Aboriginal Self-Government in Canada: Current Trends and Issues.* Saskatoon: Purich Publishing.

Somby, Á., 1999. *Juss som retorikk* [Law as Rhetoric]. Oslo: Tano Aschehoug.

Sonne, B., 1990. 'The Acculturative Role of Sea Woman: Early Contact Relations Between Inuit and Whites as Revealed in the Origin Myth of Sea Woman'. 13 *Man and Society* 1.

Wennström, B., 2002. *Rättens Kulturgräns* [The Cultural Border of Law]. Uppsala: Iustus Förlag.

Wolf, R., 1991. 'Im Fiaker der Moderne. Von den Schwierigkeiten ökologischer Gerechtigkeit'. 3 *Kritische Justiz.*

Zahle, H., 2003. *Omsorg for retfærdighed. Essays om retlig praksis* [Care for Justice: Essays on Legal Practice]. Gyldendal.

    2005. *Praktisk retsfilosofi* [Practical Legal Philosophy]. Copenhagen: Chr. Ejlers Forlag.

PART II

Public participation and access to the judiciary

6

Participatory rights in natural resource management: the role of communities in South Asia

JONA RAZZAQUE

1 Introduction

Along with Principle 10 of the Rio Declaration,[1] a number of international and regional treaties include reference to public participation in the decision-making process.[2] Although regional in scope, the 1998 UNECE Convention on Access to Information, Public Participation in Decision-Making and Access to Justice in Environmental Matters (Aarhus Convention) reflects an increased concern of the international community in transparency of environmental decision-making, and parties to the Convention are asked to consult local communities before they undertake some development activities.[3] While Asian countries are not parties to the Aarhus Convention,[4] the influence of these binding and non-binding international instruments, especially Principle 10, clearly has impacts as countries implement these instruments, and international financial institutions incorporate them into their policies.[5] Public participation requirements are increasingly attached to international loans and financing, and treaties rely on information, participation and accountability for their implementation. Recently, some of the judges from Asia recognised this influence in the Kathmandu Declaration on Environmental Justice (2004), which emphasised the importance of human rights instruments and multilateral environmental agreements (MEAs) in upholding environmental justice.[6] At the national level, the judiciary in

---

[1] Other public participation components could be found in Principles 20–2 of the Rio Declaration on Environment and Development (1992) adopted by the UN Conference on Environment and Development (UNCED), UN Doc. A/CONF.151/26 (Vol. I) (1992).

[2] Pring and Noe 2002.

[3] 1998 UNECE Convention on Access to Information, Public Participation in Decision-Making and Access to Justice in Environmental Matters, reprinted in 38 *International Legal Materials* (ILM) (1999) 515. This Convention elaborates Principle 10 of the Rio Declaration, note 1 above.

[4] However, the Aarhus Convention, note 3 above, is open to accession by any UN member with the approval of parties; see Art. 19(3).

[5] For the application of Principle 10, see the commitments form of the partners of the Partnership for Principle 10, available at www.pp10.org. Also, Petkova *et al.* 2002. For the Aarhus Convention, see the status of implementation by the parties to the Convention, available at www.unece.org/env/pp/.

[6] Twenty-one sitting judges of the Supreme and High Courts of Bangladesh, India, Pakistan, Nepal and Sri Lanka adopted this Declaration. As the name suggests, this is a non-binding document, but it does recognise that

South Asia established a substantive right to a healthy environment as part of a fundamental right to life – this move also influenced the demands for stronger participatory
tools.[7]

Participation in the decision-making process creates a sense of 'ownership' in the
decision itself, and various participatory techniques assist communities to implement
environmental justice. Across South Asia, the livelihoods of the majority are dependent on natural resources such as energy, water and forests. Yet, local users often have
no access to information concerning natural resource use planning, and no right to
participate in decision-making processes affecting their natural resource rights. The
influence of international rules (binding and non-binding) on participation has still
a long way to go in these three countries. While environmental justice demands that
there should be a right to a healthy environment for all, it also demands integration
of vulnerable (and poor) communities in the decision-making processes. In order to
strengthen environmental justice, not only is there a need to have a liberal judiciary,
strong environmental legislation and explicit constitutional provisions, there should
also be public access to decision-making and to information. New breeds of laws,
policies and regulatory techniques could allow communities to participate actively
and, in South Asia, there are some new laws and guidelines dealing with community participation. It is hoped that these new provisions will lead to transparent and
accountable decisions. Environmental justice can only be ensured through the meaningful involvement of communities in the development of laws, projects and policies
concerning natural resources.

Environmental justice has many components. Procedural justice, which is one of
the central themes in the justice discourse, relates to such issues as participation in
administrative decision-making processes on projects that may harm the environment or in judicial proceedings to challenge administrative decisions.[8] In this sense,
procedural justice is linked to the fairness of the decision-making process leading
to an accountable decision, thus creating a link between distributive and procedural
justice.[9] It leads to the understanding that fair processes would lead to a fair and
accountable outcome. In the South Asian context, the concept of environmental justice includes distributive and procedural as well as social justice. The issue of social
justice brings the racial, political and economic injustices within the broad umbrella
of environmental justice.[10] Environmental and social justice intersect when the goal
is for the people to have a right to a healthy environment and equal access to natural
resources.[11] While both the process and outcome of a decision are crucial for natural
resource management, the remit of this chapter is limited to some aspects of procedural justice in India, Pakistan and Bangladesh. In natural resource management,

---

the environmental justice issue is closely linked to poverty and empowerment. See Kathmandu Declaration
2004, available at: www.iucn.org/themes/law/pdfdocuments/LN230704declaration_final_25062004.pdf.
[7] Razzaque 2004a.   [8] Nollkaemper in Chapter 13 of this volume.
[9] Rechtschaffen 2003 at 99–100.   [10] *Ibid.* at 100.   [11] Stephens, Bullock and Scott 2001.

fair and transparent process may not always lead to a sustainable outcome nor does it ensure that communities have an equal share to their natural resources. What better procedure does is to allow communities to have an understanding of the issues involved and a say in the decision that will affect their lives and livelihood. Procedural justice can only be achieved if the affected communities are able to participate effectively in the decision-making process.

In these three countries, the concept of environmental justice was prompted initially by the human rights, poverty and development concerns rather than the ideas of conservation and resource protection.[12] Judicial activism was prominent in India where the judiciary allowed disadvantaged communities to access the courts through 'social action litigation'.[13] In the 1970s and 1980s, the focus was on poverty and inequality of human beings, and the courts were determined to provide justice to people who were socially or economically disadvantaged.[14] In recent years, the decisions of the courts integrate both social and ecological concerns with particular attention to questions of distributive justice, community empowerment and democratic accountability. In Pakistan and Bangladesh, the emphasis is more on the application of fundamental human rights, and political and social changes largely influence the development of the concept of environmental justice.[15]

In South Asia, the communities can access national courts through public interest litigation (PIL) or participate in public inquiries to protect natural resources. Participation in the decision-making process could be formal or informal. Formal procedures such as participation in policy-making include the involvement of the public in the consultation process which may also include public hearings. Informal methods include writing or calling elected officials, attending public hearings, commenting on agency rules or lobbying on specific legislation. Participation in the implementation and enforcement of decisions includes common law rights to initiate criminal or civil proceedings, statutory rights allowing citizens to bring actions against government agencies, and judicial review.

It is against this background that this chapter aims to explore the nature of community participation through regulations, and the role played by the communities in the natural resource management in South Asia. It discusses whether the participation of communities in the decision-making process effectively contributes to the objectives of environmental justice. The meaning of 'communities' used in this chapter is broad and includes environmental activists, NGOs and organised groups. While individuals can and do access the courts to protect natural resources, it is more difficult for communities, as a group, to show that they have a specific interest in bringing the action as PIL. Moreover, while accessing information and participating in the consultation process, the community has a larger role to play in gaining and disseminating the

---

[12] Razzaque 2004a, Chapter 1.   [13] Baxi 1985 at 289–315.
[14] Ahuja 1997.   [15] Khan 1993; Ahmed 1999.

information and voicing their concerns regarding resource use. Community empowerment (which is closely linked to procedural justice) requires that the community
as a whole understands that there is a violation of rights, is aware of the available
legal remedies and can identify the responsible agency. After a brief discussion, in
Section 2, on access to courts by communities to protect natural resources including
energy, water and forestry, Section 3 examines access to decision-making related to
natural resources, and Section 4 considers access to information in natural resource
management.

2 Public participation: access to courts to protect natural resources

One of the ways the communities participate in the decision making process is by challenging the decision in the court. In South Asia, PIL is a common way to challenge the
decision of the government authorities. These litigations often claim a breach of a constitutional right along with provisions of environmental regulations or guidelines.[16]
In India, Pakistan and Bangladesh, the right to life is a fundamental constitutional
right. The right to a healthy environment, on the other hand, is not an express constitutional right. Only a handful of national constitutions in Asia directly integrate
the protection of the environment or natural resources in their constitution.[17] Some
of these constitutions recognise the right to a clean environment – some of these
constitutions create a justiciable right (e.g. Philippines, Sri Lanka) and some contain
purely aspirational provisions (e.g. Afghanistan, Thailand).[18]

In India, the state has a duty to protect and preserve the environment. This is part of
the state policy and does not imply a fundamental right.[19] The Supreme Court of India
interpreted the right to life guaranteed by Article 21 of the Constitution to include
the right to a wholesome environment.[20] However, the nature and extent of this right
are not similar to the self-executory and actionable right to a healthy environment
prescribed in the constitutions of other Asian states, such as the Philippines, Mongolia
or South Korea.[21] Similarly, the Constitution of Bangladesh does not explicitly provide
for the right to a healthy environment.[22] However, its Supreme Court highlighted
that the constitutional 'right to life' does extend to include the right to a healthy
environment[23] and anything that affects life, public health and safety.[24] In Pakistan,
the right to life is guaranteed by Article 9 of the Constitution, and the Supreme Court
in *Shehla Zia's* case[25] decided that the right to life includes the right to live in an

---

[16] This part of the discussion is influenced by Razzaque 2004a.   [17] Earthjustice 2005.   [18] *Ibid.*
[19] Articles 48A and 51A(g) impose responsibility on every citizen to protect, safeguard and improve the
environment. See the Constitution (Forty Second Amendment) Act 1976.
[20] *Subhash Kumar* v. *State of Bihar*, AIR 1991 SC 420: 'Right to life guaranteed by article 21 includes the right
of enjoyment of pollution-free water and air for full enjoyment of life.'
[21] Earthjustice 2005.   [22] Articles 31 and 32 together incorporate the fundamental 'right to life'.
[23] *M. Farooque* v. *Government of Bangladesh* (1997) 49 Dhaka Law Reports (AD) 1.
[24] (1996) 48 Dhaka Law Reports, at 438.   [25] *Shehla Zia* v. *WAPDA* (1994) PLD SC 693 at 712.

unpolluted environment. Furthermore, the judiciary of Pakistan firmly established a right to safe and unpolluted drinking water as part of the right to life.[26] None of these constitutions provides a right to promote and encourage public participation in the preservation, maintenance and balanced exploitation of natural resources, or sets out that the state owns the natural resources. Nor do they ensure that the natural resources of the nation are developed, preserved and utilised for the benefit of all citizens.[27] Addressing environmental concerns and resource protection at the constitutional level means that their protection does not depend on the interpretation and nature (liberal or conservative) of the judiciary. The constitutional enactment offers an opportunity to promote environmental and resource concerns at the highest and most visible level of the legal order.

During the 1980s and 1990s, there was an influx of litigation in the Indian courts dealing with water, mining and forest conservation.[28] These litigations were brought by individuals as well as community groups.[29] In many of these cases, the court either directed the government bodies to take action as they breached a fundamental constitutional right, or set up a committee to monitor the situation and report back to the court for further action.[30] Several cases have challenged the legality of large dams,[31] and one example of such ongoing dispute is the construction of the Sardar Sarovar dam. The emphasis of this particular PIL is on the relief and rehabilitation of a landless community living around the area of the Sardar Sarovar dam along with the subsidiary issue of environmental damage.[32] Although Bangladesh and Pakistan do not have a very high number of PILs in the courts, the judiciary has taken some important decisions to protect natural resources. In Bangladesh, these cases dealt with the filling of public lakes to construct multi-storied buildings, urban development by hill cutting, the allocation of land to shrimp farmers causing salinity of water, oil and gas exploration and illegal construction around rivers.[33] In Pakistan, there are examples of cases dealing with water pollution, mining and forest conservation.[34] Many of these cases are pending in the courts for hearing, and it shows that litigation could be a lengthy and expensive process in this part of the developing world. Moreover, these litigations highlight a critical and intense relationship between poverty, development and environmental issues.

---

[26] *West Pakistan Salt Miners Labour Union* v. *The Director, Industries and Mineral Development, Lahore* (1994) SCMR 2061.

[27] In Asia, constitutional provisions related to the protection of natural resources are explicitly mentioned in the Constitution of Afghanistan, Cambodia, China, Laos, Mongolia, South Korea, Thailand and Vietnam.

[28] Rosencranz and Divan 2001.

[29] For examples of cases on mining and quarrying, forest conservation, water pollution, protection of wetlands, see Razzaque 2004a.

[30] *Ibid.*, Chapter 5.   [31] *Ibid.*, Chapter 1.

[32] *Narmada Bachao Andolan* v. *Union of India* (2005) 4 SCCC 32. More information on the Sardar Sarovar project is available at www.narmada.org/sardar-sarovar/irnoverview940525.html.

[33] Razzaque 2004a, Chapter 1.   [34] *Ibid.*, Chapter 1.

While some natural resource sectors (e.g. oil/gas sector) in Pakistan, Bangladesh and India are being privatised,[35] projects and activities undertaken by some multinational companies have been challenged in the national courts. In India, the Kerala *panchayat* took the Coca-Cola Company to the Supreme Court to stop it from drawing huge quantities of local groundwater for its bottling plant.[36] Another example can be found in Bangladesh where several NGOs brought PIL against a multinational oil company along with government bodies for two gas-blowouts in the northeastern part of Bangladesh, which caused severe infrastructure and environmental damage.[37]

One innovative way the judiciary provides protection to natural resources is by applying the 'public trust doctrine'. This common law concept, applied mainly in Indian cases, allows the public to question ineffective management of natural resources. In one case,[38] the Indian Supreme Court decided that certain natural resources like air, sea, water and forests have such great importance to people as a whole that it would be unjustified to make them a subject of private ownership.[39] In the *M.I. Builders* case,[40] the Supreme Court reconfirmed the application of public trust, as part of the right to life, in natural resource management, and asserted that public authorities should act as trustees of natural resources. It thus allowed affected communities, as beneficiaries, to access the court.

These PILs highlight some positive aspects including the power of the judiciary to monitor the execution of judgments.[41] The judiciary can appoint a socio-legal commission of inquiry to investigate the disputed facts and submit a report to the court. PIL allows local communities to take actions against decisions of public authorities. The judiciaries have also relaxed standing of communities and individuals in matters dealing with natural resource management. In these cases, the petitioner was not required to show any personal damage. These three countries follow an adversarial system, and, therefore, the loser pays the winner's costs. However, the judiciaries can apply their discretion to minimise the cost of the petitioner in a PIL, and may also decide to dispense with formal court procedures for the commencement of a PIL. Actions could be initiated by writing a letter to the court, and this would be converted into a formal petition and notice issued on the respondent.

There are critics who believe that the only purpose served by a PIL is to give the judiciary the latitude to interfere in the discretionary area of civil servants. In

---

[35] Jodhi 2000.

[36] The Supreme Court of India ordered the *Panchayat* to renew the licence of the Coca-Cola Company allowing them to extract a limited quantity of groundwater. The *Panchayat* renewed the licence with the condition that the company shall not use groundwater for industrial purposes, or for producing soft drinks, aerated carbonated beverages or fruit juice. It is of no surprise that, in early 2006, the Coca-Cola Company decided to move to another site. See www.indiatogether.org/2006/jan/env-cokesaga.htm.

[37] This case is pending before the court. Razzaque 2004b.

[38] *M. C. Mehta* v. *Kamal Nath* (1997) 1SCC 388.   [39] Razzaque 2001.

[40] *M. I. Builders Pvt Ltd* v. *Radhey Shyam Sahu*, AIR 1999 SC 2468. See also *Karnataka Industrial Areas Development Board* v. *C. Kenchappa and others*, 2006 AIR SCW 2546.

[41] Razzaque 2002.

addition to this, when courts are inaccessible to most people, PIL is nothing more than 'tokenism'.[42] Critics also highlight some negative aspects of PIL: that legal processes in South Asia could be lengthy, expensive and time-consuming; that there is no legal assistance to bring environmental cases in these three countries and no specific guidelines on cost orders; that there is a lack of implementation of the PIL judgments[43] and inadequate penalties for 'contempt of court'. It is also true that a PIL does not change the policy of the government: public authorities are free to take the same decision again for any other similar situation. The above discussion shows that access to courts may not always ensure procedural justice and a just substantive outcome. While the community can and does make a difference through accessing the court, litigation should not be the only way through which communities might want to influence the decision. In most cases, litigation may come too late and the communities may fail to influence the decision. This leads the discussion to other participatory techniques which allow communities to participate during decision-making at the project and policy level.

3 Public participation in the decision-making process

Public participation is an area that could potentially enhance public trust of government decision-making, and thus reduce subsequent litigation.[44] Public involvement in decision-making and in providing environmental information could help to achieve a better decision in the first place, negating the need to go to the court in the long run. By integrating people's voices in the decision-making process, supplying the community groups with environmental information and providing access to environmental assessment reports, the government not only can achieve better quality environmental decision, it can also offer a high quality natural resource management for the country. Though recent legislation in India, Pakistan and Bangladesh mentions public participation, the exact nature of participation is determined by government agencies at their discretion.[45] Interested members of the public may not have opportunities for sustained input that they think could change the substantive outcome of the decision. How the decisions are made can have implications for the outcomes of the decisions. Participation may also enhance the accountability, and thus acceptability, of decisions concerning resource use.[46] Participation enables the participating communities to hold public authorities accountable for implementation and improves efficiency and credibility to government processes. Greater citizen input promotes environmental justice and helps integrate ecological and social considerations in governmental decisions.[47] This part of the discussion considers the level of participation of communities

---

[42] Sathe 2002.
[43] Some of these contempt petitions involve natural resources, such as forest conservation, illegal river encroachment, industrial effluents in river water. See Razzaque 2004c.
[44] Tabb 1999 at 953.   [45] Razzaque 2004a, Chapter 3.   [46] Spyke 1999 at 263, 269–70.
[47] Lee and Abbot 2003 at 80, 82–5.

in the preparation of projects and policies related to natural resources. A number of statutes in these three countries contain procedures for consultation, hearings and complaints from the public to ensure the participation of potentially affected communities in the decision-making process.[48] Amendments in these legislations show governmental initiative to promote community participation in the implementation of national conservation strategies and environmental action plans, and assist in the monitoring of environmental policies and actions. These amendments could strengthen partnership and collaboration between government agencies, the private sector and civil society, leading to the effective management of natural resources.[49]

3.1 Participation at the project level

At the project level, communities can participate during the preparation of the environmental impact assessment (EIA) by the project proponents or by the donor organisations. It is, therefore, crucial to assess the time assigned for public comments, and the accessibility and comprehensiveness of the EIA report. Although it is argued that public participation slows down the EIA process, one underlying rationale of EIA is to ensure socially acceptable environmental results.[50] In India, the 1994 Environmental Impact Assessment Regulations provide a forum for community groups and local authorities to voice their concerns during public consultation.[51] The Ministry of Environment and Forests (MoEF) is responsible for evaluating EIA reports submitted by project proponents. The notification requires the project proponent to submit an EIA report and environment management plan, details of the public hearing and a project report to the impact assessment agency for clearance. It mandates a public hearing after screening and scoping of the proposed project.[52] For larger projects, the review is carried out in consultation with a committee of experts. The draft EIA notification (2005) amending the EIA regulation elaborates on the procedure to conduct a public hearing.[53] This allows the participation of representatives of local government and communities. There is still no provision for public involvement at the initial stage of the project's approval by the MoEF. It is only after scoping and

---

[48] In India: section 19(b) of the 1986 Environment Protection Act; 1997 National Environment Appellate Authority Act. In Bangladesh: 1995 National Environment Management Action Programme (NEMAP); section 17 of the 1927 Forest Act; section 8 of 1995 Environment Conservation Act; rule 5 of the 1997 Environment Conservation Rules. In Pakistan: section 4(2) of the 1997 Environment Protection Act.

[49] Haque 1996 at 192.   [50] Tilleman 1995.

[51] The 1994 EIA regulations apply to thirty categories of development projects, including the sectors of industry, thermal powers, river valley, infrastructure and nuclear powers.

[52] At the 'screening stage', which is an initial consideration of whether a proposal may have significant impacts on the environment, people may help identify potential impacts of the proposal. If the proposal is deemed to require an EIA, the 'scoping stage' serves to identify the range of significant impacts that need to be evaluated. This stage provides an opportunity to identify public interest and priorities for the assessment. Wood 2003; and Glasson et al. 1999.

[53] Appendix IV to the Draft EIA Notification (2005). Text available at www.elaw.org/node/1519/.

screening that communities are asked for comments and the new notification of 2005 does not clarify how the MoEF addresses concerns raised during the public hearing. Apart from officials from various government departments, public representatives or environmental groups are not part of these expert committees.[54] The successive amendments to public consultation procedures in EIA notifications have also added confusion.[55]

In Bangladesh, the rules and procedures of EIA are guided by the Environment Conservation Act 1995 and the Rules of 1997. The Department of Environment is responsible for issuing environmental clearances, and has the power to penalise anyone in breach. The 1995 Act gives the government the power to evaluate and review the EIA of various projects and activities as well as the procedure for approval. According to the Rules of 1997, the EIA procedure passes through three tiers in order to optimise the resource required for conducting EIA studies: screening; Initial Environmental Examination (IEE); and detailed EIA. These rules, however, do not mention any requirement for public consultation.[56]

In Pakistan, the 1997 Environment Protection Act deals with the EIA requirement, which is mandatory for every major project which is likely to have an environmental effect.[57] Proponents of any industrial or development activity likely to cause adverse effect on the environment will be asked to submit an EIA, and failure to submit an IEE or an EIA would be punishable with a fine.[58] In the 1997 Act, the Environment Protection Agency may itself or through appropriate government agency review the EIA and provide for public participation in the evaluation of an EIA. Any comments from the public during the hearing will be 'duly considered' by government agencies before any decision on the EIA.[59] The guidelines for public consultation put emphasis on involving affected communities at the screening stage of the project development.[60]

In these three countries, foreign aid for projects may require public participation during the preparation of EIA reports.[61] The methodology followed in these EIAs requires direct involvement of community leaders to gather basic data about the

---

[54] Appendix VI to the 2005 Notifications. Text available at www.elaw.org/node/1519/.

[55] *Athirappally Grama Panchayat* v. *Union of India and others*, decided by the Kerala High Court on 23 March 2006, concerning a hydroelectric project, is an example of how successive amendments in the procedure on public consultation in EIA regulations have impacted on the environmental clearance.

[56] Asian Development Bank 1997, available at www.adb.org/Documents/Books/Environment_Impact/Chap2. pdf; Rahman 2003 at 390–426.

[57] Section 2 of the 1997 Environment Protection Act. Under the provision, 'project' includes any activity involving any change in the environment and includes the construction of buildings, transport systems and factories; mining and quarrying; and any change of land use or water use.

[58] Sections 12 and 17 of the Act. See also the Pakistan Environmental Protection Agency (Review of IEE and EIA) Regulations 2000. Full text available at www.environment.gov.pk/act-rules/IEE-EIA-REG.pdf.

[59] *Ibid.*, section 10.

[60] Guidelines for Public Consultation, Pakistan Environmental Protection Agency 1997, available at www. environment.gov.pk/eia_pdf/e_RevPublicCon.pdf.

[61] Examples of such EIAs can be found in gas pipelines, thermal power plants, hydropower projects, water management, and biodiversity conservation sectors. See Razzaque 2004a, Chapter 8.

affected community and face-to-face surveys with community members and NGOs working in the neighbourhood of the project. In some cases, informal meetings with the local people were conducted, at which were explained the project details, its benefits and compensation in case of damage to their crops or other assets. These projects, with their detailed guidelines on public participation, show the direct influence of multilateral development banks (e.g. the Asian Development Bank) on the development of EIA process.

In India, Pakistan and Bangladesh, the law does not provide any guidance in determining what constitutes a significant impact in particular situations or what the role of the public in the consultation exercise should be. The rules allow limited participation of communities, often at later stages of the project development, and include inadequate publication requirements. It is significant that there is no requirement to update the initial environmental impact statement (EIS) prior to the final decision-making stage in response to the findings of the participation stage. Sometimes, the government bodies may opt for amending environmental regulations to evade compliance with impact assessment requirements.[62] A number of critics highlight the inadequacies of the present system of EIA in these countries. According to them, lack of legislative control of the EIA process, inappropriate procedures, lack of institutional capacity and limited public participation hamper the effectiveness of EIA.[63] It is impossible to achieve procedural justice without effective and constructive participation of communities in the EIA process, particularly concerning activities harmful to natural resources. While there are some weaknesses (e.g. the meaning of consultation, technical language, the narrow scope for participation at all levels, inadequate assessment of alternatives) of the EIA, there have been some positive developments. Recent legislative changes in India and Pakistan show that the legislators have taken into account developments in participatory rules at the international level.

3.2 Participation at the policy-making level

Human rights instruments, such as General Comment 15[64] of the UN Committee for Economic, Social and Cultural Rights,[65] assert that the formulation and implementation of strategies and plans of action on water should respect people's participation.

---

[62] See the case of Kirthar National Park in Pakistan, where the Sindh Wildlife Protection Ordinance was amended to allow pipeline construction in the park. See www.foe.co.uk/resource/press_releases/20010509131119.html.

[63] Ahammed and Harvey 2004 at 63–78; Wood 2003 at 301–21.

[64] General Comments 15. Substantive Issues Arising in the Implementation of the International Covenant on Economic, Social and Cultural Rights (Twenty-Ninth Session, Geneva, 11–29 November 2002).

[65] The Committee on Economic, Social and Cultural Rights is a body of independent experts that monitors implementation of the International Covenant on Economic, Social and Cultural Rights by its states parties. The Committee was established by an ECOSOC resolution. The Committee publishes its interpretation of the provisions of the Covenant, known as General Comments.

According to the 1992 Forest Principles,[66] governments should promote and provide opportunities for the participation of interested parties, including local communities, indigenous people, the private sector and NGOs in policy-making. Along with international and regional documents highlighting the importance of community participation,[67] national plans, programmes and policies in these three countries include provisions for communities to participate in environmental planning, conservation of shared natural resources and activities related to waste disposal, energy facilities and dams.

The environmental conservation policies in these three countries highlight the importance of community participation in the protection and management of natural resources. The National Environmental Policy (2005) of Pakistan[68] urges government agencies to promote sustainable forestry management in Pakistan, ensure the participation of women in environmental projects and develop an action plan for the protection of mangrove forests with the participation of local communities. The draft National Environmental Policy of India (2004)[69] emphasises the need for the participation of local communities in the planning and implementation of environmental projects.[70] However, this document has been criticised by many because there was no provision for the participation of communities during the preparation of the policy.[71] The problem lies in the fact that there is no agreed institutional arrangement to deliberate policies. Participatory democracy and procedural justice require that communities represent all affected groups, be involved in the actual making of policies and be part of the political debate.[72]

Community participation is a common theme in sectoral policies, such as energy, water and forestry.[73] The water policies of these three countries emphasise the importance of local community participation in the planning and management of these resources.[74] These documents encourage the participation of communities and the

---

[66] UNCED, Non-Legally Binding Authoritative Statement of Principles for a Global Consensus on the Management, Conservation and Sustainable Development of All Types of Forests 1992, availaible at www.un.org/documents/ga/conf151/aconf15126-3annex3.htm.

[67] Pring and Noe 2002 at 37.

[68] National Environmental Policy 2005. Text available at www.environment.gov.pk/nep/policy.pdf.

[69] Full text of the National Environmental Policy, 2004, available at http://envfor.nic.in/nep.htm. This document has been criticised for not reflecting specific concerns at the national level: see Geevan 2004 at 4686–8.

[70] Similar provisions can be found in the 1992 Environment Policy and the 1992 Environmental Action Plan of Bangladesh.

[71] Sharma 2004, available at www.indiatogether.org/2004/oct/env-nepolicy.htm. Acharya 2004, available at www.scidev.net/News/index.cfm?fuseaction=readNews&itemid=1789&language=1/.

[72] Richardson and Razzaque 2006 at 165–94.

[73] See India's report to the Commission on Sustainable Development, 2002, available at www.un.org/esa/agenda21/natlinfo/wssd/india.pdf. See also the National Energy Policy 1996 of Bangladesh.

[74] See the discussion on the National Water Policy (1999) of Bangladesh in Akhter 2005; the National Water Policy of India (2002), available at www.nih.ernet.in/belgaum/NWP.html; the Water Policy of Pakistan (2004), available at waterpakistan.com/OtherNationalWaterPolicy.pdf; and the Water Sector Strategy of Pakistan (2002).

private sector in the planning, development and management of water resources projects and call for an enabling environment for active stakeholder consultation in all aspects of the water sector. Similar to the water sector, the forestry sector promotes a participatory management approach, allowing the active participation and involvement of communities in forest conservation and development.[75] Forestry sector master plan encourages a massive afforestation programme through community participation and social forestry programmes. An example of such participatory management can be found in the 'Social Forestry' programme initiated under the Forest (Amendment) Act 2000 of Bangladesh, under which government agencies can establish social forestry schemes, and participants in the scheme would be responsible for afforesting, conserving or managing a piece of land.[76] In India, Joint Forest Management (JFM) had been an integral part of all forestry schemes to ensure people's participation in afforestation activities, and a large number of state governments have developed mechanisms for public participation in the management of degraded forests.[77]

India, Pakistan and Bangladesh are parties to a number of multilateral environmental agreements (MEAs),[78] most of which encourage community participation in the preparation of national plans to implement MEA obligations. Community consultation at the planning stage could ensure compliance, develop local capacity and assess the impact of measures under MEAs, including environmental effects on local communities.[79] The national reports to the secretariat of these MEAs have highlighted the need for greater participation of people at the planning and preparation of MEA national implementation plans.[80] These plans integrate obligations under these MEAs into national plans, policies and programmes. MEA national implementation plans could provide a good example of how national-level coordination with participation from all stakeholders could lead to a sustainable outcome.[81] These implementation plans involve community participation at the earliest opportunity (through village-level workshops, public hearings and consultation) allowing people to prioritise issues.[82] In Bangladesh, local communities and NGOs played an active role during the preparation of these national implementation plans. For example,

---

[75] The Forestry Sector Master Plan (1995–2015) and the Forest Policy (1994) of Bangladesh; and the National Forest Policy of Pakistan (2001).

[76] For examples of such participatory forest management in India, see Kant and Cooke 1998.

[77] Report to the Commission on Sustainable Development by India (2002), available at www.un.org/esa/agenda21/natlinfo/wssd/india.pdf.

[78] 1971 Ramsar Convention, 1992 Convention on Biological Diversity, 1992 UN Framework Convention on Climate Change, 1994 UN Convention to Combat Desertification.

[79] UNEP, Guidelines on Compliance with and Enforcement of MEAs, available at www.unep.org/DEC/docs/UNEP.Guidelines.on.Compliance.MEA.pdf.

[80] See the national reports from India, Pakistan and Bangladesh to the UN Convention to Combat Desertification, Ramsar Convention, Climate Change Convention and Biodiversity Convention secretariats.

[81] Razzaque 2005 at 282.

[82] For example, the National Biodiversity Strategy and Action Plan (NBSAP) in India, available at www.envfor.nic.in/divisions/ic/wssd/doc3/chapter1/css/Chapter1.htm.

local community-level workshops and public consultation at the national level were held throughout the preparation of the National Biodiversity Strategy and Action Plan (NBSAP) under the Biodiversity Convention[83] and National Adaptation Programme of Action (NAPA) under the Climate Change Convention.[84] Citing examples from the NBSAP process in the South Asian region, some have, however, expressed concerns as to the level of representation of local communities, women and the private sector in the consultative process.[85]

While communities can play an important role in strategic environmental assessment (SEA) of energy, water and forestry sector planning, it is not a common tool in this region.[86] SEA is undertaken much earlier in the decision-making process than EIA, and is seen as a key tool to integrate environmental, social and economic considerations during the formulation of policies, development plans and programmes. Multilateral development agencies and bilateral aid agencies play an important role in initiating SEA in developing countries. An example of this could be the World Bank financed programme to improve the state highway system in Gujarat and to prepare a long-term development strategy (Vision 2020) in Andhra Pradesh in India.[87] Further examples of SEA-type approaches can be found at the national level. One example from Bangladesh is where the involvement of communities was prioritised in the formulation of the National Environmental Management Action Plan (NEMAP).[88] NEMAP is the first national environmental plan prepared through a participatory process and involved a series of workshops with local officials, local community representatives, academics, farmers, fishermen, and women.[89] Other examples include Pakistan's water and drainage programme and the Thermal Power Generation Policy.[90] These examples where communities were consulted at the policy, programme and plan-making levels show the willingness of the government agencies to construct a meaningful working relationship with the communities, and to contribute to the development of procedural environmental justice.

Local governments could also play an important role in involving local communities in the preparation of policies aiming to achieve sustainable development. For example, Local Agenda 21 (LA21) prescribes a participatory, multi-stakeholder process to achieve the goals of Agenda 21, adopted at the 1992 UN Conference on

---

[83] The draft NBSAP (2004) is available at www.sdnbd.org.   [84] See FIELD 2004.   [85] UNDP, 2000.

[86] For examples of SEAs from other Asian countries including China, Nepal and Thailand, see Dalal-Clayton and Sadler 2005, Chapter 6.

[87] *Ibid.*, Chapter 4. See also the World Bank's Country Environmental Analysis (CEA) which examines the extent of public participation in policy-making at the national level. CEAs are being finalised in India, Pakistan and Bangladesh. Available at www.worldbank.org/.

[88] Funded by the UNDP, this programme was carried out through a series of discussions and workshops. The workshop participants identified their own environmental priorities and recommended actions that were to be taken by themselves, by the local authorities, local communities and by the national government.

[89] Haque 1996.   [90] Dalal-Clayton and Sadler 2005.

Environment and Development in Rio de Janeiro,[91] at the local level through the preparation and implementation of a long-term, strategic plan that addresses local sustainable development concerns. These processes involve consultation with community partners to create a shared vision and to identify proposals for action; and participatory assessment of local social, environmental and economic needs.[92] Examples of LA21 initiatives by local authorities include solid waste management and urban poverty reduction programmes in Bangladesh.[93] These programmes include the participation of local governmental institutes (municipalities) and local NGOs.[94] In India, government agencies encourage the participation of local communities in the planning and implementation of the renewable energy sector, particularly in rural areas.[95] At the local government level, Pakistan promotes an ecosystem approach to conserve natural resources through the participation of all sectors, especially local communities.[96]

While examples of public participation can be found in various environmental projects, plans and policies, restricted access to public hearings and the lack of elaborate guidelines on good practice makes these rules less effective. Without adequate institutional arrangements and a true opportunity to take part in the decision-making process, communities are unable to influence the outcome. In some cases, participants have to spend money in order to gain access to information, prepare submissions, attend hearings and deal with subsequent litigation. Excessive technical and bureaucratic procedures for public involvement along with financial costs make it hard for poor communities to participate effectively. If affected communities are unable to be part of the process or their inputs are not integrated into final decisions, communities will become disillusioned with the process as a whole. That will be counterproductive to achieving procedural justice.

4 Access to information to protect natural resources

Adequate access to environmental information strengthens public participation in the natural resource management and promotes procedural justice. Provisions related to

---

[91] Agenda 21 is a comprehensive plan of action in every area in which humans impact on the environment. It was adopted by more than 178 governments at the United Nations Conference on Environment and Development held in Rio de Janerio, on 3–14 June 1992, available at www.un.org/esa/sustdev/documents/agenda21/index.htm.

[92] International Council for Local Environmental Initiatives (2002).

[93] Report to the Commission on Sustainable Development by Bangladesh (2002), available at www.un.org/esa/agenda21/natlinfo/wssd/bangladesh.pdf.

[94] Report of the Government of Bangladesh (1997) to the UN Commission on Sustainable Development, Implementation of Agenda 21: Review of Progress Made Since the UNCED, available at www.un.org/esa/earthsummit/bang-cp.htm.

[95] Report to the Commission on Sustainable Development by India (2002), available at www.un.org/esa/agenda21/natlinfo/wssd/india.pdf.

[96] Report to the Commission on Sustainable Development by Pakistan (2002), available at www.un.org/esa/agenda21/natlinfo/countr/pakistan/index.htm.

access to environmental information in these three countries are found in framework environmental legislation,[97] but they do not impose any duty on the state to collect or disseminate environmental information. The public authorities also publish periodic reports on the 'state of the environment' and information related to other environmental indicators at irregular intervals.[98] Whereas some Asian constitutions provide a right to information,[99] there is no such provision in India, Pakistan or Bangladesh. All these three countries have an Official Secrets Act[100] that deals with access to information. These laws do not contain any provision on environmental information.

Apart from framework environmental legislation, the legislation on water pollution, air pollution, waste disposal and pollution from industry in India hardly provides any provision on the access to environmental information.[101] Amendments to the Environment (Protection) Rules 1994 deal with public hearings and the dissemination of information.[102] Moreover, during the EIA, the details of the project and the locations are published in the local newspaper soliciting consultation from the community. Section 20 of the Environment Protection Act 1986 enables people to receive information, reports and details on environmental pollution. However, the government can refuse to supply the required information if it considers that the passing of information will be contrary to the public interest. This gives a wide discretion to public authorities as the definition of 'public interest' is vague.

In Pakistan, communities can access information on a development project via the Environment Protection Agency. Once the EIS is presented to them for approval, the agency disseminates the information to local communities.[103] Moreover, projects funded by multilateral banks often include explicit provisions on the dissemination of information.[104] Under the Bangladesh Conservation Rules 1997, rule 15 states that any person or organisation can apply to the Environment Directorate (under MoEF) for the report or statistical data of any studies on water, waste, air or noise. A

---

[97] 1986 Environment Protection Act of India; 1997 Environment Conservation Rules of Bangladesh; 1997 Pakistan Environment Protection Act.

[98] State of the Environment, Bangladesh (2001), available at www.rrcap.unep.org/reports/soe/ bangladeshsoe.cfm; State of the Environment, India (2001), available at www.rrcap.unep.org/reports/soe/ indiasoe.cfm; Draft State of the Environment, Pakistan (2005), available at www.environment.gov.pk/ Publications.htm.

[99] For example, in the Philippines and Thailand, the right to information is recognised in the Constitution. Banisar 2004, available at www.freedominfo.org/documents/global_survey2004.pdf.

[100] The Official Secrets Act of 1923 (with necessary amendments in each country) deals with access to official information in these three countries. The emphasis of this Act is to restrict access rather than opening it.

[101] Rosencranz and Divan 2001.

[102] In evaluating a project for environmental clearance, the State Pollution Control Board (SPCB) publishes a notice of a public hearing in national newspapers. All persons including residents and environmental groups located at the project sites/sites of displacement/sites likely to be affected can participate in the public hearing or can make oral or written submissions.

[103] Guidelines for Public Consultation, Pakistan Environmental Protection Agency (1997), available at www.environment.gov.pk/eia_pdf/e_RevPublicCon.pdf.

[104] E.g. Ghazi Barotha Hydropower (1995). More information available at www.adb.org/.

nominal fee needs to be paid for such information. The 1920 Agricultural and Sanitary Improvement Act and the 1952 Embankment and Drainage Act guarantee the rights of local communities to examine and raise objections to the project being considered.[105] Although these provisions do not mention access to information, effective objection can only be possible if the community has relevant information available to them.

While India and Pakistan have an information law, Bangladesh produced a draft law on public information in 2008.[106] In India, the Supreme Court ruled in 1982 that access to government information was an essential part of the fundamental right to freedom of speech and expression.[107] The Indian Right to Information Act (2005) guarantees that the public may inspect *all* information held by government agencies. It can be presumed that environmental information falls under the wide definition, however, there is no specific mention of it in the legislation.[108] While the amount charged to access information could be excessive for some poorer communities, the government claims that the significant costs of collecting and copying so many records have forced it to charge higher fees to people seeking information.[109] In Pakistan, the Freedom of Information Ordinance (2002)[110] allows any citizen to access public records held by a public body including ministerial departments, councils, courts and tribunals, except from government-owned corporations or provincial governments. Policies, guidelines and information regarding the grant of licences and contracts and agreements by public bodies are declared as public record.[111] Similar to India, this Ordinance has been criticised by the NGOs on the ground that fees charged to inspect a document are exorbitant.[112]

For these three countries, there is no specific legislation guaranteeing access to environmental information, and there are very few opportunities for interested parties to obtain adequate information on projects and policies concerning natural resources. Public agencies have limited power and resources to collect, update or disseminate environmental information. The publication of the official data or informal reports can help the public to gather environmental information. However, accessibility of information and adequate legal and institutional mechanisms need to be in place to make any participation effective.

---

[105] Farooque and Hassan 1996.

[106] The (Draft) Right to Information Ordinance (2008), available at www.article19.org/pdfs/laws/bangladesh-draft-rti.pdf.

[107] *P. Gupta* v. *Union of India*, AIR 1982 SC 149. See Rosencranz and Divan 2001 at 157–66; Article 19, Global Trends on the Right to Information: A Survey of South Asia, July 2001, available at www.article19.org.

[108] Full text available at http://righttoinformation.gov.in.

[109] See the example in Putul 2006.

[110] Freedom of Information Ordinance 2002, No. XCVI of 2002. F. No. 2(1)/2002-Pub, Islamabad 26 October 2002, www.crcp.sdnpk.org/ordinance_of_2002.htm.

[111] The earlier Freedom of Information Ordinance of 1997 is criticised on the ground that the definition of 'public record' is unduly restrictive and left many key issues unaddressed. See Ishaque 1997.

[112] Centre for Peace and Development Initiative, 'Pakistan: Changes to Freedom of Information Law Sought', Dawn (14 February 2006), available at www.asiamedia.ucla.edu/article.asp?parentid=39190/.

5 Concluding remarks

In the absence of a strong constitutional mandate, soft laws and policies govern the regime related to 'public participation'.[113] While some sectoral legislation is available, time-limits, the nature of the project or the policy, and a dependence on financial support from donor agencies may determine the level of consultation.[114] Also, there is no participation of communities at the earlier stages of decision-making, at the monitoring of implementation, and in the review of performance. The effectiveness of public participation, in some cases, depends on sympathetic public bodies, the level of political commitment and resources invested by the local authorities. Without adequate technical and institutional support, communities may not have a meaningful voice in decisions concerning natural resources. Any reform agenda[115] (for example a separate review procedure, an information ombudsman, or a higher level of penalty for disinformation) has to be supported by a constitutional right to information and participation. The substantive right to a healthy environment, as established by the judiciary, needs to be strengthened by adequate information and participation of affected communities to protect and manage natural resources.

Before opening up natural resources to the private sector, it is necessary to have adequate law and binding compliance mechanisms. At the same time, lack of consultation at the earliest opportunity could lead to injustice (social and procedural) to the local community. Early consultation with people at the project initiation and planning level in the case of large projects such as dams and power plants, could not only legitimise the project but also forestall public complaints about the viability of the project and its likely detrimental consequences. An example could be the river linking a project in India where the riparian states were not consulted, even though the project dealt with shared natural resources, i.e. the Ganges basin.[116] It is feared that, once completed, the withdrawal of water would have serious repercussions on the climate, ecology, geomorphology, biodiversity, wetlands and navigational activities in Bangladesh, and would adversely affect more than 100 million people.[117] An SEA-type assessment or a transboundary EIA could provide the opportunity for early consultation among riparian states in the basin.[118] When a project has a potential tranboundary impact, lack of consultation with the affected community within the country and with neighbouring countries is likely to cause grave environmental injustice.

---

[113] Public participation assumes a variety of forms. It can occur through education, information dissemination, advisory or review boards, public advocacy, public hearings and submissions, and even litigation. UNECE 2000 at 85. On a definition of the 'public', see Zillman 2002.

[114] See the UNDP workshop summary, www.undp.org/bpsp/regional/S_Asia_%20NBSAPBangladesh_ %20Feb00.doc.

[115] Richardson and Razzaque 2006.

[116] India has been planning a river-linking project which would interlink major rivers with canals and construct reservoirs and embankments by 2016 to store water collected in the monsoon season for use in farming in the dry season. The River Linking Programme in India, available at www.sdnpbd.org/river_basin/index.htm.

[117] Misra *et al.* 2007 at 1361.   [118] WCD 2000.

Participatory provisions and practices are still developing, and it is difficult to assess whether these provisions can actually lead to a just substantive outcome. Although the courts of these three countries have also widened the access of community, there are no guidelines for community participation. It depends on what the judiciary defines as the 'public interest'. While the inclusion of affected parties is crucial to making the linkages between social, environmental and development concerns, the evidence from all three countries demonstrates that the best practice in respect of EIA is not always available. Most of the provisions integrated in the environmental legislation (e.g. EIA laws) deal with procedures and not so much with the end result following the consultation procedures. These laws do not dictate the 'just decisions' to be made, nor do they provide any guidelines on how the outcome of the consultation would be integrated in the final decision. Thus, the degree of public participation affects the quality of the assessment process, which in turn affects the quality of the decision.[119] Proper consultation procedure through SEA and EIA, and a coherent environmental policy guaranteeing timely and effective participation in natural resource management could ensure procedural justice.

To manage natural resources sustainably, the disadvantaged communities need to play a more direct role and be part of the whole process. While environmental law may provide participatory tools, in many cases the affected groups are not aware of these rights and may not have technical expertise to understand the impact of the decisions. Multiple languages at the national level (e.g. India, Pakistan) make it difficult to disseminate environmental information. Here, the individual activists and NGOs can play an important role to disseminate information and make communities aware of their rights.[120] Regulatory agencies and local government need to play a proactive role to ensure the involvement of community groups through regular group meetings or briefing sessions. Moreover, participatory processes do not ensure that resources will be there for the people to participate. Access to courts by marginalised communities needs to be supported by adequate public funding and legal aid.

An active role of the judiciary in South Asia could provide a valuable lesson for the judiciary in the United States and Europe in the protection of natural resources. This can be in the form of granting liberal standing to communities in cases dealing with public interest, allowing *suo motu* action, applying 'public trust' doctrine in cases involving resource rights, and issuing innovative cost orders in 'public interest' cases. Community groups would have more bargaining power at the negotiation table if they had access to the courts. At the same time, Asian countries could benefit from the detailed procedural rules found in the Aarhus Convention and adapt these rules and guidelines to their needs and constraints. A constitutional right to protect natural resources could strengthen participatory rights. One example of a country with such

---

[119] Wood 2003, Chapters 2, 3 and 5.

[120] Examples of such partnerships can be found in various dam projects in India and a Flood Action Programme in Bangladesh: see Razzaque 2004c.

a constitution is South Africa, where the Constitution includes a substantive right to water, and the water law includes a right to information, participation and remedies.[121] An explicit constitutional right would ensure that the communities would not have to depend on a liberal interpretation of a constitutional right to life. Moreover, a rights-based approach would impose a positive duty on the state to protect and preserve natural resources and the environment. It is also crucial to consider how other regions (e.g. UNECE) are sharing their experiences and how to use existing platforms, such as the Association of South-East Asian Nations (ASEAN) and the South Asian Association for Regional Cooperation (SAARC) or the Mekong River Basin initiative, to develop a regional instrument dealing with transboundary resources.

In the absence of a global treaty on procedural environmental rights, development and application of procedural rights depend a lot on the national legal system, the courts and the other government agencies of these three countries. Most public participation at the policy- and project-making level has occurred through the proliferation of administrative-based consultation, information and review mechanisms established pursuant to environmental and natural resource laws. The discussion above shows that procedural injustices at the policy- and project-making level lead to environmental injustices. Although there is an active judiciary allowing communities to access the courts, the judicial system is not always cost-effective, and legal aid is rarely available to make the legal system more accessible to community groups. Procedural environment justice requires that projects and policies reflect the views of affected communities, and that unfair administrative decisions are challenged in the courts. While it is not all gloom and doom in these South Asian countries, it is necessary to have stronger procedural regimes with adequate EIA laws, optimal institutional arrangement for consultation, and legal aid to protect resource rights and ensure environmental justice.

Bibliography

Acharya, K., 2004. '"Little Science" in India's Draft Environmental Policy', www.acidev.net/en/news/

ADB (Asian Development Bank), 1997. 'EIA for the Developing Countries'.

Ahammed, R., and Harvey, N., 2004. 'Evaluation of Environmental Impact Assessment Procedures and Practice in Bangladesh'. 22/1 *Impact Assessment and Project Appraisal* 63.

Ahmed, N., 1999. *Public Interest Litigation: Constitutional Issues and Remedies*. Dhaka: BLAST.

Ahuja, S., 1997. *People, Law and Justice: A Casebook of Public Interest Litigation*. New Delhi: Orient Longman.

Akhter, B. R., 2005. 'Pollution and Its Management Approach: Integrated Coastal Zone Management Plan Project'. Working Paper WP043.

Banisar, D., 2004. *Global Survey: Freedom of Information and Access to Government Record Laws Around the World*.

---

[121] FAO 2001.

Baxi, U., 1985. 'Taking Suffering Seriously: Social Action Litigation in the Supreme Court of India', in R. Dhavan, R. Sudarshan and S. Khurshid (eds.), *Judges, and the Judicial Power: Essays in Honour of Justice V. R. Krishna Iyer*. London: Sweet & Maxwell, 289–315.

CESCR, 2002. *Substantive Issues Arising in the Implementation of the International Covenant on Economic, Social and Cultural Rights*. Geneva: Twenty-Ninth session of CESCR, 11–29 November 2002.

Dalal-Clayton, B., and Sadler, B., 2005. *Strategic Environmental Assessment: A Sourcebook and Reference Guide to International Experience*. London: Earthscan.

Earthjustice, 2005. *Environmental Rights Report: Human Rights and the Environment: Materials for the 61st Session of the United Nations Commission on Human Rights*. Geneva: UNCHR, 4 March–22 April 2005.

FAO, 2001. *Water Rights Administration – Experience, Issues and Guidelines*. FAO Legislative Study 70, Rome: FAO, www.fao.org/003/x9419e/x9419e00.htm#Contents/.

Farooque, M., and Hassan, R., 1996. *Laws Regulating Environment in Bangladesh*. Dhaka: BELA.

FIELD, 2004. 'Strengthening the Capacity of Least Developed Countries to Negotiate and Implement the UNFCCC and the Kyoto Protocol'. Buenos Aires: Workshop Report, 3–4 December 2004.

Geevan, C. P., 2004. 'National Environmental Policy: Ascendance of Economic Factors'. 39/43 *Economic and Political Weekly* 4686–8.

Glasson, J., Therivel, R., and Chadwick, A., 1999. *Introduction to Environmental Impact Assessment*. London: UCL Press.

Haque, M., 1996. 'National Environmental Management Action Program (NEMAP) in Bangladesh', in Quddus *et al.* (eds.). *Environment and Sustainable Agriculture in Rural Development*. Dhaka: BARD.

International Council for Local Environmental Initiatives, 2002. *Local Government's Response to Agenda 21: Summary Report of Local Agenda 21 Survey with Regional Focus*. Toronto: ICLEI.

Ishaque, S, K., 1997. 'Freedom of Information or Protection of Information'. *Pakistan Legal Decisions* 22.

Jodhi, G. (ed.), 2000. *Privatization in South Asia: Minimizing Negative Social Effects Through Restructuring*. New Delhi: ILO.

Kant, S., and Cooke, R., 1998. 'Complementarity of Institutions: A Prerequisite for the Success of Joint Forest Management: A Comparative Case of Four Villages from India'. Presented at the International Workshop on Community-Based Natural Resource Management Systems, Washington DC, 10–14 May 1998.

Khan, M. H., 1993. *Public Interest Litigation: Growth of the Concept and Its Meaning in Pakistan*. Karachi: Pakistan Law House.

Lee, M., and Abbot, C., 2003. 'The Usual Suspects? Public Participation under the Aarhus Convention'. 66 *Modern Law Review* 80.

Misra, A., *et al.*, 2007. 'Proposed River Linking Project of India: A Boon or Bane to Nature'. 51 *Environmental Geology* 1361.

Petkova, E., *et al.*, 2002. *Closing the Gap: Information, Participation and Justice in Decision Making for the Environment*. Washington DC: World Resources Institute.

Pring, G., and Noe, S. Y., 2002. 'The Emerging International Law of Public Participation Affecting Global Mining, Energy and Resource Development', in D. Zillman, *et al.*, *Human Rights in*

Natural Resource Development: Public Participation in the Sustainable Development of Mining and Energy Resources. Oxford: Oxford University Press.

Putul A. P., 'Indians Find Information Too Costly', BBC News, 14 March 2006.

Rahman, A. B. M. Z., 2003. 'Environmental Aspects of Energy Exploration in Bangladesh and the Role of EIA: The Case of the Sunderbans'. 24/3 *Bangladesh Institute of International and Strategic Studies (BIISS) Journal* 390.

Razzaque, J, 2001. 'Case Law Analysis: Application of Public Trust Doctrine in Indian Environmental Cases'. 13/2 *Journal of Environmental Law* 221.

    2002. 'Human Rights and the Environment in South Asia'. 32/2 *Journal of Environmental Policy and Law* 99.

    2004a. *Public Interest Environmental Litigation in India, Pakistan and Bangladesh.* The Hague: Kluwer.

    2004b. 'Country Report: Bangladesh', in *Yearbook of International Environmental Law.* Oxford: Oxford University Press.

    2004c. 'Environmental Human Rights in South Asia: Towards Stronger Participatory Mechanisms'. Paper presented at the Roundtable on Human Rights and the Environment, Geneva: UNEP/UNHCHR, 12 March 2004.

    2005. 'Implementation of Multilateral Environmental Agreements and Integrated Water Resource Management: What Does National Co-ordination Achieve?' 26/2 *Bangladesh Institute of International and Strategic Studies (BIISS) Journal* 257.

Rechtschaffen, C., 2003. 'Advancing Environmental Justice Norms'. 37/1 *UC Davis Law Review* 95.

Richardson, B., and Razzaque, J., 2006. 'Public Participation in Environmental Decision Making', in B. Richardson and S. Wood (eds.), *Environmental Law for Sustainability.* Oxford: Hart. 165–94.

Rosencranz, A., and Divan, S., 2001. *Environmental Law and Policy in India.* Oxford: Oxford University Press.

Sathe, S. P., 2002. *Judicial Activism in India – Transgressing Borders and Enforcing Limits.* Oxford: Oxford University Press.

Sharma, S., 2004. 'Pushing an Environmental Policy', *India Together.*

Spyke, N. P., 1999. 'Public Participation in Environmental Decision-Making at the New Millennium: Structuring New Spheres of Public Influence'. 26 *Boston College Environmental Affairs Law Review* 263.

Stephens, C., Bullock, S., and Scott, A., 2001. 'Environmental Justice: Rights and Means to a Healthy Environment for All'. Special Briefing No. 7. ESRC.

Tabb, W. M., 1999. 'Environmental Impact Assessment in the European Community: Shaping International Norms'. 73 *Tulane Law Review* 923.

Tilleman, W. A., 1995. 'Public Participation in the Environmental Impact Assessment Process: A Comparative Study of Impact Assessment in Canada, the United States and the European Community'. 33 *Columbia Journal of Transnational Law* 337.

UNCED, 1992. 'Non Legally Binding Authoritative Statement of Principles for a Global Consensus on the Management, Conservation and Sustainable Development of All Types of Forests'.

UNDP, 2000. 'National Biodiversity Strategies and Action Plans – Lessons from South Asia', Workshop Summary.

UNECE, 2000. *The Aarhus Convention: An Implementation Guide.* Geneva: UNECE.

WCD, 2000. 'Environmental and Social Impact Assessment for Large-Scale Dams', Thematic
    Review.
Wood, C. M., 2003. 'Environmental Impact Assessment in Developing Countries'. 25 *International
    Development Planning Review* 301.
Zillman, D., 2002. 'Introduction to Public Participation in the 21st Century', in D. Zillman
    et al., *Human Rights in Natural Resource Development: Public Participation in the Sustain-
    able Development of Mining and Energy Resources.* Oxford: Oxford University Press.

7

Public participation and the challenges of environmental justice in China

QUN DU[*]

1 Introduction

It is commonly believed, in China, that the ultimate goal of the legal system is justice. Justice and fairness are closely intertwined in the literature, and in many respects the two terms are used interchangeably. Justice serves more like an ideology or fundamental principle in the Chinese legal context, while fairness, enlightened by justice, has been adopted as an applicable legal principle by civil law and practised widely.[1] Aristotle's theory of justice, in both its distributive and corrective aspects, has been examined by Chinese scholars and used for interpreting functions of law and the legal system.[2] Distributive justice refers to initial allocation of substantive rights or interests, procedures and opportunities by law and legal practice. Corrective justice stands first for the correction of abuse of substantive rights and interests distributed by law, public policy or private agreements; it also reflects the evolution of initially distributed rights and interests and procedures due to changes of social merits concerning overall justice. The latter mode of corrective justice could be regarded as originally distributed rights and interests.

Justice is a dynamic concept with a complex of merits; it ought to fluctuate with the changes of cultural, social and historic conditions. A combination of value in all aspects of a society constitutes a general benchmark of justice, and guides the mainstream of society in justice considerations from time to time. With the Chinese version of John Rawls' book, *A Theory of Justice*, being introduced into China in 1998,[3] a theoretical review of social justice concerning sustainable development took place in China, which obtained wide attention from society. Justice issues were aroused at that moment, not because of scholars' own interests but because of a virtual social need. In mid-1980, at the beginning of the market-oriented approach to economic

[*] This paper is an outcome of the Project (No. 40471056) of the National Sciences Foundation of PRC. Thanks to Jonas Ebbesson and Phoebe Okowa for their valuable advice and comments on an earlier draft of this chapter.
[1] Fairness is a substantial legal principle in both civil and administrative statutes, for example Art. 4 of the General Principles of the Civil Law of the PRC 1986 and Art. 5 of Administrative Permit Law of the PRC 2003.
[2] Aristotle1990 p. 103.   [3] Rawls 1998.

development, policy-makers initiated some essential principles for deeper reform, one of which dealt with the important issue of the relationship between economic efficiency and social fairness, and thus concerned justice benchmark setting. It was a new development principle called *efficiency in priority, fairness in balance.*[4] It addressed the priority of values between economic growth and social concerns, and in the following decade was commonly used as practical guidelines in mainstream society to deal with the distribution of benefits or income generated from market-oriented economic reforms. From the historic point of view, this principle largely facilitated the progress of Chinese economic reform.

In short, from mid-1980 to the present, during the period of economic reform and social development, the benchmark for justice in Chinese mainstream society was altered. Since the new millennium, it has departed from the mode of inclination to economic and efficiency priorities toward the one in favour of public welfare and social fairness. This indicates that the old distribution mode – which was coloured by the planned economy and featured policy and government-dominated decision-making as the main approaches to allocating initial development interests and opportunities – has undergone subsequent reform. As demonstrated in the past two decades, the policy-focused distributive process and government-dominated decision-making approach in public affairs (including the environment) became root-causes of unfairness and environmental injustice due to the exclusion of citizens' involvement and democratic processes. Therefore, a political and social need existed for public participation to develop as an autonomous concept in China.

As stated, when China entered the new millennium, issues of social distribution and fairness again achieved social focus. However, the increasing gap between rich and poor, rural and urban, and the social impacts of economic reforms and the principle of *efficiency in priority, fairness in balance* reveal that, while the objective of economic efficiency has been fulfilled, social fairness has not been achieved. According to the State Statistics Bureau, nationally the richest 10 per cent of people own 45 per cent of total private income, whereas the poorest 10 per cent possess only 1.4 per cent of total private income. Another source from the Ministry of Finance showed that 60 per cent of banking deposits belonged to 10 per cent of account holders. The public's view on the current *status quo* of fairness and justice through an online public survey of citizens' awareness of social fairness, was that the overall situation was worsening.[5]

---

[4] It was one of the outcomes of a study of the 'Chinese market economy and the design of social welfare institutions' in 1986, carried out by the Civil Affairs Ministry of the State Council. This new principle was soon formally adopted by the Chinese Communist Party, the ruling party, in 1987 at its 13th Party Conference. It was identical to Deng Xiaoping's well-known slogan to 'let some people get rich first'. At the end of the planned economy, commercial activities were considered to have a high political risk with uncertain gain, and people who were permitted to undertake commercial activities by this policy were allowed to use greater resources.

[5] An internet-based public survey where 'netizens' complete and submit questionnaires in an anonymous manner. See http://vote.people.com.cn/gongping (visited 19 November 2006).

Ninety per cent of interviewees were not satisfied with current social fairness; over 50 per cent of interviewees believed income distribution, individual development opportunities, political rights and public opinion releases were generally socially unfair; and more than 60 per cent of interviewees reckoned that official's neglect of duty and corruption are the main causes of social unfairness. This research found that the main causes of social unfairness were: unfair distribution of opportunities for individual development in terms of education, health care, welfare, migration rights, market access and competition; unfair and unjust policies and institutions; official corruption; and lack of public participation in decision-making and policy implementation.[6]

The rapid economic growth and the attendant disparity between rich and poor are the principal factors to be considered when re-examining Chinese development policy. Scholars like Kang Hang, the Vice President of the State Administrative College, evaluated the adoption of the principle of *efficiency in priority, fairness in balance*. He concluded that the principle was appropriate in the specific historic circumstances for its significant contribution to motivating individuals to participate in private business and market-oriented economic practices and to eliminating poverty. However, when it was demonstrated that economic prosperity also brought about high intangible social and environmental costs, this principle was widely criticised for being one of the fundamental root-causes of social unfairness and environmental injustice.[7]

As the benchmark of justice has shifted from economic efficiency to *social fairness*, justice nowadays becomes more an issue of social equity in distributing civil benefits and of individual liberty, rather than taking economic growth as the first priority. In early 2006, President Jingtao Hu proposed setting up *a fair social welfare system* which shall comply with *rights fairness, opportunities fairness, rules fairness and distribution fairness*. A socially fair democracy mechanism has also been proposed with more new distributive justice ingredients. Remarkably, in the same year, four forms of citizen rights relating to democracy and liberty were affirmed by the ruling party. These are the right to access information, the participatory right, the right to express real will and the right of inspection in all aspects of governance.[8]

Environmental justice, also a newly rising social concern in China, is a unique aspect of social fairness with regard to public environmental interests. Yue Pan, the

---

[6] The survey was also a part of a research project, the Chinese Social Fairness Issues in Economic Transition in 2005, led by Lou Jiwei, the Vice Minister of the Ministry of Finance, and sponsored by the China Development Foundation which is managed by the Research Center for Development of State Council. See S. Lu and L. Ouyang, 'The Survey Shows Social Unfairness – A Common Concern for the Public', 12 January 2006, www.phoenixtv.com/phoenixtv/83885040617914368/20060112/729091.shtml (visited 19 November 2006).

[7] China News Net, 'The Gap of the Rich and Poor Reached the Warning Line – China Reexamines the Relationship of Efficiency and Fairness', 14 July 2005, www.chinanews.com.cn/news/2005/2005-07-14/26/598914.shtml (visited 19 November 2006).

[8] Central Committee of the Chinese Communist Party, *Decisions of the 6th Meeting of the 16th Chinese Communist Party Conference*, October 2006, http://cpc.people.com.cn (visited 19 November 2006).

Vice Minister of the State Environmental Administration, has been advocating environmental justice issues in the public arena since 2004.[9]

2 Challenges of environmental justice and public participation in China

From the environmental point of view, the adverse impact of the last twenty years of rapid economic growth is a development that failed to take into account the environmental costs of development and social welfare relating to the environment. All of this provided for environmental *injustice*. The minority of rich individuals (as well as richer provinces or autonomous regions) that possessed more opportunities in business also had greater ability and resources in using the environment and its natural resources. The more the minority rich stimulated economic growth without proper regard for environmental considerations, the more the quality of the environment and natural resources was degraded, and the more the majority's benefit and public interest in the environment and natural resources were damaged. Top-down planning without adequate local participation is a root-cause of this. Specifically, there are several forms of environmental injustice widely discussed:[10]

(a) Injustice between cities and the countryside. In decades of urbanisation, political power and material resources were aimed towards urbanisation or urban development; urban areas and their inhabitants were the first to benefit from this process. The countryside and farmers were the main contributors to urbanisation, particularly through the conversion of farming land into urban land, resettlement, and providing the majority of physical labour for urban construction and livelihoods (the higher wages in cities attracted the savings and labour of rural people). The stronger position of cities enabled them to obtain almost all of the national investment in pollution prevention and pollution treatment in contrast to the limited pollution control investment in the countryside; approximately 300 million people in the countryside do not have clean drinking water. The improvements in urban environmental quality and living conditions contrast sharply with the worsening of the countryside's environment and sanitation.

(b) Injustice between regions. The developed regions (e.g. the east and south coastal areas) and the developing region (namely, the western region[11]) have intensified.

---

[9] Yue Pan, 'Environmental Protection and Social Fairness', People's Net, 28 October 2004, http://cpc.people. com.cn/GB/64093/64094/4932424.html (visited 19 November 2006).

[10] Forms of (a) and (b) have been addressed by Yue Pan. See Yue Pan, 'Environmental Protection and Social Fairness', 28 October 2004, http://cpc.people.com.cn/GB/64093/64094/4932424.html (visited 19 November 2006).

[11] The national strategy for the development of the western region commenced in 1998. The western region is a special geopolitical area consisting of six provinces (Qinghai, Gansu, Shaanxi, Yunan, Sichuan and Guizhou), five autonomous regions (Xinjiang Ugur, Inner Mongolia, Ningxia Hui, Tibet and Guangxi Zhuang) and the municipality of Chongqing. See www.chinawest.gov.cn/web/Column1.asp?ColumnId=6 (visited 12 February 2007).

It is natural that the development of land use from east to west in China shows more intensive industry, services and mixed commerce in the east, compared with more agricultural and natural resources-based activities in the west where there is much less population and infrastructure.[12] Economic development in the western region has historically been more restricted, and in certain instances prohibited outright, in order to provide the rest of the country with natural resources and to protect existing ecosystems. It is necessary for the country, in particular the eastern region of the country, to provide the western region with special payment for its contribution to ecosystem conservation. However, such a regional payment scheme has not yet been put into place, and this has led to a debate on regional distributive injustice across the country.

(c) Injustice among professionals. Taking into account the incomplete reform of healthcare and education systems in the countryside and the low income of the poor, the more affluent and urban residents have far more advantages. For example, compared with the poor the rich have more opportunities to access natural resources and more ability to protect themselves against environmental hazards.

Environmental injustice is intertwined with social fairness; further, both of them essentially caused by unfair distribution of opportunities in education, health care and welfare; less advantage in market access and competition; and unjust policies and institutions (including official corruption) for the distribution of such interests and opportunities. To cope with such distributive injustice, there are many approaches, of which two strategies are relevant to the Chinese context. The first strategy is to reform or correct the inappropriate distributive situation by using direct distributive tools in a corrective function. Such examples in China are the western region development policy,[13] the agricultural tax exemption for rural residents,[14] and the forest ecosystem conservation fund.[15] This strategy aiming to counter environmental injustice, is not the topic of this chapter but it nevertheless provides a background to the issues discussed here. The second strategy to tackle environmental injustice – the focal point of this chapter – is to create a better, reformed policy and institutional framework, in which the public is added as an independent legal personality and endowed with legal rights and procedures to participate in government-dominated governing processes. Such means include consultations with members of the public and access to review

---

[12] This land-use pattern was based on access to natural resources, development history, infrastructure and population. It was reaffirmed by the National 11th Five Year Plan (2006–10).

[13] The main policy document is the *Tenth Five-Year Comprehensive Plan of Western Region Development*: see www.chinawest.gov.cn/web/NewsInfo.asp?NewsId=34658 (visited 12 February 2007).

[14] Starting in 2006, agricultural tax, which has been imposed in China for 2,600 years, is to be phased out. See www.gov.cn/jrzg/2005-12/22/content_134606.htm (visited 12 February 2007).

[15] 'Announcement of Issuance of the Managerial Rules for the Central Fund for Forest Ecosystem Conservation'. See www.mof.gov.cn/news/20050228_1510_4037.htm (visited 12 February 2007).

procedures to correct defective administrative proceedings in environmental governance. At this point, public participation could contribute value to environmental
justice in a distributive as well as a corrective sense.

Much of the above-mentioned environmental injustice was attributed to the domination of the decision-making processes by administrative bodies and to the general
lack of an organised framework for public participation. A related weakness was: first,
the lack of distributive rights and procedures for the public to invoke in environmental
public administration; secondly, in the environmental sphere, there is a lack of public
supervision, that is, in terms of both administrative and judicial oversight. With these
shortcomings, the legal framework failed to safeguard general activity concerning
the environment and natural resources to meet the requirements of environmental
justice. If these shortcomings were redressed, then social fairness and environmental
justice would be better achieved than they are at present.

Unfortunately, there has been very little attempt in the last thirty years to redress
these shortcomings. Environmental law and regulations produced during these years
have given far more power and rights to administrative authorities than to the general
public. This top-down environmental governance has not given equal distributive
rights and resources to civil society and the public. A highly centralised administration and insufficient regulatory rules in respect of citizens' rights to the environment hinder public participation in environmental matters. This unjust distribution of individual development opportunities, political rights and public opinion
under current law and regulation, together with the dismissal of public participation in public administration and environmental governance, provide fertile soil for
official corruption. These factors jointly trigger social and environmental injustice.
Therefore, the combination of public participation with a clearly emerging concept
of participatory democracy has proven to be a reasonably effective force in coping with environmental injustice in parallel with constructing new features of social
fairness.

The following sections discuss the legal aspects of public participation in the context of environmental justice. In this chapter, the public is examined in the Chinese
legal framework as an autonomous civil subject, who participates in environmental
activities for the public interest or a collective interest rather than individual private
interests. The public, as discussed in this chapter, is thus the legal personality which
usually has unclear direct interests and rights specified by law in respect of substantive natural objects that constitute a part of the environment, but which, primarily
in a collective sense, has direct interests and public rights to diffuse environmental
value and environmental public goods. Applying this concept, the public ought to
consist of individuals at large and non-governmental organisations promoting environmental interests, and each individual and organisation should have the right to
participate in decision-making. Public participation in this sense becomes a newly
emerged element of justice in the Chinese environmental law context. Much literature

echoes this trend.[16] Although it is a mixture of distributive justice and corrective justice, as a newly initiated legal instrument, public participation in decision-making is more inclined towards distributive justice, thus emphasising a socially fair allocation of opportunities for members of the public to participate in environmental governance.

3 Distributive justice through public participation

The promotion of distributive justice in procedures for public participation has evolved in two distinct phases. The first period was characterised by the incorporation of environmental impact assessment (EIA) procedures in legislative instruments. In the second phase, more specific procedures and rights for public participation were developed, and public participation has been extended from the EIA process to all situations requiring overarching environmental protection.

The first instrument evidencing a political will to provide for public participation appeared in a 1973 document entitled *Several Opinions on the Protection and Improvement of the Environment*. This was the most important document to come out of the 1st National Conference on Environmental Protection of the State Council. It called on 'the masses' to be involved in environmental protection.[17] This legislation was a landmark, as there had been no previous public participation of any kind before 1996. The first instrument to call for public participation in explicit terms was the first amendment to the 1984 Water Pollution Control Law (WPCL) in 1995, which expressly incorporated a statutory obligation to undertake an EIA.

Environmental impact assessments have been an essential instrument to regulate acts of natural resource utilisation or contamination in order to prevent adverse impacts to the environment. The application of EIA in the USA and other Western countries demonstrated that EIA was one of the most effective mechanisms for the public to participate in regional planning, government decision-making, and for private companies involved in natural resources and the environment. It greatly enhances environmental democracy and justice. EIA was introduced into China in environmental regulations in the 1970s, and later adopted by the 1989 Environmental Protection Law (EPL) and almost by all individual laws concerning pollution control and environmental protection in areas such as water, air, solid waste and noise, etc. However, in sharp contrast to the emerging trend in international practice, EIA in China did not involve public participation before 1995. A very small but ground-breaking step was made by the 1995 amendment to the WPCL, setting out that 'the EIA report should be constituted of opinions both of the residents who live and of the entities that locate in the vicinity of the construction project'.[18] This was later reaffirmed by the 1996 Noise Pollution Control Law.[19]

---

[16] Li 2004.   [17] Jin 1990 p. 8.   [18] Art. 13(4).   [19] Art. 3(3).

However, in relation to both water and noise pollution, there was little, if any, practical mandate calling for their effective application. Moreover, the modalities for public participation remained undefined in the existing legislation. In particular, the status of residents' opinions given in the context of an EIA remained undefined. It also remained unclear how and to what extent such opinions affected the substantive outcome of an EIA proceeding. For instance, could an administrative body proceed with a project in the face of strong objections by the public? Further supporting provisions need to be enacted for dealing with these issues.

In the late 1990s, the rapidly emerging urbanisation, large-scale construction and transboundary regional planning of natural resources highlighted issues of how to balance development with environmental protection. As a consequence, the 2002 Environmental Impact Assessment Law (EIAL) was enacted with the objective of ensuring that economic growth allowed for its attendant environmental consequences. Five Articles of the EIAL specifically deal with the promotion of public participation and environmental justice. Thus, this Law provides as follows:

(a) It mandates the application of EIA to the planning of government programmes and activities. Previously, only construction projects under EIA reviews included the participation of experts and the public at large, whilst governmental programmes had internal institutional reviews. The extension of the application of EIA also extended the scope of public participation from decision-making concerning constructions to governmental decision-making on programmes and planning relating to industry, agriculture, animal husbandry, forestry, energy, water conservancy, communications, municipal construction, tourism, and natural resources development.[20]

(b) It consolidates the role of experts in EIA, which are regarded as an important pillar of public participation. An expert's view is critical to safeguarding environmental justice in the whole EIA process. The EIAL regulates the reviewing activities of experts in a more transparent manner.[21]

(c) It imposes more stringent regulations of the activities of EIA consulting firms to ensure a just and open competitive EIA service to construction projects.[22]

(d) It formally adopted 'the public' as a legal term, and for the first time endowed it in national environmental laws with an independent collective juristic personality.[23] Furthermore, it creates a substantive legal object, namely, the 'environmental rights and interests of the public' that EIAL is directed at protecting, and makes EIA value-oriented. Thus the scope of public participation in EIA is no longer

---

[20] Art. 2.   [21] Arts. 13, 11 and 21.   [22] Art. 19.

[23] Of all national-level environmental and natural resources laws promulgated by the National People's Congress of PRC, few use the term 'the public'. The Cleaner Production Promotion Law of PRC 2002 first used this term, though in a general sense of 'the masses', with no reference to a new type of legal personality, nor with clear explanation of its legal rights and interests. The Renewable Energy Law of PRC 2005 repeated the legal status of 'the public' as set out in the EIAL 2002 and confirmed the public's right to participation in EIA in renewable energy planning in principle.

defined as covering *the residents or entities surrounding the construction site*, but instead *the public at large whose environmental rights and interest are directly affected* by planning or construction activities.[24]

(e) It provides for specific procedures and the manner of conducting consultation with the public and the collection of their views (which are but not limited to arguments at conferences and public hearings). It imposes EIA obligations on planning authorities as well as on the owners of construction projects. There is an explicit obligation that EIA reports should include the public's views, and the extent to which they were accepted or rejected.[25]

These provisions are substantive improvements from the perspective of environmental democracy. The Articles relating to the inclusion of public views in EIA reports in the EIAL symbolise the legitimacy of environmental public participation and justice. There are nevertheless significant limitations in the EIAL as it stands. For example, it remains uncertain what the innovative legal term 'environmental rights and interests of the public' entails. Moreover, there are no explicit procedures or guidelines for holding consultation conferences or environmental hearings for the formulation of public opinion. Significantly, public opinions, although procedurally significant, remain legally non-binding.

The EIAL may be disappointing to some Chinese environmentalists, because the gap between this piece of legislation and best international practice in EIA is still quite wide. The Chinese experience when compared to provisions on public participation elsewhere are particularly rudimentary. Nevertheless, the EIAL is a significant milestone in the Chinese environmental law regime in recognition of the public's rights and interests in the environment. The EIAL is important in two ways. First, by recognising the legitimacy of 'the public' and the 'environmental rights and interests of the public' within a legislative and regulatory framework, it puts these rights on a sound legal footing, making it difficult for them to be ignored in practice. Secondly, by encouraging the recognition and application of these rights in the judicial system and in administrative practice, it creates a wider framework for their application in the broad environmental domain, beyond the confines of environmental impact assessment procedures.

This legislation has had a significant impact in practice. In the three years after its enactment, there was a significant increase in public participation. The EIAL provided direct legal impetus to environmental public participation. Under these statutes, environmental NGOs were enabled to participate actively in the administrative review of construction activities.

Forced by the grass-roots movements of public participation in the early 2000, the second phase of public participation was intended to create more specific legal rights and procedures, and expand it to a broader scene of environmental protection. Two

---

[24] Art. 11.   [25] Arts. 19 and 21.

ministerial-level decrees have achieved significant attention nationwide as the main legal norms on public participation in the existing Chinese environmental regime. The 2005 Provisions on Public Participation in Environmental Protection of the Shenyang Municipality (Decree No. 42 of the People's Government of Shenyang City) was the first legal document defining the rights of the public to participate in all aspects of environmental protection; it took effect on 1 January 2006. It created better defined legal concepts and jurisprudence on rights to the environment, although its jurisdiction is limited to Shanyang City. Another decree is the 2006 Interim Provisions of Public Participation in Environmental Impact Assessment of the State Environmental Protection Administration (SEPA Decree No. 2006/26).[26]

The SEPA Decree did not introduce new rights and obligations but provided implementation specifications for the EIAL concerning public participation in the EIA process. It specified time limits for information release, institutional arrangements and the principal methods of collection of public opinions on EIA. Generally, it requests the governmental authority responsible for EIA, construction project owners and EIA consulting firms to release environmental information relating to EIA, and to report to the public in an open, effective and convenient manner, and to set a minimum time limit of ten days for collecting the public's response to the EIA report. If the public's opinion is not accepted by the construction project owner or by EIA consulting firms, the public must be given specific explanation for this. Furthermore, if not convinced by this explanation, the public can report their opinion directly to the responsible governmental authority. The responsible governmental authority should verify the public's opinion and construction owner's explanation. More specific procedural guidance is given on how to organise the consultation and hearing on the EIA to facilitate the implementation of the EIAL concerning project-type EIA consultation, but not on planning-type EIA.

Nevertheless, the EIAL and the SEPA Decree did not provide very specific, though still adequate, provisions for public participation in EIA. As indicated, Chinese public participation in EIA still remains far from international practice. For instance, in China, public willingness to attend the public hearing has been limited. Moreover, the selection of representatives to the hearing has not been transparent, and they have been nominated mainly by the responsible authority, not by the affected community or group. Compare this with the EIA process of the USA, where anyone who is willing to attend the public hearing may do so and anyone who is willing to present an opinion may do so.[27] In the US EIA process, the public and environmental public authorities are powerful actors in safeguarding the public's environmental interests, for example by

---

[26] This decree was prompted by the EIA in the Yuanmingyuan Park case (concerning an engineering project on the park's lake bed), and it supplements the EIAL with procedural specifications on public participation in the EIA process.

[27] A. Moore, 'Hearings and "Due Process" in US Administrative Decisions', presentation representing the American Bar Association. Wuhan, November 2006.

initiating and negotiating alternatives for alleviating adverse environmental impacts, whereas, in China, EIA does not contain this requirement.

The 2005 Shenyang City's Decree No. 42 entrenched the jurisprudence of public participation in all aspects of environmental decision-making by defining key legal concepts such as: the public, rights of public participation in environmental protection, environmental information; the responsibility to publish public environmental information; procedures to attain environmental information; and penalties for violation. These stipulations significantly fulfil the vacuum in national legislation and provide a consolidated foundation for public participation. Shenyang City's Decree No. 42 has contributed some very interesting points in terms of consolidating distributive rights and the procedures of public participation. In particular, the Decree explains and clarifies a number of key terms that were not specifically dealt with in the EIAL. These include:

(a) Defining 'the public'. Decree No. 42 defines the public as 'the individual who has capacity to act by law, corporations and other organs'.[28] This definition clarifies that the public consists of individuals in general, corporations and other organs, particularly NGOs promoting environmental interests. Significantly, the 'rights of public participation in environmental protection' implies a right for such individuals and organisations to participate in decision-making in environmental protection in the following ways:

   (i)   to participate in environmental legislation, policy-making and planning;
   (ii) to participate in EIA;
   (iii) to acquire and use public *environmental information*;
   (iv) to comment and make suggestions on environmental governance;
   (v)   to prosecute and litigate against acts of damage or contamination of the environment;
   (vi) to appeal remedies caused by environmental pollution; and
   (vii) to report law-breaking by officials.[29]

   Among all national-level environmental and natural resources laws, which were promulgated by the National People's Congress and its Standing Committee, the concept of 'the public' was used only a few times before this local decree used it. The term 'the public' was used in the 2002 Cleaner Production Promotion Law, but it was still understood in the rather political sense of 'the masses', since it did not refer to 'the public' in the same way as it is used in our present discussion, i.e. as a new autonomous legal personality. The 2005 Renewable Energy Law repeated the legal status of 'the public' as set out in the EIAL, and in principle confirms that the public has the right to participate in the EIA of renewable energy planning. Therefore, this local decree has endowed 'the public' with a more advanced form of legal standing and substantive rights than the national law in this regard.

---

[28] Art. 3.   [29] Art. 5.

(b) Defining 'public environmental information'. This is the most important concept in Decree No. 42. It was defined as 'public-owned information regarding the environment', which thus had to be shared by the public.[30] The following 'public environmental information' ought to be open to the public:

   (i) national, provincial and municipal environmental law, regulations, decrees and other normative documents;

   (ii) national, provincial and municipal environmental policy;

   (iii) municipal environmental planning and schemes;

   (iv) various types of environmental standards and environmental function zoning;

   (v) *status quo* of enterprise's pollution discharge and treatment;

   (vi) environmental quality statement at municipal, prefecture and county levels;

   (vii) environmental management of construction projects;

   (viii) levy on pollutant discharges and its expenditure;

   (ix) by-laws on administrative penalties, standards, procedures and execution;

   (x) responsibilities of environmental authorities, regulatory procedures and service commitments; and

   (xi) key projects of environmental treatment and foreign investment projects on environmental protection.

Valid means to access environmental information are by:

   (i) oral or written request to governmental environmental authorities;

   (ii) requests to which the authorities must reply within fifteen to thirty days;

   (iii) public websites; and

   (iv) public service of newsletters and publications.[31]

These Articles are the first normative provisions defining environmental information and clearly demonstrating the public rights to access environmental information in the Chinese legal context.

(c) Institutions for public participation. The environmental authority should set up two special institutions: the Environmental Consultation Committee on which there are representatives of the public; and Environmental Inspectors selected from the public.[32] The appointed inspectors are responsible for supervising compliance with the law.

(d) Obligations of authorities and enterprises to release environmental information. First, environmental authorities are required to carry out the following obligations: to provide full and timely environmental information to the public (unless national security requires otherwise) (Art. 9); to release annual environmental quality reports (Art. 13); to report environmental incidents or accidents or emergencies where there is a high risk of environmental pollution and damage (Art. 14); and to back up citizen civil litigation for remedying damage caused by

---

[30] Art. 9.   [31] Arts. 11 and 12.   [32] Art. 8.

environmental contamination in terms of proving cause–effect links of contamination and damage (Art. 2). Among these, from an environmental justice point of view, Article 20 is most meaningful in terms of supporting disadvantaged pollution victims in claims to remedy contamination. Meanwhile, enterprises are also obliged to release information on: total amount of pollutant discharges; pollutants discharged beyond permissible levels; adverse impact of discharged pollutants; countermeasures and prevention of pollution; treatment plans and their operation; and internal environmental management schemes (Art. 15). The above environmental information is required to be published in the public media periodically (Art. 15), with a penalty for non-compliance of up to 100,000 RMB yuan (equivalent to US$12,000 (Art. 24)).

As it has been effective for only a year or so, there is very little literature or administrative practice exploring how this local decree was implemented. However, it is the first enactment in the Chinese legislative context on the public's right to access information, and is seemingly coherent with the 1998 UNECE Convention on Access to Information, Public Participation in Decision-Making and Access to Justice in Environmental Matters (Aarhus Convention),[33] the Shenyang Decree No. 42 is an advanced statute in China regarding public participation rights and procedures in overall environmental governance. It has been influential in pushing the SEPA to make efforts in improving current laws and decrees in relation to public participation and environmental information, and in initiating a special decree on the same theme but covering a broader jurisdiction.[34]

4 Corrective justice through public participation

As discussed earlier, issues of corrective justice in the environmental sphere as well as in the Chinese legal context, could be relevant to two shortcomings of current environmental governance. One is the malfunctioning of public participation in the supervision and review of the environmental administration; the other is the lack of litigation rights and procedures in respect of public interests in the judicial system. The efforts to provide for corrective environmental justice nowadays can be observed in two ways: first, by the active advocacy for public participation by citizens and NGOs in the correction of unjust governmental action usually in the planning and decision making proceedings; and, secondly, by overcoming the limitations of public interest litigation in judicial proceedings.

---

[33] 1998 UNECE Convention on Access to Information, Public Participation in Decision-Making and Access to Justice in Environmental Matters, UN Doc. ECE/CEP/43 (21 April 1998), reprinted in 38 *International Legal Materials* (ILM) (1999) 515. The Aarhus Convention was adopted in June 1998 in Aarhus, Denmark, at the Ministerial Conference on 'Environment for Europe' and entered into force in October 2001.

[34] Stepping Decree of Public Participation in Environmental Impact Assessment, Regulation for Public Participation in Environmental Protection to be drafted. See www.chinagateway.com.cn/chinese/yw/46121.htm (visited 12 February 2007).

4.1 Citizens' and NGOs' good practice

From the environmental administration point of view, in the period from the late 1990s to 2005, there appeared a series of cases showing the wrongs of environmental governance. All these instances were characterised by a general lack of public participation at all levels of the decision-making process. Civil society's reluctance to comply with the edicts of a purely command-and-control governance resulted in a failure in compliance and enforcement of the Huai River pollution treatment programme (1995–2004).[35] In Shanxi province, the mining permit process without the stakeholders' and public's participation and inspection led to repeated coal-mining accidents and tragedies, and the consequent loss of life and injuries.[36] A lack of transparency in access to information for the public during pollution incidents created great public fear with, for example, the Songhua River chemical explosion which caused a drinking water crisis in Harbin City in November 2005.[37] These cases demonstrate the malfunctioning of top-down environmental governance with its general lack of a framework for public participation in administration.

In the same period from the late 1990s to 2005, positive development occurred as a result of NGOs advocating environmental justice through the correction of ineffective environmental governance. Environmental NGOs have established new concepts of public participation and participatory rights. Much of the NGOs' advocacy in this field drew heavily on developments elsewhere, in particular international conventions such

[35] The Huai River Basin is the third largest river basin in China. Until 1994, the Huai River had been heavily contaminated by industrial waste water emission, of which more than 50 per cent was from small paper-making rural factories which contribute greatly to rural incomes. The 1994–2004 campaign of Huai River pollution treatment planned to close almost all of these small factories by command-control orders. With no alternative sources of income, both local governments and factories were reluctant to comply with the Huai River pollution treatment scheme. When flooded in 2005, the Huai River produced the same severe pollution as it did in 1994 that distributed enormous amounts of pollutants from the upper stream to the middle and down streams, and contaminated large areas of the down stream, causing a new environmental disaster only year after State Environmental Protection Agency claimed victory in a ten-year pollution treatment campaign. For more analysis, see Bai and Shi 2006 pp. 22–35.

[36] Following the energy shortage worldwide and nationwide, coal mining has become a highly profitable business in China. With the title of 'coal province', Shanxi Province has attracted large private investment in coal mining, most of which is done through joint ventures between the private sector and state-owned mining entities. In order to achieve a maximum return on their investment, private investors either take risks by cutting safety measures for mine-workers, or carry out illegal mining in non-permitted areas. As has been demonstrated in many cases, both of these would cause damage to mine-workers or residents living nearby. Privatisation of coal mining also reduces supervision. There is no access to the mining information either by mining workers or by residents or the public. See 'Shanxi Province Continuously Occurred Coal Mining Accidents', http://news.enorth.com.cn/system/2001/12/04/000196450.shtml (visited 13 February 2007).

[37] In the first three or four days, the chemicals emitted to the Songhua River polluted the drinking water of Harbin City. The municipal government of Harbin City kept the pollution secret until rumours surfaced and it became no longer possible to hide the truth. One consequence of this incident was that the Minister of State Environmental Protection Agency was removed as a part of sanctions imposed on the administration. See 'Vice Minister Zhang Lijun of State Environmental Protection Agency Interviewing News-Agents on the Songhua River Accident', http://news.xinhuanet.com/politics/2005-11/24/content_3830205.htm (visited 13 February 2007).

as the Aarhus Convention and their implementation in different contexts.[38] Victories by NGOs and citizens in, for example, the Yuanmingyuan Park public hearings in 2005,[39] the Nujiang hydroelectric power station planning in 2003–5,[40] and many others, greatly encourages members of the public to apply their participatory rights in protecting their common planet. The grass-roots movements in environmental conservation have significantly contributed to environmental corrective justice.

4.2 Limitations of citizen litigation in the public interest

The public as an autonomous legal personality, and its role in corrective environmental justice, should also exist in the judicial arena. When its intervention into environmental governance through administrative tools fail to correct the wrongs either of governments or of enterprises, the public – standing as individual citizens – should be able to approach the courts. Environmental citizen suits are thus a very effective legal approach for the public in environmental justice.[41] While such procedures exist in some countries, for example the USA, and entitle citizens to bring cases before judicial fora even in the absence of actual damage to health or property, such a developed jurisprudence of public interest litigation does not as yet exist in Chinese legislation or legal practice.[42]

---

[38] Environmental NGOs who were advocating environmental interests in these cases were (but not limited to) Green Home, Friends of the Nature, Green Islands, Earth's Villages and China Environmental Culture Promotion Society. For a comprehensive overview of environmental NGOs, see *The Public Report of Environmental Non-Governmental Organizations in China*, China Environmental Protection Union, 2006.

[39] The case of the Yuanmingyuan Park is a landmark for creating the first environmental public hearing and procedures of public participation in EIA in China. Yuanmingyuan Park is a ruined royal gardens of the Qing Dynasty. In August 2003, the Yuanmingyuan Park Administrative Division (YMYPAD) conducted a large-scale environmental improvement construction project including lake bed engineering work without undertaking an EIA. In March 2006, Professor Zhang Chunzheng, from Lanzhou University, found the lake beds engineering work to be nearly completed, and considered this engineering work destroyed national cultural heritage and the lake bed's ecological system. With no response from the YMYPAD or the Beijing Environmental Protection Bureau (BJEPB), Professor Zhang drew his conclusions to the attention of the media and NGOs. The consequent public campaign forced YMYPAD to conduct an EIA, and SEPA to pilot the first environmental public hearing and promulgated a new decree for environmental public hearings, SEPA Decree No. 2006/26. See 'Final Resolution to YMY Park's Incident', www.chinaxys.net/dajia/yuanmingyuan.html (visited 19 November 2006).

[40] The Nujiang hydroelectric power station planning campaign of 2003–5 was one of the cases in which the public used EIA to correct governmental planning proceedings. The Nujiang River is located in Yunan Province and has considerable biodiversity. It is probably the last large river in China without dams. In 2003, the provincial government approved the Nujiang hydroelectric power station. Since then, NGOs and the public nationwide have been protesting against this planning permission by arguing that the governmental planning in 2003 did not follow the EIA procedure, in particular the procedure for collecting public opinions on the project. The public and NGOs' campaign had the consequence in 2006 that the National Development and Reform Commission and the SEPA announced that it would reconsider the project. As this 'reconsideration' does not refer to any specific solution concerning dam construction, the public and environmental NGOs are still active as watchdogs in this issue. For more information, see 'Nujiang Hydroelectric Power development', www.china5e.com/focus/focus.php?type=nujiang (visited 19 November 2006).

[41] Boyle and Anderson 1998.   [42] Wall 2006.

In legislation, environmental citizen suits were regulated initially by the 1982 Marine Environmental Protection Law (MEPL). It stated: 'All units and individuals entering the sea areas under the jurisdiction of the People's Republic of China shall have the responsibility to protect the marine environment and shall have the obligation to watch and report on actions causing pollution damage to the marine environment.'[43] This statute was consolidated by the EPL, the basic law of environmental protection, which sets out that: 'All units and individuals have responsibilities to protect the environment, and rights to disclose and prosecute and sue those entities and individuals who contaminate or spoil the environment.'[44] *Prima facie* it seems that neither the MEPL nor the EPL is unequivocal in allowing environmental suits by individuals. However, they are recognised as the most appropriate legal rules. In particular, Article 6 of the EPL is considered a principal legal basis for providing rights for citizens in prosecution and in bringing public interest cases to the courts.

Due to its reference to individual litigation rights on environmental public interests, the application of Article 6 of the EPL still has to rely on special litigation laws. While two major existing litigation laws – the civil and administrative litigation laws – are applicable to environmental suits, they have in general not been very suitable for environmental citizen suits. The Civil Litigation Law restricts the cases that may be brought to court by defining citizen standing as being available only to citizens that have suffered actual damage to their property or health by the activity against which the suit is brought.[45] In relation to the Administrative Litigation Law, as interpreted by the Supreme People's Court, citizens' standing is restricted to those citizens, corporations and other organisations who have refused to comply or agree with an administrative act or decision executed by governmental authority, directed to them or their legitimate interest.[46] These citizens, corporations and other organisations must also demonstrate that they have suffered direct loss from the administrative act or decision in question or that their legitimate interests are affected even if the act or decision was not directed at them.[47]

Such legislative constraints have proved to be serious obstacles for environmental citizen suits in judicial fora.[48] In 2005, two citizens sued the Planning Bureau of Nanjin City for issuing a permit that allowed Zjingshan Administrative Bureau to build a viewing tower in a protected area. The court rejected this suit because the applicants lacked standing to bring the suit.[49] This marked reticence by the courts to

---

[43] Art. 3.

[44] Art. 6. Similar statutes with almost the same content, stipulating citizen rights of prosecution and litigation in environmental matters, have been introduced in the Marine Environmental Protection Law (1982, Art. 3; 1st Amendment 1999, Art. 4), the Air Pollution Control Law (1987, Art. 5; 1st Amendment 1995, Art. 5; 2nd Amendment 2000, Art. 5), the Water Pollution Control Law (1984, Art. 5; 1st Amendment 1996, Art. 5), the Solid Waste Control Law (1995, Art. 9; 1st Amendment 2004, Art. 9) and the Noise Pollution Control Law (1996, Art. 7).

[45] Art. 108.   [46] Art. 12.   [47] Art. 13(2) and (4).   [48] Cai 2004; Lü 2004.

[49] 'Viewing Tower Construction in Zjingshan Mount – State-Invested Capital in vain.' News on Xinhua Net, 25 January 2002, www.xinhua.net (visited 10 September 2006).

exercise its protective jurisdiction is one of the many reasons why the bulk of environmental disputes are resolved through mediation by governmental agencies rather than through litigation.[50] The actual role of the courts in alleviating environmental injustice has lagged far behind the public's expectation of what the role of the court should be.[51]

There have been ongoing debates over solutions on how to remove legislative constraints and make the judicial system provide for corrective justice in environmental matters.[52] Suggestions relevant to the above discussion are: to give some subjects special standing for environmental public interest litigation, for example the Prosecuting Office,[53] NGOs, SEPA or an environmental protection authority;[54] to provide new legislation to enlarge the class of plaintiffs entitled to commence public litigation; to rationalise the allocation of the evidential burden; and to enhance judicial practice in EIA procedures and rights of public participation.[55]

5 Conclusions

In this chapter, the position of the public was examined in the Chinese legal framework as an autonomous civil subject, equal to specific individuals and entities and governmental authorities, who have rights to participate in environmental governance in the public interest or a collective interest rather than individual interests. Public participation is a newly created institution in China that may help to combat social unfairness and environmental injustice. The introduction of participatory rights and procedures for the public to intervene in governmental decision-making and the enforcement of laws on natural resource and the environment can be seen as signs of the beginnings of environmental democracy, whereas the effectiveness of the enforcement of participatory rights and procedures still need time to be tested. The development of the right to public information at national and local level also echoes concerns and developments at the global level. In this regard, local law has advanced further in recognition of the public's right to environmental information than national law has. Environmental citizen suits, as a primary means of public participation, have not played a role as yet.[56] There is much ongoing debate over solutions on how to remove

---

[50] J. Luo and Q. Du, 'Environmental Disputes' Resolution in China', a paper for the 4th Annual Conference of the IUCN Academy of Environental Law, Pace University, available at www. pace.edu (visited 19 November 2006).

[51] *Proceedings of the International Symposium on Legislation for Environmental Damage Compensation*, 20–21 August 2004, Beijing.

[52] It was one of the findings of the debates on citizen litigation for environmental interests in the International Symposium on Legislation for Environmental Damage Compensation, China University of Politics and Law and Environmental Protection and Natural Resource Conservation Committee of the National People's Congress, 20–21 August 2004, Beijing. See note 51 above.

[53] Li 2006.   [54] Liu 2006 pp. 93–5.   [55] Shi 2006 pp. 156–60.

[56] C. F. Wang, 'Several Thoughts on Legislation Special for Environmental Disputes Resolution and Environmental Remedy', in *Proceedings of the International Symposium on Legislation for Environmental Damage Compensation* (note 51 above).

legislative constraints and make the judicial system prioritise corrective justice in environmental matters. Grass-roots movements of public participation have facilitated the formulation of national and local laws for environmental public participation.

The legal challenges in this field were noted as: inadequate rights and procedures, which prevent the public from becoming involved in environmental public administration, for example planning and decision-making; the lack of public participation in the supervision and correction of top-down government dominated environmental administration; and the absence of public interest litigation in judicial proceedings. With these shortcomings, it is difficult for the legal framework and judicial system to safeguard good governance over the environment and natural resources. Thus, it fails to achieve environmental justice. To overcome legislative obstacles and make the judiciary more responsive to corrective justice ought to be a high priority in the advocacy of environmental justice in China in the near future.

Bibliography

Aristotle, 1990. *Nicomachean Ethics* (trans.), Beijing: Chinese Social Sciences Press.

Bai, X. M., and Shi, P. J., 2006. 'Pollution Control in China's Huai River Basin', *Journal of Environment*.

Boyle A., and Anderson, M., 1998. *Human Rights Approaches to Environmental Protection*. London: Clarendon Press.

Cai, S. Q., 2004. *Policy framework of Resolution of Environmental Disputes and Enforcement of Environmental Liabilities*, Proceedings of the International Symposium on Legislation for Environmental Damage Compensation, 20–21 August 2004, Beijing.

Central Committee of Chinese Communist Party, 2006. *Decisions of the 6th Meeting of the 16th Chinese Communist Party Conference*, October 2006.

China Environmental Protection Foundation, 2006. *The Public Report of Environmental Non-Governmental Organizations in China*.

Jin, R. L., 1990. *Environmental Law Science*. Beijing: Peking University Press.

Krämer, L., 1999. 'The Citizen in the Environment – Access to Justice', 3/3 *Resource Management Journal*.

Li, C. X., 2006. 'Prosecutorate Office Intervening Public Litigation', 3 *China Lawyer*.

Li, Y. F., 2004. 'Building Legal Institutions for the Public's Participating in Environmental Protection'. 2 *Zhejiang Social Science*.

Lü, Z. M., 2004. 'Probing Environmental Litigation – Is Environmental Litigation Existing?', in Z. M. Lü, (ed.), *Environmental and Natural Resource Law Study*, vol. 3. Beijing: Law Science Press.

Pan, Y., 2004. 'Environmental Protection and Social Fairness', People's Net.

Rawls, J., 1998. *A Theory of Justice* (trans. Haihong He, Baogang He and Shenbao Liao). Beijing: China Social Science Press.

Shi, Y. C., 2006. 'An Analytical Study of Some Problems Concerning Litigation Constitutions for Public Environmental Welfare', 26/3 *Modern Law Science*.

Tao, H. Y., 1990. 'Citizen litigation in American Environmental Law', 6 *Journal of Law Review*.

Wall, M. E., 2006. 'Public Interest Litigation in the US', Paper presented at the Seminar of Comparative Study of Environmental Public Participation of Natural Resources Defense Council, 10 November 2006.

Weng, T. A., and Hu, D. C., 2004. 'Several Thoughts on the Public's Participating in Environmental Impact Assessment', 1 *Times of Law Science*.

Yutong, L., 2006. 'Standings of Environmental Public Litigation', 10 *Frontier*.

8

Environmental justice through courts in countries in economic transition

STEPHEN STEC

1 Introduction

Discussing environmental justice in any societal context, including multinational contexts relevant to globalization debates, requires an examination of fundamental principles and the disentanglement of the concept from the particular legal background. While open for slightly different understandings, a narrow, traditional notion of environmental justice would be based on the concept's obvious roots in American theory related to social or distributive justice, where the disadvantaged – in particular minorities, indigenous peoples and certain socioeconomic groups – were the beneficiaries.[1] In this form it has even been addressed by a Presidential order.[2] But, like the term 'sustainable development', environmental justice has received currency or been invoked to reinvigorate long-standing debates.[3] Thus, a concept originally focused on landfills and industrial sites has played a prominent role in critiques of globalization through its application to issues such as climate change and its intergenerational attributes.[4] In sociological or environmental studies literature, 'environment-related justice' has been invoked in terms of intra-generational distributive justice, inter-generational justice, and ecological justice (just treatment of non-human entities in nature).[5]

Certain limitations are apparent in order to ascertain a functional concept of environmental justice in the field of comparative law. As ecological justice – that

---

[1] Bullard pointed out that race was the prime factor in exposure to toxins, but that class was also a strong factor. Bullard 1990. Various surveys have pointed to specific campaigns in the US in the 1970s and 1980s, primarily involving African-American communities, as the genesis of the environmental justice movement. See e.g. Bullard and Johnson 2000 pp. 555–78; McGurty 2000 pp. 373–87; Hockman & Morris 1998 pp. 157–76.

[2] See *Federal Actions to Address Environmental Justice in Minority Populations and Low-Income Populations*, Executive Order 12898, 11 February 1994.

[3] In the European Union context, the term, for example, has been invoked to criticize infringement procedures as ineffective to compel member states to implement European Community environmental obligations. Hedemann-Robinson, 2006 pp. 312–42.

[4] Filcak debunks the criticism that US scholars did not explore broader environmental justice concerns. Filcak 2007 p. 18.

[5] Filcak 2007 p. 11.

is, a notion of justice that extends beyond human interaction to nature itself – is hardly recognized in law, a functional concept of environmental justice must rely on intra-generational distributive justice and the less-developed field of intergenerational justice. This is consistent with most literature on the subject, concerned with the just distribution within societies of environmental costs and benefits.[6] In fact, early stages of the sustainable development discourse included assertions of the basic interrelationship between social justice and sustainable development. Relevant to the notion of environmental justice, the 1987 report of the World Commission on Environment and Development, *Our Common Future* (Brundtland Report), concluded that social justice cannot be achieved without an equitable sharing of the costs and benefits of environmental protection.[7]

The debate on these topics, however, has largely taken place within a particular context that includes reasonable application of the rule of law as well as a large and empowered middle class sympathetic to a relatively small cast of disadvantaged groups. The latter moreover could avail themselves of legal procedures and secure legal and financial assistance, while corruption among authorities was kept somewhat in check by an active and free press.[8]

Richard Falk sums up a number of considerations that lead us close to the essence of environmental justice as it can be applied in any socioeconomic or political context – that is, insofar as it relates to the legitimacy and effectiveness of systems of distributive justice.[9] But the contours of distributive justice still vary widely depending on social and legal constructions as well as economic factors. The region of so-called 'countries in economic transition' bears close study and can provide insights into various discourses with relevance to a broad conception of environmental justice. Only a couple of years after the Brundtland Report, we saw the end of a system that created huge environmental burdens without equitable sharing. The collapse of scientific socialism in Eastern Europe had many causes, but certainly public rejection of the way in which the environment was managed was one of the most significant. There is now a substantial literature on the links between environmental concerns and the democratization movements of countries in transition. A major edifice built on this connection is the 1998 UN Economic Commission for Europe (UNECE) Convention on Access to Information, Public Participation in Decision-Making, and Access to Justice in Environmental Matters (Aarhus Convention).[10] Only a few remarks about the Aarhus Convention, relevant to countries in transition, will be made here. It is remarkable that the vast majority of cases brought forward under the Aarhus

---

[6] Agyeman and Evans 2004 pp. 55–164; Byrne, Martinez and Glover 2002 pp. 3–17; Baxter 2000 pp. 43–64; Low and Gleeson 1998.

[7] World Commission on Environment and Development 1987, pp. 46–9.

[8] Procedural requirements for environmental justice are treated somewhat in the literature but in terms of tinkering only, as compared to arbitrary legal systems.

[9] See Falk in Chapter 2 of this volume.   [10] 38 *International Legal Materials* (1999) 515.

Convention's compliance regime have involved countries in transition.[11] Despite the broad formulation of the Convention's access to justice provisions, the procedural rights related to access to information and public participation found in the Convention are distinct, precise and well developed, and through their acceptance as international standards on the regional level they have gone a long way towards providing a toolkit for environmental justice victims in countries in transition to use in order to defend their rights. Without a sound basis for the procedural dimension of environmental justice, progress on distributive justice can hardly be achieved, but the existence of procedures is not enough – there must also be capacity-building efforts to enable citizens to make effective use of these procedural rights.

Environmental concerns have been at the root of legal disputes that have played a role in the development of fundamental legal principles and the establishment of the rule of law in countries in transition. These legal disputes have occasionally risen to the level of written decisions of judicial or administrative bodies that may provide insight into current practices, thinking and strategies among legal professionals, whether they be advocates, prosecutors or judges. They also reveal the current state of play with respect to important issues of broad legal relevance where environmental issues have played a significant role, for example the standing of certain non-governmental organizations to bring legal action to challenge administrative decisions.

But is it at all possible to look at the collection of countries in transition today with their various developmental paths and conclude anything about environmental justice? It is true that the legislation, the ratifications of the Aarhus Convention, and the legal frameworks for access to justice can be reviewed. If these legal frameworks were fully implemented and respected, probably only a few cases would be found, where obvious mistakes had been made by the state concerned. But, what if surveys indicate that the law is not being implemented and/or respected, and yet there are still very few cases? What can be gleaned from the specific cases that are being brought to courts? Despite the concerted efforts over many years of legions of legal professionals, particularly those engaged in international assistance, to stimulate the bringing forward of test cases, these societies have remained largely non-litigious. Numerous factors may be identified as contributing to this situation, including a continued lack of trust of judicial institutions, non-identification of the public with the law, lack of individualism, procedural barriers, and social and administrative pressure to compromise on societal burdens. The result is that there are very few cases that may be examined in order to identify trends or to reach definitive conclusions about the extent to which notions of environmental justice are defended in everyday administration. This is in fact a problem for some countries that are required to show that they have

---

[11] See Fitzmaurice's contribution in Chapter 11 of this volume, where she provides a short presentation of the Aarhus Convention.

functioning judiciary systems in order to attain EU membership.[12] Although progress has been made recently, the systems in place for monitoring and collecting specific cases on particular subjects are not fully institutionalized. Therefore, it is necessary to rely on informal information flows, networks, international monitoring efforts of NGOs and IGOs, and the occasional high-profile case in order to collect environmental justice cases. Even with the best efforts, however, it is difficult to gather detailed information about more than a few cases at any given time.

2 Court cases relevant for environmental justice

A recent analysis of cases collected under the auspices of the Aarhus Convention's Access to Justice Task Force and those brought before the Compliance Committee observes the common considerations or elements of access to justice cases throughout Eastern Europe as well as some provisional distinctions based upon the different courses of development of countries in transition.[13] The present chapter represents an effort to collect and analyze particular recent examples of cases against a more explicit environmental justice framework, further testing the observations made above. The cases here presented provide opportunities to compare and contrast vastly different pictures of the ability to make use of environmental rights and of the responsiveness of state and judiciary institutions to issues raised under the rubric of environmental justice, whether express or implied.

2.1 Rosia Montana Gold Mine (Alba Iulia, Romania)[14]

The proposed project to develop the largest gold mine in Europe not far from the site of the infamous Baia Mare cyanide spill of 2000 has generated controversy and become a *cause célèbre* involving luminaries and activists. Opponents of the investment have also made use of legal means to challenge decisions related to the proposal. A series of four cases brought by Alburnus Maior Rosia Montana Goldsmiths Association, an NGO, against the Environmental Protection Agency of Alba County and the Alba Local Council provides an example of the use of legal tools in conjunction with other

---

[12] Bulgaria was threatened with non-recognition of its judicial decisions following membership because of its failure to bring certain segments of society to justice.

[13] See Stec 2000.

[14] The four cases involved are: *Asociatia Aurarilor Alburnus Maior in Rosia Montana v. Inspectoratul de Protectie a Mediului Alba* (4052/2005) (Decision No. 279/CA/2005, Alba Tribunal, Commercial and Administrative Section, 6 September 2005); *Asociatia Aurarilor Alburnus Maior in Rosia Montana v. Alba Local Council* (5199/2004) (Decision No. 349/CA/2005, Alba Tribunal, Commercial and Administrative Section, 12 October 2005); *Asociatia Aurarilor Alburnus Maior in Rosia Montana v. Inspectoratul de Protectie a Mediului Alba* (5057/2005) (Decision No. 363/CA/2005, Alba Tribunal, Commercial and Administrative Section, 26 October 2005); *Asociatia Aurarilor Alburnus Maior in Rosia Montana v. Inspectoratul de Protectie a Mediului Alba* (5132/2005) (Decision No. 14/CA/2006, Alba Tribunal, Commercial and Administrative Section, 17 January 2006).

mechanisms as an element of a highly organized and sophisticated campaign. The set of cases involved various attempts by the NGO to seek injunctions related to the issuance of environmental and construction permits for exploratory drilling, or challenging the authority's determination that the project as conceived entailed little environmental impact.

In the first place, these cases firmly established generous standing rules for environmental NGOs under Romanian law on grounds relating to the right to a healthy environment. Interestingly, the attitude towards NGO standing differed markedly depending on the judge in the case. One judge viewed NGO standing positively, the other grudgingly. The latter's denial of standing was overturned on appeal. Yet this judge found alternative grounds to deny legal standing. The plaintiff based its standing on the Romanian Law on Environment Protection which provides that 'the State acknowledges the right of all persons to a healthy environment, guaranteeing in this respect: . . . d) the right to notify, directly or by means of certain associations, the administrative or court authorities, in order to prevent or in the event of the occurrence of a direct or indirect prejudice'.[15] According to the same law, 'non-governmental organizations are entitled to initiate legal proceedings in order to preserve the environment irrespective of the prejudiced person'.[16] The judge sympathetic to the NGO's claim stated 'it is clear that, as a non-governmental organization vested with the defense of economic and social rights and freedoms of its members, it has an active procedural capacity in this case, a fact also recognized by the practice of our courts of law'.[17]

Since the Court of Appeal, in the first case, found in favour of the NGOs on the issue of standing, the trial judge on rehearing ruled that there was no recognizable legal interest because the activities had already taken place and the permit had lapsed. Hence, according to this judge, there was no further material or moral benefit that could be secured by the claim being allowed, given that the challenged permit no longer had any legal effect. In this sense, there was no remedy available, and therefore the requirement that a public interest be prejudiced could not be maintained. Thus, the court established a rule that a permit may not be challenged following the expiration of its validity. As to the NGO's argument that a finding of the illegality of the permit would be relevant to a determination of possible damages caused thereby, the court noted that such a claim may only be raised by persons having suffered material or moral damage, and held that the law does not recognize the plaintiff's standing in this respect.

In all the cases, the judges noted that the plaintiff, in order to support a claim for injunction, is required to demonstrate the concurrent and interdependent

---

[15] Law No. 554/2004 on Environment Protection, Article 5.   [16] *Ibid.*, Article 87.

[17] *Asociatia Aurarilor Alburnus Maior in Rosia Montana* v. *Inspectoratul de Protectie a Mediului Alba* (4052/2005) (Decision No. 279/CA/2005, Alba Tribunal, Commercial and Administrative Section, 6 September 2005) (on file with author).

requirements of a well-substantiated case and a danger of imminent harm. The court examined the procedure undertaken in the issuance of the environmental permit and found that there were no obvious gross deficiencies. It noted, perhaps ironically, that the fact that the plaintiff's suggestions and comments had not been fully accepted in the permitting process was not an indication of liability on the part of the permitting authority. The plaintiff's claim that the environmental permit cannot be issued without an archaeological certification was also dismissed. Thus, as the plaintiff's claims did not rise to the level of a well-substantiated case, nor was there a demonstration of potential imminent harm, they were dismissed by the court.

These cases further demonstrate that the burdens of meeting requirements for injunctive relief are nearly insurmountable in an environmental case. They also show that claims based on potential damage to the environment are often closely linked to claims based on cultural patrimony or even archaeological significance. Here, we have a close link to traditional environmental justice, since arguably the disproportionate impact of the proposed mine on the cultural sites of a particular ethnic group may be taken to be evidence of a lack of distributive justice.

Another of the Rosia Montana cases involved an attempt by Alburnus Maior to reopen the public commenting phase of the environmental permitting process on the basis of a lack of conformity of the process with Aarhus Convention requirements. The plaintiff contended that the relevant procedure was rendered ineffective through the failure of the Alba Environmental Protection Agency to notify directly those persons who had expressed an interest in providing comments on the draft proposal. The remedy sought included the direct notification of those who had requested it, together with a new deadline for commenting. The only notice had been given over the internet on the defendant's website and through newspapers, with a short commenting period, over the Christmas holidays. The plaintiff complained by letter to the defendant alleging the latter's breach of the provisions of the Aarhus Convention regarding notification and allowing sufficient timeframes for public participation. The plaintiff's letter was dated three days before the deadline for submission of comments. The NGO demanded that the defendant extend the deadline for the public to submit comments and proposals. The defendant refused the NGO's demands by letter dated after the commenting period was closed. The NGO's attempt to raise arguments relating to the inability of interested foreign persons to participate in the decision-making due to inadequate notice, and the shortcoming of only providing documentation in Romanian, was rejected. The court ruled that Alburnus Maior could not raise issues 'in connection with the potential interests of other interested individuals and legal entities'.

The court dismissed the plaintiff's claims, holding that the authority had met its obligations to provide the necessary information for participation 'both in Romania and abroad'. One interesting aspect of this part of the decision was that the court referred, as authority, to a letter sent by a European Commission official which allegedly stated that the provisions of the European Community directive concerning environmental impact assessments[18] as well as the 1991 UNECE Convention on Environmental Impact Assessments in a Transboundary Context,[19] providing for transboundary notification, had been complied with by the Alba Environmental Protection Agency. This reference to such a letter as legal authority is remarkable in any domestic legal proceeding. It is unclear for what purpose the letter was written and whether the European Commission official had any idea that it might be used in a legal proceeding.

In this particular case, the court treated the complaint letter to the authorities in an inconsistent manner. At one point, it lumped together the letter with substantive comments on the EIA to show the ways in which the public and the interested persons were informed. Yet, elsewhere, the court referred to this communication from Alburnus Maior as an administrative complaint. The court concluded its decision by observing that, even if it had admitted that the plaintiff had the possibility to comment on the mining corporation's project documentation, it 'has been provided with an answer' to its notice through the defendant's letter. The failure to determine whether the letter was a comment or an administrative complaint allowed the court to use the letter for dual purposes, in each case against the plaintiff's arguments. One may ask whether this was out of a mere lack of sympathy or an intentional disregard of procedural rights. This last case has been brought before the Aarhus Convention Compliance Committee.[20]

The opponents of the Rosia Montana gold mining project have embarked on a campaign including sophisticated legal challenges the likes of which have never before been seen in Romania. In September 2007, the Romanian Minister for Environment and Sustainable Development was forced to suspend the EIA procedure pending the resolution of legal challenges to the urbanistic certificate.

2.2 Medical Waste Incinerator (Constanta, Romania)[21]

The environmental NGO Mare Nostrum brought suit in 2002 against the Environmental Protection Agency of Constanta under the Law on Environment Protection, requesting the Constanta Court to invalidate an environmental permit related to the construction of a medical waste incinerator at Tomis Nord, where approximately 2,500 persons could be exposed to emissions, and to issue an order suspending its

---

[18] Directive 85/337/EEC on the Assessment of the Effects of Certain Projects on the Environment, *Official Journal* [1985] L175/40.

[19] 1991 UNECE Convention on Environmental Impact Assessments in a Transboundary Context, 30 *International Legal Materials* (1991) 800.

[20] Communication ACCC/C/2005/15 (Romania).

[21] *Organizatia Neguvernamentala Ecologista Mare Nostrum* v. *Inspectoratul de Protectie a Mediului Constanta* (Decision No. 1249/C, Case No. 1919/2003, Brasov Tribunal, Commercial and Administrative Section, 27 May 2004) (removed from Constanta Tribunal, Commercial and Administrative Section, Case No. 260/CA/2002).

construction. As with many environmental justice cases where there are winners and losers in terms of environmental burdens, this case was very controversial on the local level and had to be removed to another jurisdiction by order of the Supreme Court.

The court held that the mere availability of alternative sites for the incinerator in less populated areas was insufficient to invalidate the permit. The plaintiff was required to show the likelihood that the incinerator would operate outside the norms established by law, and this it had failed to do. But the case also highlights the difficulty even for plaintiffs' lawyers to get access to certain governmental decisions that might be relevant to a particular case. The plaintiff mistakenly claimed that the environmental permit for the incinerator was issued by an authority without power to do so, that is, the Constanta Environmental Protection Agency, rather than the Ministry of Waters and Environment as required by law. The legal acts delegating the relevant powers were produced in court, even though they had not been discovered through the due diligence of the attorneys. Lawyers bringing environmental justice cases in countries in transition today tend to be young, idealistic, and outside the mainstream. This is an obstacle to getting accurate information and good advice, with the result that clients are handicapped. The failure of such cases, moreover, can be pointed to as a waste of time and effort by those who are opposed to increased transparency.

2.3 Germia Park Case (Prishtina, Kosovo[22])[23]

The situation in Romania, a country that was on the verge of joining the EU, may be compared with that in Kosovo. The provisional government in Kosovo had a rather precarious existence before the establishment of UN administration of the territory. It had severed all formal contacts with Yugoslav state institutions, including the judiciary. The territory's reconstruction therefore also involved the creation of a functional judiciary almost from scratch.

A case was brought to court by a coalition of NGOs against the construction by the Kosovo Assembly of a 'protocol centre', that is, a 'high-level' meeting and conference centre, in Germia Park, the main public park in the vicinity of the capital, Prishtina. The coalition began a campaign of organized meetings, press conferences, roundtables and letter-writing in protest. The campaign comprised non-violent demonstrations, including tree-planting in the path of the construction. However, construction workers and supervisors from the Kosovo Assembly confronted protesters at the construction site and, according to the protesters, attacked them. This was allegedly recorded by media on the scene, but never broadcast.

---

[22] Kosovo refers to the territory in Serbia currently under interim UN administration.

[23] *Koalicioni 'GERMIA 2005' v. Kuvendit te Kosoves dhe Kuvendit Komunal te Prishtines (Coalition Germia 2005 v. Assembly of Kosovo and Municipal Council of Prishtina)*, Supreme Court of Kosovo (Case No. 637/2005, 17 November 2005).

The NGO coalition also used judicial means, filing cases before both the Kosovo Supreme Court and the Municipal Court of Prishtina, naming the Kosovo Assembly and the Municipal Council of Prishtina as defendants. The complaints were filed against decisions issued respectively by the Kosovo Assembly and the Municipal Council of Prishtina that either ordered or permitted the building of the Protocol Centre in a protected area. The organization asked for an immediate halt to construction and the return of the land to its previous state, claiming – besides the damage to the environment – certain social impacts of the construction, such as the need to close the park to the public for security reasons during the visits of dignitaries. At the time of writing, the Municipal Court of Prishtina still had not responded to the complaint.

The Supreme Court, however, dismissed the claim on the basis that the actions of the two authorities were not final administrative acts because they had simply disposed of public property and had not affected a right or an obligation *in personam*. According to the court, the coalition should have challenged the decisions issued by the Planning and Construction Department of Prishtina Municipality before the Executive Chief (Mayor) of Prishtina Municipality, as provided in the relevant legislative acts.

Interviews with representatives of the coalition showed a different understanding of the proceedings. They understood that their complaint had been rejected because they did not have a recognizable interest in the park, and because they did not react when the Municipal Council issued the permit for construction. While they contended that their complaint had been rejected because they had 'reacted late', they pointed to the fact that they had begun their campaigning activities before the permit was issued, but only filed the case after construction began. Thus, they tended to consider that the time of their claim should run from when they began concrete activities in the social sphere rather than from the filing of a paper with a court. Access to environmental justice requires a basic understanding of legal process. Expectations that the courts provide a podium for moral argumentation lead to disappointment and lack of trust in the judicial process.

Other questions were raised about the coalition's legal strategy. It admitted to not filing with the court a claim based on a legal opinion commissioned by it that held that ownership of public property could not be transferred to the authority of the Kosovo Assembly. According to the coalition representatives, they were content to have this point confirmed in their favour by legal counsel without pursuing it in its judicial claim. In response to a question concerning challenges to the proposal on the basis of deficiencies in environmental impact assessment procedures, the representatives replied that they 'didn't want to attack the Assembly, just protect the park'. Finally, they seemed resigned to seeing something built in the park, because so much money had already been spent and it would be 'unacceptable' to waste it. The director of a prominent international fund in Kosovo stated as follows: 'I signed the Germia petition . . . But their strategy is weak. They don't use the strongest arguments. Their advocacy is not the best. That's why they failed . . . Sometimes they're saying things that aren't true and sometimes they don't have a clue.'[24] These statements and the strategy of the coalition indicate that some societies have not embraced the idea that the full exercise of individual rights to their legal conclusion can be to society's overall benefit. This, combined with poor understanding of the legal process, makes achieving environmental justice nearly impossible in a specific case.

2.4 Fadeyeva v. Russia (European Court of Human Rights)[25]

Moving from small Kosovo to Russia – a behemoth still struggling with its judicial identity – this case was brought to the European Court of Human Rights. It involved the claim by a resident of Cherepovets, an important steel-producing centre situated about 300 km northeast of Moscow, that the operation of a steel plant in close proximity to her home endangered her health and well-being and that, by failing to relocate her to suitable housing, the authorities had violated her right to respect for privacy and family life, as set out in Article 8 of the European Convention on Human Rights (ECHR). In short, Mrs Fadeyeva sought a new flat and compensation because she allegedly suffered adverse health effects from living since 1982 in state-owned housing in the vicinity of a highly polluting steel plant. Her flat was well within the so-called 'sanitary security zone' where residential housing was not permitted. Various decrees and legal decisions beginning in 1974 took notice of the conditions there including the deterioration in public health, and obliged the authorities to resettle residents, but these were not implemented.

Mrs Fadeyeva had pursued various judicial remedies on the domestic level and had failed. Upon receiving a judgment to be placed on a 'priority waiting list', the execution warrant remained unexecuted for a long period of time, and was eventually discontinued on the ground that there was no 'priority waiting list'. In 1999, Mrs Fadeyeva brought a second action seeking immediate execution of the first judgment. She claimed additional grounds on the basis of Article 8 of the ECHR and corresponding provisions of the Russian Constitution – that systematic toxic emissions and noise from the plant violated her basic right to respect for her private life and home. She was subsequently placed on the general waiting list for new housing, as number 6820, and the court dismissed her action on the basis that that was her only available remedy. This judgment was upheld on appeal. Mrs Fadeyeva then turned to the European Court of Human Rights (ECtHR).

The case is significant regarding the Court's analysis of whether the state had struck a fair balance between the competing interests of the applicant and the community as

---

[24] Interview with Luan Shllaku, Executive Director, Kosovo Foundation for Open Society, June 2006.
[25] *Fadeyeva* v. *Russia*, ECtHR Application No. 55723/00, Judgment 9 June 2005.

a whole, as required by paragraph (2) of Article 8 of the ECHR. The Court's earlier major decision in this area – *Hatton* v. *UK*[26] – struck a balance between the harm and decisions of the state concerning the *positive* economic development of the country. In *Fadeyeva*, however, Russia's arguments on balancing the economic well-being of the country in effect were based on a kind of 'damage control' involving the thousands of people who also had the right to be resettled. In effect, granting relief to Mrs Fadeyeva would allow her to 'jump the queue' to the detriment of those with higher places on the waiting list.

This claim confronted the European Court of Human Right with a dilemma. In the *Hatton* v. *UK* case, it had struggled with the 'margin of appreciation' afforded to states in determining how to place burdens on society as a whole, and had specifically rejected a special status for environmental human rights. Yet denying relief to Mrs Fadeyeva on similar grounds would essentially uphold the arguments of the lower court in Cherepovets – that any protection of rights could be conditioned upon the availability of funds, and, where no funds could be found, no rights could be recognized. The Court was unable to reject a remedy such as the general waiting list out of hand. The Court's solution was to rest its decision on the domestic illegality of residency in the sanitary zone,[27] which Russia could not rely upon as even a temporary measure in defence of economic well-being, coupled with its failure to show that it proactively regulated the plant to control and reduce harmful emissions. The Court, in assessing whether the state had exercised due diligence and had given consideration to competing interests, focused on whether the state had exercised its authority to regulate the plant in a way that would have reduced or eliminated the impacts on the applicant. The Court concluded that the state 'did not offer the applicant any effective solution to help her move from the dangerous area'.

Significantly from an environmental justice point of view, the Russian Federation failed to meet its procedural responsibilities in the case before the Court. The Court noted that the burden is on the state, where an infringement has been established, to justify, 'using detailed and rigorous data, a situation in which certain individuals bear a heavy burden on behalf of the rest of the community' (para. 128). In this case, the state had failed to produce several important documents it referred to in support of its arguments and to explain how these documents had influenced policies towards the plant's operation. Nor could the state describe how the interests of the population had been taken into account in attaching conditions to the plant's permit (nor did it produce the operating permit itself). It did not provide specific information on enforcement actions against the steel enterprise Severstal for violations of environmental law, or on the level of sanctions imposed. The Court stated: '[I]t is

---

[26] *Hatton and Others* v. *United Kingdom*, ECtHR, Application No. 36022/97, Judgment by Grand Chamber 8 July 2003.
[27] Citing *Ivaschenko* v. *Krasnoyarsk Railways*, presented by the applicant.

not possible to make a sensible analysis of the Government's policy vis-à-vis Severstal because the Government has failed to show clearly what this policy consisted of.' In this case, adverse inferences had to be drawn.

The specific situation existing under centrally planned economies also played a role in the Court's decision. It noted that, in 1982, when Mrs Fadeyeva moved to her flat, she most likely had no choice over the place of her abode. Even after the introduction of free-market principles, her status as a life tenant in municipal housing made it financially impossible for her to enter the market and buy a new flat. The Court also considered the close relationship between the state and its former enterprises, even after privatization, when holding that Russia failed to actively enforce relevant environmental rules against Severstal. It appears that there is still insufficient separation between the regulator and the regulated, which affects the ability of the state to defend itself in international courts. The image is of a state beholden to power elites that cannot, in the words of the Court, apply 'effective solutions to help' ordinary citizens. Societies where the judiciary cannot act independently of power elites offer little prospect for defence of the rights of victims against polluters.

2.5 Judicial procedures as elements of environmental justice campaigns

In each of the cases described, the plaintiffs ultimately did not prevail on the domestic level. The ECtHR case was no exception. In the not-so-distant past, this would have been the end of it. There was no free and active press to shed a light on administrative and judicial processes. Furthermore, there were few opportunities for public manifestations, and there were significant limitations on the extent to which international standards could be applied to moderate domestic decisions. As a result of developments over the last fifteen years, cases similar to those described above are generally elements of broader campaigns, and in some cases successes or compromises can be reached. It cannot be stated for certain in these particular examples whether an adverse judicial decision actually may have contributed to the social debate on a particular issue, for example by focusing the attention of the public or certain institutions on relative injustices. However, it should be noted that a pure legal reading of each case would support conclusions that 'correct' solutions had been reached, while, as described above, subsequent events revealed that other, more socially acceptable outcomes were achievable.

For example, in the Rosia Montana case, the initial environmental impact assessment (EIA) procedure, attacked by Alburnus Maior, was suspended following media debate and public pressure, and later a new EIA procedure was initiated. In the Constanta medical incinerator case, the Constanta Environmental Protection Agency issued an order requiring the Tomis Nord incinerator to cease operation as soon as a new incinerator in a neighbouring community was completed. In the Germia case, it was elections unseating the party in power that led to a re-examination of the decision concerning the park. The scandal and public debate in the press could lead to a more just outcome, although some of the options being considered were for the Assembly *to sell the partially constructed facility* or to develop the site as a lung hospital.

2.6 Other cases (Kosovo, Bulgaria)

A well-recognized instance of an environmental justice-related case is the temporary settlement by the UN authorities in Kosovo of Roma refugees fleeing from violence in southern Kosovo during the 2002 uprising. They were placed in a highly degraded mining area within the notorious Trepca complex at Zitkovac near Mitrovica where they were exposed to critically high levels of pollutants, particularly heavy metals. On 20 February 2006, the European Roma Rights Center (ERRC) filed an action with the European Court of Human Rights alleging violations related to the right to life (Article 2 of the ECHR), prohibition of torture and inhuman or degrading treatment (Article 3), right to a fair hearing (Article 6), right to respect for private and family life (Article 8), right to an effective remedy (Article 13), and prohibition of discrimination (Article 14). In addition, the application asked for interim measures or emergency action due to the immediate need for removal of the victims from the lead-contaminated camps and medical treatment. This action was rejected by the Court on the grounds that the United Nations authority in Kosovo is not a party to the European Convention on Human Rights. Attempts to bring legal action on the domestic side are not clear, whereas it has been reported that the ERRC has threatened to file legal action against the UN in US domestic courts.[28] The classic situation in which an ethnic minority suffers disproportionate effects of environmental pollution is made even more stark by the fact that the UN placed people in harm's way in an effort to shield them against ethnic attacks.

In comparison with the gold-mining project in Romania, similar projects proposed for Bulgaria have encountered greater popular opposition. In connection with the Zlato Grad and Chelopech investment projects, public protests succeeded in halting progress on the investments. A completed EIA decision was left unsigned by the Minister for the Environment and Waters, and a legal action by the investor, Dundee Precious Metals, to compel the minister to act was rejected by the Supreme Administrative Court of Bulgaria.[29] This case demonstrates that there are some high government officials who may be receptive to environmental justice arguments, and upholds the right of such officials to block a major investment project on environmental grounds.

---

[28] Despite increasing examples of extraterritoriality in the field of human rights and regulatory legislation, such a claim would likely fail.

[29] See CEE Bankwatch Network press release dated 10 August 2006 at www.bankwatch.org/newsroom/documents.shtml?x=1915739.

3 'Social dialogue' as an alternative to injunction

3.1 *Forest reserves of Kornalovichy and Borislavsky (Ukraine)*

A large number of environmental cases in countries in transition involve attempts to motivate courts to issue injunctions. This is to be expected, as the subject matter of most such disputes involves actions that will have an impact – often inestimable or unpredictable – on the natural surroundings that may be difficult or impossible to reverse. In the vast majority of these cases, the plaintiffs fail in their efforts to seek an injunction due to the difficult burdens that they face in terms of establishing the likelihood of success of the substantive claim on the merits and of imminent harm. Not only are the matters of a technical nature that strains the resources of civil society actors, but the courts are also ill-equipped to review determinations of responsible authorities. Courts in countries in transition (and other countries as well) cannot be relied upon by civil society to exercise their powers of review in the same manner as in some judicially activist countries. One tool to aid in this situation and which may be increasing in frequency is an elaborate social dialogue process. Proponents of this mechanism claim that it cannot work without media attention to ensure that the 'more influential party' does not dominate the decision-making process and ignore stakeholders.

In Ukraine, an environmental NGO (WETI) provides an example of how alternative methods of dispute resolution can be more effective in challenging environmentally harmful activities than administrative or judicial process. It involved attacks on a decision removing from protected status about 4,000 hectares of mostly forested land in eleven protected areas, thus opening the land to commercial forestry. In accordance with law, the proposal was supported by scientific studies and was approved by the local department of the Ministry of Environment and Natural Resources of Ukraine. Protests against the action began almost immediately. However, it was only when old oak forests in the former Kornalovichy reserve began to be cut, and some scientists raised their voices in alarm, that sustained media attention was brought to bear. The alliance between scientists and NGOs was supported by an environmental legal NGO, which compiled a detailed legal critical analysis of the decision-making process and the scientific basis thereof and submitted this to the competent authorities.

In early 2005, WETI organized a tour of Kornalovichy and Borislavksy for around forty journalists, scientists, governmental officials, prosecutors, NGO representatives and foresters that resulted in broad media coverage. The day following the tour, one of the prosecutors began to inspect the areas for possible legal violations. Another result was the initiative to organize a 'roundtable' discussion, ultimately held in July 2005. The roundtable discussion included representatives of the state-run forestry enterprise as well as those opposed to the exploitation of the forests, and scientists on both sides of the issue. They ultimately reached consensus that a part of the old oak forest that had not been cut should be returned to protected status.

In lieu of an injunction, the NGOs convinced the state-run forestry enterprise to agree to a moratorium on forest cutting during the social discussion. As a result, only around 30 per cent of the forest area was cut. The NGO representatives considered the media attention generated by the press tour as having led directly to the enterprise's interest in participating in social discussions. The social discussions themselves were covered by the press. The same level of media attention may not have been applied to a court case. The NGOs' restraint in not filing a court case appears also to have had some value in their negotiations. According to an NGO representative, 'We understand that if the Decision of 1999 was admitted as illegal several people responsible for it might be punished. But our main priority was to save valuable natural territories as soon as possible because every day of delay cost us a decrease in territory of old growth oak forest. Even if some people were punished we would never be able to return trees that were cut.'[30] The informality of the proceedings lowered the stakes, while the transparency resulting from media attention helped to undermine the influence of powerful local interests over the forestry experts and scientists, who, despite their dependency on these institutions, in the words of one NGO representative, 'did not want to lose face or credibility'. The proactive exercise of citizens' environmental rights, despite the lack of legal proceedings, produced a comparatively democratic and transparent result, avoiding the kinds of environmental injustices that would have occurred if power elites could have acted with impunity. The legal background was still present and had an influence on the process. Without legal guidance through international standards and the possibility of administrative responsibility, such an outcome could hardly have been expected.

4 Conclusion

This chapter has looked at environmental justice cases from countries in transition that are in very different stages of development. Not so long ago, all of these countries were nominally under a socialist legal structure in which the notion of a distributive type of environmental justice simply did not exist, as socialist legal theory held that socialism was in harmony with nature. Today, however, the application of environmental justice has different aspects if examined against the background of rapid European Union membership of some countries versus the emergence of societies with limited experience in self-determination from the ruins of crumbled empires. Other differentiating factors have also come to the fore. In some countries, there are distinct minority groups such as the Roma, bearing a disproportionate environmental burden and presenting a classic environmental distributive justice situation. The state of societies in transition, their inherent flux, especially with respect to application of the rule of law, and in some cases the rapid reorganization of societies, raise questions as to whether standard notions of environmental justice should be modified for

---

[30] Statement of Hanna Hopko, WETI.

application in each situation. For example, Kosovo is unique among transitional societies because of the long period of time during which the majority of its population boycotted official institutions, and the corresponding *tabula rasa* upon which new institutions and relationships have been built.

Nevertheless, there is a unifying factor among all the countries of transition. That is, the residue of the nominally egalitarian, single-class societies, that consisted of an elite class ruling over a bureaucratic polity. An aspect of this residue consists of the efforts of elites to keep their positions in society and by a new entrepreneurial class to seize such positions. In countries in transition, environmental justice often involves challenges to actions of those in power who increase their wealth or status at the expense of others. There, the environmental justice concept is most relevant when it is applied to situations where power elites govern in the absence of sufficient legal controls, taking advantage of gaps in legal processes and standards and the flux in application of the rule of law to grant themselves privileges. The victims are the general population, rather than particular disadvantaged groups. When it is observed that power relationships in society under scientific socialism were pervaded by a general waste of resources, an inability to maintain infrastructure, and environmental degradation on a large scale, then the link between environmental justice issues and larger issues about the governed and the governing, the promise of the future and the disappointing reality (leading to concerns of intergenerational equity) can clearly be seen. In that sense, environmental justice can be a force for defining the relationship between those in power and the governed, and developing respect for the law and overall notions of justice and equity.

One statement made during the gathering of these cases seems to illustrate the intended practical effect of environmental justice cases on these societies, through combining environmental, social, economic, and political issues. Concerning the Germia park case in Kosovo, one influential citizen observed: 'There are at least twenty bigger hotspots, but these NGOs chose a case where the government violated the trust of the people and didn't respect either nature or its own procedures.' This case is a good example of how the self-mobilization of society on environmental issues is often less about the protection of nature *per se*, and more about the building of institutions and the relationship between the state and the people.

It has been seen that, despite the fact that environmental justice has proven to be elusive, court cases are still being brought in hopes of achieving a measure of environmental justice. In most of the cases analyzed, the final decisions went against those seeking environmental justice. The *Fadeyeva* case was no exception at any rate with regard to the issues raised before the Russian court, although the outcome was different from an environmental justice point of view at the European level. In the Rosia Montana cases, at least one judge appears to have felt no compunction against issuing a decision contrary to well-established law, which was overturned on appeal. In terms of achieving relative justice, decisions of courts do not compare well with other types of campaigns. There appears to be a lack of sympathy among the judiciary for citizen plaintiffs in environmental cases. The *Fadeyeva* case also illustrates the influence of economic factors in environmental justice. Factors external to administrative and legal processes continue to play a major role in the supervision of such processes. The Russian Federation government refrained from producing potentially exculpatory evidence that related to the operations of a powerful firm. As this occurred before an international tribunal, inferences can be drawn about the proceedings at the domestic level, which were anything but transparent.

In light of this, it is not surprising that recourse to the courts has usually been seen by NGOs and concerned individuals as a strategy of last resort. The judicial decision, even one resulting in an adverse outcome, may nevertheless expose the weaknesses in current state structures and the rule of law. Judicial proceedings may also serve as stimulus for other campaigns and alternative mechanisms for the resolution of the disputes in the manner and form more receptive to environmental justice arguments. In at least one example, a campaign for the restoration of the protected status of a forest took place through an elaborate social dialogue process that included legal elements, without resorting to the courts to seek an injunction. The large number of failed cases in domestic courts, compared to the successes that have been achieved through non-formal dispute resolution mechanisms and media pressure, indicates that much work needs to be done to ensure that the judicial system can play a meaningful and proper role in determining solutions to societies' environmental problems.

An analysis of resort to the courts to determine issues of environmental justice in countries in transition gives some practical description, if not a definition, of environmental justice that may be applied generally to various sets of power relationships. This description includes the recognition that environmental justice is a struggle that takes place against the background of the different capabilities of particular societies to achieve substantial justice. More fundamentally, it pinpoints the struggle as one to reduce environmental risks on a broad societal level through the resolution of individualized cases. The development of procedural guarantees, substantive rules, and transparency makes it more difficult for the economic and political elites to shift risk to less powerful actors, resulting in a lower level of overall acceptable risk. Environmental justice is essentially about developing and maintaining the best achievable legal mechanisms for managing environmental risks through individual empowerment in order to ensure a fair and equitable distribution of such risks and burdens throughout society.

Bibliography

Agyeman, J., and Evans, B., 2004. '"Just sustainability": the emerging discourse of environmental justice in Britain?' *Geographical Journal* 170 (2): 155–64.

Baxter, B. H., 2000. 'Ecological Justice and Justice as Impartiality'. *Environmental Politics* 3 (Autumn): 43–64.

Bullard, R. B., 1990. *Dumping in Dixie: Race, Class, and Environmental Quality.* Boulder, CO: Westview Press.

Bullard, and Johnson, 2000. 'Environmental Justice: Grassroots Activism and Impact on Public Policy Decision Making'. *Journal of Social Issues* 56 (3): 555–78.

Byrne, J., Martinez, C., and Glover, L., 2002. 'A Brief on Environmental Justice', in J. Byrne *et al.* (eds.), *Environmental Justice: Discourses in the International Political Economy*. Rutgers, NJ: Transaction Publishers, 3–17.

Filcak, R., 2007. 'Environmental Justice in the Slovak Republic: The Case of Roma Ethnic Minority'. Dissertation, Department of Environmental Sciences and Policy, Central European University, Budapest.

Hedemann-Robinson, M., 2006. 'Article 228(2) EC and the Enforcement of EC Environmental Law: A Case of Environmental Justice Delayed and Denied? An Analysis of Recent Legal Developments'. *European Environmental Law Review* 15 (11): 312–42.

Hockman, E. M., and Morris, C. M., 1998. 'Progress Towards Environmental Justice: A Five-Year Perspective of Toxicity, Race and Poverty in Michigan 1990–1995'. *Journal of Environmental Planning and Management* 41 (2): 157–76.

Low, N., and Gleeson, B., 1998. *Justice, Society and Nature – An Exploration of Political Ecology*. London: Routledge.

McGurty, E. M., 2000. 'Warren County, NC, and the Emergence of the Environmental Justice Movement: Unlikely Coalitions and Shared Meanings in Local Collective Actions'. *Society and Natural Resources* 13: 373–87.

Stec, S., 2000. '"Aarhus" Environmental Rights in Eastern Europe'. *Yearbook of European Environmental Law* 5: 1.

World Commission on Environment and Development, 1987. *Our Common Future*. Oxford: Oxford University Press.

9

Environmental justice through environmental courts? Lessons learned from the Swedish experience

JAN DARPÖ

1 Introduction

The concerns of environmental justice in general involve more than the substantive content of environmental law. Furthermore, institutional and procedural aspects of decision-making are particularly instrumental in promoting a fair distribution of goods and burdens – thus making it possible for those concerned to influence such decision-making. This is true in any social context, but perhaps even more so in the environmental field, which is characterised by a strong imbalance of power between actors.

In the environmental procedure, private persons, neighbours and others, can find themselves in the position of challenging large companies (often multinational) and public enterprises. On the one side large organisations with vast resources and all kinds of technical, economic and legal expertise, as well as considerable experience in such things as permit-procedures, appeal cases and trials for damages, are ranged against the other side, made up of one-shot litigants with no such financial resources, and often with little or no access to legal or scientific advice. Despite increased involvement in litigation on the part of non-governmental organisations (NGOs) over the past few decades, the picture has not changed. Essentially, the work of such organisations is based upon voluntary effort.

One would expect that the necessary alignment to reduce such imbalances in environmental procedures would be seen by all as a matter of course, something of fundamental value in any democratic society. However, as evidenced by the continuing debate on the implementation of the Aarhus Convention[1] – which expresses basic standards on information, public participation in decision-making and access to justice in environmental matters – a more complex picture emerges. In a way, Aarhus-related ideas are in collision with the traditions of strong society in Western Europe and the belief in public authorities as being the sole defenders of environmental

---

[1] UNECE Convention on Access to Information, Public Participation in Decision-Making and Access to Justice in Environmental Matters (UN Doc. ECE/CEP/43 (1998)) signed in Aarhus, Denmark, on 25 June 1998, reprinted in 38 *International Legal Materials* (1999) 515.

interests. Concerned individuals and NGOs are sometimes viewed as 'outsiders' with no particular right to participate in decision-making procedures.

The aim of this chapter is to accentuate certain aspects of 'access to justice'. To some extent, this discussion concerns the role of the court in relation to the environmental area. This topic has generated considerable interest over the past decade, and in some countries, such as the United Kingdom, strong arguments have emerged in favour of establishing specialised tribunals or 'environmental courts'. Today, Sweden is the only country in Western Europe where such courts exist, at least from an organisational viewpoint.

Accordingly, this discussion will begin with a brief description of the main features of the Swedish system. This will then be taken as the starting-point with which to reflect upon certain procedural aspects in relation to public participation and access to justice in the environmental area. Of course, one is only too well aware that first and foremost the cardinal issues relate to such things as money: court fees, costs for lawyers and technicians, bonds etc. But for the moment, the pecuniary aspects of access to justice will be set aside. My intention is merely to initiate a discussion on other procedural issues that are vital when considering the possibilities of 'third party interests' having their say in environmental decision-making. In doing so, the presumption is that a *broad consideration* of issues, at an *early stage* of decision-making, where *all actors* are able to have their say and *all interests can be invoked*, is crucial to bringing about environmental justice. When applying this presumption on environmental cases – where both the legislation and the technical and natural scientific issues can be extremely complicated – it becomes evident that special demands must be made on the procedure. It must be transparent and easily intelligible to ordinary citizens. Attention must be paid to the imbalance between the parties. For example, the deciding body should have a duty to investigate the particulars of the case and the weaker parties should be able to benefit from legal and technical aid. The system must also be effective. In this respect, it is crucial that decisions are easily enforceable and that enforcement is accessible to all. Actors of the environmental procedure, broadly defined as operators, public concerned, stakeholders, NGOs and *ad hoc* groups, must be treated equally. This is important in the decision-making, but also when it comes to appeal. To my understanding, it is also crucial for effective access to justice that appeals have suspensory effect and that the appellate body can replace the challenged decision with a new and better one. These views will be expounded in the chapter.

2 Environmental law and institutions of Sweden

2.1 The 1999 Environmental Code

Since 1999, Sweden has had a 'universally' applicable Environmental Code,[2] which replaced some fifteen older pieces of legislation, and harmonised the general rules

---

[2] Government Bill 1997/98:45. The Environmental Code is published in English on the Swedish Ministry of the Environment's website, www.regeringen.se/English/Publications/2000:61/.

and principles in this field. In addition, this legislation also introduced new concepts, principles and procedures. Some parts of the Code apply to all activities and measures, whereas others concern only special areas. The main core is administrative law, that is, rules that express the demands that environmental authorities can make upon persons intending to undertake any activity or measure that entails a risk for man or the environment. The Code, however, also contains some private law elements, such as provisions concerning compensation for damages and injunctions based upon neighbourhood law.

Both the objectives and scope of the Environmental Code are extensive. Its aim is to protect human health and the environment against damage or nuisance, to protect and conserve valuable natural and cultural environments, and to secure good management of natural resources and waste. The Code applies to all human activities that might harm the environment and it is, in principle, immaterial as to whether it is a question of commercial or private operations or measures. However, certain activities, such as infrastructure installations, are also regulated in special pieces of legislation.

The Environmental Code sets out well-established environmental principles, such as the precautionary principle, the polluter pays principle, the principle of best available technologies, and the substitution principle. However, these rules only apply to the extent that the demands made by them cannot be regarded as being unreasonable. This is decided by balancing different interests, mainly the benefit and cost of the measures required. The general parts of the Code also contain provisions providing for environmental quality norms as well as environmental impact assessments. Certain listed industrial undertakings, quarries and other environmentally hazardous activities are subjected to permit or notification requirements. The Code also contains provisions for the protection of nature, flora and fauna. Obviously, vital parts of the Code reflect European Community environmental law.

On supervision and sanctions, the Code reflects traditional public law enforcement. The main instrument of enforcing environmental law in Sweden is that of administrative orders, which can be combined with administrative fines (*astreinte*[3]). Other sanctions of the Code are sanction fees and criminal penalties.

2.2 Institutions for decision-making

The reform following the introduction of the Environmental Code also brought a new system for permits and appeals. Environmental courts replaced the National Licensing Board, the water courts and the administrative courts.[4] The court system of today

---

[3] Administrative fines are not the same as (civil) penalties. Instead, they are individually calculated by the deciding authority and set down in advance as a threat. In case of disobedience, the authority can ask the court to decide on the execution of the fine.

[4] As in Germany and Finland, Sweden has administrative courts for the retrial of administrative decisions and ordinary courts for civil and criminal cases. The ordinary courts have three levels: district courts, courts of appeal and the Supreme Court.

involves five regional environmental courts sitting as courts of first instance.[5] The Environmental Court of Appeal is the court of second instance, and the final instance in the line of appeal is the Supreme Court.

In relation to administrative authorities with special responsibility for the environment, the municipalities[6] and the Local Environmental Boards (LEBs) act as supervisory authorities. Formally speaking, the LEBs are political bodies entrusted with the task of applying environmental law, and acting independently of the government and the central agencies. Thus, no state agency can instruct them on how to apply the law against individual subjects, but their decisions can be appealed. The County Administrative Board[7] (CAB) is responsible for 'green' issues and for supervision concerning water-related activities and integrated pollution prevention and control (IPPC) activities. A special body within the CAB – the Regional Licensing Board – issues permits for environmentally hazardous activities and landfills. CABs also issue permits for waste transportation and disposals, chemical activities and more. Unlike the municipalities, CABs are part of the governmental powers. However, as with the municipalities, they cannot be ordered in an individual case concerning the exercise of authority.

Installations and activities involving a substantial environmental impact must obtain a permit from the Environmental Court. The same goes for all kinds of water operations. In such cases, the Environmental Court is effectively a court of first instance for the purposes of permit applications. The Environmental Court also has jurisdiction in cases concerning damages and injunctions against hazardous activities, as well as appeals in cases relating to sanction fees.

The Environmental Court consists of one professional judge, one environmental technician and two expert members. Industry and central public authorities nominate the last two. The underlying philosophy is that experts will contribute with their experience of municipal or industrial operations or public environment supervision. The Environmental Court of Appeal comprises three professional judges and one technician. Here, too, all members of the courts have equal votes. The Supreme Court has no technicians.

2.3 The line of appeal

The Swedish route for appeals in cases concerning the environment is always the same and quite simple: Local Environmental Board → County Administrative Board → Environmental Court → Environmental Court of Appeal → Supreme Court. If appealed, all environmental decisions follow this route, although the

---

[5] In fact, the Environmental Courts are sections within five ordinary district courts. However, their jurisdiction in environmental matters is regional.

[6] There are 290 municipalities in Sweden with populations ranging from a couple of thousand up to almost one million (Stockholm).

[7] Sweden is divided into twenty-one counties.

starting-point and terminus differ. 'Administrative' cases, starting with a decision by an authority, may be brought to the Environmental Court, and finally to the Environmental Court of Appeal. Cases starting in the Environmental Court can be appealed to the Environmental Court of Appeal and the Supreme Court.[8] Thus, from an organisational point of view, Sweden has a court system for environmental appeals. However, looking at the *procedures, examination,* and *scope of decision-making* in appeal cases, it is more true to say that the environmental courts work within the system of administrative procedure.[9]

On appeal, the actors are the usual ones in environmental cases. On the one side, resides the applicant for a permit or the addressee of an administrative decision. On the other, there are the third party interests of both an individual and a public nature. The former are neighbours and other individuals 'concerned' by the decision. In Sweden, the central authorities traditionally represent the public interest. On the environmental scene, the National Environmental Agency, of course, plays a leading role. To some extent, the Agency can challenge environmental decisions by municipal authorities as well as the lower levels of the administration.

With the Environmental Code came the potential for certain non-governmental organisations to appeal decisions in environmental cases. However, the requirements for 'standing' are strict: 2,000 members, activity in Sweden for three years and applicable to only certain kinds of non-profit associations. In practice, only one or two organisations can meet those requirements and neither Greenpeace nor WWF is one of them.

The most positive effect of the introduction of the Environmental Code is that almost all environmental issues are decided 'in one line'. All types of cases are ultimately dealt with by the same environmental courts: permits, supervisory decisions, all kinds of charges, enforcement (*astreinte* and sanction fees), cost recovery and damages. The uniformity of case law in the Swedish system is also strengthened by the role of the Environmental Court of Appeal. In practice, judgments of this Court have a great and expedient impact.[10] Almost 80 per cent of all cases are 'administrative' and cannot proceed further. The Environmental Court of Appeal is also quite willing to grant leave to appeal, while the opposite applies for the Supreme Court. Whereas the former

---

[8] When the Environmental Court of the Appeal or Supreme Court is the final instance, cases require leave to appeal.

[9] However, some cases are dealt with in a different manner. Decisions by the County Administrative Board concerning wider land-use and planning – such as the appointment of national parks, nature reserves and areas exempt from shore protection – are appealed to government. As with any governmental decision, the legality of those positions can be challenged by the public concerned by launching a judicial review in the Supreme Administrative Court (SAC). A further example of a different mode of 'appeal' in environmental matters is one where all members of a local community have the authority to challenge the legality of any municipal decision by launching 'legality control' procedures in the administrative courts.

[10] The most important judgments and decisions from the Environmental Court of Appeal (Miljööverdomstolen) are published within two or three months on the website of the National Court Administration, at www.rattsinfosok.dom.se, but only in Swedish.

opens the door to almost 25 per cent of appeal cases (out of 300 per year),[11] in contrast the Supreme Court grants leave in perhaps five or six cases a year.

The most acknowledged disadvantage of the court system is its increasing formality in procedure. Courts are not as service-oriented as administrative authorities. Another negative observation is that the environmental courts have had difficulty in adapting both to the new environmental principles set out and to the notions reflected in the Environmental Code. In fact, some of the traditions from the old Water Right Act of 1918 still prevail – for example, the curious fact that water-related cases can live on for twenty or even thirty years after the first permit decision. Obviously, such a system can find itself at variance with both EC law and the ideas of Aarhus.

3 Procedural aspects on participating and access to justice

3.1 Introduction

No common understanding exists within the legal systems of Europe in relation to the notion of 'environmental procedure'. The processes for decision-making, including appeals and enforcement in this area of law, can be, and in fact are, based upon administrative, civil or criminal law procedures. Furthermore, these different approaches can even be found within the same legal system. However, there are substantial differences in terms of procedural obstacles and access to justice between, on the one hand, an appeal system where the court acts in the ordinary course of appeal and has the authority to review the decision in its entirety, and, on the other, where the court may only scrutinise a particular case on issues of legality. As described below, the procedural principles applied in decision-making, and on appeal, are also crucial from the viewpoint of environmental justice.

Within the provisions of the Aarhus Convention, the essential requirements of access to justice are expressed in Article 9. While Article 9(1) concerns access to a review procedure in cases of denied access to environmental information, Article 9(2) calls for access to a review procedure before a court, or another impartial body, to 'challenge the substantive and procedural legality' of decisions to permit certain, listed activities. In Article 9(3), access to administrative or judicial procedures is required 'to challenge acts and omissions by private parties and public authorities which contravene provisions of national law concerning the environment'. Under Article 9(4), there is a requirement for procedures that provide adequate and effective remedies, including injunctive relief. The process should be fair, equitable and not prohibitively expensive. The terms expressed in the Aarhus Convention largely relate to civil law procedure. This is also true of much of what is written in the Implementation Guide of the Convention.[12] However, the fifteen years of hard work that gave birth to

---

[11] Beside these, the Environmental Court of Appeal also hears about 130 cases a year that do not require leave.
[12] UNECE 2000, pp. 123–36.

EC Directive 2004/35/EC on environmental liability have shown that one must not be misled by legal labels, concepts or expressions. Therefore, an international convention on access to justice should be neutral with regard to the kind of instruments the legal system offers, as long as they are effective.

The main core of European environmental law, decision-making and procedure belong to what is considered to be administrative law. In addition, most legal systems also allow the affected public to go direct to court with claims against the operator concerned, usually in the form of a request for an injunction against a particular activity. These private law remedies are valuable alternatives to the administrative procedures, but they often entail high costs, procedural obstacles (such as a mandatory counsellor at the higher levels of the judicature) as well as a requirement that certain thresholds of injury be attained, or that the risk complained of was imminent. Finally, some systems also allow for the possibility for the public to initiate criminal proceedings. In most European countries, including Sweden, the power to prosecute is the prerogative of the Attorney General. In other legal systems, the potential for public prosecution is wider. In England and Wales, in cases relating to the environment, the role of the Attorney General is usually taken on by the Environment Agency, but also by private parties in situations where the authorities have been passive.[13] Spain is another country where *actio popularis* exists for criminal law.[14]

So, in order to illustrate access to justice in environmental matters in a particular country, one must consider all these aspects of law and procedure. The scope of the following discourse, however, is narrower, focusing on procedural issues affecting the various possibilities open to the concerned public to *challenge administrative decision-making* in the environmental area. The discussion will be on the structure of the different appeal systems and the role of the courts (section 3.2), the scope of review in the appeal (section 3.3), the outcome of the proceedings and the relationship between different decisions (section 3.4) as well as the procedural rights of different actors (sections 3.5 and 3.6). The intention is to stimulate debate rather than to make a thorough analysis of these subjects.

3.2 The system

It is crucial that any legal system is transparent and easily intelligible to ordinary citizens if there is to be successful access to justice. Too many routes of appeal will

---

[13] Perhaps the most famous is *Anglian Water*, where the operator was convicted in the Crown Court and had to pay a record £200,000 in sewage fines, although reduced to £60,000 in the Court of Appeal ([2004] Env LR 10). On this case and private prosecutions in the UK, see Environmental Data Services (ENDS) 326, March 2002, 54; and Jones and Parpworth 2004, pp. 220ff.

[14] See Bonet 2002 p. 364. Also Milieu 2007, p. 6, which provides an executive summary of the inventory of EU member states' measures on access to justice in environmental matters.

have a constraining effect on such access.[15] Other disadvantages exist with a divided and disintegrated system. Where several organs are involved in the different stages of an environmental dispute, there will be divergences in case law. A familiar example of producing the opposite of the desired effect is when an administrative order is accepted on appeal, but – sometimes years later – quashed in the stage of enforcement. The 'one-line-system', of course, counteracts such a phenomenon but brings about other demands and challenges.

Environmental decisions invariably involve 'civil rights and obligations' within the meaning of Article 6 of the European Convention on Human Rights (ECHR). Thus, somewhere in the line of appeal there has to be a court or another 'independent and impartial' body. There is also a demand for a 'fair trial' which implies the right to request a public hearing before that body.[16] The complexity of environmental cases, the necessity to include and consider all interests, preferably with the involvement of a public hearing, as well as the need to gain approval for the decision, are all factors tending to suggest that the 'court' appears at an early stage of any decision-making.

However, a system where ordinary courts act as decision-makers of first instance can conflict with the basic features of environmental decision-making. For instance, the nature of environmental decision-making strongly suggests that the burden of investigation lies on the deciding body. This in turn requires the decision-making body to include independent and impartial technicians. Both these elements are crucial for the environment *per se*, and also for the weaker parties not to be entirely dependent on technical consultants and lawyers. That is the main reason why the Swedish administrative decision-making is based upon the 'inquisitorial principle', meaning that the deciding body of first instance is responsible for any examination. It will have to ascertain that the activity in question will take place in accordance with the legal requirements, whatever the parties claim. The Swedish viewpoint is that, at this stage of an environmental case, the principle also means – together with the principle of transparency[17] – that anybody can participate in the procedure before the decision-making. The deciding body is also obliged to consider his or her opinion.

However, in the Swedish experience, the court reform has debilitated the inquisitorial principle in environmental cases. Being familiar with the civil procedure, the environmental courts are reluctant to undertake their own investigations in the case. Even when an application for a permit is decided by a court of first instance, the findings reveal that the case is looked upon as a two-party conflict under non-mandatory law. An example of this is when the court finds that the authorities and the public concerned 'have failed to prove' that certain precautions or protective measures are

---

[15] In the debate on public accessibility, the English system has been mentioned as a deterrent example, with more that fifty routes of appeal in environmental cases. See Macrory 2003, para. 5.2.

[16] *Allan Jacobsson (No. 2)* v. *Sweden*, ECtHR, 19 February 1998.

[17] The principle of transparency is regarded as a constitutional principle of good governance, promoting accountability by exposing administrative decisions and relevant documents to public scrutiny.

required as conditions. This is an unfortunate development, given that environmental cases can be extremely complicated in technical and scientific matters. My belief is that the inquisitorial principle must be upheld by bodies well equipped with technicians and nature scientists, and that such experts should be present at all stages of decision-making. The features of environmental conflicts are so specific when compared with ordinary issues of criminal and civil law, that the appreciation of judges as 'generalists' can be a hindrance to effective decision-making. In the field of environmental decision-making, 'general knowledge' may easily turn into 'general ignorance'.

On the one hand, the need for a non-bureaucratic procedural order and the complexity of cases suggest that environmental decisions should be appealed to bodies external to the ordinary courts system, while, on the other, bodies so created should satisfy the requirements of Article 6 of the ECHR. However, the jurisprudence of the European Court of Human Rights shows that a number of tribunals outside the ordinary courts system, dealing with different areas of law, have generally satisfied the formal requirements of Article 6. The Court regards the expression 'tribunal' as an autonomous concept, meeting certain criteria.[18] First, the tribunal must be established by law and undertake its functions of determining matters within its competence on the basis of rules of law, following proceedings conducted in a prescribed manner.[19] Secondly, its members must be independent and impartial. The independence of a body is to be determined in the light of the manner of appointment of its members, the duration of their terms of office, and guarantees against outside pressures. It is also important whether or not the body is seen to be independent by impartial spectators.[20] Lay assessors are generally acceptable, but in specific cases their objectivity can be questioned.[21] Furthermore, it is acceptable that the first decision in a case is taken by an authority, so long as the possibility exists of having that decision appealed to a court, without restriction on the scope of examination. Finally, the decision of the court must be binding, prohibiting the government or other authorities to have it set aside.[22]

Drawing on this jurisprudence, a procedural order where environmental cases of all kinds are decided by tribunals assembled with lawyers, technicians, nature

---

[18] Thus, the following tribunals were accepted by the European Court of Human Rights: a board for deciding compensation for criminal damage in Sweden, *Rolf Gustafsson* v. *Sweden*, ECtHR, 1 July 1997; an authority for real estate transactions in Austria, *Sramek* v. *Austria*, ECtHR, 22 October 1984; a prison board for visitors in the UK, *Campbell and Fell* v. *UK*, ECtHR, 28 June 1984; and an appeals council of the Medical Association of Belgium, *Le Compte et al.* v. *Belgium*, ECtHR, 22 June 2000.

[19] *Sramek* v. *Austria*, note 18 above, para. 36. See also *Coême and others* v. *Belgium*, ECtHR, 22 June 2000.

[20] *Campbell and Fell*, note 18 above, para. 78.

[21] In the case of *Langborger* v. *Sweden*, ECtHR, 22 June 1989, the Housing and Tenancy Court was not accepted in a case concerning the right of the applicant to stay outside the organisations that had nominated the lay assessors. However, in this case, the European Court also commented that such members 'appear in principle to be extremely well qualified to participate in the adjudication of disputes between landlords and tenants and the specific questions which may arise in such disputes' (para. 34).

[22] *Zander* v. *Sweden*, ECtHR, 25 November 1993.

scientists and other fields of expertise, together with lay judges with experience derived from differing areas of society, seems to be compatible with the ECHR. Preferably, such a tribunal could even be employed on appeal, although the need for laymen becomes less pronounced at the later stages of cases. As the Swedish environmental court system shows, the capability exists of adjusting the procedural rules to make it possible for administrative, private and criminal law cases to be dealt with in the same line of appeal. Such a solution would surely improve both the legal certainty and the 'environmental effectiveness' of the system, as well as accessibility for the public concerned. Furthermore, demands for legal protection of rights and obligations under the ECHR would be made possible.

3.3 Scope of review

Another issue of vital importance for the success of third party interests to be heard relates to those matters that can be decided on appeal. More precisely, what types of decision can be appealed, and to what extent? In this respect, there is much variety in the environmental procedures of European countries. This issue is closely related to the 'result' of an appeal, where one can distinguish between a reformatory and a cassatory procedure.

Again, Swedish law serves as an example. Most decisions of the environmental authorities are subject to appeal before the Environmental Courts and the procedure is reformatory. The essence of such a procedure is that the appellate body has the authority to replace the decision with a new one. To apply an expression of English law, the court 'sits in the chair' and decides the case in question on its merits. Of course, there can be restrictions due to the particulars of the case, such as who made the appeal, and what it was about. For example, if somebody complains on a permit with regard exclusively to conditions on noise, the appellate body cannot change the conditions on discharges in water. Furthermore, if the deciding authority has rejected an application for a permit, the 'two-instances principle' causes difficulties for the appeal body to issue the permit.[23] If the applicant makes a successful appeal, the case will accordingly be referred back to the deciding authority. On the other hand, if the case is 'open' – meaning that both sides have appealed and the complaints are about the permissibility of the activity as a whole – the decision can be anything between rejection of the application and full success for the applicant.

In Sweden and Finland, a reformatory procedure is prevalent, meaning that the appellate body can change to decision on the merits. However, in most countries, the first step of appeal is made within the administration, usually to the government, or to governmental agencies. Thus far, the proceedings and scope of review in these

---

[23] However, that is the principal rule. Certain kinds of 'permits' can be characterised as yes- or no-decisions (e.g. exemptions from the prohibition to build in protected areas) and in such cases the appellate body is free to grant the applicant what he or she wants.

countries is still complete and reformatory, whereas the subsequent court examination is commonly a judicial review or a pure legality control. Principles of civil procedure are often applied, which can be decisive on the burden of proof and litigation costs. The procedure is cassatory, meaning that the reviewing court cannot replace the contested decision with a new one, only accept or quash it. Such an approach is found in the United Kingdom, where environmental decisions can be the subject of judicial review in the High Court. In Germany, the corresponding review is undertaken by the administrative courts,[24] and the German court examination, as well as the French, is restricted to a legality control which does not, with some exceptions, include a full review.[25] Finally, unlike the administrative appeal, the application for judicial review commonly does not have a suspensive effect on the decision. Admittedly, the applicant can ask for an injunction. However, such a move can be met with a demand for bonds or undertakings in damages, which sometimes render the appeal meaningless.[26]

The prospects of success for members of the public to challenge an administrative decision are evidently greater if the possibility exists of a full trial, invoking all interests at stake. When combined with the potential to challenge an omission on behalf of the administration in charge of protecting the environment, this has proved to be quite an effective means for frustrated stakeholders. This issue has been raised in relation to the EC environmental liability directive, which states that the public concerned – including NGOs – shall have access to court to challenge the procedural and substantial legality of decisions, acts or failures to act of the competent authority under the directive.[27] If a polluter party does not abide by the requirements of the competent authority, to undertake the *necessary* remedial measures (including risk assessment), the authority *may* undertake the measures itself.[28]

But what if the competent authority is asked by a member of the public to order a polluter to undertake specific measures, but the authority declares that it will not intervene or that the measures already undertaken are 'necessary' and therefore sufficient? Not only are such 'zero-decisions' not challengeable in all systems, but also the possibility for the court to determine what is 'necessary' or 'adequate' or what poses a 'risk' is clearly limited if only the legality of a decision is to be reviewed. Even with an all-European tendency for the courts to broaden the scope of review and the concepts of legality, these remedies still have their inherent restrictions. The opposite is true when concerned parties can force an authority to take a decision that can

---

[24] See Rehbinder 2002 pp. 241f.   [25] See Prieur and Makowiak 2002 p. 229.

[26] This happened e.g. in the famous case, C-44/95, *R* v. *Secretary of State for the Environment, ex parte Royal Society for the Protection of Birds* (Lappel Bank case), [1996] ECR I-3805, where the Royal Society for the Protection of Birds (RSPB) launched a judicial review of the decision to build a parking lot in the area in question. The House of Lords asked for a preliminary ruling by the ECJ, but at the same time refused interim relief. When the ECJ ruled on the matter in favour of the RSPB, the parking lot had already been built. See Castle *et al.* 2004, p. 38.

[27] European Community Directive 2004/35/EC on Environmental Liability with Regard to the Prevention and Remedying of Environmental Damage, [2004] *Official Journal* (OJ) L143/56, Art. 13(1).

[28] *Ibid.*, Arts. 6 and 7, and Annex II.

then be challenged on its merits in a reformatory procedure. On appeal, the public concerned can request the appellate body to review the position of the particular authority and from the same or subsequent facts decide either to intervene directly, or to remit the case back for a fresh decision. Thus, the appellate body makes its own estimation on what is necessary and imposes a risk on its own investigation.

3.4 Scope of decisions

Another characteristic of environmental decision-making with a considerable effect on the possibilities open to the public to participate in decision-making, relates to the fact that the decisions concerning an activity or installation are often made in stages. In particular, larger undertakings often comprise several phases of administrative decisions from planning to the actual issuance of a permit. In Sweden, the government first decides the permissibility of some larger projects (infrastructures, mines and so on), and that decision is binding for the subsequent permit procedure. At the same time, the government's decision can be taken at such an early stage that stakeholders cannot be identified and therefore deprived of the potential to launch a judicial review on the initial decision.[29] To my understanding, this state of affairs is incompatible with both the ECHR and the Aarhus Convention.

Situations also occur of slicing or 'sectioning' that may be technically motivated and not controversial. However, there are other examples, such as where the application for a permit is narrowed down to the extreme to avoid litigation costs and the legal impediments associated with larger projects. Disintegration and sectioning of decision-making can be related to different activities within the same installation (an activity within a larger operation is sometimes given a separate licence, despite the rather clear technical link to the main activity) or different locations (a permit is given for dredging operations in one place and another for the disposal of the sludge two kilometres away in the same watercourse). Furthermore, different disturbances and environmental impacts from an activity can be regulated by several authorities and decisions. This can be made both on traditional reasons and by way of modern 'smart licences', that is, permits that only cover certain aspects of the activity.

From the applicant's viewpoint, the main reason for sectioning is, of course, to gain time and save costs by narrowing the scope of examination. It is often more convenient from both the operator's and society's point of view to examine only that part of the activity/installation intended to be developed, reconstructed or changed. Sectioning of the permit procedure is sometimes also preferable for the permit body itself, as time and costs for the authority will be reduced if there is a chance of submitting parts of the case to another decision-maker. No matter what the motives for sectioning are, such an order can drastically weaken any hope of the public concerned to participate in and challenge such decision-making. To employ salami-slicing tactics to avoid the

---

[29] [2004] *Regeringsrättens årsbok* (RÅ) Ref. 108.

demand for a consultation process in accordance with the EIA directive, or to avoid permit procedures in order to get away from a decision that is challengeable by NGOs, are two examples.[30]

In relation to access to justice, the position of the public concerned is affected by disintegrated decision-making. Such a disintegrated approach makes it practically impossible to reach a holistic evaluation of the likely consequences of a particular decision from the perspective of environmental protection. One aspect of a project might seem defensible in environmental justice terms if it were to be considered in isolation, but the advantage is lost if all the interrelated aspects of the decision are considered together. Therefore, in order to enhance the acceptance of decisions, the aim should be to include the interests of the public concerned as early as possible in such decision-making.

3.5 Actors I: private parties

In any article on access to justice, something must be said of the actors. The rules on standing were a much-contested issue in the deliberations leading to the 1998 Aarhus Convention, as well as the aftermath in relation to the procedures for its implementation. In addition to the deeper analyses that have been made on the issue, it is appropriate here to contribute a few remarks. The Swedish position can serve as a starting-point.

Those affected by an environmental decision involving activities generating a disturbance to their surroundings should possess the means of challenging it. In relation to traditional hazardous activities and water operations, the determination of the class – those 'concerned' – is straightforward, and depends on the kinds of disturbance (discharges into air and water, noise, odour, traffic and so on) that the person in question can be affected by, and at what distance. An extensive case law from the Swedish Supreme Court and the Environmental Court of Appeal illustrates this.[31] Once the 'concern' of the individual has been established, the scope of review is complete, meaning that he or she can refer to both individual and public interests in favour of the cause. No arguments are precluded.

The definition of who is concerned differs from one national legal order to another. Obviously, this goes for the delimitation of those who are affected by disturbances from different activities, something that is regularly decided in national case law. The comparison is also complicated by the fact that 'environmental cases' cover a wide range of different activities that are regulated in different ways; from neighbourhood

---

[30] In both the Aarhus Convention, note 1 above, Art. 9(2), and the new provisions on access to justice in EC law (e.g. the IPPC Directive and the EIA Directive), the possibilities open up for NGOs to challenge environmental decisions connected to the permit procedure.

[31] [2004] *Nytt juridiskt arkiv* (NJA) 590. See also the decisions by the Environmental Court of Appeal, MÖD 2002:92, MÖD 2 May 2003; M 438-03, MÖD 2003:98, MÖD 2003:99, MÖD 3 December 2002; M 9885-02, MÖD 2003:56; see note 10 above.

issues to major IPPC-activities, from pesticides and chemicals to discharges in water, nature conservation and endangered species. Although there are differences between the national approaches on who constitute the 'public concerned', some general observations can be made.

Generally speaking, one may say that the wider the possibilities to challenge a decision, the narrower the scope of the trial. On the one hand, in jurisdictions allowing *actio popularis* in environmental cases, the scope of trial is usually limited to the legality of the decision in a rather narrow sense. On the other hand, when the scope of review is full, only the 'concerned parties' can take such an initiative. Even within this category, the scope of persons can differ. This is especially true with regard to persons invoking 'competing interests'. In many countries, they are regarded as 'third parties' with no say, but there are also examples showing the opposite. Thus, in a Swedish case, invoking competing interests concerning the exploitation of a natural resource (a gravel pit for the extraction of gravel or for recharging groundwater) was sufficient to constitute a right to appeal.[32] In other countries, even competitors in business can invoke their interest. In the English case, *Rockware Glass Ltd* v. *Chester City Council*, a competitor of the company that obtained a permit for glass production was granted leave to launch a judicial review in relation to that decision. The High Court quashed the permit, stating that the permit body had misinterpreted the technical standards for the discharges of NO_x, which could distort the market for glass.[33]

Moreover, different categories of persons involved in an environmental case can be treated differently. This seems to be particularly distinct in countries with a traditional view on the actors involved in environmental cases, for example concerning permits. According to that administrative tradition, the case is primarily between the applicant (the operator) and the authority. All others are outsiders. An example of this can be found in the United Kingdom, where only the applicant can make an administrative appeal (to the Secretary of State). The public concerned can challenge the legality of the decision only by way of an application for judicial review.[34]

However, one of the most significant restrictions from an environmental point of view is to be found in the protective law theory ('*Schutznormentheorie*'). It was originally developed in German jurisprudence but has also been employed in varying degrees in many other countries. According to this theory, a private party can only rely on his or her own interests in bringing a case: the interests of others affected by the decision – including public interests – cannot be invoked. In the German version, the concerned person cannot invoke such 'other' interests even when he or she has been

---

[32] MÖD 2003:3; see note 10 above.

[33] Administrative Court/High Court, 24 October 2005, [2006] *Environmental Law Review* (ELR) 30. The applicant for the permit, Quinn Glass Ltd, appealed before the Court of Appeal, but was dismissed, Court of Appeal, 15 June 2006, [2007] ELR 3. There is a similar case in the Netherlands, where an outlet retailer in Roosendaal was allowed to appeal a planning permit to open a competing discount warehouse in Leyland, Raad van State (ABR) 2007-0307 in Case No. 200606317/1.

[34] The applicant can also launch a judicial review of the decision of the Secretary of State.

allowed to challenge a decision on the basis of the existence of individual interests.[35] In other countries, the protective law principle may instead determine who should be allowed to appeal in certain cases.[36] The most common situation occurs in cases concerning nature conservation and biodiversity, which are not considered to concern private interests and therefore cannot be challenged by individuals.[37]

3.6 Actors II: environmental NGOs

Generally speaking, third-party interests in environmental cases are represented by concerned individuals, *ad hoc* groups and established environmental organisations. *Ad hoc* groups are locally founded and concentrate on a single environmental issue. Among the established NGOs, there are both national (for example, the Swedish Society for Nature Conservation, the RSPB in the United Kingdom, and the Dutch Stichting Natuur en Milieu) and international ones (such as Greenpeace, Friends of the Earth, and WWF).

The attitudes in different jurisdictions differ with regard to NGOs, for example, in terms of the types of organisation allowed to participate and/or appeal. There are also differences on what kinds of decision can be challenged by them. Environmental NGOs in Sweden cannot *initiate* any cases with regard to environmental matters, but can only appeal certain permit decisions.[38] As mentioned earlier, the delimitation of NGOs in Sweden is strict and only a few are let into the environmental arena. *Ad hoc* groups have no standing at all.[39]

The possibilities open for the established NGOs in Sweden's neighbouring countries, Denmark and Norway, are much wider, as they are in most other European countries. However, the Aarhus Convention leaves room for national differences, although in accordance with the spirit of the Convention. It must be seen to be highly questionable as to whether the Swedish order meets this requirement. The Netherlands and the United Kingdom can be taken as the opposite, where access to justice for organisations is particularly wide. In these countries, both *ad hoc* groups and very small organisations have a standing so long as they are defending an environmental interest according to their statutes and previous activities. Finally, in other countries,

---

[35] See Rehbinder 2002 pp. 233f.   [36] For Swedish cases, see MÖD 2001:29, MÖD 2005:8, note 10 above.

[37] This line of argument can also be found in European Community law. In C-127/02, *Landelijke Vereniging tot Behoud van de Waddenzee and Nederlandse Vereniging tot Bescherming van Vogels* v. *Staatssecretaris van Landbouw, Natuurbeheer en Visserij* (Waddenzee case) [2004] ECR I-7405, paras. 140–4, Advocate General Kokott suggested that direct applicable provisions of EC directives be divided into two categories: those that carried rights of prohibition and those that gave grounds for entitlements. Only in relation to the latter are member states obliged to offer a procedural entrance for concerned parties. For the provisions that carried rights of prohibition, individuals may rely on the EC provision only in so far as avenues of legal redress against infringements were available under national law.

[38] Chapter 16, section 13, of the Environmental Code, MÖD 2007:17.

[39] However, both *ad hoc* groups and established NGOs – irrespective of the numbers of members – can initiate certain class actions in civil law cases according to the Environmental Code.

a common solution is to list or register those NGOs acceptable for making environmental challenges. Germany and Finland are examples of this order, which generally excludes *ad hoc* groups from standing.[40]

The solution reached in EC Regulation No. 1367/2006 on access to justice in environmental matters to EU institutions and bodies involves the following criteria: independent and non-profit-making according to national law, a stated objective of promoting environmental protection, and being in existence for more than two years. Provisions will be adopted by the Commission to ensure a transparent and consistent application (Article 11). It is reasonable to believe that these criteria will have an indirect impact on views on this issue in the member states. It should be noted, though, that this order excludes *ad hoc* groups, which can be seen as a major shortcoming from the viewpoint of environmental justice.

Another interesting issue from a justice point of view is the possibility open to organisations to represent concerned individuals in environmental cases. In that way, the resources and expertise of the NGOs would contribute to justice for the individual. At the same time, the organisation in question would still draw up its own priorities on what cases should be taken on. Friends of the Earth UK has chosen this way of working, having achieved 'Specialist Quality Mark' which enables them to represent individuals who benefit from legal aid. In the German understanding of the Aarhus Convention, the demand for NGO standing is essentially met by widening the extent of the possibility for them to represent concerned individuals, a viewpoint that has been heavily criticized.[41]

Finally, the position of the NGOs is an issue not only for the national systems. In many countries, the 'monistic' approach to international conventions leads to immediate effects. But, even in those EU member states that are dualistic, the Aarhus Convention and the subsequent EC directives can have effects that are perhaps unexpected. The main reason for this is the development of the doctrine of 'direct effect' in EC law. Traditionally, this has only been given to unconditional and sufficiently precise provisions in EC directives that entail individual rights. The development of case law in the European Court of Justice (ECJ) shows, however, that the concept of direct applicability is applied in a broader sense. This 'primacy of EC law' can be described as follows: 'Direct effect is the obligation of the court or another authority to apply the relevant provision of Community law, either as a norm which governs the case or a standard for legal review.'[42] This is taken to mean that the courts of the member states shall apply those provisions of EC directives that are unconditional and sufficiently clear, irrespective of any 'individual rights'.[43] However, this effect is worthless if no one can initiate it. In the light of the Aarhus Convention and the need for conformity of EC law in all twenty-seven member states, it would not be too

---

[40] See Milieu 2007, pp. 8–9 and Table 1. Also, Dross 2005 p. 68f; Kuusiniemi 2002 pp. 187ff.
[41] See Milieu 2007 p. 10 and Table 4.   [42] Prechal 2005 p. 241.
[43] See e.g. the judgement by the ECJ, C-237/07, *Dieter Janecek* v. *Freistaat Bayern* of 25 July 2008 (n.y.r.).

surprising if the ECJ in the near future found that the NGOs were the ones carrying these interests and for whom the national legal systems, therefore, should offer the chance of challenging any infringement before the courts.[44] I suggest it is a matter of personal preference whether or not one could call this 'to have a right'.

4 Concluding remarks

At the outset, I began with the presumption that, when it comes to environmental decision-making, a *broad consideration* of issues at an *early stage*, when *all actors* can have their say and *all interests can be invoked*, is crucial to bringing about environmental justice. I am aware that strong NIMBY factors[45] in the environmental area render this presumption controversial. Evidently, well-educated and financially strong neighbours possess greater opportunities to make their voices heard and thereby block a particular project, regardless of its societal benefits. In the Swedish debate, fierce local opinions against wind-farms have been used as an example. However, I do believe that this is a phenomenon that has to be dealt with in a democratic society with other means, such as alternative dispute resolution (ADR) and similar mechanisms for gaining approval. In the long run, widened public participation and access to justice in decision-making procedures are necessary in our societies and are also prerequisites for the effectiveness of environmental legislation, at both national and international levels.

In this article, I have discussed certain procedural issues that are vital if a broad access to justice is to be achieved in more than merely the formal sense. The following conclusions can be drawn:

- The system: Too many routes of appeal will have a constraining effect on the possibilities open to challenging environmental decisions. It also creates divergences in case law. The complexity of environmental law suggests that the deciding bodies (tribunals and courts) must be well equipped with both lawyers and technicians. Preferably, this body should lie outside the ordinary courts system. At the same time, the criteria of 'fair trial', in accordance with the ECHR, have to be met. A need also exists for an environmental procedure whereby the duty to investigate the particulars of a case lies primarily on the deciding bodies, in order to secure the protection of the environment and to avoid weaker parties becoming entirely dependent on technical consultants and lawyers.

---

[44] However, this may be an over-optimistic hope. Recently, the European judiciary has delivered two judgments that show that the court can be extremely traditional in its views on access to justice issues: T-94/04, *European Environmental Bureau* v. *Commission of the European Communities* (Paraquat case), [2005] ECR II-4919; and C-216/05, *Commission* v. *Ireland* [2006] ECR I-10787. The Aarhus Convention Compliance Committee has taken the contrary position by stating that 'some members of the public' must have access to justice in such cases (Communication ACCC/C/2006/18 (Denmark), ECE/MP.PP/2008/5/Add.4).

[45] NIMBY ('Not In My Backyard') is a term describing the general truth that no one wants 'disturbing activities' in their vicinity.

- Scope of review: The prospects of success for members of the public in challenging an administrative decision is evidently greater if the possibility exists of a full trial, invoking all interests. No arguments should be precluded. If an appeal is made, the decision at stake should be suspended. Modern thinking in environmental law strongly suggests that a case should not be decided until the last word is spoken, unless the appellate body says differently. Another vital factor lies in the appellate body being able to replace the authority's decision with a new one, thereby being able to effectively control whether the authorised decision is in accordance with environmental legislation.
- Scope of decision: A disintegrated approach counteracts a holistic evaluation of the likely consequences of the decision from the perspective of environmental protection. Therefore, in order to enhance the acceptance of decisions, the aim should be to include the full interests of the public concerned at the earliest possible time in the decision-making procedure.
- Actors: An important factor from the justice perspective is that individuals who are concerned by an environmental decision should have the possibility open to them to challenge it, irrespective of what kind of activity it concerns. The delimitation of the class of 'public concerned' should be wide, and preferably include directly involved competitors to counteract distortions in the market. Third parties should be treated on equal terms with other parties to the case. Finally, the procedure should allow all kinds of environmental organisations defending an environmental interest to participate and have access to justice. From a democratic point of view, it is not acceptable that only the larger and more established NGOs are invited. *Ad hoc* groups play an important role as defenders of environmental justice.

The Aarhus Convention has been met with enthusiasm from environmentalists, lawyers representing third party interests, environmental NGOs and academics. The response from the governments of the EU member states has been less positive. According to some of these, there is no urgent need to discuss such matters in an EU context, except for certain minor issues. This attitude is probably the true reason why the proposed Directive on Access to Justice in Environmental Matter[46] will never be realised, except perhaps in a watered-down version. There have even been some efforts in the internal discussions among politicians on how to decrease possibilities for the public concerned to participate in environmental decision-making. Applying the national scope in Article 2(5) of the Aarhus Convention to make more stringent the conditions for environmental NGOs is just one example. Another is the introduction of different fees and other economic barriers for weaker parties. Both Ireland and Denmark have – after signing the Convention – introduced fees for those wishing to participate in decision-making or to make an appeal in environmental cases.[47] The

---

[46] COM (2003) 624 final.
[47] According to the ECJ judgment in the *Irish fees* case (see note 43 above), this is acceptable so long as the fees are not fixed at a level that would hinder EC law from being fully effective.

strong resistance by Swedish industry to any proposal increasing the possibilities open to environmental NGOs to participate in judicial proceedings is another worrying tendency. These examples show what is perhaps self-evident, that there is an unbroken and uninterrupted need to keep alive the discussion on access to justice!

Bibliography

Bonet, M. T., 2002. 'Public Environmental Law in Spain', in R. Seerden, M. Heldeweg and K. Deketelaere (eds.), *Public Environmental Law in the European Union and the United States: A Comparative Analysis*. The Hague, London and Boston: Kluwer Law International.

Castle, P., Day, M., Hatton, C., and Stokes, P., 2004. 'The Environmental Justice Project', available at www.wwf.org.uk/filelibrary/pdf/envirojustice.pdf.

Dross, M., 2005. 'Germany', in N. de Sadeleer, G. Roller and M. Dross (eds.), *Access to Justice in Environmental Matters and the Role of the NGOs*. Groeningen: Europa Law Publishing, 65.

Jones, B., and Parpworth, N., 2004. *Environmental Liabilities*. Crayford (Kent, UK): Shaw & Sons.

Kuusiniemi, K., 2002. 'Finland', in J. Ebbesson (ed.), *Access to Justice in Environmental Matters in the EU – Accès à la justice en matière d'environnement dans l'UE*. The Hague, London and New York: Kluwer Law International, 177.

Macrory, R., 2003. *Environmental Tribunals*. London: Department for Environment, Food and Rural Affairs.

Milieu, 2007. *Summary Report on the Inventory of EU Member States' Measures on Access to Justice in Environmental Matters*. Brussels: Milieu Ltd, also available at http://ec.europa.eu/environment/aarhus/study_access.htm.

Prechal, S., 2005. *Directives in EC Law*. 2nd edn, Oxford: Oxford University Press.

Prieur, M., and Makowiak, J., 2002. 'France', in J. Ebbesson (ed.), *Access to Justice in Environmental Matters in the EU – Accès à la justice en matière d'environnement dans l'UE*. The Hague, London and New York: Kluwer Law International.

Rehbinder, E., 2002. 'Germany', in J. Ebbesson (ed.), *Access to Justice in Environmental Matters in the EU – Accès à la justice en matière d'environnement dans l'UE*. The Hague, London and New York: Kluwer Law International.

UNECE, 2000. *The Aarhus Convention: An Implementation Guide*. New York and Geneva: United Nations.

10

Environmental justice in the European Court of Justice

LUDWIG KRÄMER

1 The discussion on environmental justice in the United States

The notion of environmental justice, as far as can be seen, has never been used in European Community (EC) environmental legislation or, indeed, by the European judiciary, i.e. the European Court of Justice (ECJ) or the Court of First Instance (CFI). In trying to explain the reason for this, it is necessary to have a look at the origin of this notion. It is obvious that it does not stem from (continental) European law, but that it was developed in the United States, thus in the context of Anglo-Saxon law. Moreover, the notion seems to stem from social science rather than law.

The concept of environmental justice first appeared at the US federal level in the Presidential Executive Order 12898 of 1994.[1] This Order, entitled 'Federal actions to address environmental justice in minority populations and low income populations', asked the federal administration to address the impact of environmental measures on minority populations and low-income groups.[2] It was a reaction to the fact that studies, reports and publications since the early 1970s had linked the siting of waste facilities with race. They had also shown that poor people and people of colour in the United States suffered disproportionately from environmental risks or pollution, and that they had greater difficulties in accessing information, in participating in decision-making and in accessing courts in environmental matters. Subsequently, public policy addressed these issues. For example, the US Environment Protection Agency (EPA) defined environmental justice as:

> the fair treatment and meaningful involvement of all people regardless of race, colour, national origin, or income with respect to the development, implementation, and enforcement of environmental laws, regulations and policies... It will be achieved, when everyone enjoys equal access to the decision-making process to have a healthy environment in which to live, learn and work.[3]

[1] Executive Order 12898 of 11 February 1994.
[2] *Ibid.*, section 1-101: '[E]ach Federal agency shall make achieving environmental justice part of its mission by identifying and addressing, as appropriate, disproportionally high and adverse human health or environmental effects of its programs, policies and activities on minority populations and low income populations in the United States.'
[3] Environment Protection Agency, www.epa.gov/environmentaljustice/index.html.

Of course, since the mid-1990s, the discussion in the United States has evolved. There are in particular two trends which appear to have gained influence in the discussion. On the one hand, there is less emphasis put on the aspects of social, ethnic or racial discrimination of minority groups in environmental policy matters and more focus on the rights of all citizens to a clean and healthy environment. An example of this tendency might be the Sierra Club's 'Environmental Justice Principles' of 2001.[4] These principles support the precautionary principle, favour an end to pollution and then put the main emphasis on the human right to a clean and healthy environment which they substantiate in eight 'rights'.[5] As regards the social aspects, these principles are rather discreet. For example, under the right to participate, they mention that '[b]arriers to participation (cultural, linguistic, geographic, economic, other) should be addressed', and, under the right to equal protection, it is stated that: 'Laws, policies, regulations, or criteria that result in disproportionate impact are discriminatory, whether or not such a result was intended, and should be corrected.' The right to equity states that: 'Environmentally degrading land uses should be avoided, but when such uses occur, they should be equitably sited taking into account all environmental and community impacts.' Finally, the principles oppose efforts to dispossess indigenous people of their lands, their cultures, and their right to self-determination. As can be seen from this short presentation, social injustice in environmental policy is only addressed in an indirect way.

On the other hand, the increasing discussion on globalisation has turned the attention to social aspects of environmental policies at the global level. In these discussions, increasing attention was given to the topics of climate change, the effects of free trade on the social conditions of third world countries, the depletion of tropical forests, and the impacts of genetically modified seeds, plants and products on local agriculture and trade. Overall, these global subjects turned some attention away from the 'environmental justice for minority groups' discussions within the United States.

'Environmental justice' in the United States discussion is thus understood here as the request for environmental justice, voiced by low-income and other minority groups, in particular of ethnic groups. This request was progressively transformed into attempts to improve decision-making and access to information, and to take better into consideration the concerns of minority groups. At present, the notion of environmental justice seems to have lost its cry for more justice, but is being turned into a more general request for better environmental protection.

---

[4] Sierra Club, www.sierraclub.org/policy/conservation/justice.asp.
[5] Sierra Club (note 4, above). The most significant for the purposes of the present chapter are: (1) the reduction of corporate influence; (2) the right to equal protection and the avoiding of disproportionate charges to certain groups; (3) the right to enjoy natural resources; (4) the rights of indigenous populations; (5) the siting of facilities and infrastructure projects (the right to equity); (6) intergenerational equity; (7) the right to know; (8) the right to participate in decision-making.

2 Environmental justice in the European Union

If one puts the question to a European lawyer who does not know the discussion in the United States and its evolution during the last thirty years, of what he or she understands by environmental justice, the answer would probably be that environmental justice is the attempt to do justice to the environment by ensuring that, in the outcome of conflicts of interest in administrative – and private – decision-making, the environment is not permanently and systematically the loser. It is more than unlikely that the European lawyer would link the notion to the environmental situation of people of colour or low-income groups, thus of minority groups, of the population. It is submitted that in the European Union, there is no perception of any problem that links the social status – ethnic, religious, low-income or other minority – of certain groups of the population to the concerns for environmental injustice in decision-making, enforcement or other activities of the administration. Of course, the European Union also has minority groups, such as immigrants from Africa, Asia or Eastern Europe, ethnic or religious minorities; and, while, officially, the policy in most EU member states is to favour social integration and not to accept social, ethnic or religious segregation, it is a fact that there are low-income quarters in European agglomerations as well.

Practically nothing is known about any disproportionate effect of environmental laws, regulations and activities on such neighbourhoods. Social science and political science research lack in this regard, and the effect of general, EC-wide or at least national-wide legislation certainly has the effect that low income or other minority groups also profit from such legislation. An example might be the EC directive which requires that all urban agglomerations with more than 2,000 persons be equipped with urban waste water treatment installations.[6] It would be difficult to differentiate investments according to the social composition of agglomerations, even though planning decisions are taken at local, regional or national, but not at the European level; there is no information available which would suggest that poorer agglomerations have seen investments for urban waste water treatment not made or made later than wealthier agglomerations. Other examples concern the quality of drinking water or waste collection by municipalities. Despite harmonised EC legislation on drinking water since 1985,[7] it is still advised not to drink tap water in Southern Europe in summer. However, this is due to general implementation and enforcement problems of environmental law and does not differentiate according to special socially underprivileged groups. And, as the public collection of household waste is perceived as a general interest service,[8] any court in Europe would probably immediately interfere for reasons of

---

[6] Directive 91/271/EEC Concerning Urban Waste Water Treatment, [1991] *Official Journal* (OJ) L135/40.

[7] Directive 80/778/EEC on the Quality of Drinking Water, [1980] OJ L229/11.

[8] Article 16 of the EC Treaty might be mentioned, which states that, 'given the place occupied by services of general economic interest in the shared values of the Union as well as their role in promoting social and territorial cohesion, the Community and the Member States, each within their respective powers and within

discrimination (equality of citizens before the law), if waste were not collected from certain groups or quarters – independently from the question whether this relates to environmental justice or not.

Of course, the EC also knows the notion of NIMBY.[9] The siting of waste incinerators, nuclear waste landfills, chemical industries etc., but also of infrastructure projects such as airports or motorways, poses problems in almost all EU member states. And it would be an illusion to believe that the procedures for town and country planning do not lead to planning decisions that are influenced by social and political interests of persons or groups which are better organised, represented and protected than those of minority groups. Overall, though, even among minority groups, there appears to be no perception of sites for facilities being targeted to minority neighbourhoods. This might be due to the policy of more than one hundred years of age to separate, if possible, the residential and industrial areas and concentrate (polluting) industries and infrastructure projects away from places where people live. Other reasons might be the fact that environmental policy in Western Europe – at least in the past – laid down its standards for environmental emissions mainly in legislative instruments, which gave citizens the impression of equality before the law.

Whether this short analysis is correct or not, it seems that over the last thirty years there were no significant complaints on the territory of the European Union that claimed environmental justice for minority groups and argued that the siting of polluting or hazardous facilities had deliberately been organised in a way that minority or low-income groups had been disproportionately affected.

Talking about environmental justice and the European Court of Justice thus leads into a dilemma: either the notion is understood in the sense of US Executive Order 12898, to ensure that environmental policies, programmes or activities do not discriminate against minority or low-income groups. Then this contribution can quickly be brought to an end. Indeed, there are no cases decided by the Court of Justice in this regard; and, according to what was said above, there was no political or societal concern in this regard within the European Union.[10] This conclusion is only logical: no national court felt the need to submit such cases to the Court of Justice, as such cases did not either occur at national level. And, for the same reason, the European Commission which brings approximately 75 per cent of all environmental cases before the Court of Justice,[11] had not become aware of such cases either.

---

the scope of application of this Treaty, shall take care that such services operate on the basis of principles and conditions which enable them to fulfil their missions'. It is generally accepted that this provision may also justify impediments to free trade within the EC.

[9] NIMBY ('Not In My Backyard') describes the attitude of citizens who oppose polluting or hazardous facilities in their neighbourhood.

[10] See also de Sadeleer in Chapter 23 of this volume.

[11] See L. Krämer, 'Statistics on Environmental Judgments by the EC Court of Justice' (2006) *Journal of Environmental Law* 407.

The alternative to this approach, which will be followed hereafter, is to adopt a broader view of 'environmental justice', following in large measure the description of the US Environmental Protection Agency or the principles of the United States Sierra Club. The rulings of the European judicature are therefore to be examined, in order to assess to what extent the principles of environmental justice, as formulated by the Sierra Club, are reflected in its jurisprudence.

Before this analysis starts, however, it needs to be underlined that cases are brought before the Court of Justice mainly by the European Commission or by national courts.[12] The action of the Commission is mainly addressed to Member States, where national legislation or practice does not conform to EC law. Individuals and environmental organisations may only apply to the Court of Justice, where they are the addressees of an administrative decision, or where such a decision is of direct and individual concern to them. This means that standing for minority groups before the Court of Justice is very difficult to obtain. Furthermore, there is no contingency fee system in the EC. This has the consequence that the legal advocates are not willing to take, at their own risk, cases to the Court, in order to challenge a traditional interpretation where the likelihood of success is particularly uncertain. This is a significant difference to the structure of the United States, where the contingency fee system is an embedded aspect of litigation, which generally supports access to courts in borderline cases.

3 The European Court of Justice and environmental justice

3.1 *The constraining of corporate influence*

In a number of judgments, the Court of Justice has discussed the limits for member states to give specific interest groups a specific advantage in environmental protection matters. In view of the continued importance of agricultural policy at the EC level, it is of no surprise that farmers were the first interest group affected by environment protection. In 1979, the EC introduced legislation to protect wild living birds and their habitats.[13] Activities which could significantly disturb birds in those habitats were forbidden. Germany tried to maintain a provision which had existed for decades in Germany, according to which ordinary agricultural activity did not constitute a significant disturbance. The Court declared that provision incompatible with the objective of the protection of habitats.[14]

When the Community limited the effluents from agriculture into waters, it asked member states to designate zones where there was a risk of exceeding the nitrate levels. For such zones, member states had to take measures in order to contain that

---

[12] From 1976 to 2006, of a total of 471 cases in environmental matters before the Court of Justice, the Commission submitted 328 and national courts 97: see Krämer (note 11 above).

[13] Directive 79/409/EEC on the Conservation of Wild Birds [1979] OJ L103/1.

[14] Case C-412/85, *Commission* v. *Germany* [1987] ECR 3503.

risk and had eventually even to limit the number of animals per hectare.[15] The Court condemned Spain and France for not having designated such vulnerable zones – which then would not require them to take measures.[16] For France, the consequence of omitting the taking of measures led to further condemnations, because the high nitrate levels in water were found to have returned to the surface waters and drinking waters in Brittany.[17] Furthermore, the Court rejected the argument of some farmers that the limitation of livestock constituted an expropriation; rather, it saw the EC legislation dealing with the exercise of property as being proportionate to the objective pursued.[18]

The attempt to give special protection to farmers was also at the root of another case against Germany. Germany had prohibited the import of live crayfish, but had at the same time given very generous derogations to local cultivators and traders. It was therefore not based on the argument that the import ban was necessary to protect indigenous species.[19]

In the industrial area, the EC legislation required that persons who exercised a dangerous or polluting activity needed a permit. Normally, a permit contains the conditions under which the activity may be exercised, in order to allow the administration, the public and the holder of the permit to know precisely what rights and obligations existed under the permit. For industrial activities, a tacit permit is advantageous, because no restrictions other than those that are laid down in the legislation, apply in such a case, and the activities would be less controlled. In view of protecting the environment, however, the Court considered it incompatible with EC law that a permit could be given tacitly, upon an application and the administration's omission to react within a certain time-span.[20]

The attempts to allow industry to work without a permit were particularly numerous in the waste sector. This was mainly practised through efforts to declare the material which was treated, not to be 'waste', but to be 'products', 'by-products', 'secondary raw materials' or otherwise. The Court very largely resisted these attempts and held that recoverable, recyclable materials, materials which had an economic value or were traded at stock-exchanges constituted waste.[21] Recently, however, it considered pig slurry which was to be spread on land, not to be waste, but a 'product' so that

---

[15] Directive 91/676/EEC Concerning the Protection of Waters Against Pollution Caused by Nitrates from Agricultural Sources, [1991] OJ L375/1.

[16] Cases C-71/97, *Commission* v. *Spain* [1998] ECR I-5991 and C-258/00, *Commission* v. *France* [2002] ECR (2002) I-5959.

[17] Cases C-505/03, *Commission* v. *France*, judgment of 28 October 2004, unpublished.

[18] Case C-293/97, *Standley* [1999] ECR I-2603.

[19] Case C-131/93, *Commission* v. *Germany* [1994] ECR (1994) I-3303.

[20] Cases C-360/87, *Commission* v. *Italy* [1991] ECR I-791; C-230/00, *Commission* v. *Belgium* [2001] ECR I-4591.

[21] Cases C-206 and 207/88, *Vessoso and Zanetti* [1990] ECR I-1461, C-359/88, *Zanetti* [1990] ECR I-1509, C-304/94 a.o., *Tombesi and others* [1997] ECR I-3561, C-444/00, *Mayer Parry* [2003] ECR I-6163, C-457/02, *Niselli* [2004] ECR I-10853.

no permit was needed – a judgment which tries to be good to farmers and industrial agriculture.[22]

In order to protect certain activities, member states sometimes provided for local, regional or national monopolies or prevented the export of materials. The ECJ held that such practices were incompatible with EC law in the area of waste oils[23] and recoverable hazardous waste,[24] but allowed the monopoly in the case of a local harbour de-pollution activity and for the recycling of building waste.[25]

Sometimes, the efforts of the ECJ to protect the environment and health are frustrated by successful lobbying by industry of the legislature. Thus, the Court had upheld a provision in EC environmental law, according to which manufacturers, in order to prevent major industrial accidents, had to designate a competent person on the spot who was responsible for the safety of the specific plant.[26] This provision, disliked by industry, was deleted when the relevant legislation was revised in 1996.[27] In 2004, the Court held that soil, which had been contaminated by a leaking tank in a petrol station, constituted 'waste' and could lead to the liability of the petrol company which owned the petrol station.[28] When, in 2005, the Commission proposed a revision of the relevant directive, it suggested the exclusion of unexcavated contaminated soil from its application,[29] as industry had heavily tackled the judgment.

In the nuclear sector, EC law provided that member states had to consult the Commission before they authorised the discharge of waste water from nuclear installations into the water. The ECJ decided to extend the period of such consultations, in order to make them meaningful.[30] Furthermore, it stipulated that the EC was also competent for safety standards for nuclear installations, even though the Euratom Treaty did not explicitly provide for this.[31]

Overall, the Court of Justice successfully resisted attempts to allow groups with vested interest, including local or regional administrations, not to respect EC environmental provisions in a given case, by interpreting any legislative derogation in a restricted way and by letting the general interest of environmental protection prevail.

3.2 Disproportionate charges over certain groups of the population

EC legislation provided that disputes for compensation of damage suffered were to be submitted to the national court of the place where the damage was caused. This

---

[22] Case C-416/02, *Commission v. Spain* [2005] ECR I-7215.
[23] Cases C-172/82, *Inter-Huiles* [1983] ECR 555, C-295/82, *Syndicat national* [1984] ECR 575, C-173/83, *Commission v. France* [1985] ECR 491.
[24] Case C-203/96, *Dusseldorp* [1998] ECR (1998) I-4075.
[25] Cases C-343/95, *Calì* [1997] ECR I-1547, C-209/98, *FFAD* [2000] ECR I-4313.
[26] Case C-190/90, *Commission v. Netherlands* [1992] ECR I-3265.
[27] Compare on the one hand Directive 82/501/EEC, [1982] OJ L230/1, and on the other hand Directive 96/82/EC on the Control of Major-Accident Hazards Involving Dangerous Substances, [1997] OJ L10/13.
[28] Case C-1/03, *van de Walle* [2004] ECR I-7613.
[29] Commission, Proposal for a Directive on Waste, COM(2005) 667 of 21 December 2005.
[30] Case C-187/87, *Saarland* [1988] ECR 5013.   [31] Case C-29/99, *Commission v. Council* [2002] ECR I-11221.

provision became relevant in a dispute between Dutch farmers and French industries which discharged waste from potassium extraction into the River Rhine. The Rhine water became too salty and caused damage to Dutch farmers. The ECJ was asked to decide whether the rule on jurisdiction – referring to the court where the harmful event occurred[32] – should be understood as meaning the court where the damaging act was done (thus the French court), or the court where the damage was caused (thus the Dutch court). It was foreseeable that the outcome of the dispute would depend on the competent court which was likely to apply its national law. The ECJ took a rather Solomonic decision: it gave the persons harmed the possibility to choose either court.[33] This judgment, on the surface quite neutral, in fact enabled the Dutch farmers to obtain compensation; it finally led to a political solution concerning the residues of the French potassium mines.

In 1992, the ECJ upheld an import ban from other member states for hazardous waste which was adopted by the Belgian region of Wallonia. The Court was of the opinion that past uncontrolled imports of waste risked creating serious problems for the Wallonian environment. It found a number of arguments to justify this import ban,[34] in part setting aside its own earlier judgments which had, among other things, stated that such national measures were not allowed to treat EC member states differently. Obviously, the will to protect the Wallonian population against too many imports prevailed over other legal arguments.

Also, the judgment in Case C-293/97, *Standley*, mentioned above, can be cited as belonging to those cases where the Court had to pronounce itself with regard to the argument of a group, that it was disproportionately charged with the costs of pollution.[35] The Court indicated that farmers were not obliged to bear all the costs of water pollution by nitrates, but only those costs that had been caused by their activities. In support of that, the Court used the principle of proportionality and the polluter pays principle, and asked member states to take these principles into consideration in their measures to implement EC legislation.

In general, the Court successfully avoided the situation where some groups, regions or even member states were disproportionately charged with environmental impairment, and succeeded in balancing the diverging interests.

3.3 The right to enjoy the environmental benefits of natural resources

There are numerous decisions where the Court of Justice, in the conflict between the natural resources and other interests, decided in favour of the environment. Only

---

[32] Cf. 1968 Brussels Convention on Jurisdiction and the Enforcement of Judgements in Civil and Commercial Matters (Consolidated version), Article 5(3), [1998] OJ C27/1. The 1968 Brussels Convention has been replaced for most of the EU member states by the EC Regulation No. 44/2001 on Jurisdiction and the Recognition and Enforcement of Judgements in Civil and Commercial Matters, [2001] OJ L12/1.

[33] Case C-21/76, *Mines de potasse* [1976] ECR 1735.

[34] Case C-2/90, *Commission v. Belgium* [1993] ECR I-4431.   [35] Case C-293/97, *Standley* [1999] ECR I-2603.

some can be mentioned here. But it should be underlined that, in particular as regards the legislation on the protection of animals and of habitats, the protection of the environment has largely been ensured, over the last twenty-five years, through the jurisprudence of the Court of Justice which fine-tuned the rather rudimentary provisions of EC legislation, generally trying to protect the environment against the greed of administrations or economic operators.

In Case C-272/80, *Biologische Produkten*, the ECJ decided that a member state was not obliged to allow the free trade of a pesticide which had received an authorisation for marketing in another member state. Rather, the member state was entitled to examine whether its own environmental (soil, water) conditions were different from those which had served for the original testing of the pesticide. If that was the case, the member state was entitled to request a new testing.[36]

In Case 412/85, *Commission* v. *Germany*, the ECJ accepted that a work within a protected European birds habitat could exceptionally be authorised, even if it constituted a significant disturbance of the birds. However, this was only possible if the objective of the work was of an overriding general interest.[37] The criteria which the Court laid down in that judgment have served, for about twenty years, to delimit the protection of natural habitats and economic activities.

In 1993, the ECJ had to decide a case where Spain had not identified a bird habitat and had undertaken work within that area. The Court declared that Spain had disregarded its obligations to identify the area in question. It therefore had to be treated as if it had complied with its obligations. The projects realised within the area in question were thus illegal and had to be taken away.[38] In this as well as in another, subsequent case,[39] the Court established the principle that the consequences of an illegal impairment of the environment had to be eliminated, a principle that is nowhere explicitly laid down in EC law.

EC legislation established requirements for fresh waters needing protection in order to support fish life, but left it to member states to designate the waters to which the directive should apply. The Court decided that, while the member states had a large discretion, such designations could not remain limited to some regions but had to cover the whole national territory.[40]

Finally, according to EC legislation on the protection of habitats and wild fauna and flora,[41] member states may, under certain conditions, authorise measures which significantly disturb the protected species, provided they examine alternatives. In Case C 239/04, *Commission* v. *Portugal*, Portugal had examined some alternatives. However,

---

[36] Case 272/80, *Biologische Produkten* [1981] ECR 3277.
[37] Case 412/85, *Commission* v. *Germany* [1987] ECR 3503.
[38] Case C-355/90, *Commission* v. *Spain* [1993] ECR I-4221.
[39] Case C-365/97, *Commission* v. *Italy* [1997] ECR I-7773.
[40] Case C-322/86, *Commission* v. *Italy* [1988] ECR I-3995.
[41] Directive 92/43/EEC on the Conservation of Natural Habitats and of Wild Fauna and Flora, [1992] OJ L206/7.

the ECJ considered that an alternative which was objectively a reasonable alternative, had not been examined and therefore concluded that Portugal had not examined alternatives.[42]

There is thus a clear line in the Court's reasoning to extend the protection of the natural environment as far as possible under existing legislation and, in the interest of all, to defend the natural environment even against the interests of planning administrations, local interests or specific uses.

3.4 Protection of the indigenous population and its environment

There are only a few cases where the ECJ had to weigh the interest of the local population to be protected and to see its local environment preserved with regard to economic interests. In Case 182/89, *Commission* v. *France*,[43] France had granted import licences for the import of wild cats from Bolivia, but there was a lingering suspicion by the international community[44] that the export licences issued by the Bolivian authorities were not always in conformity with national Bolivian nature protection laws. France had relied on positive advice from its own scientific authorities. The Court held that the French authorities were not entitled to rely on the opinion of their authorities which was not considered to be relevant under the relevant EC legislation. Furthermore, that opinion was not as unambiguous as France thought. What mattered was the situation in Bolivia, not in France. With these arguments, the French measures were declared illegal.

In 1998, Spain looked for a clarification whether it was entitled to decide on the use of the water resources of its rivers and lakes or whether the EC could, in the case of transboundary watercourses, decide by majority decision on the repartition of water. While Spain lost the concrete case in question,[45] it obtained the desired confirmation by the Court: EC decisions on the quantitative management of water resources required unanimity; thus, each member state had the possibility to veto EC decisions in this regard.

In Case T-37/04, *Azores* v. *Council*, fishermen from the Azores Islands (Portugal) asked the Court of First Instance for interim measures against a decision by the Council of Ministers of the EC to authorise the EC fishery fleet to fish in the Azores waters. They argued that the vulnerable Atlantic fauna and flora would be irreversibly destroyed by the fishing methods used. While the Court of First Instance[46] held that the conditions for taking interim measures were not fulfilled, the arguments discussed by the Court were considered sufficiently reasonable by the Council to amend its legislation.

---

[42] Case C-239/04, *Commission* v. *Portugal*, judgment of 26 October 2006, not yet reported.
[43] Case 182/89, *Commission* v. *France* [1990] ECR I-4337.
[44] Under the CITES Convention on trade in endangered species, a warning had been issued in this regard.
[45] Case C-36/98, *Spain* v. *Council* [2001] ECR I-779.
[46] Case T-37/04P, *Azores* v. *Council* [2004] ECR II-2153.

In Case T-366/03, *Land Oberösterreich*,[47] an Austrian region tried to keep its region 'GMO-free', in view of the vulnerable Alpine fauna and flora, and the large number of small farmers and organic farming. The Court of First Instance did not consider questions of land use, but examined the application almost exclusively from the perspective of the free circulation of genetically modified products. It concluded that the regional legislation was incompatible with EC law. The appeal was rejected.

In this group of judgments may also be counted case 252/85, *Commission* v. *France*,[48] where the European Commission had applied to the ECJ with the argument that EC legislation was intended to protect all wild living birds and permitted derogations only under very strict conditions. Traditional bird hunting, as practised with lime and nets in France, was not selective and thus prohibited. France argued that traditional hunting methods in France were part of the cultural heritage. The Court rejected the Commission's application, arguing that the Commission had not proven that the conditions for a derogation were not fulfilled. The political character of this judgment becomes obvious when one considers that the Court did not accept traditional hunting methods in any other member state as a defence.[49]

In Case 42/89, *Commission* v. *Belgium*,[50] the ECJ had to deal with the question whether EC legislation on drinking water also applied to private water wells. This was doubtful, as the relevant legislation referred, on the one hand, to 'all' water, regardless of its origin, and, on the other hand, to water that was 'supplied' or used by industry. The Court was of the opinion that private water wells were mainly used by a limited number of persons in rural areas and that the stringent requirements of EC law did not apply to them.

The jurisprudence on the protection of local populations thus does not show a very clear picture. Sometimes, the protection of local interests is allowed to prevail; in other judgments, the interests of local populations are subordinated to the general concern of protecting the environment.

3.5 *Siting of facilities, and intergenerational equity*

The ECJ has never had to decide a case where the siting of a facility or an infrastructure project had been questioned, because it had been located in a place which disproportionately burdened low-income or minority groups. There were a number of cases, where the planning permission for facilities or projects had been challenged. However, these cases all concerned arguments where the project as such was questioned, not its siting at a specific place – though it is obvious that the above-mentioned notion of NIMBY played a certain role in the discussions.

---

[47] Case T-366/03, *Land Oberösterreich* [2005] ECR II-4005.
[48] Case 252/85, *Commission* v. *France* [1988] ECR 2243.
[49] Cases C-334/89, *Commission* v. *Italy* [1991] ECR I-93, C-118/94, *WWF* v. *Veneto* [1996] ECR I-1223, C-79/03, *Commission* v. *Spain* [2004] ECR I-11619, C-135/04, *Commission* v. *Spain* [2005] ECR I-5261.
[50] Case 42/89, *Commission* v. *Belgium* [1990] ECR I-2821.

Nor has the concept of intergenerational equity received any explicit consideration in the jurisprudence of the European judiciary. It is possible to argue that the Court of Justice, in the above-mentioned cases – when it held that an illegal activity not only had to stop, but that the consequences of this activity also had to be repaired and the impaired environment to be restored – was nevertheless implicitly concerned with intergenerational aspects. However, as the Court did not in any instance mention future generations, this seems too far-fetched. Also, no Court decision has, until now, discussed in any detail the notion of sustainable development, which might have given it an opportunity to consider the concerns of future generations.

3.6 The right to know

The citizens' right to know has, throughout the jurisprudence of the Court of Justice, played a considerable role. Perhaps the most important of all was the jurisprudence on the legal form which Community environmental measures had to take. It should be remembered that, in the European Union and in the great majority of member states, the protection of the environment is placed in the hands of the administration. And it was frequent in the early days of environmental policy that the administration – at local, regional or national level – took administrative measures in order to protect the environment. Such measures were addressed to the administration, but did not have the force of law that could oblige or entitle all citizens.

With regard to European legislation, the ECJ decided that, at least in those cases where environmental legislation created rights or obligations for private persons, these persons were entitled to see such provisions in the relevant statute books and that administrative measures – circulars, internal instructions etc. – were not sufficient. This jurisprudence was linked to the Court's findings, that emission limit values or quality standards for discharges into the air, the water or the soil, also had the objective to protect human health and therefore meant to create 'rights' for private persons. For these reasons, the Court did not allow member states to transpose EC environmental legislation through administrative acts, but requested legislative measures.[51] In the meantime, member states have largely abandoned attempts to transpose EC environmental legislation through administrative provisions. The citizens' right to know was also underlying the judgments where the ECJ held that the tacit granting of a permit was not permitted; since then, more recent EC legislation expressly requires that applications for permits and the decisions on permits be made public.

Since 1990, the EC has adopted legislation on the free access to information on the environment.[52] The jurisdiction of the ECJ in interpreting this legislation was

---

[51] Cases 262/85, *Commission* v. *Italy* [1987] ECR 3073, 131/88 *Commission* v. *Germany* [1991] ECR I-825, 361/88, *Commission* v. *Germany* [1991] ECR I-2567, 59/89, *Commission* v. *Germany* [1991] ECR I-2607, 13/90, *Commission* v. *France* [1991] ECR I-4327.

[52] Directive 90/313/EEC on the Free Access to Information on the Environment, [1990] OJ L158/56.

rather mixed. It was striking that the Court never even tried to base its interpretation on the individual right to know, though the title of the directive and several other provisions clearly indicated[53] that the Community legislature had intended to place this right in the direct neighbourhood of a human right. The ECJ decided that technical advice which an environmental administration gave to another administration, was information relating to the environment and that citizens were entitled to have access to such advice.[54] In contrast to that, the ECJ was of the opinion that information on the number of controls with regard to GMO products did not constitute environmental information.[55] The Court of First Instance also accepted the European Commission's argument that access to letters of formal notice and to reasoned opinions which the Commission, having formally decided on that, addressed in environmental matters to member states, were better kept confidential.[56] Finally, the Court of First Instance was of the opinion that a clause in the EC legislation which entitled a member state to veto access to environmental information which the member state had sent to the Commission, prevailed over the citizens' right to know.[57]

Overall, the jurisprudence of the European judiciary with regard to citizens' right to know, is rather disappointing. It has not succeeded in putting the words of Article 1 of the Treaty on European Union, that 'decisions are taken as openly as possible and as closely as possible to the citizen' into practice, by extrapolating the access to information in a broad way and restricting the numerous attempts by administrations to keep access to environmental information restricted.

3.7 Participation in environmental decision-making

The jurisprudence of the European judiciary is also ambiguous in the area of citizens' participation in environmental decision-making. On the one hand, there are attempts to enlarge citizens' participation in decision-making. Thus, in 1993, the Court decided that member states had to inform other member states of measures which they intended to take with the purpose of combating air pollution, in order to allow the participation of citizens in consultations and deliberations of such measures.[58] In the same vein are the Court's efforts to oppose member states' attempts not to provide for environmental impact assessments for infrastructure and other projects that would have included participation of the public in that procedure.[59]

---

[53] *Ibid.* The title mentions 'free access'; Article 1 mentions as the objective 'to ensure freedom of access to information on the environment'. The right is given to any person, not only to EC citizens; this may be compared to the general access to documents established by Article 255 of the EC Treaty which gives such a possibility only to EC citizens.

[54] Case C-321/96, *Mecklenburg* [1998] ECR I-3809.   [55] Case C-316/01, *Glawischnig* [2003] ECR I-5995.

[56] Case T-105/95, *WWF* v. *Commission* [1997] ECR II-313.

[57] Case T-168/02, *IFAW* v. *Commission* [2004] ECR II-4135. On appeal, this judgment was reversed: see Case C-64/05P, *Sweden* v. *Commission*, judgment of 18 December 2007.

[58] Case C-186/91, *Commission* v. *Belgium* [1993] ECR I-851.

[59] Cases C-396/92, *Bund Naturschutz* [1994] ECR I-3717, C-201/02, *Wells* [2004] ECR I-723.

On the other hand, the Court of First Instance overlooked the existence of Directive 85/337/EEC on environmental impact assessment,[60] which provides for the 'public concerned' the right to participate in the environmental impact assessment.[61] This led the Court to decide that the applicants who opposed the construction of power plants in their neighbourhood, were not individually and directly concerned and therefore had no standing. On appeal, the ECJ found another, hardly more convincing construction not to grant standing to the applicants.[62]

In Case C-216/05, *Commission* v. *Ireland*,[63] the ECJ was of the opinion that member states were entitled to raise fees for citizens' participation in the environmental impact assessment procedure. Again, there was no attempt to make Article 1 of the Treaty on European Union operational and to consider the participation rights of citizens as a fundamental right which had to be interpreted under general auspices of environmental justice. Indeed, with the same reasoning as used by the Court, it would be possible to charge fees for participation in political elections, in referenda or in other expressions of citizens' participation in the democratic life of society.

3.8 Access to the courts

Returning to the different forms of the right to a clean and healthy environment, as formulated by the Sierra Club, two aspects seem to lack: a specific right to the protection of health and safety, and a right to access to the courts (standing) for the purpose of enforcing recognised environmental rights. The European Court of Justice handed out a considerable number of judgments on the right of persons (and animals and plants) to health and safety which will not be commented in detail here, as they overlap with the area of consumer law and workers' protection.

As regards access to justice, the Court was originally very innovative. In a judgment of 1991, it ruled that environmental standards also aimed at the protection of human health. Persons therefore had the right to access courts in order to ensure that the environmental standards were respected.[64] This jurisprudence, in theory, opened the door wide for access to justice for persons, local citizens' groups and environmental organisations, though it was hardly ever made use of in subsequent years. And the administration of the member states and the Community institutions was intelligent

---

[60] Directive 85/337/EEC on the Assessment of the Effects of Certain Public and Private Projects on the Environment, [1985] OJ L175/40, Article 6: 'Member States shall ensure that *the public concerned* is given the opportunity to express an opinion before the project is initiated' (emphasis added). As the Directive elsewhere mentions the 'public', there is a legal difference between 'public' and 'public concerned'.

[61] Case T-585/93, *Greenpeace and others* v. *Commission* [1995] ECR II-2205.

[62] Case C-321/95P, *Greenpeace and others* v. *Commission* [1998] ECR I-1651.

[63] Case C-216/05, *Commission* v. *Ireland*, judgment of 9 November 2006, not yet reported.

[64] Case C-131/88 (note 51 above).

enough to draft environmental standards in such a way that their enforcement by private persons or bodies became impossible.[65]

In 1998, the ECJ had to decide on an appeal by Greenpeace and others against the judgment of the Court of First Instance in Case T-585/93, *Greenpeace* v. *Commission*, mentioned above.[66] The question in dispute was whether an environmental organisation had standing in the general interest, when environmental decisions were taken by a Community institution. The Court insisted that standing only existed when the matter was of 'direct and individual concern' (Article 230(4) of the EC Treaty) to it, and argued that any change of this interpretation would need an amendment of the EC Treaty.[67] This landmark decision was maintained in subsequent years. As the environment is not anybody's property, it had the consequence that organisations – and individual persons – hardly have any access to the European Court in environmental matters. In fact, there is not one single case where an environmental organisation has ever been granted standing before the Court of Justice.

Overall, the Court of Justice is rather conservative as regards the right of standing in environmental matters. It does not even discuss the question whether justice for the environment would not need a broader interpretation of the rules on standing. The Court does not question the classical concept of court litigation of the nineteenth and twentieth century that there be an applicant and a defendant in court and that justice is found by carefully listening to both sides. It does not consider that this concept does not work in environmental matters, as the environment has no voice.

4 Some concluding remarks

Looking at the jurisdiction of the Court of Justice, one has the impression that a rather environmentally friendly interpretation of the EC Treaty and of secondary environmental legislation prevailed in the 1980s and the beginning of the 1990s. However, since then, the Court of Justice has reduced its enthusiasm for the environment and has instead fallen back into considering the environment as one of the many interests in question. During the last years, there was practically not one single consideration of the environment being of a different nature, as it is an interest without a group that could – this observation is limited to the judicial aspect – bring actions to the Court and thus protect, defend and enlarge the interests in question. Farmers and their organisations have, of course, standing to tackle agricultural decisions. Industries and their groups are allowed to tackle, before national courts, any barrier to the free circulation of goods. Where the use of a pesticide is prohibited by the European

---

[65] Examples are standards such as 'best available technique' for installations (Directive 96/61/EC on industrial installations, [1996] OJ L257/26), 'good environmental quality' for waters (Directive 2000/60/EC on waters, [2000] OJ L327/1) or the compliance with quality requirements during an average period of four years for bathing waters (Directive 2006/7/EC, [2006] OJ L64/37).

[66] Case T-585/93, *Greenpeace and others* v. *Commission* [1995] ECR (1995) II-2205.

[67] Case C-321/95P, *Greenpeace and others* v. *Commission* [1998] ECR I-1651.

Commission, the producer of the pesticide may tackle that decision before the Court of Justice; but, when the pesticide is authorised and an environmental group considers that this causes too much harm to the environment, it has no standing. Examples of this kind could be multiplied. In fact, there is, within the European Union, a structural imbalance concerning access to courts, and it is a poor consolation to find that this applies to access to national courts – at least of most member states – as well as to access the Court of Justice. The judiciary itself has not done much to rebalance this situation.

In 1998, the Aarhus Convention on access to information, participation in decision-making and access to justice in environmental matters was adopted. As the EC adhered to it,[68] it became, under Article 300(7) of the EC Treaty, an integral part of EC law. Subsequently, the EC adopted legislation to adapt member states' laws to the requirements of the Aarhus Convention[69] and adopted a specific regulation in order to adapt the law governing the EC institutions to the requirements of the Aarhus Convention.[70] The rules of access to the Court of Justice were not changed, though.

It is not the subject of the present contribution to assess where present EC law and national law is incompatible with the provisions of the Aarhus Convention. It must suffice to mention that the Aarhus Convention tries to enter into the orientation of an open society, where decisions are taken in public, with full participation of all interested citizens. And, in order to have the same state of knowledge as the administrations, it gives citizens and their organisations the right of access to the same information on the environment as the administration has. Finally, in cases of litigation on the respect of environmental law, it grants access to courts, beyond existing provisions – though this last point is heavily contested. We must wait to see whether the Court of Justice takes up the letter, and in particular the spirit, of the Aarhus Convention and strengthens the right to information for persons, the right to participate and the right of access to justice. Full implementation of the letter and spirit of the Aarhus Convention would constitute a big step towards environmental justice – towards an adequate protection of the environment with the means of law.

---

[68] Decision 2005/370, [2005] OJ L124/1.

[69] Directive 2003/4/EC on Public Access to Environmental Information, [2003] OJ L41/26; Directive 2003/35/EC Providing for Public Participation in Respect of the Drawing up of Certain Plans and Programmes Relating to the Environment, [2002] OJ L156/17. A Proposal for a Directive on Access to Justice in Environmental Matters, COM (2003) 624 of 22 October 2003, was not adopted, as the Council was of the opinion that access to justice should be dealt with by member states individually.

[70] EC Regulation No. 1367/2006 on the Application of the Provisions of the Aarhus Convention to Community Institutions and Bodies, [2006] OJ L264/13.

11

Environmental justice through international complaint procedures? Comparing the Aarhus Convention and the North American Agreement on Environmental Cooperation

MALGOSIA FITZMAURICE

1 Complaint procedures and environmental justice in a new world order

The subject-matter of this chapter relates to the achieving of environmental justice through international complaint procedures. These procedures can be seen as a part of the fabric of the new world order, governed by international law, in which justice for an individual is accomplished through expanding public participation of civil society (non-governmental organisations). Therefore, one may suggest that, by means of analogy, the theories of deliberative democracy – according to which the validity and legitimacy of norms directly depend on the participation of citizens in their formation and application[1] – are relevant also in a global community, which is 'a community of states and, simultaneously, . . . community of persons'.[2] In this new order, and in the arena of international and national law relating to the environment and nature resources management, the role of non-governmental organisations (NGOs) has increased dramatically.[3]

While these post-national processes are unclear and ambiguous, this increasing influence of non-state actors indicates that the legitimacy of international law may be assured, or at least promoted, by popular processes of will-formation through transnational networks of communication.[4]

Provided that legitimacy is about procedural systems enabling the application of law, do these systems also 'satisfy the participants' expectations of justifiable distribution of costs and benefits'?[5] With this question in mind, the complaints mechanisms in question will be assessed from the point of view of their suitability as a tool to achieve procedural justice and perhaps corrective justice. These complaint procedures are based on the 1998 UNECE Convention on Access to Information, Public

---

[1] Habermas 1996 at 228.   [2] Franck 1995 at 13.

[3] One such example, linking democratic aspirations and environmental protection, is the important role of environmental NGOs in the democratic process in the post-Communist countries. See Pring and Noé 2002; Barton 2002 at 71–2; Stec 2005 at 1–23.

[4] Habermas 2001 Chapters 3–4. For critical comments, see Giesen 2004 at 1–13; Murphy 2005 at 143–56.

[5] Franck 1995 at 7.

Participation in Decision-Making and Access to Justice in Environmental Matters (Aarhus Convention)[6] and the 1993 North American Agreement on Environmental Cooperation (NAAEC).[7] Relevant factors from the point of view of justice (procedural and corrective), when assessing the international complaint mechanisms, are public participation, the independence of the complaint mechanism as well as the time-frame, transparency and openness in which they operate.

Drawing in part from sociological philosophers concerned with the legitimacy of political regimes (Weber, Teubner and Habermas),[8] scholars in the field of environmental law argue that public participation 'promotes the legitimacy, and thus the acceptability, of decisions concerning resources and the environment'.[9] These factors are important from the point of view of legitimacy, in particular public participation. As Jonas Ebbesson observes:

> Public involvement serves to legitimize environmental decisions, partly because of environmental arguments. However, factors relating to democratic decision-making are just as important. The trust in public authorities and the acceptance of decisions are enhanced if the members of the public have a say – not only by voting – in the development, application, implementation, and enforcement of legal norms and policies, as well as in decision-making concerning specific projects.[10]

Public participation in decision-making thus 'reflects an expansive notion of democracy',[11] which cannot be achieved solely by states' involvement in decision-making. In these procedures, 'the emphasis in reasoning and the reappraising of interests indicates that legitimacy is, like accountability, a substantive rationale as well as a procedural one'.[12] Thus, from a practical point of view, by resulting in less

---

[6] 1998 UNECE Convention on Access to Information, Public Participation in Decision-Making and Access to Justice in Environmental Matters, 38 *International Legal Materials* (ILM) (1999) 517, entered into force 2001. The text of the Convention, as well as information relating to the different cases, may be found at the UNECE website, www.unece.org/env/pp/. There are at present some forty parties to the Convention. Among the numerous articles dealing with this Convention, see e.g. Koester 2005 at 31–45; Walters 2005 at 2–11; Morgera 2005; Marshall 2006 at 123–54; Lee and Abbot 2001 at 83.

[7] The 1993 North American Agreement on Environmental Cooperation, 32 ILM (1993) 1480, entered into force 1994. The parties are the same as in the NAFTA, that is, Canada, Mexico and the United States of America. The text of the Agreement can also be found on the website of the Commission on Environmental Cooperation, at www.cec.org. For more details of the mechanisms and NAAEC procedure, see e.g. Fitzmaurice 2003. See also Bowdery 2006; Goldschmidt 2002 at 343; Knox 2004 at 359–87; Knox 2001; Block 2003; Raustiala 2004 at 389–413; Markell 2005; Markell 2004; Baily 2004.

[8] Barton 2002 at 105; Ebbesson 1997; Ebbesson 2007 at 75.

[9] Barton 2002 at 105; Pring and Noé 2002 at 11–76; Ebbesson 2007 at 681–703.   [10] Ebbesson 2007 at 687.

[11] Ebbesson 2007 at 687. The same author notes that participatory rights (access to information and access to justice) drew from the institutions adopted in human rights: *ibid.*, p. 687. See also Lee and Abbot 2001 at 83, arguing that public participation in environmental decision-making within the domestic context may improve procedural legitimacy, 'tempering unease with the democratic condition of environmental decision-making'.

[12] Barton 2002 at 105.

disruption, public participation in a decision-making process is the most fundamental in achieving legitimacy. Strong presence, legal and factual, of non-governmental organisations representing civil society within the structure both in the NAAEC and in particular the Aarhus Convention contributes to legitimisation of non-compliance procedures set up under these instruments. Legitimacy is a factor closely related to justice, although it is beyond the scope of the present essay to cover in-depth the issues relating to the link between them. Environmental justice, in the context of complaint procedures, can probably be understood as a type of procedural justice, which should ensure fair proceedings, i.e. impartiality, consistency and transparency.[13] Therefore, mechanisms under the Aarhus Convention and NAAEC will be assessed from these points of view. Through their jurisprudence they may form a certain common legal order, at least in so far as environmental justice is concerned.

2 The international complaint procedure under the Aarhus Convention

2.1 The Aarhus Convention Compliance Committee

The Aarhus Convention, adopted within the framework of the UN Economic Commission for Europe (UNECE), draws on Principle 10 of the 1992 Rio Declaration on Environment and Development.[14] The Aarhus Convention sets out minimum standards to be ensured by the parties with regard to access to information, public participation in decision-making, and access to review procedures. This Convention has the potential of becoming a global regime by being open in principle to all states members of the UN, but also by requiring the parties to promote the application of the Aarhus Convention principles in international environmental decision-making processes and in international organisations regarding matters relating to the environment. The most significant and innovative feature of the Convention is the extent of public participation and the role played in this by civil society, not least by environmental NGOs. Such NGOs have a right to participate in environmental decision-making as parts of the 'public concerned', without having to demonstrate a specific interest or prove that they are likely to be affected by the environmental decision-making, as long as they meet the requirements under national law.[15] Nor do these organisations have to prove a sufficient interest or the impairment of a right in order to benefit from the right of access to justice.[16] While the Aarhus Convention allows the parties to somehow limit the range of persons with a right to participate in decision-making and with a right of 'access to justice' (although such limitations must comply with the prescribed minimum standards),[17] there is hardly any limitation at all as far as the right of access to environmental information is concerned.[18]

---

[13] Maiese 2004.
[14] 1992 United Nations Declaration on Environment and Development, 31 ILM (1992) 876.
[15] Aarhus Convention, note 6 above, Art. 2(5).   [16] *Ibid.*, Art. 9(2).
[17] Ebbesson 1997 at 85.   [18] Ebbesson 1997 at 92.

The Aarhus Convention complaint procedure is based on an enabling clause contained in Article 15. This provides for the creation by the Meeting of Parties, on a consensual basis, of an optional system of a non-confrontational, non-judicial and consultative nature for reviewing compliance with the provisions of the Convention. The Compliance Committee was established at the first Meeting of Parties in Lucca, Italy, in 2002.[19] Although the Committee shares some fundamental features with like procedures under other multilateral environmental agreements for reviewing non-compliance,[20] the Aarhus Convention Compliance Committee was endowed with certain distinct characteristics which are particularly well suited to promote legitimacy and justice in environmental decision-making.

In particular, this is the first compliance system which permits members of the public to lodge a claim against a state. Members of the Compliance Committee serve in a personal capacity, thus securing its independence. Moreover, NGOs promoting environmental protection, and who come within the scope of Article 10(5) of the Aarhus Convention can nominate candidates for election as the Committee members following exactly the same method as parties and signatories do. The functioning of the Compliance Committee is based on the principles of transparency.[21] The Compliance Committee consists of eight members, who are independent experts, and considered to be of high moral character with recognised competence in the fields to which the Convention relates, including persons having legal experience.[22]

Receiving communications directly from members of the public is one of the main functions of the Compliance Committee, which is likely to foster legitimacy and democracy by involving a non-statist element.[23] This procedure is innovative, different from other, similar mechanisms and also reflects the procedural human rights-based approach underlying the Aarhus Convention. On ratification, each party was given the option of delaying, for a period of up to four years, the possibility of members of the public to submit complaints to the Compliance Committee.[24] The fact that no party made use of that possibility is in itself a sign which strengthens the legitimacy of the mechanism.

---

[19] Decision I/7 of the First Meeting of the Parties, ECE/MP.PP/2/Add.8, 2, available at www.unece.org/env/pp/documents/mop1/ece.mp.pp.2.add.8.e.pdf; see also Decision II/5 on general issues of compliance: Report of the Second Meeting of the Parties, Addendum, ECE/MP.PP/2005/2/Add.2, adopted at Almaty, Kazakhstan, 2005, available at www.unece.org/env/documents/2005/pp/ece/ece.mp.pp.2005.2. add.6.e.pdf.

[20] Compliance mechanisms of quite different compositions and competence can be found e.g. in the 1987 Montreal Protocol on Substances that Deplete the Ozone Layer, the 1997 Kyoto Protocol, and the 1989 Basel Convention on the Transboundary Movement of Hazardous Wastes.

[21] Marshall 2006 at 127.   [22] Decision I/7, note 19 above, Annex, paras. 1–10 and 16–19.

[23] The other functions include: (a) to consider submissions by parties, referrals by the Secretariat and communications from the public; (b) to prepare a report on compliance with or implementation of the Convention for the Meeting of Parties; and (c) to monitor, assess and facilitate implementation of and compliance with each party's obligation to regularly report on their implementation of the Convention; see Decision I/7, note 19 above, Annex, para. 13. According to Decision I/7, the Compliance Committee may also examine compliance issues and make recommendations on its own initiative.

[24] Decision I/7, note 19 above, Annex, para. 18.

When deciding on the establishment of the Compliance Committee and setting out the conditions governing the receipt of complaints, the Meeting of Parties followed the approach of the European Convention on Human Rights on the question of prior exhaustion of local remedies. It relaxed the strict rule that bringing the case before international judicial or quasi-judicial bodies requires prior full exhaustion of local remedies, which helps to speed up the procedure. Having determined that the communication from the public is admissible, the Compliance Committee has the duty to notify the party as soon as possible about the submission.[25] Considering the lengthy procedures before other international judicial and quasi-judicial bodies, the time-limits for response for a party in alleged breach are relatively short (maximum five months as regards communication from the public; six months as regards referral or submission), which may promote the efficiency of the procedure.

Full access to information furthers transparency. In this respect, it must be noted that one of the most important functions of the Compliance Committee is information gathering.[26] Furthermore, the principle of transparency is fulfilled by the right for members of the public to participate in the formal discussion at the meetings of the Compliance Committee. To facilitate such participation at the hearings, financial assistance may be offered to assist communicants and eligible governments. After the public discussion stage, the Committee starts its deliberation in closed session, which leads to the adoption of the decision.

Since the compliance procedure was established to improve compliance with the Convention, rather than to redress violations of individual rights, the Compliance Committee does not consider itself limited or confined to consideration of the legal arguments or factual arguments provided by members of the public in their communications or by parties submitting cases of non-compliance. The same considerations underlie the decision of the Committee, not to address all the arguments presented in submissions, referrals or communications, but rather to concentrate upon what it decides to be the most relevant.[27] Still, the difference (or contrast) between the decisions on compliance with the Convention and the redress of human rights is very fine, and in some cases almost difficult to distinguish, in particular if one regards the Aarhus Convention as a human rights-based treaty. Therefore, the arbitrary decision of the Committee as to what is most relevant, in spite of the parties' convictions, is not a course of action, in the view of the present author,

---

[25] Decision I/7, note 19 above, Annex, para. 22.

[26] The Committee has the right to: (a) request further information on matters under its consideration; (b) undertake, with the consent of any party concerned, information gathering on the territory of that party; (c) consider any relevant information submitted to it; and (d) seek the advice of experts and advisors as appropriate.

[27] Marshall 2006; also the Report of the Compliance Committee to the Meeting of Parties, Second Meeting, available at www.uncee.org/env/documents/2005/pp/ece.mp.pp2005.13.e.pdf.

which adds to legitimacy of the Compliance Committee in the discharging of its duties.

If the Compliance Committee makes a provisional finding, that the party in question is not in compliance with the Convention, it will consider and propose possible 'measures'[28] and 'recommendations'[29] in order for that party to improve its compliance. The former regards the actions, which may be adopted by the Committee itself, pending the next Meeting of Parties, while the latter relates to measures recommended by the Committee to the Meeting of Parties for the adoption at its next meeting. Transparency is also observed by the Committee, by sending its draft findings, measures and recommendations to the parties concerned for comments. After the expiry of the period of time for receiving of comments, the final findings of the Committee are completed and the comments are taken into account.

Measures adopted by the Compliance Committee are meant to bridge over to the next Meeting of Parties. The findings have a character of a dialogue with parties, again based on full transparency, which can be said to be the fundamental premises on which the Convention is founded.[30] Transparency is also ensured by the general rule, that all information kept by the Compliance Committee is within the public domain and cannot be kept confidential.[31] All submissions, referrals and communications, replies, draft findings and recommendations, as well as the final ones are accessible on the Commission's website. As already mentioned, the meetings of the Committee are open to the public, save in certain cases when confidentiality is requested and when the Committee is in deliberation of drafts on findings, measures and recommendations.

---

[28] Decision I/7, note 19 above, Annex, para. 25. They consist of the following: (a) in consultation with the party concerned, it may provide advice and facilitate assistance to individual parties regarding implementation of the Convention; and (b) subject to the agreement of the party concerned it may: (i) make recommendations to that party; (ii) request the party to submit a strategy, including a time schedule regarding the achievement of compliance and to report on the implementation of the strategy; (iii) in cases of communications from the public, make recommendations to the party concerned on the specific measures to address the matter raised by the public.

[29] The Compliance Committee may recommend to the Meeting of Parties one or more of the following measures: (a) provide advice and facilitate assistance to individual parties regarding the implementation of the Convention; (b) make recommendations to the party concerned; (c) request the party concerned to submit a strategy, including a time schedule, to the Compliance Committee regarding the achievement of compliance with the Convention and to report on the implementation of this strategy; (d) in cases of communications from the public, make recommendations to the party concerned on the specific measures to address the matter raised by the member of the public; (e) issue declarations of non-compliance; (f) issue cautions; (g) suspend, in accordance with the applicable rules of international law concerning the suspension of the operation of a treaty, the special rights and privileges accorded to the party concerned under the Convention; (h) take such other non-confrontational, non-judicial and consultative measures as may be appropriate; see Decision I/7, note 19 above, Annex, para. 37.

[30] Marshall 2006 at 133–4.

[31] Decision I/7, note 19 above, Annex, paras. 26 and 28–9, which also provide for certain limitations of transparency.

2.2 Analysis of selected cases

In the first three years of its activity, the Compliance Committee received a total of seventeen communications from members of the public (the first one in February 2004) and only one submission from a party in respect of another party's non-compliance. During this period, there was no submission from a party reporting its own non-compliance, nor were there any referrals from the Secretariat.[32]

The Compliance Committee has described its own complaint procedure as 'a dialogue with a party concerned in each particular case and throughout the procedure is essential to ensure the consultative nature of the process of reviewing and facilitating compliance', and that 'its main objective is to facilitate compliance in a non-judicial way and this can be best realised if any findings and/or recommendations stem from a dialogue with the Party'.[33] It is thus clear that the complaints procedure as implemented in the structure of the Aarhus Convention has two main features: it is conceived as a dialogue and as a consultative process, in which all parties are treated equally, on the basis of the principle of transparency. This can be best illustrated by a case study, such as the one concerning Turkmenistan, which encompasses all relevant elements characterising this process. Drawing from this example, certain observations regarding the general question of environmental justice (procedural and corrective) within this system will be made.

The case was initiated by a Moldovian NGO on the basis of the communication alleging that the new Turkmenistan's Law on Public Association was in breach of the Convention articles concerning the recognition and support of environmental NGOs, and non-discrimination as to citizenship, nationality and domicile of the members of the public.[34] This case was brought by a Moldovian NGO on behalf of the public of Turkmenistan.

The communicant observed several restrictions, which the law of Turkmenistan imposed on the freedom of public association, and it noted the possibility for a public association to be liquidated by a court decision with no right of appeal. It was further alleged that the new legislation provided the basis for the Ministry of Justice to abolish the majority of environmental NGOs in Turkmenistan, and the only remaining NGO was headed by the Turkmen Deputy Prime Minister. The Compliance Committee made a preliminary decision on admissibility and the communication was forwarded to Turkmenistan for a reply, which was not delivered. At the meeting of the Committee, in the absence of both the communicant (the environmental NGO) and the

---

[32] The communications from the public were as follows: in respect of Kazakhstan (four); Hungary (two); Armenia (two); Poland (two); Ukraine (one communication and one submission); Lithuania (two); and Turkmenistan, Belgium, Albania, Romania (one). For information on the cases, see the UNECE website, at www.unece.org/env/pp/compliance.htm. The Compliance Committee reported its findings to the second Meeting of Parties in 2005, and the Meeting of Parties gave full support to the work of the Committee and its procedures.

[33] Report of the Compliance Committee, ECE/MP.PP/2005/13. p. 7.

[34] Aarhus Convention, note 6 above, Arts. 3(4) and (9).

party concerned (Turkmenistan), the decision was reached that Turkmenistan was in breach of the relevant articles. The Committee also found that Turkmenistan had failed to comply with the general requirements of establishing a clear, transparent and consistent framework, by legislation and other measures, to implement the Convention.[35] The Committee adopted a set of recommendations, which were submitted to the Meeting of Parties, and adopted as it stood by the Meeting of Parties, with Turkmenistan absent.[36] Turkmenistan submitted a letter to the Compliance Committe in which it disagreed with its finding and recommendations, expressing, however, a wish to engage in further dialogue. This suggestion was accepted by the Committee, which extended an invitation to Turkmenistan to attend the next meeting in order to review its implementation of the recommendations. The representatives of Turkmenistan attended the meeting of the Compliance Committee. It was agreed to consider how to implement the recommendations of the Meeting of Parties, and the Turkmen representative indicated the willingness of Turkmenistan to accept assistance from the Committee, which 'might be useful in the process of implementing the recommendations'.[37] Transparency was upheld and all the issues were discussed in open session with all parties present and observers participating. The discussion also involved the development of the awareness of the public as to the use of the rights granted by the Convention, which includes enquiries about the progress made and a timeline. Turkmenistan was also granted the possibility to address the Compliance Committee for assistance. Therefore, the above case clearly indicates constitutive elements of justice: strong NGO participation; transparency for all parties involved, openness and fairness. The Committee made all possible efforts to involve Turkmenistan, despite its initial reluctance.

Another case illustrates that the component of legitimacy and public participation is very strongly upheld by the Compliance Committee. In a communication against Hungary,[38] the communicant alleged that Hungary's recent Act on Public Interest and Development of the Expressway Network failed to meet the requirements of public participation. The communicant argued that the new Act had the consequence of further reducing opportunities for public participation when compared to the original Act. It thus was in breach of the Aarhus Convention, with regard to public participation in decision-making as well as access to justice.[39] The Compliance Committee

---

[35] *Ibid.*, Art. 3(1).

[36] The recommendations included a request that Turkmenistan amend its Act on Public Associations with a view to bringing all its provisions into compliance with the Convention; a recommendation to immediately take appropriate interim measures to ensure compliance with the Convention; a recommendation to carry out these measures with the involvement of the public, and, in particular, relevant national and international organisations, including non-governmental organisations; and an invitation to submit a report to the Meeting of Parties, through the Compliance Committee, on the measures taken to implement the recommendations.

[37] ECE/MP/.PP/C.1/2006/4.

[38] ACCC/C/2005/13, submitted by Mr András Lukács, President, Clean Air Action Group.

[39] Cf. Aarhus Convention, note 6 above, Arts. 6 and 9(2) and (4).

did not uphold the complaint. It found that the Act in question had not reduced the possibilities of public participation to the extent of breaching the Convention. However, it observed that the consequences of the changes in the legislation as regards compliance might depend on their practical application. Therefore, the Committee made a recommendation of a more general character to the Meeting of Parties: (a) urge parties to refrain from taking any measures which would reduce existing rights of access to information, public participation in decision-making and access to justice in environmental matters, even if such measures would not necessarily involve any breach of the Convention; and (b) recommend to parties having already reduced rights to keep the matter closely under review. This recommendation was adopted by the 2005 Meeting of Parties.

This case shows that the Compliance Committee, while adopting decisions within the law, advocates the full participatory rights of civil society even if the limitations made by the party in question were considered to be within the remit of the Aarhus Convention. It is suggested that this decision has a far-reaching importance for environmental justice as it does go beyond *de minimis* standards in the application of the Convention. This includes the issue of exhausting domestic remedies,[40] which is assessed at the stage of preliminary determination of admissibility. The rules of procedure require that the Committee takes into account, at all stages, any available domestic remedy, unless the application is unreasonably prolonged or does not yield an effective and sufficient measure of redress.[41]

3 The international complaint procedure under the NAAEC

Although NAAEC is a side agreement to the North American Free Trade Agreement (NAFTA), it is in fact an independent treaty. The Commission on Environmental Cooperation (CEC) is the organ of the NAAEC entrusted with the function of investigating alleged breaches in enforcement of environmental legislation in member states. It is composed of three bodies: the Council, the Joint Public Advisory Committee (JPAC) and the Secretariat. The Council is the governing body of the CEC and consists of the top environmental administrator of the national environmental agency of the three member states.[42] The Secretariat consists of qualified professionals and is the operational, technical and administrative arm of the CEC.[43] The JPAC is composed of fifteen private citizens from divergent backgrounds, five of which represent each of three member states. The JPAC is an advisory body (a voice of the public) established to give advice to the Council and to support the Secretariat.

The main tool for civil society participation is the so-called Citizen Submissions Procedure under Articles 14 and 15 of the NAAEC. In order to trigger the procedure, a private entity – in most cases an individual or NGO – sends a submission to the

---

[40] Marshall 2006 at 152.   [41] Marshall 2006 at 152–3.
[42] NAAEC, note 7 above, Art. 10.   [43] *Ibid.*, Art. 11.

CEC Secretariat in Montreal. The requirements governing submissions are strict. The procedure is only intended to deal with cases involving the failure by states to enforce environmental regulations (thus it excludes acts by private subjects). If the Secretariat decides that the matter was not addressed satisfactorily by the party in question (that there are still pending legal or factual issues), it may request the Council to prepare a factual record. The Council adopts the resolution by two-thirds vote authorising the Secretariat to do so.[44] Transparency and openness is fulfilled, at least pro forma, by the competence of the Secretariat to take into consideration all available information. This includes 'any relevant technical, scientific or other information' that is publicly available, submitted by interested NGOs or JPAC, or developed by the Secretariat or independent experts.[45] The Secretariat can also obtain the information from the parties and take it into account.[46] Since the Secretariat is impartial,[47] the parties are forbidden to unilaterally influence the Secretariat in the performance of its responsibilities. Still, any party can provide any comments on the draft as to its accuracy.[48] Upon the completion of the factual report, the Council must vote by two-thirds majority on whether or not to make the record public, which puts in doubt the requirement of transparency, as two parties may block the release of factual record.[49] The publication of the factual record is the final and only result of this procedure.

The institutional system set up under the Agreement was meant to secure the independence of the Secretariat and its important role for citizens' submissions.[50] However, the statistics are not impressive: since 1995, fifty-seven submissions were received; only eleven factual records were publicly released; and there are forty-five closed files and twelve active ones. As far as timeframes are concerned, it takes about six years to complete the case – obviously a factor which does not contribute to maintaining of environmental procedural justice.

There are several reasons for this state of affairs. The most important appears to be the tension and power struggle between the Council and the Secretariat, which became public in the context of the Resolutions passed by the Council in 2001, which had an impact on the delimitation of jurisdictional authority between these two organs. As it is explained by Markell, the actions of the Council in relation to this resolution are of paramount importance since factual records are 'at the heart of the citizen's submissions and spotlighting process.'[51] The Resolutions of the Council changed in a very substantial way the focus of the factual records asked for by the submitters and recommended by the Secretariat. It limited and redefined the scope of the record, from the broad and programmatic issues, indicating the widespread failures, as suggested by the Secretariat, to focusing on some isolated examples, which

---

[44] The Council adopt a resolution by two-thirds vote authorising the Secretariat to do so.
[45] NAAEC, note 7 above, Art. 15(4).   [46] *Ibid.*, Art. 21.   [47] *Ibid.*, Art. 14(4).   [48] *Ibid.*, Art. 15(5).
[49] *Ibid.*, Art. 15(7).   [50] Markell 2004 at 345.   [51] Markell 2004 at 767.

were given by the submitters just to illustrate the wider failures.[52] This practice undermines the legitimacy of the process, as it distorts the whole picture and has a negative impact on environmental justice by inhibiting transparency.

A very good example of this problem is the *Migratory Birds* submission.[53] The factual record recommended by the Secretariat focused on the alleged general failure of the United States to enforce the 1916 Migratory Birds Treaty Act (MBTA) on a nationwide basis.[54] However, the Council's Resolution limited the factual record to two isolated instances of alleged failures to effectively enforce the MBTA, which were largely ignored by the Secretariat in its draft factual record. The submitters only referred to these two instances in a single paragraph and the United States in its response did not even mention them. One of the authors of the submission stated that '[w]ithout question, the submitters would have never prepared Migratory Birds if they had known the Council would, in an arbitrary and unexplained fashion, limit the record to two specific instances cited only as examples of widespread government non-enforcement'.[55] Such arbitrary action makes it difficult for environmental NGOs to determine whether the factual records they request will in the end address the issues of their concern, 'since the Council could apparently limit them even to the point of uselessness'.[56] The Recommendations of the Council were also subject to strong criticism from the JPAC, which recommended the Council to refrain in the future from such an encroachment on the jurisdiction of the Secretariat.[57] There is at present not enough evidence to express the view that the Council has changed its methods of functioning.

There are, however, some indications for a more optimistic assessment of the Council's actions. For example, in recent submissions, it authorised a broad approach to the factual records without an attempt to narrow them down. This makes it difficult to assess the real impact of the factual records.[58]

The *Cozumel* submission provides a good example of this. After the release of record, the Mexican general environmental legislation improved. However, the government failed to stop the erection of the second cruise ship pier in the environmentally sensitive coral reefs area of the Gulf of Mexico, which was the subject-matter of the case. The government established the area as a national marine park and expressed its intent to implement a management plan for the park and to initiate an ecological management study of Cozumel Island. There is a disagreement, however, whether the statement of the government resulted from the submission to the CEC, or whether it did not have any influence at all.[59] If this is the case, the victory was at best the paper one.[60]

---

[52] Markell 2004 at 770–1.
[53] CEC, A 14/SEM-99-002/01/SUB, 1999, at www.cec.org. Example cited in Markell 2004 at 776–7.
[54] Markell 2004 at 772.   [55] Wold 2004 at 415.   [56] Bowdery 2006 at 13.
[57] JPAC, Advice to Council No. 030-05. at www.cec.org/files/pdf.JAPC/Advice03-05_EN.pdf.
[58] Markell 2004 at 357.   [59] Goldschmidt 2002 at 393.
[60] On the case, see Johnson 1997 at 203–7; Kibel 2001 at 469.

As this case indicates, the procedure provided by the NAAEC may increase publicity, mostly through the participation of NGOs, and at times such public criticism has resulted in changes in policy.[61] There is also quite a considerable influence exercised through the process of 'shaming', 'sun-shining' or 'spotlighting', which brings 'the environmental problems and enforcement failures of a given nation to the attention of its neighbours and closest trading partners and thereby embarrass them into reform'.[62] It must be noted, however, that the submissions are mainly filed by Mexican and Canadian citizens and environmental NGOs.[63] The reasons for this lie in the domestic legal systems. The US legal system is based on a strong participation of environmental NGOs already in its own legal system, making appeals to external bodies largely unnecessary. Mexican environmental NGOs are weaker and have less participatory options than those in the US.[64] Another reason is that US litigators, used to the US legal culture, prefer a binding determination 'that leads to definite and enforceable results and set precedents'.[65]

4 A comparison of two complaint regimes, and their strengths and weaknesses: do they promote environmental justice?

The two complaints systems described are of a ground-breaking character by creating a certain type of a legal system (post-national, cosmopolitan), the fabric of which is not primarily made by states, but also by individuals and civil society. These processes of law-making and decision-making present a formidable challenge to the traditional notion of sovereignty, as enshrined in the Westphalian statist structure.[66] For, ultimately, how decisions relating to the environment are made is not just a matter for domestic concern, but can also be subject to external scrutiny. In principle, both systems have the basic potential structure to strengthen and promote environmental justice (both procedural and corrective), and may provide a 'potential model for accountability and governance' and a 'positive response to globalisation that gives citizens a voice in the often impenetrable affairs of international organisations'.[67] However, it can be questioned whether these structures work in practice and in reality strengthen environmental justice and democratic processes. The complaint procedure under the Aarhus Convention, as it has been implemented thus far, appears to promote environmental procedural justice through the processes of full environmental NGO participation and transparency. The growing number of governments, willing to cooperate with the Compliance Committee and review their behaviour, may also lead to the conclusion that this procedure fulfils, at lease to a certain extent, requirements of corrective justice.

---

[61] Bowdery 2006 at 26.   [62] Bowdery 2006 at 27.
[63] Until 1 November 2006, there were nineteen submissions from Canada, ten from the US and twenty-eight from Mexico.
[64] Baily 2004 at 325–6.   [65] Bowdery 2006 at 21.
[66] See Knox 2004 at 386 and 388. See also Raustiala 2004 at 392.   [67] Wold 2004 at 416.

NGOs can be champions of the interests of individuals lacking the capacity to bring a case and when the state authorities fail to represent the interests of the public.[68] The role accorded to environmental NGOs under the complaint procedure of the Aarhus Convention is very broad. Not only do they have a right to nominate members of the Compliance Committee, but, most importantly, they have the right to lodge complaints. The possibility of bringing a case even concerning failures of compliance by another country, as in the case described above, enhances the process of democratic accountability not just domestically but to all parties to the Convention. The Compliance Committee also acts with full transparency and openness, allowing environmental NGOs as observers. Moreover, it can be said that transparency and the participation of civil society which should take place in formal and informal forums, are the elements which fulfil the idea of Habermas of validating and legitimising of norms.[69] Even in cases of states disagreeing with the assessment of the Compliance Committee, it takes on the useful role of an institution within which a mutual, constructive dialogue can be conducted. The significant role of the Compliance Committee in promoting environmental justice is particularly visible in relation to environmental and other NGOs within former Communist countries and in Central Asia, as the case law clearly indicates. It may even be said that the complaint procedure of the Aarhus Convention has had the indirect effect of raising awareness amongst the environmental NGOs in these regions, of their potential contribution to democratic accountability as well as to the promotion of environmental justice. The two-tier procedure under the Aarhus Convention compliance regime, which requires the approval of Compliance Committee recommendations by the Meeting of Parties, also contributes to the implementation of democratic governance. Due to the fact that this procedure involves all of the parties to the Convention (not only the members of the Compliance Committee), it contributes to environmental justice by making the process even more transparent and fair as regards concerned parties.

The situation in North America and the Commission on Environmental Cooperation is different. The members of the CEC are the cabinet members and therefore not as truly independent as in the Aarhus Convention Compliance Committee. Legitimacy and democratic governance can formally be furthered by the existence of the JPAC, which acts as a 'watchdog'. It oversees the activities of the other two organs of the CEC – the Council and the Secretariat – and represents the public. However, the JPAC has only a weak advisory capacity and its advice is often ignored. It may also be said that the power struggle between the Council and the Secretariat, which resulted in curbing the scope and impact of citizens' submissions by the Council,

---

[68] See more on the role of NGOs in Ebbesson 2007 at 693–6.

[69] Habermas 1996 at 165–6. He further explains that diverse interests in society must find a compromise through bargaining, 'that is, negotiation between success oriented parties who are willing to cooperate' (at 165) and 'the discourse principle, which is supposed to secure an uncoerced consensus can thus be brought to bear only indirectly, namely, through procedures that *regulate* bargaining from the stand point of fairness' (at 166).

also undermines the democratic process and legitimacy of the procedure. This also casts doubt on the validity of the CEC as a citizens' forum, where debates can be held. All this leads to marked disillusionment as regards the CEC as the beacon of legitimacy and democratic processes in an international context. It may be said that it is the international dimension of this issue, which makes it special. It has even been suggested that the decisions of the Council have 'eroded public confidence' for the procedure.[70] Unlike the complaint procedure under the Aarhus Convention, parties involved in the CEC process treat it as an adversarial process rather than a cooperative endeavour.[71] Furthermore, the value process has been undermined by obstructionist practices of the three governments.[72] The very substantial delays in the CEC response to cases submitted to it – sometimes up to six years – do not foster confidence in the system. As was also pointed out, while citizens of the three parties can report breaches in enforcement of national laws in all three states, regardless of nationality, this procedure is used very sparingly against the US. With only three parties, this lack of application against the US further weakens the importance of the CEC as a general forum. In all, therefore, this complaint procedure, as it stands at present, cannot be said to embody or further the principles of environmental justice. The limited advantages of this procedure do not compensate for the severe shortcomings described. Although it is open to all residents of the three states and relatively easy to follow, the above-mentioned drawbacks – as well as the lack of cooperative spirit by the three governments – render the complaint system in many cases ineffective.

The erratic and unreliable decision-making process thwarts the possibility for the creation of a coherent body of law between the parties. A number of suggestions on how to turn citizens' submissions into a legitimate process have been put forward. First of all, the Council must release 'its grip' on the complaint process, i.e. grant wider autonomy to the Secretariat. Furthermore, the parties must serve their functions as 'stewards' of the NAAEC and approach the citizens' submissions process as a 'collaborative process'. Some kind of a follow-up procedure as regards factual records has to be put in place in order to monitor their implementation. In general, public confidence must be restored.[73] It thus appears that the NAAEC process is too political, and in order to gain legitimacy and the confidence of the parties it should be 'depoliticised'.[74]

The next question is how the two compliance procedures relate to environmental justice (procedural and corrective). While it may be said that the Compliance Committee under the Aarhus Convention fosters legitimacy and environmental justice, the NAAEC mechanism has a potential to do so, but at present (due to the serious flaws in the functioning of the system) it does so only to a very limited extent.

---

[70] Wold 2004 at 417.   [71] Wold 2004 at 417.   [72] Wold 2004 at 433.   [73] Wold 2004 at 441–2.
[74] See Ebbesson 2007 at 694, who correctly assesses the CEC as being far more politicised than the Aarhus Convention Compliance Committee.

5 Concluding remarks and lessons learned

From a formal point of view, both complaint mechanisms have considerable potential to foster environmental justice (procedural and corrective) through the participation of environmental NGOs and the legal framework for challenging the decisions of states. Both are potential forums for fruitful dialogues, and the decision-making may influence states' law-making, thereby contributing to the formation of transnational law at least at the regional level.

The analysis of the practice of the two bodies clearly indicates that only the Aarhus Convention complaints regime furthers legitimacy, due to its structure, the rigorous observance of transparency, the grant of full participatory rights to environmental NGOs (including the right to nominate the members of the Compliance Committee), and the short timeframes for responding to complaints. The Compliance Committee performs the role of a friendly, non-adversarial discussion forum, which initiates and facilitates constructive dialogue. The Committee also adopts measures and recommendations which aim at giving assistance, thereby encouraging confidence in the system. We may therefore conclude that this body plays an important role in furthering environmental procedural and even, perhaps, corrective justice.

The NAAEC regime fails due to the usurping of power by the Council, thereby depriving the Secretariat of its statutory rights to decide on the content of the factual record and the lack of transparency in which its decision is adopted. The absence of elements which contribute to environmental justice resulted in loss of confidence by environmental NGOs in the CEC as a forum, which was specially set up to promote environmental justice.

There are broader lessons – beyond the specific regions – to be drawn from the critical analysis of these two regimes. Despite the above criticisms of the complaint mechanisms, one may agree with the view that the two systems, even that of the NAAEC, 'go well beyond other international environmental arrangements in providing access to a review procedure for members of the public', and that in the 'effectiveness and relevance of these mechanisms much depends not only on the legal basis and rules of procedure but also on self-perception of the review bodies – their engagements, integrity, and the use they make of their discretionary powers in interpreting and applying the rules concerned . . . Such decisions and findings exert a political pressure on the failing state to comply with applicable rules and standards, and may induce other treaty parties to initiate international dispute settlement procedures against it. Findings and recommendations by an international review body may be used by non-state actors as evidence of a legal or factual nature in domestic procedures against the government of the failing state.'[75]

[75] Ebbesson 2007 at 694.

In concluding this chapter, it may be asked if and how these two international complaint procedures provide for justice in cases relating to the environment. As it was explained in the introductory remarks, environmental justice was understood as a type of procedural and corrective justice. In the view of the present author, the complaint mechanism under the Aarhus Convention appears to conform with parameters of environmental justice. The independence of the members of the Compliance Committee, fair hearings, and the participation of NGOs ensure that environmental justice is achieved.

The NAAEC has developed a mechanism which has a potential to foster environmental justice (within a narrower scope, in relation to the limited number of parties). However, the politicised environment in which the North American complaint mechanisms works casts severe doubts on the role of the NAAEC in achieving environmental justice in practice.

Bibliography

Baily, K., 2004. 'Citizen Participation in Environmental Enforcement in Mexico and the United States; A Comparative Study'. 16 *Georgetown International Environmental Law Review* 323.

Barton, B., 2002. 'Underlying Concepts and Theoretical Issues in Public Participation in Resources Development', in D. Zillman, A. Lucas, and G. Pring (eds.), *Human Rights in Natural Development, Public Participation in the Sustainable Development of Mining and Energy Resources*. Oxford: Oxford University Press.

Block, J., 2003. 'Trade and Environment in the Western Hemisphere: Expanding the North American Agreement on Environmental Cooperation into the Americas'. 33 *Environmental Law* 501–45.

Bowdery, C., 2006. 'The CEC's Citizen Submission Procedure: Innovative Model Institution of the Toothless Tiger?', American Bar association, www.abanet.org/environ/committees/lawstudents/pdf/Bowdery.pdf (visited 15 November 2007).

Ebbesson, J., 1997. 'The Notion of Public Participation in International Environmental Law'. 8 *Yearbook of International Environmental Law* 75–81.

2007. 'Public Participation', in J. Brunneé, D. Bodansky and E. Hey (eds.), *Oxford Handbook of International Environmental Law*. Oxford: Oxford University Press.

Fitzmaurice, M., 2003. 'Public Participation in the North American Agreement on Environmental Cooperation'. 52 *International and Comparative Law Quarterly* 333–68.

Franck, T., 1995. *Fairness in International Law and Institutions*. Oxford: Oxford University Press.

Geisen, K.-G., 2004. 'The Post-National Constellation: Habermas and "the Second Modernity"'. 10 *Res Publica* 1–13.

Goldschmidt, M., 2002. 'The Role of Transparency and Public Participation in International Environmental Agreements: The North American Agreement on Environmental Cooperation'. 29 *Boston College Environmental Law Review* 343.

Habermas, J. (trans. W. Rehg), 1996. *Between Facts and Norms*. Cambridge, MA: MIT Press.

2001. *The Postnational Constellation: Political Essays*. Cambridge, MA: MIT Press.

Johnson, P. M., 1997. 'The Commission for Environmental Co-operation and the Cozumel Case'. 6 *Review of European Community and International Environmental Law* 203–7.

Kibel, P. S., 2001. 'The Paper Tiger Awakens: North American Environmental Law after the Cozumel Reef Case'. 39 *Columbia Journal of Transnational Law* 469.

Knox, J. H., 2001. 'A New Approach to Compliance with International Environmental Law'. 28 *Ecology Law Quarterly* 1–122.

2004. 'Separated at Birth: The North American Agreements on Labor and the Environment'. 26 *Loyola of Los Angeles International and Comparative Law Review* 359–87.

Koester, V., 2005. 'Review of Compliance under the Aarhus Convention: A Rather Unique Compliance Mechanism'. 11 *Journal of European Environmental and Planning Law* 31–45.

Lee, M., and Abbot, C., 2001. 'The Usual Suspects? Public Participation under the Aarhus Convention'. 66 *Modern LawReview* 83.

Maiese, M., 2004. 'Procedural Justice', Beyond Intractability, www.beyondintractability.org/essay/procedural_justice/ (visited 15 November 2007).

Markell, D. L., 2004. 'The North American Commission for Environmental Cooperation after Ten Years: Lessons about Institutional Structure and Public Participation in Governance'. 26 *Loyola of Los Angeles International and Comparative Law Review* 341–57.

2005. 'Governance of International Institutions: A Review of the North American Commission for Environmental Cooperation's Citizen Submissions'. 30 *North Carolina Journal of International Law and Commercial Regulation* 759–93.

Marshall, F., 2006. 'Two Years in the Life: Pioneering Aarhus Convention Compliance Committee 2004–2006'. 1 *International Community Law Review* 123–54.

Morgera, E., 2005. 'An Update on the Aarhus Convention and Its Continued Global Relevance'. 14 *Journal of European Environmental and Planning Law* 138–47.

Murphy, M., 2005. 'Between Facts, Norms and a Post-National Constellation'. 12 *Journal of European Public Policy* 143–56.

Pring, G., and Noé, S. Y., 2002. 'The Emerging International Law of Public Participation Affecting Global Mining, Energy, and Resources Development', in D. Zillman, A. Lucas, and G. Pring (eds.), *Human Rights in Natural Development, Public Participation in the Sustainable Development of Mining and Energy Resources*. Oxford: Oxford University Press.

Raustiala, K., 2004. 'Police Patrols and Fire Alarms'. *Loyola of Los Angeles International and Comparative Law Review* 389–413.

Stec, S., 2005, 'Aarhus "Environmental Rights" in Eastern Europe'. 5 *Yearbook of European Environmental Law*.

Walters, J., 2005. 'The Aarhus Convention: A Driving Force for Environmental Democracy'. 11 *Journal of European Environmental and Planning Law* 2–11.

Wold, C., 2004. 'The Inadequacy of the Citizen Submission Process of Articles 14 and 15 of the North American Agreement on Environmental Cooperation'. 26 *Loyola of Los Angeles International and Comparative Law Review* 415.

PART III

State sovereignty and state borders

12

Environmental justice in situations of armed conflict

PHOEBE OKOWA

1 Introduction

Questions of environmental justice, whether in the form of procedural rights or corrective remedies, as such, have on the whole not featured prominently in the legal developments governing the conduct of war. One of the unintended consequences of the Gulf War of 1991 was that it brought to the fore in profound and unexpected ways the seriousness of environmental damage caused by warfare. International conferences,[1] United Nations agencies[2] and the academic literature[3] immediately started treating the issue as one of some urgency, requiring coherent and comprehensive action at the international level. There were even suggestions that a third Additional Protocol to the Geneva Conventions specifically dedicated to preventing environmental damage should be enacted.[4] Central to these debates was the realisation that the existing normative framework did not contain procedural and substantive constraints for preventing environmental damage. The debates also revealed other significant gaps in the substantive content of responsibility for war-related damage, which had not, until now, addressed the question of who should bear responsibility for environmental damage and what form the distribution of burdens and risks should take.

This chapter takes as its starting point the inevitability of war as an activity, which although not always sanctioned by international law is nevertheless regulated by it,

---

[1] 'First International Conference on Addressing Environmental Consequences of War: Legal, Economic, and Scientific Perspectives', www.eli.org/pdf/annotated.pdf; International Council of Environmental Law, 'Law Concerning the Protection of the Environment in Times of Armed Conflict, Final Report of the Consultation of December 13–15 1991'; Plant 1993; United Nations Decade of International Law, 'Report of the Secretary General on the Protection of the Environment in Times of Armed Conflict', UNGAOR, 48th Session, Provisional Agenda Item 44, UN Doc. A/48/269 (1993); Gasser 1995 at 637.

[2] Conclusions by the Working Group of Experts on Liability and Compensation for Environmental Damage Arising from Military Activities (hereinafter 'Conclusions by UNEP Working Group'), in Timoshenko 1998 at paras. 39–42.

[3] Grunawalt *et al.* 1996.

[4] There were already two Additional Protocols to the 1949 Geneva Conventions on the Laws of War. The first Protocol expands and develops the general context of the law: Protocol Additional to the Geneva Conventions of 12 August 1949, and Relating to the Protection of Victims of International Armed Conflicts (Additional Protocol I), available at www.unhchr.ch/html/menu3/b/93. The second Protocol applies to civil wars: Protocol Additional to the Geneva Conventions of 12 August 1949 and Relating to the Protection of Victims of Non-International Armed Conflicts (Additional Protocol II), available at www.unhchr.ch/html/menu3/b/94.htm.

in particular, in terms of minimising its effects. A number of chapters in this volume consider participatory rights as the most developed medium for the realisation of environmental justice. These process rights are an important feature of the major environmental conventions and have been implemented in diverse forms in a number of regions.[5] However, the decision to go to war and the precise modalities of executing it has never been subjected to public scrutiny even in democracies committed to a process of accountability either before or in the course of hostilities.[6] Although historically the concept of 'justice' was in fact central to the law on use of force, with many of the earlier writers regarding war as only legitimate if it was for a just cause, in reality the concept of just or unjust war did not have much of a constraining effect.[7] It had much to do with 'a good reason for military operations' and did not itself seek to determine the legality or otherwise of a proposed military activity. In modern parlance, concerns for corrective justice, in the sense of an equitable formula for apportioning who should bear responsibility for war-related damage was quite simply not part of the regulatory landscape. A war under this doctrine did not become unjust on account of consequential damage (which would today include environmental damage), although there were also in place developed rules against wanton destruction of property or pillage.[8] For instance in the writings of Augustine, wars were just if directed at obtaining satisfaction for injuries received or to restore what had been unjustly taken.[9] In Islam, war was just if taken in defence, or as punishment, or when taken against non-Moslems.[10] In this sense, it was possible to see the concept of 'just war' as an ethical minimum insisted upon before war could be regarded as legitimate. But it was not much of a constraint since the state itself was the ultimate determinant of the justness or otherwise of a cause, and it was frequently possible for war to be just on both sides![11] So long as war was considered the prerogative of sovereigns, objective justness of the cause in whose name the action was taken was generally considered inappropriate. In the literature, it was nevertheless accepted that a war waged ruthlessly and with a view to vengeance could become unlawful so that things captured may not be rightfully retained. In any event, the overriding consideration was one of military necessity, and even disproportionate action was frequently legitimised on account of the military gains resulting from it.

---

[5] See Razzaque, Du, Bugge and Fitzmaurice in, respectively, Chapters 6, 7, 21 and 11 of this volume.

[6] White 2003. In a landmark ruling, the German Constitutional Court observed that the modalities, duration and form of military operations were a prerogative of governments not subject to parliamentary control, BVerfGE, Vol. 90, (1994) 106 ILR 321 at 350; Nolte 2003.

[7] Walzer 1997; Green 2000; Brownlie 1963.

[8] Hague Regulations on the Laws and Customs of War 1907.

[9] *Quaestiones in Heptateuchum*, VI. 10 b, cited in Brownlie 1963 at 5.

[10] Khadduri, *War and Peace in the Law of Islam* (London 1940), cited in Brownlie 1963 at 6.

[11] See generally Brownlie 1963 at Chapter 1.

In terms of contemporary regulation, in a number of countries, the use of force is subjected to processes of parliamentary oversight, but even these forms of scrutiny are confined to the constitutional legitimacy of the use of force in a broad sense and the political consequences of such use.[12] They do not concern themselves with the modalities of the operation or consequential damage in general or damage to the environment in particular.[13] Within the environmental justice debate, the central question addressed in this chapter, is one of the extent to which the enforceable content of the law of armed conflict requires states to ensure that their military operations conform with national and international law for the protection of the environment. Put in another way, it is an enquiry into what procedures and opportunities are in place for the public to challenge planned military action on the basis of the potential environmental risks that they entail. Secondly and more importantly, it evaluates the normative content of *jus in bello* (the law of war), and the extent to which its regulatory content is directed at the protection of the environment. It examines the extent to which environmental values permeate decision-making in military operations, in particular, in the calculation of what are acceptable risks or not. In the latter sense, it involves a consideration of the role and place of corrective and restorative discourses of justice in the law of war. Thirdly, it involves an assessment of the extent to which existing institutional frameworks address the question of responsibility for environmental damage. This involves an inquiry into the distribution of war-related environmental losses and methods of calculating them. But it also involves an inquiry into criminal processes that may be in place for dealing with transgressions. It is suggested that it is only in relation to the last two incidents, that the law of war attempts to incorporate in any meaningful way the concept of corrective or remedial justice.

In focusing on these issues, the chapter is, strictly speaking, confined to the environmental consequences of war. It is not concerned as such with the large body of questions arising out of the inequitable allocation of environmental resources, namely, wars caused by unjust or inequitable allocation of scarce resources of which water wars, conflicts over the exploitation of fishery resources and land degradation as a result of unsustainable patterns of resource use are prime examples.[14] The limitation may appear unduly restrictive, but it is the inevitable consequence of the very marginal role that law can play in the resolution of these problems. They in large part involve distributive political choices for the communities concerned and are strictly speaking not amenable to resolution through legal processes *per se*.[15]

---

[12] White 2003.

[13] In Germany, the Constitutional Court has decided that the government alone has the prerogative to decide on the modalities of the operation once launched: see Nolte 2003 at 231; see also Shibata 2003; Nustad and Thune 2003.

[14] Wald 1997; Gleick 1993; Homer-Dixon 1994; Collier 2000.   [15] Homer-Dixon 1991 at 76–116.

2 Environmental damage in war

The negative consequences of war on the environment have now been extensively and authoritatively documented in the literature.[16] The damage caused by armed conflict to ecosystems, air quality and water supply have been systematically analysed in different studies.[17] Others such as the impact of refugees which exacerbate pre-existing land use tensions leading to further environmental degradation are increasingly being recognised.[18] The most spectacular example in recent times is the deliberate setting on fire of Kuwaiti oil wells by the Iraqi authorities during the 1991 Gulf War. It is estimated that Iraqi troops set on fire as many as 700 Kuwait oil wells, extensively damaging 600 of them. The immediate environmental consequences were catastrophic, resulting in black rain which was felt across a number of countries. The ignited oil wells also extensively damaged desert soil and contaminated the water table. In addition, Iraq also deliberately discharged a substantial amount of crude oil into the Gulf, with all the predictable consequences for the marine environment. Recent studies have also indicated the emergence of respiratory diseases that are most likely attributable to the toxic fumes released into the environment at the time of the conflict.[19]

Equally significant are the documented accounts of the hazardous substances released into the environment as a result of the aerial bombardments of oil installations during NATO's Kosovo campaign.[20] This also resulted in the extensive contamination of the Danube, although the impact on aquatic life was reported to be insignificant. Of the most significant allegations both in the context of Kosovo and the ongoing hostilities in Iraq, is the suggestion that NATO forces in the case of Kosovo and the coalition in Iraq, have used depleted uranium in their military operations. These allegations have persisted notwithstanding the conclusion of a Special Committee established on 14 May 1999 to look into NATO's compliance with international humanitarian law that the damage to the natural environment was collateral, unintended and in all material respects proportionate to the desired military outcome.[21] In addition to the environmental consequences of war, war, especially internal conflict, also exacerbates

---

[16] Stockholm International Peace Research Institute/United Nations Environment Program, *Environmental Hazards of War*. London: 1990; United States Department of Defense, *Conduct of the Persian Gulf War: Final Report to Congress* (Washington DC: United States Government Printing Office, 1992) at 624; Kuwaiti Environmental Protection Council, 'State of the Environment Report: A Case Study of Iraqi Regime Crimes Against the Environment'; Westing 1976; Westing 1982 at 363–89.

[17] Omar *et al.* 2000; Abdulraheem 2000; McNeely 2000; Hulme 1997; Austin and Bruch 2000.

[18] Biswas and Tortajada-Quiroz 1996 at 403–9; see generally McNeely 2000 at 353.

[19] Leaning 2000 at 384.

[20] Regional Environmental Center for Central and Eastern Europe, 'Assessment of the Environmental Impact of Military Activities during the Yugoslavia Conflict: Preliminary Findings' (June 1999), available at www.rec.org/REC/Announcements/yugo/contents.html; International Criminal Tribunal for the Former Yugoslavia (ICTY), 'Final Report to the Prosecutor by the Committee Established to Review the NATO Bombing Campaign against the Federal Republic of Yugoslavia', 39 ILM (2000) 1257; Sinha 2001.

[21] International Criminal Tribunal for the Former Yugoslavia (ICTY), 'Final Report to the Prosecutor by the Committee Established to Review the NATO Bombing Campaign against the Federal Republic of Yugoslavia', 39 ILM (2000) 1257; Sinha 2001.

environmental damage by encouraging unsustainable patterns of resource use. One of the defining features of the many recent conflicts of the last three decades, especially those in Angola, Sierra Leone, Liberia and more recently the Great Lakes region of Africa, is the fact that they have been perpetuated through illegal exploitation of extractive resources. Although much of the attention has turned on ostentatious natural resources such as diamonds, there is also substantial evidence of environmental damage caused by unsustainable resource exploitation such as the logging of timber. For instance, from 1989 until his formal indictment before the Special Court for Sierra Leone, Liberia's former president, Charles Taylor, had financed his rebellion by using revenue generated by the sale of natural resources. The Revolutionary United Front (RUF) in Sierra Leone effectively became his surrogate in Sierra Leone's long-running civil war. He provided it with arms in return for diamonds. In the event, the source of diamonds was curtailed as a result of a UN-imposed embargo, he turned to illegal logging of timber to fund his activities.[22] In Cambodia, it is also now clear that the Khmer Rouge largely funded their operations by illegal trade in timber.[23]

Refugees and internally displaced people are frequently settled in resource-scarce areas also substantially impacting on already fragile ecosystems with serious consequences for biodiversity. It has been shown for instance that the decision of the Congolese government to site refugee camps in the aftermath of the 1994 Rwanda genocide on the edge of the Virunga National Park led to the deforestation of 113 square kilometres of the park with all the attendant consequences in biodiversity terms.[24] The war has also had a substantial impact on Congo's forests, yet this is a unique ecosystem containing 47 per cent of Africa's forest resources. The Congo basin has eighteen protected areas, including seven national parks, of which five have been classified as part of the 'common heritage of mankind'. Many of these species are also protected by existing conventions including the Biodiversity and CITES Conventions. Much of the implementation of biodiversity programmes, for instance in war-torn societies, has invariably been undertaken by NGOs but many of these are unable to operate once civil war takes place.

The problem is not marginal or insignificant when one takes into account the fact that at least one-third of the countries in Africa for instance have undergone armed conflict in the last ten years. In most cases, such as in the Great Lakes region, the conflict has lasted for more than five years and impacted on the natural resources not just of the Congo but also of the nine neighbouring states. Thus, although the

---

[22] See Security Council Resolution S/Res/1521 (22 December 2003) imposing timber sanctions on Liberia. See also the documented accounts of the role of timber and other natural resources in perpetuating the Burmese conflict, Environment News Service, 'Myanmar's Ancient Forests Stripped by Military Government', www.ens-newswire.com/ens/oct 2003/2003-10-08-02.

[23] See Global Witness, 4 February 2003, www.globalwitness.org.

[24] Central African Region Program for the Environment (CARPE 1), 'Conservation in a Region of Civil Instability: The Need to Be Present and Assist', http://carpe.umd.edu/products/carpe-cd-02/CARPE-Briefs/Congo-22.html.

contexts in which the question of environmental damage in war arises are infinitely varied, they all raise, at their core, an overarching concern for justice, especially in a corrective sense for the communities affected. They specifically call for a systematic framework for preventing unsustainable exploitation of resources and for making good war-related environmental damage.

3 The substantive legal framework for environmental justice in armed conflict

3.1 Constraints under peacetime environmental treaties

To what extent do peacetime environmental obligations provide an appropriate yard-stick by which to assess justice considerations in armed conflict? In what ways does the existing framework of legal regulation support either directly or indirectly possible claims for environmental justice? The inadequate nature of the legal regime for the protection of the environment in the conduct of war has been extensively noted in the legal literature.[25] The enforceable content of *jus in bello* has in general not been concerned with natural resource protection. They in large part reflect the increased public sensitivity to human rights values that followed in the immediate aftermath of the Second World War. The radical shift in the importance of sustainable use of natural resources that followed in the wake of the 1972 Stockholm Conference was not, however, accompanied by any coherent framework for their protection in situations of armed conflict or an attempt to address the aggravation of issues of resource protection in the context of an armed conflict.[26] The conventions that emerged out of the Rio Conference do not exhibit any particular sensitivity to their application in situations of armed conflict.[27] Natural resource/environmental protection broadly construed thus remained an afterthought even when the opportunity arose to revise the Geneva Conventions in the two Additional Protocols of 1977.[28] It appears that, even in 1977, the international community was not sufficiently sensitised to the pos-sible catastrophic effects of environmental damage in the conduct of war and the significant likelihood of the loss of biodiversity through unsustainable patterns of

---

[25] See, for instance, Falk 2000 at 137; Schmitt 2000. For the view that the existing legal framework provides a comprehensive framework of protection, see Roberts 2000 at 47.

[26] Declaration of the United Nations Conference on the Human Environment (Stockholm), UN Doc. A/CONF/48/14/REV.1.

[27] 1992 Declaration of the UN Conference on Environment and Development, UN Doc. A/CONF.151/26/Rev.1, Report of UNCED Vol. 1 (New York: United Nations); Framework Convention on Climate Change, 31 ILM (1992) 851; Convention on Biological Diversity, 31 ILM (1992) 818; Non-Legally Binding Authoritative Statement of Principles for a Global Consensus on the Management, Conservation and Sustainable Devel-opment of All Types of Forests, 31 ILM (1992) 881.

[28] Protocol Additional to the Geneva Conventions of 12 August 1949, and Relating to the Protection of Victims of International Armed Conflicts (Additional Protocol I), note 4 above; Protocol Additional to the Geneva Conventions of 12 August 1949, and Relating to the Protection of Victims of Non-International Armed Conflicts (Additional Protocol II), note 4 above.

resource exploitation. In fact, the many environmental treaties ratified in the imme-diate aftermath of the Stockholm Conference tended to focus on traditional concerns of transboundary harm. Curiously, the tectonic shift in the science of environmental damage leading up to the 1985 Vienna Convention on the Protection of the Ozone Layer,[29] the 1992 Climate Change Convention and the 1992 Convention on Biolog-ical Biodiversity was not accompanied by any attempt to address the aggravation of these issues in situations of armed conflict. There was already and still is a marked reluctance on the part of many states to accept the very modest obligations imposed on them by environmental conventions. To aggravate the seemingly intrusive restric-tions demanded by the new environmental regimes by further restrictions on their military operations would have done untold damage to the environmental agenda. In this regard, the 1997 UN Watercourses Convention is unique, in making explicit provision for its continued application during the outbreak of hostilities.[30]

Several chapters in this volume have addressed participatory and corrective aspects of justice as found in a number of international instruments. Juridically, there is of course nothing in the substantive content of these general environmental obligations to restrict their application to peacetime. The rigid distinction maintained in the last century between the law of war and the law of peace is generally regarded as having fallen into desuetude.[31] Since states no longer have an unrestricted right to use force, they can no longer claim an unfettered freedom to suspend their obligations on account of recourse to force. As a matter of principle, the obligations continue to apply in their entirety subject to excuses recognised under the law of state responsibility and to the extent that they are not incompatible with the more specific provisions of the laws of war as *lex specialis.*

In the *Advisory Opinion on the Legality of the Threat or Use of Nuclear Weapons,* the International Court of Justice rejected the argument put forward by a number of states that obligations for the protection of the environment were intended to be obligations of total restraint. By reference to nuclear weapons, these states had argued that the use of any weapon was impermissible as a matter of general international law, if it entailed long-term environmental damage.[32] After noting that the general obligation of states to ensure that activities within their jurisdiction and control respect the

---

[29] Vienna Convention on the Protection of the Ozone Layer 1985, UNEP Doc. IG.53/5, 26 ILM (1987) 1529, entered into force 22 September 1988.

[30] United Nations Convention on the Non-Navigational Uses of International Watercourses, 36 ILM (1997) 700.

[31] See Greenwood 1999.

[32] A similar line of reasoning may also be detected in the 1995 case brought by New Zealand against France, in which New Zealand argued that environmental obligations, especially the duty to carry out environmental impact assessment, enjoined France from carrying out underground nuclear tests unless she had carried out environmental impact assessments which were objectively verifiable and which demonstrated conclusively that no environmental damage would result. See *Request for an Examination of the Situation,* 21 August 1995, *Nuclear Tests Cases* at www.icj-cij.org. See also New Zealand Ministry of Foreign Affairs and Trade, *French Nuclear Testing in the South Pacific* (Wellington, 1996).

environment of other states or areas beyond national control is now part of the corpus of international law relating to the environment, the Court went on to consider the general effect of environmental treaties, and observed that:

> the treaties in question could not have been intended to deprive a state of the exercise of its right of self-defence because of its obligations to protect the environment. Nonetheless, states must take environmental considerations into account when assessing what is necessary and proportionate in pursuit of military objectives. Respect for the environment is one of the elements that go to assessing whether an action is in conformity with the principles of necessity and proportionality.

After referring to General Assembly Resolution 47/37 of 25 November 1992 on the protection of the environment in times of armed conflict, the Court affirmed that environmental considerations constitute one of the elements to be taken into account in the implementation of the applicable law of armed conflict. It observed that destruction not justified by military necessity and carried out wantonly is clearly contrary to existing international law. It is, however, significant that the Court did not regard environmental obligations whether conventional or derived from customary law as having an absolute constraining effect on military operations during armed conflict. In each case, there had to be deference to the more specific rules of armed conflict. Although the judgment of the Court was specifically directed at nuclear weapons, there is no doubt that the issue of principle was formulated with such generality as to make it equally applicable to conventional weapons.

The effect of war on peacetime obligations has also received explicit attention by the International Law Commission (ILC) in the context of its work on the 'Effect of Armed Conflict on Treaties'. Taking its cue from the *Advisory Opinion on the Legality of the Threat or Use of Nuclear Weapons*,[33] the ILC was of the view that in general the outbreak of an armed conflict does not as such involve the termination or suspension of a treaty unless a contrary intention was indicated.[34] The ILC's Special Rapporteur also regarded environmental treaties as those which by necessary implication, judging from their object and purpose, were intended to apply even during the operation of an armed

---

[33] See *Legality of the Threat or Use of Nuclear Weapons*, Advisory Opinion, (1996) ICJ Reports 226 at 240, para. 25; see also Advisory Opinion on the *Legal Consequences of the Construction of a Wall in Palestinian Occupied Territory*, (2004) ICJ Reports 136 at 178, para. 106; Greenwood 1999.

[34] Draft Article 3 adopted by the ILC reads as follows:
Non-automatic termination or suspension
The outbreak of an armed conflict does not necessarily terminate or suspend the operation of treaties as:
(a) Between the parties to the armed conflict;
(b) Between one or more parties to the armed conflict and a third state.

See also *Annuaire de l'Institut de Droit International*, Vol. 61 (II), pp. 278–83.

conflict.[35] But it also conceded that such application must give way to the *lex specialis* of *jus in bello*.[36] It therefore seems inevitable that the substantive and procedural justice considerations surveyed in this volume, in so far as they are based on peacetime obligations, will only be of marginal relevance in situations of armed conflict – being overridden in almost all cases by the law of war. For instance, it is inconceivable that the detailed provisions of the Aarhus Convention on public participation were intended to apply in the conduct of war so as to serve as a constraint on a state's choice of weapons or targets. Moreover, even if it is conceded that peacetime environmental obligations continue to apply, the precise mode and effect of application remains problematic. For instance, what level of environmental damage is acceptable in a military operation? How significant should the military advantage be to offset the assault on the environment? Do developed concepts of international environmental law such as the precautionary principle have any operating influence in deciding what is an acceptable level of harm in a military operation? Is there a distinct role for pre- and post-conflict environmental impact assessment as part of the balancing exercise on which the rule presumably rests? In so far as the answer to all these questions is at the present stage of the development of international law in the negative, it is further evidence that claims of environmental justice remain on the periphery of the law on armed conflict.

There are of course explicit references to environmental protection in the context of war in a number of non-binding instruments. For instance, Principle 26 of the 1972 UN Conference on the Human Environment states that: 'Man and his environment must be spared the effects of nuclear weapons and all other means of mass destruction. States must strive to reach prompt agreement in the relevant international organs on the elimination and complete destruction of such weapons'.

Protection of the environment in armed conflict is also provided for in form in the 1982 World Charter of Nature. It states that 'nature shall be secured against the degradation caused by warfare or other hostile activities' and military activities damaging to nature are to be avoided. Principle 24 of the Rio Conference, after noting that there was an inherent conflict between sustainable development and warfare, called on states to respect international law for the protection of the environment during armed conflict. However, these instruments did not envisage a specific programme of enforcement, nor do they concern themselves with apportioning responsibility or redressing environmental harm. They are more a recognition of the importance of the environment from both the legal and the political perspective than a mandatory obligation to ensure that corrective/remedial measures are taken to ensure that warfare

---

[35] Third Report, Draft Article 7; see also Voneky 2000 at 190.

[36] The ILC's Draft Article 6 provided that: 'The application of standard-setting treaties, including treaties concerning human rights and environmental protection, continues in time of armed conflict but their application is determined by reference to the applicable *lex specialis*, namely, the law applicable in armed conflict. Third Report on the Effect of Armed Conflict on Treaties, 59th Session, A/CN.4/578.

is not destructive of the environment or that the burdens are equitably distributed. They do not therefore advance the arguments much further by considering how the burdens of environmental protection can be accommodated within the existing body of *jus in bello* to support claims of injustice.

3.2 Protection of the environment in jus in bello stricto sensu

Two provisions of Additional Protocol I specifically concern themselves with environmental damage in warfare, and to that extent incorporate *lex specialis* rules for environmental protection in warfare. The provisions also attempt to balance the competing claims of environmental protection and military necessity. However, these provisions are set at such a high threshold, and allow states a wide margin of appreciation, making them practically irrelevant as effective constraints in most international conflicts.

Article 35(3), for instance, provides that: 'it is prohibited to employ methods or means of warfare which are intended or may be expected to cause widespread, long-term and severe damage to the natural environment.' And Article 55 provides that:

> (1) Care shall be taken in warfare to protect the natural environment against widespread, long-term, and severe damage. The protection includes a prohibition of the use of methods or means of warfare which are intended or may be expected to cause such damage to the natural environment and thereby prejudice the health or survival of the population.
> (2) Attacks against the natural environment by way of reprisals are prohibited.

The restriction to harm that is widespread, long-term and severe is a significant constraint, and, if the restrictions are intended to be cumulative, they will be inapplicable in most conflicts as the assessment of the severity and long-term nature of damage may be very difficult to calculate. It would seem that, in the calculation of who should bear the burdens of environmental harm, the law of armed conflict is heavily biased in favour of belligerent's freedom of action. In justice parlance, it takes the view that it is not particularly inequitable that the losses should lie where they fall or that the protection of the environment should be secondary to calculated military advantages.

Rudimentary as they are, the provisions of *jus in bello* that have some bearing on the protection of the environment are in any event largely state-centred – they are mainly directed at imposing obligations on states in inter-state conflicts, a type of conflict that is increasingly the exception rather than the rule.[37] Secondly, even in the context of inter-state conflicts, they only apply to protect the territory of the other belligerent, leaving states largely unconstrained in relation to what they do on their own territory.[38] The recent conflicts in Liberia and Sierra Leone, outlined

[37] Roberts 2000.   [38] Bothe 1991.

in the introduction, have only peripherally involved national armies subject to an organised command structure and would clearly fall outside the scheme of protection in these treaty provisions. Moreover, although the bulk of the provisions of Additional Protocol I are generally regarded as having customary law status, the environmental provisions of Additional Protocol I are taken to be only binding *qua* treaty, and they in general have no effect as a matter of general international law.[39] It seems trite but worth re-emphasising that in general only states are parties to these treaties.

The ENMOD Convention[40] was another milestone in the attempt to incorporate discretely environmental values in the substantive content of *jus in bello*. This Convention is, however, pregnant with limitations. The restriction of the Convention to the modification of the environment's natural processes as a technique of warfare, has meant that it has largely been irrelevant to most forms of environmental harm arising in the context of armed conflict. Although the Convention has been widely ratified, there is little consensus that its provisions are binding *qua* custom. A further significant limitation from a restorative justice perspective is that none of the conventions referred to make any reference to post-conflict environmental impact assessment procedures.

Moreover, although Additional Protocol II applies to internal conflicts, there are no provisions equivalent to Articles 35 and 55. Any assessment of claims of either procedural or corrective justice under the instrument flounders for the simple reason that their substantive content does not as such protect the environment. Additional Protocol II applies exclusively to internal conflicts; however, even in those limited situations where Additional Protocol II imposes obligations on belligerents, these are subject to the requirement that the territorial state has ratified the treaty in question. In other words, obligations imposed on belligerents, for instance under the provisions of Common Article 3 of those instruments, remain obligations of states in disguise. It also remains an open and an unresolved question whether the environmental provisions of these armed conflict treaties apply to United Nations forces.

4 Security Council powers under Chapter VII

A second set of rules of considerable relevance in the exploitation and sustainable use of national resources in armed conflict emanate from Security Council powers under Chapter VII of the UN Charter. In the exercise of these powers, the Security Council has taken a wide range of measures, which, although they have as their desiderata the maintenance of international peace and security, also play a secondary role of protecting and preserving natural resources in conflict zones. The powers can

---

[39] Roberts and Guelff 2003.
[40] 1976 UN Convention on the Prohibition of Military or Any Other Hostile Use of Environmental Modification Techniques, 16 ILM (1977) 88.

be directed at corporations, states and non-state actors alike.[41] The measures most frequently adopted are in the nature of commodity sanctions which are primarily directed at preventing trade in commodities that are identified as a primary source of revenue for the warring parties. On the whole, the range of commodities targeted has been restrictive and mostly confined to ostentatious items such as diamonds and in some cases timber. The Security council has also made wide use of expert panels whose reports on the linkages between natural resources and armed conflicts, has been widely used in the United Nations as a means of publicly condemning and bringing pressure to bear on those involved in illicit trade in conflict zones. The panels' potential as instruments of remedial justice is, however, limited. These panels are not judicial bodies and their mandates preclude them from making conclusive determinations on questions of guilt or innocence.[42]

Moreover, once participation in illegal exploitation or non-compliance with national and international norms of corporate governance and ethics are identified, it is left to national governments to take appropriate measures. Not surprisingly, the record of compliance has been far from impressive. Many governments have correctly or disingenuously maintained that they lack the resources or institutional capacity to monitor compliance with these UN-imposed measures. As Chapter VII measures, they carry the authority of that instrument, and by virtue of Article 25 of the UN Charter are automatically binding on all members.[43] Moreover, under the terms of Article 103 of the UN Charter, Chapter VII measures override any pre-existing treaty commitments the governments may have. The record of compliance with these measures has on the whole been patchy and subject to the political factors that dominate all UN initiatives in the field of international peace and security. Moreover, as the Council's constitutional mandate is closely intertwined with the maintenance of international peace and security, it lacks the power to adopt broad thematic sanctions for the sole purpose of preserving natural resources as a 'right of peoples'. To that extent, the role of the Council as an instrument of restorative justice is bound to be limited. The continuation of conflicts in the face of commodity sanctions is further testimony to the ineffectiveness of these measures in most contexts.

The Chapter VII powers of the Security Council have also been used to provide indemnity for war-related consequential damage in at least one instance. The Security Council passed a resolution in the aftermath of the Gulf War, holding Iraq responsible for all the consequences of damage resulting from the conflict. Resolution 687 provided that:

---

[41] Le Billon 2007.

[42] See, for instance, Final Report of the UN Panel of Experts Reports on Illegal Exploitation of Natural Resources and Other Forms of Wealth of the Democratic Republic of Congo, UN Doc. S/2002/1146, 16 October 2002; see also Final Report of the Judicial Commission of Inquiry into Allegations of Illegal Exploitation of Natural Resources and Other Forms of Wealth in the Democratic Republic of Congo, UN Doc. S/2002/146, 16 October 2002.

[43] Le Billon 2007.

Iraq, without prejudice to the debts and obligations of Iraq arising prior to 2 August 1990, which will be addressed through the normal mechanisms, is liable under international law for any direct loss, damage, including environmental damage and the depletion of natural resources, or injury to foreign governments, nationals and corporations as a result of Iraq's unlawful invasion and occupation of Kuwait.

The resolution expressly indicated that it extended to environmental damage. While this was heralded as a very bold move on the part of the Council, commentators have also noted the very partisan nature of the resolution. It confined itself to Iraqi war damage and failed to impose any responsibility for the alleged harm inflicted by coalition forces – damage which it has been suggested included extensive environmental damage as a result of the widespread use of depleted uranium. The United Nations Compensation Commission (UNCC), the institutional machinery set up by the Security Council for the purpose of processing these claims, confined its jurisdiction to claims by foreign governments, environmental damage being strictly limited to that incurred by these governments directly. The difficult question of responsibility for environmental damage in Iraq as a result of actions by coalition forces or the Iraqi government was not addressed. Moreover, the Iraqi precedent does not advance the law on the protection of the environment in war much further – the penalties were considered justifiable on account of the Council's prior determination that Iraq's invasion of Kuwait was illegal. It remains uncertain what the precise content of obligations for the protection of the environment is, say, in a war of self-defence.

5 Permanent sovereignty and inequitable exploitation patterns in armed conflict: lessons from the Congo case

A third set of rules of relevance to natural resource protection may be discerned from residual principles of general international law, which, although not developed specifically with natural resources in mind, remain relevant; this includes in particular the concept of permanent sovereignty, although the content and potential reach of this principle remains in material respects heavily contested.[44] This concept, which developed out of the political processes of decolonisation, rests on the idea that the resources of a territory belong to its population, and not government. It postulates a broad governmental stewardship of resources which must be exploited, managed and disposed of for the benefit of the population. In so far as it provides a yardstick for contesting and challenging decisions which are not in the interest of a population, it carries within it enormous potential for remedial or corrective justice. Governmental management of natural resources in peace or war may be challenged or invalidated for the simple reason that unsustainable stewardship of resources cannot be for the

[44] Crawford 2001 at 7; Schrijver 1996.

benefit of the population.[45] However, outside the framework of the law on belligerent occupation, international law has in general not developed a coherent framework for protection of extractable natural resources in situations of armed conflict. In terms of state practice, the concept has remained in effect an instrument at the hands of national governments or UN bodies in the context of non-self-governing territory to take action against foreign economic interventions which are not for the benefit of the population. What is for the benefit of the population even in situations where access to public power is deeply contested has remained with national governments. The law in the context of belligerent occupation in part builds on a fairly stable body of obligations applicable to non-self-governing territories.[46]

In assessing arguments based on permanent sovereignty, the case brought by the Democratic Republic of Congo (DRC) against Uganda provides a useful focal point, as it is the first time that decidedly legal arguments based on the concept have been raised outside the context of decolonisation or non-self-governing territories, and within the specific context of an armed conflict involving at least six national armies and twenty-one other armed groups.[47] The decision therefore involved, at least potentially, a consideration of the normative value of the concept, if any, and whether its application placed any constraints on a belligerent's use of national resources in the context of an armed conflict. In other words, were the resolutions in question intended to impose specific duties in relation to the use of natural resources or were they merely statements of political value?

In the Congo case, the DRC had argued that illegal exploitation of Congolese mineral resources, in addition to violating Congo's sovereignty, also contravened international law principles in the field of self-determination, in particular a people's permanent sovereignty over natural resources, and the principle of non-intervention in matters that are reserved for the domestic domain. In the written pleadings, Congo had provided extensive evidence of Ugandan involvement in the illegal exploitation of gold, diamonds and (of relevance to the present inquiry) forest resources of the DRC. In oral arguments, Philippe Sands' submissions on the point of permanent sovereignty were as follows:

> The detailed rules of the law of armed conflict in relation to the exploita-
> tion of natural resources have to be considered against the background of
> this fundamental principle of permanent sovereignty over natural resources.
> The acts which occurred while Uganda occupied large parts of the DRC were
> wholly inconsistent with the General Assembly's landmark resolution 1803 of

---

[45] General Assembly Resolution 1803 (XVII) of 14 December 1962: the resolution described the concept of permanent sovereignty as a basic constituent of the right of self-determination. It further declares in para. 1 that 'the right of peoples and nations to permanent sovereignty over their natural wealth and resources must be exercised in the interest of their development and well-being of the State concerned'.

[46] See, for instance, Security Council Resolution 687 (1991) on Iraq; see more generally, Report of the Security Council Informal Working Group on General Issues of Sanctions (2006).

[47] Armed Activities in the Territory of the Congo, Judgment of 19 December 2005, www.cij-icj.org.

1962 – more than 40 years ago – on permanent sovereignty over natural resources. That resolution confirmed explicitly the right of peoples and nations to permanent sovereignty over their natural wealth and resources and that the exploitation of such resources had to be exercised in the interest of the well being of the people of the State concerned. These rights and interests continue to apply at all times, including during occupation. There is no question that an occupying power is entitled to exploit resources for its own benefit. And nor may it permit – or fail to prevent, or turn a blind eye to – the exploitation of resources by its armed forces for personal benefit. The principle of permanent sovereignty is an alienable right of all states.[48]

Sands also cited other General Assembly resolutions as supporting the application of the concept of permanent sovereignty during times of occupation and armed conflict. In particular, he cited General Assembly Resolution 3005 (XXXVII) of 15 December 1972 concerning Israel and the occupied territories. He noted that this resolution affirmed in material respects 'the permanent sovereignty of the population of the occupied territories over their natural wealth and resources'. And General Assembly Resolution 3171 (XXVIII) of the following year, in 1973, expressed the General Assembly's resolute support for states under foreign occupation in their struggle to regain effective control over their natural resources.

The suggestion here was that all decisions involving the use and disposal of resources including in armed conflict could only be just if ultimately, they were for the benefit of the population. Unsustainable exploitation of forests could not on any view be regarded as just by reference to permanent sovereignty. Although the challenge in the Congo case primarily focused on the use of natural resources by rebel forces and foreign governments, it is suggested that the concept may also be invoked to challenge expedient government decisions, such as those involving the sale of resources for the perpetuation of an unpopular war. On this view, successive Congolese governments or those regimes in Liberia and Sierra Leone that had used the resources of their territories to perpetuate conflicts could be made accountable by invoking the concept. As a potential instrument for the realisation of the ends of justice, its chief weakness lies in the general absence of institutional machinery which can be utilised by aggrieved populations to challenge governmental decisions and those of foreign entities not for the benefit of the population. As is widely known, dispute settlement machinery in the international system is notoriously state-centred. Since those responsible for the most serious environmental damage in war also control access to institutions for redress, any meaningful concept of environmental justice does not fare well in the existing structure of international law.

[48] Arguments of Sands, *ibid.*, CR 2005/5, p. 18, para. 8.

6 Environmental justice in the practice of the United Nations Compensation Commission

The preceding discussion has demonstrated the very rudimentary character of the substantive obligations that putatively apply to the environment. For this reason, it is doubtful that they create an appropriate framework for redress in the event of violation, in any but the most straightforward of cases. Compensation for environmental damage arising out of the 1991 Gulf War remains an isolated although highly effective example of how existing institutions can be utilised for the ends of justice.[49] The United Nations Compensation Commission, to which reference has been made, was established as a subsidiary organ of the Security Council in 1991. Its mandate was to resolve and process claims by individuals, governments and international organisations arising from Iraq's invasion and occupation of Kuwait.

The circumstances leading to its creation were, however, unique. Iraq had admitted its responsibility for the consequences of the aggression, including its liability under international law 'for any direct loss, damage, including environmental damage and depletion of natural resources'. Furthermore, the enforcement procedure had the full backing of the Security Council's Chapter VII powers.[50] The compensation regime was therefore clearly grounded on the illegality of Iraq's conduct under *jus ad bellum*, rather than the law of war. It left open the question whether a state using force in self-defence or on the authority of the Security Council could be made liable for consequential damage including environmental damage. The payment of compensation totalling billions of dollars to the governments of Kuwait, Jordan and Saudi Arabia indicates that, in the presence of political will, international law is capable of redressing environmental damage in situations of armed conflict.

However, there are many operational aspects of the Compensation Commission that raise questions about their compatibility with general rules of fairness and substantive justice. First, the Commission's rules allowed for very limited participation by Iraq or other claimants. Secondly, the rules made no provision for review or appeal from decisions of the Council, both of which represent significant departures from conceptions of justice as found in national and international legal systems.

In so far as the Commission did not concern itself with claims by Iraqi nationals or losses and damage incurred on account of the coalition forces' own conduct, of which the most significant was damage allegedly caused by the use of depleted uranium, its contribution to the development of a comprehensive framework of civil accountability for war-related environmental damage is bound to be insignificant. Moreover, a partisan application of responsibility of that kind significantly undermines the legitimacy of the system in so far as it is seen as a particular application of victor's justice. It is particularly significant that the Iraqi precedent has not been followed in

---

[49] Sand 2005 at 244.
[50] See letter from Iraq accepting its responsibility for the aggression and its consequences, UN Doc. S/22480 (1991); UN Security Council Resolution 687 (3 April 1991). For a full account, see Kazazi 2001.

other conflicts. Yet claims of damage to natural resources and the environment have been a significant feature of the recent conflicts in Kosovo, Congo and East Timor. However, in the cases brought by the government of Yugoslavia against the nineteen NATO states for their bombing campaign in Kosovo in 1999, the government of Yugoslavia, in addition to the claims for a declaration that the NATO operation violated its sovereignty, also made a specific claim for NATO responsibility for environmental damage, although the precise basis of this claim was not sufficiently developed in the pleadings.[51] In the event, the International Court of Justice was unable to give a judgment on the merits, finding in each of the cases that it manifestly lacked jurisdiction to proceed to give a judgment on the merits.

7 Justice through criminal law processes

The possibility of using criminal law processes by way of dealing with wilful or significant environmental harm has generated much interest in the international arena. At the inter-state level, the idea of holding states criminally responsible has a long and chequered history in the context of the work of the International Law Commission (ILC) on state responsibility. The ILC had proposed that, in addition to the normal delictual consequences of responsibility, serious and wilful pollution of the environment – a conduct which is particularly likely to be encountered in the context of war – should also attract the criminal responsibility of the wrongdoing state.[52] In putting forward this proposal, successive Special Rapporteurs of the ILC were influenced by the belief that an effective deterrent system could only be achieved if delictual responsibility was supplemented by penal accountability. It was felt that a penal regime, in addition to stigmatising the wrongdoing state would also reflect the seriousness that the international community attached to the obligations in question. The proposal met with strong and persistent opposition both within the ILC and in the Sixth Committee as unrealistic and incapable of meaningful implementation.[53] As a result, the Draft Articles adopted in 2001 contain no provisions on state criminality for serious conduct including environmental damage.

The idea that serious environmental damage should attract penal consequences was more successful in the context of the emerging regimes of individual criminal responsibility for heinous conduct.[54] Article 8(2)(b)(iv) of the ICC Statute specifically criminalizes serious damage to the environment as a war crime. It provides that:

---

[51] Application Instituting Proceedings Submitted by *Serbia and Montenegro* v. *Belgium*, 29 April 1999, www.icj-cij.org.

[52] Brownlie 1983 at 32–3; Gilbert 1990 at 360. In the Sixth Committee of the General Assembly, a number of state representatives expressed reservations at the inclusion of environmental pollution in the category of international crimes. See oral and written comments by Bulgaria, Byelorussia, China, Federal Republic of Germany, Hungary, Indonesia, Syria, Ukraine, the United Kingdom, the United States and Russia, UN Doc. A/C.61/SR.26, para. 25, and UN Doc. A/C.6/SR.21, paras. 34–5.

[53] See Crawford 2002 at 17–20.   [54] See, for instance, Drumbl 2000 at 620.

> Intentionally launching an attack in the knowledge that such attack will cause
> incidental loss of life or injury to civilian objects or widespread, long-term, and
> severe damage to the natural environment which would be clearly excessive in
> relation to the concrete and direct overall military advantage anticipated.[55]

The overriding consideration in this provision of the Rome Statute is the proportionality of the measures anticipated. If the measures in question are deemed proportionate in light of the anticipated military advantage, then no criminality will attach to the conduct notwithstanding the fact that the resulting damage was widespread, long-term and severe. In weighing the competing claims, the provision is thus heavily tilted in favour of military advantage and against environmental protection. Moreover, the peculiarly criminal law restrictions requiring that the person must have acted with knowledge and intention of the environmental consequences will also restrict its application in many cases. Furthermore, the provision is intended to apply only to inter-state conflicts as the relevant provisions of the Rome Statute that apply to internal conflicts do not penalise environmental damage.[56]

8 Conclusions

It is unfortunate that the central importance of environmental protection has wholly been sidelined in much of the contemporary discourses on armed conflict. As a result, any discussion of justice considerations, whether in the sense of broad-based participatory rights, or in the form of remedial measures for environmental damage, is largely illusory since the substantive framework as such is not supportive of such claims. The structural and institutional deficits in this regard are not insurmountable. The failure to embrace environmental values is due to a lack of political will rather than the inherent non-justiciability of the rights involved.

The partial success of the United Nations Compensation Commission set up in the aftermath of the 1991 Gulf War, for all its shortcomings, bears testimony to the fact that environmental claims for restorative justice are not inherently non-justiciable. The Commission was able to come up with workable formulae for compensating for environmental damage including detrimental alteration of environmental quality which was not directly linked to a diminution of property value. The claims for compensation for environmental damage outlined in the Yugoslavia pleadings and in the cases brought against the nineteen NATO states, and the very public calls for investigation of environmental damage resulting from NATO's Kosovo operation, bears further testimony to an increasing perception that even the conduct of war is not and should not be inherently immune to claims for remedial justice.

However, apart from these limited examples, there is no doubt that this whole area has been mostly accompanied by legislative and institutional inertia. There has been

---

[55] Rome Statute of the International Criminal Court, in force 1 July 2002, www.un.org/law/icc/index.html.
[56] Drumbl 2000 at 630.

no comprehensive attempt to create a broad-based framework of public participation in pre-war decisions, which ostensibly could ensure that the conduct of war is sensitive to possible damage to the environment. The near total immunity accorded to governments in this area is a particular handicap in any attempt to inject discretely environmental values into military operations.

Moreover, to the extent that the enforceable content of the law of armed conflict provides protection for the environment, it is largely rudimentary, not having kept pace with developments in international environmental law. Its preoccupation with inter-state conflicts, in the face of overwhelming evidence that the majority of conflicts since 1945 are within states, remains an anomaly but one which requires urgent action. The modalities for bringing in this structural change are far from easy. Despite profound changes in the international economic order as a result of globalisation and the end of the Cold War, the international system and its institutions remain predominantly state-oriented. To the extent that only a small proportion of actors are within the normative reach of the law, this serves as a considerable limitation in any evaluation of environmental justice considerations in armed conflict. Clearly, as far as rebels and multinationals are concerned, the most obvious and likely institutional instrument for remedial justice is through the medium of international criminal responsibility. However, this will require a coherent normative framework that would meet the international law standards of criminal liability. The Rome Statute of the International Criminal Court has already provided a lead by criminalising deliberate and wilful damage to the environment, but there is no reason why the regime of criminal liability cannot extend to all forms of excessive assaults on the environment in inter-state as well as intra-state conflicts.

Despite the general acceptance in the literature and the case law that the principle of permanent sovereignty is a principle of international law, the preceding discussion has attempted to indicate that there is still much normative uncertainty at the heart of the principle. The thesis advanced here, that the concept has a particular resonance beyond decolonisation, does not necessarily mean that there are international standards which can be applied to annul action taken by governments or rebel groups in the exploitation and use of resources at present. In terms of state practice, the concept has remained in effect an instrument at the hands of national governments or UN bodies, in the context of non-self-governing territories, to take action against foreign economic intervention which is not for the benefit of the population. What is for the benefit of the population even in cases where access to public power is deeply contested has primarily rested with *de facto* governments.

It is suggested that, in the majority of cases, the autonomy given to national governments will prevail, and permanent sovereignty will remain a principle to be interpreted, applied and achieved primarily at the national level. However, the thesis advanced here is a call for international definition and oversight in the application of the principle in extreme cases, of which the conflicts outlined in the DRC, Sierra Leone, Liberia and Sudan would be prime examples. These situations clearly call for a displacement of the presumption that the national governments act in the interest of their populations allowing the populations to challenge governmental action inimical to the environment and ultimately securing justice.

Bibliography

Abdulraheem, M. Y., 2000. 'War Related Damage to the Marine Environment in the ROPME Sea Area' in J. Austin and C. Bruch (eds.), *The Environmental Consequences of War*. Cambridge: Cambridge University Press.

Austin, J., and Bruch, C. (eds.) 2000. *The Environmental Consequences of War*. Cambridge: Cambridge University Press.

Biswas, A. K., and Tortajada-Quiroz, C., 1996. 'Environmental Impacts of the Rwandan Refugees on Zaire'. 25 *Ambio* 403–9.

Bothe, M., 1991. 'The Protection of the Environment in Times of Armed Conflict: Legal Rules, Uncertainty, Deficiencies and Possible Development'. 34 *German Yearbook of International Law* 54.

Brownlie, I., 1963. *International Law and the Use of Force by States*. Oxford: Clarendon Press.
    1983. *State Responsibility*. Oxford: Oxford University Press.

Collier, P., 2000. *Economic Causes of Civil Conflict and Their Implications for Policy*. Washington DC: World Bank.

Crawford, J., 2001. 'Right of Self-Determination in International Law', in Philip Alston (ed.), *People's Rights*. Oxford: Oxford University Press.
    2002. *The International Law Commission's Articles on State Responsibility*. Cambridge: Cambridge University Press.

Drumbl, M. A., 2000. 'Waging War Against the World: the Need to Move from War Crimes to Environmental Crimes' in J. Austin and C. Bruch (eds.), *The Environmental Consequences of War*. Cambridge: Cambridge University Press.

Falk, R., 2000. 'The Inadequacy of the Existing Legal Approach to Environmental Protection in Wartime', in J. Austin and C. Bruch (eds.), *The Environmental Consequences of War*. Cambridge: Cambridge University Press.

Gasser, H.-P., 1995. 'For a Better Protection of the Natural Environment in Armed Conflict: A Proposal for Action'. 89 *American Journal of International Law*.

Gilbert, G., 1990. 'The Criminal Responsibility of States'. 39 *International and Comparative Law Quarterly*.

Gleick, P., 1993. 'Water and Conflict: Freshwater Resources and International Security'. 18 *International Security*, No. 1.

Green, L. C., 2000. *The Contemporary Law of Armed Conflict*. 2nd edn, Manchester: Manchester University Press.

Greenwood, C., 1999. 'Jus ad Bellum and Jus in Bello in the Nuclear Weapons Advisory Opinion', in Laurence Boisson de Chazournes and Philippe Sands (eds.), *International Law, the International Court of Justice and Nuclear Weapons*.

Grunawal, R. J., *et al.* (eds.), 1996. *The Protection of the Environment During Armed Conflict*. Newport, RI: Naval War College.

Homer-Dixon, T. F., 1991. 'On the Threshold: Environmental Change as Causes of Acute Conflict'. 16 *International Security* 76.

1994. 'Environmental Scarcities and Violent Conflict: Evidence from Cases'. 19 *International Security*.

Hulme, K., 1997. 'Armed Conflict, Wanton Ecological Devastation and Scorched Earth Policies: How the 1990–91 Gulf Conflict Revealed the Inadequacies of the Current Law to Effective Protection and Preservation of the Natural Environment'. 2 *Journal of Armed Conflict Law* 45.

Kazazi, M., 2001. 'Environmental Damage in the Practice of the UN Compensation Commission', in M. Bowman and A. Boyle, *Environmental Damage in International and Comparative Law*. Oxford: Oxford University Press.

Le Billon, P., 2007. 'Natural Resources, Armed Conflicts, and the UN Security Council', paper presented at the Seminar on Natural Resources and Armed Conflicts, United Nations Headquarters, New York.

Leaning, J., 2000. 'Tracking the Four Horsemen: The Public Health Approach to the Impact of War and War Induced Environmental Destruction in the Twentieth Century', in J. Austin and C. Bruch (eds.), *The Environmental Consequences of War*. Cambridge: Cambridge University Press.

McNeely, J., 2000. 'War and Biodiversity: An Assessment of Impacts', in J. Austin and C. Bruch (eds.), *The Environmental Consequences of War*. Cambridge: Cambridge University Press.

Nolte, G., 2003. 'Ensuring Political Legitimacy for the Use of Military Forces Requiring Constitutional Accountability', in C. Ku and H. K. Jacobson (eds.), *Democratic Accountability and the Use of Force*. Cambridge: Cambridge University Press.

Nustad, K. G., and Thune, H., 2003. 'Norway, Political Consensus and the Problem of Accountability', in C. Ku and H. K. Jacobson (eds.), *Democratic Accountability and the Use of Force*. Cambridge: Cambridge University Press.

Omar, S. A. S., *et al.*, 2000. 'The Gulf War Impact on the Terrestrial Environment of Kuwait: An Overview', in J. Austin and C. Bruch (eds.), *The Environmental Consequences of War*. Cambridge: Cambridge University Press.

Plant, G., 1993. 'Environmental Protection and the Law of War: A "Fifth Geneva" Convention on the Environment in Time of Armed Conflict?'. 42 *International and Comparative Law Quarterly* 976.

Roberts, A., 2000. *The Law of War and Environmental Damage*, in J. Austin and C. Bruch (eds.), *The Environmental Consequences of War*. Cambridge: Cambridge University Press.

Roberts, A., and Guelff, R., 2003. *Documents on the Laws of War*. Oxford: Oxford University Press.

Sands, P. H., 2005. 'Compensation for Environmental Damage from the 1991 Gulf War'. 35 *Environmental Policy and Law* 244.

Schmitt, M., 2000. 'War and the Environment: Faultlines in the Prescriptive Landscape', in J. Austin and C. Bruch (eds.), *The Environmental Consequences of War*. Cambridge: Cambridge University Press.

Schmitt, M., and Green, L. C. (eds.), 1998. *The Law of Armed Conflict: Into the Next Millennium*. Newport, RI: Naval War College.

Schrijver, N., 1996. *Sovereignty over Natural Resources*. Cambridge: Cambridge University Press.

Shibata, A., 2003. 'Japan: Moderate Commitment within Legal Strictures', in C. Ku and H. K. Jacobson (eds.), *Democratic Accountability and the Use of Force*. Cambridge: Cambridge University Press.

Sinha, K., 2001. 'Protection of the Environment During Armed Conflicts: A Case Study of Kosovo'. *ISIL Yearbook of International Humanitarian and Refugee Law* 1.

Timoshenko, A. (ed.), 1998. *Liability and Compensation for Environmental Damage: Compilation of Documents.* UNEP.

Voneky, S., 2000. 'Peacetime Environmental Law as a Basis of State Responsibility for Environmental Damage Caused by War', in J. Austin and C. Bruch (eds.), *The Environmental Consequences of War.* Cambridge: Cambridge University Press.

Wald, P., 1997. 'Water as a Source of Conflict: Cross-Border Water Problems in the Middle East'. *Development and Cooperation* 2.

Walzer, M., 1997. *Just and Unjust Wars.* New York: Basic Books.

Westing, A. H., 1976. *Ecological Consequences of the Second Indochina.* Stockholm: International Peace Research Institute.

1982. 'The Environmental Aftermath of Warfare in Vietnam', in *World Armaments and Disarmament: SIPRI Yearbook.*

White, N. D., 2003. The United Kingdom: Increasing Commitment Requires Greater Parliamentary Involvement', in C. Ku and H. K. Jacobson (eds.), *Democratic Accountability and the Use of Force.* Cambridge: Cambridge University Press.

13

Sovereignty and environmental justice in international law

ANDRÉ NOLLKAEMPER

1 Introduction

In this chapter, I will examine one narrow aspect of the potential contribution of the notion of 'environmental justice' to the body of international law aiming to protect the environment. I will address the question of to what extent 'environmental justice' may qualify or limit states' sovereign powers under international law to use and destroy their environment as they see fit, as long as it does not cause damage to other states.

For two reasons, this focus may strike the reader as counter-intuitive. First, it might be said that this focus is of limited practical relevance since, if one takes into account transboundary effects as well as the effects on the commons of many activities, not much would be left of states' sovereign rights to exploit their own resources pursuant to their own environmental and developmental policies. Is not everything connected to everything? However, this can easily be exaggerated. The argument would neglect the critical role of thresholds such as 'significant harm' in the definition of states' rights and obligations in regard to environmental harm.[1] It also would understate the degree to which environmental degradation continues largely to be of a local nature.

A second reason why the focus on domestic effects may strike the reader as counter-intuitive is that environmental justice originated as a concept of domestic law, and was used to criticise the domestic environmental policies and laws of some states, notably the United States.[2] It responded to particular specific, local concerns over environmental degradation.[3] Indeed, justice issues traditionally concern themselves with the distribution of burdens and benefits within a state.[4] The prime reason that *international* law takes an interest in issues of environmental justice seems to be the fact that environmental burdens and benefits may be distributed in an unjust manner *between* states, rather than within states.[5] For most people, the prime connotation of 'environmental justice' in international law therefore will be its application to transboundary issues like transboundary movement of hazardous waste, climate change, and more generally issues concerning the distribution of environmental burdens and benefits between states.[6]

---

[1] Sachariew 1990.   [2] Cole and Foster 2000.   [3] Falk in Chapter 2 of this volume.
[4] Caney 2005a.   [5] Adealo 2000.   [6] Caney 2005a at 748.

However, the aim of this chapter is to take the debate one step further and to consider the question how, if at all, notions of environmental justice may be relevant for states' powers under international law in regard to the environment within their territory. This question is of obvious relevance. International law has become increasingly concerned with the way in which states protect the environment within their borders, irrespective of immediate transboundary effects. One of many recent examples is the 2003 African Convention on the Conservation of Natural Resources, which stipulates obligations to protect the environment without much regard to transboundary issues.[7] The question, on which views will sharply differ, is whether it is desirable to take this development further and to progressively prescribe on the level of international law how a state should, in its domestic system, make choices between environmental, developmental, social and other values. The question before us is whether the notion of environmental justice provides any leads for the interpretation and further development of international law in this regard.

The answer to the question of whether the notion of environmental justice is relevant to a state's sovereignty over its environmental resources of course largely will be determined by the definition of the concept of 'environmental justice' employed. Defining environmental justice in terms of the distribution of environmental burdens and benefits over states or people (whether between or within states)[8] will lead to a radically different outcome for our purposes, than if we would construe it in terms of requirements for living in harmony with the natural world.[9] This article does not opt for one or the other definition, and does not attempt to debate the merit of particular positions of moral philosophy in connection to environmental protection.[10] Rather, it will explore alternative conceptions of environmental justice and examine how these may underpin developments in international law that impinge on the sovereignty of states in regard to the protection of 'their' environment.

The chapter's main argument is that the concept of 'environmental justice', although not a direct source of rights and obligations, indeed can underlie and induce development of international law to curtail the power of states under international law to destroy environment as they see fit as long as there are no significant transboundary effects. The concept may define the contours for the political contestation over environmental protection. However, the article also argues that contestation largely will continue to proceed at domestic, rather than at the international level.

The chapter proceeds in four parts. Section 2 will discuss the continuing dominance of territorial sovereignty. Section 3 will discuss four alternative conceptions of environmental justice, respectively linked to justice towards the environment, distributive justice, intergenerational justice, and social justice. Section 4 argues that, while some of these conceptions indeed may qualify states' powers with regard to

---

[7] www.africa-union.org/root/AU/Documents/Treaties/Text/nature%20and%20natural%20recesource.pdf (visited 4 July 2007).
[8] Caney 2005a.   [9] Mickelson in Chapter 15 of this volume.   [10] Dobson 1999.

their own environment, the scope and object of such qualification is highly contextual and will allow for wide differences between and within states. Section 5 contains the conclusions.

2 The continuing dominance of state sovereignty in regard to the environment

The starting point of our analysis is that international law traditionally has been neutral towards the protection by states of their own environment. International law protects states' right to determine for themselves whether to protect or destroy their environment. Principle 2 of the Rio Declaration affirms the basic sovereign right of states to exploit their own resources pursuant to their own environmental and developmental policies, as long as no transboundary effects or effects for the commons occur.[11]

The much heralded principle that a state must ensure that activities within their jurisdiction or control do not cause damage to the environment of other states, formulated by the tribunal in the *Trail Smelter Case*,[12] and repeated in the Rio Declaration, in itself is agnostic about protection of the environment, even though the net result of its application may well benefit the environment. It is just an application of the more general 'no-harm' principle that the International Court of Justice (ICJ) formulated in the *Corfu Channel Case*.[13] The justification and aim of this no-harm principle is to protect the sovereignty of other states. In the *Corfu Channel Case*, Albania had to protect the sovereign rights of the United Kingdom. In the *Trail Smelter Case*, Canada had to ensure that the activities of the smelter at Trail (in the Canadian province of British Columbia) did not cause injury to the United States. But just as international law would have been neutral to any act by the United Kingdom that would have destroyed its own warships, it was neutral to any act of the United States that would be destructive of its own environment. Of course, the Trail Smelter Tribunal was not asked to rule on that latter matter. But, if it had been asked to do so, it would have said that international law did not contain a prohibitive rule. Certainly, in that respect, any transfer of principles of domestic United States law pertaining to the protection of natural resources (that the tribunal laid as the foundation of its main holding on interstate pollution) would have been unwarranted.[14]

The no-harm principle is not some ancient principle that is part of the history of international (environmental) law. To this day, it is the only obligation pertaining to the protection of the environment that the ICJ has expressly recognised. The Court did so in its 1996 Advisory Opinion on the *Legality of the Threat or Use of Nuclear*

---

[11] Rio Declaration on Environment and Development 1992, UN Doc. A/CONF.151/26/Rev.1, 31 *International Legal Materials* (ILM) (1992) 874.

[12] *Trail Smelter Arbitration* (*United States* v. *Canada*), 3 RIAA (1938) 1911, reprinted in 33 *American Journal of International Law* (AJIL) (1939) 182, and 3 RIAA (1941) 1938, reprinted in 35 AJIL (1941) 684.

[13] *Corfu Channel Case* (*United Kingdom* v. *Albania*), (1949) ICJ Reports 22–3

[14] For a recent discussion on the jurisprudence of the tribunal and its history, see Brapties and Miller 2005.

Weapons,[15] and more recently in its Order in the *Pulp Mills on the River Uruguay* case.[16] Much has been made of the ICJ's broader concerns for the environment, expressed in both these cases and also in the *Gabcikovo–Nagymaros Project Case.*[17] In *Legality of the Threat or Use of Nuclear Weapons*, the Court said 'the environment is not an abstraction but represents the living space, the quality of life and the very health of human beings, including generations unborn'[18] – a formula it also cited with approval in *Pulp Mills on the River Uruguay.*[19] In *Gabcikovo*, the Court said:

> Owing to new scientific insights and to a growing awareness of the risks for mankind – for present and future generations – of pursuit of such interventions at an unconsidered and unabated pace, new norms and standards have been developed, set forth in a great number of instruments during the last two decades. Such new norms have to be taken into consideration, and such new standards given proper weight, not only when States contemplate new activities but also when continuing with activities begun in the past. This need to reconcile economic development with protection of the environment is aptly expressed in the concept of sustainable development.[20]

Though acknowledging the more general importance of protection of the environment, the Court did not suggest that states would be under an obligation to protect their environment, irrespective of any transboundary effects on the sovereignty of other states. Certainly, in *Gabcikovo* and *Pulp Mills*, this was determined by the nature of the facts before the Court. But the categorical restriction by the Court of obligations to a transboundary setting suggests that general international law indeed limits itself to concern with transboundary issues and, by inference, to protection of states' rights to protect or destroy the environment, rather than with the protection of the environment as such.

Traditional international environmental law has one notable exception to its primary concern with protection of sovereignty. This is the principle that a state may not cause damage to the environment of areas beyond national jurisdiction.[21] It might be said that that rule is not informed by the wish to protect states' sovereign rights and would reflect a concern with the environment as such. Arguably, states could agree to this principle because this concern over the environment would not have to be balanced with their territorial sovereignty. However, one also might argue that

---

[15] *Legality of the Threat or Use of Nuclear Weapons* (Request by the General Assembly), (1996) ICJ Reports 226, para. 29 (stating that '[t]he existence of the general obligation of States to ensure that activities within their jurisdiction and control respect the environment of other States or of areas beyond national control is now part of the corpus of international law relating to the environment').

[16] *Pulp Mills on the River Uruguay* (*Argentina* v. *Uruguay*) (Request for the Indication of Provisional Measures), para. 72.

[17] *Gabcikovo–Nagymaros Project* (*Hungary* v. *Slovakia*), (1997) ICJ Reports 78, para. 140.

[18] Note 15 above, para. 29.   [19] Note 16 above, para. 72.   [20] *Ibid.*

[21] Principle 2 of the Rio Declaration (note 11 above), also referred to by the ICJ in *Legality of the Threat or Use of Nuclear Weapons*, note 15 above, para. 29, and *Pulp Mills*, note 16 above, para. 72.

the hidden ambition of this rule is to preserve the equal rights of all states to make use of areas beyond national jurisdiction, and that these equal rights should not be pre-empted by acts of any single state that cause pollution. The rationale of that rule would then not be much different from the rationale of the rule that a state may make no territorial claims over areas beyond national jurisdiction. In any case, this exception is a relatively narrow one and is not further considered in this chapter.[22]

All this does not mean that international law has nothing to say about the question whether a state does or does not protect the environment within its borders. Rather, the combination of the fundamental principle of territorial sovereignty and the absence of a prohibitive rule means that international law actually protects states' rights to make their own decisions in regard to the environment. As noted by David Kennedy, international environmental law is not synonymous with environmentally protective rules. There is also a catalogue of international law norms that enable or even encourage despoliation.[23] International law is not silent on environmental protection within a state's sovereignty, but regulates it by leaving a liberty. Given states' historical record in using that liberty, this can hardly be called a neutral position.

This construction of the relevance of international law to environmental policies is not to be confused with a blanket adoption of the *Lotus* principle that 'restrictions upon the independence of States cannot . . . be presumed' and that international law leaves to states 'a wide measure of discretion which is only limited in certain cases by prohibitive rules'.[24] The sovereignty of states is restricted by the 'principles and rules of international law'.[25] In this respect, it would be too narrow to say that a state can do what it likes as long as there is no prohibitive rule. However, this is not the same as saying that a state can only destroy its environment if there is a permissive rule. The key question is whether the 'principles and rules' of international law, apart from treaty obligations, limit a state's power with regard to the protection of its own environment. In the dominant understanding of the state of international law, the answer to that question is still a negative one. It is against this background that we will consider the potential contribution of the notion of environmental justice to the development of international environmental law.

3 Competing conceptions of environmental justice

In order to assess the relevance of international justice for the principle of state sovereignty with regard to the environment, this section will explore four alternative conceptions of (environmental) justice: environmental justice as distributive justice, justice towards the environment, environmental justice as intergenerational justice, and environmental justice as social justice. This overview of possible

---

[22] Joyner 2001 at 354.   [23] Kennedy 2004 at 143.
[24] *SS Lotus* (*Turkey* v. *France*), PCIJ Series A, No. 10, 18, 19.
[25] *Legality of the Threat or Use of Nuclear Weapons*, note 15 above, para. 22.

interpretations of environmental justice is by no means exhaustive. Conceptions of environmental justice that are not discussed, even though they may have some relevance to the qualification of state sovereignty in respect of the protection of the environment, include procedural justice[26] and corrective justice.[27]

3.1 International distributive justice

Environmental justice has come to international law along two strands. In either strand, environmental justice is predominantly distributive justice. The first strand is an extension of the domestic environmental justice debate, primarily taking place in the United States, to international law. This discourse was essentially on matters of distribution. Environmental justice concerns emerged as a result of the disproportionate burden of environmental hazards or undesirable land uses borne by low-income and minority communities.[28]

The second strand is an extension of the justice discourse in relation to international society[29] and international law[30] to (international) environmental law. This discourse naturally was concerned with issues of distribution: international justice seeks to ensure that resources are distributed in a fair way across peoples or states. Much of the discourse on justice in international relations and international law is a direct challenge to state sovereignty. From the perspective of international justice, state sovereignty can be said to be *prima facie* unjust because it is at odds with resource distribution that is necessary for a just world.[31]

In both strands, justice discourse focuses on distribution between states, collectivities and/or individuals: how should a society or group (or the international community) allocate its scarce resources or products among individuals with competing needs or claims[32] and seek the alleviation of poverty and the diminution of inequality (or at least certain dimensions of it) as a matter of justice?[33]

The approach that international law has taken towards (environmental) justice as distributive justice has been ambiguous. While much has been done to promote development and the redistribution of resources,[34] the international legal system as a whole remains pitted against a more equitable distribution. For instance, it empowers non-representative governments that borrow funds from international financial markets and place their governments more in debt with Western investors

---

[26] Notably the 1998 UNECE Convention on Access to Information, Public Participation in Decision-Making and Access to Justice in Environmental Matters, Aarhus, 25 June 1998, 38 ILM (1999) 517. Note also that, in some interpretations, it is held that the 'right to a healthy environment' has procedural aspects, including the right to information, the right to participate and the right to effective remedies. See also Giorgetta 2002.

[27] The no-harm principle in inter-state relations can in its compensatory aspects be seen as an application of the corrective justice principle. See Bugge in Chapter 21 in this volume.

[28] Gunn 1996 at 1227–45.   [29] Nagel 2005 at 113; Caney 2005b.

[30] Brilmayer 1996 at 611; Franck, 1989; Shelton in Chapter 3 of this volume.   [31] Beitz 1975.

[32] Roemer 1996.   [33] Jackson 2005 at 281–2.   [34] See e.g. the essays in Weiss, Denters and De Waart 1998.

for projects that may not have the backing of the local population. Thereby, it may do as much to sustain an unjust system of distribution as it may do to curb that.[35]

What the concept of environmental justice brings to this established debate on distributive justice is that it factors in environmental burdens and benefits in the equation of things that should be distributed. Environmental justice is concerned with the undue imposition of environmental burdens on innocent communities that are not parties to the activities generating such burdens.[36] Global environmental justice then refers to the global distribution of environmental burdens and benefits.[37]

This construction of environmental justice may be of much significance for the development of international environmental law on global issues and indeed may be said to underlie much of modern development of international environmental law. But it does not seem helpful if we would seek a qualification of the sovereign right of states to exploit their own resources pursuant to their own environmental and developmental policies. It might even be said that it would have a reverse effect. The main environmental degradation has occurred in the states and societies that have been able to develop mostly – it is the otherwise *advantaged* communities that generally have caused and suffered the worst environmental consequences. In distributional terms, we then should be concerned with the right of underdeveloped states to develop and to deplete their resources in a way that 'the West' has done. Environmental justice then might even be used as a basis for the entitlement to pollute.

There is an alternative interpretation. Even though the bulk of environmental degradation has taken place in the West, the negative effects of economic development in developing states have been sizable and, moreover, often, directly or indirectly, are caused by development elsewhere, for instance by activities of multinational corporations and/or Western states and/or international organisations. Movement of hazardous waste to developing countries and the general pattern of shifting of environmental burdens to developing countries indeed may well be analysed from this concept of environmental justice.[38] Several principles and rules in regard to such issues as climate change, protection of the ozone layer and transboundary movement of hazardous waste then may be said to seek to counteract such distributive injustice.

However, in both interpretations such rules of international law are quite agnostic about the protection of the environment that otherwise lies within the domain of a state's sovereignty. It may be that certain rules of international law disallow a Western state or a transnational corporation based in an industrialised state to cause pollution in an African state,[39] but such a rule would not really be concerned with the question whether that African state protects its environment itself. The large number of treaties concerned with transboundary water pollution,[40] transboundary air

---

[35] Pogge 2001 at 334–43.   [36] Adealo 2000.   [37] Caney 2005a at 748.
[38] This is the main focus of Anand 2004.   [39] See Ebbesson in Chapter 14 of this volume.
[40] United Nations Convention on the Law of the Non-Navigational Uses of International Watercourses, 21 May 1997, 36 ILM (1997) 700.

pollution[41] or transboundary movement of waste[42] or chemicals[43] essentially seek to prevent one state from causing injury to the environment of other states without the consent of that latter state, thereby foreclosing the sovereign options of that latter state. The prior informed consent principle, contained in the 1998 Rotterdam Convention, is a conspicuous example of this category: as long as a state consents to receive the hazardous waste of chemicals, international law is, irrespective of the effects, agnostic. Indeed, they may be said to aim at the protection of the territorial state's sovereignty to decide in its own manner how to handle its natural resources.

The larger point here is that distributive justice is largely a global process that has no immediate aims and effects for how states arrange their internal affairs. It has been extrapolated from the domestic sphere to the international level, but the principles that have been adjusted for application to the international level are not easily transferred back within the domestic domain of a state.

Largely the same applies when we do not focus on the distribution of impacts of environmental harm, but on the distribution of burdens imposed by international environmental law. For instance, in international climate policy, debates over fairness predominantly concern the equitable distribution of the costs of emissions-reduction measures rather than consideration of equity in the burden of impacts. Such concerns of environmental justice are to some extent being addressed by modern international environmental law, for instance by the principle of 'common and differentiated responsibilities'.[44] The purport of this set of principles is to ensure that the developing countries, that have not yet had the possibility to develop in a way that the West has had, are not required to carry equal costs of prevention.[45] But such principles in themselves largely seek more to achieve some form of distributive justice by keeping open the door to future development, and in themselves offer little to curb state sovereignty.

3.2 Justice towards the environment?

The second construction of the notion of 'environmental justice' is justice between people and the environment as such. This construction could provide the basis for the obligations of states to protect the environment as such, and not just to protect the environment if that would harm the sovereignty of other states. That construction thus could lead to a fundamental qualification of the first leg of Principle 2 of the Rio Declaration.

---

[41] United Nations Convention on Long-Range Transboundary Air Pollution, Geneva, 13 November 1979, 18 ILM (1979) 1442 and its various protocols.

[42] Basel Convention on the Control of Transboundary Movements of Hazardous Wastes and Their Disposal, Basel, 22 March 1989, 34 ILM (1995) 850.

[43] Rotterdam Convention on the Prior Informed Consent (PIC) Procedure for Certain Hazardous Chemicals and Pesticides in International Trade, Rotterdam, 11 September 1998, 38 ILM (1999) 1.

[44] See generally Brunnée and Mickelson in, respectively, Chapter 16 and Chapter 15 of this volume.

[45] Stone 2004.

International law now contains a wide variety of obligations to protect the environment as such, irrespective of the harmful effects on states or other entities. These include the Biodiversity Convention,[46] regional nature conservation treaties, in particular in Africa and Europe,[47] and also modern watercourse treaties, in particular in Europe.[48] These treaties do express a common concern that has little to do with the protection of sovereignty and oblige states to take protective measures, irrespective of effects on other states. Even though most of these treaties are fundamentally tilted to the protection of the rare and exotic over the protection of the environment as such (members of a species are entitled to protection if the species threatens to be extinct, but not so the member of an abundantly available species), one may discern a trend in these treaties of moving beyond the sovereignty paradigm. It has even been argued that, also under general international law, states would now have an obligation to prevent environmental harm, apparently for the sake of the environment, rather than for the sake of preventing physical injury to other states.[49]

It is contested whether the concept of justice can provide a proper basis for obligations towards the environment as such. Brian Barry notes that the concept of justice cannot 'be deployed intelligibly outside the context of relations between human beings'.[50] He adds:

> justice and injustice can be predicated only on relations among creatures who are regarded as moral equals in the sense that they weigh equally in the moral scales.[51]

Treaties aiming at the protection of the environment as such, and the alleged general obligation to prevent harm, could be premised on notions other than (environmental) justice – such as on the existence of moral obligations towards nature, existing independently of considerations of justice,[52] rather than on environmental justice as such.

This position has been criticised by other scholars.[53] We can in this legal analysis leave aside the merits of both positions in moral philosophy. It can be noted, though, that the concept of environmental justice in this interpretation is rather one-dimensional and would not provide a basis for resolving the competing economic, social and environmental claims that are at the heart of decisions of policy and law affecting the environment.

---

[46] Convention on Biological Diversity, Rio de Janeiro, 5 June 1993, 1760 UNTS 143.

[47] For Africa, see note 7 above; for Europe, see Convention on the Conservation of European Wildlife and Natural Habitats, Bern, 19 September 1979, ETS No. 104, 19 September 1979.

[48] Convention on the Protection and Use of Transboundary Watercourses and International Lakes, Helsinki, 17 March 1992, 31 ILM (1992) 1312.

[49] Trouwborst 2002 at 35–6.   [50] Barry 1999 at 95; Rawls 1973; Dobson 1999.

[51] Barry 1999 at 95.   [52] Barry 1999 at 115.

[53] Garner 2003, arguing that Rawls illegitimately excludes animals as beneficiaries of the deliberations in the original position.

3.3 Intergenerational justice

A third construction of environmental justice is environmental justice as part of intergenerational justice.[54] In a certain sense this is a variant on distributive justice as discussed above. It maintains the distributional element that is inherent in justice.[55] However, rather than focusing on distribution within the present generations (whether groups, peoples or states), it focuses on distribution between different generations.

For our purposes, this focus leads to a fundamentally different outcome. Whereas, in the distributive justice discourse, it is in principle immaterial how a state treats its domestic environment, for intergenerational justice this is critical. Although the concept of intergenerational equity often is applied to transboundary or commons issues (for instance, to climate change),[56] responsibilities towards future generations do not distinguish between the territorial loci of environmental harm.

The concept or principle of sustainable development, that implements the concept of intergenerational justice in the international legal system, indeed lacks any restriction on its territorial scope. Sustainability generally is seen as a necessary condition of intergenerational justice:[57] we should at least leave people in the future with the possibility of not falling below our level. Though this concept raises a variety of problems (e.g. if the future population is larger, should we forego our needs to allow satisfaction of the vital needs of future generations?),[58] the territorial scope is not among those. The principle is not contingent on a transboundary nature of environmental harm, and it applies fully to environmental degradation located within a state's boundary. This conclusion may be supported by the fact that, of course, we do not know today the state borders of tomorrow.

This territorially unlimited concept of sustainable development has had a clear influence in positive international law pertaining to sovereignty and environmental law. A notable example is the African Charter of Human and Peoples' Rights, stating in its preamble that: 'States are responsible for protecting and conserving their environment and natural resources and for using them in a sustainable manner with the aim to satisfy human needs according to the carrying capacity of the environment.' It also underlies the Convention on Biological Diversity – similarly unbothered by transboundary issues.[59] Also noteworthy is the International Law Association's New Delhi Declaration on Sustainable Development (2000), referring to the duty of states to ensure sustainable use of natural resources. This would mean that states are under a duty to manage natural resources, 'including natural resources within their own territory or jurisdiction, in a rational, sustainable and safe way so as to contribute to the development of their peoples, with particular regard for the rights of indigenous

---

[54] Brown Weiss 1989; Shelton in Chapter 3 of this volume.   [55] Barry 1999 at 94.
[56] Caney 2005a; Page 1999 at 53–66.   [57] Barry 1999 at 106; Howarth and Norgaard 1972 at 473–7.
[58] Barry 1999 at 111–12. See critically, Beckerman 1997.
[59] Convention on Biological Diversity, note 46 above.

peoples, and to the conservation and sustainable use of natural resources and the protection of the environment, including ecosystems'.[60]

In its manifestation in the concept of sustainable development, intergenerational equity requires the reconciliation between economic development and protection of the environment.[61] This principle does not provide by itself the legal answers to the balancing processes between development and environmental protection. But it may fulfil a role as a background principle that informs the development and interpretation of the law.[62] It also may play a more independent role in the balancing of interests. The Indian Supreme Court held in the *Narmada* case that:

> when the effect of the project is known then the principle of sustainable development would come into play which will ensure that mitigative steps are and can be taken to preserve the ecological balance. Sustainable development means what type or extent of development can take place which can be sustained by nature/ecology with or without mitigation.[63]

3.4 Social justice

In the fourth interpretation, environmental justice is considered as being part of a broader concept of social justice. Though social justice is essentially distributive in nature and thus overlaps with the second construction, the focus here is a different one. Whereas distributive justice as used in international law is essentially distribution between states or groups, social justice refers also to justice within a state's sovereign domestic sphere.

What distinguishes this construction from the construction of justice towards the environment[64] is that environmental justice is not seen here as a justice relationship between humans and the environment, but as one element in the distribution of goods and benefits between human beings.

Though traditionally international law has been quite neutral on how states consider and balance social aspects, there is little doubt that international law indeed influences in many ways domestic social justice. Leaving aside the intended or unintended consequences of apparent neutrality on the actual balances struck within states,[65] human rights, in particular social and economic rights, are obviously a constituent component of social justice.[66] As such, social justice squarely is a concern for modern international law.

---

[60] New Delhi Declaration of Principles of International Law Relating to Sustainable Development, in ILA, *Report of the Seventieth Conference, New Delhi* (London: ILA, 2002).

[61] *Gabcikovo–Nagymaros Project* (*Hungary* v. *Slovakia*), note 17 above para. 140.   [62] Lowe 1999 at 36.

[63] *Narmada Bachao Aandolan* v. *Union of India and Others*, ILDC 169 (IN 2000), para. 143.

[64] See section 3.2 above.   [65] Cf. Kennedy 2004.

[66] M. Glendon, 'Social Justice and Human Rights', available at www.vincenter.org/97/glendon.html (visited 4 July 2007).

There seems increasing support for considering the interests of protection of the environment as part of the considerations of social justice. It has been said that environmental injustice and human rights violations are inextricably interwoven.[67] It has also been suggested that the concept of sustainable development, that initially mainly was seen in terms of a reconciliation between environment and economic development, should be understood as also encompassing social interests.[68] The ILA New Delhi Declaration on Sustainable Development (2000) postulated the principle of integration and interrelationship, in particular in relation to human rights and social, economic and environmental objectives.[69]

There is much merit in making these connections. International environmental policies cannot be separated from social objectives and policies. An important illustration of this approach is the judgment by the South African Constitutional Court in the case of *Fuel Retailers Association of Southern Africa* v. *Director-General*.[70] The case involved an application for a filling station in White River, Mpumalanga. In assessing the legality of the decisions of the administration on the application, the Court expressly considered the principle of sustainable development under international law. It said that 'economic development, social development and the protection of the environment are now considered pillars of sustainable development',[71] and that '[t]he integration of economic development, social development and environmental protection implies the need to reconcile and accommodate these three pillars of sustainable development'.[72] The Court used this construction, in both international and domestic law, as the basis for its interpretation of the applicable statute to the effect that the environmental authority includes the consideration of socio-economic factors as an integral part of its environmental responsibility.[73]

4 Sovereignty, environmental justice, and diversity

It follows from the above that the constructions of environmental justice as justice towards the environment, as intergenerational justice and as social justice each may underlie the development of the law in a direction that qualifies the scope of states' sovereign powers over their domestic environmental policies. However, it is clear that such qualification will proceed only at a highly abstract level. Already, the notion of justice between states has to allow for diversity of policies and economic and social

---

[67] Adealo 2000; Hendrick 2006.

[68] For connection between sustainable development and social justice, see also Dobson 1999.

[69] New Delhi Declaration, note 60 above.

[70] *Fuel Retailers Association of Southern Africa* v. *Director-General: Environmental Management, Department of Agriculture, Conservation and Environment, Mpumalanga Province and Others*, Case CCT 67/06 (decision of 7 June 2007), available at www.constitutionalcourt.org.za/uhtbin/cgisirsi/20070918181710/SIRSI/0/520/J-CCT67-06.

[71] *Ibid.*, para. 53.   [72] *Ibid.*, para. 55.   [73] *Ibid.*, para. 62.

choices.[74] This applies *a fortiori* to what international law would have to say on the balances between environmental, developmental and social factors within states.

Linking social justice issues with the environment is only the starting point of critical political choices and does not in itself provide any answers. The difficulties were illustrated in the 2002 Johannesburg summit, where the already difficult tension between environment and development was further complicated by the infusion of social values, and it proved impossible to agree on universal standards that determined the triangle between environment, development and social issues.[75] International law does not resolve in any substantive way the conflicts between economic, social and environmental claims within states. Rather, it formulates the authoritative concerns and values – but how any claims are resolved has to be determined contextually – largely beyond the reach of international environmental law and of any abstract notions of environmental justice.[76]

International law does not appear able, and perhaps we should not want it to be able, to resolve in any substantive way the conflicts between economic, social and environmental claims within states. While it formulates the authoritative concerns and values, such concerns and values may and do compete. How any competing claims are resolved has to be determined contextually – and is often only partially determined by international environmental law or abstract notions of environmental justice.[77]

The fact that international law has traditionally protected states' 'internal sovereignty' to determine their own environmental and developmental policies is not based on some immoral principle that, for the greater benefit of environmental protection, should as quickly as possible be limited. It is inherent in the notion of self-determination, a notion which is valued by international law.[78] This is not to say that the principle of self-determination would oppose the formulation of more or less uniform international legal standards. But there is a limit to the extent to which international law can prescribe outcomes of very context-specific balancing processes between environmental, developmental and social factors. Sovereignty and self-determination protect the freedom of communities to take their own path, against existing inequalities of power that otherwise would govern and that would determine what should be the proper balance between developmental, environmental and social values.[79] Of course, such balancing has to take place within the limits of international law. However, precisely in the area of reconciling economic, social and environmental concerns, such limits are highly unlikely to be specific.

---

[74] Rawls 2001 at 124, 126, referring to 'reasonable pluralism' and 'democratic unity in diversity'.
[75] Koskenniemi 2004. [76] *Ibid.* [77] *Ibid.*
[78] Art. 1 of the United Nations Covenant on Civil and Political Rights, New York, 16 December 1966, in force 23 March 1976, 999 UNTS 171; and United Nations Covenant on Economic, Social and Cultural Rights, New York, 16 December 1966, in force 3 January 1976, 993 UNTS 3; *Legal Consequences of the Construction of a Wall in the Occupied Palestinian Territory*, Request for Advisory Opinion, (2004) ICJ Reports, para. 88.
[79] Kingsbury 1998.

Any qualification or limitation of the first leg of Principle 2 of the Rio Declaration requires a contextual assessment, also involving the wide range of values relevant in the implementation of the right of self-determination.[80] This already holds for transboundary issues (for example, equitable balancing in the law of international watercourses) and the administration of treaties like the Kyoto Protocol, and it certainly holds for domestic environmental issues. International law leaves substantial room for political contestation in the domestic arena, within the context of the emerging normative considerations identified in the previous section.

On the one hand, the room for domestic political contestation is inherent in the use of open and contextual norms, as illustrated by the Biodiversity Convention. On the other hand, this development is spurred in part by the use of non-legal norms, for instance in the form Forest Principles.[81] Forest management is one of the most obvious examples of a resource management issue that in many respects essentially is within the domestic jurisdiction of states. It involves in most cases a triangle of interest of an environmental, developmental and social nature. Any attempts to prescribe in a meaningful way at the international level how states should strike that balance have come to nothing – as exemplified in the impossibility to agree on a formal legal text. This does not mean that international law has nothing to say on the matter. It has become common to refer to the use of 'soft law' as a sign of the rich variety of normativity, but it equally continues to protect states' pre-existing legal powers. It does provide for a set of general legal principles, objectives and procedures that defines the parameters and establishes the ground rules of what can be termed 'global forest law'.[82] This consists of a combination of widely ratified multilateral conventions that directly or indirectly deal with forestry issues, a number of international principles of the use of natural resources and an increasing body of non-legally binding texts that formulate the normative concerns at stake. However, the decisions to balance these various principles essentially remains at the domestic level.

The resulting picture of an international recognition of generally recognised parameters that have to compete at the domestic level shows that there can be some agreement as to the direction of balances and the relevant issues to be considered. However, inevitably this will result in different outcomes in different states. This can also be seen as fragmentation between different regimes. The phenomenon of fragmentation is mostly located at the international level between different international regimes, but is even more dominant when applied at the domestic level, where domestic actors continue to be entitled to project the rule resulting from the colliding values with legal meaning.[83]

---

[80] Koskenniemi 2004 at 211, noting that the universal level 'only identifies the authoritative concerns and actors, while material regulation will be decided contextually, often by setting up an informal "regime" to manage the problem'.

[81] Non-Legally Binding Authoritative Statement of Principles for a Global Consensus on the Management, Conservation and Sustainable Development of All Types of Forests, UN Doc. A/CONF.151/26 (Vol. III).

[82] Brunnee and Nollkaemper 1996.   [83] Koskenniemi 2004 at 206.

Much of this is illustrated by the struggles between social, environmental and economic issues over the Narmada dam. The Indian plans, originating in the early 1960s, to build a dam on the Narmada river, involved a balancing of economic development and environmental protection, and the rights of people threatened by dislocation and the rights of access to drinking water. In *Narmada Bachao Aandolan* v. *Union of India and Others*,[84] brought by what the Court described as an 'anti-dam organisation', the Indian Supreme Court could rely on all sides of the equation on some (soft) international norm. Sustainable development might have protected the environment and the people threatened with dislocation. The interest of access to water, recognised by the General Assembly of the United Nations,[85] might have been taken to protect the interest of other stakeholders. The latter prevailed, but it can hardly be said that at some general level this means that the human right to water prevails over the interests of sustainability. If anything, the case illustrates the feeble power of international law to strike at the heart of the sovereign right of states to determine their own environmental policies.

5 Conclusion

The notion of 'environmental justice' is open to a variety of meanings and applications. At least some of those (in particular, intergenerational justice and social justice) are relevant as a conceptual basis for qualifying states' sovereign rights to formulate their environmental and developmental policies as long as there are no significant transboundary effects.

One may question whether environmental justice has anything to add to the principles of sustainable development, equity and integration that, from different angles, appear to aim for similar goals. However, none of these other principles are well established in themselves. Environmental justice can be seen as one largely overlapping concept, working in the same direction. The emergence of environmental justice simply points in the same direction and thereby may underpin our thinking, and perhaps our policies on integration of social, economic and environmental spheres.

However, we have also seen that the concept of environmental justice in itself does not provide any answers to the required levels of forms of environmental protection. Rather, it provides the parameters for actual contestation of values that may overlap but may just as well compete. The key question is not only what these values are, but also who is endowed with the authority to decide on collisions. International law continues to confer that power largely on the domestic level. In that respect, environmental justice provides contours for the exercise of states' sovereign rights to determine their own developmental and environmental policies, while it does not and cannot dictate the outcomes.

---

[84] Note 63 above.   [85] GA Res. 32/158 (1977).

Bibliography

Adealo, F. O., 2000. 'Cross-National Environmental Injustice and Human Rights Issues'. 43 *American Behavioral Scientist* 688.

Anand, R., 2004. *International Environmental Justice: A North South Dimension.* Aldershot: Ashgate Publishing.

Barry, B., 1999. 'Sustainability and Intergenerational Justice', in Andrew P. Dobson (ed.), *Fairness and Futurity: Essays on Environmental Sustainability and Social Justice.* Oxford: Oxford University Press.

Beckerman, W., 1997. 'Debate: Intergenerational Equity and the Environment'. 5 *Journal of Political Philosophy* 392.

Beitz, C. R., 1975. 'Justice in International Relations'. 4 *Philosophy and Public Affairs* 371.

Brapties, R., and Miller, R., 2005. *Transboundary Harm in International Law: Lessons from Trail Smelter.* Cambridge: Cambridge University Press.

Brown Weiss, E., 1989. *In Fairness to Future Generations: International Law, Common Patrimony, and Intergenerational Equity.* New York: Transnational Publishers.

Brilmayer, L., 1996. 'International Justice and International Law'. 98 *West Virginia Law Review* 611.

Brunnee, J., and Nollkaemper, A., 1996. 'Between the Forests and the Trees – An Emerging International Forest Law'. 23 *Environmental Conservation* 307.

Bullard, R. B., 2005. *Environmental Justice: Human Rights and the Politics of Pollution.* San Francisco: Sierra Club.

Caney, S., 2005a. 'Cosmopolitan Justice, Responsibility, and Global Climate Change'. 18 *Leiden Journal of International Law* 749.

2005b. *Justice Beyond Borders: A Global Political Theory.* Oxford: Oxford University Press.

Cole, L. W., and Foster, S., 2000. *From the Ground up: Environmental Racism and the Rise of the Environmental Justice Movement.* New York: New York University Press.

Dobson, A., 1999. *Justice and the Environment: Conceptions of Environmental Sustainability and Dimensions of Social Justice.* New York: Oxford University Press.

Franck, T., 1989. 'Is Justice Relevant to the International Legal System?' 64 *Notre Dame Law Review* 945.

Garner, R., 2003. 'Animals, Politics and Justice: Rawlsian Liberalism and the Plight of Non-Humans'. 12 *Environmental Politics* 3.

Giorgetta, S., 2002. 'The Right to a Healthy Environment, Human Rights and Sustainable Development'. 2 *International Environmental Agreements: Politics, Law and Economics* 171.

Gunn, W. A., 1996. 'From the Landfill to the Other Side of the Tracks: Developing Empowerment Strategies to Alleviate Environmental Justice'. 22 *Ohio Northern University Law Review* 1227.

Hendrick, P. M., 2006. 'The Theory of Legal Relativity: Environmental Justice in the Context of Doctrinal Durability'. 32 *University of Toledo Law Review* 180.

Howarth, R., and Norgaard, R., 1972. 'Environmental Valuation under Sustainable Development'. 2 *American Economic Review, Papers and Proceeding* 473.

Jackson, B., 2005. 'The Conceptual History of Social Justice'. 3 *Political Studies Review* 356.

Joyner, C. C., 2001. 'Global Commons: The Oceans, Antarctica, the Atmosphere, and Outer Space', in P. J. Simmons and C. de Jonge Oudraat (eds.), *Managing Global Issues: Lessons Learned.* Washington DC: Carnegie Endowment.

Kennedy, D., 2004. *The Dark Sides of Virtue: Reassessing International Humanitarianism.* Princeton: Princeton University Press.

Kingsbury, B., 1998. 'Sovereignty and Inequality'. 9 *European Journal of International Law* 601.

Koskenniemi, M., 2004. 'International Law and Hegemony: A Reconfiguration'. 17 *Cambridge Review of International Affairs* 211.

Lowe, L., 1999. 'Sustainable Development and Unsustainable Arguments', in A. Boyle and D. Freestone (eds.), *International Environmental Law and Sustainable Development: Past Achievements and Future Challenges.* Oxford: Oxford University Press.

Nagel, T., 2005. 'The Problem of Global Justice'. 33 *Philosophy and Public Affairs* 113.

Page, E., 1999. 'Intergenerational Justice and Climate Change'. 47 *Political Studies* 53.

Pogge, T., 2001. 'The Influence of the Global Order on the Prospects for Genuine Democracy in the Developing Countries'. 14 *Ratio Juris* 334.

Rawls, J., 1973. *A Theory of Justice.* 6th edn, Cambridge, MA: The Belknap Press of Harvard University Press.

2001. *The Law of Peoples.* Cambridge, MA: Harvard University Press.

Roemer, J., 1996. *Theories of Distributive Justice.* Cambridge, MA: Harvard University Press.

Sachariew, K., 1990. 'The Definition of Thresholds of Tolerance for Transboundary Environmental Injury under International Law: Development and Present Status'. 37 *Netherlands International Law Review* 193.

Stone, C. D., 2004. 'Common but Differentiated Responsibilities in International Law'. 98 *American Journal of International Law* 276.

Trouwborst, A., 2002. *Evolution and Status of the Precautionary Principle in International Law.* The Hague, Boston and London: Kluwer Law International.

Weiss, F., Denters, E., and De Waart, P. J. I. M. (eds.), 1998. *International Economic Law with a Human Face.* Dordrecht: Martinus Nijhoff.

14

Piercing the state veil in pursuit of environmental justice

JONAS EBBESSON

1 Environmental law and justice across state borders

State borders do not mark out correctly who is concerned by decisions, acts and omissions – whether by public authorities or private entities – that affect health and the environment. Nor do state borders adequately define how far pursuits for justice should go in such cases. Rather, basic legal conceptions of state sovereignty and responsibility, jurisdiction and civil liability are challenged by transboundary effects on health and the environment and by transboundary corporate structures; and these features trigger particular concerns of procedural, distributive and corrective justice across state borders.

Situations of transboundary *effects* on health and the environment range from local settings, where only two neighbouring countries are involved, to global contexts; and they pertain to pollution, use of natural resources, stress on ecosystems, and trade in hazardous goods and wastes. These transboundary features reflect the current paradigm of international environmental law, which is primarily focused on inter-state concerns. Yet, as I will argue, it is not sufficient to consider these cases as inter-state only. From a justice viewpoint, it should be considered which interests are taken into account and who is capable of participating in decision-making and challenging decisions concerning activities with transboundary impact. Are they the interests only of those persons in the state of the activity or also those affected across state borders? And in which state, that of the activity or that of the harm, should justice be pursued?

The expansion of transnational corporations, fuelled by economic globalisation, also raises transboundary justice considerations, but of a different kind. In these cases, the transboundary element is found in the *corporate structure* and *subjectivity* of the actor responsible for the harm. From a justice perspective, the main concern is whether the locals – i.e. those affected *in* the state of the activity/harm – may make the transnational corporation responsible, so as to prevent or remedy harm, through legal proceedings *outside* that state, for example in the home state of the parent company.[1] If no such opportunities are available, or if international law so prevents,

---

[1] I discuss the transboundary dimensions of corporate responsibility in Ebbesson 2006. See also Schwartz in Chapter 22 of this volume with regard to transnational mining corporations in Sierra Leone.

transnational corporations can benefit from inadequate national institutions and laws, and abuse jurisdictional borders so as to avoid taking appropriate measures to prevent, restore or compensate for harm. Moreover, if the units in a corporation – the parent company and its subsidiaries – are perceived as distinct legal persons in all respects, splitting a corporation into several bodies in different jurisdictions may help the parent company to circumvent responsibility and liability over its subsidiaries, even though it maintains full *de facto* control of the activities. In other instances, a foreign company, which imposes overwhelming *de facto* control on a local sub-contractor, making the latter virtually dependent upon the former, may escape responsibility for harm. Although this situation is most likely to occur in states with inadequate legislation and institutions, it may arise also in states with effective laws and institutions if the operator has no assets in that state to compensate for or remedy the harm caused.[2] In either situation, the justice implications are clear.

This essay has the dual purpose of identifying legal hurdles for pursuing justice in transboundary contexts, and examining the relevant legal principles and concepts in such cases from a justice point of view. I first discuss why justice considerations in transboundary cases should not be limited to inter-state concerns, but should take individual members of the public (and possibly also non-human species) into account. I then examine whether state sovereignty and accepted principles of jurisdiction preclude pursuits for justice across state borders. In that context, I also consider the possible choices of law in transboundary context. This is followed by an analysis of how international law responds to justice issues that arise in different constellations of the (likely) harm, the cause and the forum to resolve the conflict related to health and the environment.

2 Individuals rather than states as the measure

Deliberations of procedural, distributive and corrective justice in transboundary contexts hinge on whether states (or peoples) or individuals are the measure of justice. Taking states as the unit means focusing on the procedural opportunities, the distribution of burdens and benefits, and corrective effects *of and between states only*, while effectively leaving justice concerns within each state at its own discretion.[3] The alternative, a more cosmopolitan conception of justice, is to place members of the public at the centre also in transboundary justice deliberations.[4]

---

[2] One such case is the mine in Aznalcóllar, Spain, which at the time of the severe collapse in 1998 was operated by a subsidiary of the Swedish corporation Boliden. After various legal procedures in Spain, the corporation did not have enough assets in Spain to cover the clean-up costs. A concise account of the case and its aftermath is given by Moreno 2006–7.

[3] This is further debated by Nollkaemper in Chapter 13 of this volume.

[4] I leave aside at this stage that individual non-human species also should be considered subjects to justice deliberations. See Nussbaum 2006 at 325–407.

The state-centred approach is in line with John Rawls' theory of the 'law of peoples', which he distinguishes from the principles of justice for individuals within a fixed society.[5] Rawls rejects the notion of cosmopolitan justice or global justice for all persons in part because he thinks it requires too much of states; some degree of toleration is needed and all states cannot be expected to be liberal democracies.[6] Instead of expanding his theory of justice to transboundary cases and putting individuals in the 'original position', he replaces them in a 'second original position' by representatives of peoples (states). Peoples, he argues, have equal reciprocal rights of recognition, and their representatives 'will want to preserve the equality and independence of their own society'.[7] In essence, this means that justice considerations stop at the state borders in favour of the law of peoples, whereas justice considerations are left to the discretion of each state. Apparently, this much resembles the logic of the traditional conception of international law.

Rawls has been strongly criticised for keeping his theory of justice to 'closed societies' rather than transcending it across state borders. As argued by Martha Nussbaum, his analogy fails on several accounts because it fundamentally assumes incorrect features of states. First, many nations of the world do not have governments that represent the interest of the people as a whole. Second, states and their basic domestic structures are not as fixed as Rawls presumes, and groups within states may turn to international norms in order to change domestic injustices. Third, by making a too close analogy with the domestic relations of individuals, Rawls assumes that each society is effectively self-sufficient, while in real life the situation is often different. He is not troubled by multinational corporations and does not pay much attention to international or supranational organisations.[8] Nor does he take into account the interdependence of states in other ways, in particular that many 'Southern' states are affected by 'domestic' events in certain, predominantly 'Northern', states.[9] Thus, by insisting on this analogy and thus disregarding essential facts, Rawls 'loses useful contact with reality'.[10]

These shortcomings of course matter for justice appraisals in transboundary cases of harm to health and the environment. There are numerous real life situations where harm is caused to human health and the environment in transboundary settings, without the government(s) acting so as to limit the harm to citizens on either side of the border. There are also situations where transnational corporations operate in

---

[5] Rawls 1999. Also Rawls 1972 at 7–8.   [6] Rawls 1999 at 82–3.

[7] Rawls 1999 at 23–30 (where he describes why he prefers the term 'people' to 'state', although many similarities remain), *ibid.* at 32–5 (where he explains the second original position) and *ibid.* at 41 (quote).

[8] Nussbaum 2006 at 230–8.

[9] Pogge 1989 at 256 and 262, where he gives the illustrative example of how the changes in US interest rates or certain domestic speculative trades can have tremendous impact on poor states that have significant foreign debt and rely on certain exports.

[10] Nussbaum 2006 at 233. Similar criticism is put forth by Twining in Chapter 4 of this volume.

states with weak governments as well as weak, or even non-existing, environmental legislation and control.

From a justice viewpoint, the ideal situation of environmental decision-making should as far as possible include the interests of *all* individuals (and possibly also non-human species) who are affected or concerned by decisions regarding the distribution of burdens and benefits, whether within or outside a particular state. This is not the case in real life. While territorial borders constitute the dominant, formal delimitations of societies in international law, state borders do not mark correctly who is concerned or affected by decisions, acts and omissions with regard to health or the environment. Nor should they prevent us from taking individuals as the measure in justice deliberations, for instance when examining international law and international institutions.

Thomas Pogge, when 'globalising the Rawlsian conception of justice', convincingly shows how the theoretical starting-point for cosmopolitan justice, that transcends state borders, can be founded on Rawls' social contract theory (although Rawls did not do that himself).[11] Cosmopolitan justice requires that the influence of, opportunities for and effects on each and every individual concerned be taken into account. Policies, decisions, acts and omissions cannot be justified only by referring to the positive effects for certain groups, while the interests of others are ignored. Thus, decisions, acts and omissions within a territory – regardless of the form or effects of the ruling – are not immune from justice considerations simply by reference to the sovereignty of that state.

Placing individuals rather than states as the measure for justice calculations in transboundary contexts does not rule out the value of self-determination and some conception of state sovereignty, provided it is not perceived as absolute. Rather, it should be understood as equal self-determination and autonomy of states, with possibilities of permeating the veil in certain cases.[12] When outlining the global application of the Rawlsian 'original position' as the test for justice deliberations, Pogge argues:

---

[11] Pogge 1989 at 211–79. Cosmopolitan claims for justice can also be founded on the notion of certain basic entitlements – 'human capabilities' – to be given to all individuals across national borders. Nussbaum 2006 at 69–95 draws on notions of natural law, and takes human capabilities as the core measure of justice, rather than utility or the distribution of resources to individuals. Sen 1999 at 54–86 considers freedom as the foundation for justice, and sees 'capability' as the substantive freedoms of a person to achieve alternative lifestyles. He contrasts this with, for example, Rawls' priority of liberty.

[12] Cf. Cohen 2005, who argues in favour of adapting the conception of sovereignty so as to be compatible with cosmopolitan principles inherent in human rights norms. Pogge 1989 at 271–2, without referring to state sovereignty, when considering the global application of the Rawlsian 'original position' as the test for justice deliberations, argues that '[t]he global parties are not constrained by any prior criterion of domestic justice; and they will then specifically decide how much room to leave for differences in national institutional arrangements and in national conceptions of domestic justice'. Cf. Nussbaum 2006 at 316, who suggests that '[n]ational sovereignty should be respected, within the constraints of promoting human capabilities'.

> The global parties are not constrained by any prior criterion of domestic justice; and they will then specifically decide how much room to leave for differences in national institutional arrangements and in national conceptions of domestic justice. Seeing how the original position is described, the parties decide this question by balancing two desiderata . . . : They want to enable citizens to choose and revise their own domestic constitution, even their own conception of domestic justice, so long as such choice results from and guarantees for the future free and informed decisions. Yet they also want to preclude institutions that tend to produce severe deprivations or disadvantages for some participants.[13]

Nor does a cosmopolitan conception of justice imply that norms and policies from one region or state can be imposed on others without any justifiable reason; that would amount to environmental imperialism rather than pursuing environmental justice. The crux is to agree on the leeway for national self-determination, while ensuring due respect for the opportunities and interests of all persons concerned by decision-making.[14]

The limits for self-determination are reflected not only in the constraints for domestic institutional arrangements and conceptions of justice, but also in the extent to which states accept overlapping competences and jurisdictions. For transboundary pursuits of justice in environmental matters, the element of overlapping jurisdictions, and whether such overlapping amounts to unacceptable interference, is most relevant. Fairness and justice require that, in cases of *transboundary effects* to health and the environment, those affected have access to adequate decision-making procedures and remedies in the state of the activity or elsewhere. It also requires that, in cases of *transnational corporations*, if there is no opportunity to take part in decision-making or to challenge the harmful conduct of private corporations in the state of the harm and activity, those affected have access to remedies abroad.[15]

Despite my emphasis on the opportunities for the persons concerned to engage themselves in the decision-making, as an essential element in the conception of justice, this does not preclude other institutional arrangements to promote the protection of health and the environment. On the contrary, such institutional arrangements may in many cases promote justice when health and the environment are at stake; and sometimes more effectively than when individuals act alone. Public authorities in the state of the activity and/or the state of the harm are often better equipped to deal with

---

[13] Pogge 1989 at 271–2.

[14] For Nussbaum 2006 at 316, '[n]ational sovereignty should be respected, within the constraints of promoting human capabilities'. Cohen 2005 suggests adapting the conception of sovereignty so as to be compatible with cosmopolitan principles in human rights norms.

[15] Cf. Pogge 1989 at 245–6, arguing that persons abused by their own governments have no official remedies and must rely on the willingness of other governments or agents to intercede in their behalf, and that, if Rawls' notion of 'original position' were to be applied to persons in an international context, 'the parties would prefer international law to afford some remedies to persons against abuse by their own governments, some incentives for societies to reform themselves'.

transboundary effects and act against powerful operators than the persons affected by the activity. Thus, establishing public environmental authorities, or allowing non-governmental organisations to initiate or participate in decision-making, may be instrumental to providing distributive or corrective justice for individual members of the public. Moreover, while the distinction between private and public inter-ests is often blurred in environmental matters, a functioning public administration is necessary to ensure the effective protection of public environmental interests, such as public health and nature conservation.

3 Procedural, distributive and corrective justice in transboundary contexts

All forms of environmental decision-making – for example, the issuance of per-mits and concessions for harmful activities, approval of plans and environmental impact assessments, administrative requests for safety measures, banning of harmful substances, litigation for compensation or injunctive relief, protection of sensitive ecosystems, initiation of criminal procedures, and request for judicial review – have justice implications, in many cases across state borders. The first aspect of justice con-cerns the procedural opportunities to initiate or participate in such procedures and influence the decision-making: how is the group of persons with such opportunities defined, and to what extent do state borders matter for this delimitation? The second issue, decisive for the distribution of burdens and benefits, regards the interests to be considered and their relative weight: which interests are given priority when balanced against other interests, and again to what extent do state borders matter in these balances?

As stated, procedural justice also requires that persons on the other side of the border, potentially affected by environmental laws and policies, are given a right to participate and be represented in the law-making processes.[16] Although beyond the scope of this essay, similar arguments can be raised for the legitimacy, i.e. the general acceptance,[17] of laws in a transboundary context. If the legitimacy of national laws in democratic states rests on the understanding that citizens are the 'authors' of the law,[18] then we face a lack of democratic legitimation in situations where national

---

[16] Cf. Fraser 2005 at 82, who sees in the 'all-affected principle' the most promising candidate for a 'postwest-phalian mode of frame-setting', meaning that all those affected by a given social structure or institution have moral standing as subjects of justice in relation to it. Thus, she argues, 'what turns a collection of people into fellow subjects of justice is not the geographical proximity, but their co-imbrication in a common structural or institutional framework, which sets the ground rules that govern their social interaction, thereby shaping their respective life possibilities in patterns of advantage and disadvantage'.

[17] Cf. Habermas 1979 at 178: 'Legitimacy means that there are good arguments for a political order's claim to be recognized as right and just: a legitimate order deserves recognition. *Legitimacy means a political order's worthiness ro be recognized*'. Emphasis in orginal.

[18] Cf. Habermas 2001 at 101: 'The citizens of a democratic legal state understand themselves as the authors of the law, which compels them to obedience as its authors.' The theoretical premises for this is further set out in Habermas 1996.

laws affect subjects and interests across state borders that have not been represented. A weak form of such legitimation may be provided by increasing the participation of civil society not only in international negotiations (mainly through NGOs), but also by the transboundary participation of civil society in environmental decision-making.[19] While increasing opportunities for such participation concerning plans, programmes and activities with transboundary impact may not meet the standards for 'cosmopolitan democracy',[20] it would at least promote a cosmopolitan conception of justice. To do so, equal opportunity must be provided for transboundary participation as for domestic participation, but mere *non-discrimination* would not be sufficient: it would also require some *minimum standard* for procedural opportunities.[21] Thus, a state with no or only marginal opportunities for its own citizens would not meet the standard of justice simply by providing equally poor opportunities to those concerned across the border.

In international environmental law, 'access to justice' has come to refer largely to the *procedural* and informational aspects of justice, including the possibility of challenging decisions, acts and omissions by public authorities and private persons, with a bearing on health or the environment. The assumption, one may say, is that procedural justice is instrumental to achieving justice also in the distributive and corrective senses.[22]

While these opportunities should primarily be available at the place of the decision, act or omission that may affect health or the environment, in some situations alternative procedural opportunities should also be available elsewhere. When the case involves a transboundary effect or risk of an activity, the most relevant alternative would be to prevent or remedy the situation in the state where the harm occurs. When transnational corporations are involved, and the corporate structure of the operator constitutes the transboundary element, the alternative would be to pursue the case in the state to which the corporation has some link, for example by means of nationality, registration, ownership (parent company) or *de facto* control. In either case, to

---

[19] In this respect, the 1998 UNECE Convention on Access to Information, Public Participation in Decision-making and Access to Justice in Environmental Matters (Aarhus Convention), 38 *International Legal Materials* (ILM) (1999) 515, is a special case. While requiring the parties to ensure certain minimum participatory rights also in the drafting of general norms, they are also not allowed to discriminate, on the basis of domicile, citizenship etc., when providing the public with participatory opportunities.

[20] Cf. Habermas 2001 at 107–12.

[21] This draws on the Rawlsian conception of 'equality of opportunity', although he refers to constitutional rights and liberties of a fundamental political character within a society rather than the detailed design of environmental decision-making in transboundary contexts; cf. Rawls 1972 at 195–201, 228–34. For Rawls 1972 at 60–1, 83–90, the fair equality of opportunity has to match certain basic civil and political liberties and rights. Cf. Nussbaum's (2006 at 76–7) claim for 'minimum core social entitlements', which she describes as central human capabilities, also includes some minimum standards of a procedural kind. While Rawls comes close to civil and political human rights, without any detail on how to consider environmental issues, Nussbaum's list stretches further as it also includes social, economic and environmental elements.

[22] See Ebbesson 2002 at 1, 7–8 and 12–15.

provide adequate opportunities, the institutional arrangements must not be so complicated, time-consuming and costly that, while available in principle, the persons concerned are effectively barred for economic or social reasons from making use of them.

The decision-making procedures mentioned involve different considerations with regard to the *distribution* of burdens and benefits, and the balancing of interests and priorities, for instance how the interests of the applicant to run the harmful activity are to be balanced against the interest of protecting health and the environment. In part, the *corrective* concerns overlap the distributive aspects. Claims for civil liability and torts, where harm is compensated for, and other reparative and remedying claims such as clean-up, may also produce corrective effects, and so can criminal liability for harm to health and the environment.

4 Sovereignty, jurisdiction and environmental policy

Since self-rule and self-determination are fundamentals for political legitimacy and justice considerations in decision-making procedures, the quest for justice outside the state of the harm/activity needs to be balanced against the imperative of not generally imposing the law on a people from outside. If the law for using natural resources or permitting harmful activities is decided by other states or peoples, those concerned *in* the state of the activity would have no say in how the burdens and benefits should be allocated. As argued, such a lack of opportunities for the persons concerned to be engaged in law-making would rather amount to a kind of environmental imperialism, where standards are imposed from abroad. Even so, there are cases where those concerned have legitimate reasons to seek justice outside, because the government in the state of activity does not in fact represent the peoples in that state or because there is no functioning legal or administrative system to provide means for preventing, remedying or redressing cases of harm to health or the environment.

The fear for having external laws and regulations imposed was critical for the newly independent states in the 1960s and 1970s, as reflected in the 1962 UN Resolution on Permanent Sovereignty over Natural Resources:

> The exploration, development and disposition of such resources should be in conformity with the rules and conditions which the peoples and nations freely consider to be necessary or desirable with regard to the authorization, restriction or prohibition of such activities.[23]

In addition to pronouncing the self-determination of states *vis-à-vis* each other, the resolution also stresses the duty of foreign companies to abide by the national laws where the activities are carried out. Full and permanent sovereignty over natural

---

[23] UNGA Resolution 1803 (XVII) on Permanent Sovereignty over Natural Resources (1962), para. 2.

resources, 'including possession, use and disposal', over natural resources, is also set out in the 1974 UN Resolution on the Charter of Economic Rights and Duties of States, which is even more elaborate than the 1962 resolution. Thus, it declares the right of each state to 'regulate and supervise the activities of transnational corporations within its national jurisdiction and take measures to ensure that such activities comply with its laws, rules and regulations and conform with its economic and social policies'.[24]

Not surprisingly, the newly independent states, when freed from European colonial powers, perceived sovereignty as a shield against European and American dominance and power, and a means to preserve their independence and self-determination, but also as a means to promote economic and social development and fair distribution of wealth.[25] This mind-set was evident in the context of the New International Economic Order (NIEO),[26] proclaimed by developing countries at that time. It is reflected in international human rights treaties, such as the UN covenants on civil and political rights as well as economic, social and cultural rights,[27] and in numerous international environmental agreements, policy documents and decisions of normative weight, adopted since the 1970s.[28] Thus proclaims the 1992 UN Declaration on Environment and Development (Rio Declaration):

> States have, in accordance with the Charter of the United Nations and the principles of international law, *the sovereign right to exploit their own resources pursuant to their own environmental and developmental policies*, and the responsibility to ensure that activities within their jurisdiction and control do not cause damage to the environment of other States or of areas beyond the limits of national jurisdiction.[29]

When analysing its impact on transboundary pursuits for justice, we need, again, to distinguish between situations of transboundary effects and cases where transnational corporations are involved without any apparent transboundary effects on the environment. As far as transboundary *effects* on health and the environment are concerned, it follows from the quoted principle that a state is not immune from claims or interference by other states when its policies or use of natural resources may harm the persons or the environment outside its territory. Yet, even taking the interests

---

[24] UNGA Resolution 3281 (XXIX), Charter of Economic Rights and Duties of States (1974), Art. 2.

[25] Rajagopal 2003 at 79–81.   [26] See Shelton in Chapter 3 of this volume.

[27] See 1966 International Covenant on Civil and Political Rights, 999 UNTS 171, Art. 1(2); 1966 International Covenant on Economic, Social and Cultural Rights, 6 ILM (1967) 368, Arts. 1(2) and 25; 1981 African Charter on Human and Peoples' Rights, 21 ILM (1982) 59, Art. 21.

[28] See e.g. 1992 Convention on Biological Diversity, 31 ILM (1992) 818, Art. 3; 1992 Statement of Principles for a Global Consensus on the Management, Conservation and Sustainable Development of All Types of Forests, 31 ILM (1992) 881, para. 1a; 1994 UN Convention to Combat Desertification in Those Countries Experiencing Serious Drought and/or Desertification, Particularly in Africa, 22 ILM (1994) 1328, Preamble; and 1991 Convention on Environmental Impact Assessment in a Transboundary Context, 30 ILM (1991) 800, Preamble.

[29] 1992 United Nations Declaration on Environment and Development, 31 ILM (1992) 876, Principle 2. Cf. 1972 United Nations Declaration on the Human Environment, 11 ILM (1972) 1416, Principle 21.

of other affected *states* into account is no guarantee for cosmopolitan justice or for fair consideration of the individuals potentially affected. This would still depend on whether there are institutions in place for the persons concerned to somehow pursue their case – either in the state of the activity or elsewhere.

In cases of transboundary effects, the *territorial connection*, which is the most significant jurisdictional basis, can be invoked by the state of the activity as well as by the state suffering the harm.[30] In environmental settings, the 'territorial principle' applies for instance when the state of the activity issues a permit or imposes its environmental protection standards or tort law on national and foreign companies operating within its territory. It also applies when a claim for compensation is brought to a court in the state of the harm rather than the state of the activity. Whereas administrative decision-making (permits, requests by supervisory authorities) will largely take place in the state of the activity, a possibility of choosing the forum may arise in private law litigation concerning transboundary effects on health and the environment.[31] In theory, either route may promote justice, although the choice of forum will be determined not only by the possibility of a positive outcome, but also by the means of enforcement.

The situation is different when a transnational corporation or its subsidiary is brought by the locals affected to a court outside the state of the harm/activity. In these situations, without transboundary effect, the jurisdictional basis for the court to decide on the corporation's activity mainly consists in the *personality* or *nationality* of the corporate wrongdoers; and this is compatible even with a rather orthodox reading of sovereignty.[32] The 'nationality principle' provides a pertinent basis for jurisdiction when transnational corporations operate in states with inadequate legal or institutional structures to effectively handle cases of harm to health or the environment. In such cases, the court of the company's home country may try claims for compensation and maybe even apply injunctive measures. While the personality link to the home country of the transnational corporation may appear weaker when it operates through local subsidiaries in the state of the activity, there is still a legitimate jurisdictional basis from an international law point of view as the subsidiary operated under *de facto* control of the parent company.

As a jurisdictional basis, the personality link outside the state of the activity (with no adequate environmental laws and institutions) appears weaker if the company in question is owned by several foreign corporations, none of which has the majority of shares. Yet, in these cases, jurisdiction can be established in the home country of the

---

[30] For general accounts of the territorial principle, see e.g. Lowe 2006 at 342–4; Shaw 2003 at 572; and Malanczuk 1997/2002 at 109.

[31] See Case 21/76, *Bier* v. *Mines de Potasse d'Alsace* [1976] *European Court Reports* (ECR) 1735. The distinction between public law and private law is admittedly not that clear, and what is seen as a private law remedy in one state may be functionally equivalent to a public law remedy in another state.

[32] It is for each state to decide on the criteria for a corporation's nationality, e.g. registered seat, main business and tax payment.

shareholder with *de facto* control of the subsidiary. If no such owner can be identified, even partial ownership (or simply access to assets) may suffice to establish jurisdiction, although the personality link is weak. This would imply overlapping jurisdictions, still without amounting to universal jurisdiction. Apparently, the weaker the personality link between the accused corporation and the state of the court, the more important becomes the lack of adequate laws and institutions in the state of the harm/activity as a ground for claiming jurisdiction to try a case for compensation for harm to health or the environment.

From the perspective of justice in cases concerning health and the environment, *universal* jurisdiction – i.e. jurisdiction without any particular link at all to the state where the case is tried – may seem appealing as it would, in effect, expand the opportunities for remedies and procedures for those affected. Increasing the possibility for persons affected to claim compensation or ask for injunction or mandamus action could thus promote justice and the protection of health and the environment. However, universal jurisdiction is problematic from a legitimacy as well as from a justice point of view, since it means that some states or regions – without any link to the issue at stake – may impose their laws onto another people. Unless some international normative consensus exists regarding corporate behaviour, universal jurisdiction may be perceived as imposing laws from outside onto a people. There is indeed some international consensus with regard to a limited number of activities, such as the production of CFCs, transboundary shipment of hazardous wastes, and the dumping of such wastes at sea, and it may also be possible to establish some common elements in compensation schemes.[33] Still, universal jurisdiction should be limited to rather severe cases, where the host state fails to ensure even minimum standards of human rights related to health and the environment.[34] Today, universal jurisdiction is generally accepted only for a limited number of serious acts, such as piracy, war crimes and hijacking.

This said, to preclude any such opportunities to bring the claims abroad, by reference to state sovereignty, would in certain cases amount to *déni de justice*, which is as such incompatible with the notion of a human right to a fair trial. Whereas some gross violations of human rights may even justify interventions on the basis of humanitarian law (when approved by the UN Security Council),[35] our concern is rather if, and when, recourse can be had to remedies abroad in cases of harm to health and the environment. This is the sovereignty versus justice test; and in severe situations pursuits for justice require that the state of the activity cannot claim

---

[33] See Boyle 2006 at 559, 570–83.

[34] I leave aside the more contested bases for jurisdiction, e.g. the 'protective principle' (with respect to acts by aliens abroad that threaten the state in question) and the effects doctrine. While in theory they could be useful in the pursuit for justice, a too far-reaching 'effects doctrine' would not be compatible with the principle of self-rule. See Akehurst 1972–3 at 157–9, and Lowe 2006 at 344–5 and 347–8.

[35] See Cohen 2005 for a critical account on cosmopolitan justice in cases of violations of humanitarian law.

exclusive jurisdiction even if there is no link of territoriality or personality to any other particular state.

These concerns were not addressed in the 1962 or 1974 UN resolutions. Rather, these resolutions were intended to clarify that foreign ownership does not deprive the host state of its right to regulate or control the activities of foreign companies,[36] and under what circumstances the host state may even nationalise or expropriate foreign investments without violating international law. Both NIEO resolutions focus on the laws and regulations of the host state, but do not expressly tackle the question whether a foreign corporation can – also – be held responsible outside the host state, presumably in its home state, for causing harm to health or the environment in the host state. When proclaiming the sovereign right of states or peoples to pursue their own environmental and developmental policies, the NIEO resolutions, human rights treaties and international environmental instruments (such as the Rio Declaration), presume that there are national environmental laws, regulations and institutions in place in the state of the activity. They do not refer to lawless situations or cases where the state fails to control foreign corporations. In such situations, accepting overlapping jurisdictions, so as to allow some courts outside the state of the harm/activity to decide on compensation or injunctive measures, does not amount to thwarting the economic policy or self-determination of the people in the state of the harm/activity.[37]

5 Choice of law

In most cases of administrative decision-making and adjudication in environmental matters, the choice of law is not really an issue, since the activity, the harm and the forum to decide the case are located within the same jurisdiction. In transboundary contexts, however, the situation is different, and the choice of law becomes an issue.

Possible options for the choice of law, depending on the forum as well as the issue at stake, are the law of the place of the court (*lex fori*), the law of the place of the activity and/or harm (*lex loci delicti*), or resort to international or generally accepted standards. In cases involving transboundary effects, the presumption would be to apply the law of the place of the harm/tort.[38] Yet, in such settings the place of the harm may refer to either the place where the harmful activity or the harmful effects occurred; and the court, or the plaintiff,[39] will have to choose between the law of the state of the activity and the law of the state of the harm. In the alternative setting, of a transnational corporation brought to court in its home country, the court, if it accepts jurisdiction, may decide to try the case according to the law of the state of

---

[36] P. Malanczuk 1997/2002 at 236.   [37] Cf. Akehurst 1972–3 at 189.

[38] As argued by Briggs 2002 at 176–8, alternative approaches to *lex loci delicti* have been applied for torts, such as a 'test of the closest connection'.

[39] The possibility for the plaintiff to choose the law to be applied in cases of harm to the environment is set out in European Community Regulation (EC) No. 864/2007 on the Law Applicable to Non-contractual Obligations (Rome II), [2007] *Official Journal* (OJ) L199/40, Art. 7.

the activity/harm. As mentioned, applying the environmental law of the state of the court, rather than the state of the activity/harm, implies imposing foreign standards on the people affected. Therefore, provided rules on the protection of health and the environment actually exist in the state of the activity/harm, it may be preferable to apply this law since it may somehow reflect the values, preferences and principles for the distribution of burdens and benefits among those concerned. There is no general principle of international law on the choice of law in cases like this. Determining the responsibility of transnational corporations may involve yet another choice of law issue when considering holding the parent company responsible for the activities of its subsidiaries overseas. While corporate matters are usually determined by the law under which the corporation was created (*lex incorporationis*),[40] courts may also avoid entering into such deliberations simply by allocating the responsibility to the parent company without further ado about piercing the corporate veil.

The choice of law has justice implications, because the distribution of burdens and benefits as well as the opportunities for participation etc. depend on the values and priorities reflected in the law to be applied. For instance, different laws weigh in different ways the interests of the operator of a hazardous activity against the interests of those who are adversely affected by the activity. This balance of interest may be based on the application of general principles (e.g. the precautionary principle, the polluter pays principle and proportionality), but also follow from emission standards, technical standards (including the standard of best available technology) and ambient standards intended to protect health and the environment. The principles for compensation for harm (e.g. strict or fault-based liability) also differ depending on the choice of law to be applied.

6 Premises for pursuits across state borders

6.1 Three constellations

Remaining at a rather abstract level, we can identify three possible groupings of the harm(s), its cause (i.e. the activity) and the decision-making forum in transnational contexts. Of course, the complexity of a case depends on the number of causes and spreading of harms as well as the distance between the cause and the harm(s). Yet, from a typology point of view, they can be reduced to the following constellations:

1. *Cause* and *forum* in State A, *harm* in State B.
2. *Cause* in State A, *harm* and *forum* in State B.
3. *Cause* and *harm* in State A, *forum* in State B.

Harm refers to harm to the environment as well as harm to health and damage sustained by persons or property in relation to harm to the environment. It also

---

[40] Briggs 2002 at 245–9.

includes possible future harm, i.e. situations of prevention and risk of harm. The *cause* is the activity or installation which entails the nuisance, harm or risk of harm. The cause may be a polluting industry, but also an activity that uses natural resources in a harmful way. Depending on the kind of decision-making, the *forum* may be an administrative authority, which decides on whether to permit the activity, or a court which either reviews the administrative act (or omission) or decides on compensation, enforcement or criminal sanctions. While, in theory, the forum for transboundary claims regarding health and the environment could be an international institution of some sort, such a forum remains yet to be established.[41] Therefore, from a justice point of view, it is essential to consider whether recourse can be had to fora – courts, other tribunals, or competent administrative bodies – established under some national law and jurisdiction.

In all cases with some transboundary reach, the question arises not only as to which state(s) can decide and whether there are procedural opportunities across state borders, but also about enforcement and recognition of decisions. To be worthwhile from a justice point of view, a decision concerning environmentally harmful activities must also be enforceable somewhere and somehow.

6.2 Case I: pursuing justice in the state of the cause (activity)

The first case refers to situations where the harm occurs outside the state of the cause (activity), but the affected members of the public across the border take part in decision-making or initiate legal actions in the state of the cause.

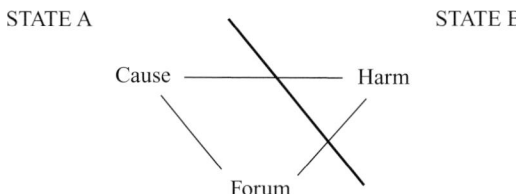

Figure 14.1 Case I: pursuing justice in the state of the cause

This is the situation when persons potentially affected by transboundary harm seek to participate in a permit procedure or an environmental impact assessment

---

[41] If the operator causing the harm so accepts, it would be possible to refer a dispute between non-state actors to an *ad hoc* arbitral tribunal, e.g. in accordance with the procedures set out by the Permanent Court of Arbitration. To my knowledge, however, no such transboundary conflict between the non-state actors concerned by environmentally harmful operations and the operator has ever been settled by arbitration. See Hey 2000. The Aarhus Convention Compliance Committee has no power to remedy any harm caused. Rather, it is intended to be forward-looking with regard to the implementation of the Convention, and can only address the issue of non-compliance of a state party to the Convention (although this includes cases where the party failed to control private companies). See Fitzmaurice in Chapter 11 of this volume, and Koester 2005 at 31.

procedure in the state of the activity, or appeal such decisions. Possible claims in such procedures are the denial of a permit or the requirement that certain precautionary measures be taken by the applicant in order to avoid adverse effects. Alternatively, if procedures involve actions in court, the plaintiffs may claim compensation, injunctive measures and enforcement with regard to activities already in place. There is solid jurisdictional support, based on the territorial principle, for the forum in the state of the activity (State A) to deal with either cases.[42] While outside the scope of this chapter, these are situations where the neighbouring state might also initiate diplomatic or legal measures against the state of the activity for violations of international law. Such inter-state proceedings may provide for just outcomes as far as the distributive and corrective aspects are concerned, although what is just for the government of a state in such a dispute is not necessarily just for the affected individuals in that state.[43]

For this particular constellation some development of international law has taken place, in particular by the increasing recognition of *non-discrimination and equal access* as a legal principle.[44] Non-discrimination and equal access imply that the forum deciding the case must apply no less favourable rules and principles on standing, participation in decision-making and access to justice to subjects outside the territory of the state of the court than to like subjects within that state. As to the examination on the merits, non-discrimination, for example when issuing a permit or trying a claim for compensation, also implies that the interests and concerns on the other side of the border should be treated no less favourably than like interests and concerns in the state of the activity. Thus, criteria for defining the group of persons with standing may well relate to the distance from the installation and possible impact on those concerned, but not to the state borders. If the criterion for standing refers to sufficient interest, the same test should apply across the border. If certain non-governmental organisations have standing in the state of the activity, non-discrimination implies standing also for like organisations in the affected state.

While non-discrimination and equal access have achieved global recognition as a legal principle (although its practical implementation in many countries and regions

---

[42] On jurisdictional principles and *forum non conveniens* in general, see McLachlan and Nygh 1996.

[43] Indeed, in the 1941 *Trail Smelter* award, concerning an air pollution dispute between Canada and the US, the tribunal was asked to 'reach a solution just to all parties concerned'; and it was to this end that the tribunal concluded the principle that 'no State has the right to use or permit the use of its territory in such a manner as to cause injury by fumes in or to the territory of another or the properties or persons therein, when the case is of serious consequence and the injury is established by clear and convincing evidence': 3 RIAA 1905, at pp. 1908, 1963–6. Still, such settlements are scarce and they do not necessarily provide for just outcomes for the persons affected by transboundary nuisance. That would in part depend on the claims made by the affected state, and the extent to which it truly represented the persons concerned.

[44] I have dealt elsewhere with the non-discrimination principle in international environmental law, see e.g. Ebbesson 2007, and more substantially in Ebbesson 1998 81–7. A yet lengthier analysis of the non-discrimination principle, with regard to the 1974 Nordic Environment Protection Convention, 13 ILM (1974) 591, is found in Ebbesson 2003.

can be questioned), this is not the case with international minimum standards for procedural opportunities. Some minimum standards for public participation and access to justice have been established in international law, but this development is basically limited to Europe, parts of Asia and North America. The most advanced regime for this purpose is the 1998 Convention on Access to Information, Public Participation in Decision-making and Access to Justice in Environmental Matters (Aarhus Convention), which applies to the UNECE region.[45] Despite the strong endorsement of public participation in environmental decision-making at the 1992 Rio Conference, this has not yet been incorporated in any international agreement of broader geographical coverage. Although human rights instruments, if seriously implemented, would promote procedural justice also in environmental cases, they may not generally ensure procedural opportunities in cases related to health and the environment, and in particular not in transboundary contexts. Thus, with the possible exception of the Aarhus Convention, international law does not provide for procedural justice across state borders. The minimum procedural opportunities in transboundary cases therefore essentially depend on the national law of the state of the cause (activity).

When the case is tried in the state of the cause (activity), the court or administrative body most likely applies the law of that state (possibly influenced by international law). The court may decide to apply foreign law, for example the law of the state of the harm – at least to the extent that it does not lead to less favourable result for the subjects and concerns abroad as to like concerns in the state of the activity.[46] An alternative approach to the choice of law is found in European Community law, which leaves it to the injured party to choose the law to be applied – either the law of the place of the activity or of the place of the harm.[47] From a justice point of view, this appears to be a satisfactory solution, and it does not amount to imposing the law from outside the context.

---

[45] 1998 UNECE Convention on Access to Information, Public Participation in Decision-Making and Access to Justice in Environmental Matters, 38 ILM (1999) 515. See Ebbesson 1998 and 2007. The Aarhus Convention sets out such minimum requirements for access to information, public participation in decision-making and access to review procedures. However, it does not apply to the US, Canada or Russia. Some such internationally defined minimum requirements also apply to North America, through the 1993 North American Agreement on Environmental Cooperation, 32 ILM (1993) 1480.

[46] Cf. the 1974 Nordic Environment Protection Convention, note 44 above, Art. 3, which seems to be drafted on the assumption that *lex loci delicti* is the general principle providing for the choice of law. For that reason, it sets out that, if the law of the state of the harm is less generous to the plaintiff than that of the state of the activity, the latter should apply.

[47] See European Community Regulation (EC) No. 864/2007 on the Law Applicable to Non-contractual Obligations (Rome II), [2007] OJ L199/40, Art. 7: 'The law applicable to a non-contractual obligation arising out of environmental damage or damage sustained by persons or property as a result of such damage shall be the law determined pursuant to Article 4(1) [i.e. the law of the country in which the damage occurs], unless the person seeking compensation for damage chooses to base his or her claim on the law of the country in which the event giving rise to the damage occurred.'

While transboundary procedures in cases of environmental harm will always be complicated, generally speaking bringing them to the state of the cause is the least complicated route of procedure.

6.3 Case II: pursuing justice in the state of the harm

While the state of the activity has a solid support for jurisdiction in just about all cases, and should take the transboundary matters into account on the basis of non-discrimination, this does not preclude overlapping jurisdiction. There are transboundary cases where other routes of procedure appear more promising from the perspective of the persons potentially harmed. The most relevant alternative is to bring the claims to a forum in the state of the harm. The reason for doing so may be that there is no competent forum or adequate remedy available in the state of the cause (activity). This makes the following constellation:

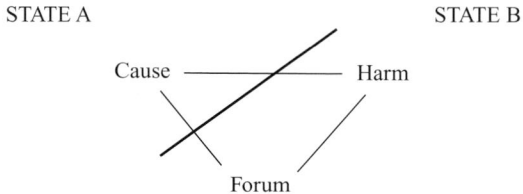

Figure 14.2 Case II: pursuing justice in the state of the harm

Jurisdiction can clearly be established on the territorial principle also in the state of the harm, and international law does not generally preclude such jurisdiction. Even so, there may be situations where litigation in the state of the harm, depending on the implications of the decisions in/for the state of the cause (activity), is considered to interfere too much with the domestic policies of the latter. While of little interest for this essay, it would, for instance, clearly amount to an unacceptable interference in the domestics of State A if a court or an administrative authority in State B were to grant permits for activities in State A without State A's approval. The situation is different, though, if members of the public in State B claim compensation for harm or injunctive measures in a court of State B against an activity in State A. For such claims, international law does not preclude jurisdiction also for State B.

In effect, however, the most complicated issue with pursuing justice in the state of the harm (State B) instead of the state of the cause (State A) relates to enforcement rather than jurisdiction. While states may agree through bilateral and multilateral treaties to recognise court decisions in other states, there is no general and consistent practice among states on the recognition of court decisions on compensation, let alone on injunctive measures, made in another state. For that reason, in terms of effective remedies, running the procedure in the state of the cause would often be preferable, because the court decision can easily be enforced against the operator of the activity.

This will have to be balanced against the possible advantages for the plaintiffs to bring the case to the court in State B, where they live, whether from a procedural, distributive or corrective point of view.

Even though international law does not generally block jurisdiction for the state of the harm, national law in that state may do so – with a negative impact from a justice point of view. There is no common position among states on how to decide in cases like these. In some states, courts may dismiss the case on the basis of *forum non conveniens* or other discretionary reasons, even if it has jurisdiction. In other states or regions, jurisdiction in these cases also is mandatory. A promising development from a justice point of view, in line with the notion that state borders should not block pursuits for justice, can be found in the European Union, where the persons affected *can choose* whether to bring the claim for compensation and injunctive measures to a court in the state of the activity or the state of the harm. This possibility was previously based on an international agreement between the EU member states, but it is now based on European Community law.[48] The states concerned are also obliged to recognise and even enforce court decisions made in the other EU member states. Moreover, the plaintiff can decide on the choice of law regardless of whether the case is brought to a court in the state of the activity or the state of the harm.[49] This is a rather unique development without any parallel on a global scale, so here, too, the effectiveness of bringing the case to court in the state of the harm depends on the national law of the particular state of the harm as well as on the law of the state of the cause; with obvious impact for the pursuit of justice.

6.4 Case III: pursuing justice outside the states of the cause and the harm

The third constellation occurs when a transnational corporation is held accountable outside the state of the activity/harm for harm caused either by itself or its subsidiaries. As mentioned, this situation differs from the previous two by the lack of transboundary effects; while the cause and harm largely remain in the same state, the case is brought to a forum outside that state for a decision regarding the harmful activity.

The concerns for such pursuits for justice are driven by the fact that, if no such opportunities are available, there are situations where transnational corporations may cause severe harm to health and the environment without any possibility to make them accountable. This is particularly the case when transnational corporations operate in countries with inadequate, if any, administrative institutions, laws and participatory opportunities for the persons concerned to prevent or remedy harm to health and the environment. Yet, as mentioned, it may arise also in states with effective laws and

---

[48] See Regulation (EC) No. 44/2001 on Jurisdiction and the Recognition and Enforcement of Judgments in Civil and Commercial Matters, [2001] OJ L12/1. This Regulation replaced the 1968 Brussels Convention on the same matter. Case 21/76, *Bier* v. *Mines de Potasse d'Alsace* [1976] ECR 1735; and Case C-343/04, *Land Oberösterreich* v. *ČEZ as* [2006] ECR I-4557.

[49] See note 47 above.

institutions if the operator has no assets in that state to compensate for or remedy the harm caused.

STATE A

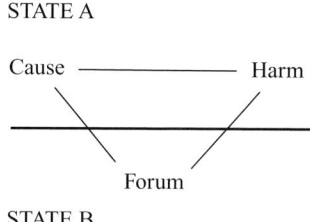

Figure 14.3 Case III: pursuing justice outside the state of the cause and the harm

Corporations organise themselves in multiple ways when acting across state borders, and this matters for jurisdictional considerations. Most transnational corporations have some national basis, but some companies are active in many countries without a particular link to any particular 'home country'. Some corporate structures are organised as even more diffused international networks or clusters of firms, sub-units, suppliers and sub-contractors.

Some policy documents and guidelines concerning corporate accountability in transboundary contexts have been adopted by international organisations, such as the UN,[50] the OECD[51] and the ILO.[52] Apart from that, however, there has been only little effort at a global scale to harmonise the laws or secure some minimum degree of responsibility of transnational corporations for harm to health and the environment. While outside the scope of this chapter, certain transboundary initiatives through 'self-regulation', corporate codes of conduct, voluntary auditing and management schemes etc., have taken place, and they may influence also administrative decision-making and legal reasoning.[53] Yet, these voluntary or legally non-binding instruments are not themselves enforceable against the corporation in case of a conflict.

The lack of an international legal framework does not mean that international law prevents a state from deciding cases concerning the activities of its nationals in other states, provided that it does not generally thwart the economic policy of that state. Different positions and policies on jurisdiction for corporate activities abroad are employed in different regions and states. One of the few efforts at harmonisation can

---

[50] Agenda 21, UN Doc. A/Conf.151/26; UN Global Compact, at www.unglobalcompact.org (visited 15 November 2007); Sub-Commission on the Promotion and Protection of Human Rights, Norms on the Responsibilities of Transnational Corporations and Other Business Enterprises with Regard to Human Rights, UN Doc. E/CN.4/Sub.2/2003/12/Rev.2 (2003).

[51] OECD, Guidelines for Multinational Enterprises 2001, reprinted in OECD 2001a; also at www.oecd.org (visited 15 November 2007).

[52] ILO Tripartite Declaration of Principles Concerning Multinational Enterprises and Social Policy (3rd edn, 2001), available at www.ilo.org (visited 15 November 2007).

[53] See e.g. OECD 2001b.

again be found in the European Union, as it opens the doors to the European courts in cases where European companies are involved outside Europe. Under European Community law, the exclusive forum in international cases concerning civil and commercial matters is the court of the state where the defendant is domiciled, i.e. where the corporation has its statutory seat, central administration or principal place of business.[54] In principle, this makes it possible to bring a European company to the court in the company's home state also in cases when the company operates its harmful activity in a country outside Europe.[55]

If the operation is carried out by a local corporation which is owned and/or controlled by a transnational corporation, the local corporation may, formally speaking, be a separate legal person. Even so, the court in the parent company's home country should have to look through the corporate veil to determine whether the parent company has maintained *de facto* control of the subsidiary. If not, this corporate divide, however artificial, may be abused in a similar way as national jurisdictions in order to do away with accountability for harms to health and the environment. Corporate structures, including the possibility of piercing the corporate veil, is yet another issue for which there is hardly any international effort of coordination, let alone harmonisation.[56] Due to the different perceptions of corporate structures, the possibility of pursuing these kinds of cases will depend on the national laws of the states involved.[57] Yet, while there is no international framework for harmonising the laws on corporate structures and responsibilities, international law does not preclude national courts from piercing the corporate veil in a case for preventing or remedying harms to health and the environment.[58]

In determining the responsibility of the transnational corporation, the choice of law is all the more important, taking into account the distance between the states concerned – the home state and the host state – and the possibility of differing laws and regulations in these states. While in these cases the presumption should be to apply the law of the state of the harm,[59] provided such laws and institutions exist, this rule could possibly be set aside if the standards in the state of the activity/harm

---

[54] See Regulation (EC) No. 44/2001 on Jurisdiction and the Recognition and Enforcement of Judgments in Civil and Commercial Matters, [2001] OJ L12/1. This Regulation replaced the 1968 Brussels Convention on the same matter.

[55] See Case C-281/02, *Owusu* v. *Jackson et al.* [2005] ECR I-1383; Case C-343/04, *Land Oberösterreich* v. *ČEZ as* [2006] ECR I-4557.

[56] Ebbesson 2006.

[57] A thorough analysis of corporate groups and their legal responsibilities is given by Antunes 1994, in particular pp. 64–80.

[58] Even if such opportunities are available, this may not resolve cases where the harmful company is owned by several corporations from different countries, and none of them is particularly dominant. Apparently, international law does not provide much guidance. One possibility would be to bring the case to the state of the most dominant owner, another to accept jurisdiction where any of the major owners has assets. Yet, this is not established in international law.

[59] Again, see Regulation (EC) No. 44/2001 on Jurisdiction and the Recognition and Enforcement of Judgments in Civil and Commercial Matters, [2001] OJ L12/1, Art. 7.

are obsolete or manifestly unacceptable. Of course, if there is no applicable law in the state of the harm/activity this may not only be a sufficient reason to bring the case out of the country, but also a reason for not applying *lex loci delicti*.

The almost unlimited jurisdiction of states to legislate and try cases of criminal and tort law on the basis of nationality provides a potentially useful entry for pursuits of justice in transboundary cases, although it has not yet been widely used for this purpose. The legal developments in Europe go in this direction, but there are few signs of such developments in international law at the global scene. While this area of law is developed without coordination through international law, there are some examples, for example in the US and the UK, where pursuits for justice in the home country of the transnational corporation have been acknowledged.[60]

7 Effective cosmopolitan justice without environmental imperialism

Procedures to remedy violations of performance standards and harm to health and the environment are often most effective, efficient and available for members of the public if they take place near the area of the activity or harm. Too remote procedures, geographically, economically or socially, make it difficult, if not impossible, for many people to participate in, let alone initiate, proceedings. For this reason, if possible, it makes good sense to run the procedure in the state where the activity is carried out, and, if that does not seem appropriate, in the state of the harm. Moreover, the application of local laws and the use of local proceedings ideally implies more of self-rule and self-determination than applying distant laws. This includes establishing principles for the distribution of burdens and benefits. Provided such opportunities exist in the state of the activity, non-discrimination and equal access for those concerned outside that state may add to achieving fair distributive and corrective outcomes also in transboundary contexts.

Still, as I have argued, there are numerous such situations where procedures to deal with environmental or health issues in the state of the activity are inadequate or simply not available – and thus cannot be used by members of the public who are at risk of suffering harm. In these cases, increasing procedural opportunities outside the state of the cause (activity) may be instrumental for justice. Failing international institutions for individuals to prevent or remedy harm to the environment, recourse must be had to national fora in other states. Such an overlapping of jurisdiction – in some cases in the state of the harm, in others in the state to which the corporation

---

[60] Numerous claims have been brought to US courts against corporations with some link to the US for harm caused 'abroad' on the basis of the Alien Tort Claims Act (28 USC section 1350 (2000)). While most claims have been dismissed on jurisdictional grounds (including *forum non conveniens*), there are also cases where the jurisdiction has been acknowledged, resulting in out-of-court settlements; see e.g. Crook 2005. In the UK, the House of Lords decided to try a case concerning claims for injuries from asbestos in South African mining where British corporations were involved; see Muchlinski 2001.

has some link – may promote pursuits for justice, by complicating for corporations engaged in harmful activities to shield behind state borders. While recognising the positive effects of overlapping jurisdiction in these transboundary contexts, some caveats, already mentioned, are in place.

The first regards the effectiveness of proceedings outside the state of the activity. While the jurisdictional basis for such decision-making may be perfectly fine, the decision on, say, compensation or precautionary measures may not be enforceable in the state of the activity. Unless the company has assets in the state of the proceedings or the decision can be formally recognised in the state of the activity, bringing the case outside the state of the activity may have little immediate legal effect (although it may still have a political effect).

The second concern is more principled and refers to justice versus imperialism. The point made – that the rules and principles for procedural opportunities as well as the distribution of burdens and benefits should as far as possible be decided by those concerned – matters for jurisdictional allocation as well as for the choice of law. Overlapping jurisdiction does not imply universal jurisdiction; and for the said reason, while some overlapping may promote pursuits for justice, universal jurisdiction is not optimal even from a justice point of view. Just outcomes would require some common perception of what is accepted or unaccepted behaviour. Once a case is brought out of the country of the activity/harm, some caution is required in terms of jurisdiction as well as the choice of law, in order to avoid a sense of imposing protection standards from one state or region onto another, and of disregarding the moral weight of self-determination and autonomy of the people concerned. Even so, these concerns should be weighed against the lack of remedies – laws and/or institutions – for those harmed by the corporate misdeeds, and against the fact that the case is actually brought abroad by the affected persons themselves. If there is no law or institution for the protection of health or the environment in the host state, then there would be no articulated self-rule to interfere with in the first place, and possibly no means for those affected to articulate it either, unless proceedings could be triggered abroad. What would remain in such a situation is just a lack of decent government. Moreover, in some of these cases, the corporate activity is likely to violate international norms, for example international human rights law, labour law or environmental law standards. If so, values and norms, at least if part of general international law, would not really be imposed from one territory to the other. In construing such principles for allowing pursuits for justice outside the state of the cause, much can be built on already existing notions for jurisdictional claims.

Third and final concern, re-conceptualising the transboundary situations and relaxing the impact of state borders in a formal, legal sense is not in itself sufficient to ensure fair proceedings. Justice, also in these contexts, requires that existing institutions actually make it possible for those concerned to participate in decision-making or to initiate legal proceedings. While, in most states, participating in environmental decision-making is free of charge,[61] bringing a case to court, either as a private suit or as an appeal, is costly. Economic constraints may completely block any access to transboundary proceedings even if they are formally open and available. To be fair, procedures for challenging acts and omissions with a bearing on the environment should 'provide adequate and effective remedies... and be fair, equitable, timely and not prohibitively expensive'.[62] This applies in the national contexts, but is equally important in transnational situations.

Bibliography

Akehurst, M., 1972–3. 'Jurisdiction in International Law'. 46 *British Yearbook of International Law* 145.

Antunes, J. E., 1994. *Liability of Corporate Groups.* Deventer and Boston: Kluwer.

Boyle, A. E., 2006. 'Globalising Environmental Liability: The Interplay of National and International Law', in G. Winter (ed.), *Multilevel Governance of Global Environmental Change.* Cambridge: Cambridge University Press, 559.

Briggs, A., 2002. *The Choice of Law.* Oxford: Oxford University Press.

Cohen, J., 2005. 'Whose Sovereignty?: Empire versus International Law', in C. Barry and T. Pogge (eds.), *Global Institutions and Responsibilities: Achieving Global Justice.* Malden: Blackwell, 159.

Crook, J. R., 2005. 'Contemporary Practice of the United States Relating to International Law (Tentative Settlement of ACTA Human Rights Suits Against Unocal)'. 99 *American Journal of International Law* 497.

Ebbesson, J., 1998. 'The Notion of Public Participation in International Environmental Law'. 8 *Yearbook of International Environmental Law* (1997) 51.

2002. 'Comparative Introduction', in J. Ebbesson (ed.), *Access to Justice in Environmental Matters in the EU – Accès à la justice en matière d'environnement dans l'UE.* The Hague, London and New York: Kluwer Law International, 1.

2003. *Den nordiska miljöskyddskonventionens relevans och framtid [The Relevance and Future of the Nordic Environment Protection Convention], TemaNord 2003:522.* Copenhagen: Nordic Council of Ministers.

2006. 'Transboundary Corporate Responsibility in Environmental Matters: Fragments and Foundations for a Future Framework', in G. Winter (ed.), *Multilevel Governance of Global Environmental Change: Perspectives from Science, Sociology and the Law.* Cambridge: Cambridge University Press, 200.

2007. 'Public Participation', in D. Bodansky, J. Brunnée and E. Hey (eds.), *Oxford Handbook of International Environmental Law.* Oxford: Oxford University Press, 681.

Fraser, N., 2005. 'Reframing Justice in a Globalized World'. 36 (November–December) *New Left Review* 69.

Habermas, J., 1979. *Communication and the Evolution of Society.* Oxford: Polity Press.

---

[61] See, however, Case C-216/05, *Commission* v. *Ireland* [2006] ECR I-10787, where the European Court of Justice accepted the Irish system, where the court did not consider the charge of €20 and €45 respectively as constituting an obstacle to the exercise of the rights of participation as set out in European Community law.

[62] Aarhus Convention, note 19 above, Art. 9(4).

1996. *Between Facts and Norms*. Cambridge, MA: MIT Press.

2001. *The Postnational Constellation: Political Essays*. Cambridge: Polity Press.

Hey, E., 2000. *Reflections on an International Environmental Court*. The Hague: Kluwer.

Koester, V., 2005. 'Review of Compliance under the Aarhus Convention: A Rather Unique Compliance Mechanism'. 2 *Journal of European Environmental and Planning Law* 31.

Lowe, V., 2006. 'Jurisdiction', in M. Evans (ed.), *International Law*, 2nd edn, Oxford: Oxford University Press, 335.

Malanczuk, P., 1997/2002. *Akehurst's Modern Introduction to International Law*, 7th edn, London: Routledge.

McLachlan, C., and Nygh, P. (eds.), 1996. *Transnational Tort Litigation: Jurisdictional Principles*. Oxford: Oxford University Press.

Moreno, A.-M., 2006–7. 'Miljöskador och transnationella företag: olyckan i Aznalcóllar och dess svenska anknytning' [Environmental Damage and Transnational Corporations: The Accident in Aznalcóllar and Its Swedish Connection]. 18 *Juridisk tidskrift* 339.

Muchlinski, P., 2001. 'Corporations in International Litigation: Problems of Jurisdiction and United Kingdom Asbestos Cases', 50 *International and Comparative Law Quarterly* 1.

Nussbaum, M. C., 2006. *Frontiers of Justice: Disability, Nationality, Species Membership*. Cambridge, MA: Harvard University Press.

OECD, 2001a. *Annual Report 2001: Guidelines for Multinational Enterprises – Global Instruments for Corporate Responsibility*. Paris: OECD.

2001b. *Corporate Responsibility – Private Initiatives and Public Goals*. Paris: OECD.

Pogge, T., 1989. *Realizing Rawls*. Ithaca: Cornell University Press.

Rajagopal, B., 2003. *International Law from Below: Development, Social Movements and Third World Resistance*. Cambridge: Cambridge University Press.

Rawls, J., 1972. *A Theory of Justice*. Oxford: Oxford University Press.

1999. *The Law of Peoples*. Cambridge, MA: Harvard University Press.

Sen, A., 1999. *Development as Freedom*. New York: Anchor Books.

Shaw, M. H., 2003. *International Law*, 5th edn, Cambridge: Cambridge University Press.

PART IV

North–South concerns in global contexts

15

Competing narratives of justice in North–South environmental relations: the case of ozone layer depletion

KARIN MICKELSON

1 Introduction

We live in a time in which issues of environmental protection and human poverty are near the top of the international agenda. Concerns about justice and injustice are inextricably linked with both. There is often a tendency to separate out the two, so that justice in the environmental context is seen as relating to the proper relationship between humans and the natural world, while justice in the human context is seen as relating to the bonds that unite us to those of our own species within and across borders. Furthermore, these issues are sometimes seen as competing for scarce resources, so that some of those seemingly concerned about Third World poverty view it as an excuse to delay or avoid action on the environmental front. Such views go back to the time of the 1972 Stockholm Conference on the Human Environment. In her statement at the Conference, then Indian Prime Minister Indira Gandhi asserted:

> We do not want to impoverish [the] environment any further . . . [but] we can-
> not forget the grim poverty of large numbers of people. When they themselves
> feel deprived how can we urge the preservation of animals? How can we speak
> to those who live in villages and in slums about keeping the oceans, rivers and
> the air clean when their own lives are contaminated at the source. Environment
> cannot be improved in conditions of poverty.[1]

Gandhi's language encapsulates what many have perceived as the traditional stance of the global South or Third World with regard to environmental concerns. Development must be prioritized over the environment; to the extent that justice is a concern, it must be justice for humans before we can attempt to achieve justice as between humans and the environment.

This chapter proceeds on the assumption that such a simplistic characterization fails to adequately account for the different – and competing – narratives of justice

---

[1] Anand 1980 at 10.

that underlie the approaches to international environmental law and policy taken by the North and the South.[2] In order to explore these differences, I will begin with a brief survey of how various understandings of justice might apply in an international context. I will then proceed to evaluate some of the debates surrounding the Montreal Protocol on Substances that Deplete the Ozone Layer[3] in order to ascertain whether they reflect different narratives of justice, and how the resulting regime might be said to represent an attempt to develop consensus around what justice requires in international environmental affairs.

2 Theories of justice: a framework

The classic account of the forms of justice, found in Aristotle's *Nicomachean Ethics*, distinguishes between corrective and distributive justice.[4] Corrective justice deals with the rectification of a wrong or injustice committed by one person against another; the purpose of justice is to reestablish the condition that existed previously. Distributive justice, in contrast, deals with the distribution of those things that can be divided amongst members of a political community. For Aristotle, according to Ernest Weinrib, 'justice in both these forms relates one person to another according to a conception of equality or fairness. Injustice arises in the absence of equality, when one person has too much or too little relative to another.'[5]

The literature on international justice, though drawing on a long tradition of normative analyses of the international sphere such as natural law theory and just war doctrine, has only fairly recently received significant attention. Below, I briefly consider how distributive and corrective justice have been applied in an international setting, along with an alternative notion of justice known as environmental justice.

2.1 Distributive justice

Much of the literature on justice in international affairs has been concerned with distributive justice, in particular, questions of the extent of responsibilities towards others located across international boundaries. Some of this literature has built on the work of John Rawls, whose seminal work, *A Theory of Justice*, was published in

---

[2] Given the tremendous diversity that characterizes the states that would usually be included in the global South, it may seem problematic to speak of 'a Southern approach' to international environmental law and policy. As I have argued elsewhere, however, one need not assume that the South is monolithic in order to identify a shared set of perceptions and commitments. See generally Mickelson 2000 at 52–81. See also Mickelson 1998 at 353–419.

[3] Protocol on Substances that Deplete the Ozone Layer, 16 September 1987, 1522 UNTS 3, reprinted in 26 ILM (1987) 1550.

[4] Aristotle 1962.   [5] Weinrib 2002 at 349.

1971. While Rawls had little to say about international affairs in that work,[6] other scholars have taken some of his insights on distributive justice and transferred them nearly wholesale from the domestic to the international level.[7] In essence, these so-called 'cosmopolitan liberals' have argued that individuals within an international community should be able to expect similar kinds of protections to those enjoyed by individuals within a domestic community.

Martha Nussbaum has criticized both Rawls and the cosmopolitan liberals, whose analysis she regards as fundamentally flawed because of its reliance on social contract theory.[8] According to Nussbaum, among other weaknesses, the idea of a social contract fails to provide an adequate foundation for a sense of international community, since the contract is understood as one that is entered into for mutual advantage, with advantage being defined in traditional economic terms. It thus reduces cooperation to its lowest common denominator, by viewing it as the outcome of self-interest rather than fellowship. Nussbaum, noting that '[w]e live in a world in which it is simply not true that cooperating with others on fair terms will be advantageous to all',[9] insists that we should reject this account of cooperation. Pointing out that we have much more profound understandings of cooperation, among others in the natural law tradition, she argues, 'a central part of our own good, each and every one of us – insofar as we agree that we want to live on decent and respectful terms with others – is to produce, and live in, a world that is morally decent, a world in which all human beings have what they need to live a life worthy of human dignity.'[10] Nussbaum espouses a 'capabilities' approach, about which she has written along with Amartya Sen.[11] By focusing on human capabilities, and designing institutions that allow human beings to have those capabilities or to be in a position to claim them, we will be able to live in a world such as she describes above.

2.2 Corrective justice

In contrast to the many discussions of distributive justice, there has been relatively little analysis of corrective justice in the international context. In her chapter in this volume, Dinah Shelton argues that the principle of common but differentiated responsibilities 'provides a corrective justice basis for obliging the developed world to pay for past harms as well as present and future harms'.[12] Paul Harris, in an analysis of international equity and global environmental politics, includes 'righting past wrongs' as a principle of international equity, and links it not to common but differentiated responsibilities

---

[6] Rawls himself expanded his discussion of the international aspects of justice in a 1993 article that he later reworked into a book. See Rawls 1999. However, he severely restricted distributive justice among peoples, and has been criticized for that reason. Twining, in Chapter 4 of this volume, characterizes his position in this work as 'a huge disappointment' from a global perspective.

[7] See e.g. Beitz 1983 at 591–600; Pogge 2002.   [8] Nussbaum 2006.

[9] Nussbaum 2006 at 273.   [10] Nussbaum 2006 at 274.   [11] See Nussbaum and Sen 1993.

[12] Shelton in Chapter 3 of this volume. See also Mickelson 2000 at 69–77.

but to the polluter pays principle. He notes: 'If we accept that the affluent countries are indeed responsible for a disproportionate share of (or even most) global pollution, then the debate can move to questions of what to do about it. The so-called "polluter-pays principle" is an accepted standard in the affluent countries. Interpretations of international equity based on causality and responsibility suggest that this principle ought to be applied among national communities, not just within them.'[13] Harris' argument is reinforced when one considers the important role that the polluter pays principle plays in allocating environmental costs fairly, as discussed by Hans-Christian Bugge in his chapter in this volume.[14] Further, as Shelton notes, a corrective justice approach does not have to focus exclusively on past wrongs. Rather, as Henry Shue has argued with regard to climate change, justice may be said to require that the bulk of the costs associated with addressing environmental problems be borne by those who can more easily afford them.[15] Imposing the costs on the developed countries, according to Shue, may now be 'necessary to avoid committing fresh injustices in future'.[16] He notes: 'Even in an emergency one pawns the jewelry before selling the blankets... [W]hatever justice may positively require, it does not permit that poor nations be told to sell their blankets in order that rich nations may keep their jewelry.'[17]

2.3 Environmental justice

In contrast to the preceding approaches, environmental justice did not begin as an abstract set of principles, but instead grew out of grassroots responses to situations of environmental injustice, specifically the unequal and inequitable distribution of environmental risks and benefits based on race and class. At one level, then, environmental justice as a movement calls for an acknowledgment of the injustices of the past, and demands a fairer model of distribution for the future. At a deeper level, however, the environmental justice movement calls for a more equitable and sustainable social order, and insists that a society cannot be socially harmonious without existing in harmony with the natural world. While it poses a fundamental challenge to what it characterizes as a narrow mainstream understanding of environmentalism, it also goes beyond environmentalism itself by linking environmentalism to other social movements aimed at combating injustice in a variety of contexts.

Environmental justice does not fit neatly into the dichotomy between corrective and distributive justice. It draws on aspects of each, and perhaps goes beyond both in seeking to transform relationships through a call to justice. At its core, it may reflect an Aristotelian notion of justice as founded in equality – an equality, however, which extends beyond the social realm to encompass the ecosphere as well.

---

[13] Harris 2001 at 35.   [14] Bugge in Chapter 21 of this volume.   [15] See e.g. Shue 1992.
[16] Shue 1992 at 396.   [17] Shue 1992 at 397.

3 North–South debates in the development of the Montreal Protocol

The ozone regime provides a useful case study to evaluate the differing understandings of justice underlying Southern and Northern perspectives on international environmental law and policy. North–South tensions and debates have arguably played a more important role in other environmental regimes, notably the climate change and desertification regimes explored by Jutta Brunnée and Bo Kjellén in this volume.[18] Nevertheless, I have chosen to focus on the Montreal Protocol for three main reasons. First, its status as the main international environmental 'success story' gives it tremendous symbolic importance. Second, some of the cleavages that can be perceived among developing countries with regard to other issues (including climate change and desertification) have not been as apparent in the ozone context. Finally, and perhaps most importantly, concerns about fairness were inextricably linked with the debates surrounding the Protocol almost from the very beginning, as will be seen below.

The debate regarding ozone depletion began in the North, and developing countries played a fairly minor role in the negotiations resulting in the 1985 Vienna Convention for the Protection of the Ozone Layer.[19] While the Convention included two minor references to developing countries,[20] a more intriguing reference is found in the resolution that the Vienna Conference adopted on a protocol to the Convention dealing with chlorofluorocarbons (CFCs).[21] The Resolution echoed the Preamble in noting that the Conference is 'mindful that special consideration should be given to the particular situation of developing countries', but then added that it was 'mindful also of the relationship between the level of industrialization of a State and its responsibilities for the protection of the ozone layer'. It may well be that this language represented no more than a political compromise, included so as to garner support for the resolution from the developing countries at the Vienna Conference. Nonetheless, this was a theme that was to resonate throughout the debates regarding the Montreal Protocol itself.

The protocol discussions themselves were informed by a sense of urgency, as the need for prompt and effective action to reduce the production of ozone-depleting substances became clear.[22] It was also becoming increasingly clear that the solution to

---

[18] Brunnée in Chapter 16, and Kjellén in Chapter 17 of this volume.

[19] Convention for the Protection of the Ozone Layer, 22 March 1985, UNEP Doc. IG.53/5, reprinted in 26 ILM (1987) 1529, also available at http://untreaty.un.org/English/UNEP/ozone_english.pdf (hereinafter Vienna Convention).

[20] The Preamble notes that the parties take 'into account the circumstances and particular requirements of developing countries'; the requirement to consider the needs of developing countries is again brought up in the context of technology and knowledge transfer in Article 4(2); Article 4 as a whole deals with 'Cooperation in the Legal, Scientific and Technical Fields'.

[21] 'Resolution on a Protocol Concerning Chlorofluorocarbons', UNEP Doc. IG.53/5, note 19 above.

[22] The Vienna Convention itself was largely an agreement to cooperate; it committed its parties individually to a series of largely procedural obligations concerning exchange of information, and collectively to monitor the situation with a view to taking further measures as required. This sense of relative complacency ended

the problem could not come purely from the North. Although developing countries were minor producers and consumers of CFCs and other ozone-depleting substances, there was a growing demand for these substances as *per capita* incomes rose. CFCs, in particular, had the enormous advantage of being both safe (non-reactive and non-toxic) and inexpensive. This, of course, was precisely what had made them so popular in the North since their invention in the late 1920s. They were not only used in a wide range of industrial processes, but were also important components of consumer goods, notably refrigerators. Developing countries came to realize that the phase-out being proposed could have a significant impact on their own domestic development processes, and lost no time in voicing their concerns in the negotiation process.

The efforts to ensure developing country participation in the ozone regime can be characterized as involving two stages, both of which reflect major themes in South–North environmental relations: the focus on the negotiation of differentiated obligations, and the focus on the provision of financial resources to facilitate compliance.[23] The first stage came during the negotiations for the Montreal Protocol itself, and involved the commitment to a different schedule for meeting phase-out requirements for developing countries. The second stage is reflected most clearly in the negotiations of the London Revisions to the Protocol, which resulted in the establishment of the Multilateral Fund.[24]

3.1 Stage One: differentiated obligations

The Vienna Group, the *ad hoc* working group entrusted with the task of elaborating a protocol,[25] treated the situation of developing countries as one of the key issues that had to be resolved in its work. Developing country participation increased steadily from the first to the third sessions of the Group,[26] and representatives from developing countries, notably Argentina and Egypt, played a vocal role from the start. While expressing concern for the environmental problem represented by ozone depletion, both raised the 'special situation' of developing countries, and their need for

---

with the publication in May 1985 of British research data indicating the existence of what came to be known as the 'hole in the pole', a significant seasonal thinning of the ozone layer over Antarctica.

[23] Mickelson 2000 at 72–3.

[24] It should be noted that the two-stage analysis refers to the theme which dominated discussions; as will be seen, the provision of financial resources was already a concern during the negotiations for the Protocol, but only came to be seen as a central concern by all parties once wider participation by key developing states became crucial for the overall success of the regime.

[25] Formally, the Ad Hoc Working Group of Legal and Technical Experts for the Preparation of a Protocol on Chlorofluorocarbons to the Vienna Convention for the Protection of the Ozone Layer. Documents relevant to the Vienna Group's work have been made available online by the Ozone Secretariat at http://ozone.unep.org/Meeting_Documents/adhoc/5Jii_Adhoc_vienna_group.shtml.

[26] Six were represented in the first session, rising to eleven in the third.

'financial and technical support to enable them to comply with any regulatory measures adopted'.[27]

At the first session of the Group, a debate took place concerning two alternative proposals regarding control measures, one put forward by the United States, the other by Canada. The US proposed a straightforward gradual reduction of 'aggregate annual emissions' (roughly production plus imports minus exports) from 1986 levels over a period of time to be agreed upon by the parties, culminating in 95 percent reductions from 1986 levels. The Canadian proposal, on the other hand, involved the establishment of two different levels of emissions limits. The first was a global emission limit (GEL), defined as 'the total quantity of ozone modifying substances that can be released per annum without causing irreversible harm to the ozone layer'.[28] The second was a national emission limit (NEL), to be determined on the basis of a formula by which 25 percent of the GEL would be apportioned among countries based on their share of world population, while 75 percent would be apportioned on the basis of the relative size of their gross national product (GNP).[29]

At this stage, concerns about justice began to be articulated, as the representatives of developing countries began to express significant reservations based on the view that the proposals being discussed were 'unfair to the less developed world'.[30] One expert noted that a production limit would affect the ability of developing countries that currently imported CFCs to produce those substances in the future. Another criticized the Canadian formula, arguing that it was 'discriminatory against countries having a low GNP which was not compensated for by the population element'. He argued that 'the burden of cost for protecting the ozone layer should fall on the major producing and consuming countries', and raised the spectre of developing country non-involvement by asserting that 'any agreed protocol should be fair and not contain clauses unacceptable to particular groups which would inhibit their becoming a party to the protocol and result in its less than universal acceptance'. He also noted that the need for the development of CFC alternatives should be included in the Protocol. Canada, in response, insisted that its proposal was 'fair to all countries and would initially be most severe on the major producing countries'.[31]

At the second session of the Vienna Group, the plenary discussion was structured around a number of questions, including the question, 'How can it be ensured that

---

[27] Ad Hoc Working Group of Legal and Technical Experts for the Preparation of a Protocol on Chlorofluoro-carbons to the Vienna Convention for the Protection of the Ozone Layer (Vienna Group), Draft Report of the Ad Hoc Working Group on the Work of Its First Session (UNEP/WG.151/L.4), 1–5 December 1986, p. 6, para. 13.

[28] Vienna Group, Draft Protocol on Chlorofluorocarbons or Other Ozone-Modifying Substances: Proposal Submitted by Canada (UNEP/WG.151/L.1), 29 October 1986, p. 2, Art. I.

[29] *Ibid.*, p. 7, Annex, Schedule B.

[30] Vienna Group, Draft Report on First Session, note 27 above, p. 8, para. 21.

[31] *Ibid.*, p. 9, para. 22. Earlier, the Canadian representative had spoken of the need for 'an equitable apportion-ment of the global responsibility to protect the ozone layer' (Draft Report on First Session, note 27 above, p. 5, para. 12).

a protocol on CFCs will be fair to developing countries?'[32] A number of approaches to the issue of justice to developing countries can be identified in the discussion that followed:

- *A balanced approach.* Developing countries must be encouraged to join in taking measures to protect the ozone layer, and their potential contribution to ozone layer depletion must be ascertained. However, they have a right to benefit from the use of ozone-depleting substances.
- *An exclusionary approach.* Since the contribution to ozone depletion by developing countries was minimal, their needs could be met by excluding them from regulation; criteria would have to be established to determine the threshold at which regulatory measures would apply.
- *An incremental approach.* Although the initial costs of taking regulatory action should be borne by the developed countries, all nations would eventually have to assume responsibility for ozone layer protection.
- *A facilitative approach.* While developing countries should be allowed to increase their use of regulated substances consistent with their own development plans, and national emissions of developed countries should be adjusted accordingly in order to maintain global emissions at an agreed level, the Protocol should also ensure that developing countries could take advantage of new technology and CFC alternatives.

Also at the second session, an Ad Hoc Working Group on the Special Situation of Developing Countries was set up and met to discuss a number of issues of concern to developing countries. A paper included as an annex to its report, prepared by a sub-group and considered and amended by the working group on developing countries as a whole,[33] reflects the debates that took place. It is divided into three sections: (1) basic principles and objectives, (2) considerations, and (3) options. The first and third sections are particularly telling. The first, on principles and objectives, strikes a delicate balance between the acknowledgment of the importance of the overall objective of the Protocol to protect and restore the ozone layer, and the assertion of the developmental aspects of the use of CFCs and other ozone-modifying substances. It begins by emphasizing the former, stating that the recognition and accommodation of the needs of developing countries is necessary in order to ensure full participation in the Protocol. It then immediately addresses the latter, and states that those needs are 'essential and vital' to economic growth and development goals. However, that assertion is itself qualified by the principle that follows, which provides that identification of those needs 'should be based upon the concept of the essential use of the substances and their relationship to the important interests of the country'; in other words, there

[32] Vienna Group, Report of the Ad Hoc Working Group on the Work of Its Second Session (UNEP/WG.167/2), 4 March 1987, p. 13.
[33] *Ibid.*, pp. 27–9, Annex B to the Report of the Ad Hoc Working Group on the Special Situation of Developing Countries.

appears to be a rejection of an unquestioning embrace of ozone-modifying activities as a developmental imperative. The fourth and final principle refers to the importance of facilitating access to alternative substances and technologies, in order '[t]o give developing countries the opportunity to respond fully to the responsibility under the Protocol'.

The final section, on options, sets out the various proposals on how to accommodate developing countries that had been considered:

1. The establishment of maximum permissible volumes of annual consumption of CFCs shall not be extended to developing countries.
2. The developing countries will be permitted to have growth in use up to the current average per capita/use in the world.
3. Any developing country which does not produce the regulated substances is entitled to produce an amount which does not exceed its aggregate 1986 consumption level.
4. During a first phase of reduction, any party whose emissions do not exceed the average per capita consumption in the world should be exempted from reduction requirements.

The section concludes by pointing out that, given that the needs of developing countries have not yet been identified, it is extremely difficult to evaluate whether a particular option takes those needs into account.

At the third session, there appeared to be concern among some states about the possibility of certain states being excluded from its control measures. In his remarks to the group, Mostafa Tolba, the then Director General of UNEP, set out UNEP's goals for the meeting, stating that: 'UNEP wanted to see an international agreement reached at that meeting whereby rates of production and use in the developed world, and by any major producers or users in the developing countries, would be frozen at current levels and reduced to a very small fraction of the frozen levels within the next decade.'[34] The US government stated that it 'remained determined to arrive at an international protocol that would protect the ozone layer, including the maximum possible number of participating States, and also make it unprofitable for those countries which did not accept their share of responsibility'.[35] The Swedish representative, in addition to noting that the new instrument should be simple, effective, and provide a clear indication to producers that they should seek alternatives to CFCs, asserted that it was 'equally important . . . that the instrument should address the responsibility of every country to decrease its use of CFCs and shift to other products and methods'.[36]

Argentina and Egypt, on the other hand, again taking a vocal role in the opening statements, continued to emphasize the importance of differentiated treatment, and to link it to concerns about justice. The representative of Argentina expressed

---

[34] Vienna Group, Report of the Ad Hoc Working Group on the Work of Its Third Session (UNEP/WG.172/2), 8 May 1987, p. 2, para. 3.
[35] *Ibid.*, p. 5, para. 10.   [36] *Ibid.*, p. 8, para. 19.

satisfaction regarding the progress that had been made at the second session, 'particularly with the general consensus among countries as to the need to give special consideration to the situation of the developing countries as regards control measures to be adopted in the protocol, which should not run counter to their development needs'.[37] He reiterated that equity 'should enjoy priority in the adoption of control measures', noting again the dramatic difference in levels of per capita consumption of ozone-depleting substances as well as the overall responsibility of industrialized countries for atmospheric pollution.[38] He also called attention to the report of the sub-group on the Special Situation of Developing Countries, and its emphasis on 'the importance of providing the developing countries with assistance in the fields of research, development and exchange of information', and the need for 'measures to facilitate access of the developing countries to new technologies and substitute products'.[39] The representative of Egypt emphasized the need for 'flexible and fair' treatment of developing countries, pointing out that allowing for exemption from control measures 'would not by itself increase dramatically the emission of CFCs'.[40] He noted that there had been consensus in the working group on developing countries regarding assistance to developing countries, but went on to point out that the real challenge would be to find ways of helping developing countries access alternative substances and technologies.

Following the opening plenary, the sub-group on the Special Situation of Developing Countries met. Its starting point was the report on its own work during the second session of the Vienna Group.[41] In contrast to the broad discussion that had taken place during the second session, there appears to have been a much narrower focus on developing a specific proposal for the consideration of governments. The result was the following: states whose annual per capita level of consumption of the substances controlled in the Montreal Protocol was less than a certain amount (the proposal had both 0.1 kilograms and 0.2 kilograms in brackets) would be given an exemption period (again, five years and ten years were both mentioned as possibilities), following which they would be 'subject to controls in a manner parallel to other members of the protocol'.[42] There was also a provision stating that: 'Protocol members shall make all possible efforts to assist those countries exempted to make expeditious use of environmentally safe alternative chemicals and technologies.'[43]

Given the complex debates that had preceded it, this compromise, which proved to be the foundation for the reduction commitments of the Montreal Protocol, is a miracle of simplicity. It reflects an even narrower version of the fourth option for the treatment of developing countries that had been proposed and canvassed by

[37] *Ibid.*, p. 6, para. 12.   [38] *Ibid.*   [39] *Ibid.*   [40] *Ibid.*, p. 7, para. 14.

[41] Report of the Ad Hoc Sub-Working Group on the Special Situation of Developing Countries, *ibid.*, p. 20, para. 1. Canada also put forward a proposal for an article on low-consuming countries.

[42] *Ibid.*, p. 22, Annex, 'Article on the Special Situation of Low Consuming Countries', Submitted by the Ad Hoc Sub-Working Group on the Special Situation of Developing Countries, para. 2.

[43] *Ibid.*, p. 22, para. 3.

the sub-group in the second session. The report does not reflect how and why this compromise was reached; perhaps some clue can be found in the statement that '[d]iscussions took place in a spirit of co-operation and understanding of the special situation of developing countries on the one hand, and on the other, of the common objective of all participants to protect the ozone layer'.[44] It is not presented in an exclusive way; the group recommended that it 'along with other relevant options discussed during the previous sessions of the Vienna Group . . . should be used by Governments for carrying out further analysis of this issue prior to the next round of negotiations'.[45] Furthermore, the report reflects some differences of opinion, noting that some experts suggested that at some future date a level be fixed above which exemption would not be authorized (as was to be the case in the final version of the relevant provision), while others supported including at a future date a requirement for periodic revision.[46] The group also noted that 'in finalizing the protocol it would be necessary to take account of agreed conclusions reached during the second session of the Vienna Group on questions concerning assistance to be received by developing countries and on financial matters'.[47]

It was at Montreal itself that the details regarding differentiated obligations were finally hammered out, in a working group chaired by Ambassador Essam-El-Din Hawas, who had played an important role in the Vienna Group meetings.[48] Developing countries whose annual level of consumption of the substances controlled in the Protocol was less than 0.3 kilograms per capita were essentially given an extra ten years to meet their phase-out obligations; over that ten-year period they were allowed to increase consumption so as to be able to meet their 'basic domestic needs', so long as it remained below 0.3 kilograms.[49] While this may appear to have been a fairly generous concession, at the time it required developing countries to remain far below the levels of consumption of the developed world. Richard Benedick, a lead US negotiator, points out that 0.3 kilograms 'represented approximately 25 to 30 percent of the existing per capita consumption in Europe and the United States and about 50 or 60 percent of the targeted level in the industrialized countries after their cutbacks were effected in the same period'.[50]

3.2 Stage Two: resources for the transition to ozone-friendly technologies

Both developed and developing states involved in the negotiations of the Montreal Protocol recognized that a longer phase-out schedule was only a partial solution to the problem of ensuring that developing states could meet their obligations. A number of developing states had proposed that the Protocol include a provision creating a financial mechanism that could be accessed in order to facilitate the switch

---

[44] *Ibid.*, p. 20, para. 1.   [45] *Ibid.*, p. 21, para. 4.   [46] *Ibid.*, p. 21, para. 3.   [47] *Ibid.*, p. 21, para. 2.
[48] Benedick 1998 at 93.   [49] Montreal Protocol, note 3 above, Art. 5(1).   [50] Benedick 1998 at 93.

to CFC alternatives. This proposal was opposed by the majority of the developed countries, however, and, as a compromise, the Montreal Protocol encouraged parties to 'facilitate access to environmentally safe alternative substances and technology', and to make funds available for such alternatives.[51] However laudable the sentiments, they were clearly insufficient to allay the concerns of many developing states. By the time the Montreal Protocol entered into force on 1 January 1989, it had been ratified by only six developing nations.[52] At workshops held later that year, both China and India presented papers that discussed the costs of a shift to alternative technologies; the Indian paper characterized the Protocol as 'iniquitous'.[53] Justice appeared to be a fundamental concern; it seemed that these and other countries felt that they were being asked to assume a burden with unknown and potentially huge economic costs, in order to address a problem to which they had contributed relatively little. As Maneka Gandhi, the head of the Indian delegation at the London meeting, later explained, 'Asked whether I was prepared to stand out and destroy the ozone layer, I said, "we did not destroy the ozone layer; you have done that already. Don't ask us to pay the price."'[54]

At the same time, it had become clear even before the Montreal Protocol came into force that more drastic control measures were necessary. The need to increase the effectiveness of the Protocol meant not only that the most populous developing nations must participate, but also that their transition beyond ozone-depleting technologies must be made as quickly as possible. At the first Meeting of the Parties (MoP), held in Helsinki in May 1989, it was already clear that some kind of assistance would have to be made available, and the idea of a fund 'was supported by several delegations'.[55] Between the Helsinki meeting and the London meeting a year later, a series of formal and informal gatherings of experts and government officials took place in order to hammer out a consensus on financial mechanisms and technology transfer. In order to prepare for the first meeting of the formal Open-Ended Working Group established by the MoP, UNEP convened an informal working group of experts, which met in Geneva in July 1989. The group canvassed many of the themes that were to resonate throughout the meetings over the following year. In particular, it identified criteria that would be critical to the acceptability of any financial mechanism to many developing countries.[56] One basic requirement was that control of the mechanism should be balanced between developed and developing countries rather than being weighted in favour of the former. In addition, however, the group stipulated that:

---

[51] Montreal Protocol, note 3 above, Art. 5(2) and (3).
[52] These were Egypt, Kenya, Malta, Mexico, Nigeria and Uganda.
[53] Andersen and Sarma 2002 at 100.   [54] Andersen and Sarma 2002 at 126.
[55] First Meeting of the Parties to the Montreal Protocol on Substances that Deplete the Ozone Layer (UNEP/OzL.Pro.1/5), 6 May 1989, para. 26.
[56] Report of the Informal Working Group of Experts on Financial Mechanisms for the Implementation of the Montreal Protocol (UNEP/OzL.Pro.Mech.1/Inf.1), 16 August 1989, para. 17.

- the basis of the funding should not be loans; the group noted that 'many countries...argue strongly for an outright transfer of resources on the grounds of equity'; and
- the resources made available through the mechanism should be additional to existing aid.

Both of these issues reflected a concern about justice as between developed and developing nations. The group also pointed out that the financial mechanism developed for the Montreal Protocol could be a forerunner to a mechanism designed to deal with greenhouse gases, pointing out that the latter would require 'much larger volumes of funding'.[57] This notion of potential precedent, again, would prove to be a significant topic in discussions leading up to the London revisions of the Protocol.

3.3 Basis of funding

Interestingly, the basis upon which funding would be made available was not a major point of contention throughout the negotiations. The G-77 and China, in its opening statement, emphasized that 'agreed incremental costs for developing countries would have to be met as a grant from a multilateral fund under the control of the Parties'. In the discussions that followed, there was 'wide understanding that the flow of funds should be on a concessionary basis', with some delegations advocating that funding be made available on a grant basis.[58] Closely linked to the question of the basis upon which funding would be made available was the issue of who would contribute to the fund, and how contributions would be assessed. There was general agreement that contributions should come primarily from official government sources in developed countries.[59] In later meetings, there was some discussion of whether contributions should come from both developed and developing countries.[60] While there was some support for this, a number of delegations argued that only developed countries should contribute.[61] By the third meeting, support for making funds available as a grant appeared to be increasing, with a number of delegations taking the position that 'the agreed incremental costs for any developing country should be met as a grant, in all cases, if they result in a net financial burden on that country'.[62]

---

[57] *Ibid.*, para. 20.
[58] Open-Ended Working Group of the Parties to the Montreal Protocol, First Session, Final Report (UNEP/OzL.Pro.WG.I(1)/3), 25 August 1989, p. 7, para. 25.
[59] *Ibid.*, p. 7, para. 24.
[60] Open-Ended Working Group, Report of the Second Session of the Second Meeting of the Open-Ended Working Group of the Parties to the Montreal Protocol (UNEP/OzL.Pro.WG.II(2)/7), 5 March 1990.
[61] *Ibid.*, p. 11, para. 36.
[62] Open-Ended Working Group, Report of the Second Session of the Third Meeting of the Open-Ended Working Group of the Parties to the Montreal Protocol (UNEP/OzL.Pro.WG.III(2)/3), 22 May 1990, p. 5, para. 22.

3.4 Additionality

Developing countries were adamant that the funds to be provided to them under the ozone regime would have to be additional to existing financial flows of development aid and financing.[63] During its first meeting, in the course of its deliberations on sources of financing, the Working Group noted the difficulty in defining the concept of 'additionality', but agreed that 'the totality of funds flowing to developing countries should show an increase'.[64] At the second meeting, following further discussion of definitions, 'all delegations approved the principle of additionality'.[65] However, this consensus was to come under attack at the third meeting, when the United States stated that it would support a financial mechanism within the World Bank and that funds for the mechanism would come from the Bank's existing resources, such that no additional funding would be required.[66] The statement caused an uproar; many participants expressed 'concern and disappointment', while every other delegate who addressed the issue 'supported the principle of additionality as agreed at the second session of the second meeting'.[67] The G-77 and China, in a joint statement, 'expressed their deep dismay' over the US position, and urged the US delegation 'to quickly review its position and join the global efforts to save the ozone layer, by shouldering its obligations'.[68] The World Bank representative present at the meeting gave the US position an even more significant blow, stating that the Bank was willing to participate in efforts to protect the ozone layer, but that this willingness 'was based on the understanding that funding would be additional and on grant or concessional terms', and went on to state that 'the Bank could assume responsibility and accountability for the success of these programmes only on the basis of additional funding'.[69]

3.5 The fund as precedent

As noted previously, the potential precedent represented by the financial mechanism being developed in the ozone context was recognized and discussed from the outset. Many of the developed countries may have had concerns in this regard, but the United States was particularly worried about the implications for the climate change regime, and voiced its reservations in the clearest and indeed most vehement fashion. At the beginning of the fourth and final meeting of the Open-Ended Working Group,

---

[63] The notion of financial additionality had a long history by the time the London Revisions were being negotiated. Principle 12 of the Stockholm Declaration on the Human Environment, for example, had referred to the need to make 'additional international technical and financial assistance' available to developing countries for the purpose of preserving and improving the environment.

[64] Report of the First Meeting, note 58 above, p. 7, para. 26.

[65] Report of the Second Meeting, note 60 above, p. 12, para. 41.

[66] Report of the Third Meeting, note 62 above, p. 4, para. 17.

[67] Ibid., p. 4, para. 18.　　[68] Ibid., p. 4, para. 19.　　[69] Ibid., p. 4, para. 20.

just before the MoP, the US delegation released a statement setting out the conditions under which it would join the consensus regarding the fund, which provided in part:[70]

> The limited and unique nature of the Fund must be explicitly confirmed making clear that the Fund is appropriate because:
>
> i. There is a scientifically documented connection between the substances controlled by the Protocol and ozone depletion;
> ii. The Fund and the actions being financed through it can reasonably be expected to address the problem of ozone depletion;
> iii. The amount of funds needed is limited and reasonably predictable;
> iv. Any financial mechanism set out here does not prejudice any future arrangements the Parties may develop with respect to other environmental issues.

In the end, an extraordinary statement was included in the amendments to the effect that the new financial mechanism was 'without prejudice to any future arrangements that may be developed with respect to other environmental issues'.[71]

4 Narratives of justice in the ozone context

It is clear from the preceding overview of the debates surrounding differentiated obligations and the provision of financial resources that notions of justice and fairness were invoked on all sides from the beginning of the negotiations for the Montreal Protocol, frequently in competing ways. While a full analysis of the dynamics at play in these negotiations is beyond the scope of this chapter, I will focus on a few specific examples from the discussions surrounding each issue.

The survey of the discussions regarding differentiated obligations reveals a number of points. First, there did not appear to be a significant attempt on the part of developing countries to set up a stark opposition between concern for the ozone layer, on the one hand, and concern for development, on the other.[72] Developing country representatives frequently invoked environmental concerns, referred to the need to develop alternatives to ozone-modifying substances, and often discussed differentiated obligations in partly instrumental terms, as helping to encourage developing countries to adhere to the Montreal Protocol. Second, it was clear from the very first session and its discussion of the US and Canadian proposals for control measures, and in

---

[70] 'Statement of the US Delegation Regarding the Financial Mechanism', 20 June 1990, at www.unep.org/ozone/Meeting_Documents/adhoc/other-meetings/us_statement-financial_mechanism.90-07-00.pdf.

[71] Second Meeting of the Parties to the Montreal Protocol on Substances that Deplete the Ozone Layer (UNEP/OzL.Pro.2/3), 29 June 1990, Annex II, Amendment to the Montreal Protocol on Substances that Deplete the Ozone Layer, Art. 10(10), p. 36.

[72] At the second session of the Vienna Group, the representative of Thailand, which had not been involved in the first session, came closest to this when he noted that 'his country shared the common concern for the risks posed for the ozone layer. However, in addressing the problem there was a need to balance national development needs against other concerns.' Vienna Group, Report of the Second Session, note 32 above, pp. 6–7, para. 13.

particular the claims that the proposals were 'unfair to the less developed world', that the issue of fairness to developing countries was regarded as critical to the negotiation process.[73] It is noteworthy that the Canadian representative felt compelled to insist that its proposal was 'fair to all countries and would initially be most severe on the major producing countries'.[74] The importance of the issue is reflected in the decision to include it as one of the questions for plenary discussion in the second session of the Vienna Group, as well as the decision to set up the Ad Hoc Working Group on the Special Situation of Developing Countries.[75]

Third, despite the apparent consensus regarding the importance of ensuring that the Protocol was fair to developing countries, there was no agreement on how to achieve that goal. Nowhere is this more clearly reflected than in the third session's discussion of the prospect of some countries being excluded from control measures altogether. This was obviously deeply troubling to many participants, as reflected in the statements made by Mr Tolba from UNEP and the US and Swedish representatives. Neither the US's rather threatening invocation of the notion of making it 'unprofitable for those countries which did not accept their share of responsibility', however, nor the Swedish statement about 'the responsibility of every country to decrease its use of CFCs and shift to other products and methods', addressed the notion that there might be different shares of responsibility for protection of the ozone layer. The statements made by Argentina and Egypt, on the other hand, see responsibility itself as being differentiated. The representative of Argentina talked about the need for equity in control measures, and again emphasized differences in per capita consumption of ozone-depleting substances and the fact that industrialized countries have a greater responsibility for atmospheric pollution overall. The Egyptian representative talked about flexibility and fairness, and implied that the real responsibility for enabling developing countries to protect the ozone layer rests with those in the position to help those countries access alternative substances and technologies.

Against this backdrop, and given the very real possibility of excluding developing countries from any form of control measures that seemed to be mentioned on an ongoing basis, it is more than a little surprising that the final provisions in the Montreal Protocol regarding developing countries reflected so little of the concerns about fairness that had been raised by developing country participants. As noted previously, the formula required that developing countries' per capita consumption of ozone depleting substances remain far below the levels in developed countries, with no binding obligation on developed countries to facilitate access to alternatives or to provide funding. In contrast, the immediate insistence on the establishment of a funding mechanism by developing countries should have come as no surprise whatsoever. In fact, one might argue that the negotiation of differentiated obligations and the funding mechanism cannot be separated out in principle, since both must be seen as fundamental requirements to ensure justice for developing countries.

[73] See note 30 above.   [74] See note 31 above.   [75] See note 33 above.

Concerns about fairness continued to dominate the discussions regarding a funding mechanism. To a large extent, by the time the decision was reached at Helsinki to set up a working group it was already clear that a fund would have to be established. Here again, developing countries argued that their demands for transfer of resources were based on equity rather than expediency. Furthermore, at this stage they seemed to make it clear that this was not a demand for distributive justice, but for corrective justice. In the informal working group, it was emphasized that the problems with the ozone layer were largely the responsibility of developed countries, who had been able to use CFCs for a long period without having to pay any cost for the damage caused. Furthermore, it was noted that the costs of complying with the Protocol would be higher for developing countries, relative to the benefits they would receive from it, than for developed countries.[76] Similarly, at the first meeting of the formal Working Group, two main purposes for financial or other support were recognized: 'first, compensation for the incremental costs of transition to substitutes of the ozone depleting substances, and, second, support which would serve as an incentive to ensure adherence to the Protocol.'[77] The language of 'compensation', whether or not deliberately chosen, clearly invokes notions of corrective justice rather than distributive justice (or mere expediency). The discomfort that this overall approach may have caused some of the developed country parties is clearly reflected in numerous references to discussions about whether contributions to the fund should be mandatory, or voluntary on an assessed basis.

The debates regarding the fund as precedent also reflected fundamental differences in view, with the United States making every effort to ensure that the Multilateral Fund would be seen as a one-off arrangement, tailored to the specific and limited characteristics of the ozone-depletion problem. In the end, the US insistence that the new financial mechanism was 'without prejudice' to any future environmental issues, in addition to being legally unnecessary, was of dubious political value. Arguably, the developing countries had in fact succeeded in changing the terms of the normative debate; the obligations of developed countries were now understood to encompass not only their domestic phase-outs but also their support to the capacity of developing countries to meet their own phase-out requirements. In her statement at the London MoP, the then British Prime Minister Margaret Thatcher asserted that participation by all countries was necessary for the Montreal Protocol to be successful, and pointed out that developing countries had 'understandable concerns about adverse effects on their economic growth'. Thus, she asserted, it was 'the duty of industrialized countries to help them with substitute technologies and with financing the additional costs involved'.[78] A clearer statement could not be possible. This could be said to represent

---

[76] Informal Working Group Report, note 56 above, para. 18.
[77] Open-Ended Working Group, Report of the First Meeting, note 58 above, p. 7, para. 22.
[78] Report of the Second Meeting of the Parties to the Montreal Protocol (UNEP/OzL.Pro.2/3), 29 June 1990, para. 6.

the new consensus regarding the involvement of developing countries in international environmental regimes, reflected in later agreements such as the Framework Convention on Climate Change[79] and the Convention on Biological Diversity,[80] which link the effective implementation of the obligations of developing country parties to the fulfillment of the obligations of developed country parties with regard to the provision of financial resources and technology transfer.

What is particularly noteworthy about the outcome of the ozone negotiations is that they cannot be explained only by reference to traditional notions of justice. From the perspective of the South, this did not appear to have been a demand for distributive justice, although it seems to have been regarded as such by at least some developed country representatives. While representatives of developing countries referred to existing flows of development aid in the context of the discussion of additionality, there appears to have been a clear distinction drawn between aid and the kind of financial resources to be made available through the funding mechanism. Nor could Southern concerns be reduced to a demand for corrective justice, although this was certainly a significant component of the Southern approach throughout the negotiation process. I would argue that the conception of justice which comes closest to capturing the stance taken by the South in the ozone context is environmental justice, with its insistence that an effective response to environmental challenges must go beyond minimizing human impacts on the biosphere. It requires a broader and more inclusive vision of environmental protection and sustainability that encompasses concerns about social justice as well as ecological integrity.

Bibliography

Anand, R. P., 1980. 'Development and Environment: The Case of Developing Countries'. 24 *Indian Journal of International Law* 1–19.

Andersen, S. O., and Sarma, K., 2002. *Protecting the Ozone Layer: The United Nations History 100.* London: Earthscan.

Aristotle, 1962. *Nicomachean Ethics*, Book Five. Martin Oswald, trans., Indianapolis: Library of Liberal Arts.

Beitz, C., 1983. 'Cosmopolitan Ideals and National Sentiment'. 80 *Journal of Philosophy* 591.

Benedick, R. E., 1998. *Ozone Diplomacy: New Directions in Safeguarding the Planet*, enlarged edn, Cambridge, MA: Harvard University Press.

Harris, P. G., 2001. *International Equity and Global Environmental Politics: Power and Principles in US Foreign Policy*. Aldershot: Ashgate.

Mickelson, K., 1998. 'Rhetoric and Rage: Third World Voices in International Legal Discourse'. 16 *Wisconsin International Law Journal* 353.

[79] United Nations Framework Convention on Climate Change, UN Doc. A/AC.237/18 (Part II)/Add.1, 1771 UNTS 107, reprinted in 31 ILM (1992) 849, Art. 4(7).

[80] Convention on Biological Diversity, 2 June 1992, UN Doc. DPI/130/7 (1992), 1760 UNTS 79, reprinted in 31 ILM (1992) 818, Article 20(4).

2000. 'South, North, International Environmental Law and International Environmental Lawyers'. 11 *Yearbook of International Environmental Law* 52.

Nussbaum, M., 2006. *Frontiers of Justice, Disability, Nationality, Species, Membership.* Cambridge, MA: Belknap Press of Harvard University Press.

Nussbaum, M., and Sen, A., 1993. *The Quality of Life.* Oxford: Clarendon Press.

Pogge, T., 2002. *World Poverty and Human Rights: Cosmopolitan Responsibilities and Reforms.* London: Polity Press.

Rawls, J., 1999. *The Law of Peoples.* Cambridge, MA: Harvard University Press.

Shue, H., 1992. 'The Unavoidability of Justice', in Andrew Hurrell and Benedict Kingsbury (eds.), *The International Politics of the Environment.* Oxford: Clarendon Press, 373.

Weinrib, E. J., 2002. Corrective Justice in a Nutshell. 52 *University of Toronto Law Journal* 34.

16

Climate change, global environmental justice and international environmental law

JUTTA BRUNNÉE*

[W]e need to be constantly skeptical of the universalist 'we' who talks loftily about the principles of global justice.

Andrew Hurrell[1]

I don't find justice either a useful decision-making tool or a recognizable objective for international law.

Judge Rosalyn Higgins[2]

[I]nternational law exists as a promise of justice.

Martti Koskenniemi[3]

[T]he future will see increasing efforts to form international [environmental] regimes, often with profound effects on nonparticipants... Principles of global justice... are going to be among the most important topics of the new world.

Christopher D. Stone[4]

1 Introduction

Climate change is a global problem. The emission of greenhouse gases or destruction of carbon sinks anywhere in the world affects the Earth's climate.[5] Similarly, while the nature and severity of impacts may vary geographically, no state can insulate itself from the consequences of global climate change. Climate change is also an inter-temporal problem. The actions and omissions of the present will have implications for climatic conditions in the future, just as activities undertaken in the past have had impacts on today's climate. Historically, emissions of greenhouse gases have been far greater in the

---

* I gratefully acknowledge the financial support of the Social Sciences and Humanities Research Council of Canada (SSHRC), and the excellent research assistance provided by James Hunter.
[1] Hurrell 2001 at 46.   [2] Higgins 2006.   [3] Koskenniemi 2003 at 77.   [4] Stone 1993 at 265–6.
[5] For the purposes of this chapter, I assume that anthropogenic changes to the global climate are occurring and will occur in the future. See Intergovernmental Panel on Climate Change (IPCC), *Fourth Assessment Report*, Vol. I (Climate Change 2007: The Physical Science Basis), February 2007; Vol. II (Climate Change 2007: Impacts, Adaptation and Vulnerability), April 2007; and Vol. III (Climate Change 2007: Mitigation of Climate Change), May 2007. All at www.ipcc.ch.

industrialized countries. The emissions of Northern countries still significantly exceed those of developing countries,[6] although the emissions share of the developing world and the emissions of some large developing countries are projected to rise sharply over the next two decades.[7] The impacts of climate change are likely to disproportionately affect Southern, developing countries, many of which are especially vulnerable to such impacts.[8] Northern countries have vastly larger economic and technological capacity not only to mitigate greenhouse gas emissions, but also to adapt to its consequences.[9]

These well-known features of global climate change obviously complicate the quest for effective responses to the problem. But they have also prompted many observers to assert that climate change raises serious issues of global environmental justice, which must be addressed if policy, economic, technological or legal measures are to succeed. Relevant questions pertain to participation in and processes of decision-making about responses to global climate change, and to the allocation of the benefits and burdens of greenhouse gas emissions, mitigation measures and adaptation to climate change impacts, especially as between Southern and Northern countries.[10]

Perhaps surprisingly, the legal literature has not devoted much detailed attention to the 'justice' dimension of climate change issues and its implications for international environmental law.[11] The relatively modest goal of this essay is to help fill this gap by reflecting on three sets of issues. First, can principles of justice apply at a global level and to inter-generational issues? Secondly, is environmental justice a viable, or 'recognizable', objective for international law? I will answer these two questions affirmatively. The key to both global climate justice and its pursuit through international environmental law, I will argue, is to pay attention to the interplay between procedural and substantive (distributive) justice and to build genuine shared understandings in international society. Thirdly, I explore the role of the concept of 'common but differentiated responsibilities' (CBDR), which has assumed a prominent position in international environmental law,[12] and which engages many of the features of the climate change problem that I highlighted above. I argue that the concept plays an important role in framing a debate *about* global climate justice; but it does not currently constitute a global principle *of* justice. I conclude that it is all the more important to ensure procedural justice. Only if global decision-making and

---

[6] This is true for total, per capita and, especially, historic global emissions. See e.g. Baumert and Pershing 2004 at 4 (share of global emissions), 11 (per capita emissions) and 13 (cumulative CO_2 emissions 1850–2000), at www.pewclimate.org/global-warming-in-depth/all_reports/.

[7] *Ibid.* at 15–16.   [8] *Ibid.* at 17–18.   [9] *Ibid.* at 17–20.

[10] For an extensive, interdisciplinary literature review, see Gardiner 2004. See also Adger 2001; Ikeme 2003; Shukla 1999; and Roberts and Parks 2007.

[11] Notable exceptions include: Biermann 1999; Caney 2005 at 747; Melkas 2002 at 115; Rajamani 2000 at 120, Adger, Paavola, Huq and Mace 2006; see also Karin Mickelson in Chapter 15 of this volume.

[12] See e.g. Cullet 2003; French 2000; Rajamani 2000; Stone 2004 at 276; Mickelson in Chapter 15 of this volume.

law-making processes are widely seen as legitimate, will the conditions exist in which a more ambitious global understanding of climate justice could be cultivated.

Before I proceed, two caveats are in order. First, my exploration of climate justice issues is conceptual; it does not examine the particulars of the climate change regime. Secondly, the discussion will be focused on inter-state issues. It has rightly been pointed out that, within all states, poor and minority populations are likely to be disproportionately affected by climate change.[13] However, in light of other contributions to this volume,[14] questions of domestic environmental justice or transnational questions of environmental justice between individuals and states or other international actors will not be considered in this article.

2 Global environmental justice

A first step in any effort to grapple with the implications of environmental justice for international environmental law and climate change must be to clarify the meaning of the concept of 'environmental justice'. A second step must be to ask whether the concept can be applied to a global and inter-temporal problem like climate change.

2.1 The concept of environmental justice

As is well known, the idea of environmental justice originated in the United States in the 1980s and was inspired by local activism against environmental impacts.[15] The American environmental justice movement, like comparable movements in many Southern countries, has sought to connect concern for environmental integrity with demands for social justice.[16] In particular, the movement has been preoccupied with the disproportionate imposition of environmental burdens on low-income communities or communities of color.[17] Emphasis has also been placed on the need for equal application and enforcement of environmental laws, as well as for full access to and participation in decision-making in environmental matters. In other words, the focus of domestic environmental justice movements has been on both substantive, primarily distributive, and procedural justice.[18]

---

[13] See Harper and Rajan 2004, available at www.peri.umass.edu/Publication.236+M53cb8b79b72.0.html.

[14] See Darpö, Kameri-Mbote, Razzaque and Schwartz in, respectively, Chapters 9, 20, 6 and 22 of this volume.

[15] See Mickelson 2007 at 262.

[16] Prominent Southern movements include, for example, Brazil's rubber tappers or India's Chipko movement. See Mickelson in Chapter 15 of this volume.

[17] Anand 2002 at 248–54.

[18] See *ibid.* at 249–50. See also the definition of environmental justice provided by the US Environmental Protection Agency (EPA), which established an 'Office of Environmental Justice' under the Clinton Administration: Environmental Justice is the *fair treatment* and *meaningful involvement* of all people regardless of race, color, national origin, or income with respect to the development, implementation, and enforcement of environmental laws, regulations, and policies. US EPA, 'Environmental Justice: Basic Information', available at www.epa.gov/compliance/basics/ejbackground.html.

In the international environmental policy literature, the term 'justice' is often used in conjunction with other terms, such as equity, fairness, procedural justice, distributive justice, or corrective justice. However, the linkages and distinctions between these concepts are not always drawn very clearly. The concept of 'equity', for example, is sometimes conflated with 'justice'.[19] Others limit equity, correctly in my view, to matters of distributive justice, which constitute only one dimension of the broader concept of justice.[20] The latter concept encompasses procedural, distributive or corrective aspects. Fairness is another term that is often employed in relation to distributive questions.[21] A more nuanced framework can be found in Thomas Franck's influential work on international fairness. It distinguishes between procedural fairness, which is treated under the rubric of legitimacy, and substantive fairness, which demands distributive justice.[22]

For the purposes of this chapter, 'environmental justice' will be understood as a blend of procedural and substantive considerations. This understanding is in keeping with the most common conceptualization of the domestic root concept as well as with much of the internationally focused literature on the topic.[23]

2.2 Can environmental justice be global and inter-temporal?

The salience of procedural issues is not questioned in the literature on international environmental justice. But strong emphasis on procedural justice is found primarily in discussions of environmental justice from a Southern standpoint.[24] Similarly, corrective justice arguments tend to be advanced in developing country perspectives on the topic.[25] Whereas domestic environmental movements emphasize ecological integrity in addition to social justice, there is little explicit reference to this dimension in the international environmental and climate justice literature. The predominant focus in the international environmental justice literature, and certainly in the literature on climate change, from both Southern and Northern perspectives, is upon matters of distributive justice.[26]

2.2.1 Global distributive justice?

One of the most prominent conceptions of distributive justice is without doubt John Rawls' *A Theory of Justice*. It proceeds from the principles upon which members of

---

[19] See Kütting 2004 at 120. See also the discussion of conceptual issues in Shelton 2007 at 639; and in Chapter 3 of this volume.

[20] Ikeme 2003 at 200; Shukla 1999 at 145.   [21] See Linnerooth-Bayer 1999 at 44.   [22] Franck 1995 at 7.

[23] Anand 2002 at 254–7; Ikeme 2003 at 200; Paavola and Adger 2002, available at: www.tyndall.ac.uk/ publications/working_papers/wp23.pdf.

[24] Ikeme 2003 at 201–2; Najam 2004 at 225.   [25] Ikeme 2003 at 201; Stone 1993 at 248–51.

[26] Caney 2005 at 748; Linnerooth-Bayer 1999; Shukla 1999; Paavola and Adger 2002 at 3 (commenting on the 'tendency among political and economic theorists to frame all moral dilemmas narrowly as questions of just distribution').

a society, without knowing their own position within that society, would agree to order their affairs. Among these principles, argues Rawls, would be equal distribution of wealth and income. Unequal distributions could be just, however, as long as the least well off in society would be better off than they would otherwise be.[27] Rawls himself did not consider that these principles of distributive justice could prevail between states, due to widely divergent values and the absence of a global community. One people cannot be expected to shoulder the costs of decisions made by another.[28] Political community and agreement on common principles for the basic structure of a society, according to Rawls, must precede agreement on principles of justice.[29]

Various commentators agree that, in the absence of a community and basic common understandings of justice, the moral preconditions for distributive justice do not exist at the international level.[30] Others go further, adding that the quest for global justice is not only futile but actually dangerous because it would merely serve to extend the influence of already dominant states.[31] Thus, Chandran Kukathas argues that the international order should be based only on 'a commitment to mutual toleration'.[32] This perspective resonates to some extent with the classical realist view that justice cannot play a central role in international politics,[33] which is ultimately a struggle for survival and power.[34]

However, for a majority of commentators, representing a broad spectrum of theoretical perspectives, principles of distributive justice are appropriately deployed at the international level. Iris Marion Young, for example, argues that responsibility for injustice arises not from membership in a community but from social connection through 'a system of interdependent processes of cooperation and competition through which we seek benefits and aim to realize projects' and which produces structural injustice.[35] Cosmopolitans base the argument for global distribution upon the imperative to extend justice equally to all human beings across the globe, combined with the effects of globalization on national political communities.[36] Yet others agree that the increasing breadth and density of independence entailed by processes of globalization has impacted on the role of states.[37] But the primary concern of some of these commentators remains with states,[38] cautioning that some cosmopolitans' focus on justice within states neglects the influence precisely of the transnational dynamics of globalization on global inequalities.[39] For many of these commentators, with whom I align myself for the purposes of this chapter, the key consideration is that an international society with shared expectations of justice has in fact been emerging,

---

[27] Rawls (revised edition) 1971/1999 at 7–8; Rawls 2001.
[28] However, Rawls does contemplate certain duties of assistance that may flow from unequal resource endowments. See Rawls 1999 at 115–19. For a discussion see Beitz 1999 at 276, 278.
[29] Rawls 1971/1999 at 110.   [30] See Walzer 1983; Miller 1999 at 187.   [31] Kukathas 2006 at 8.
[32] *Ibid.* at 5–7.   [33] See Cohen 1985 at 3.   [34] See Wight 1966 at 17.   [35] Young 2006 at 119.
[36] See Barry 1998 at 144; Buchanan 2004; Pogge 2002.   [37] Hurrell 2001 at 35; Linklater 1999 at 473.
[38] Hurrell 2001 at 38.   [39] *Ibid.* at 48.

the global diversity of views and circumstances notwithstanding.[40] In any case, it is pointed out by some, diversity exists also *within* most polities.[41] Thus, overarching principles of justice either should be disqualified nationally as well,[42] or there is no compelling reason not to apply them internationally.[43]

2.2.2 Inter-temporal justice

Even assuming the validity of global distributive justice considerations, a number of theorists object that principles of intra-generational justice cannot be applied to inter-generational questions.[44] For some, the difficulty rests in the fact that subsequent generations cannot actually be identified in any meaningful sense, given that all actions of a previous generation will affect the identity of subsequent generations in some way or another.[45] For others, a key consideration is that present generations should not be responsible for decisions in which they did not participate, or for decisions that were made at a time when the harmful consequences of actions could not be known.[46]

My sympathies lie with those who argue that these objections overdraw the concerns that they raise. Concerns pertaining to the impossibility of responsibilities towards those one does not know, and whose identity cannot be known, have analytical bite when the argument is about individual responsibility. However, when the focus is on collective entities like states, their purchase is greatly diminished.[47] Similarly, the objection that responsibility can flow only from decisions and from actions that resulted in knowable harm has some force with respect to corrective justice arguments, which focus on responsibility for wrongs.[48] But, as Young suggests, the 'liability model' of responsibility is not the only way to conceptualize global justice; a 'social connection' model offers a broader account that can better capture the realities of a globalized world.[49] Others argue that, to the extent that current generations derive benefits from past actions, they should also be responsible for the costs.[50] Concerns about lack of knowledge, of course, apply only as long as harmful consequences are indeed unknowable. In the case of climate change, for example, this argument has been difficult to make for some time now.[51]

2.3 Procedural and substantive justice

The fact that a case for global and inter-generational distributive justice considerations can be made does not necessarily imply that salient principles have emerged

---

[40] *Ibid.* at 1, 46; Franck 1995 at 19.   [41] Linnerooth-Bayer 1999 at 46.

[42] Pogge 2002 at 105; Kukathas 2006 at 4, 9–10 (arguing that, given the diversity of opinions and communities within national societies, the pursuit of justice is not desirable even at this level; just as at the international level, justice risks being either diluted or shaped by the interests of powerful actors).

[43] Beitz 1997 and 1999 at 138–9, 141.

[44] Rawls, for example, argues that not the difference principle, but a 'just savings' principle, should apply in this regard. See Rawls 1999 at 251–8.

[45] Caney 2005 at 757 (discussing Derek Parfit's 'non-identity problem').

[46] *Ibid.* at 760–2; and Stone 1993 at 248–51.   [47] Caney 2005 at 756–60.   [48] Shue 1999 at 536–7.

[49] Young 2006 at 115–18.   [50] Shue 1999 at 536.   [51] *Ibid.*

or will emerge. The diversity of outlooks in international society presents significant obstacles. Procedural justice therefore plays a particularly important role in the international context, and in working towards even modest global understandings of substantive environmental justice.

3 Global environmental justice and international law

Most international lawyers would readily accept that procedural justice is an important aim for international law.[52] But many would question international law's ability to promote genuinely global substantive justice. For example, Rosalyn Higgins, who is quoted at the beginning of this chapter, observed that '[b]eyond due process, what is just to one person is totally unfair to another. And so it is with states.'[53] Indeed, for positivists, questions of substantive justice are not an appropriate domain for legal inquiry. Especially in the international arena, the separation of law from morality and politics is seen as crucial to international law's ability to mediate the diverse interests and values in international society.[54] Of course, certain matters of substantive justice, such as human rights standards, the concept of self-determination, or 'just war' principles, have come to be expressed in positive international law. But critical international law theorists argue that the positivist project of separating these legal standards from politics is futile. Martti Koskenniemi has famously suggested that international law is inevitably political, whether it strives to track the practice and thus interests of states, or purports to reflect universal values.[55] Either way, hegemonic processes are bound to shape international law's postulates.[56] Ironically, for Koskenniemi, the best defense against the domination of world society by powerful states is a 'culture of formalism', which insists upon the 'validity' of rules as measured by the consent of sovereign states.[57]

Both perspectives raise weighty concerns. But each also provides an incomplete account of the functioning of law in international society, including the role that it can play in promoting international justice. Positivism is overly optimistic about the extent to which rules enshrined through formal 'sources' reflect genuinely shared international norms. The critical perspective, in turn, is often unduly pessimistic about the possibility of arriving at such norms, rather than just at 'utopian justice' or 'an apology of actual power'.[58] In some of his recent work, Martti Koskenniemi himself appears to read the inevitable tension between apology and utopia that he so famously attributed to international law in somewhat more optimistic terms. International law, he posited, 'exists as a promise of justice'. Although this promise will never be fully realized, '[i]n the gap between positive law and justice lies the necessary (and impossible) realm of the politics of law'.[59]

Like Koskenniemi, I believe that international law does hold a promise of justice. However, I do not believe that the role that law can play in this regard is limited to its

---

[52] See e.g. Higgins 2006.   [53] *Ibid.*   [54] Hall 2001 at 272.   [55] Koskenniemi 2005 at 17, 63–7, 539.
[56] *Ibid.* at 597.   [57] *Ibid.* at 616.   [58] *Ibid.* at 539.   [59] *Ibid.* at 111.

formalism.[60] Rather, the limitations of positivist optimism and critical pessimism are confronted head-on precisely when we look beyond the formal validity of norms and understand law-making in part as an enterprise of building up shared understandings. Without basic understandings about the appropriate role of law in international society, international law cannot emerge. These basic understandings can be cultivated through pre-legal interaction in informal and formal institutions, through the work of norm entrepreneurs, through the engagement of epistemic communities and issue networks, and through other processes of socialization affecting the self-perception and identity of actors.[61] Legal norms, however, must be constructed and applied in a manner that meets procedurally oriented criteria of legality. These include the requirements that rules are compatible one with another, that they ask reasonable things, that they are transparent and relatively predictable, and that known rules actually guide decision-making.[62] When norms meet these criteria, they are infused with a particular legitimacy, in important part because they enable states and other international actors to communicate, to organize their interactions, and to reason from law to pursue their objectives.[63] For these reasons, law also constrains actors, including powerful ones. In this sense, legal norms are premised upon reciprocity and interaction. The more they meet the criteria of legality, the more they will garner respect and the more will violations or self-serving interpretations be resisted. Conversely, the less norms conform to the criteria, the more likely they are to be reshaped through their application by states and other international actors.

In other words, law-making quite appropriately does have a moral dimension but, crucially, the underlying conception of morality is largely procedural. This conception of what Lon Fuller famously referred to as the 'internal morality of law'[64] is particularly helpful in international society. It accommodates the prevailing diversity of outlooks and priorities and allows interaction without the need for prior agreement on a common view of the world. Yet, as diverse actors interact through law, opportunities do arise to deepen shared understandings, provided that all relevant actors can participate in the process and are able to do so in meaningful fashion.[65] Around certain concrete issues, such as climate change, it may then be possible to venture from procedure to substance and to cultivate a normative community. In that process, due to their

---

[60] See *ibid.* at 110 (arguing that 'the pure form of international law provides the shared surface . . . on which political adversaries recognize each other as such and pursue their adversity in terms of something shared').

[61] On the importance of pre-legal normativity and the evolution of 'contextual regimes,' see Brunnée and Toope 1997 at 31–7, 58.

[62] These criteria build upon Lon Fuller's eight tests of legality or, as he called them, the 'inner morality' of the law. See Fuller 1969 Chapter 2. For a detailed discussion in the context of the climate change regime, see Brunnée 2002.

[63] See Brunnée and Toope 2000; Brunnée and Toope 2001.

[64] Fuller insisted that his criteria were not just about the efficiency of law, but were moral because they upheld and promoted individual autonomy. For a helpful discussion see Murphy 2005 at 239.

[65] Of course, this is a significant proviso, especially in the context of North–South interaction. See Gupta 2000a; Roberts and Parks 2007 at 14–19.

above-mentioned constraining effects, adherence to the criteria of legality helps ensure that substantive commitments emerge from a genuine normative community and not merely enact powerful actors' preferences. I quite consciously use the phrase '*helps ensure*'. It would be foolish to deny the influence of power on international law-making.[66] But that does not mean that we should neglect the opportunities that do exist to build at least modest normative communities and an inclusive international legal order.

4 International environmental law and the elements of global climate justice

So far, I have suggested that the idea of global climate justice is conceptually defensible, and that international law can play a role in the pursuit of this idea. Against this backdrop, I now turn to the question whether a globally shared conception of environmental justice has in fact emerged in international climate change law. I begin with a look at the concept of common but differentiated responsibilities and the distributive justice issues that it engages, and conclude by returning to the importance of the interplay between process and substance.

4.1 The concept of common but differentiated responsibilities

The concept of common but differentiated responsibilities has found prominent expression in the international climate change regime, and in other pivotal international environmental instruments.

The preamble to the United Nations Framework Convention on Climate Change opens with the acknowledgment that 'change in the Earth's climate and its adverse effects are a common concern of humankind'.[67] It goes on to note:

> that the largest share of historical and current global emissions of greenhouse gases has originated in developed countries, that per capita emissions in developing countries are still relatively low and that the share of global emissions originating in developing countries will grow to meet their social and development needs.[68]

It also acknowledges:

> that the global nature of climate change calls for the widest possible cooperation by all countries and their participation in an effective and appropriate international response, in accordance with their common but differentiated responsibilities and respective capabilities and their social and economic conditions.[69]

---

[66] See Gupta 2000b. And, more generally, Krisch 2005 at 369; Barnett and Duvall 2005.
[67] United Nations Framework Convention on Climate Change (UNFCCC), reprinted in 31 *International Legal Materials* (ILM) (1992) 849, Preamble, 1st recital.
[68] *Ibid.*, 3rd recital.   [69] *Ibid.*, 6th recital.

Finally, Article 3(1) of the Climate Change Convention reads:

> The Parties should protect the climate system for the benefit of present and future generations of humankind, on the basis of equity and in accordance with their common but differentiated responsibilities and respective capabilities. Accordingly, the developed country Parties should take the lead in combating climate change and the adverse effects thereof.[70]

The closest thing to a definition of the CBDR concept is provided not in the Climate Change Convention but in Principle 7 of the 1992 Rio Declaration on Environment and Development:

> States shall cooperate in a spirit of global partnership to conserve, protect and restore the health and integrity of the Earth's ecosystem. In view of the different contributions to global environmental degradation, States have common but differentiated responsibilities. The developed countries acknowledge the responsibility that they bear in the international pursuit to sustainable development in view of the pressures their societies place on the global environment and of the technologies and financial resources they command.[71]

It is tempting to see the CBDR concept as the easy answer to questions about global climate justice, at least as far as matters of distributive justice are concerned. However, it is not enough that the concept is contained in salient international instruments. The crucial question is whether it represents a globally shared understanding of distributive justice in the face of climate change. An authoritative answer to this question would require a thorough empirical enquiry. In the context of this essay, I can only offer some tentative conclusions.

It seems fair to say that there is wide agreement on the basic idea that animates the CBDR concept in the present context: that addressing climate change and its consequences is a common responsibility of states, but that states' attendant individual responsibilities are differentiated.[72] There also appears to be a shared sense that capacity differences among states are relevant to that differentiation of responsibilities. Finally, states seem to agree that industrialized countries should take the lead in combating climate change.[73] Beyond these very basic parameters, however, the common ground between states does not run very deep. A brief examination of three issue clusters may suffice to illustrate the point.

The first cluster revolves around the types of responsibilities that CBDR entails for industrialized countries. While it would appear that Northern states' responsibilities

---

[70] *Ibid.*, Art. 3(1).
[71] Rio Declaration on Environment and Development, reprinted in 31 ILM (1992) 876.
[72] See Rajamani 2003 at 31.
[73] This idea also animated the Kyoto Protocol, which imposes emission reduction commitments only upon developed countries.

encompass emission reductions and other climate change mitigation measures, it is not so clear that they demand assistance to developing countries in their mitigation or adaptation efforts. Developing countries, to be sure, assert that industrialized countries bear this responsibility, and some Northern countries may well agree.[74] But many industrialized countries prefer to see assistance as a matter of pragmatism or benevolence, rather than an outgrowth of CBDR.[75] The references to CBDR in the Climate Change Convention and Rio Declaration do not address this issue. The preamble to the Climate Change Convention, for example, speaks broadly of cooperation by all states and 'participation in an effective and appropriate response'.[76] To be sure, Article 4(7) of the Convention ties the extent of effective implementation by developing countries of their commitments to the effective implementation by developed countries of their financial and technical assistance commitments. The provision also notes that developing countries' implementation efforts 'will take fully into account' their development priorities.[77] Still, while this phrasing may resonate with the CBDR concept, it must also be noted that Article 4(7) is set apart from the Convention's statements on CBDR.

Secondly, understandings of CBDR's implications also diverge when it comes to the responsibilities of developing countries. Industrialized countries tend to assume that, albeit with some delay and with appropriate differentiation, developing countries too must take on emission mitigation commitments.[78] However, at least some developing countries insist that their responsibility is merely to cooperate in promoting sustainable development or adaption to climate change, through national emission inventories, or through devices such as the clean development mechanism.[79] Many developing countries also maintain that the concept of CBDR does not apply amongst developing countries, but only as between developing countries and industrialized countries.[80] The articulations of CBDR in the Climate Change Convention and Rio Declaration neither support nor discredit these diverging views.

The third cluster of issues concerns the thorny question of historical contributions to climate change. Developing countries see this aspect, along with capacity, as the central reason, and criterion, for differentiation.[81] Indeed, past contributions to climate change are seen as just one aspect of a much larger grievance about the historical and economic injustices inflicted on the South by Northern states.[82] Thus, for many developing countries, industrialized states must correct a wrong, having claimed an unfair share of the atmosphere's capacity to absorb greenhouse gases. Principle 7 of the

---

[74] Rajamani 2003 at 31.   [75] Ikeme 2003 at 202–3.   [76] See UNFCCC, note 67 above, Preamble, 3rd recital.
[77] *Ibid.*, Art. 4(7).   [78] Rajamani 2000 at 128.   [79] *Ibid.*   [80] *Ibid.*   [81] Ikeme 2003 at 201.
[82] See Rajamani 2003 (highlighting the impact of the developing countries' aspiration for a 'New International Economic Order' on environment and development debates). See also Roberts and Parks 2007 at 23 (arguing that climate negotiations must be seen 'in the context of an ongoing development crisis and what the global South perceives as a pattern of Northern callousness and opportunism in matters of international political economy').

Rio Declaration and the preamble to the Climate Change Convention certainly make reference to developed countries' past and present emission patterns. But at least some industrialized countries resist the notion that their past emissions are relevant to their share of climate-related responsibilities. The Climate Change Convention carefully avoided a direct linkage, mentioning historical and current emissions in a preambular paragraph, but not in conjunction with references to CBDR. While the Kyoto Protocol to the Climate Change Convention imposes emission reduction commitments only on industrialized countries and countries with economies in transition, it also suggests that, at least amongst industrialized countries, historical contribution is not a central factor. In relating industrialized countries' emission reduction commitments to their 1990 emission levels, the Protocol effectively grandfathered earlier emissions.[83] Principle 7 of the Rio Declaration does not shed much further light on the implications of CBDR. It merely averts to the pressures that industrialized societies currently place on the global environment. The attendant responsibility is also forward-looking, relating to the international pursuit of sustainable development and not a correction of past actions. The United States, for one, has consistently resisted any implication of legal responsibility for past actions, and has repeatedly lodged interpretative statements to that effect.[84]

In sum, at the present time, the concept of CBDR raises at least as many questions about climate justice as it answers. It represents the nucleus of an emerging framework for global burden sharing. But an internationally shared understanding of how and why mitigation and adaptation burdens should be allocated has yet to solidify.[85] Perhaps more importantly, it is not clear that all participants in the climate change debate actually treat it as a debate about global justice. This conclusion should not be surprising, given precisely the fundamental nature of the debate. The recognition of historical responsibility and differentiation would have significant implications beyond merely questions of cost allocation and burden sharing, and beyond the context of climate change. Politically, the recognition of a principle of historical responsibility and differentiation in international environmental law could set a precedent with much broader reach.[86] Conceptually, it touches the deep structures of international law, including the sovereign equality of states and,[87] potentially, the law of state responsibility, which

---

[83] Kyoto Protocol, reprinted in 37 ILM (1998) 22, Art. 3(1). And see Shukla 1999 at 153.

[84] Pallemaerts 2003 at 8–9; Mickelson 2000 at 70–2 (showing that developing countries very much conceived of the questions as one of legal responsibility when Principle 7 of the Rio Declaration was negotiated).

[85] On the many differences among states in reading the principle, see also Biniaz 2002 at 362–3.

[86] Consider in this context the efforts of industrialized countries, notably the United States, to contain references to CBDR in the texts emerging from the 2002 World Summit on Sustainable Development. See Rajamani 2003 at 29–32; Pallemaerts 2003 at 7–9. And see Roberts and Parks 2007 at 46–7 (on the long-standing US opposition to 'any recognition of compensatory justice as a generalized principle').

[87] Melkas 2002 at 123; Hanqin 2003 at 324.

assumes the equality of consequences of all breaches of international law, regardless of differences between states.[88]

4.2 The interplay between process and substance

These rather sobering conclusions about CBDR as a principle of global distributive justice lead me back to my earlier observations regarding the interplay between the procedural and substantive dimensions of environmental justice. Legitimate international decision-making and regime-building processes are crucial to enabling the interaction of all relevant actors and to creating the conditions in which substantive understandings can emerge or evolve.[89] That is why Northern states, whether they see CBDR as a matter of distributive justice or not, must take seriously Southern states' insistence on equal participation in decision-making and fair process. For an illustration of this point, one need only look to recent efforts to frame climate change as a security issue. In April 2007, the United Kingdom took the unprecedented step of bringing climate change before the UN Security Council, calling it a question of 'collective security in a fragile and increasingly interdependent world'.[90] Many of the more than fifty states participating in the debate welcomed the effort to reframe the issue so as to highlight its importance and urgency. But many also questioned that the Security Council, with its limited membership, was an appropriate forum. In particular, many developing countries saw the move as following a familiar pattern, threatening their full participation in policy-making and raising the specter of decisions being imposed on them.[91]

As for the substantive contribution of international law, formal enactment of a given principle alone will not promote the pursuit of global environmental justice. The example of the concept of CBDR only serves to underscore this point. The understanding of international law that I sketched out in the previous section highlights the opportunities that nonetheless exist. Yet, it does not imply an optimistic vision of the inevitability of global environmental justice through law. Rather, it highlights just how much work is required to build and re-build international law. Whether the goal is to promote global climate justice or to address climate change in pragmatic fashion, constant efforts must be made to ensure that certain conditions are met. Norms must be developed and applied in keeping with the criteria of legality that generate law's

---

[88] But note that precisely this potential impact of the concept has, so far, been contained by developed countries. See note 84 above and the accompanying text.

[89] Hurrell 2001 at 39 (arguing that institutions 'reflect, but also actively shape, communities'), at 42–3 (on the impact of international institutions on the evolution of shared understandings), at 44 (on elements of procedural justice), at 47 (on the interplay between process and substance), and at 55 (noting that institutions and their processes must be legitimate in order to be effective).

[90] UN Security Council, Press Release SC/9000, 17 April 2007, available at www.un.org/News/Press/docs/2007/sc9000.doc.htm.

[91] See *ibid.*

legitimacy and enable it to shape conduct, and they must resonate with widely shared understandings in international society.

5 Conclusion

I share Christopher Stone's sense that principles of global justice will be among the most important topics in international regime building. Such principles can be developed and international law can play an important role in the process. Global climate change is one issue area in which states must face up to what Henry Shue has termed the 'unavoidability of justice'.[92] Some important steps have been taken. Notably, the concept of common but differentiated responsibilities sketches the parameters of a debate *about* global climate justice. However, it does not currently constitute a genuine principle *of* global justice. If justice is to be pursued through the climate change regime, the hard work of international law has only just begun.

Bibliography

Adger, W. N., 2001. 'Scales of Governance and Environmental Justice for Adaptation and Mitigation of Climate Change'. 13 *Journal of International Development* 921.

Adger, W. N., Paavola, J., Huq, S., and Mace, M. J. (eds.), 2006. *Fairness in Adaptation to Climate Change*. Boston: MIT Press.

Anand, R., 2002. 'International Environmental Justice: A North–South Dimension'. 1 *International Journal of Politics and Ethics* 241.

Barnett, K., and Duvall, J. (eds.), 2005. *Power in Global Governance*. Cambridge: Cambridge University Press.

Barry, B., 1998. 'International Society from a Cosmopolitan Perspective', in David R. Mapel and Terry Nardin (eds.), *International Society: Diverse Ethical Perspectives*. Princeton: Princeton University Press.

Baumert, K., and Pershing, J., 2004. *Climate Data: Insights and Observations*. Washington, DC: Pew Center on Global Climate Change.

Beitz, C., 1979 and 1999. *Political Theory and International Relations*. Princeton: Princeton University Press.

  1999. 'International Liberalism and Distributive Justice: A Survey of Recent Thought'. 51 *World Politics* 269.

Biermann, F., 1999. 'Justice in the Greenhouse: Perspectives from International Law', in F. Tóth (ed.), *Fair Weather? Equity Concerns in Climate Change*. London: Earthscan.

Biniaz, S., 2002. 'Common But Differentiated Responsibility – Remarks', in *Proceedings of the Annual Meeting*. American Society of International Law.

Brunnée, J., 2002. 'Coping with Consent: Lawmaking under Multilateral Environmental Agreements'. 15 *Leiden Journal of International Law* 1.

Brunnée, J., and Toope, S. J., 1997. 'Environmental Security and Freshwater Resources: Ecosystem Regime Building'. 91 *American Journal of International Law* 26.

---

[92] Shue 1992 at 373.

2000. 'International Law and Constructivism: Elements of an Interactional Theory of International Law'. 39 *Columbia Journal of Transnational Law* 19.

2001. 'Interactional International Law'. 3 *International Law FORUM de droit international* 186.

Buchanan, A., 2004. *Justice, Legitimacy and Self-Determination: Moral Foundations for International Law*. Oxford: Oxford University Press.

Caney, S., 2005. 'Cosmopolitan Justice, Responsibility, and Global Climate Change'. 18 *Leiden Journal of International Law* 747.

Cohen, M., 1985. 'Moral Skepticism and International Relations', in Charles R. Beitz, Marshall Cohen and A. John Simmons (eds.), *International Ethics*. Princeton: Princeton University Press.

Cullet, P., 2003. *Differential Treatment in International Environmental Law*. Brookfield, VT: Ashgate Publishing Co.

Franck, T. M., 1995. *Fairness in International Law and Institutions*. Oxford: Clarendon Press.

French, D., 2000. 'Developing States and International Environmental Law: The Importance of Differentiated Responsibilities'. 49 *International and Comparative Law Quarterly* 35.

Fuller, L. L., 1969. *The Morality of Law*. revised edn, New Haven: Yale University Press.

Gardiner, S. M., 2004. 'Ethics and Global Climate Change'. 114 *Ethics* 555.

Gupta, J., 2000a. 'North–South Aspects of the Climate Change Issue: Towards a Negotiating Theory and Strategy for Developing Countries'. 3 *International Journal of Sustainable Development* 115.

2000b. *Climate Change: Regime Development and Treaty Implementation in the Context of Unequal Power Relations*. Amsterdam: Institute for Environmental Studies.

Hall, S., 2001. 'The Persistent Spectre: Natural Law, International Order and the Limits of Legal Positivism'. 12 *European Journal of International Law* 269.

Hanqin, X., 2003. *Transboundary Damage in International Law*. Cambridge: Cambridge University Press.

Harper, K., and Rajan, S. R., 2004. 'International Environmental Justice: Building the Natural Assets of the World's Poor', Working Paper No. 87, Political Economy Research Institute, University of Massachusetts Amherst.

Higgins, R., 2006. Plenary Address to the 2006 Annual Meeting of the American Society of International Law (Theme: 'A Just World Under Law'), Washington, DC, 31 March 2006 (notes on file with author).

Hurrell, A., 2001. 'Global Inequality and International Institutions'. 32 *Metaphilosophy* 34.

Ikeme, J., 2003. 'Equity, Environmental Justice and Sustainability: Incomplete Approaches in Climate Change Policies'. 13 *Global Environmental Politics* 195.

Koskenniemi, M., 2003. 'What Is International Law For?', in Malcolm D. Evans (ed.), *International Law*. Oxford: Oxford University Press, 89–114.

2005. *From Apology to Utopia: The Structure of International Legal Argument*. Reissue with a new Epilogue, Cambridge: Cambridge University Press.

Krisch, N., 2005. 'International Law in Times of Hegemony: Unequal Power and the Shaping of the International Legal Order'. 16 *European Journal of International Law* 369.

Kukathas, C., 2006. 'The Mirage of Global Justice'. 23 *Social Philosophy and Policy* 1.

Kütting, G., 2004. 'Environmental Justice. Book Review Essay'. 4 *Global Environmental Politics* 115.

Linklater, A., 1999. 'The Evolving Spheres of International Justice'. 75 *International Affairs* 473.

Linnerooth-Bayer, J., 1999. 'Climate Change and Multiple Views of Fairness', in F. Toth (ed.), *Fair Weather? Equity Concerns in Climate Change*. London, Earthscan.

Melkas, E., 2002. 'Sovereignty and Equity within the Framework of the Climate Change Regime'. 11 *Review of European Community and International Environmental Law* 115.

Mickelson, K., 2000. 'South, North, International Environmental Law, and International Environmental Lawyers'. 11 *Yearbook International Environmental Law* 52.

2007. 'Critical Approaches', in Daniel Bodansky, Jutta Brunnée and Ellen Hey (eds.), *Oxford Handbook of International Environmental Law*. Oxford: Oxford University Press.

Miller, D., 1999. 'Justice and Global Inequality', in Andrew Hurrell and Ngaire Woods (eds.), *Inequality, Globalization and World Politics*. Oxford: Oxford University Press.

Murphy, C., 2005. 'Lon Fuller and the Moral Value of the Rule of Law'. 24 *Law and Philosophy* 239.

Najam, S., 2004. 'The View from the South: Developing Countries in Global Environmental Politics', in Regina S. Axelrod, David Leonard Downie and Norman J. Vig (eds.), *The Global Environment: Institutions, Law and Policy*. 2nd edn, Washington, DC: CQ Press.

Paavola, J., and Adger, W. N., 2002. 'Justice and Adaptation to Climate Change', Tyndall Centre Working Paper 23.

Pallemaerts, M., 2003. 'International Law and Sustainable Development: Any Progress in Johannesburg?'. 12 *Review of European Community and International Environmental Law* 1.

Pogge, T., 2002. *World Poverty and Human Rights*. Malden, MA: Polity Press.

Rajamani, L., 2000. 'The Principle of Common But Differentiated Responsibility and the Balance of Commitments under the Climate Regime'. 9 *Review of European Community and International Environmental Law* 120.

2003. 'From Stockholm to Johannesburg: The Anatomy of Dissonance in the International Environmental Regime'. 12 *Review of European Community and International Environmental Law* 23.

Rawls, J., 1971/1999. *A Theory of Justice*. Revised edn, Cambridge, MA: Harvard University Press.

1999. *The Law of People*. Cambridge, MA: Harvard University Press.

2001. *Justice as Fairness: A Restatement*. Cambridge, MA: Harvard University Press.

Roberts, J. T., and Parks, B. C., 2007. *A Climate of Injustice, Global Inequality, North South Politics and Climate Policy*. Cambridge, MA: MIT Press.

Shelton, D., 2007. 'Equity', in Daniel Bodansky, Jutta Brunnée and Ellen Hey (eds.), *Oxford Handbook of International Environmental Law*. Oxford: Oxford University Press, 639.

Shue, H., 1992. 'The Unavoidability of Justice', in Andrew Hurrell and Benedict Kingsbury (eds.), *The International Politics of the Environment: Actors, Interests, and Institutions*. Oxford: Clarendon Press, 373.

1999. 'Global Environment and International Inequality'. 75 *International Affairs* 531.

Shukla, P. R., 1999. 'Justice, Equity and Efficiency in Climate Change: A Developing Country Perspective', in F. Tóth (ed.), *Fair Weather? Equity Concerns in Climate Change*. London: Earthscan.

Stone, C. D., 1993. *The Gnat Is Older Than Man: Global Environment and Human Agenda*. Princeton: Princeton University Press.

2004. 'Common But Differentiated Responsibilities in International Law'. 98 *American Journal of International Law* 276.

Walzer, M., 1983. *Spheres of Justice.* Oxford: Blackwell.

Wight, M., 1966. 'Why Is There No International Theory?', in Herbert Butterfield and Martin Wight (eds.), *Diplomatic Investigations: Essays in the Theory of International Politics.* London: Allen & Unwin.

Young, I. M., 2006. 'Responsibility and Global Justice: A Social Connection Model'. 23 *Social Philosophy and Policy* 102.

17

Justice in global environmental negotiations: the case of desertification

BO KJELLÉN

1 Experiences from Chairing the Negotiations of the Desertification Convention

This chapter is based on the practice of diplomacy, rather than academia, and it is not intended to break new theoretical ground. It is an effort to draw some conclusions from practical experience as an active participant in negotiations on sustainable development over the last fifteen years. More particularly, it deals with the 1994 UN Convention to Combat Desertification in those Countries Experiencing Serious Drought and/or Desertification, Particularly in Africa (Desertification Convention),[1] where I served as chairperson of the UN committee that negotiated the Convention.

Some people might say that the Desertification Convention is not really an environmental instrument, but rather a multilateral treaty on development cooperation. However, the borderlines are not very clear, since the Desertification Convention is one of the three conventions established in connection with the Rio Conference on Environment and Development in 1992.[2] Together with its sister conventions on, respectively, climate change and biodiversity, it is part of a major effort to tackle global environmental problems in such a way that the effort of reducing poverty in developing countries and secure equitable growth is not hampered. In fact, the UN World Commission on Environment and Development, known as the Brundtland Commission, in its 1987 report, *Our Common Future*,[3] not only launched the concept of 'sustainable development', but also brought environment and development closely together through its insistence not only on *inter-generational equity* but also on *intra-generational equity*. This means that we need to combine our efforts to improve living conditions all over the planet today with the daunting realization that we are the first generation with the capacity to impact on the whole global natural system.

---

[1] Negotiation concluded in Paris, 17 June 1994, 33 *International Legal Materials* (ILM) (1994) 1328. The signing ceremony took place in Paris in October 1994, and the Convention entered into force in 1996. The first Conference of Parties was held in Rome in September–October 1997.

[2] The documentation from the 1992 Rio Conference is reprinted in Johnson 1993.

[3] World Commission on Environment and Development 1987.

It is this knowledge that challenges our reflection on global justice and fairness in ways which seem to require new thinking among academics and new attitudes among policy-makers and opinion-builders. In terms of international relations, it is now clear that the existence of concrete global threats to the future, such as global warming, has created a new brand of diplomacy, with specific characteristics. Before commenting more in detail on the Desertification Convention, this chapter first discusses the concept of a new diplomacy for sustainable development.[4]

2 A new diplomacy for sustainable development

Traditional diplomacy deals with security policy in a broad sense. During the Cold War, the primacy of the national state was extreme in the relations between the superpowers; the immense dangers of a global disaster caused by a nuclear war were ever present. Now this danger seems to have subsided – though certainly not totally – but instead man's impact on, for example, climate can lead to consequences with catastrophic global effects. For the individual, it is extremely difficult to visualize disasters of this dimension; they fall outside our normal frames of reference. But responsible governments must continue to calculate different courses of action in order to manage the dangers.

So now governments need to recognize threats of a different character, long-term and diffuse. There is no concrete enemy, the threat is nowhere and everywhere. The threat is also within the very fabric of our societies, often linked to material progress. In all countries, it is difficult to make this kind of threat credible in order to get the support of public opinion that permit funds to flow and action to be taken. We may right now witness such a process in relation to climate change, but the movement is still uncertain and slow.

It is clear that new dimensions are added to traditional diplomacy. The threat is absolute, but there is no adversary on the other side of the table who can be bullied or subtly convinced to postpone the execution of the threat or accept the terms of a compromise: potentially disastrous global change will happen unless countries can agree on common action to be taken to modify certain practices, such as excessive emissions of carbon dioxide. Furthermore, we are uncertain about the character of the threat; we are facing absolute limits of a kind, but we do not know where these limits are. And we are also dealing with systemic effects of a tremendously complicated nature. When and where will the sensitive fabric of global resilience tear apart?

Policy-makers in capitals and the negotiators – these middlemen between the desirable and the possible – are caught in a dilemma: on the one hand they are operating within the boundaries of traditional methods of multilateral negotiation, and on the other hand they are negotiating about problems of a totally new kind. The long-term threats are real, though diffuse; but in the short term very concrete

---

[4] Kjellén 2008.

and very important economic and other interests are challenged, as we move from vision to action. The overall impression is that all the actors in these processes are still on a learning curve, trying to understand better how the international negotiating framework could be better adapted to this new kind of problem.

This new diplomacy requires a very broad vision, and the courage to consider the very long term in a concrete way. We see now how governments are setting targets for greenhouse gas emission reduction for periods stretching into the 2050s, far beyond traditional policy planning. These are fundamental parameters for the new diplomacy, but there are also some more specific elements that characterize it. One of them is the emergence of new international actors that normally play a subordinate role in international affairs. One example is constituted by the small island states whose vulnerability to sea-level rise makes them very active participants in climate negotiations.[5] Another is the intense, and high-quality participation of the West African countries in the negotiations on desertification.[6]

But we have also seen how other stakeholders than governments are close to the negotiations, even if they are not negotiating parties. Non-governmental organizations (NGOs) and other representatives of civil society are following the talks very closely, and they have many ways of making their voices heard. But still more important is the impact of research, in particular as the natural sciences provide the basis for negotiation and action; science paved the way for the negotiations on the ozone layer, and the successive assessment reports of the Intergovernmental Panel on Climate Change (IPCC) have been an important basis for the climate negotiations.[7] And a direct reference to the desertification negotiations shows that a great number of scientists have given important inputs, in particular through the Panel of Experts that was associated with the convention secretariat during a crucial phase of the negotiation.

It is true that desertification and land degradation in general are problems of a different nature from climate change, or the depletion of the ozone layer. Climate change and ozone layer depletion are really global problems: the gases go into a global atmosphere that knows no borders, even if response measures of different kinds have to be taken at the national or local levels. Desertification, or water shortages, or the disappearance of species, are rather problems of global significance, with different kinds of effects appearing at the local, national or regional levels, whereas their combined impact becomes a global concern. And this reality certainly makes them part of the new diplomacy.

---

[5] Kjellén 2003.   [6] Kjellén 2008.

[7] The first assessment report of the IPCC was published in 1990, just before the beginning of the negotiations leading up to the Framework Convention on Climate Change. Subsequent reports were issued in 1995 and 2001. The Fourth Assessment Report (AR4) was published in 2007. Its findings with regard to scientific evidence about climate change, its impacts, and possible response measures, have had a deep impact on public opinion and on the climate negotiations. The IPCC brings together more than 2,000 researchers in an extensive network, evaluating and quality-checking climate research.

Values, and ethical considerations of many different kinds, are important in this connection. As was pointed out in the beginning, it is therefore natural that the question of justice is inherent in the practice of the new diplomacy, with its constant need to consider environmental threats and social conditions in an integrated way. And the desertification issue raises important questions in this regard, which becomes clear, as we now turn back to the central subject of this chapter.

3 The background to the Desertification Convention

At the time of the Rio Conference, in 1992, the developing countries had a strong fear that the concept of sustainable development would not do justice to their quest for development and growth. These concerns had in fact already been voiced at the first big UN Conference on the Human Environment, in, Stockholm in 1972. At that time, Prime Minister Indira Gandhi of India, as the main spokesperson of the South, insisted that there must be an absolute priority for the combat of poverty, a theme that has ever since been an essential part of all global negotiations on environment and sustainable development. And, in fact, the concept of sustainable development itself is defined as encompassing not only environmental, but also economic and social sustainability. All this means that environmental justice has become closely linked to the notion of social and economic equity in a globalizing world. The Rio process, and the Rio conventions, are illustrative in this regard.

Looking back at the Rio Conference in 1992, and the way in which desertification was negotiated, it is worth recalling two developments as far back as the 1970s which influenced the positions of the South. One was of a general nature, and the other was specifically related to the case of desertification.

First, the elusive saga of the New International Economic Order, linked to the first oil crisis and the enhanced importance of OPEC in world affairs. The oil scare forced the major industrialized countries to propose negotiations in the so-called North–South dialogue, which brought together high-level representatives of the two camps for very extensive talks in Paris for a period of more than two years.[8] But nothing really came out of this effort, and, as the pressure on oil markets was reduced, things returned to normal, and the world experienced the reverse oil shock with extremely low prices by the mid-1980s. This lack of result in the dialogue increased frustration in the G-77, and certainly increased the quest for environmental justice and fairness. In Rio, the South simply had to obtain concessions from the industrialized countries to give substance to their negotiating stance.

The second element was the experience of the UNEP Plan of Action to Combat Desertification. This plan had its origins in the terrible drought that hit the Sahel in West Africa in the early 1970s. This was a human, social and economic disaster of epic proportions, and it triggered the kind of humanitarian reactions that normally

---

[8] For an interesting account of this now forgotten story, set in a systemic perspective, see Hansen 1979 at 19–43.

appear in such situations. But, beyond disaster relief, the international community deemed it necessary to establish structures for longer-term efforts to avoid similar disasters in the future. The newly established UN Environment Programme was given a central role, and UNEP organized the UN Conference on Desertification in Nairobi in 1977.[9] One of its main purposes was to establish a programme to combat desertification, and therefore the agreement on a Plan of Action to combat desertification was welcomed by the affected countries. However, while the Conference succeeded in placing desertification on the international environmental agenda, implementation of the plan was insufficient to accomplish its goals; and the Plan was unable to attract any substantially increased financial resources to enable it to make a real impact.

Therefore, the story of the Plan of Action is an example of how human solidarity and a sense of justice can raise an issue to the level when international awareness is sufficient to reach a potentially important agreement. But it also shows that it is difficult to sustain such action over time, as other crises and problems claim the attention of the international community.

4 Desertification in the 1992 Rio Conference on Environment and Development

As the Rio Conference was prepared, the developing countries in the G-77 (by that time more than 130) strongly emphasized the absolute need to combat poverty and promote equity and justice. In particular, the industrialized countries were called upon to increase their development assistance; and a new formula was coined which came to be used widely in the Rio process: the principle of common but differentiated responsibilities.[10]

Since conditions continued to be bad in the Sahel region, it was not surprising that the arguments based on justice and equity would be brought forward with particular strength as the Conference approached the question of drought and desertification; and it soon became a central issue for all the African countries. The two elements discussed in the previous section were very much on the minds of African negotiators, and the question of justice was present all the time: How could the world accept such poverty and despair without taking stronger action? But different factors also worked in other directions. Many developing countries had other priorities and concerns, and it seemed that the rich countries and environmental NGOs were giving central attention to problems such as climate, forests, and biological diversity.

---

[9] United Nations Conference on Desertification (UNCOD): Round-up, Plan of Action and Resolutions, 29 August–9 September 1977. New York: United Nations, 1978.

[10] One typical example is the UN Framework Convention on Climate Change, 31 ILM (1992) 849, Art. 3(1): 'The Parties should protect the climate system for the benefit of present and future generations of humankind, on the basis of equity and in accordance with their common but differentiated responsibilities and respective capabilities. Accordingly, the developed country Parties should take the lead in combating climate change and the adverse effects thereof.'

As Chairman of the plenary Working Group I of the Preparatory Committee for the 1992 Rio Conference, I quickly got a strong sense of these tensions. The Sahelian countries were disappointed and frustrated, they felt that no one was really interested in justice for them. At the time of the PrepCom's third session in the autumn of 1991, with the Conference just nine months away, this frustration reached crisis point. As a Chairman of the Working Group, one also felt that the African countries had a valid point, and a promise was made to give priority to the issue of desertification and drought at the fourth and final session of the Prepcom, to be held in March 1992. My decision to go to some of the Sahel countries for consultations before that session – a trip to Mauretania and Mali – turned out to be productive.[11] At this point, G-77 support was also strengthened: desertification was now seen as a central issue for all developing countries, not just for the African group. In the last six months before the Rio Conference, several events contributed to raise the priority of desertification.[12]

African Ministers of the Environment took the lead as they managed to agree on the principle of a convention to combat desertification as one of the concrete elements to be included in Agenda 21. The African group, at high political level, felt that the interests of other regions were met by the two conventions on climate and on biological diversity, to be signed in Rio. The developing world, especially the African countries, needed something in return. This clear political stance was of great importance, and as Chairman of the Working Group, I welcomed this initiative and encouraged the African group to present a concrete draft proposal on what would ultimately become Chapter 12 of Agenda 21 (Managing *Fragile Ecosystems: Combating Desertification and Drought*) including the proposal for a convention. This text was on the whole well received, and almost all of it was agreed at the final session of the Preparatory Committee. Without going into the details of the text, it may be noted that the Agenda 21 chapter managed to agree on a very difficult question, namely, the definition of desertification as 'land degradation in arid, semi-arid and sub-humid areas, resulting from various factors, including climatic variations and human activities'. As attention after Rio moved on to the negotiation of the Convention, this definition survived and avoided some potentially very difficult discussions.

However, at the time of the final session of the Preparatory Committee, the developed countries were not ready to agree on the proposal for a convention to combat desertification. The main argument was that it would be an unnecessary legal instrument, since the issue was not really of a global nature, and thus of a different character from climate change, the ozone layer, or the loss of biological diversity. Desertification was accepted as a problem of global significance, but one not well suited to a global convention. This negotiating stance was thus defended on the ground of practical convenience. Behind this position many observers could feel another concern, namely, that, since most countries suffering from desertification and drought were very poor,

[11] Kjellen 2003.
[12] For more detailed descriptions of this process, see Corell 1999 and Kjellén 2003 and 2008.

a convention would increase pressure on the North for more official development assistance (ODA). The issue was further complicated by the fact that a number of developed countries at the time expressed rather keen interest in negotiating a forest convention, which was opposed by the G-77. The possibility of bargaining around these different interests with a view to achieving some kind of a package deal lingered in the corridors; and the net result was that the Working Group had to put the references to a convention to combat desertification in brackets, for decision at the Rio Conference itself.

In Rio, the controversy continued, and it took major efforts by the Chairman of the General Committee, the very competent Ambassador Tommy Koh of Singapore, to secure an agreement on the principle of a convention, to be negotiated quickly, 'by June 1994'. In the end, everyone had to recognize that a forest convention was not within reach, while the Conference could agree on a 'Non-Legally binding Authoritative Statement of Principles for a Global Consensus on the management, conservation and sustainable development of all types of forests'. The developed countries continued to resist the Convention, but the turning point came when the United States agreed to support the proposal and the pressure became too strong for the European Union. The US change of position probably had a political background: the Americans tried to avoid conveying a negative image of their role in the Rio Conference and did not wish to oppose the African countries. The text in Agenda 21, Chapter 12, Article 12.40, reflected the difficulties of negotiation: 'The General Assembly ... should be requested to establish, under the aegis of the General Assembly, an intergovernmental negotiating committee for the elaboration of an international convention to combat desertification in those countries experiencing serious drought and/or desertification, particularly in Africa, with a view to finalizing such a convention by June, 1994'. This convoluted and complicated labelling of the Convention has been with us ever since, reflecting the difficulties of negotiation. However, the Africans did win a diplomatic victory, and several African representatives later confessed that for them this was the most significant outcome of the whole Conference. But the tensions and doubts about the whole issue, particularly in the group of OECD countries, have continued to complicate negotiations and reduce the impact of the Convention. In particular, the financial support has been lacking. Nevertheless, the Convention exists, and it has the potential to play a significant role in improving the conditions in the dry-lands, not only in Africa.[13] A new ten-year strategic plan to enhance the implementation of the Convention was adopted in 2007.

5 The Desertification Convention and its significance for equity and justice

Negotiations for the Convention started in earnest in May 1993, so there was a need for a quick negotiation if agreement would be reached by June 1994. In the capacity

[13] Details of the negotiations have been presented in Corell 1999, who also makes reference to Johnson 1993. The negotiations were also covered in various issues of the *Earth Negotiations Bulletin*.

of elected chairman of the negotiating committee, one had serious concerns about the possibility of our reaching the desired result. The first negotiating meetings were also very difficult and progress was slow. However, with the help of many skilled and constructive negotiators, and an excellent Secretariat, led by the resourceful and imaginative Arba Diallo of Burkina Faso, the negotiating team managed to move the negotiation up to a final session in Paris in June 1994, which turned out to be a real thriller, with final agreement uncertain until the original deadline had been passed by several hours. Not surprisingly, the financial provisions of the Convention did create these final problems, and it is quite obvious that the outcome was less than satisfactory in that regard.[14] In terms of environmental justice, it is certainly not satisfactory that the financial provisions of this Convention, which was designed to support some of the poorest countries on the planet, particularly in Africa, would have a weaker financial mechanism than the other Rio Conventions: the ultimate compromise on the Global Mechanism did not include any concrete commitments for funding. The G-77 also resisted the deal to the last moment, but finally decided – at ministerial level – that the Convention should not be rejected since even with its weaknesses it represented an important step forward. The financial structure has also been improved later, particularly with the increased involvement of the Global Environmental Facility (GEF). But more remains to be done, not least in light of the expected consequences of climate change for the dry-lands.

Rather than reviewing the negotiations in detail, or analyzing the full contents of the Convention, focus is now given to provisions which are particularly significant for the perspective of environmental justice. As we have just noted, the essential financial package of the Convention did not live up to expectations on justice grounds, and the examples given below certainly demonstrate that the agreed language often lacks precision and clarity. However, this is a common problem with many international agreements among many parties, and one must often rely on the incremental and dynamic character of the treaties. The Rio conventions are to a large extent process conventions with ample opportunities for improvements over the years. A new ten-year strategy for the Desertification Convention has been adopted, and this work might lead to more precision in the many aspects of environmental justice that are part of the original text.

As a background to these comments, it is useful to make one initial reflection on the definition of environmental justice at different scales, comparing the global to the national or local, David Schlosberg argues that 'most theories of environmental justice are inadequate', and that 'a thorough notion of global environmental justice needs to be locally grounded, theoretically broad, and plural, encompassing recognition,

---

[14] During the negotiations, I made a great number of statements to the Negotiating Committee and in other fora, highlighting various aspects of the negotiations. These can be found in various issues of the *Earth Negotiations Bulletin*. Verbatim accounts are difficult to find, but see the essays reflecting my views on the negotiations and on the Desertification Convention itself, in Kjellén 2003 and 2008.

distribution and participation'.[15] In that perspective, he considers John Rawls' theories with their focus on distribution inadequate. Looking at the evolution of the new diplomacy, and in particular the negotiations on desertification, through that prism, it seems rather obvious that the focus on justice at the UN level is on distribution. The right to development is a cornerstone of the position of the G-77, and the uneven distribution of income and wealth is the background argument as the combating of poverty is given the highest priority. But, behind this central theme, broader issues appear, since global problems and problems of global significance need to be tackled at other levels as well. The Desertification Convention is a case in point, which is made clear in a number of its preambular paragraphs, for instance:

> Noting ... that desertification is caused by complex interactions among physical, biological, political, social, cultural and economic factors,

> Considering the impact of trade and relevant aspects of international economic relations on the ability of affected countries to combat desertification adequately,

> Conscious that sustainable economic growth, social development and poverty eradication are priorities of affected developing countries, particularly in Africa, and are essential to meeting sustainability objectives,

> Mindful that desertification and drought affect sustainable development through their interrelationships with important social problems such as poverty, poor health and nutrition, lack of food security, and those arising from migration, displacement of persons and demographic dynamics,

> Stressing the important role played by women in regions affected by desertification and/or drought, particularly in rural areas of developing countries, and the importance of ensuring the full participation of both men and women at all levels in programmes to combat desertification and mitigate the effects of drought ...

These examples show that the Desertification Convention is ambitious in its approach to issues of environmental and social justice. In fact, this was a natural consequence of the shared conviction among negotiators that desertification could only be countered effectively through a broad range of different measures, going well beyond 'technical' action of tree-planting and dune containment.

Article 2 of the Desertification Convention sets out the objective and reflects these ambitions with a reference to 'an integrated approach' which is consistent with Agenda 21. Article 2(2) merits a full quotation:

> Achieving this objective [i.e. to combat desertification] will involve long-term integrated strategies that focus, simultaneously in affected areas, on improved

---

[15] Schlosberg 2005.

productivity of land, and the rehabilitation, conservation and sustainable management of land and water resources, leading to improved living conditions, in
particular at the community level.

Article 3 deals with principles, and underlines in particular the importance of
participation:

> (a) the Parties should ensure that decisions on the design and implementation
> of programmes...are taken with the participation of populations and local
> communities and that an enabling environment is created at higher levels to
> facilitate action at national and local levels,
>
> ...
>
> (c) the Parties should develop, in a spirit of partnership, cooperation among all
> levels of government, communities, non-governmental organizations and land-
> holders to establish a better understanding of the nature and value of land and
> scarce water resources in affected areas and to work towards their sustainable
> use.

Furthermore, in Article 9, which states the basic approach for the establishment of
action programmes, the principle of participation is emphasized:

> ...Such programmes shall be updated through a continuing participatory pro-
> cess on the basis of lessons from field action, as well as the results of research...

This brief review of a number of features of the Convention shows that a broad
approach to justice, in particular to the principle of participation, permeates the text.
A comparison with the Conventions on Climate Change and Biological Diversity, as
well as the Montreal Protocol, demonstrates that these treaties did not go as far in
this respect. This is largely due to the fact that they were negotiated before or during
the Rio preparations, whereas the Desertification Convention came out as a direct
result of the Rio Conference, which in many ways underlined the importance of broad
public participation in decision-making.

Thus, the distributional aspects of environmental justice, which played – and continue to play – a central role in all global environmental negotiations, were also
supplemented with strong calls for participatory justice in the documents agreed at
the Rio Conference. Having been an actor in the process, it is easy to recall my initial statements as the chairman of the International Negotiating Committee, which
underlined that the negotiation provided the first chance after the Rio Conference to
reflect the centrality of people's participation. As has been pointed out by Elisabeth
Corell, there was indeed widespread agreement from the start of the negotiations that
the Convention should use a bottom-up approach.[16]

Seen from the perspective of the chairman during the sometimes difficult negotiation rounds that followed until the Desertification Convention was finally agreed in

---

[16] Corell 1999.

June 1994 and signed in October that same year, the impression is that the importance of a bottom-up approach was never questioned. Furthermore, the presence of a great number of grass-root NGOs, particularly from Africa, underlined the participatory character of the process.[17] It was felt by those who participated that this was an endeavour to create an international instrument with innovative features, which could break some new ground in multilateral diplomacy in the post-Rio period. The question of people's participation as an essential element of justice was always present in the negotiations. This approach was well summed up in an article by the then UN Secretary-General Kofi Annan on the tenth anniversary publication of the Convention:

> Policies and national action plans can indeed contribute to relevant action on the ground. But it is only by taking into full consideration local populations' initiatives and empowering them with real responsibility that a true change in the degradation of natural resources can be secured. It is only on the basis of such legitimacy that the real conditions of an optimized local level management can be achieved.[18]

This link between the local level and justice was also underlined in my concluding statement, as Chairman of the Negotiating Committee, to the first Conference of Parties (CoP) to the Desertification Convention, held in Rome in October 1997, that, 'while the CoP should be satisfied with the results of their endeavours, if the Convention fails to have a daily impact on the people of the drylands, the job is not complete'.[19]

The question of justice has thus played a significant role in the elaboration of the Convention and in defining its place among other international legal instruments. In that context, the bottom-up approach, as a method of promoting participatory justice, has had more than just symbolic value; at the same time, we have to realize that it is the practical implementation of the principle that matters, and that conditions vary significantly between different countries.

There is quite a significant literature on desertification and the effects of drought, from colonial times to the present day. However, most authors tend to concentrate on the physical conditions in the drylands, even if social aspects are also given due attention. In the context of this paper, it has not been possible to make a full review of the literature, in order to clarify to what extent the justice point of view has been elaborated on. As an example of a positive approach in this regard, it is useful to refer to an issue paper published by the International Institute for Environment

---

[17] One example is the Senegal-based NGO, ENDA, which for many years has published a newsletter entitled *La Circulaire sur la Désertification*, which is available in French at www.enda.sn.

[18] *Preserving Our Common Ground. UNCCD 10 Years On.* Geneva: United Nations, 2006.

[19] 4/116 *Earth Negotiations Bulletin*, p. 9.

and Development, which clearly indicates that justice arguments should be used in designing development cooperation programmes.[20]

6 Reflections on the implementation of the Desertification Convention and its relevance for the concept of environmental justice

The hopes and expectations on the Convention have only been partially fulfilled. On the one hand – as pointed out by the then UN Secretary-General Kofi Annan on the occasion of the tenth anniversary of the Convention – it enjoys a truly universal membership of 191 parties, and it plays an important role in efforts to eradicate poverty, achieve sustainable development and reach the Millennium Development Goals.[21] But at the same time it has had difficulties in establishing itself as an international legal instrument at the same level as its sister conventions.

This is not due to flaws in its legal construction. The negotiators did a good job and the innovative method of creating regional implementation annexes to recognize the important differences in approach that would be needed in different parts of the world, seems to have been successful. The national action programmes have been designed to 'specify the respective roles of government, local communities and land users and the resources available and needed'.[22] In order to ensure participation, the Convention obliges the parties in a rather precise way to 'provide for effective participation at the local, national and regional levels of non-governmental organizations and local populations, both women and men, particularly resource users, including farmers and pastoralists and their representative organizations, in policy planning, decision-making and implementation and review of national action programmes'.[23] In the text there are also clear recommendations to developed country parties to support the establishment and implementation of action programmes.

The language on action programmes thus reflects an intention to give substance to some of the lofty considerations of environmental justice in the earlier Rio documents. There are now a large number of such programmes in operation, which in most cases have been supported through bilateral development cooperation funds.

Nevertheless, the continuing difficulty to mobilize financial resources within the Convention itself has given the G-77 the feeling that this Convention is not taken seriously enough by the industrialized countries, confirming their fear that this instrument directly designed to tackle problems of least developed countries is still considered second-rate in comparison with, for example, the Climate Change Convention.

---

[20] Evers 1994.
[21] United Nations General Assembly, Resolution 55/2, 'United Nations Millennium Declaration' (A/55/L.2, 18 September 2000). The Millennium Development Goals were agreed at a special High-Level Meeting of the General Assembly in 2000. They set targets for e.g. poverty reduction, access to clean water and education, mostly with the time horizon of 2015. There is also a general reference to sustainable development.
[22] Desertification Convention, note 1 above, Art. 10(2).   [23] *Ibid.*, Art. 10(2)(f).

Thus, the impact of the Desertification Convention on justice in distribution can still be questioned. The difficulties in negotiating the financial sections of the Convention foreshadowed these particular problems. As already stated, there was no way of agreeing on any precise amounts, and the institutional structure became unwieldy, since the OECD countries at the time were unwilling to establish a financial mechanism of the same kind as that existing in other conventions. Instead of appointing a financial operator such as the Global Environment Facility (GEF) to manage designated funds, the last-minute compromise only permitted the creation of a hybrid body called the Global Mechanism, with no resources of its own. This solution subsequently created a number of institutional tensions and was not conducive to the raising of new funds. However, in 2003, the GEF was established as a financial mechanism for the Convention.

In conclusion, the role of the Convention in the continuing struggle to combat poverty and improve global distributive justice is still unclear. However, the establishment of the Millennium Development Goals and the increasing attention to Africa's development problems would seem to be favourable elements. The Desertification Convention is seen by many of the poorest countries in the world as their Convention, which is not surprising, since a large number of these countries belong to the driest regions of the planet. Furthermore, the ever increasing concern for humanly induced climate change, and the probable reduction in rainfall in these parts of the world, would highlight their predicament and the role of the Convention in improving their prospects. Similarly, the risks for uncontrollable migratory movements caused by poverty and drought-linked environmental disasters should make it easier to mobilize funding for desertification projects.

In establishing the National Action Programmes foreseen in the Desertification Convention, the participatory character has been of importance, even if there are variations between countries and regions. A study of a number of these plans, including Mali, South Africa, Brazil, Vietnam, and Kazakhstan, reveals considerable differences in the way local populations and local authorities have participated actively in their elaboration. This is certainly not surprising, given the great differences in background and political structures between the countries. It should be noted, though, that the Convention Secretariat has spent considerable resources and time on efforts to promote participation in the process to work out the national programmes. The clear emphasis on participation and the corresponding possibilities of reaching people in the villages might make donors more willing to release funds.

At the more general level, it seems established that the Convention has been relatively successful in reaching local groups, including women's groups, and achieving the cooperation of various types of NGOs. As far as participatory justice is concerned, it might therefore be reasonable to consider the Convention as a relative success. Furthermore, its explicit ambition to integrate social factors in the range of actions to combat desertification, has added an important dimension to international and national action.

Nevertheless, since the implementation of the Convention still needs improvements, it has been deemed desirable to re-emphasize some of its fundamental principles, and review its operation, thereby strengthening the role of the Convention as an instrument for improving conditions in the dry-lands and underlining important aspects of environmental justice. To this end, the Conference of Parties has established an Intersessional Working Group with the task of preparing a ten-year strategic plan to enhance the implementation of the Convention and to establish a North–South dialogue to find a common vision for such a strategy. It is expected that this Working Group would be able to conclude its work in the summer of 2007. Its report would then form the basis for further consideration by the Conference of Parties.[24]

It is obviously not possible at this stage to have a clear view of the future potential of the Convention to really combat desertification. At this point in time, the main attention on issues related to global change is rightly concentrated on the climate issue. However, it is logical to recall the original reasons why desertification became an issue in the Rio process, namely, the sense of exclusion by a number of poor countries, suffering from drought and desertification. Their situation has not improved much, and there are strong indications that climate change will make the dry-lands even drier. The responsibility of the world community is engaged, and, when looking at Africa, the industrialized world, not least the European Union, has to recognize that its support should be seen as an act of enlightened self-interest. Recent problems with uncontrolled migration from Africa to Europe are symptoms of a severe crisis. But land degradation and desertification are certainly not only African problems. However, the fact that so many of the countries suffering from these phenomena are poor, directly engages the sense of justice and fairness. Principle 1 of the Rio Declaration states that: 'Human beings are at the centre of concerns for sustainable development. They are entitled to a healthy and productive life in harmony with nature.'

As I stated in my capacity as chairman at one of the sessions of the Intergovernmental Negotiating Committee for the Desertification Convention: 'This Convention has qualities beyond the reality of the fast-moving modern world. It is a Convention dealing with the fundamentals: sand, sun, water, food, and people.'[25]

No doubt, the negotiators of the Convention were inspired by general considerations of fairness and justice, but it is fair to state that the justice debate *per se* had a limited impact on proceedings. The African Ministers of Environment, who launched the idea of a convention, were above all driven by practical concerns related to the limited results of previous international efforts and the perceived need to improve living conditions in the dry-lands. From there on, the issue became part of the much broader considerations related to the Rio process, driven by the double ambition raised by the Brundtland Commission, namely, inter-generational *and* intra-generational equity.

---

[24] For more details on this review process, see the Desertification Convention website, www.unccd.org.
[25] Personal recollection by the author.

Since the negotiation of the Convention could benefit from the ideas and principles raised in the Rio process, among them those related to fairness and justice, it was not surprising that such fundamental aspects would influence the general approach to the Convention text. On the other hand, all those involved in multilateral negotiations know that the reality outside the negotiation rooms does not always permit rapid or effective implementation of agreements based on heavily negotiated texts. But the Desertification Convention exists and it has already made an impact, albeit still more limited than could have been expected. In the continued quest for effective implementation, there is no doubt that an increased concern for justice and fairness in the international arena will support a gradual strengthening of the Convention.

Bibliography

Binns, T. (ed.), 1995. *People and Environment in Africa.* New York: John Wiley and Sons.

Corell, E., 1999. *The Negotiable Desert.* Linköping: Department of Water and Environmental Studies, Linköping University.

Evers, Y. D., 1994. *Dealing with Risk and Uncertainty in Africa's Drylands: The Social Dimensions of Desertification.* London: International Institute for Environment and Development.

Glantz, M. H. (ed.), 1994. *Drought Follows the Plow.* Cambridge: Cambridge University Press.

Hansen, R. D., 1979. *Beyond the North–South Stalemate.* New York: McGraw-Hill.

Johnson, S., 1993. *Earth Summit.* London: Graham & Trotman.

Kjellén, B., 1997. 'The Desertification Convention: Towards creating a Multilateral Framework for Coping with Global Threats', in (eds.), M. Rolén, H. Sjöberg, and U. Svedin, *International Governance on Environmental Issues.* Dordrecht: Kluwer Academic Publishers.

2003. 'The Saga of the Convention to Combat Desertification: The Rio/Johannesburg Process and the Global Responsibility for the Drylands'. 12 *Review of European Community and International Environmental Law* 127.

2005. 'Diplomacy and Governance for Sustainability in a Partially Globalised World', in J. Paavola and I. Lowe (eds.), *Environmental Values in a Globalising World: Nature, Justice and Governance.* Abingdon and New York: Routledge.

2008. *A New Diplomacy for Sustainable Development: The Challenge of Global Change.* London and New York: Routledge.

Raynaut, Claude, *et al.*, 1997. *Societies and Nature in the Sahel.* London and New York: Routledge (SEI Global Environment and Development Series).

Schlosberg, D., 2005, 'Reconceiving Environmental Justice', in J. Paavola and I. Lowe (eds.), *Environmental Values in a Globalising World.* Abingdon and New York: Routledge.

World Commission on Environment and Development, 1987. *Our Common Future.* Oxford: Oxford University Press.

PART V

Access to natural resources

18

Distributive justice and procedural fairness in global water law

ELLEN HEY*

1 Introduction

One billion individuals lack access to safe and affordable water, 2.6 billion individuals lack access to sanitation, and 1.8 million children die of water-related diseases annually.[1] These hardships affect especially the poor in urban slums and marginal rural areas, who often are not connected to water and sanitation networks. Amongst the poor, women and children suffer disproportionately from water shortages.[2] Given that the task of fetching water is mostly allocated to women and girls, they lose opportunities to engage in education, childcare or earning an income. While the United Nations Development Programme (UNDP) sets the minimum daily amount of water for basic needs at 20 liters, many of the over 1 billion people who do not have proper access to water use as little as 5 liters, with the affluent in the same region using significantly more, and North Americans on average accessing over 400 liters and Europeans over 200 liters.[3] On average, the poor – not connected to municipal systems and having to buy water from private sellers – pay ten times more for water than the more affluent.[4] Increases in population and economic growth have been predicted to lead to increased water consumption and under a business-as-usual scenario it is estimated that in 2025 'some 3 billion women and men will live in countries – wholly arid or semiarid – that have less than 1.700 cubic metres per capita, the quantity below which one suffers from water stress'.[5]

It is generally acknowledged that the water crisis is not due to a lack of water, but rather is distributional in nature. The World Water Commission (WWC) estimates that, in order to address the water crises, investments of US$100 billion annually are required in developing countries, until 2025, in addition to the US$70–80 billion

* I thank Eibe Riedel for his comments on an earlier version of this text, and Gijs van der Velden and Paul Simpelaar, my student assistants, for helping me find the materials used in this chapter. The usual disclaimer applies.

[1] UNDP 2006 at 2–3.

[2] The World Health Organization (WHO 2003) estimates that, of the 1.3 billion people living in extreme poverty, 70 percent are women; WHO 2003 at 16 and 22–6.

[3] UNDP 2006 at 5 and 25.   [4] UNDP 2006 at 7.   [5] Cosgrove and Rijsberman 2000 at 5.

currently invested annually.[6] Pricing water, and thus reducing subsidies, and private sector investment are, according to the WWC, the way to reduce water consumption and the manner in which sufficient financial resources can be obtained to address the water crisis.[7] UNDP, however, emphasizes the need for public sector involvement in particular, to secure access to water for the poor.[8] It also points out that the water-related Millennium Development Goal (halving by 2015 the amount of people who do not have adequate access to drinking water and basic sanitation[9]) could be met if US$10 billion, 'five days of global military spending and less than half what rich countries spend each year on mineral water', were invested annually in lowest-cost sustainable technology.[10] The World Bank holds that both public and private sector investments are required if the water crisis is to be addressed.[11]

This chapter explores the manner in which international rules and standards seek to address the water crises. It argues that the nature of international water law has changed during the past decades, meriting the use of the term 'global water law'. Most noteworthy, global water law has moved beyond the inter-state paradigm, the 'trade-mark' of classical international water law. Global water law emphasizes the functional, over the discretionary, role of states, i.e. it requires states to fulfill certain duties instead of underlining the sovereignty of states and their independent decision-making powers. Global water law seeks to protect the interests of individuals and groups in society, and international institutions operate as relatively independent actors within this body of law. It is these characteristics and the fact that generally applicable rules and standards apply within this body of law that justify the use of the term global water law, not the geographical coverage of the law involved, global water law, as illustrated below in many cases being applicable only to a certain region or to certain states. Global water law, moreover, as the figures above illustrate, is not necessarily law that meets standards of fairness.[12]

This chapter traces the development of global water law by discussing changes in classical international water law and the International Court of Justice (ICJ), the 1992 Convention on the Protection and Use of Transboundary Watercourses and

---

[6] *Ibid.* at 60.   [7] *Ibid.* at 19–20 and 61–4.   [8] UNDP 2006 at 9–10.

[9] Initially, the water-related Millennium Development Goal referred only to access to safe drinking water, but the Johannesburg summit added access to sanitation. See para. 19, first bullet, of the Millennium Development Goals, UN General Assembly Resolution 55/2, 8 September 2000, www.un.org/millenium/declaration/ares552e.htm (accessed 26 July 2006), and paras. 8 and 25 of the Johannesburg Plan of Implementation; see also para. 18 of the Johannesburg Declaration. For the Johannesburg summit documents, see UN Doc. A/Conf.199/20, www.un.org/jsummit/html/documents/documents.html, accessed 26 July 2006.

[10] UNDP 2006 at 8.   [11] See section 5 below.

[12] In this chapter, the terminology as developed by Thomas Franck is used. Franck 1995 asserts that fairness involves both procedural fairness and distributive justice. Procedural justice, furthermore, in this essay is understood as 'good processes' as employed by Lon Fuller (Fuller 1969) and elaborated by Brunnée and Toope 2000. Good process is what distinguishes law from other normative systems. It entails a process that enables the constant construction and reconstruction of legal rules in inter-action between actors, and determines the extent to which rules attract compliance.

International Lakes (Helsinki Convention) and its protocols,[13] the right to water, and World Bank involvement in water management. In each of these sections, the rules and standards involved will be characterized in terms of the changes that they introduce into the international legal system. Thereafter, by way of conclusions, the discussion will focus on how these developments relate to fairness in global water law.

2 Changes in classical international water law and the International Court of Justice

Classical international water law focuses on inter-state relations regarding transboundary waters. These relations are governed by principles of customary law and by treaties that riparian states may have concluded for a specific transboundary water. Relevant principles are those concerning equitable and reasonable utilization, the obligation not to cause significant harm, and the duty to consult in case of planned activities that may result in significant adverse effects. These principles have been incorporated in the 1997 Convention on the Law of the Non-Navigational Uses of International Watercourses (Watercourses Convention).[14]

Two aspects of the Watercourses Convention are noteworthy. First, riparian states are not obliged to conclude cooperative agreements for an international watercourse. Instead, Article 3(3) of the Watercourses Convention provides that states parties 'may enter into' such agreements and in so doing may 'apply and *adjust*' (emphasis added) the provisions of the Convention. This provision entails that the Watercourses Convention, as such, does not provide minimum standards that states parties must meet in their cooperative endeavors regarding an international watercourse.

Secondly, the Watercourses Convention focuses on inter-state relations. Its consultation procedure does not provide for participation by actors other than states.[15] Its provision on damage to natural or juridical persons who have suffered transboundary harm determines that states shall not discriminate in terms of nationality or residence in providing access to judicial or other procedures.[16] The Convention, thus, does not establish minimum standards on access to justice. Moreover, vital human needs, such as access to drinking water and sanitation, are not given absolute priority. The Convention only provides that '[i]n the event of a conflict between uses ... it shall be resolved with reference to articles 5 and 7, with *special regard* being given to the requirements

---

[13] 1992 Convention on the Protection and Use of Transboundary Watercourses and International Lakes, 31 ILM (1992) 1312 (adopted 17 March 1992, in force 6 October 1996); and 1999 Protocol on Water and Health to the 1992 Convention on the Protection and Use of Transboundary Watercourses and International Lakes, 29 *Environmental Policy and Law* (1999) 200. These treaties are also available at www.unece.org/env, accessed 23 July 2006. All UNECE documents referred to in this chapter and information pertaining to these documents are available at www.unece.org/env/(accessed 23 July 2006).

[14] UN General Assembly Resolution 51/229, 21 May 1997, not in force, 36 ILM (1997) 700. For further information, see McCaffrey 2001 and Tanzi and Arcari 2001.

[15] Watercourses Convention, note 14 above, Arts. 11–19.   [16] *Ibid.*, Art. 32.

of vital human needs' (emphasis added).[17] Harm also is conceived primarily in terms of 'harm to other watercourse States',[18] even if a broader approach is adopted where the protection of the environment is concerned. In that case, states are to 'individually and where appropriate, jointly' 'protect and preserve the ecosystems',[19] 'prevent the introduction of species, alien or new',[20] and 'prevent, reduce and control ... pollution ... that may cause significant harm to other watercourse States or their environment, including harm to human health or safety, to the use of the waters for any beneficial purposes or the living resources of the watercourse'.[21] While the Watercourses Convention indicates how states might cooperate towards the protection of an international watercourse, it only imposes on riparian states the obligation to consult, at the request of any one of them. Only with respect to the regulation of the flow of water in an international watercourse does the Convention provide an obligation to cooperate, albeit under the proviso 'where appropriate'.[22]

That states, however, are not completely free to proceed as they deem appropriate in their cooperative endeavors regarding the protection of the environment is evidenced by the 1997 decision of the ICJ in the *Gabčikovo–Nagymaros* case.[23] In its decision, the ICJ determined that general provisions on the protection of the environment and nature, included in a 1977 bilateral treaty applicable between the parties, gave rise to a 'joint responsibility' to determine on a continuous basis the environmental risks and to translate such risks into specific obligations by way of consultation and negotiation.[24] The ICJ held this to be the case, because, as it had declared in the *Legality of the Threat or Use of Nuclear Weapons* case,[25] 'the environment is not an abstraction but presents the living space, the quality of life and the very health of human beings, including generations unborn'.[26] These findings clearly emphasize the duty of states to protect the environment for the benefit of individuals and groups in society. The ICJ also held that the provisions in the 1977 Treaty require the parties to apply new norms and standards in evaluating the environmental risks of both new activities and activities begun in the past.[27] I suggest that this reasoning of the ICJ also is applicable to the environmental provisions of the Watercourses Convention, in spite of Article 3(3) of the Convention. In other words, the environmental provisions of the Watercourses Convention give rise to a joint responsibility to protect the environment, provide minimum standards for and require the incorporation of new norms and standards into the cooperative endeavors that states engage in.

In terms of fairness, classical international water law, thus, focuses on attaining inter-state fairness and reflects a discretionary role of states in determining what is fair in the context of a particular international watercourse. The ICJ decision in the *Gabčikovo–Nagymaros* case, however, suggests that, where the protection of the

---

[17] *Ibid.*, Art. 10(2). Arts. 5 and 7 refer, respectively, to the principle of equitable and reasonable use and the principle of no significant harm.
[18] *Ibid.*, Art. 7.   [19] *Ibid.*, Art. 20.   [20] *Ibid.*, Art. 22.   [21] *Ibid.*, Art. 21(2).   [22] *Ibid.*, Art. 25(1).
[23] (1997) ICJ Reports 3.   [24] *Ibid.*, para. 112.   [25] (1996) ICJ Reports, para. 29.
[26] (1997) ICJ Reports, para. 112.   [27] *Ibid.*, para. 140.

environment is concerned, this discretion is limited in the interest of present and future generations.[28] As a result of this approach, the ICJ introduced a new element into classical international law: the functional role of states in the interest of individuals and groups in society.

3 The Helsinki Convention and its Protocols

The adoption of the Helsinki Convention within the United Nations Economic Commission for Europe (UNECE) marked a move away from classical international water law in the UNECE region.[29] However, the 2003 decision of the states parties to open participation in the Helsinki Convention to states beyond the UNECE region entails that the Convention may attain wider geographical relevance.[30]

The Helsinki Convention imposes minimum standards for the management of transboundary waters upon its parties and further specifies those standards for parties sharing a particular transboundary water.[31] It, for example, provides that '[Parties] shall take appropriate measures to prevent, control and reduce any transboundary impact'[32] and sets out standards that provide the contours within which states should undertake such action, including, the principle of inter-generational equity[33] and the application of 'low- and non-waste technology'.[34] While the foregoing are examples of provisions that apply to all parties individually, the Convention also provides more specific obligations that apply to riparian parties sharing a transboundary water. Riparian states, for example, are under an obligation to conclude agreements or arrangements and adapt existing ones in order to implement the Convention.[35] The Helsinki Convention also determines that these agreements shall establish joint bodies, and specifies the tasks of these bodies, including the elaboration of joint monitoring programs and joint water-quality objectives and criteria.[36] The Convention

---

[28] See the text at note 26 above.

[29] For references, see note 13 above. The UNECE region encompasses the European Union, non-EU Western and Eastern Europe, South-East Europe and the Commonwealth of Independent States (CIS) and North America. Note, however, that North American states are not parties to most of the treaties mentioned in this chapter.

[30] Decision III/1, Amendment to the Water Convention, adopted 28 November 2003, Doc. ECE/MP.WAT/14, 12 January 2004. Other states may accede to the Helsinki Convention upon approval of the Meeting of the Parties. Such approval shall only be considered once the amendment has entered into force for all parties to the Convention on the date of the adoption of the amendment. The amendment was not in force at the time of writing.

[31] The Helsinki Convention includes both surface and groundwater, including confined groundwater, within its ambit of application (Art. 1(1)); the Watercourses Convention applies to surface water and groundwater connected to surface water only (Art. 2(a)).

[32] Helsinki Convention, note 13 above, Art. 2(1).   [33] *Ibid.*, Art. 2(5)(c).

[34] *Ibid.*, Art. 3(1)(a).   [35] *Ibid.*, Art. 9(1).

[36] *Ibid.*, Art. 9(2). Also see Annex III to the Helsinki Convention, which provides guidelines on how such objectives and criteria can be developed. Annexes I and II fulfill a similar role by providing, respectively, the definition of the term 'best available technology' and Guidelines for Developing Best Environmental Practices.

thus limits the discretionary power of its parties and imposes minimum standards on those parties, both individually and jointly, in the interest of the protection of the environment.

The 1999 Protocol on Water and Health to the Helsinki Convention builds on the approach adopted in the Convention.[37] The Protocol, unlike the Convention, applies to all waters within the territory of a party.[38]

The Protocol on Water and Health imposes the obligation on parties to secure the provision of 'adequate supplies of wholesome drinking water' and 'adequate sanitation', with the aim of protecting human health (and in case of sanitation) also the environment.[39] The Protocol also indicates how parties are to implement these duties by providing general principles and the type of measures to be adopted. The general principles include, besides a number of principles of international environmental law, such as the precautionary principle,[40] the following: 'Water has social, economic and environmental values and should therefore be managed so as to realize the most acceptable and sustainable combination of these values'; '[e]fficient use of water should be promoted through economic instruments and awareness-building'; and '[e]quitable access to water, adequate in terms of both quantity and quality, should be provided for all members of the population, especially those who suffer a disadvantage or social exclusion'.[41] The Protocol also provides that, among other measures, parties shall improve, establish and maintain collective systems,[42] formulate targets and set target dates,[43] review and assess progress,[44] and take measures to enhance public awareness.[45]

The Protocol also requires parties to cooperate with respect to transboundary waters, but also to cooperate and assist each other in the adoption of international measures that further the objectives of the Protocol,[46] and, upon request, in the development of national and local plans that implement the Protocol.[47] The adoption of international measures refers to general cooperation among the parties to implement the Protocol through, for example, the establishment of joint or coordinated surveillance systems, the development of integrated information systems or exchanges of

---

[37] For references, see note 13 above. Adopted 17 June 1999, in force 4 August 2005.

[38] Art. 3 of the Protocol on Water and Health, note 13 above, lists the following waters: surface freshwater; groundwater; estuaries; coastal waters which are used for recreation or for the production of fish by aquaculture or for the production or harvesting of shellfish; enclosed waters generally available for bathing; water in the course of abstraction, transport, treatment or supply, and waste water throughout the course of collection, transport, treatment and discharge or reuse.

[39] Protocol on Water and Health, note 13 above, Art. 4(2)(a) and (b). According to the UNECE, in the European part of the UNECE, that is, the UNECE region without North America, 'an estimated 120 million people, i.e. one person in every seven, do not have access to safe drinking water and adequate sanitation' and 30 million cases of water-related disease occur annually. See www.unece.org/env/water/text/text_protocol.htm, accessed 25 July 2006.

[40] Protocol on Water and Health, note 13 above, Art. 5(a).   [41] Ibid., Art. 5, paras. (g), (h) and (l) respectively.

[42] Ibid., Art. 4(2)(a) and (b).   [43] Ibid., Art. 6.   [44] Ibid., Art. 7.   [45] Ibid., Art. 9.

[46] Ibid., Art. 11(a).   [47] Ibid., Art. 11(b).

information.[48] The provision on cooperation and assistance enables developing parties to request assistance from more affluent parties in developing national and local policies to implement the Protocol.[49]

The Protocol, in three distinct ways, distances itself from the classical inter-state paradigm. It imposes minimum obligations on its parties, its central objective is the interest of individuals and groups in society in drinking water of sufficient quality and quantity and water for sanitation, and it places the responsibility for protecting that interest not only on individual parties within their own territory and with respect to their inhabitants, but also on parties jointly. The Protocol, as the Helsinki Convention, hereby emphasizes the functional role of states, which are to act in the interest of individuals and groups in society and the protection of the environment.

The Protocol, moreover, stresses the importance of access to information, participation and access to justice.[50] In this respect, the Helsinki Convention and the Protocol on Water and Health should be regarded in the context of other UNECE environmental conventions, in particular, the 1991 Convention on Environmental Impact Assessment in a Transboundary Context (Espoo Convention)[51] and the 1998 Convention on Access to Information, Public Participation in Decision-making and Access to Justice in Environmental Matters (Aarhus Convention).[52] The Espoo Convention provides standards regarding citizens' participation in assessing the possible transboundary negative effects of planned activities. The Aarhus Convention provides standards on access to information, participation and access to justice and enables individuals and groups to submit a claim of non-compliance to its Compliance Committee, if a party does not meet those standards. The provisions on access to information, participation and access to justice in all these instruments aim to increase procedural fairness in decision-making, both within a state and in a transboundary context.[53]

The 2003 Protocol on Civil Liability and Compensation for Damage Caused by the Transboundary Effects of Industrial Accidents on Transboundary Waters (Civil

---

[48] *Ibid.*, Art. 12. Note the establishment of the International Water Assessment Centre (IWAC), in 2000 at the Netherlands Institute for Inland Water Management and Waste Water Treatment (RIZA). IWAC assists UNECE governments and joint bodies in the implementation of the Convention, particularly in monitoring and assessment (www.unece.org/env/water/services/serv.htm, accessed 25 July 2006).

[49] Protocol on Water and Health, note 13 above, Art. 14. Note the establishment of the Capacity for Water Cooperation Project (CWC) for Eastern Europe, the Caucasus and Central Asia (EECCA). The CWC assists the twelve states in the EECCA region in strengthening capacity for transboundary water management, in particular, through training. The project is supported by individual donors and the Global Environment Facility (www.unece.org/env/water/cwc.htm, accessed 25 July 2006).

[50] Protocol on Water and Health, note 13 above, Artt. 5(i), 6(2), 8(1)(a)(iii), 9 and 10. Also see Art. 16 of the Helsinki Convention.

[51] 30 ILM (1991) 800. Adopted 25 February 1991, in force 10 September 1997. Decision II/4, adopted 27 February 2001, not yet in force, will open the Espoo Convention to participation by states outside the UNECE region.

[52] 38 ILM (1999) 515. Adopted 25 June 1998, in force 30 October 2001. Art. 19(4) of the Aarhus Convention opens the Convention to participation by states outside the UNECE region.

[53] See Ebbesson 2007 at 681.

Liability Protocol) is also relevant to the rights of individuals and groups in society.[54] It is a protocol to both the Helsinki Convention and the 1992 Convention on the Transboundary Effects of Industrial Accidents,[55] also adopted under the auspices of UNECE. The Protocol on Civil Liability makes operators strictly liable for transboundary damage caused by industrial accidents in a transboundary water. It also imposes fault-based liability on individuals, subject to national law on servants and agents.[56] It enables the claimant to bring an action for compensation in the courts of the party where the 'damage was suffered, the industrial accident occurred or where the defendant has his or her habitual residence, or, if the defendant is a company or other legal person or an association, where it has its principal place of business, statutory seat or central administration'.[57] The Protocol on Civil Liability also offers persons involved in a dispute regarding damages the option of settling it, if all parties to the dispute agree, by means of final and binding arbitration pursuant to the Permanent Court of Arbitration's Optional Rules on Arbitration of Disputes Relating to Natural Resources and/or the Environment (PCA Rules).[58] States also in this case are regarded as functional entities that are to ensure that individuals or groups in society have access to appropriate procedures for claiming compensation if they suffer transboundary damage. This entails that relevant actors in seeking compensation are not dependent on the discretion of states to commence inter-state responsibility procedures.

The Helsinki Convention and its protocols can be characterized as instruments that focus on the interests of individuals and groups in society and treat states as functional entities that are to ensure that those interests are protected. That as such is a departure from classical international water law. A further departure from that body of law consists in the emphasis that these instruments place on the joint responsibility of states, not only with respect to transboundary waters but, more generally in the provision of access to clean and sufficient water and adequate sanitation.

4 The right to water

The most comprehensive formulation of the right to water is found in General Comment 15, adopted by the Committee on Economic, Social and Cultural Rights (CESCR) in 2002.[59] Earlier formulations of the right to water are either less

---

[54] Available at www.unece.org. Adopted 21 May, 2003, not yet in force.

[55] 31 ILM (1992) 1330. Adopted 17 March 1992, in force 19 April 2000.

[56] Civil Liability Protocol, note 54 above, Arts. 4 and 5.   [57] *Ibid.*, Art. 13.

[58] *Ibid.*, Art. 14. For further information on the PCA Rules, see www.pca-cpa.org/ENGLISH/BD/ (accessed 8 August 2006) and Ratliff 2001.

[59] General Comment 15(2002), 'The Right to Water (Arts. 11 and 12 of the International Covenant on Economic, Social and Cultural Rights)', UN Doc. E/C.12/2002/11, 20 January 2003 (General Comment 15). All CESCR general comments are available at www.ohchr.org/english/bodies/cescr/comments.htm, accessed 3 July 2006. General comments, adopted by the CESCR as well as other human rights bodies, are legally non-binding documents that constitute authoritative interpretations of the rights contained in human rights

elaborate,[60] conceive of the right to water as part of other rights,[61] or place the right to water in a subsidiary position to other considerations.[62] The right to water is also included in the final outcomes of the 1977 United Nations Water Conference,[63] the 1992 United Nations Conference on Environment and Development,[64] and the 1994 United Nations International Conference on Population and Development.[65] Subsequent summit documents, such as the 2000 United Nations Millennium Declaration, the 2002 Johannesburg Declaration and Plan of Implementation, and the 2005 World Summit Outcome, however, do not refer to the right to water. Instead, they include the commitment to reduce by 50 percent by 2015 the amount of people without access to safe drinking water and sanitation.[66] The 2006 Human Development Report emphasizes the importance of the right to water.[67]

The CESCR links the right to water to Articles 11 and 12 of the International Covenant on Economic, Social and Cultural Rights (ESCR Covenant), respectively, on the right to an adequate standard of living and on the right to the highest standard of health.[68] General Comment 15 formulates the human right to water as follows:

> The human right to water entitles everyone to sufficient, safe, acceptable, physically accessible and affordable water for personal and domestic uses. An adequate amount of safe water is necessary to prevent death from dehydration,

instruments. See Langford, Khalfan, Fairstein and Jones 2004, available at www.cohre.org/water, accessed 26 July 2006; McGaffrey 2005 at 93; and Riedel 2006 at 19.

[60] The European Charter on Water Resources, para. 5, adopted by the Committee of Ministers of the Council of Europe, Recommendation (2001)14, www.coe.int, accessed 15 July 2006. See Herrero de la Fuente 2005 at 285.

[61] Art. 14(2) of the 1979 Convention on the Elimination of All Forms of Discrimination Against Women (CEDAW), adopted 16 December 1979, in force 3 September 1981; and Art. 24(2) of the 1989 Convention on the Rights of the Child, adopted 20 November 1989, in force 2 September 1990. CEDAW conceives of the right to water as part of the right to enjoy adequate living conditions for women living in rural areas; the Convention on the Rights of the Child as part of the right to health. Both conventions are available at www.ohchr.org/english/law/index.htm, accessed 8 August 2006.

[62] Principle 4 of the 1992 Dublin Statement on Water and Sustainable Development links the right to water to and places it in a subsidiary position to water as an economic good: see www.wmo.ch/web/homs/documents/english/icwdece.html, accessed 23 July 2006.

[63] Preamble, Mar del Plata Action Plan, quoted in Langford, Khalfan, Fairstein and Jones 2004 at 31.

[64] Para. 18.45 of Agenda 21, www.un.org/esa/sustdev/documents/agenda21/index.htm, accessed 26 July 2006.

[65] Principle 2 of the Programme of Action of the United Nations International Conference on Population and Development, also see its paragraph 8.10, www.iisd.ca/Cairo/html, accessed 26 July 2006.

[66] See note 9 above, and para. 3, 2005 World Summit Outcome, UN General Assembly Resolution A/RES/60/1, 24 October 2005, www.un.org/millenniumgoals, accessed 26 July 2006.

[67] UNDP 2006 at 60–1.

[68] 1966 International Covenant on Economic, Social and Cultural Rights, 6 ILM (1967) 368. General Comment 15, note 59 above, para. 3. Also see Committee on ESCR, General Comment 4(1991), 'The Right to Adequate Housing (Art. 11(1))', UN Doc. E/1992/23, 1992, in particular, para. 8(b); and General Comment 14(2000), 'The Right to the Highest Standard of Health (Art. 12)', UN Doc. E/C.12/2000/4, 1992, in particular, para. 15.

to reduce the risk of water-related disease and to provide for consumption, cooking, personal and domestic hygienic requirements.[69]

General Comment 15 thus addresses the need to ensure the availability of water in both quantitative and qualitative terms and addresses the accessibility and affordability of water,[70] also for vulnerable groups.[71] General Comment 15 further specifies the right to water in terms of obligations to respect,[72] protect,[73] and fulfill,[74] as well as international[75] and core obligations.[76] Among the obligations to fulfill, is the obligation to 'adopt comprehensive and integrated strategies and programmes to ensure ... sufficient and safe water for present and future generations'.[77] The core obligations relate to physical access to water; personal security while accessing water; participation and transparency in developing national water strategies and plans of action; monitoring; the adoption of low-cost water programs; and measures to prevent, treat, and control diseases.[78]

General Comment 15 limits the human right to water, by encompassing within its ambit only personal and domestic uses to prevent death from dehydration, reduce the risk of water-related disease and to provide water for consumption, cooking and personal and domestic hygienic requirements. The CESCR stresses that, while access to water is relevant in the context of other human rights, priority must be given to the uses mentioned in its definition of the right and that other water uses must be accomplished within the ambit of other rights guaranteed in the Covenant.[79] Relevant rights are the right to gain a living,[80] the right to culture,[81] the right to food,[82] and the right to education.[83]

General Comment 15 also provides that '[w]ater should be treated as a social and cultural good, and not primarily as an economic good'[84] and that financial resources should be so allocated to avoid discrimination, for example, by also investing in lower cost water supply services and facilities that are likely to benefit larger parts of the population.[85] In terms of obligations to protect, General Comment 15 points to the responsibility of states in case water services are operated or controlled by private parties and provides that: 'States parties must prevent them [private parties] from compromising equal, affordable, and physical access to sufficient, safe and acceptable

---

[69] General Comment 15, note 59 above, para. 2.   [70] *Ibid.*, para. 12.   [71] *Ibid.*, para. 16.

[72] *Ibid.*, paras. 21 and 22.   [73] *Ibid.*, paras. 23 and 24.   [74] *Ibid.*, paras. 25–9.   [75] *Ibid.*, paras. 30–6.

[76] *Ibid.*, paras. 37 and 38.   [77] *Ibid.*, para. 28.   [78] *Ibid.*, para. 37.

[79] *Ibid.*, para. 6. Also see WHO 2003 at 18–21.

[80] ESCR Covenant, note 68 above, Art. 6.   [81] ESCR Covenant, note 68, Art. 15.

[82] ESCR Covenant, note 68, Art. 11. Also see Committee on ESCR, General Comment 12, 'The Right to Adequate Food (Art. 11)', UN Doc. E/C.12/1999/5, 1999.

[83] ESCR Covenant, note 68 above, Art. 13, and CESCR General Comment 13(1999), 'The Right to Education (Art. 13)', UN Doc. E/C12/1999/10, 8 December 1999, in particular, para. 55 on child labor.

[84] General Comment 15, note 59 above, para. 11. Also see para. 2 of the European Charter on Water Resources, note 60 above, which provides that 'water must be equitably used in the public interest'.

[85] General Comment 15, note 59, para. 14.

water.'[86] Moreover, in terms of obligations to fulfill, General Comment 15 provides that water must be affordable and that '[a]ny payment for water services has to be based on the principle of equity, ensuring these services, whether privately or publicly provided, are affordable for all, including socially disadvantaged groups'.[87] These provisions are illustrative of the caution with which the CESCR approaches privatization and the pricing of water. The part on international obligations reflects similar caution. It provides that states should take steps, both legal and political, 'to prevent their own citizens and companies from violating the right to water of individuals and communities in other countries'[88] and 'should ensure that the right to water is given due attention in international agreements and, to that end, should consider the development of further legal instruments'.[89] Moreover, the same paragraph provides that 'agreements concerning trade liberalization should not curtail or inhibit a country's capacity to ensure the full realization of the right to water'.[90]

These obligations are noteworthy due to the indirect manner in which they address privatization and trade liberalization in relation to water.[91] They, however, also merit attention because they formulate commitments for states, other than the state of residence. This approach is based on the importance accorded to international cooperation, assistance, and joint and separate action in Articles 2(1), 11(1), and 23 of the ESCR Covenant.[92] Other examples of similar provisions are those requiring states to refrain from imposing measures, such as embargoes, that would prevent the supply of water or otherwise use water as a measure of political or economic pressure;[93] to facilitate realization of the right to water in other countries, subject to available resources, and with a special responsibility for developed states to assist developing states;[94] and to ensure that 'international financial institutions, in particular the International Monetary Fund and the World Bank, and regional development banks take steps to implement the right to water'.[95] This approach has also been integrated in the section on core obligations, which provides 'that it is particularly incumbent on States parties, and other actors in a position to assist, to provide international assistance and cooperation ... which enables developing countries to fulfil their core obligations'.[96]

In a separate section, entitled 'obligations of actors other than states', General Comment 15 directly addresses the obligations of international institutions.[97] It points to the need of the United Nations and institutions concerned with water as well as

---

[86] *Ibid.*, para. 24.   [87] *Ibid.*, para. 27.   [88] *Ibid.*, para. 33.   [89] *Ibid.*, para. 35.   [90] *Ibid.*, para. 35.

[91] For critical accounts of the possible effects of the commodification of water, see Brown Weiss 2005 at 61 and Cossy 2005 at 117.

[92] General Comment 15, note 59 above, para. 30. Also see CESCR, General Comment 3(1990), 'The Nature of States Parties Obligations (Art. 2, par. 1)', UN Doc. E/1991/23, 1991, in particular, paras. 13 and 14.

[93] General Comment 15, note 59 above, para. 32. Also see CESCR, General Comment 8(1997), 'The Relationship Between Economic Sanctions and Respect for Economic, Social and Cultural Rights', UN Doc. E/C.12/1997/8, 12 December 1997, in particular, para. 3.

[94] General Comment 15, note 59 above, para. 34.   [95] *Ibid.*, para. 36.   [96] *Ibid.*, para. 38.

[97] *Ibid.*, para. 60. Also see ESCR Committee, General Comment 2, 'International Technical Assistance Measures (Art. 22)', UN Doc. E/1990/23.

those concerned with trade, such as the World Trade Organization, to cooperate with states in the implementation of the right to water, and provides that '[t]he international financial institutions, notably the International Monetary Fund and the World Bank, should take into account the right to water in their lending polices'. This section also provides that, in 'examining the reports of State parties and their ability to meet the obligations to realize the right to water, the Committee will consider the effects of the assistance provided by all actors'. Lastly, under this heading, General Comment 15 refers to the importance of the Red Cross and Red Crescent Societies, relevant international institutions and non-governmental organizations and other associations in times of emergencies, and provides that priority be given to supplying the most vulnerable or marginalized groups with water. Interestingly, the comment here addresses non-governmental organizations directly, and not via states, as it does with regard to the private sector.[98]

It is clear from the above that the right to water addresses fairness, and, in particular distributive justice, at national and international levels. Moreover, the CESCR stresses the need for the accessibility of information, public participation, and transparency at the national level, and thus procedural fairness at that level.[99]

This manner of approaching rights and duties related to water clearly differs from classical international water law and shows parallels with the approach adopted in the Helsinki Convention and its protocols. First, it addresses the rights and interests of individuals and groups in society, and, in particular, vulnerable groups – the poor in general, and women and children in particular. Secondly, it addresses responsibilities of states in realizing the right to water. Importantly, it also addresses the responsibility of states other than that of residence, by formulating the responsibility of developed states to transfer resources to developing states and so assist them in implementing the right to water. Thirdly, it addresses the responsibility of international institutions, both directly and via states acting within these institutions. Moreover, indirectly via states, General Comment 15 addresses the responsibility of the private sector, both individuals and companies who invest in water-related projects abroad.

5 The World Bank and water management

During the past decade, about 16 percent of World Bank lending was devoted to water-related projects.[100] In order to guide its work, the World Bank has adopted strategies, programs, operational guidance and procedures, and bank policies, which contain guidelines and sometimes rules and standards that are to guide the bank and recipients in designing, selecting, and implementing projects. Only operational procedures and Bank policies, together known as safeguard policies, contain rules and

---

[98] See the text quoted in note 88 above.
[99] E.g. General Comment 15, note 59 above, paras. 12(c)(iv) and 16(a).
[100] World Bank 2004 at 1. World Bank instruments related to water are available at web.worldbank.org (under topics, water supply and sanitation, strategy and policy), accessed 1 August 2006.

standards that bind the Bank's personnel internally; other instruments provide policy guidelines.

In 2004, the World Bank adopted its Water Resources Sector Strategy, which replaces earlier water-related policy documents.[101] This strategy seeks to implement the Dublin Principles,[102] and focuses on water resources management and the connections between resource use and management.[103] It addresses the institutional framework, management instruments, the development and management of infrastructure, and the political economy of water.[104] The focus thus is not on the water-using sectors, which are addressed in other Bank instruments.[105]

Where privatization is concerned, the strategy provides that 'there is now a broad consensus among developing countries that, while public funds have and will remain dominant and indispensable, the required infrastructure cannot be built with public funds alone and that the private sector has an important role to play in financing water infrastructure'.[106] In addition to emphasizing the need for public–private partnerships, the strategy, as well as other related strategies and programs, stresses the importance of pricing water and the role of private sector involvement in attaining both sufficient financial resources[107] and more efficient water and sanitation sectors.[108] It also provides that water resources management is a 'significant public good'[109] and points to present difficulties in attracting private sector funding for the water sector.[110]

Moreover, the strategy refers to the need for participation, for example through user associations,[111] the interests of the poor,[112] the accountability of water-service providers, and management institutions,[113] and is critical of the past policies of the Bank regarding major infrastructural works, in particular dams.[114] The strategy, however, rejects[115] the World Commission on Dams 'prior informed consent' approach to the participation of affected individuals and groups and indigenous peoples in decision-making and the recommendation that financial institutions disengage from projects if riparian states do not engage in good faith negotiations.[116] The World Bank finds that this approach to prior informed consent would amount to a veto for such groups over potential projects and 'undermine the fundamental right of the state to make decisions in the best interest of the community as a whole'.[117] It prefers its own policies on inter-state consultation, 'based on proactive engagement

---

[101] World Bank 2004.   [102] See note 62 above.   [103] World Bank 2004 at 12.

[104] World Bank 2004 at 12–13.

[105] See Strategies for Water Supply and Sanitation concerning Rural Development, Private Sector Development, Urban and Local Government and Environment; also see operational guidelines on Public and Private Sector Roles in Water Supply and Sanitation Services and the World Bank Group's Program for Water Supply and Sanitation.

[106] World Bank 2004 at 43.   [107] World Bank 2004 at 44.   [108] World Bank 2004 at 45.

[109] World Bank 2004 at 42.   [110] World Bank 2004 at 44.   [111] World Bank 2004 at 13 and 15.

[112] World Bank 2004 e.g. at 10.   [113] World Bank 2004 e.g. at 19.   [114] World Bank 2004 at 7–8.

[115] World Bank 2004 at 38 and Appendix I.

[116] See 'A Set of Guidelines for Good Practice', in World Commission on Dams 2000 at 278–307.

[117] World Bank 2004 at 38.

rather than disengagement from countries that are not already negotiating with their neighbors'.[118]

The World Bank's own policies on participation and inter-state consultations are contained in a number of safeguard polices. Where participation is concerned, the safeguard policy on environmental assessment, for example, requires consultation with project-affected groups and local NGOs and requires that relevant information be made available in a timely manner and in a form and language relevant to those consulted.[119] The policy, further, determines that, if a borrower objects to the Bank releasing an environmental impact assessment report, Bank staff will refrain from further processing the project, if it is being considered for financing by the International Development Agency, and, if it is being considered for financing by the International Bank for Reconstruction and Development, will submit the project to the Executive Directors for further consideration.[120] The safeguard policy on indigenous peoples requires the borrower to engage in free, prior and informed consultation with indigenous people who may be affected by a project and determines that the Bank shall only engage in projects where such consultations 'result in broad community support to the project by the affected Indigenous Peoples'.[121] The World Bank's safeguard policies on consultation with affected and indigenous peoples, even if not specifically concerned with water-related projects, clearly address the manner in which states are to engage individuals and groups in water management within their territory and extend beyond the participatory rights that classical international water law offers individuals and groups.

The safeguard policy on international waterways contains the World Bank's policy on inter-state consultations in the context of transboundary waters. 'The Bank requires the beneficiary state … formally to notify other riparians of the proposed project and Project Details.' If the state informs the Bank that it does not wish to provide such information, 'normally the Bank itself does so'. If the borrower objects, 'the Bank discontinues processing of the project'.[122] In case another riparian state raises an objection, the Bank may appoint one or more independent experts to examine the issue, and, where the Bank decides to proceed with the project despite objection from another riparian state, the Bank shall inform that state of its decision.[123] The

---

[118] World Bank 2004 at 38.

[119] Paras. 14–18 of Operational Policy 4.01: Environmental Assessment, 1999. All World Bank safeguard policies are available at www.worldbank.org (under projects and operations, under safeguard policies), accessed 1 August 2006.

[120] *Ibid.*, para. 18.

[121] Para. 1 of Operational Policy 4.10: Indigenous Peoples, 2005. Also see Bank Procedure 4:10: Indigenous Peoples, para. 2, which further specifies the notion of 'free, prior and informed consultation'.

[122] Para 4 of Operational Policy 7.50; Projects on International Waterways, 2001. Also see Bank Procedure 7.50, Projects on International Waterways, 2001, para. 3, which specifies the type of information to be submitted to other riparian states.

[123] Para. 6 of Operational Policy 7.50. Also see Bank Procedure 7.50, paras. 8–12, which set out the procedure regarding the appointment of independent experts.

World Bank's policies on consultation among riparian states, I suggest, would figure positively as an implementation mechanism of the provisions of the Watercourses Convention on consultation between riparian states, even if that process itself is limited because it does not require the participation of individuals and groups. In case of the World Bank, the provisions on participation in the safeguard policies on environmental impact assessment and indigenous peoples, however, provide a basis for such participation, even if at the national level and not with individuals and groups located in another state.

In terms of procedural fairness, the World Bank's safeguard policies provide for consultation at the inter-state level and for participation at the level of individuals and groups within a state and thus address issues of procedural justice. Bank policies also emphasize the need to ensure access to water for the poor, thus addressing distributive justice; they, however, do not refer to the right to water, but in implementing the Dublin Principles subsume the right to water as an economic good.[124] The manner in which access to water is to be attained remains controversial, with the World Bank voicing strong support for market mechanisms and privatization, where, for example, the CESCR and UNDP voice caution. It must also be noted that the Bank's concern with water is broader than that of the right to water, which as noted above focuses on water for essential private uses, while the Bank focuses on water management in general.

One aspect of procedural fairness merits consideration in case of the World Bank. It relates to the legitimacy of the World Bank itself. How legitimate are the decision-making processes and procedures in the World Bank, with developed states holding a majority of the votes and developing and economy-in-transition states experiencing the effects of the Bank's policies? Given these voting arrangements, how legitimate is the policy initiative announced by the World Bank to develop lending options that would permit the provision of assistance to sub-national entities without central government involvement,[125] as is ongoing on an experimental basis through the Municipal Fund, established in 2003?[126] Such a step signifies a significant departure from the classical inter-state paradigm, but whether it meets standards of procedural fairness might be doubted.

A related point of concern is the fact that the World Bank has developed a large amount of rules and standards that it applies in its relationships with developing countries and economy-in-transition states. Thus, while the Watercourses Convention is not in force, something very similar to its consultation procedure is being applied in the relationships between riparian developing and economy-in-transition states through the safeguard policies of the Bank. Likewise, standards on what the

---

[124] See the text at and notes 62 and 102 above.

[125] See World Bank, Operational Guidance on Public and Private Sector Roles in Water Supply and Sanitation Services, note 105 above, at 16.

[126] For further information, see www.ifc.org/ifcext/municipalfund.nsf, accessed 8 August 2006.

World Bank considers to be efficient water management are applied to those same states. Moreover, rules and regulations on the participation of affected individuals and groups and indigenous peoples have been developed by the Bank and, if a state seeks support from the Bank, will have to be applied by that state. One might thus conclude that there is a body of law, or at least a set of rules and standards, at the global level that applies to how developing and economy-in-transition states manage their water resources. That body of law, however, came about through the decision-making processes of the World Bank and not through the processes and procedures associated with classical international law. In other words, this body of law marks another departure from the inter-state paradigm that is central to classical international law, including classical international water law. It also marks a departure from the discretionary role of states, at least for developing and economy-in-transition states. What is that discretionary role replaced with? I suggest that it is replaced with a more functional role for developing and economy-in-transition states and a discretionary role for the Bank, meaning that the Bank holds decision-making powers without being bound by, for example, duties to secure an adequate supply of water, while developing states have to operate within the rules and policies set by the Bank.

6 Conclusions: systemic change and fairness

This chapter illustrates that water-related rules and standards adopted at the international level have moved beyond the inter-state paradigm. I suggest that the relevant rules and standards merit qualification as 'global water law', even if some of the standards discussed at present apply only in a specific region – the Helsinki Convention and its protocols – or only to developing and economy-in-transition states – World Bank rules and standards – and some rules and standards do not qualify as international law under the classical definition – General Comment 15 and the rules and standards adopted by the World Bank. I, however, suggest that it is their nature, as generally applicable normative rules and standards, that justifies the denomination 'global water law'.

Global water law has moved beyond the inter-state paradigm in five distinct ways. First, global water law is concerned not only with how states manage transboundary waters, but also with how states manage their waters more generally. Secondly, global water law provides minimum standards on how states are to manage their water resources, both individually and jointly, and includes efforts to develop the right to water. Thirdly, global water law formulates obligations not only for states in respect of their territory or their inhabitants, but also for states more generally and for international institutions. Fourthly, the express objective of global water law is to further the interests of individuals and groups in society. Fifthly, international institutions, or at least the World Bank, operate as rather independent actors within global water law.

These characteristics entail that the transition from international to global water law involves systemic change. These changes can be characterized as follows. First, the functional, as opposed to the discretionary, role of states is emphasized. Secondly, the relevant rules and standards in question no longer, as in classical international law, have the characteristics of contractual undertakings between states; instead, they more closely resemble general legislative acts of a public law nature.[127] Thirdly, the interests of individuals and groups in society are the objectives of this body of law, which provides relevant actors with language in which to present their claims, *vis-à-vis* their state of residence, other states and international institutions, instead of such interests being mediated through the state of nationality or residence, as in classical international law.[128] Fourthly, some international institutions, such as the World Bank, apply their own rules and standards to states, or at least to developing and economy-in-transition states, instead of functioning as platforms through which states coordinate shared interests.

Global water law thus encompasses a diverse number of interrelationships, including inter-state relations, as well as relationships between individuals and groups and states, between individuals and groups and international institutions, and between international institutions and states. It is thus a multifaceted body of law in which fairness can only be assessed through a multifaceted approach, taking into account the various interrelations involved.

Besides the obvious lack of distributive justice in global water law, as set out in the introduction to this chapter, two other aspects related to fairness stand out. First, the role that private sector financing and privatization are to play in water management merits consideration. Secondly, the discretionary role of the World Bank in water management *vis-à-vis* developing and economy-in-transition states requires attention.

As to the role of private financing and privatization, most institutions involved agree that there can and should be a role for private sector involvement in water management but that such involvement should be encompassed in proper public sector policies and that the private sector should be subject to the rule of law. Moreover, as UNDP asserts, large-scale private sector infrastructure development in the water sector is not necessarily the only or even the best way to ensure access to water and sanitation for the poor.[129] Furthermore, the World Bank has also voiced criticism of its own past policies regarding lending for large infrastructural water-related projects.[130] These considerations suggest that the scale of water management projects, including private sector involvement, have to be commensurate with what the public sector is able to control. The first responsible public sector is of course the national public sector. However, the international public sector, both international institutions and other states, also may have a role to play in this respect, in ensuring both that projects

---

[127] Hey 2004.
[128] See Permanent Court of International Justice, *Mavommatis Palestine Concessions (Greece* v. *Great Britain)*, PCIJ, Series A, No. 2, 30 August 1924, at 12.
[129] UNDP 2006.   [130] See notes 114 and 115 above.

are commensurate with what the national public sector can control and that private actors meet their responsibilities. In the latter case, rules and standards that address the responsibility of the private sector in water management could be developed. This would be a step forward, especially if home states and international institutions, in addition to host states, would cooperate in enforcing such rules and standards. Procedural fairness would of course require that such rules and standards be decided on with the participation of all involved, including host states. Private sector involvement, however, also should be critically assessed with a view to the consequences that the commodification of water may have in terms of international trade law. As Edith Brown Weiss suggests, it is time that the World Trade Organization concentrate on developing an understanding that would mitigate any possible negative effects.[131]

The discretionary role of the World Bank *vis-à-vis* developing and economy-in-transition states is problematic, in terms of fairness. The World Bank in these cases exercises what may be referred to as public power, albeit of an international nature. However, the international level of decision-making lacks the checks and balances and accountability mechanisms generally associated with the exercise of public powers at the national level, at least in democratic societies governed by the rule of law. While the World Bank Inspection Panel offers an accountability mechanism within the Bank, individuals and groups in society may base their complaints only on the safeguard policies. The panel thus is not a body where complaints can be submitted regarding, for example, violations of human rights, such as the right to water. In terms of procedural fairness, larger formal involvement in World Bank decision-making procedures of developing and economy-in-transition states is what seems to be necessary as well as the expansion of the accountability mechanism available at the Bank. In the context of the latter, consideration might be given both to an expansion of the rules and standards on which individuals and groups may base their complaints before the Inspection Panel as well as to the expansion of accountability mechanisms for private sector actors engaged in World Bank projects. In order to enhance distributive justice, the World Bank should consider the adoption of a safeguard policy on the right to water.

This chapter illustrates that global water law is not necessarily law that is fair, neither in terms of distributive justice nor in terms of procedural fairness. Global water law, as Martti Koskenniemi points out with respect to international law in general, [132] serves a variety of functions. It offers a means for dominant actors to further their interests and a platform on which weaker actors can present their claims, it is 'the shared surface' on which adversaries can engage in debate without engaging in '"outlawry" – of the other', and it 'exists as the promise of justice'. While much needs to be improved, I suggest that global water law, more than classical international water law, offers the weak a voice and exists as the promise of justice. The formulation of the right to water and the

---

[131] See note 91 above.
[132] Koskenniemi, 2006 at 77–8 (all quotations in this paragraph are taken from these pages).

focus on providing access to drinking water and sanitation are particularly important in this respect. As Koskenniemi points out, the surface provided by international law is a 'fragile surface'. I suggest that this is also true for global water law. Moreover, if the promise of justice is to be strengthened and global water law is to become fairer, I suggest that it is this surface that needs to be strengthened. In other words, procedural fairness needs to be enhanced in global water law by introducing a degree of formalism, associated with the rule of law, in decision-making procedures, both to ensure that the outcomes are fair in terms of distributive justice at the level of both states and individuals, but also to enhance, what Lon Fuller found distinguishes law from other normative systems, good process.[133]

Bibliography

Brunnée, J., and Toope, S., 2000. 'International Law and Constructivism: Elements of an Interactional Theory of International Law'. 39 *Columbia Journal of Transnational Law* 19.

Cosgrove, W. G., and Rijsberman, F. R., 2000. *World Water Vision: Making Water Everybody's Business*. London: World Water Council, Earthscan Publications.

Cossy, M., 2005. 'Water Services and the WTO', in E. Brown Weiss, L. Boisson de Chazournes and N. Bernasconi-Osterwalder (eds.), *Fresh Water and International Economic Law*. Oxford: Oxford University Press.

Ebbesson, J., 2007. 'Public Participation', in D. Bodansky, J. Brunnée and E. Hey (eds.), *Oxford Handbook of International Environmental Law*. Oxford: Oxford University Press.

Franck, T. M., 1995. *Fairness in International Law and Institutions*. Oxford: Oxford University Press.

Fuller, L., 1969. *The Morality of Law*. Revised edn, New Haven and London: Yale University Press.

Herrero de la Fuente, A. A., 2005. 'El derecho al agua en el orden internacional', in L. Caflisch, R. Bermejo García, J. Díez-Hochleitner and C. Gutiérrez Espada (eds.), *El Derecho Internacional: Normas, Hechos y Valores*. Madrid: Servicio Publicaciones Facultad Derecho, Universidad Complutense Madrid.

Hey, E., 2004. 'International *Public* Law'. 6 *International Law FORUM du droit international* 149.

Koskenniemi, M., 2006. 'What Is International Law For?', in M. Evans (ed.), *International Law*. 2nd edn, Oxford: Oxford University Press.

Langford, M., Khalfan, A., Fairstein, C., and Jones, H., 2004. *Legal Resources for the Right to Water: International and National Standards*. Geneva: Centre on Housing Rights and Evictions.

McCaffrey, S. C., 2001. *The Law of International Watercourses*. Oxford: Oxford University Press.

2005. 'The Human Right to Water', in E. Brown Weiss, L. Boisson de Chazournes and N. Bernasconi-Osterwalder (eds.), *Fresh Water and International Economic Law*. Oxford: Oxford University Press.

Ratliff, D. P., 2001. 'The PCA Optional Rules for Arbitration of Disputes Relating to Natural Resources and/or the Environment'. 14 *Leiden Journal of International Law* 887.

Riedel, E., 2006. 'The Human Right to Water and General Comment No. 15 of the Committee on Economic, Social and Cultural Rights', in E. Riedel and P. Rothen (eds.), *The Right to Water*. Berlin: BWV Berliner Wissenschafts-Verlag and the Ministry of Foreign Affairs.

---

[133] See note 12 above.

Tanzi, A., and Arcari, M., 2001. *The United Nations Convention on the Law of International Water-courses: A Framework for Sharing*, International and National Water Law and Policy Series 5, London, The Hague and Boston: Kluwer Law International.

UNDP, 2006. *Human Development Report 2006, Beyond Scarcity: Power, Poverty and the Global Water Crises.* Basingstoke and New York: Palgrave Macmillan (also available at www.undp.or.in, accessed 17 November 2006).

Weiss, E. B., 2005. 'Water Transfers and International Trade Law', in E. Brown Weiss, L. Boisson de Chazournes and N. Bernasconi-Osterwalder (eds.). *Fresh Water and International Economic Law.* Oxford: Oxford University Press.

WHO, 2003. *The Right to Water.* Geneva: World Health Organization (also available at www.who.int/water_sanitation_health/righttowater/en, accessed 26 July 2006).

World Bank, 2004. *Water Resources Sector Strategy.* Washington, DC: World Bank.

World Commission on Dams, 2000. *Dams and Development, A New Framework for Decision-Making: Report of the World Commission on Dams.* London: Earthscan (also available at www.dams.org, accessed 8 August 2006).

19

Environmental justice in the use, knowledge and exploitation of genetic resources

PHILIPPE CULLET

1 Introduction

Access to and use of genetic resources have become increasingly contentious at the national and international levels over the past couple of decades. The importance of genetic resources in law and policy debates in recent years has largely been linked to their new-found economic importance in the context of the development of agricultural and pharmaceutical biotechnology. As a result, questions concerning transfers of and trade in genetic resources as well as questions concerning the protection of knowledge related to genetic resources have been given a lot of attention by policy-makers.

This has resulted in a flurry of new rules and regulations fostering the use of genetic resources, for instance, as a raw material for biotechnology products. In particular, the use of genetic resources in transgenic products has been encouraged by the progressive introduction in most countries of patents on life forms in the context of the implementation of the Agreement on Trade-Related Aspects of Intellectual Property Rights (TRIPS).[1]

While legal incentives for the use of genetic resources in industrial applications have rapidly developed over the past couple of decades, much less has been done with regard to the protection of the rights and interests of the holders of genetic resources and associated knowledge concerning their useful characteristics. Nevertheless, a number of initiatives have been taken in different contexts. The 1992 Convention on Biological Diversity ('Biodiversity Convention') has been one of the focal points for addressing some of the concerns related to access to and use of genetic resources.[2] Rules and principles, such as prior informed consent concerning transboundary movement of genetic resources, have been introduced. Further, in the context of Article 8(j) of the Convention, concerns of indigenous peoples with regard to genetic resources have been debated, such as the *sui generis* protection of individuals' and groups' knowledge

---

[1] Agreement on Trade-Related Aspects of Intellectual Property Rights, Marrakech, 15 April 1994, 33 *International Legal Materials* (ILM) (1994) 197 (hereafter TRIPS Agreement).
[2] Convention on Biological Diversity, Rio de Janeiro, 5 June 1992, 31 ILM (1992) 818.

related to genetic resources.[3] Finally, the Convention has been one of the most active frameworks where the question of benefit sharing has been debated leading to the decision to prepare the first binding legal instrument on access and benefit sharing by 2010.[4]

The development of rules concerning access to genetic resources, the sharing of associated benefits and the asymmetrical protection of knowledge all raise questions concerning the equity of existing legal frameworks. Two main issues arise in this context. First, the legal protection of knowledge as well as compensation mechanisms such as benefit sharing raise distributive justice concerns.[5] Indeed, one of the main questions that arise concerns the uneven benefits that different contributors to knowledge creation receive in law. This raises the need to develop new conceptual bases for knowledge protection frameworks, something which can, for instance, be achieved through the development of *sui generis* protection of traditional knowledge.[6] Secondly, existing and proposed knowledge protection frameworks have important international law dimensions either because they are adopted at the international level, as in the case of the TRIPS Agreement, or because they concern transboundary transactions. In the context of international law agreements, where different countries are in different situations with regard to their capacity to benefit from the legal framework in place, the concept of differential treatment needs to inform the development of these agreements.[7] In other words, international legal frameworks in this field need to incorporate provisions that take into account that full reciprocity will not lead to results that are substantively equal and that specifically benefit developing country member states.

2 Access and benefit sharing

The question of access and benefit sharing refers to two distinct questions. The former refers to the conditions under which genetic resources and related knowledge can be obtained. The latter refers to a form of compensation meant to reward holders of genetic resources and related knowledge for their contribution to the development of products which are eventually commercialised by other actors, often in another country. In theory, the regulation of access and the introduction of a compensation system called benefit sharing are independent of each other. They are considered in the same section here because they have been discussed as a single subject in international policy-making circles for at least a decade.

---

[3] See e.g. Section E, Decision VIII/5. Article 8(j) and Related Provisions, in Report of the Eighth Meeting of the Conference of the Parties to the Convention on Biological Diversity, UN Doc. UNEP/CBD/COP/8/31 (2006).

[4] Decision VII/19 D, Access and Benefit-Sharing as Related to Genetic Resources (Article 15), in Report of the Conference of the Parties to the Convention on Biological Diversity, Seventh Meeting, UN Doc. UNEP/CBD/COP/7/21 (2004).

[5] Aristotle 1991.   [6] See section 3.   [7] See generally Cullet 2003.

2.1 Access to genetic resources and associated knowledge

The issue of access to genetic resources as well as related knowledge concerns the conditions under which individual and collective holders of such resources or knowledge can control their transfer outside of their local environment. From an international law perspective, access refers to the conditions that states can put on the use of genetic resources and related knowledge found under their jurisdiction.

The introduction of access regimes is related to the increasing dissatisfaction in the 1980s with the open access system that prevailed at the time. On the one hand, countries seeking to develop agro-biotechnology products had started to push for the introduction and strengthening of patents on life forms at the international level.[8] On the other hand, countries hosting most biodiversity, a large number of which are from the South, determined that the only immediate response they could give to the proposed commodification of knowledge was to propose restrictions on access to genetic resources found under their jurisdiction.

The Biodiversity Convention formalised what is in effect a new conception of equity in international law. The open access system that prevailed in the context of agricultural research was often *de facto* applicable for wild biodiversity, in view of the lack of specific national or international regulation. However, this system was replaced by a system where each developing country hosting genetic resources is given the right to control access by foreigners to its resources. This constituted a significant change which has generally been interpreted as being of benefit to developing countries in general. The reason is that the introduction of sovereign rights over biological resources gives countries of origin more control over the use that is made of resources found within their jurisdiction.

Even though the principle of sovereign rights has been accepted by all states parties to the Biodiversity Convention, this does not provide an unconditional right for countries of origin to restrict access to their resources. In fact, countries of origin have a duty to facilitate access to their resources because biodiversity is legally recognised as a common concern of humankind.[9] More specifically, countries of origin have to ensure that there is a regulatory framework allowing users of genetic resources to access them. The specific operative legal principle for access is that of prior informed consent which implies that holders of genetic resources should give their approval to transboundary movements.[10]

The legal regime that prevails today at the international level gives countries of origin a fair measure of control over transboundary movements of genetic resources. This must be seen in the context of the search for increased commodification of research outputs, which includes the introduction of patents for transgenic seeds or plant breeders' rights for plant varieties that has until now benefited mostly

---

[8] Cf. Hamilton 2001 at 88.   [9] Biodiversity Convention, note 2 above, Art. 15 and preamble.
[10] On prior informed consent, see *ibid.*, Art. 15(5).

countries, individuals and companies in the North. The introduction of an access regime constitutes one way to rebalance the legal framework in favour of countries of origin.

The equity dimension of the existing access regime is limited by at least two factors. First, the existing international law regime is unclear concerning access to knowledge. Thus, there are clear stipulations that the access regime applies to physical resources such as seeds, but there is much less clarity with regard to the knowledge embodied in seeds. In fact, the Bonn Guidelines on Access to Genetic Resources and Fair and Equitable Sharing of the Benefits Arising out of their Utilization specifically recognise that there is no congruence between access to genetic resources and access to related traditional knowledge which should be sought separately.[11] This is problematic because there are many cases where specific genetic resources are accessed because they are known to have specific characteristics or properties. These properties are what make the physical resource valuable from the point of view of the person accessing it. Further, in a situation where control over the final product, which may be derived from the genetic resource accessed, is mostly through intellectual property rights such as patents, it is important to ensure that not only the physical resource but also related knowledge is formally acknowledged in the access transaction. The existing draft of the proposed international legal regime seems to acknowledge this problem.[12]

Secondly, while the existing access regime gives countries of origin relatively strong rights to control transboundary movements, it does little for individuals and groups that are the actual holders of genetic resources and related knowledge. Some countries, like India, have interpreted the Biodiversity Convention mandate as the grant of a permission to governments to assert control over transboundary movements in genetic resources and related knowledge at the expense of individuals and groups that actually developed them.[13] This tends to further weaken the position of farmers and other traditional knowledge holders that are denied rights of full control over their knowledge and physical resources.

2.2 Benefit sharing

Benefit sharing is a relatively new notion which has been developed as a consequence of the rapidly changing paradigm concerning claims over genetic resources, traditional

---

[11] Section 31, Bonn Guidelines on Access to Genetic Resources and Fair and Equitable Sharing of the Benefits Arising out of their Utilization, in Report of the Sixth Meeting of the Conference of the Parties to the Convention on Biological Diversity, UN Doc. UNEP/CBD/COP/6/20 (2002).

[12] The situation remains unclear because of the amount of bracketed text in the current draft. See Decision IX/12, Access and Benefit-sharing, in Report of the Eighth Meeting of the Parties to the Convention on Biological Diversity, Bonn, 19–30 May 2008, DOC. UNEP/CBD/COP/9/29.

[13] The access process involves no more than the national and state authorities consulting local biodiversity management committees while taking decisions on access requests. Section 41(2), India, Biological Diversity Act, 2002, No. 18 of 2003, *Gazette of India Extraordinary* Part II, Section I (5 February 2003) (hereafter Biological Diversity Act – India).

knowledge and the strengthening of intellectual property rights to accommodate life patents. Benefit sharing is the response given to the fact that holders of genetic resources and traditional knowledge are not granted rights to control the use of their resources and knowledge but only rights to put conditions on access by outsiders. In other words, benefit sharing has evolved as an indirect recognition that traditional knowledge holders can, for instance, not directly benefit from the strengthening of the intellectual property rights system even where their knowledge constitutes the basis for a product or process which can be protected under existing intellectual property rights.

Benefit sharing is generally offered to actors who can at best negotiate the conditions under which their resources or knowledge are accessed. The situation of traditional knowledge holders under existing intellectual property rights systems needs to be compared with the situation of patent holders. The latter are in a position to stop others from using their inventions, can decide whether to license the invention to another individual or not and can independently commercialise the product without facing competition in the market place for the duration of the rights granted. In comparison, traditional knowledge holders do not have the same rights. In cases where the prior informed consent of traditional knowledge holders for accessing genetic resources or traditional knowledge is a legal requirement,[14] the latter can be said to have a right to control access to their knowledge, especially if this also involves the right to deny or withdraw access.[15] However, even in cases where prior informed consent is required from the holders themselves, the respective legal frameworks do not provide for any form of control after access has been granted. Benefit sharing is the compensation mechanism which has been introduced as an additional indirect control mechanism that prolongs the access regime.

Benefit sharing can be understood from two different perspectives. First, before the coming into force of the Biodiversity Convention, there was no international legal regime directly regulating transfers of genetic resources and traditional knowledge. As a result, bioprospecting took place in a legal vacuum. At best, parties involved would have signed a bilateral contract, as was the case in the Merck–INBio agreement which happened shortly before the entry into force of the Biodiversity Convention.[16] At worst, as must have been the case in many situations before the 1990s, there was no contract at all. From this point of view, the institutionalisation of benefit sharing is an improvement which formalises the need to compensate holders of genetic resources and traditional knowledge for their contribution to the evolution of plant varieties for instance.

---

[14] See e.g. Article 6, Peru, Law Introducing a Protection Regime for the Collective Knowledge of Indigenous Peoples Derived from Biological Resources, Law No. 27811, *Official Journal*, 10 August 2002 (hereafter Collective Knowledge Law – Peru).

[15] See e.g. Section 7, Ethiopia: Proclamation 482/2006 to Provide for Access to Genetic Resources and Community Knowledge and Community Right, 2006.

[16] Sittenfeld and Gámez 1993 at 69.

Secondly, benefit sharing can be seen as a response to the introduction and strength-ening of life patents and the general move towards sovereign and private appropriation of physical resources and knowledge. Previously, at least in countries where patents on life forms and patents on products related to food were prohibited, there was no appropriation by either traditional knowledge holders or other actors since they could not get patents on any products related to food, such as seeds. Today and increasingly so in the future, patent applicants can assert rights over a range of products and processes which were previously unpatentable. This has not been accompanied by a similar change concerning traditional knowledge holders. In this sense, benefit shar-ing can be criticised as institutionalising the absence of property rights for traditional knowledge holders.

Benefit sharing is on the whole a tool which has been found acceptable to developed and developing countries, though for partly different reasons. For countries that have strong genetic engineering industries, benefit sharing is more restrictive than the pre-Biodiversity Convention system which would have allowed freedom to choose the mode of access and compensation. However, it was a necessary part of the bargain that led developing countries to accept the facilitated access provisions now in place. For countries of origin, benefit sharing has proved to be until now an avenue through which governments can acquire more authority towards other countries and towards holders of genetic resources and traditional knowledge. For countries of origin, benefit sharing has the advantage of providing a role for the state in managing genetic resources and the compensation that comes in return.

The proposal to share benefits has gained wide acceptance in principle. Nevertheless, there is little consensus regarding the specific benefits that should be offered in individual cases. As a result, existing frameworks do no more than list possible forms of benefits without ordering them hierarchically. The most usual form of benefits offered is a form of financial compensation. This can take the form of access fees, royalty payment, licence fees or contributions to be paid to special financial mechanisms set up for this purpose. Other proposed benefits include participation in the development of products or transfer of technologies such as novel technologies which may be developed on the basis of the resources or knowledge accessed. Other benefits which can also be shared include the training of local people, access to scientific information and institutional relationships to allow local or national institutions in the country of origin to foster their own research.

One of the ongoing problems is the difficulty to conceive of benefit sharing exclu-sively at the national level. This is because countries of origin are not in a position to impose extraterritorial measures on users. Therefore, an effective benefit sharing system for transboundary transactions must either involve an international law frame-work or be coordinated between all countries. Countries of origin can take measures at the point of access of the resources but it is often difficult to judge at the outset what exact use will be made of the resources and what benefits will be eventually derived. Further, even when an estimate is made, if respect for the benefit sharing arrangement is not made a condition of patentability or commercialisation of derived products, it becomes much more difficult to enforce benefit sharing arrangements.

On the whole, benefit sharing can be seen as fostering a weak form of distributive justice in favour of provider countries. In certain cases, according to the legal frameworks adopted by specific countries or regions, benefits will reach individuals or communities that are the providers of the genetic resources or knowledge, but often the benefits will be channelled into general funds that are administered by the state.[17] Further, at present benefit sharing is conceived mostly as a bilateral instrument between providers and users, and thus may contribute to asymmetrical negotiations between unequal 'partners'. Certain countries have taken into account the fact that contracts between a large university or company and a single farmer or a group of local farmers may lead to unsatisfactory results for the farmers. This is why the South African Biodiversity Act proposes, for instance, that negotiations should involve not only the holders themselves but also the government.[18]

Benefit sharing as a mechanism for compensation can be improved, for instance, through the adoption of a binding international regime. There is, in fact, hope that such a regime will be adopted by 2010 in the context of the Biodiversity Convention and that countries will be willing to widely accept it.[19] However, even if an international legal regime is eventually adopted and implemented, there remain problems which are intrinsically linked to the concept of benefit sharing. Indeed, benefit sharing fails to address the imbalance built into the existing legal framework for the protection of knowledge. On the one hand, different options exist to appropriate the results of research undertaken in formal laboratories through intellectual property rights. On the other hand, the protection through rights frameworks for holders of traditional knowledge is at best still in its infancy. In other words, while benefit sharing is a form of compensation for the use of resources and knowledge, it does not address the much more important issue of the protection of traditional knowledge through rights frameworks.

3 *Sui generis* protection

Besides the forms of compensation that benefit sharing can offer, there have been efforts for a number of years to pursue more elaborate options to protect the interests of providers of genetic resources and traditional knowledge holders. One such option is the introduction of a special or *sui generis* regime for the protection of traditional knowledge. This has the advantage of seeking to conceptually put on a par the rights

---

[17] See e.g. Section 27, National Biodiversity Fund, Biological Diversity Act – India, note 13 above; and Section 45, National Gene Fund, India, Protection of Plant Varieties and Farmers' Rights Act, 2001, No. 53 of 2001, *Gazette of India Extraordinary* Part II, Section 1 (30 October 2001) (hereafter Plant Variety Act – India).

[18] Section 82, South Africa, National Environmental Management: Biodiversity Act 2004.

[19] For the existing draft of the regime, see Draft International Regime, note 12 above.

granted to individuals and companies that benefit from the existing intellectual property rights regime and other holders of knowledge, such as farmers developing their
own plant varieties or healers developing plant-based medicines.

   Sui generis intellectual property protection has been the object of significant attention since the coming into force of the TRIPS Agreement.[20] This is linked to a negotiating compromise concerning plant variety protection whereby the TRIPS Agreement
imposes the introduction of plant variety protection in all member states, but gives
member states the possibility to choose the form of protection they want to introduce. Thus, Article 27(3)(b) specifically requires all member states to 'provide for the
protection of plant varieties either by patents or by an effective *sui generis* system or
by any combination thereof'.[21] The introduction of the *sui generis* concept reflects
two broad elements. First, a number of countries in the North and the South rejected
the compulsory introduction of plant variety patents. Secondly, negotiators did not
manage to agree on one specific alternative to patents. As a result, TRIPS gives member
states a margin of appreciation in determining how to implement their obligation to
introduce plant variety protection.

   The *sui generis* option constitutes a form of flexibility which is of some benefit
to European countries that refused to introduce patents to protect plant varieties to
maintain their existing system of plant breeders' rights formalised under the International Convention for the Protection of New Varieties of Plants (UPOV).[22] The UPOV
Convention is a *sui generis* regime under the terms of Article 27(3)(b) of the TRIPS
Agreement, but it is only one among many possible alternatives to patents on plant
varieties that can be adopted by states. In fact, the lack of specificity of this clause
means that the main theoretical beneficiaries of the existing flexibility are developing
countries that wanted to introduce neither plant variety patents nor plant breeders'
rights. From this perspective, the *sui generis* option is a form of differential treatment
in favour of developing countries that are given the liberty to decide which system of
protection is best suited to their needs.

   Over the past decade, a number of countries have attempted to take advantage of the
flexibility offered by Article 27(3)(b). In particular, a number of countries determined
that the introduction of plant variety protection laws provided an opportunity to
formalise the notion of farmers' rights. This is, for instance, reflected in the African
Model Legislation for the Protection of Rights of Local Communities, Farmers, and
Breeders and for the Regulation of Access to Biological Resources.[23]

---

[20] Cullet 2005 at Chapter 8.   [21] TRIPS Agreement, note 1 above.
[22] International Convention for the Protection of New Varieties of Plants, Geneva, 19 March 1991
   (Geneva: UPOV Doc. 221(E), 1996), also available at www.upov.int/en/publications/conventions/1991/
   pdf/act1991.pdf.
[23] African Model Legislation for the Protection of Rights of Local Communities, Farmers, Breeders and for
   the Regulation of Access to Biological Resources, endorsed by the Organization of African Unity in 2000,
   available at www.grain.org/brl_files/oau-model-law-en.pdf.

Debates around *sui generis* plant variety protection have largely been triggered by the necessity to introduce 'a' form of plant variety protection under the TRIPS Agreement. From an intellectual property protection point of view, one of the main contributions of more than a decade of thinking about plant variety protection has been the more prominent role given to farmers' rights. Nevertheless, *sui generis* plant variety protection need not be conceived only as an intellectual property protection mechanism. In fact, the reason why there was no consensus in the TRIPS Agreement negotiations over the introduction of patents over plant varieties is that agriculture has always been seen as a field that must be addressed separately. This is due to the fact that agriculture directly contributes to meeting humankind's food needs, to the links between agricultural production and environmental conservation and to the fact that agriculture remains the primary source of employment and livelihood in most of the South. As a result, plant variety protection provides an apt entry point not only to introduce farmers' rights but also to associate intellectual property protection with food security, agro-biodiversity conservation and sustainable use of resources as well as the realisation of the human right to food.

The introduction of a legal regime where farmers are given substantially the same rights as commercial breeders, as is the case under the Indian plant variety and farmers' rights legislation, constitutes a significant advance over a system of compensation like benefit sharing.[24] Such a *sui generis* system constitutes an acknowledgment that the contribution that farmers have made and are making to agriculture, food security and livelihoods is as important as that made by commercial actors. From a legal point of view, it also constitutes an attempt to put in perspective two different bodies of knowledge that have never been put on the same level. On the one hand, there is the knowledge that qualifies for protection under intellectual property rights such as patents and plant breeders' rights. On the other hand, there is every other knowledge which does not qualify for protection under existing intellectual property rights laws and is therefore deemed to be part of the public domain and freely available for all to use. This dichotomy is the root cause of existing imbalances that deprive farmers and other traditional knowledge holders of the legal means to control their own knowledge. One of the consequences of the absence of positive protection for traditional knowledge has, for instance, been a series of high-profile cases of knowledge appropriation through patents that was in fact public domain knowledge in other countries.[25] These cases of biopiracy have contributed to raising awareness about the need for benefit sharing, but the real underlying problem is the lack of knowledge protection, something that *sui generis* systems can contribute to remedying.

While the debate over *sui generis* intellectual property protection focused for several years mostly on plant variety protection, because of the specific need to comply with the TRIPS Agreement provisions, the issue is in fact much broader. It is not only plant variety-related knowledge which needs to be protected but all knowledge which is

---

[24] Plant Variety Act – India, note 17 above.   [25] On biopiracy, see Schuler 2004 at 159.

generally qualified as traditional knowledge. In the context of the TRIPS Agreement, traditional knowledge is knowledge which does not qualify for intellectual property rights protection. This includes, for instance, knowledge related to the medicinal properties of genetic resources and various aspects of the cultures of communities such as indigenous peoples.[26]

At present, a few countries such as Peru and the Philippines have made attempts to introduce laws for the *sui generis* protection of traditional knowledge.[27] These are noteworthy efforts, since they indicate that there is scope to go beyond mainstream intellectual property rights frameworks that are fundamentally incapable of providing an answer to the interests and rights of farmer-innovators, local healers and individual or collective traditional knowledge holders in general.

Despite the efforts of selected countries to provide alternatives to the existing intellectual property rights system and to strengthen the position of traditional knowledge holders at the national level, such efforts can only be effective if they are supplemented by an international law level legal instrument. Indeed, many of the problems that have surfaced over the past fifteen years concern transfers of genetic resources and knowledge from the South to the North. As a result, while existing *sui generis* regimes constitute useful first steps in the development of alternative legal regimes, these must be complemented by regional and preferably international law level regimes that constitute an effective way to ensure greater fairness in knowledge-related protection regimes.

4 Equity for genetic resources and traditional knowledge

The existing legal regime for the protection of knowledge is largely imbalanced because it only rewards one particular type of contributor to knowledge, such as the person recognised as the inventor under patent law, and gives this person or entity exclusive or monopolistic control over the use of the knowledge. This is based on a conception of knowledge creation which privileges the person or entity that comes at the end of the production process and makes the final improvements to a product or process. It has been increasingly questioned whether this model is appropriate in the context in which it was developed, namely, industrial and post-industrial knowledge creation in the North, for instance, where 'overpatentability' has the potential to stifle innovation.[28] In any case, this model is an inappropriate tool to take into account the different

---

[26] For a definition put together in the context of WIPO, see e.g. WIPO, Composite Study on the Protection of Traditional Knowledge, IGC, Fifth Session, Doc. WIPO/GRTKF/IC/5/8 (2003), para. 61.

[27] Collective Knowledge Law – Peru, note 14 above; and The Philippines, An Act to Recognize, Protect and Promote the Rights of Indigenous Cultural Communities/Indigenous Peoples, Creating a National Commission on Indigenous Peoples, Establishing Implementing Mechanisms, Appropriating Funds Therefor, and for Other Purposes, 28 July 1997, Doc. S. No. 1728/H. No. 9125.

[28] Barton and Berger 2001, available at www.issues.org/17.4/barton.htm.

contributions to the development of a specific product like a transgenic seed that may have been made by the farmer developing the original farm-level variety, a national research institute working on the same variety and the scientists working for the multinational company that ends up patenting the transgenic seed derived from the farm-level variety. This is a problem which can surface at the national level as well as at the international level. In fact, it needs to be addressed concurrently at both levels because many governments of the South are not particularly keen to strengthen the rights of traditional knowledge holders. They would rather provide incentives for the commercial use of knowledge which seems to be a more attractive option in the short term. In other words, because of the specificities of intellectual property law which remains largely territorial in its practical application but is largely dominated by the minimum standards of the TRIPS Agreement, the justice implications of intellectual property law need to be addressed simultaneously at the national and international levels.

In view of the shortcomings of the existing legal regime, there is a need to consider alternative proposals. These must be conceived in such a way that they contribute to achieving differential treatment at the international level and distributive justice at the national level. In the context of an intricate subject that covers both the use of the physical resources and related knowledge, different suggestions can be put forward. This section does not seek to provide an overview of all possible proposals fostering substantive equality, but limits itself to examining three different options which may be considered separately or jointly.

4.1 Further commodification

One of the changes that have taken place over the past couple of decades is the increasing place given to the appropriation of physical resources and knowledge by private actors and by the state. This is reflected in the fast expanding scope of intellectual property rights protection that received a tremendous boost with the adoption of the TRIPS Agreement. This imposed, on all developing countries members of the WTO, the introduction of minimum standards of intellectual protection that were much higher than most national laws in the 1990s. Appropriation by the state is best reflected in attempts to progressively restrict the scope of the principle of the common heritage of humankind and the assertion of sovereign rights over biological and genetic resources.

Changes that have taken place over the past couple of decades make today's world a place where much more can be privately appropriated and owned than twenty years ago. Focusing on agriculture, the past couple of decades have seen the introduction of life patents in most developing countries. This has paved the way for the direct or indirect patentability of transgenic seeds as well as the introduction of plant breeders' rights for non-transgenic seeds in many countries. These are fundamental changes for most developing countries where no intellectual property rights in agriculture existed before the adoption of the TRIPS Agreement.[29] The overall results of these changes is that the legal landscape has been completely modified. Today, commercial breeders and agro-biotechnology companies benefit from a number of options to protect their knowledge in most developing countries. These changes have not necessarily been accompanied by attempts to strengthen the rights of non-commercial holders of knowledge. As a result, in most countries farmers' knowledge is today legally part of the public domain that can be freely appropriated by anyone, while the knowledge protected by plant breeders' rights and patents is not freely available.

The inequity of a system which protects certain types of knowledge with exclusive or monopoly rights, while deeming all other knowledge to be part of the public domain that can be freely appropriated by anyone, has not gone unnoticed. The development of schemes of benefit sharing is in fact a response to this fundamental dichotomy between protectable and freely available knowledge. However, as noted above, benefit sharing has generally been conceived as a compensatory mechanism which does not address the underlying problem of knowledge protection.

The introduction of *sui generis* traditional knowledge protection, as attempted in certain countries, is a much more effective way to address this imbalance. However, while the conceptual framework for providing a more equal knowledge protection system is known, much more needs to be done to make it a reality. First, in the few countries that have attempted to introduce protection for farmer knowledge or indigenous people knowledge, the focus of the laws adopted is usually relatively specific. Thus, in India, it is only farmer knowledge which is protected and not traditional knowledge in general.[30] In Peru, it is only the collective knowledge of indigenous peoples which is protected.[31]

Secondly, it is insufficient to introduce national laws in a context where resources and knowledge are increasingly often the object of transboundary movements. While the Biodiversity Convention has introduced an international regime which binds all its member states, the same cannot be said with regard to the protection of knowledge. On the one hand, there is no uniformity in intellectual property rights standards of protection because countries can choose to go beyond the minimum requirements of the TRIPS Agreement. This implies that there is scope for asymmetrical knowledge appropriation in different countries. In other words, even if a developing country uses some of the restrictions on life patents allowed in the TRIPS Agreement, that same knowledge may still be patentable in the United States or another jurisdiction that does not have the same restrictions. On the other hand, the absence of an international treaty for the protection of farmer knowledge and traditional knowledge in general means that even traditional knowledge holders who can assert some rights

---

[29] For instance, most African countries, with the exception of a handful – Kenya, South Africa, Zimbabwe – had not even introduced plant breeders' rights before the adoption of the TRIPS Agreement.
[30] Plant Variety Act – India, note 17 above.   [31] Collective Knowledge Law – Peru, note 14 above.

at the national level would not be in a position to effectively enforce them in other countries.

Overall, a system of traditional knowledge protection constitutes one way to redress imbalances in the existing legal regime for knowledge protection. This is, however, only one option which builds on the ongoing worldwide trend seeking to give specific actors such as states, private companies and individuals control over an increasing array of resources and knowledge.

4.2 An open access system

Among the various alternatives that can be proposed to a system which suggests further commodification as a response to existing commodification, a system that reverts back to open flows of resources and knowledge is one option. The best example is the open access system for plant genetic resources that constituted the basis for the development of an effective international research network on plant genetic resources for food and agriculture. The reason why agriculture was given this special treatment up to the 1980s was based on the direct link between agriculture and food security, or in other words between agriculture and the eradication of hunger.

A system which privileges open access for plant genetic resources and for improved seeds is legally based on the principle of common heritage of humankind.[32] It recognises that there is a community of interests among all states to share their resources and knowledge to contribute to the development of plant varieties that can contribute to the eradication of hunger. The sharing of plant genetic resources is in nearly every country's interest since an overwhelming majority of countries are mostly dependent on germplasm from other countries for their main food crops.[33] Since there is a dichotomy between countries that are rich in agro-biodiversity and countries which have the resources to foster the development of new plant varieties, a consensus position that suits everyone has to provide not only for the free access to plant genetic resources but also to the improved varieties developed on the basis of existing varieties. This is in fact what was recognised in the International Undertaking of 1983.[34] The reason why this system promptly collapsed was that some developed countries had already invested at that time substantial sums in the development of agro-biotechnology. The refusal of these countries to accept a completely open system eventually led countries of origin to also reject an open system and assert sovereign rights over their genetic resources.

Today, the legal regime for plant genetic resources for food and agriculture embodied in the 2001 FAO International Treaty on Plant Genetic Resources for Food and Agriculture ('Plant Gene Treaty') reflects the various compromises that have been

---

[32] MacDonald 1995.   [33] Flores Palacios 1997.
[34] International Undertaking on Plant Genetic Resources, Resolution 8/83, Report of the Conference of FAO, 22nd Session, Rome, 5–23 November 1983, Doc. C83/REP.

reached over the past two decades. On the one hand, states' sovereignty over plant genetic resources is recognised.[35] Further, the legitimacy of intellectual property rights over products derived from plant genetic resources is also recognised.[36] On the other hand, in recognition of the need to share plant genetic resources and in recognition of the fact that hunger is still prevalent in many parts of the world, certain plant genetic resources collections have been maintained in the public domain.[37]

Existing compromises are unsatisfactory for most countries. First, developed countries would have wanted to keep all plant genetic resources freely available to ensure easier access for agricultural research centres or private companies. Secondly, developing countries would have wanted much stronger restrictions on intellectual property rights in agriculture to ensure easier access to products developed on the basis of plant genetic resources that originate in developing countries.[38] Thirdly, the Plant Gene Treaty provides limited additional mechanisms to recognise the contribution of farmer innovators. There is, for instance, a benefit sharing mechanism put in place. However, it provides that access to plant genetic resources is in itself to be seen as a major benefit. This leaves little place for farmers themselves to be compensated.[39] It also mentions farmers' rights, and much hope was pinned on the fact that negotiators would strengthen the clause adopted in the context of the revised International Undertaking in 1989.[40] However, the Plant Gene Treaty does not go further than largely restating the 1989 position and giving pointers to member states on ways in which they can develop farmers' rights regimes at the national level.[41]

On the whole, the Plant Gene Treaty fails to take a clear conceptual line. It advocates an open access position as traditionally advocated by the agricultural community but makes a number of significant compromises to ongoing commodification. An effectively open access system would therefore not look like the existing Plant Gene Treaty. Rather, it would seek to rebalance equities in a different way. An open access system would first be based on free flows of plant genetic resources as well as related knowledge. It would not differentiate between knowledge which is deemed 'traditional' or in the public domain and knowledge which can be protected by intellectual property rights. It would further not recognise barriers to transfers such as sovereign rights or intellectual property rights. As a result, there would be no place for any exclusive rights over knowledge.

Such a system is fundamentally opposed to the legal regime which is currently in place and which many countries want to further strengthen. There is therefore

---

[35] Article 10, International Treaty on Plant Genetic Resources for Food and Agriculture, Rome, 3 November 2001, available at ftp://ftp.fao.org/ag/cgrfa/it/ITPGRe.pdf (hereafter Plant Gene Treaty).
[36] Arts. 12(3)(f) and 13(2)(b)(iii).   [37] Art. 11.   [38] Cooper 2002.
[39] Plant Gene Treaty, note 35 above, Art. 13(1).
[40] Resolution 5/89, Farmers' Rights, Report of the Conference of FAO, 25th Session, Rome, 11–29 November 1989, Doc. C89/REP.
[41] Plant Gene Treaty, note 35 above, Art. 9.

little chance that it will be accepted in the near future at the international level. It is nevertheless necessary to consider it as an alternative, given that the present system seems unable to ensure differential treatment among states and distributive justice among the different actors involved in agriculture and health. A fully open access system may have faults and shortcomings that will need to be addressed. Nevertheless, while an open access system may not be 'the' panacea for all equity-related issues in the field of plant genetic resources, historical experience shows that it did more for hunger than what the current commodified system is achieving. Thus, while major food-security-related gains were achieved through the development of high-yielding varieties of rice and other food crops until the 1980s,[42] the agro-biotechnology industry is yet to develop products that are meaningful from a food security point of view.[43] While some useful genetically modified food crop will probably be developed in years to come, it is unwise to expect major hunger-related products because the type of incentives that drive the development of new plant varieties now are fundamentally different from what they were a couple of decades ago. Today, private companies do most of the research in new (genetically modified) plant varieties. The incentives that private companies have for the development of new plant varieties are the commercial benefits they can derive from them, largely through the protection offered by intellectual property rights. Given that intellectual property rights as conceived in the TRIPS Agreement make few concessions to food security and hunger,[44] it would be unwise to expect private companies to develop a significant number of new food crops directly targeted at people who suffer from hunger. This is, in fact, not something that the existing incentive system can be expected to produce even though some *ad hoc* measures, such as incentives for research focusing on orphan crops can be introduced within the existing intellectual property rights regime.

4.3 A broader conception of protection

One of the main shortcomings of the existing legal regime is to focus nearly entirely on the commercial benefits that can be derived from the use of genetic resources and the commercial aspects of knowledge related to genetic resources. This is the case in the context of intellectual property rights regimes whose main concern it is. In the context of the Biodiversity Convention and related instruments, broad statements that go beyond commercial aspects are repeatedly used, but the focus of access and benefit sharing negotiations has, for instance, been mostly on commercial and economic aspects. This is not surprising since governments are the main players

---

[42] Sharma and Poleman 1994.
[43] The product in focus is the so-called golden rice. See Dawe, Robertson and Unnevehr 2002; and the website, www.goldenrice.org. On the controversies surrounding it, see Sharma 2005.
[44] See e.g. TRIPS Agreement, note 1 above, Arts. 7 and 8.

in the debates on access and benefit sharing, while the actual holders of resources and traditional knowledge are at best given a limited role. There are a number of good reasons why governments from the South and the North are focusing mostly on the economic and commercial aspects of the use of genetic resources and related knowledge. In part, access and benefit sharing can be reduced to one additional trade opportunity. Considering the importance given to international trade in the recent past as a vector of economic development, access and benefit sharing can be seen from a narrow perspective as contributing to the development opportunities created by international trade.

Nevertheless, the focus on the commercial aspects of the use of genetic resources and related knowledge is inappropriate given the subject matter. First, holders of genetic resources and traditional knowledge may have a number of reasons to seek to control the use made of their resources and knowledge. The lure of financial benefits is in many cases an important element which fits within the existing access and benefit sharing regime. Other reasons are, however, also present. These include cultural and religious reasons which may, for instance, prohibit the transmission of knowledge outside of the local context or may prohibit the use of certain religious symbols in other contexts.[45]

More broadly, it cannot be assumed that all farmers, healers and other traditional knowledge holders want to control the use made of their resources and knowledge only because they hope to derive a commercial benefit. Further, it remains unclear how extensive overall commercial benefits may be. In fact, there are situations where people simply want to protect their resources and knowledge against its commercial exploitation by outsiders. Thus in the case of the biodiversity register of Pattuvam village in Kannur district (Kerala, India), the rationale for producing the register was partly to avoid biopiracy, partly to bring together all known knowledge and partly to allow exchange of information with other farming communities on a non-commercial basis.[46] In other words, the register was conceived as an instrument to rule out the commercial use of the resources and knowledge found within the village while not excluding the sharing of information and resources with other farmers or villages elsewhere.

Beyond the need to recognise the broad array of factors which may motivate people in seeking to control the use made of their knowledge and resources, it is necessary to consider the fact that access regimes, as they have been conceived until today, are insufficiently evolved. Indeed, at best, communities are given the right to refuse access to their resources and knowledge for cultural, spiritual, social, economic and other

---

[45] Concerning the use of symbols having an important role in aboriginal ceremonies on an Australian banknote, see *Terry Yumbulul* v. *Reserve Bank of Australia*, Federal Court of Australia Northern Territory District Registry, 25 July 1991, 21 IPR 481.

[46] Interview with Mohan Kumar, Pattuvam.

motives.[47] Yet, even in such a situation, the access regime remains a framework that gives comparatively limited rights to resource and knowledge holders.

Where the access regime is compared with existing intellectual property rights, the divide that separates the two becomes obvious. Nevertheless, this does not mean that a more evolved protection regime for genetic resources and traditional knowledge holders should be based on existing intellectual property rights regimes. In fact, they should preferably be conceived separately so that they can be much more broadly based. What is required is a novel way to consider the protection of genetic resources and knowledge. The main rationale for introducing a new type of protection is to acknowledge the fact that different subject matters require different approaches. Control over genetic resources and related knowledge may need to be partly privatised to ensure that the current holders of these resources and knowledge can control the use that is made of them. At the same time, the control regime that is introduced should recognise that such resources and knowledge are not always individually held and that a private property rights model may not be an appropriate model. Further, the control regime should be tailored to the specific uses made of genetic resources and acknowledge the direct link between genetic resources, the realisation of the rights to food and health and the livelihoods of hundreds of millions of people more generally. This broader framework constitutes one way to introduce more equity to the legal regime concerning genetic resources and related knowledge.

5 Conclusion

In the context of sustainable development law, it has been recognised that equity should be a primary consideration in the development of a just and effective legal regime. This is, for instance, reflected in the differential treatment which is granted to developing countries in various environmental treaties and in the development of the principle of common but differentiated responsibilities which provides an acknowledgment that the legal regime should take into account the different positions of different countries.[48]

As far as access to genetic resources is concerned, the legal regime which is embodied in the Biodiversity Convention seeks to balance the different interests of provider and user countries by recognising the sovereign rights of countries of origin but imposing on them the introduction of a regime of facilitated access. No such attempt has yet been made at the international level with regard to knowledge related to genetic resources. At present, the legal regime is skewed in favour of certain types of knowledge and in favour of the commercial use of this knowledge. The existing intellectual property rights regime makes little, if any, space for the protection of any knowledge apart from the knowledge which can be protected through patents or plant breeders' rights.

---

[47] Art. 66, Costa Rica, Biodiversity Law, 1998.
[48] See Shelton, Brunnée, and Mickelson in, respectively, Chapters 3, 16 and 15 of this volume.

Efforts to redress imbalances in knowledge protection have already been made. These include the development of benefit sharing. This is limited by the fact that it is not directly linked to the grant of patents and plant breeders' rights at the international level.[49] The other option is the development of *sui generis* knowledge protection regimes. This constitutes a first step towards rebalancing the legal regime but can only be effective if an international legal framework to this effect is adopted.

While the introduction of *sui generis* farmer and traditional knowledge protection regimes provides an avenue to ensure more equitable outcomes in knowledge protection legal regimes, this must be looked at from a broader perspective. *Sui generis* protection is a response to the increasing commodification of knowledge at the international level and is conditioned by the development of an intellectual property rights framework. There exist alternatives, like the development of an open access framework which could provide similarly or more equitable outcomes.

Bibliography

Aristotle, 1991. *The Nicomachean Ethics* 112, trans. D. Ross, revised by J. L. Ackrill and J. O. Urmson, Oxford: Oxford University Press.

Barton, J. H., and Berger, P., 2001. 'Patenting Agriculture'. *Issues in Science and Technology Online.*

Cooper, H. D., 2002. 'The International Treaty on Plant Genetic Resources for Food and Agriculture'. 11 *Review of European Community and International Environmental Law* 1.

Cullet, P., 2003. *Differential Treatment in International Environmental Law.* Aldershot: Ashgate.
   2005. *Intellectual Property Protection and Sustainable Development.* New Delhi: Butterworths/Lexis-Nexis.

Dawe, D., Robertson, R., and Unnevehr, L., 2002. 'Golden Rice: What Role Could It Play in Alleviation of Vitamin A Deficiency?'. 27 *Food Policy* 541.

Flores Palacios, X., 1997. *Contribution to the Estimation of Countries' Interdependence in the Area of Plant Genetic Resources.* Rome: Commission on Genetic Resources for Food and Agriculture.

Hamilton, N. D., 2001. 'Legal Issues Shaping Society's Acceptance of Biotechnology and Genetically Modified Organisms'. 6 *Drake Journal of Agircultural Law* 81.

MacDonald, R. St. J., 1995. 'The Common Heritage of Mankind', in U. Beyerlin *et al.* (eds.), *Recht Zwischen Umbruch und Bewahrung.* Berlin: Springer, 153.

Schuler, P., 2004. 'Biopiracy and Commercialization of Ethnobotanical Knowledge', in J. M. Finger and P. Schuler (eds.), *Poor People's Knowledge: Promoting Intellectual Property in Developing Countries.* Oxford: Oxford University Press.

Sharma, D., 2005. 'Rice in a Private Grip'. 113 *South Bulletin* 532.

---

[49] The need for a link has been the object of contentious debates in the context of the TRIPS Council for several years, but no compromise has yet emerged. See e.g. a recent communication by a group of developing countries and the response of the United States. Council for TRIPS, Bolivia, Brazil, Colombia, Cuba, India and Pakistan, The Relationship Between the TRIPS Agreement and the Convention on Biological Diversity (CBD) and the Protection of Traditional Knowledge, WTO Doc. IP/C/W/459 (2005). Council for TRIPS, Communication from the United States, Art. 27.3(b), Relationship Between the TRIPS Agreement and the CBD, and the Protection of Traditional Knowledge and Folklore, WTO Doc. IP/C/W/469 (2006).

Sharma, R., and Poleman, T. T., 1994. *The New Economics of India's Green Revolution: Income and Employment Diffusion in Uttar Pradesh.* New Delhi: Vikas.

Sittenfeld, A., and Gámez, R., 1993. 'Biodiversity Prospecting by INBio', in W. V. Reid *et al.*, *Biodiversity Prospecting: Using Genetic Resources for Sustainable Development.* Washington, DC: World Resources Institute.

20

Law, gender and environmental resources: women's access to environmental justice in East Africa

PATRICIA KAMERI-MBOTE

1 Introduction

Concern for the environment has increased over the years since the United Nations Conference on the Human Environment in 1972. Many countries have signed, acceded to or ratified many international instruments providing for access to justice for the citizenry generally and in environmental decision-making specifically. Alongside this has been the growth of the women's rights movement beginning with the Women's Conference in Mexico in 1975 and the coming into force of the Convention on the Elimination of All Forms of Discrimination Against Women (CEDAW) in the early 1980s. Christopher Stone, in his seminal article written in 1970, entitled 'Should Trees Have Standing', analogised the quest for the rights of trees to that for women's rights and the resistance that such quests elicit from the entities that have the power to bestow rights. Explaining the resistance, he noted that 'until the rightless thing receives its rights, we cannot see it as anything but a thing for the use of us. It is hard to see it and value it for itself until we can bring ourselves to give it rights.'[1]

Access to environmental justice (EJ) by persons at all levels is mediated by the power relations between different actors. Since environmental management shapes decisions and actions on how resources are developed and to whom they are provided, lack of equity in what choices and what resources are provided to whom is an EJ issue. Yet the people most likely to be affected by environmental management are not included in the processes often enough. Exclusion of women in decision-making on environmental matters and property ownership and control systems that exclude women contribute to environmental injustice.

Paradoxically, the environmental movement and the women's rights movement have moved on parallel tracks even as gendered encounters with environmental resources at local and national levels have been noted. The perception in many instances has been that environmental issues are elite issues and not women's issues in the way that political participation and the right to health, work and education are. On the environment side, there is the perception that environmental concerns

---

[1] Stone 1972.

are human concerns and not women's concerns. Yet herein lies the paradox, because the state of the environmental resources impacts on women's work, health and education, and the gendered social ordering of society mitigates human encounters with the environment. Constrained access to resources, lack of ownership rights and the vesting of control of land and resources in men has implications for women's performance of their duties. In similar vein, marginalisation, outlawing or demeaning of women's ways of managing environmental resources (as well as the introduction of technologies that obliterate women's roles) impacts on women's work and their political leverage as they become more dependent on new forms of knowledge that are owned and controlled by others.[2]

In the quest for a template for procedural rights in the environmental realm, human rights have proved to be particularly useful for a number of reasons.[3] The recognition that women's rights are human rights, though implicit in the recognition of the human right to a healthy environment, requires greater articulation to address gender biases in access, control and ownership of environmental resources as well as women's participation in environmental decision-making.

The most succinct statement on procedural rights is the Rio Declaration on Environment and Development.[4] The states parties to the Declaration commit themselves to grant the right of access to information held by public authorities to each individual citizen, the opportunity to participate in decision-making processes, and effective access to judicial and administrative proceedings, including redress and remedy.[5] Increasingly, these rights have been adopted in international treaties on the environment such as the Convention on Biological Diversity and its Cartagena Protocol,[6] and also in domestic legislation.

At the national level, the context for promotion of environmental justice is intrinsically intertwined with the respect for human rights as provided for in national constitutions, framework environmental laws and sectoral statutes. It is within this context that discourses on EJ have been canvassed. These discourses have focused on the disproportionate environmental burdens and hazards borne by lower income communities and racial minorities and the efforts made to address this imbalance. US writers on the subject have addressed the disproportionate burden borne by racial minorities with respect to the location of dumping sites in a context where the more affluent communities are able to organise and resist the location of the dumps in their backyards. For our purposes, we view EJ as a useful tool in addressing environmental

---

[2] Sandy Thomas, 'Gender and Biotechnology', unpublished discussion paper prepared for the International Development Research Centre, 2004, on file with the author.

[3] Boyle and Anderson 1996.

[4] United Nations Conference on Environment and Development, Rio Declaration on Environment and Development, Rio de Janeiro, Brazil, 31 *International Legal Materials* (ILM) (1992) 874.

[5] Principle 10 of the Convention on Biological Diversity, Rio de Janeiro, Brazil, 31 ILM 818 (1992).

[6] 1998 Convention on Biological Diversity, 31 ILM (1992) 818; 2000 Cartagena Protocol on Biosafety to the Convention on Biological Diversity, 39 ILM (2000) 1027.

entitlements, human vulnerability and environmental management. We define it to mean that environmental risks and hazards as well as investments, benefits and natural resources are equally distributed, without direct or indirect discrimination, at all jurisdictional levels. We also define it to include access to information, participation in decision-making and access to justice for all in environmental matters.

Environmental injustice therefore exists when members of disadvantaged, ethnic, minority or other groups suffer disproportionately at the local, regional (sub-national) or national levels from environmental risks or hazards, and/or suffer disproportionately from violations of fundamental human rights as a result of environmental factors, and/or are denied access to environmental investments, benefits and/or natural resources, and/or are denied access to information, and/or participation in decision-making, and/or access to justice in environment-related matters.

In African countries, the context for EJ is nuanced by legal pluralism with the official legal system recognising several other legal orders and providing an operating environment for them. Many constitutions provide for the operation of religious and customary laws for particular religious or ethnic groups in some instances where such laws are not repugnant to justice and morality (a vague and indeterminate notion that is left to judicial interpretation). These operate alongside state law which is the ultimate authority and dominates other plural legal orders.

Environmental resources are managed at much more localised levels where customary law determines ownership, access and control of resources. The hallmark of African customary law is the dominance of older male members over the property and lives of women and their juniors. The family, not the individual, is the reference point. It includes ascendants and descendants and more than one wife in polygamous unions. Women-unfriendly customary law has gradually developed as African societies have undergone change towards the individual as the locus for resource control, ownership and access.[7] Women and children have become very vulnerable with the removal of guaranteed access to environmental resources. This is despite the fact that women continue to play critical roles of reproduction and production. It is noteworthy that rural women contribute substantially to food production.[8]

It is within this context that this chapter looks at women's rights in environmental law. It avers that, while laws on environmental and natural resources are largely gender-neutral, ownership, control and access to these resources is gendered. Noting that access to justice in the environmental realm means involving stakeholders in the management of the resources, decision-making on issues pertaining to the resources and avenues of redress in the event of non-observance of their rights, it argues that this entails going beyond the dictates of formal equality espoused in gender-neutral laws and addressing the situation and needs of the subjects of law through substantive equality to foster meaningful access to resources. It also underscores the role of law as either facilitating or constraining access to resources at the international,

---

[7] Armstrong 1996.   [8] Khasiani 1992.

regional, national and local levels and the extent to which environmental policies and interventions have taken on board the strategic interventions identified in the Nairobi Forward Looking Strategies (NFLS) and the Beijing Platform for Action (BPFA) in relation to the environment. In assessing the role of law, the paper will identify the dominant paradigm in the management and control of environmental resources and suggest ways of engaging that paradigm with a view to enhancing women's rights.

The second section of this chapter lays out the conceptual and analytical framework for the discussion on women and the environment. The third section highlights EJ issues for women in context. The fourth section highlights EJ interventions proposed by international and regional instruments. The fifth section assesses the extent to which legal and policy initiatives take women's EJ concerns into account in framing environmental entitlements and environmental management initiatives. The sixth section is the conclusion. It proposes ways of engendering environmental law and management.

2 Conceptual framework

Women have an essential role to play in the development of sustainable and eco-logically sound consumption and production patterns and approaches to natural resource management. This has been recognised at the United Nations conferences on both the environment and women's rights. Indeed governments have expressed their commitment to creating a new development paradigm that integrates environmental sustainability with gender equality and justice within and between generations as contained in Chapter 24 of Agenda 21.

At a conceptual level, there is, for instance, a growing body of literature on ecofem-inism which seeks to combine different feminist theories and relate them to environmental issues. Ecofeminists explore gender oppression and environmental degradation, mainly caused by men, and hold that women have a responsibility to stop this male domination over both. It was borne out of disillusionment with prevailing discourses on the environment which lacked a feminist analysis.[9] Ecofeminists are at the forefront of developing a deeper analysis of the woman/nature dynamic and challenge all kinds of subjugation which leads to environmental degradation.

Elaborating on the woman/nature relationship, Bina Agarwal notes that gender oppression and environmental degradation are mainly caused by male Western dominance; women are more related to the environment than men who relate to culture that subjugates both the environment and women; male oppression of women and nature have occurred simultaneously and women have a responsibility to challenge it; and ecofeminism combines feminism and ecological thought, both working towards egalitarian, non-hierarchical structures. Ecofeminists argue that both women and

---

[9] Merchant 1992.

nature could be liberated together.[10] Ecofeminism has not informed women's quest for access and control of natural resources in Africa, and some scholars hold that the framing of the ecofeminist debate is abstract and removes an essentially grassroots movement from its main constituency, the rural women.[11]

The Women, Environment and Development (WED) approach has also scrutinised the correlation between the oppression of women and the oppression of the environment.[12] Apart from characterising women as the main victims of environmental degradation, WED emphasises the special bond that exists between women and the environment: women are seen as the privileged bearers of a special knowledge imported to them by nature. According to this view, women are assumed to be caring, nurturing and selfless beings committed to both future generations and the environment.[13]

Environmental laws, policies and interventions that fail to factor in the gender dynamic contribute to environmental degradation while accentuating women's poverty and increasing their workload where they depend on environmental resources as fuels and food. In similar vein, tenurial arrangements that favour men over women also impact on reforestation and afforestation if women are not accorded rights to the trees they plant on account of their not owning the land they plant them on.[14]

3 Environmental justice for women

Environmental justice for women is an issue of concern in many subsistence economies. Women have organised themselves to protect the environment and promote EJ in their communities, in national organisations, in international networks, working on issues such as biodiversity, land rights, access to water and sanitation, sustainable energy and climate change. All over the world they are major agents for environmental action, prompting others to work on the basis of the linkages of environmental sustainability, gender equality and poverty reduction. In certain regions women are generally the most stable members of the community, as men pursue work in distant locations leaving women to safeguard the natural environment and ensure adequate and sustainable resource allocation within the household and the community.[15]

Women's participation in environmental decision-making is, however, limited and their knowledge and interests are not incorporated in such decisions and in development planning. EJ is thus nuanced by the social construction of gender where roles

[10] Agarwal 1997.
[11] M. Businge, 'The Legal Aspects of Ecofeminism as a Vehicle for Implementing Sustainable Development in Kenya', unpublished Master's thesis submitted to the Faculty of Law, University of Nairobi, 2005, on file with the author.
[12] Diamond and Orenstein 1990.   [13] *Ibid.*
[14] Rocheleau and Edmunds 1997 at 1356.   [15] Women and Natural Resource Management 1996 at 60–1.

and realms of operation of men and women are set and translated into power relation-ships and masculinity and femininity denote differentiated entitlements to resources. Indeed gender mediates environmental encounter, use, knowledge, and assessment. Further, gender roles, responsibilities and the division of labour shape all forms of human relationships to the environment.[16]

As pointed out above, there are different legal orders governing resources. Law can empower or disempower its subjects in the quest for EJ. Formal legal equality may result in substantive inequality where the prevailing situation of legal subjects as influenced by cultural and social norms – as is the case with gender – is not taken into account. For instance, the patriarchal social ordering of many societies in African countries makes access to resources under customary law tilted in favour of male members of society. In this regard, laws intended to grant equal access for men and women must engage the gendered context if they are to be effective.[17]

At another level, globalisation, technological development and privatisation of environmental resources impact on EJ for women. For instance, as new technologies are adopted, women's ways of managing resources such as saving seed are sidelined even as the technologies are not made readily available to women.[18] The net effect is the alienation of environmental managers from the environmental resources.[19] This impacts on both food security and sustainable environmental management.

The trend towards privatisation of resources and formalisation of land rights has made women's access to EJ more tenuous, yet equitable access to land and envi-ronmental resources is one way to achieve overall national development.[20] Feminist critiques of development have identified the marginalisation of women from the means of production as a critical factor in the subordination of women.[21] EJ may be negated by lack of ownership, access or control of land and environmental resources which is critical because these resources constitute an essential validation of social and political autonomy. For women, it is a means of moving from reproductive roles to production.[22]

It is noteworthy that gender-neutral laws on land and environmental resources have not resulted in more women owning these resources because of structural barriers, such as access to credit and the prevalence of the myth that women cannot own land. Women are under-represented in institutions that deal with land and environmental resources, their rights under communal ownerships and ranches are not defined, and this allows men to dispose of family land freely. Few women have land registered in their names.[23] Similarly, state control of environmental resources has not resulted in equitable access to the resources for all. In instances where resources such as grazing areas and forests are vested in communities, equal access for all members of the community is not always guaranteed.

---

[16] Seager and Hartmann 2005.   [17] Dahl 1987. See also Mackinnon 2005.   [18] Shiva 1989.
[19] Mies and Shiva 1993.   [20] Ikdahl et al. 2005.   [21] Mies 2003.   [22] Ibid.   [23] Ikdahl et al. 2005.

The Nairobi Forward Looking Strategies,[24] the Beijing Platform for Action[25] and the Optional Protocol to the African Charter on Human and Peoples' Rights on the Rights of Women in Africa[26] identify the need to upscale women's participation in environmental decision-making as a strategic action in the improvement of the overall status of women. On the environment side, Agenda 21[27] and the Convention on Biological Diversity[28] also identify women as key allies in sustainable environmental management. If effectively implemented, these instruments would go a long way in securing EJ for women.

4 The Nairobi Forward Looking Strategies and the Beijing Platform for Action

Both the Nairobi Forward Looking Strategies (NFLS) and the Beijing Platform for Action (BPFA) put women at the centre of the quest for sustainable environmental management while underscoring the importance of these resources for women's empowerment.

4.1 Nairobi Forward Looking Strategies

With regard to the NFLS, the themes of the Nairobi meeting, 'Equality, Peace and Development', have nuances that relate to EJ. Equality in access to and participation in environmental resources is critical for women's emancipation. Paragraph 12 of the NFLS underscores the need for a holistic approach to development taking into account all aspects of human life including material resources and the physical environment. It is interesting to note that this paragraph points to the need to have environmentally sustainable technology responsive to the needs and rights of the individual. It seems to implicitly affirm the nature–women connection promoted by ecofeminists.

With regard to peace, there is growing literature on the environment as a cause of conflict on the one hand and as a pathway to peace on the other. Changes in the environment have implications for peace at different levels. In places where environmental resources provide both a subsistence and an economic lifeline, such changes impact directly on gender relations. In many parts of the world, there is a growing

---

[24] Report of the Third United Nations International Conference on Women, Nairobi, 15–26 July 1985, reviewing and appraising the achievements of the United Nations Decade for Women: Equality, Development and Peace, New York, 1995.

[25] Report of the United Nations Fourth World Conference on Women, Beijing, China, September 1995, Action for Equality, Development and Peace, Platform for Action, 1995.

[26] See African Union Protocol to the African Charter on Human and Peoples' Rights on the Rights of Women in Africa, adopted by the Conference of Heads of State and Government on 11 July 2003 in Maputo, Mozambique, in force November 2005. It is a Protocol to the African Charter on Human and Peoples' Rights, OAU Doc. CAB/LEG/67/3 Rev.5 (1981), entry into force 12 October 1986 (with the 26th instrument of ratification).

[27] Report of the United Nations Conference on Environment and Development, United Nations, Rio de Janeiro, 3–14 June 1992, UN Doc. A/CONF.151/26/Rev.1 (Vol. 1), Annex II.

[28] For references, see note 6 above.

appreciation among conflict policy-makers of the environmental origins of conflict. Conflicts in Africa, for instance, though often linked to political and communal differences, are now understood to have potentially important linkages with environmental factors.[29] Given the roles that women play in relation to environmental resources, they are in a position to contribute to peace-building initiatives.[30] Where the environment is degraded or natural resources destroyed as a consequence of war, the capacity and ability of women to perform the tasks expected of them is impacted on. Paragraph 62 of the NFLS specifically points out that agrarian reform measures 'should guarantee women's constitutional and legal rights in terms of access to land and other means of production and should ensure that women will control the products of their labour and their income as well as benefits from agricultural inputs, research, training, credits and other infrastructural facilities'.

Paragraph 74 requires that all women, particularly married women, be vested with the right to own, administer, sell or buy property independently as an aspect of their equality and freedom under the law. This provision has implications for ownership, control, access and management of environmental resources by women. Paragraphs 174–88, dealing with food, water and agriculture, underscore the need to recognise and reward women for their performance of tasks hereunder; to equip them with the resources necessary to perform the tasks; and to ensure that they actively participate in the planning, decision-making and implementation of programmes. Paragraph 182 specifically requires that rural women's rights to land be secured to ensure that they have access to land, capital, technology, know-how and other productive resources that they need. This action is critical for women's access to environmental resources.

On science and technology, the requirement at paragraph 200 of full and effective participation of women in the decision-making, priority setting for research and development, choice and application would avoid instances where technology adversely impacts on women's performance of their tasks or leads to their marginalisation. This is very relevant in the realm of genetic engineering where new varieties of food may be developed and promoted without taking into account the time and fuel required to cook the food. While the new food variety may be high yielding, it may lead to more demands on the women's time.

On energy, women's participation in energy needs assessment; technology and energy conservation management and maintenance will ensure that women's energy needs are taken into consideration in planning.[31] Additionally, the initiation of farm woodlot development involving men and women, proposed at paragraph 222, would balance the needs of women for fuel wood on the one hand and sustainable development on the other.

Paragraphs 224–7 deal explicitly with the interface between the environment and women's empowerment. Paragraph 224 recognises that:

---

[29] Kameri-Mbote 2004.   [30] *Ibid.*   [31] Nairobi Forward Looking Strategies, note 25 above, para. 220.

> Deprivation of traditional means of livelihood is most often a result of envi-
> ronmental degradation resulting from such natural and man-made disasters as
> droughts, floods, hurricanes, erosion, desertification, deforestation and inap-
> propriate land use . . . Most seriously affected are women . . . These women
> need options for alternative means of livelihood. Women must have the same
> opportunity as men to participate in . . . irrigation and tree-planting.

Other issues addressed include improvements in sanitary conditions and drinking
water and the home and work environment. Paragraph 226 points to the need for:

> Awareness by individual women and all types of women's organisations of
> environmental issues and the capacity of men and women to manage their
> environment and sustain productive resources . . . All sources of information
> dissemination should be mobilised to increase the self-help potential of women
> in conserving and improving their environment. National and international
> emphasis on ecosystem management and the control of environmental degra-
> dation should be strengthened and women should be recognised as active and
> equal participants in this process.

Paragraph 227 requires environmental impact assessment of policies, programmes
and projects on women's health and activities.

It is clear from the above that EJ issues cut across a number of areas addressed
in the NFLS. The measures identified are broad and encompass key gender concerns
in the environmental realm. Considering that the NFLS predates the major international policy pronouncements that are contained in the Rio Conventions, there is no
doubt that the realisation that women's empowerment is predicated on sustainable
management of environmental resources has informed the quest for women's rights
for a long time.

4.2 The Beijing Platform for Action

In preparation for the 1995 Beijing conference, the United Nations Environment
Programme (UNEP) hosted an International Seminar on Gender and Environment,
at which it was urged that environmental policies and programmes should reflect
gender equality and empowerment as both the means and the goals of sustainable
environment and development. This has been followed by calls to foster and encourage the ability of women to contribute to effective environmental management in
line with the strategies announced at the Fourth World Conference on Women, in
Beijing in 1995. In seeking to engender environmental work, UNEP has worked with
the Women's Environment and Development Organization (WEDO) in convening
meetings of women environmental activists and scholars.

The BPFA clearly articulates the linkage between women's empowerment and sustainable environmental management. It reiterates the principle that human beings are

at the centre of concerns for sustainable development.[32] More specifically, the BPFA points out that:

- Women's empowerment is being sought against the background of resource depletion, natural resource degradation and pollution of the environment by dangerous substances. These conditions are displacing communities, especially women, from productive activities (paragraph 246).
- Women have a role to play in sustainable development as consumers, producers, caretakers of families, educators of current and future generations and there is a commitment by governments to integrate environmental sustainability with gender equality and justice (paragraph 248).
- Environmental degradation has specific impacts on women.
- Poverty eradication and peace are integral to sustainable development (paragraph 247).
- Women's work related to natural resources is often neither recognized nor remunerated (paragraph 247).
- Women remain largely absent at all levels of policy formulation and decision-making in natural resource and environmental management, conservation, protection and rehabilitation and their experience and skill in advocacy for and monitoring of proper natural resource management are marginalised in policy-making and decision-making bodies, educational institutions and environment-related agencies (paragraph 249).
- Women are rarely trained as natural resource managers and, even when trained, they are under-represented in formal institutions with policy-making capacities at the national, regional and international levels (paragraph 249).
- Women's non-governmental organisations have weak links with national environment management institutions (paragraph 249).
- Women play leadership roles in environmental conservation and management; are well placed to influence sustainable consumption decisions; are involved in grassroots campaigns to protect the environment; have (especially indigenous women) particular knowledge of ecological linkages and fragile ecosystem management (paragraph 250).

The BPFA recognises that there is a need for a holistic, inter-sectoral approach to environmental management. It is also imperative that men and women are involved in sustainable development policies (paragraph 251). It calls for the need to mainstream gender in all policies and programmes and an analysis of the gender-differentiated impacts of such policies and actions before decisions are taken (paragraph 252).

Three strategic objectives are identified for action by governments, regional and international organisations and non-governmental organisations:

---

[32] Sustainable development is defined as development that meets the needs of current generations without compromising those of future generations. See WCED 1987 at 8.

- The need to involve women actively in environmental decision-making at all levels.
- Integration of gender concerns and perspectives in policies and programmes for sustainable development.
- Strengthening or establishing mechanisms at the national, regional and international levels to assess the impact of development and environment policies on women.

These proposed interventions proceed from the premise that women have been excluded from available opportunities and that such exclusion impacts negatively not just on women but on society and resources. To deal with this problem, gender mainstreaming is needed at different levels. First, there is a need for gender mainstreaming in the normative legal and policy frameworks governing these resources. The aim here is to include women's concerns in the laws and policies. Secondly, women need to be involved in the institutions charged with shepherding these norms. An effective mainstreaming strategy, according to Seager and Hartman,[33] seeks to bring women into positions where they can take part on an equitable basis with men in determining the institution's values, directions and the allocation of resources. It also seeks to ensure that women have the same access as men to resources within the institution. Effective gender mainstreaming facilitates participation of women as well as men to influence the entire agenda and priorities and culture of the organisation.[34]

It is reassuring to note that the Optional Protocol to the African Charter on Human and Peoples' Rights on the Rights of Women in Africa[35] pays particular attention to the rights of women to land and environmental resources. Article 19, dealing with sustainable development, exhorts states parties to promote 'women's access to and control over productive resources such as land and guarantee their right to property'.

At the normative level, it is clear from the above that EJ considerations have permeated international and regional women's rights instruments. This is done implicitly, as the instruments do not address EJ directly.

5 The place of women in legal initiatives for sustainable environmental management

5.1 International and regional contexts

The multilateral environmental agreements concluded in the last two decades seek to establish a legal framework for environmental resources management and also to create a favourable environment for sustainable and equitable development. They have implications on EJ, poverty reduction and food security. Access to land and natural resources is important in ensuring that the citizenry contributes to and benefits from economic growth. Poverty reduction in East Africa, for example, is largely predicated

---

[33] Seager and Hartmann 2005.   [34] *Ibid.*   [35] Note 26 above.

on land productivity in addition to access to basic services, markets, education and health care.

Furthermore, secure rights to land and other resources underpin secure liveli-hoods and shelter by reducing vulnerability to shocks, guaranteeing a level of self-provisioning and supplementary incomes from basic food stuffs and enabling easier access to basic infrastructure, employment, markets and financial services. Direct access to environmental resources by all people including women is therefore critical in ensuring economic growth, which is environmentally sustainable.

International instruments such as Agenda 21 outline the role of women in envi-ronmental management.[36] It identifies the following actions as critical to sustainable development:

- full, equal and beneficial integration of women in all development activities includ-ing national ecosystem management and control of environmental degradation;
- increase in the proportion of women decision-makers, planners and technical advis-ers, managers, extension workers in the environment and development fields;
- elimination of constitutional, legal, administrative, cultural, behavioural, social and economic obstacles to women's participation in sustainable development;
- passing relevant knowledge to women through curricula in formal and non-formal education;
- valuation of roles of women; and
- ensuring women's access to property rights and agricultural inputs.

The Convention on Biological Diversity also recognises the role that women play in the management of biological resources and calls for facilitation of women in the performance of those critical roles.[37] Similarly, Principle 20 of the Rio Declaration[38] states that:

> Women have a vital role in environmental management and development. Their
> full participation is therefore essential to achieve sustainable development.

The World Summit on Sustainable Development (WSSD) Plan of Action in 2002 also identified women as key to the attainment of sustainable development.[39] It explicitly states that women need to be provided with access to agricultural resources and that land tenure arrangements should recognise and protect indigenous and common property resource management systems. This is in recognition of the critical role that agriculture plays in addressing the needs of a growing global population, its inextricable link to poverty eradication, especially in developing countries and the

---

[36] Report of the United Nations Conference on Environment and Development, note 27 above.
[37] Convention on Biological Diversity, note 6 above, Arts. 8(j) and 10(c).
[38] Note 4 above.   [39] WSSD Plan of Action, 2002.

realisation that enhancing the role of women at all levels and in all aspects of rural development, agriculture, nutrition and food security is imperative.[40]

Paragraph 38(i) points to the need to:

> Adopt policies and implement laws that guarantee well defined and enforceable land and water use rights, and promote legal security of tenure, recognizing the existence of different national laws and/or systems of land access and tenure, and provide technical and financial assistance to developing countries as well as countries with economies in transition that are undertaking land tenure reform in order to enhance sustainable livelihoods.

Paragraph 38(f) identifies the need to enhance the participation of women in all aspects and at all levels relating to sustainable agriculture and food security. With regard to women's knowledge on environmental conservation and natural resource management, paragraphs (g) and (h) are relevant. They point to the need to:

> Integrate existing information systems on land-use practices by strengthening national research and extension services and farmer organizations to trigger farmer-to-farmer exchange on good practices, such as those related to environmentally sound, low-cost technologies, with the assistance of relevant international organizations; and Enact, as appropriate, measures that protect indigenous resource management systems and support the contribution of all appropriate stakeholders, men and women alike, in rural planning and development.

It is noteworthy, however, that regional environmental agreements in Africa such as the revised African Convention on the Conservation of Nature and Natural Resources adopted by the African Union in July 2003[41] and the Lusaka Agreement on Wildlife[42] do not have any provisions on women's participation in environmental management. They are largely gender-neutral. While this is to be expected on account of the fact that international law guides states on measures to put in place at the municipal levels, the failure to guide states on the need to involve women as critical actors in the quest for sustainable development is a grave omission.

5.2 National contexts

5.2.1 Constitutions

Chapter III of Tanzania's Constitution, at Article 14, provides for the right to life and its protection by society. The High Court of Tanzania, on two occasions, has ruled that

---

[40] Para. 38.

[41] See African Convention on the Conservation of Nature and Natural Resources, adopted at Maputo, July 2003, African Union EX/CL/50 (III). Art. III on Principles, includes both the right to a satisfactory environment favourable to development, the duty of states to ensure the enjoyment of the right to development and the duty of states to ensure that developmental and environmental needs are met in a sustainable, fair and equitable manner.

[42] Adopted at Lusaka, 8 September 1994.

the said right includes the right to live in a clean and healthy environment.[43] These cases show that the right to a clean and healthy environment, though not explicitly enshrined in the country's Constitution, has been found to exist in Article 14 of Tanzania's Constitution by the judiciary.

In Uganda, the Constitution, as the supreme law, enshrines basic principles and rights upon which public involvement in environmental decision-making is premised. These include the right to a clean and healthy environment: Article 39 of the Constitution provides that 'every Ugandan has the right to a clean and healthy environment'. Additionally, the Constitution of Uganda provides that the state holds the natural resources as trustee for the people of Uganda.

In Kenya, the current Constitution[44] does not have direct environmental provisions. It does, however, place importance on the right to life, and experts argue that this right to life encompasses the right to a clean and healthy environment.[45] The Proposed National Constitution of Kenya that was rejected in a referendum in November 2005 contained explicit provisions on the right to a healthy environment.[46]

It is important to point out that, whether the right to a healthy environment is provided for implicitly (Kenya and Tanzania) or explicitly (Uganda), the provisions are gender-neutral. There is no provision in any of the Constitutions pointing to the right of women to environmental resources or for access to EJ for women. This impacts adversely on women because of the gender division of labour. Women provide the bulk of the labour for tending resources but are not engaged in decision-making. If they are unfairly denied access to resources, they have no avenues for airing their grievances as the available avenues are male dominted and favour men.

5.2.2 Land laws

Land rights have implications for EJ, since land hosts environmental resources. Land law in the three countries has been undergoing changes. The Constitutions of the three countries are gender-neutral with regard to property rights including land rights. They accord men and women the same status. Objective XV of the National Objectives and Directive Principles of State Policy of the Constitution of the Republic of Uganda 1995 recognise the significant role women play in society. This Constitution guarantees the rights of all to own property without bias as to gender or marital status.[47] In view of this constitutional right, whatever provision is made under the 1995 Constitution should not be seen to deprive the proprietor or owner of land in whatever manner of his/her interest in the said property. The rights of spouses to matrimonial property are also safeguarded. Furthermore, the national gender policy addresses gender concerns which need to be incorporated into national development processes. The

---

[43] See *Joseph Kessy and Ors* v. *Dar es Salaam City Council*, Civil Case No. 299 of 1989, High Court of Tanzania at Dar es Salaam (unreported); and Misc. Civil Case No. 91 of 1991, High Court of Tanzania at Dar es Salaam (unreported).

[44] Act No. 5 of 1969, last amended in 1992, and revised in 1998.

[45] Wamukoya and Situma 2000 at 2.   [46] Proposed National Constitution of Kenya, 2005.   [47] Art. 21(2)C.

land sector strategic plan recognises the vulnerability in relation to security of tenure of women. One of its strategies is to mainstream gender in all land sector activities. The Land Act tackles practices of customary tenure that do not observe the Constitution. The Act provides that no person shall sell, mortgage or give away land on which she/he ordinarily resides with his/her spouse and from which they derive sustenance except with the prior written consent of the spouse. Ugandan communities are, however, patrilineal and most women gain access to land through marriage. Despite the progressive land and inheritance laws, widows are frequently evicted and children disinherited by family members.

While the role of women is recognised in agriculture in Kenya and efforts have been made to ensure that women own land, the practical implementation of this laudable goal remains to be attained. Land has been and continues to be the most significant form of property in rural Kenya and is a critical determinant of economic well-being, social status and political power. Since Kenya's independence in 1963, the government has pursued programmes to transform customary land tenure to statutory freehold tenure through land adjudication and registration. The problem is that the titled land is being transferred almost exclusively to male individuals, thereby leaving no provision on how women's access rights are to be defined. Land title deeds do not only increase men's control over distribution of land, but also create dependency of women on men since the former now do not have legal access to the land.[48] The rejected Proposed National Constitution contained provisions for the state to define and keep under review a National Land Policy ensuring equitable access to land and associated resources, and the elimination of gender discrimination in regulations, customs and practices related to land and property in land.[49] It had also included the principle of equality and equity among women and men as a fundamental human right for all citizens stating that 'women and men have equal right to inherit, have access to and manage property' and that 'any law, culture, customs or tradition that undermines the dignity, welfare and interest or status of women or men is prohibited'. The draft National Land Policy also requires that mechanisms be put in place to ensure gender equity in land allocation and ownership. One of its core issues is to address insecure land tenure, in particular of the urban and rural poor and for women as a vulnerable group. This remains a draft, and, in light of the rejection of the impasse on constitutional review, it is doubtful that the policy's goals of ensuring gender equity in land ownership and management will have firm grounding.

With the rejection of the draft Constitution in the November 2005 referendum, the issue of women's ownership of land has become one of the eight most contested issues on the draft. The situation therefore remains that, though land law is gender-neutral and allows for both men and women to own land in Kenya, the patrilineal nature of the society mediates the application of the law and dictates that men are the main

---

[48] Nzioki 2006.   [49] Draft Constitution of Kenya; section 75(a) and (f). Kenya Gazette Supplement, 2005.

owners and controllers of land. In the circumstances, women access land through male fiduciaries (husbands, fathers, sons and other male relatives).

The Kenya National Policy on Gender and Development was adopted in 2006. The overall objective of the policy is 'to facilitate the mainstreaming of the needs and concerns of men and women in all areas in the development process in the country'. Among the critical areas identified in the policy is the economy, poverty, law, education and training, health and population, the media, and political participation. The environment is not identified as a critical area.

In Tanzania, the Land Acts seek to guarantee gender equality. In reality, however, they have been criticised as discriminating against women in access/ownership of land, participation in decision-making and with regard to inheritance and divorce.[50] Non-governmental organisations such as Hakiardhi, the National Land Forum (NALAF), also known as UHAI (Ulingo wa kutetea haki za ardhi), and the Land Tenure Study Group (LTG) working on land, recommended that the administration of land should involve the full and effective participation of women; the dispute settlement machinery should fully entrench women's rights to own and control land without harassment and insecurity; and that ownership certificates of family land should include the names of both spouses and land should not be transferred without the consent of both of them. The patrilineal ordering of societies in Tanzania, however, militates against the attainment of these objectives.

5.2.3 Framework environmental laws and sectoral environmental laws

The framework environmental laws of Kenya, Uganda and Tanzania are gender-neutral. The sectoral environmental laws (water, fisheries, wildlife and forest legislations) are also gender-neutral. Environmental laws do not recognise the roles of women and facilitate their performance thereof. Indeed, wildlife, forest, water and agriculture laws are gender-neutral. The only innovation that has recently been introduced in a bid to decentralise natural resource management is the involvement of communities in resource management.[51] This, however, does not guarantee women either access to environmental resources or involvement in their management. Moreover, it is not yet clear how or whether women are engaged in environmental decision-making at the national levels and whether their interests inform the operations of national, regional and local environmental institutions within the countries. In Kenya for instance, there is no requirement that women be included among the members of the board of the National Environment Management Authorities and other institutions established under the Environment Management and Coordination Act.

---

[50] Critiques of the Report II: Gender and Land in Issa; Shivji 1998 at Chapter 3.
[51] Government of Kenya (2005), Forests Act.

6 Conclusion

As pointed out above, the environmental and women's rights movements have moved on parallel tracks and only converged coincidentally. While there is increasing recognition of women's roles in environmental management and attempts are being made to include women in sustainable development initiatives, EJ for women continues to be a mirage in terms of accessing substantive entitlements as well as participating in decision-making processes. There is a gap between the gender and sustainable environmental management discourses, with the perception that the latter is not a concern for women. This militates against the quest for EJ. The absence of gender disaggregated indicators of environmental integrity, vulnerability and sustainable trends, nominal participation of women in environmental decision-making, and the continued emphasis of traditional women's domains thus reinforcing gender stereotypes remain a challenge in the quest for engendering EJ.

Gender-neutral statutory law on land and environment and their interplay with customary, religious and other social norms have impacted significantly on EJ for women. This calls for other interventions. It is important to develop tools for mainstreaming gender into environmental management and to develop expertise in gender and environment issues. This needs to be done through, first, holding governments accountable for domesticating provisions in multilateral environmental and women's rights agreements to provide a basis for EJ at the municipal law level. This entails ensuring that women participate in decision-making on environmental resources and have access to the remedies provided for in the event that their rights (substantive and procedural) are infringed upon. Secondly, women's enjoyment of substantive EJ provisions should be promoted and facilitated even where these are couched in gender-neutral terms. Thirdly, efforts should be made to promote the full participation of women at all levels, particularly in decision-making and identifying the impact of the macro-context on women and their participation in sustainable environmental management. Fourthly, there is a need to engage and challenge customary and traditional norms that validate women's subordinate position through legal and non-legal methods. Education on the need for EJ for all should accompany the domestication of norms facilitating EJ contained in international and regional agreements. Finally, access to EJ for women in East Africa is unlikely to be achieved across the board if women's access to land and environmental resources is not secured since these provide the means of livelihood as well as economic prosperity.

Bibliography

Agarwal, B., 1997. 'Environmental Management, Equity and Ecofeminism: Debating India's Experience'. 5 *Journal of Peasant Studies* 4.

Armstrong, A., 1996. 'Customary Law in Southern Africa: What Relevance for Action', *WLSA Newsletter*, No. 1.

Boyle, A., and Anderson, M. (eds.), 1996. *Human Rights Approaches to Environmental Protection.* New York: Oxford University Press.

Dahl, T. S., 1987. *Women's Law: An Introduction to Feminist Jurisprudence*, trans. Ronald L. Craig, Oslo: Norwegian University Press.

Diamond, I., and Orenstein, G. F. (eds.), 1990. *Reweaving the World: The Emergence of Ecofeminism.* San Francisco: Sierra Club.

Ikdahl, I., *et al.*, 2005. *Human rights, Formalisation and Women's Land Rights in Southern and Eastern Africa.* Studies in Women's Law No. 57, Oslo: Institute of Women's Law, University of Oslo.

Kameri-Mbote, P., 2004. 'Gender, Conflict and Regional Security', in Makumi Mwagiru (ed.), *African Regional Security in the Age of Globalisation.* Nairobi: Heinrich Böll Foundation.

Khasiani, S., 1992. *Groundwork: African Women as Environmental Managers.* Nairobi: African Centre for Technology Studies Press.

Mackinnon, C., 2005. *Women's Lives, Men's Laws.* Cambridge, MA and London: Harvard University Press.

Merchant, C., 1992. *Radical Ecology.* New York: Routledge, Chapman & Hall Inc.

Mies, M., 2003. *Patriarchy and Accumulation on a World Scale: Women in the International Division of Labour.* London: Zed Books.

Mies, M., and Shiva, V., 1993. *Ecofeminism.* Halifax: Fernwood; and London: Zed Books.

Nzioki, A., 2006. *Land Policies in Sub-Saharan Africa.* Nairobi: CLEAR.

Rocheleau, D., and Edmunds, D., 1997. 'Women, Men and Trees: Gender, Power and Property in Forest and Agrarian Landscapes'. 25 *World Development* No. 8.

Seager, J., and Hartmann, B., 2005. *Mainstreaming Gender in Environmental Assessment and Early Warning.* Nairobi: United Nations Environment Programme, Division of Early Warning and Assessment.

Shiva, V., 1989. *Staying Alive: Women, Ecology and Development.* London: Zed Books.

Shivji, G., 1998. *Not Yet Democracy: Reforming Land Tenure in Tanzania.* Dar es Salaam: International Institute for Environment and Development, Hakardhi.

Stone, C., 1972. 'Should Trees Have Standing? Toward Legal Rights for Natural Objects'. 45 *Southern California Law Review* 450.

Wamukoya, G., and Situma, F. (eds.), 2000. *Environmental Management in Kenya: A Guide to the Environmental Management and Coordination Act, 1999.* Nairobi: Centre for Research and Education Environmental Law (CREEL).

WCED, 1987. *Our Common Future.* Oxford and New York: Oxford University Press.

Women and Natural Resource Management, 1996. *The Overview of a Pan-Commonwealth Training Module.* London: Commonwealth Secretariat.

PART VI

Corporate activities and trade

21

The polluter pays principle: dilemmas of justice in national and international contexts

HANS CHRISTIAN BUGGE

1 Introduction

The Polluter Pays Principle (PPP) is one of the internationally recognized principles that influence the shaping of environmental policy at both the national and international level. As one of the environmental principles that have developed 'from political slogans to legal rules,'[1] it is also increasingly reflected in national and international law.[2]

It is seen and analyzed both as a principle of environmental economics and as a principle of environmental law. In environmental economics, it is discussed as an efficiency principle of internalization of environmental costs. As a legal principle, it is usually treated as a principle for the allocation of the cost of pollution prevention, and for liability and compensation for environmental damage.[3]

In general, it is regarded as an important and 'right' principle in the perspective of environmental protection. It is often mentioned together with other major environmental principles such as the precautionary principle, the principle of prevention and the principle of integration.

The PPP is expressed in numerous international recommendations and treaties.[4] For example, it was included in the EC Treaty in 1987 in Article 130R of the Single European Act (now Article 174 of the EC Treaty), which states that the policy of the Community 'should be based on the principle... that the polluter should pay'.[5] It is also expressed in the 1992 Declaration of the UN Conference on Environment and Development ('Rio Declaration') as Principle 16.[6] The meaning of the principle in international instruments is not always clear, and it differs. The same goes for national law. On the one hand, the *explicit* term 'Polluter Pays Principle' has several meanings. On the other hand, many rules *implicitly* lay down substantive parts of the principle

---

[1] Sadeleer 2000 at 23–32.   [2] Macrory 2004.

[3] For a more thorough discussion, see Bugge 1996 at 53–90.

[4] For a nearly complete list, see Bugge 1996 at 56; and Sadeeler 2000 at 23–32.

[5] However, the principle was introduced into EC environmental policy in 1973, in the first Environmental Action Programme. It is also included in several environmental EC directives.

[6] Report of the UNCED, Doc. A/CONF.151/26/Rev.1 (Vol. 1), Annex II (1992).

by – in various ways – allocating responsibility and costs to the one that causes pollution. A closer analysis reveals that the principle has several dimensions or 'functions'[7]
to which we shall revert.

Although generally acclaimed, the PPP is not uncontroversial. It is in fact subject
to doubts and criticism in economic theory as well as in politics. One indication of
this is the rather reserved wording of Principle 16 in the Rio Declaration:

> National authorities should endeavour to promote the internalization of envi-
> ronmental costs and the use of economic instruments, taking into account the
> approach that the polluter should, in principle, bear the cost of pollution, with
> due regard to the public interest and without distorting international trade and
> investment.

As will be shown in the following, the ambivalence that is reflected in this formulation may at least partly be explained by considerations of justice[8] and fairness.[9]

The various dimensions or functions of the principle become apparent when considering the core content of the rule: That the '*polluter*' shall '*pay*' excludes others
from the duty to pay. A normal interpretation points to the following negations of the
principle:

- The *victim* of pollution shall not pay. Here, PPP appears as a principle for allocation
  of costs of pollution prevention and for liability for pollution damage.
- The *taxpayer* shall not pay. In this relation, PPP is a principle that excludes that the
  costs of pollution prevention or clean-up of existing pollution is covered by public
  budgets.
- *Society at large* shall not pay. This means that the social costs of pollution have to
  be covered, in some way or another, by the polluter; they have to be internalized
  into the polluter's production costs. In legal terms, this may also be defined as a
  fundamental duty to avoid pollution, and even expressed as 'no right to pollute'.
  It follows from this that the polluter normally is not entitled to any compensation
  from the state because its polluting activity is restricted or prohibited.
- *Nature itself* shall not pay. As with social costs, damage to nature has to be compensated or repaired – whether or not there are measurable economic consequences of
  the pollution for people or society.
- *Future generations* shall not pay. Costs of preventive, compensatory and restoring
  measures must be covered by the present polluter – and the present generation –
  and not be left to our descendants.

---

[7] See Bugge 1996; and Pagh 1998 at 253–8.
[8] Recognizing fully the complexities of the concept of 'justice' from both a legal and philosophical point of
view, I deliberately use it in a broad and general meaning in most of this chapter. In some parts of the analysis,
a distinction between corrective justice and distributive justice is necessary.
[9] The first critical, in-depth analysis of the principle, and of its possible social consequences, was made by
Rehbinder 1972.

A closer look at the principle reveals that it is even more complex. Many difficult questions appear: *Who* is the 'polluter' in the many situations where the causes of pollution are several, or in 'chains' of production or uses of a polluting product? *When* must the polluter pay and on what basis and criteria? Are there exceptions and situations where the polluter is not obliged to pay? *What* is to be paid or paid for – and *to whom*? And what is meant by '*principle*'? What is its legal meaning and 'strength' relative to other and possible contradictory legal principles and considerations?

Whether in its explicit or implicit form, it usually only regulates the question of allocation of what may be called 'the primary costs': the obligation to pay for preventive or compensatory measures *in the first instance*. The principle does not deal with the possibility for the polluter to have the costs covered by increased price on the products, or – in case of an accident – by insurance. As a principle of economic efficiency, it presumes that the cost of pollution prevention may lead to increases in the price of products. However, whether this will be the case depends on price elasticity and other market conditions. If the increased price is still competitive, *the consumer* – and not the polluter in the strict sense – is the one who ultimately 'pays'. Therefore, the principle may be seen as a *presumption* or a principle for allocation of primary responsibility and thus the economic *risk*: the polluter has to pay to the extent that the cost burden cannot be transferred to and ultimately carried by the consumer or other clients, an insurance company or another actor.

When all these various aspects are taken into account, the principle becomes indeed very complex. It may be understood in many different ways, and it has to be amplified and nuanced. It may even be more adequate to describe the principle in plural, as 'polluter pays *principles*', although with connections and overlaps, and a common core.[10]

The purpose of this chapter is to take a look at this principle – or these principles – from the perspective of environmental justice. The question to be discussed is: 'Is it a just principle?' or rather: 'How does the principle work from the perspective of fairness and justice?' Clearly, the PPP raises issues of justice of both a distributive and corrective nature, and in several relations: the distribution of environmental quality between social groups; the allocation of benefits and costs between the one that causes the pollution and the pollution victims, between several actors that cause pollution, between the polluter and society at large, between the human society and nature, and between the present generation and future generations.

While a full analysis of the issue would be far too complex here, I shall take an 'environmental justice look' at three main 'versions' of the PPP:

- PPP in the 'narrow' (or 'standard') sense as a principle for allocating the cost of preventing and reducing pollution to an acceptable level;

---

[10] Bugge 1996.

- PPP in the 'wide' (or 'extended') sense as a principle for full internalization of environmental costs; and
- PPP as a principle of liability and compensation for environmental damage.

2 The polluter pays principle in the 'narrow' sense: the costs of measures to prevent pollution should be borne by the polluter

This is the 'original' version of the PPP, as it was defined and recommended by the OECD in 1972 as a guideline for national environmental policy. It resulted from discussions among economists on how to allocate pollution prevention costs in order to achieve an efficient environmental policy. In addition, an important political objective was to avoid national differences that could create unequal competition conditions for industry between OECD member states. The first recommendation aimed in particular at limiting state aid to clean-up measures in polluting industry, and emphasized the PPP as a 'no-subsidy principle'.[11] It is 'narrow' because – although it contributes to the internalization of the environmental externalities of polluting activities – it does not aim at a full internalization of social and environmental costs of the (remaining) pollution.

The PPP in this sense is intuitively viewed as a 'just' principle: Since pollution above a certain level is harmful to people and the environment, it is 'natural' that the cost of reducing pollution to an acceptable level is covered by the one that causes the harm. However, the question is not quite as simple as this. While it is true that pollution may be harmful, it is not generally prohibited. Most often, pollution is a negative side-effect of an otherwise useful and desirable activity. Some people depend on that activity for their living. Others need the products or services it provides. Depending on technical and economic conditions, the prevention of pollution may entail considerable costs, and may even lead to the closing of the activity, to the detriment of those who are benefiting from it. Who loses, and who gains from this development? And are these consequences just?

Two commonplace examples illustrate the dilemma:

Case A: The emission from a factory is a serious nuisance to people in the neighbourhood. Smoke and stench reduce the value of the properties in the area. When the factory is ordered to reduce its pollution, it may have to close down for economic reasons and the workers lose their jobs and income. The neighbours, on the other

---

[11] Recommendation on Guiding Principles Concerning International Economic Aspects of Environmental Policies, C(72)128, OECD, 1972. Its para. 4 reads: 'The principle to be used for allocating costs of pollution prevention and control measures to encourage rational use of scarce environmental resources and to avoid distortions in international trade and investment is the so-called 'Polluter-Pays Principle.' This principle means that the polluter should bear the expenses of carrying out the above mentioned measures decided by public authorities to ensure that the environment is in an acceptable state. In other words, the cost of these measures should be reflected in the cost of goods and services which cause pollution in production and/or consumption. Such measures should not be accompanied by subsidies that would create significant distortions in international trade and investment.'

hand, see an increase in value of their properties. Is it fair? Or would it in such a case be more just if the *victim* of the pollution pays for the measures from which they get a clear benefit? There are clearly arguments of fairness in favour of a 'beneficiary pays principle'.[12]

The polluter–victim relationship appears more clearly in the context of the classical issue of compensation for neighbour nuisance, to which we shall revert.

Case B: A factory is the main economic basis of a small community. Most of the families depend on the factory for their livelihood. The factory emits substances that are not harmful to the community itself, but contributes – together with many other sources – to regional or even global pollution problems. In order to reach national emissions reduction targets, the factory must reduce the emissions. If the PPP is applied fully, the costs are prohibitive, and the factory has to close down with serious social consequences in the community. Is it fair that the local community shall bear such a burden?

In order to avoid these consequences, the authorities must either exempt the factory from the restriction and accept the pollution, or cover parts of the costs through financial support in some form or another.

So, there may be arguments of justice *against* the PPP in the narrow sense, due to its distributive consequences. And, in fact, exceptions to the PPP are found to be politically necessary in order to avoid serious pollution problems without unreasonable economic and social effects. From the very beginning, the OECD accepted state aid to clean-up measures as exceptions to the PPP, and adopted guidelines that draw the limits for state aid to pollution control measures. These were followed up by similar guidelines within the EC, which – with later modifications – are still in force.[13]

A weakness – from an environmental point of view – of this version of the PPP as defined by the OECD, is that it does not in itself imply a strict pollution control policy. The polluter shall bear the expenses of 'measures decided by public authorities to ensure that the environment is in an acceptable state'. It is left to each state to define the 'acceptable' environmental quality and thus the strictness of environmental measures. Therefore, its effect as a principle of international harmonization of environmental policy is limited. Unless it is supplemented by international rules and standards that apply internationally, it may in fact contribute to a 'race to the bottom'. In the perspective of global environmental justice, the principle itself does not protect poor people in developing countries from being exposed to more pollution than people in developed countries with a stricter environmental policy.

Another weakness, or limitation, is that it limits the burden of the polluter to the abatement measures. The burden of the remaining pollution must be borne by the society – or nature itself. Generally speaking, this is neither economically efficient nor just. This is exactly what the PPP in the wide sense is intended to correct.

---

[12] There may of course be nuances to this, from a distributive justice point of view, depending on social conditions, etc. One discussion of a 'victim pays' approach is found in Meissner 1985 at 197–207.

[13] Community Guidelines on State Aid for Environmental Protection (2008/C82/01) of 1 April 2008.

3 The polluter pays principle in the 'wide' sense: a principle of internalization of social costs of pollution

The starting point here is the general efficiency objective of welfare economics,[14] and the economic view of pollution as (rational) use of the environment as a resource for harvesting, recreation and renovation. To economists, the challenge is to find the efficient or 'optimal' level of environmental quality – or the optimal pollution level – that is, the level which gives the maximum difference between the total social value of the environment as a resource and the total social costs of protecting it.[15]

In order to reach the efficient level of pollution, the full social costs of pollution as an external effect must be internalized into the polluter's cost. The 'basic' version of the PPP in the 'wide' sense as an economic efficiency principle is simply this: the polluter shall bear all social costs – including the environmental costs – of the pollution it causes.[16]

Although it is rational in an economic sense, this version of the PPP raises numerous technical difficulties, as well as serious problems of justice and fairness. In general, the efficient level of resource use is reached through the market mechanism. The problem here is that important environmental values and resources are what economists call 'free goods'. As they have no price in the market, they have to be estimated. To estimate the full social costs of pollution is a huge challenge. There is a rich economic theory on the issue,[17] and considerable practical experience.

This is where problems of distributive justice come in. Some of the methods used will inevitably result in higher environmental value of areas where property prices are high, than of areas where property prices are low. It will obviously be more costly to destroy or damage more valuable properties than less valuable properties. Although, depending on the level of environmental quality, thresholds of environmental and health effects in the areas etc., the social costs of (more) pollution will most often be relatively higher in clean areas than in areas that are already deteriorated by pollution. Hence, to put it somewhat bluntly, it is generally more costly to damage the environment of wealthy people than that of poor people. In this way, economic efficiency may easily contribute to maintaining and even increasing, environmental injustice in the sense of different environmental quality. This effect can be analyzed – and be observed – within a city, within a country and, not least, globally. Needless

---

[14] I use 'efficiency' in the meaning of static, 'Kaldor-Hicks efficiency'.

[15] Or the level of pollution that gives the maximum difference between total benefits of pollution abatement measures and the total costs of these measures.

[16] Also *partial* internalization may be regarded as being in accordance with the principle, since it contributes towards a higher degree of efficiency than if no internalization took place. This distinction is underlined in OECD 1992, which focuses on the PPP: 'Partial internalization is an internalization limited to certain categories of costs. Full internalization is an internalization of all categories of costs. In practice full internalization is rarely achieved because, at best, the polluter bears the cost of full compensation of the damage instead of full social cost of damage.'

[17] See e.g. Freeman 2003; and Garrod and Willis 1999. For earlier introductory literature on the topic see, among others, Pearce, Markandya and Barbier 1989; Pearce and Turner 1990; Tietenberg 1994; and Pearce 1995.

to say, the PPP is not the cause of unequal social conditions. Neither is this problem exclusively linked to the application of the PPP. It is first and foremost a general problem with cost–benefit analyses of projects that may have negative environmental effects: The same environmental effects in physical terms may have very different economic costs in areas with different property value. Hence poor areas are preferred as sites for polluting activities. This is a key factor behind problems of environmental (in)justice. Nevertheless, one side-effect of the PPP in the wide sense is that poverty becomes a competitive advantage.

Here, we are clearly faced with a dilemma. It is basically right from the point of view of protecting the environment to put a value on the environment and thus a cost on the destruction of the environment, and to let the polluter cover this cost. At the same time, however, it may contribute to undesirable social consequences. In order to avoid these problems of distributive justice, serious considerations have to be given to the pricing of environmental values and environmental damage. Measures to correct the unfair social effects must be developed. The 'wide' PPP and instruments to apply it must be supplemented by substantial rules such as environmental quality standards, emission limits, and material and procedural environmental rights.

The next question is *how* the external costs can be internalized into the polluter's costs. This is one of the classical issues in environmental economics. The usual answer is *taxes and charges* on the polluting activity. This raises new questions: What exactly should be taxed? Who should pay the tax? What is the right tax level? These are typical issues of environmental economics in the perspective of efficiency and cost-effectiveness.

Environmental taxes raise difficult issues of distributive justice. Who bears the burden of environmental taxes? The problem is particularly evident when a tax system is applied to everyday activities of ordinary families. Examples are tax on energy consumption/electricity, transport, or waste disposal. The tax increases the price in order to reduce demand – in energy consumption, car use or waste production. The objective is reduced pollution from these sources. But, in a social perspective, the tax may be problematic. The increased costs are relatively more burdensome for some people than for others. Charges on energy consumption will be particularly burdensome for big families with poor income. It is necessary for poor families to reduce their expenses and thus their consumption. It is not equally necessary for wealthy families. Hence, *most of the environmental effect of taxes is achieved through the sacrifices of the poorest segment of the population.* The well-to-do can afford the increased price, and continue their high level of energy consumption, car use and waste generation. Although rational from a purely economic view, the effect of the PPP as a principle of internalization of costs becomes its caricature: 'Those who can pay may pollute.'[18]

---

[18] The PPP in the narrow sense may, of course, indirectly have the same effect, since it normally leads to increased prices of the products produced by the polluting activity. However, the economic and hence social effects of taxes and charges are more direct and evident.

The distributive effects of environmental taxes are strengthened by the application of economic theory on these instruments. The efficiency objective of taxes is to get the polluter to adapt its activity to the 'optimal' level of pollution. According to economic theory, the correct tax level is not equal to the social costs, including environmental costs, but must correspond to the *marginal* social cost at the 'optimal' level. This so-called 'Pigovian tax'[19] has the somewhat surprising effect that the polluter must pay considerably more than the full social costs of the pollution. This is shown in the 'classical diagram' of environmental economics. Here, it may illustrate a factory's abatement cost, at an efficient emission level, the social damage cost caused by the emission, and the factory's cost when a Pigovian tax is applied as an incentive to reach the efficient emission level.[20]

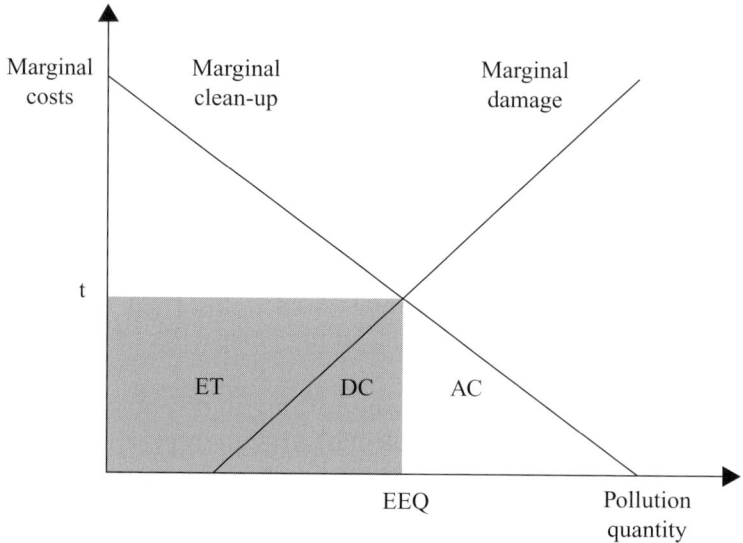

Figure 21.1 Pigovian tax: relationship between clean-up costs and social costs of pollution

EEQ = the efficient emission quantity
T   = the level of emission tax that leads to the efficient emission quantity
AC   = the abatement costs to be covered by the polluter under the PPP in the narrow sense
DC   = the damage cost of the remaining pollution
ET   = the extra tax amount – in addition to the damage cost – to be paid by the polluter through a 'Pigovian tax'

Figure 21.1 illustrates the relationship between clean-up costs and social costs of pollution. It may be applied, for example, to the costs related to pollution from a

---

[19] Developed by the British economist in Pigou 1924.   [20] Source: Eide and Stavang 2005.

factory. If the factory's clean-up costs are zero, the pollution from the factory is at its maximum, and so are the social damage costs of the pollution. It shows how the economic burden of a polluter, in order to reach the efficient or optimal level of pollution (EEQ), varies considerably with different policy instruments and meanings of the PPP. If the polluter has to pay for abatement costs under the PPP in the narrow sense, the cost is AC. If he must pay a 'Pigovian tax', the cost is DC + ET.

The extra burden on the polluter of a Pigovian tax strengthens the incentive effects of the taxes towards efficiency, but aggravates the distribution problems of taxes. For polluting firms, it may entail production costs and other distributive effects which are simply too high to bear. The effect of this may be the closing down of factories, the loss of jobs and social problems. Intuitively, it is difficult to understand why a polluting factory has to pay a tax which may be several times higher than the social costs entailed by its pollution. In short, it is very problematic in a distributive justice perspective.[21]

It should be noted that PPP in this sense has limitations and is disputed as an efficiency principle. The 'Pigovian tax' solution presupposes that the pollution problem is 'unilateral'; that the victims of the pollution are not in a position to adjust to the pollution or in other ways influence the consequences and thus the social costs. This is the case with many of today's pollution problems, most clearly with chemical air pollution from diffuse sources. However, some environmental problems can correctly be described as *reciprocal relationships*: they are caused by conflicting or incompatible uses of the same environmental resource. Both parties may be in a position to avoid the problem. Cases in point are discharge of biodegradable waste into a fjord with aquaculture, and airport noise in a housing area. The economically efficient solution to the problem may be to continue aquaculture and air traffic, but remove the aquaculture installations to the neighbouring fjord, and insulate the houses to reduce the noise nuisance. It is thus the '*principle of the cheapest cost avoider*' that leads to efficiency, not the PPP, which may imply that the *victim* and not the polluter should pay for necessary preventive measures.

The conception of pollution problems as reciprocal relationships – conflicting or incompatible uses of the same resource or environment – is the point of departure for Ronald H. Coase's discussion of the problem of social costs.[22] The 'Coase theorem'[23] is another challenge to the PPP as a principle of economic efficiency. If the victim is in a position to influence the consequences of the pollution, Coase shows that the parties will negotiate the efficient solution regardless of the initial distribution of rights and obligations. If the rights of the parties are clearly defined, and transaction costs are zero, an efficient result will be reached regardless of whether the rule is

---

[21] See the discussion on this, *inter alia*, in Pearce and Turner 1990 chapter 6.

[22] Coase 1960; repeated in Coase 1998.

[23] The Coase theorem is worded in several different ways. A straightforward definition is found in Polinski 1989 at 12: 'If there are zero transaction costs, the efficient outcome will occur regardless of the choice of the legal rule.'

that the polluter pays or that the victim pays. If it is profitable for the polluter to continue the pollution, while compensating the victim for his damage, the polluter will seek that solution. If, on the other hand, the damage of the pollution to the victim is such that it is better for the victim to avoid it by paying the polluter to stop pollution, the victim will seek that solution. The end result will depend on the strengths of interests on both sides.

As an (efficiency) principle of internalization of social costs, the PPP in the wide sense does not imply compensation to victims of pollution. The income from environmental charges and taxes shall not be used to compensate the victims. Compensation may in fact lead to an inefficient solution, as it may remove the incentive for victims of pollution to avoid the problem.

However, rules on liability and compensation for pollution damage are often claimed to be a fulfilment of the PPP. One may even maintain that PPP in a legal sense means (strict) liability and compensation for pollution damage. This version of the principle, and some connected issues of justice, will now be discussed.

4 The polluter pays principle as a principle of liability and compensation for pollution damage

As a principle of liability and compensation, PPP implies that the person that causes pollution is usually liable for pollution damage regardless of *culpa*, and consequently also for the costs of preventing such damage. In many countries this has old roots in tort law. This is also perceived as a 'natural' legal solution, based on considerations of fairness or justice. It is conceived, intuitively, as a 'normal' or 'just' principle: Nobody should have the right to damage others without a duty to compensate the victim. This appears as particularly reasonable where the polluter earns money from the polluting activity and pollution is a normal and foreseeable effect of the activity. The polluter is seen – and legally defined – as the one who brings about negative changes through emissions and thus 'causes' the problem – the 'tortfeasor'. The PPP in this sense becomes a clear principle of *corrective justice*, even an ethical principle.

This is clearly valid as the main rule and the starting point for the analysis. But, again, a closer look at different situations shows that the PPP is not always a just principle in a corrective justice perspective. Let us take a closer look at some aspects of this issue.

First, there must be some limitations to the liability at the outset. We must all accept some pollution, because society – and actually life itself – cannot function without a certain level of pollution. We are all contributing to pollution through our daily activities, so we are at the same time polluters and victims of pollution. A certain level of pollution is always accepted by society. So, corrective justice must mean that only pollution damage over and above a certain acceptable or 'usual' limit – to which not 'everybody' contributes – should be compensated. Here, the concept of a tolerance limit comes into play.

In the traditional neighbour law of many Western countries, there is a 'tolerance limit' which limits liability for neighbour nuisance. The nuisance has to exceed a certain threshold before it entails compensation to the neighbour. This threshold is usually not only a physical factor. It may also be linked to the question of probability and predictability: What can be expected? What is my future position likely to be? If you choose to live close to a motorway, you must expect traffic noise at night. You have to tolerate more noise than the person who settles in the remote countryside. This influences both the corrective justice assessment and the solution to the compensation issue.

In many cases, the victim accepts the pollution or risk of pollution. She buys an apartment close to a noisy road or a stinking factory. This choice may be hard, and 'voluntary' only in a theoretical sense. She may simply not be able to afford to settle in a pollution-free area. For others, the choice may be more real: the victim prefers the nuisance and thus lower housing costs in order to afford and enjoy other goods. It may even be maintained that she herself *causes* her problem when she moves into the polluted area. In this case, one may argue that full compensation for the damage caused to her by the pollution is neither necessary nor reasonable from a corrective justice point of view. In reality, rules on liability for neighbour nuisance are often based on a 'time priority rule': neighbours who moved into the area after the polluting industry have no – or only limited – right to compensation.[24]

This is just a simple example among many that shows that PPP as a principle of compensation for damage is not always evident from a *corrective justice* aspect. Instead, corrective justice may require an *exception* to the PPP.

But what about the *distributive justice* perspective here? A closer look reveals that we are again faced with a dilemma.

On the one hand, if compensation is excluded on the basis of a time priority rule, it works to uphold differences in environmental quality and social conditions. More pollution in an already polluted area – where poorer groups of the population live – is not compensated. The polluter has no incentive to improve the situation. Hence, the time priority rule works to the effect that bad conditions are kept bad, and it may even entail a worsening of the situation – to the further detriment of the weaker part of the population. This touches the core of the environmental justice problem as a social issue.

From this perspective, *the PPP can be used as an argument in favour of distributive justice*, with a view to modifying the traditional neighbour law by giving less weight to time priority.

But this is not the whole story. There are also situations where *distributive* justice goes against the PPP solution, because of social conditions. Take the example of a polluting factory close to a living area with well-to-do people. The factory strives to

---

[24] In Norwegian law, time priority is important, but not always entirely decisive according to the Neighbour Act of 16 June 1961 No. 15, section 2.

survive, with the risk of unemployment for the (less affluent) workers if it has to compensate the rich community for the reduced property value due to the emissions from the factory. An extreme case is the following: In New Delhi in India, the people living in the wealthy part of town, with electrical heating, are said to have once complained about nuisance from smoke from Old Delhi. This smoke came from small fires lit by the poor people, living in the slum areas, who could not afford electricity. Would it be just that the poor people should compensate the rich people for their damage, or be forced to end fire burning? Most people will probably answer no, regardless of time priority.

Let us now go back to questions of corrective justice as a challenge to PPP. It is, for example, not evident that PPP is always a just principle if the effect of a certain emission is *excusably unknown* to the polluter. For example, the possible harmful effects of a substance may have been totally unknown even to scientists in the field.[25] Another example is what is known as 'regulatory compliance defence'.[26] Here, the pollution is in compliance with the law and regulations. Society has struck a balance between the interests of the polluter and the environment, and the polluter respects the restrictions which have been laid down by the authorities. It is still reasonable and fair – in many situations – that the victim of the remaining pollution is compensated for the damage and loss. But is it fair that the compensation is to be paid by the polluter? It is possible to argue in favour of a different solution: that the compensation is paid by the society, since the society has defined the limit between the legal and illegal pollution and thus also brought about – and accepted – the harm to the victim of pollution. Needless to say, there are also arguments in favour of polluter liability also for the remaining pollution. One important argument is that this will be an incentive for further emissions reductions.

Yet, this illustrates a general viewpoint: corrective justice may require that the victim of pollution is compensated. But must the compensation necessarily be paid by the polluter? In his profound analysis of compensation and justice, Jules L. Coleman[27] shows that this is not necessarily so. If the main argument for compensation is that a wrongful act has been carried out to the detriment of others, then corrective justice implies that compensation is paid by the tortfeasor – in our case, the polluter. But, if we instead concentrate on the harm and see the need for compensation to the victim as the main reason for compensation, *who* pays compensation is less important from a *corrective justice* point of view. In our case, it might be a state budget, an insurance company or other financial sources instead of the polluter.

The examples mentioned are possible exceptions to the PPP as a principle of liability and compensation for pollution damage, which are not insignificant. Still, a broad and intuitive corrective justice assessment implies strict liability for the polluter.

---

[25] The fairness problem of PPP faced with 'excusable ignorance' is one of the issues discussed with reference to climate change and mitigation of greenhouse gas emissions in Caney 2005 at 747–75.

[26] Or 'permit defence' if the pollution is legal on the basis of a permit.   [27] Coleman 1992.

5 The PPP as a principle of allocation of costs between states

Turning to the PPP as a principle of allocation of costs between states, we are faced with many of the same dilemmas of fairness and justice as have been described above. Here, they refer to relations between states instead of between citizens and other actors at the national level, and the core issue is the relationship between rich and poor countries. Let us take a closer look at how the three main versions of the PPP work in the perspective of justice between states:

- The PPP in the narrow sense: each state should bear its own costs to abate pollution.
- The PPP in the wide sense: the polluting state should internalize the environmental (damage) costs in other states in its pollution control policy.
- The PPP as a principle of liability and compensation for environmental damage: the polluting state should be liable for pollution damage in other states.

5.1 The PPP in the narrow sense

Looking first at the PPP in the narrow sense, one problem has to be highlighted: the striking difference in environmental policy between most of the rich and most of the poor countries, not least related to pollution control. As mentioned, PPP in the narrow sense does not in itself work to reduce this difference. Rather, on the contrary, without substantive international rules to harmonize pollution control policy, it may stimulate a 'race to the bottom'. It does not in itself promote environmental justice in the sense of improved environmental conditions for poor people in poor countries.

The soft wording of Principle 16 of the Rio Declaration reflects a certain ambivalence. This may partly be explained by the fact that most industrial countries still give some state aid to clean-up measures, as illustrated by the OECD and EC guidelines on state aid for environmental protection. It may also reflect the recognition of a more profound global problem: the lack of resources for pollution abatement in many developing countries, and the need for financial support from the industrialized countries.

As a matter of fact, this need was recognized as early as the 1972 UN Stockholm Conference on the Human Environment. Principle 12 of the Stockholm Declaration[28] stated that necessary resources should be made available, 'taking into account the circumstances and particular requirements of developing countries and any costs which may emanate from their incorporating environmental safeguards.' However, for a long time, the issue was not really pursued.

The World Commission on Environment and Development elaborated on the topic in its report in 1987. The Commission strongly recommended that 'a larger portion of total development assistance should go to investments needed to enhance the environment and the productivity of the resource sectors' in developing countries,

---

[28] Report of the UN Conference on the Human Environment, UN Doc. A/CONF.48/14/Rev.1 (1972).

mentioning such tasks as reforestation, watershed protection, soil conservation and low-cost sanitation measures.[29] It also argued for the active support of the industrialized countries to strengthen the technological capabilities in developing countries.[30] On the other hand, it criticized developing countries for the lack of measures to reduce pollution, which gave these countries a competitive advantage on the world market for 'pollution-intensive goods'. The Commission added:

> Yet it is in the developing countries' own long-term interest that more of the environmental and resource costs associated with production be reflected in prices. Such changes must come from the developing countries themselves.[31]

Faced with the critical situation of the ozone layer, urgent action was needed also in developing countries. The 1987 Protocol on Substances that Deplete the Ozone Layer (Montreal Protocol)[32] to the Vienna Convention for the Protection of the Ozone Layer[33] established a 'financial mechanism', including a 'multilateral fund'.[34] The mechanism 'shall meet all agreed incremental costs' of the developing countries 'in order to enable their compliance with the control measures of the Protocol'. An important point is that contributions to the mechanism shall be *additional* to other financial transfers. This was probably the first major exception from the PPP in a state-to-state context.

In 1990, the environmental economist David W. Pearce acknowledged the need to adjust the PPP for development purposes when he wrote:

> Finally, sustainability requires a reconsideration of the international economic order. Where critical ecosystems are in the possession of the developing world the richer cannot expect their conservation, with consequent benefits to the developed world, without paying for those benefits. This will mean rethinking the 'polluter pays principle', since a country degrading its forests (the polluter) will not pay those suffering the loss of carbon-fixing values (the polluted). International conservation financing must become a key focus for the last decade of the 20th century.[35]

This approach was broadened and strengthened in the 'Rio process', and since then it has marked the North–South debate on the environment and sustainable development. In the United Nations Declaration on Environment and Development (Rio Declaration) and the 1992 Framework Convention on Climate Change, the issue was given a general application through the principle of 'common but differentiated

---

[29] World Commission on Environment and Development 1987 at 77.   [30] *Ibid.*, 88.   [31] *Ibid.*, 84.
[32] 1987 Protocol on Substances that Deplete the Ozone Layer, reprinted in 26 *International Legal Materials* (ILM) (1987) 1550. Adopted on 16 September 1987 at Montreal.
[33] 1985 Convention for the Protection of the Ozone Layer, UNEP Doc. IG.53/5, reprinted in 26 ILM (1987) 1529. Adopted on 22 March 1985 at Vienna.
[34] Montreal Protocol, note 32 above, Art. 10, later to become the Global Environment Facility (GEF). On which see Mickelson, in Chapter 15 of this Volume.
[35] Pearce 1990.

responsibilities'.[36] Special multilateral financial instruments have been developed to this effect, the most important being the Global Environmental Facility (GEF). The consequences of this are, at least on the surface, an important deviation from the PPP in the narrow sense as a principle for allocation of costs between states.

'Common but differentiated responsibilities' is considered as a principle of justice and equity in international relations.[37] This is indirectly expressed in Principle 7 of the United Nations Declaration on Environment and Development (Rio declaration):

> States have common but differentiated responsibilities. The developed coun-
> tries acknowledge the responsibility that they bear in the international pursuit
> of sustainable development in view of the pressures their societies place on
> the global environment and of the technologies and financial resources they
> command.

However, this can also be seen as an expression of the Polluter Pays Principle in a broad and general sense, and based on justice and equity: the industrialized states have already polluted the atmosphere too much, and must pay for necessary measures to clean it up, even measures taken by developing countries.[38]

5.2 The PPP in the wide sense

This point of view is strengthened when we move to an analysis of the PPP in the wide sense, related to transfrontier pollution. According to this, a polluting state has an obligation to internalize the cost of pollution damage in other states when regulating polluting activities within its borders. This coincides with another principle of international environmental law: the principle of 'non-discrimination'. Environmental effects in other countries shall be assessed and considered similarly, and be given the same weight when decisions are taken, as effects within the national borders.[39]

The economic efficiency objective behind the PPP in the wide sense applies in principle to any economic unity. The need to internalize all social costs to reach efficiency is no less when the pollution is transboundary than when it is kept within

---

[36] United Nations Declaration on Environment and Development, UN Doc. A/CONF.151/26/rev.1 (1992), 31 ILM (1992) 876, Principle 7; United Nations Framework Convention on Climate Change, reprinted in 31 ILM (1992) 849, Art. 4.

[37] Whether it is always a good principle from an environmental protection point of view is another matter, and remains controversial. A discussion of this in relation to the international climate regime is found in Kokott 1999. See also Brunnée and Shelton in, respectively, Chapters 16 and 3 in this volume.

[38] This is, from necessity, a simplification. It may, for example, be discussed whether it is fair that the members of the present generation should pay for effects that have been caused by earlier generations' actions. Caney offers a thorough and critical analysis of these and other problems of fairness in the distribution of costs of climate change mitigation and adaptation measures. See Caney 2005.

[39] The principle was first expressed in the Environment Convention of 19 February 1974, between Denmark, Finland, Iceland, Norway and Sweden (Nordic Environment Convention), 13 ILM (1974) 591.

the borders of a nation state.[40] However, to reach efficiency in a transboundary pollution context raises special methodological and institutional problems. One may again argue that the principle of common but differentiated responsibilities is one way of at least partly implementing the PPP in the wide sense. This viewpoint seems particularly valid for those international environmental problems which are mainly caused by the developed countries, such as climate change, the problem of the ozone layer, and the global spreading of toxic, persistent chemicals.

This leads into the third issue.

5.3 The PPP as a principle for liability and compensation for transfrontier pollution damage

The principle of state sovereignty in customary international law implies that a state has the right to use its natural resources according to its own decisions, while at the same time have the the responsibility to ensure that activities within their jurisdiction or control do not cause damage to the environment of other states or of areas beyond the limits of national jurisdiction.[41]

It is the last part of this principle which is of interest here. In many ways it can be compared to the general prohibition of harmful pollution in national law. It is generally understood as also implying a duty of the polluting state to compensate the damaged party, as was expressed in the *Trail Smelter* case.[42] Unfortunately, this rule is unclear, both in its content and its status. For example, it is unclear whether the state is liable if it has shown 'due diligence' and done whatever seemed reasonable to prevent the damage. It is also unclear where the liability 'threshold' lies, and what types of damage should be compensated. There is agreement in international law that a state must accept some nuisance or damage without having the right to compensation, but the borderline between what is acceptable and what is not acceptable is quite unclear. And, thirdly, a general 'proportionality principle' may apply in the sense that the damage done to the victim state should be compared to the polluting state's costs of preventing the damage. These and other questions make it quite unclear what exactly constitutes a breach of international law.[43]

---

[40] Baumol and Oates 1988, chapter 16, analyzing international environmental economics, underline that the general analysis of environmental economics 'is fully applicable to the regulation of transnational pollution'. The transfrontier pollution problem is not different from an ordinary problem of externalities among a small group of individuals.

[41] See 1972 United Nations Declaration on the Human Environment (Stockholm Declaration), UN Doc. A/CONF/48/14/Rev.1 (1972), 11 ILM (1972) 1416, Principle 21. Repeated with a slight modification ('environmental policies' changed to 'environment and development policies') in Principle 2 of the Rio Declaration of 1992, note 36 above, and expressed in the preambles to or operative parts of several global environmental conventions.

[42] 33 *American Journal of International Law* (AJIL) (1939) 182; and 35 AJIL (1941) 684.

[43] State responsibility for transfrontier damage is a complex issue in international law. Since 1978, the International Law Commission has been working on the topic of 'International Liability for Injurious Consequences

It is definitely a just rule, but it is difficult to apply. Transfrontier pollution takes place every day without any protests or legal actions by the state victim. As the principle is interpreted, it is not applicable to true global problems like climate change and the dispersion of toxic substances. The PPP could be used as an argument for strengthening and sharpening this general rule of international environmental law.

To sum up with the problem of global warming as the clear case. It is certainly in accordance with environmental justice that those parts of the world where the main sources to the problem are found shall cover their own costs of preventing further emissions, seek to internalize the global costs of climate change in their policy, and pay compensation for the damage done elsewhere.

It must be recognized, however, that the complexities of both the most important environmental problems and the international economic relations make the application of the principle difficult. Increasingly, all states are at the same time polluter and victim of pollution, as they together contribute to climate change and the deterioration of the global biodiversity. The globalization of business, trade and the economy, and the intricate web of multinational companies, makes it often very difficult, if not impossible, to identify 'the polluter' and 'victims', and allocate responsibilities and costs in accordance with conceptions of fairness and justice.

6 Conclusion

The Polluter Pays Principle has several meanings, and I have looked into three versions of the principle from a justice perspective. The main conclusion is that the principle is a just principle both as a principle for the allocation of costs to prevent pollution, a principle of internalization of the social costs of pollution, and of compensation to victims of pollution. I have mainly dealt with local situations. However, as shown in section 5 above, the PPP is basically a just principle also as a principle of the allocation of the costs of pollution and pollution abatement between states.

However, exemptions and modifications are required in order to avoid clearly unreasonable results from both a corrective justice and a distributive justice point of view. In particular, it must be applied with due account of its possible unreasonable distributive effects. And, in the perspective of global justice, it must work together with the principle of common but differentiated responsibilities. The PPP should be seen as exactly that: a principle, a starting point, a 'presumption' or 'main rule' – with modifications and exceptions required by considerations of corrective and distributive justice.

Arising out of Acts not Prohibited by International Law'. The work includes both prevention of transboundary damage from hazardous activities, and international liability in case of loss from transboundary harm arising out of hazardous activities. Three more recent consecutive reports by the Special Rapporteur, Mr P. S. Rao, are illustrative: see ILC Report A/53/10 (F), 1998, Chapter IV (B), ILC Report A/54/10 (F), 1999, Chapter IX (B), and ILC report, A/55/10, 2000, Chapter VIII. For the theoretical discussion, see also, *inter alia*, Birnie and Boyle 2002 at 181–200.

Bibliography

Baumol, W. J., and Oates, W. E., 1988. *The Theory of Environmental Policy*. 2nd edn, Cambridge: Cambridge University Press.

Birnie, P., and Boyle, A., 2002. *International Law and the Environment*. 2nd edn, Oxford: Oxford University Press.

Bugge, H. C., 1996. 'The Principles of "Polluter Pays" in Economics and Law', in Erling Eide and Roger van den Bergh (eds.), *Law and Economics of the Environment*, Oslo, 53–90.

Caney, S., 2005. 'Cosmopolitan Justice, Responsibility, and Global Climate Change'. 18 *Leiden Journal of International Law* 747.

Coase, R. H., 1960. 'The Problem of Social Cost'. 3 *Journal of Law and Economics* 1–44.

   1998. 'Notes on the Problem of Social Cost', in R. H. Coase, *The Firm, the Market, and the Law*. Chicago: University of Chicago Press.

Coleman, J. L., 1992. *Risks and Wrongs*. Cambridge Studies in Philosophy and Law, Cambridge: Cambridge University Press.

Eide, E., and Stavang, E., 2005. *Rettsøkonomi*. Oslo: Cappelen Akademisk Forlag.

Freeman, A. M., 2003. *The Measurement of Environmental and Resource Values: Theory and Methods*. 2nd edn, Washington, DC: Resources for the Future.

Garrod, G., and Willis, K. G., 1999. *Economic Valuation of the Environment – Methods and Case Studies*. Edward Elgar Publishing.

Kokott, J., 1999. 'Equity in International Law', in F. L. Tóth (ed.), *Fair Weather: Equity Concern and Climate Change*. London: Earthscan.

Macrory, R. (ed.), 2004. *Principles of European Environmental Law*. The Avosetta Series 4, Groningen.

Meissner, W., 1985. 'Prinzipen der Umweltpolitik', in Rudolf Wildeman (ed.), *Umwelt, Wirtschaft, Gesellschaft – Wege zu einem neuen Grundverständnis*. Baden-Württenberg.

OECD, 1992. *The Polluter-Pays Principle*. Paris: OECD.

Pagh, P., 1998. *Miljøansvaret*. Copenhagen.

Pearce, D., 1990. 'Being Fair to the Future', in *Towards an Ecologically Sustainable Economy*, FRN Rapport 90:6, Stockholm.

   1995. *Blueprint 4: Capturing Global Environmental Value*. London: Earthscan.

Pearce, D., and Turner, R. K., 1990. *Economics of Natural Resources and the Environment*. New York.

Pearce, W., Markandya, A., and Barbier, E., 1989. *Blueprint for a Green Economy*. London: Earthscan.

Pigou, A. C., 1924. *The Economics of Welfare*. London: Transaction Publishers.

Polinski, A. Mitchell, 1989. *An Introduction to Law and Economics*. 2nd edn, Boston and Toronto: Little, Brown & Co.

Rehbinder, E., 1972. *Politische und rechtliche Probleme des Verursacherprinzips*. Berlin.

Sadeleer, N. D., 2000. *Environmental Principles: From Political Slogans to Legal Rules*. Oxford: Oxford University Press.

Tietenberg, T., 1994. *Environmental Economics and Policy*. New York: Addison Wesley.

World Commission on Environment and Development, 1987. *Our Common Future*. Oxford: Oxford University Press.

22

Corporate activities and environmental justice: perspectives on Sierra Leone's mining

PRISCILLA SCHWARTZ

1 Introduction

This chapter explores the concept of justice in environmental law in relation to the regulation of transnational corporate activities from a developing country perspective. First, it will identify the internationally recognised principles of justice in environmental law. Second, it will illustrate the legal character and context in which justice is provided for in the conduct of corporate development activities. Having marked out the different permutations of justice in environmental law, the chapter goes on to examine its practical operation, taking the legal system of Sierra Leone as a case study. The aim here is to determine the extent to which the current legal and institutional structure for regulating corporate activities conforms with generally agreed concepts of justice. A cross-section of the country's mining laws, agreements, corporate initiatives and methods of implementation will form the backdrop for the evaluation. The chapter will also highlight the extent of international influences on corporate mining in Sierra Leone as part of the process for the realisation of environmental justice.

Sierra Leone gained recent prominence on the international arena as a result of the long civil war that engulfed the country between 1991 and 2002. That war, and the setting up of a Special Court to try those responsible for some of the worst atrocities committed during the conflict, has continued to be of interest to the international community. The role of diamonds in funding and perpetuating the conflict has also received significant attention through what has widely become known as the Kimberley Process Certification Scheme. This scheme is an innovative, voluntary system that imposes extensive requirements on participants to ensure that shipments of rough diamonds are not illegally obtained by rebel movements to finance wars against legitimate governments.[1] The operation of this scheme has, however, not been free from controversy. Even here, the role of foreign corporations as international links for marketing 'conflict diamonds' in exchange for ammunitions was uncovered. While

---

[1] See www.kimberleyprocess.com.

the Sierra Leone economy has benefited from these certification processes, this chapter is concerned with justice for the peoples and communities of Sierra Leone who have endured the adverse environmental and social effects of mining. These consequences result from corporate abuses by transnational enterprises (TNE),[2] legal uncertainty, administrative prejudices and institutional weaknesses in the regime governing the exploitation of mineral resources.

Sierra Leone has an impressive reservoir of mineral resources, and has persistently sought development through mineral exploitation, notably in the mining of diamonds, rutile, gold, bauxite, iron ore and platinum. Petroleum exploration and granite mining are recent additions. For over seventy years, such activities have been and continue to be predominantly carried out by TNEs, in particular in rural regions outside the western area. TNEs operate in the country usually as direct foreign investors, but also as locally incorporated companies, subsidiaries or as affiliates of companies based or operating in other countries. They operate upon concessionary agreements with the government which are selectively ratified as laws and maintain strong international linkages. Such is the case of Sierra Rutile Limited (SRL) and Koidu Holdings Limited (KHL), which are currently engaged in the development of rutile and kimberlite diamonds. The rest of this chapter considers in detail the agreements and activities of these two companies in Sierra Leone.

These companies maintain very few links with the domestic economy. Their exploitation of mineral resources is largely externally controlled, with outflows of wealth largely dominated by the export of 'raw' or unprocessed minerals.[3] Their activities are also influenced by policies of international financial institutions as project financiers, guarantors or insurers, while remaining elusive and subservient to weak local jurisdiction. The TNE legal regime is made more complex especially in determining their environmental responsibility, accountability and appropriate enforcement mechanisms given their transboundary character.[4]

The environmental impacts of corporate mining activities in Sierra Leone have extensive effects beyond physical damage to the natural environment and extend to severe impact on social and cultural well-being of mining communities. These communities have among other things been deprived of their traditional way of life. They have also been subjected to the inequitable allocation of resources and distribution of mining proceeds, pollution of the environment, health hazards, and enforced physical relocation with all the attendant economic and social consequences.

---

[2] The term 'TNE' is used here (as opposed to MNC or MNE or 'transboundary corporations') in relation to mining entities and companies owning or controlling production, sale or services, or otherwise engaged in direct investments internationally, and includes domestic firms and joint ventures that export part of their output; and is not limited to incorporated business entities based on parent–subsidy relations alone.

[3] Cleeve 1997 at 6.

[4] For a discussion of state borders and transnational corporations in the context of environmental justice, see also Ebbesson in Chapter 14 of this volume.

The most devastating effects are borne by the natural environment, the silent subjects of systematic abuse and mismanagement.[5]

These negative impacts of corporate mining in Sierra Leone are aggravated by the fact that, in the past, no established mechanism existed to direct responsible mining to guarantee environmental protection or invest in critical mine-related social issues. Also, no individual or corporate entity has been found legally culpable for environmental atrocities since the commencement of mining in the 1930s. Equally, no arm of government has accepted responsibility for mining-related social deprivation consequent upon development policies, nor has there been any judicial determination on the subject. Even today, despite the inclusion of environmental and social commitments in recent mining policy,[6] corporate environmental abuses are still prevalent. There is systematic exclusion of the members of the public affected by mining in decision-making, enforcement processes and benefit-sharing. Evidently, the conduct of mining has not brought about the desired objective of development as the country is rated among the least developed, amidst severe environmental degradation and adverse social consequences of such activities.

Nowhere does the concept of 'justice' in environmental law find more immediate relevance than in Sierra Leone's mining industry. The adverse environmental effects of mining not only undermine peoples' health, their ability to earn their livelihood, but do bear a direct relationship with poverty. It is therefore essential to re-evaluate these activities from an environmental justice point of view. In reaction to calls for justice for all peoples adversely affected by corporate environmental abuses including communities in Sierra Leone, there is now an overwhelming and growing international consensus that development activities must be carried out in a sustainable manner. This consensus is evidenced in the pronouncement by the international community of environmental principles which, as argued in this chapter, represent a putative programme for the realisation of the ends of justice in environmental law.

In this chapter, a distinction will be made between, on the one hand, formal methods of environment protection and, on the other hand, distributive justice, participatory (procedural) justice, corporate accountability, and cooperative justice. The chapter will examine the extent to which the current legal and institutional structures of Sierra Leone, with regard to corporate activities and mining operations, draw upon these concepts of justice. In doing so, it will focus on a cross-section of the country's mining laws, agreements, corporate initiatives and methods of implementation. Moreover, it will highlight the scope of international influences on corporate mining in Sierra Leone in order to see whether the operations meet the requirements of environmental justice.

---

[5] Such adverse effects are well documented in Schwartz 2006 at 33–7.
[6] See Core Mineral Policy (CMP), Ministry of Marine Resources, Freetown, available at www.minmines-sl.org.

2 Approaches to environmental law and justice in the context of Sierra Leone mining

2.1 Concept, movement or ideology?

'Environmental justice' has been defined by the United States Environmental Protection Agency to mean 'the fair treatment of people of all races, cultures, and incomes with respect to the development, implementation, and enforcement of environmental laws and policies, and their meaningful involvement in the decision-making processes of the government'.[7] This definition is relevant to Sierra Leone, to the extent that it advocates fairness in the application of environmental laws and policies and participation of people in the decision-making processes, especially development-related ones which are likely to impact on them.

According to David McDonald, the term concerns itself with *environmental injustices* as a complex web of political, economic and social relationships and the ways and means of rectifying or avoiding them.[8] Put more succinctly by another author, 'environmental justice' serves to highlight disproportionate impacts on minority communities, discrimination during the siting of unwanted land uses, social justice and civil rights concerns with potentially discriminatory application of environmental laws.[9] As an ideology, 'environmental justice' has been branded by three distinct labels of 'environmental equity', 'environmental racism' and 'environmental justice', the latter focusing on determinations of distribution of benefits and burdens.[10]

As a movement it has been understood in terms of the acceptance of 'grassroots political organising', a social justice movement that combines the principles of civil rights and environmental protection.[11] In fact, the articulated seventeen 'Principles of Environmental Justice' upon which a justice movement was founded aimed to address the ecological threats facing minority and disadvantaged communities.[12] But, elsewhere, 'environmental justice' has been deemed a misnomer where it is expressed largely in terms of uneven distributions of or exposure to environmental threats, but is understood instead to relate to uneven distribution of risk.[13]

Beyond this categorisation, justice is said to involve a balance of three interlinked elements of 'recognition', 'distribution' and 'participation', and moves beyond the focus on the state alone for remedies.[14] Thus, over and above an emphasis on the equal protection of laws, the corporate role in 'environmental justice' bears special significance in the sense of the disproportionate impact of lawful pollution attributable to private sector operational policies, decisions, practices and production activities, and is as much an issue for corporate social responsibility.[15] It is therefore advocated

---

[7] C. Todd Whitman, 'EPA's Commitment to Environmental Justice'. Memorandum 9 August 2004, available at the US Environmental Protection Agency website, at www.epa.gov; Popescue and Gandy 2004 at 143; Dobson 2002, 84.
[8] McDonald 2002 at 3.   [9] Monsma 2006 at 444–5.   [10] Popescue and Gandy 2004 at 145.
[11] Monsma 2006 at 445 and 451.   [12] Pinney in Monsma 2006 at 470.   [13] Stallworthy 2006 at 363.
[14] Schlosberg 2005 at 105.   [15] Monsma 2006 at 469.

that salient particulars of environmental justice principles be incorporated with the emerging global standards for corporate social responsibility and social accountability.[16]

There remain, however, marked variations in definition, terminology, mode of application and targeted subjects of 'environmental justice'.[17] This has inhibited the development of a universal model applicable to all countries. Yet this fact has been regarded as its strength, affording it the potential of a comprehensive integrated movement for justice in multiple overlapping forms. To insist on uniformity is to limit the diversity of stories of injustice, the multiple forms it takes and the variety of situations it calls for.[18] Perhaps its contribution to our understanding of justice is its inherent anthropocentric reasoning of what is 'environmental', focusing on human beings as the 'centre of concern' for protection and defining unified global and national movements in concerted action to demand justice for it. It would be wrong, however, to assume that the environmental justice movement is an autonomous concept within national legal systems.[19]

From another viewpoint, 'environmental justice' is in varying degrees derived from certain principles in international environmental law contained in the Stockholm, Rio and Johannesburg Declarations, that seek to address the increasing awareness of the damage being done to the human and natural environment as a result of development activities.[20] Concerns with justice in this context are squarely rooted, *inter alia*, in principles requiring countries to ensure that benefits from the employment of non-renewable resources are distributed, and to create formal legal redress mechanisms in the form of liability and compensation regimes for environmental damage, as well as to use international cooperation as a means of enhancing the process of justice. States must adopt common but differentiated responsibilities in environmental matters, and encourage the use of EIA, public participation, polluter responsibility and corporate accountability.[21]

In relation to Sierra Leone, these principles have implications for securing justice for victims of corporate environmental abuses in the context of mining, over and above the civil liberty or racial connotations that depict 'environmental justice' in American versions. They speak to justice through overarching objectives geared towards ensuring rights and obligation through law, administrative and judicial processes, distributive justice and more modern concepts as processes of acquiring justice, namely,

---

[16] Stallworthy 2006 at 498.
[17] See generally Low and Gleeson 1998, 201–26; Bullard 1996 at 34–5; Goldman 2006 at 122–41.
[18] Schlosberg 2004 at 116–18.   [19] Popescue and Gandy 2004 at 143.
[20] The Stockholm Declaration on the Human Environment, adopted 16 June 1972, UN Doc. A/CONF.48/141/Rev.1 at 3, 11 ILM (1973) 1416; Rio Declaration on Environment and Development, 13 June 1992, adopted by the UNCED, UN Doc. A/CONF.151/26 (Vol. 1) ILM (1992) 874; Johannesburg Declaration and Plan of Implementation UN Doc. A/CONF.199/20/Rev.1, Annex at 1–5, and 2, Annex at 7–77, both available at wwwjohannesburgsummit.org (Johannesburg Principles).
[21] Stockholm Declaration, Principles 5, 22 and 24; Rio Declaration, Principles 7, 10, 16 and 17; Johannesburg Principles.

corporate accountability and participatory and cooperative justice. The concept of environmental justice in Sierra Leone corporate mining activities does draw heavily on this paradigm. The following section will determine the extent to which the formal rules, institutions, corporate practices and international influences shape or guarantee justice for Sierra Leone's mining communities. The version of environmental justice adopted is anthroprocentric, being the most relevant in analysing the protection of Sierra Leone's mining industry.

2.2 Formal or traditional methods of protection (instrumentalism)

Environmental justice has a formal component that advocates the creation of 'rights' and obligations for the protection of humans and the natural environment. It aims to guarantee such protection in the context of appropriate legal systems to facilitate it, through the promulgation or adoption of environmental treaties, laws and regulations, enabling procedures and effective institutions (administrative or judicial). Also implicit in this articulation is the concept of equality to legal rights.[22] It should be clarified that, while formal methods of protection may not refer to justice as such, they represent approaches which may have different implications for justice, either with regard to procedure or distributive effects. In this sense, justice is understood in terms of 'moral permissibility'[23] distinguished by the kind of entity to which it is applied, rather than a specific kind of moral concern. The implementation process of this justice mechanism has been summed up as 'localisation', 'legalisation' and 'institutionalisation' and the role of sovereign states becomes paramount in effecting it.[24]

Sierra Leone does provide for formal rights of protection in corporate mining activities through the Mines and Minerals Act of 1994, the Sierra Rutile (Ratification) Act 2002 (SRA) and the Koidu Project Mining Lease (Modification and Ratification) Act 2002 (KPML) in respect of rutile and kimberlite mining.[25] Note that the Minerals Act is the parent legislation that regulates mining activities in Sierra Leone. But the SRA and the KPML were ratified by parliament upon no legal basis other than stipulations in the agreements themselves. These shall now be examined, including the institutions of the mines and environmental departments and the judiciary, to determine the extent to which the system affords or inhibits the process of justice for its mining communities. As noted by Jonas Ebbesson in this volume, the state's role in this matter is an essential justice consideration *vis-à-vis* overcoming 'environmental imperialism'.[26]

---

[22] Almond 1995 at 8–10.
[23] P. Valentyne, 'Distributive Justice', available at http://web.missouri.edu/~umcasklinechair/on-line%20papers/distributive%20justice%20(handbook).doc (last visited May 2007).
[24] Schwartz 2006.
[25] Act No. 5 of 1994 (Minerals Act); Act No. 4 of 2002 (SRA); Act No. 6 of 2002 (KPML) respectively.
[26] Ebbesson in Chapter 14 of this volume.

2.3 The Minerals Act, the SRA and the KPML

The Minerals Act contains general provisions that contemplate damage caused by mining activities to the natural and social environment, including the welfare of communities. It restricts mining in protected areas in order to protect community values and welfare. The Act also creates rights for mining communities to share benefits from such activities through taxes, licences, rents, royalties and the creation of annual funds for agricultural and community development.[27] The Act further provides an obligation to conduct EIA for holders of mining leases, creates a criminal offence and liability for breach of environmental conditions and the cancellation of mineral rights on the occurrence of environmental harm or gross violations of standards.[28]

The SRA and the KPML impose obligations and specific responsibilities on companies to minimise the adverse effects of mining on the communities where the mines are located. Both aim to ensure this through provisions that prohibit, restrict or prevent pollution or the prejudicial use of water enjoyed by communities, or to require the provision of alternative adequate water supplies to any village affected by a company's adverse use of water and to limit damage and disturbance to the local environment and population.[29] Other guarantees of community rights over and above resource allocation include provisions for contributions to development funds and non-profit foundations, compensation for damage, protection of living conditions, and the provision of resettlements programmes.[30]

On another level, the KPML indirectly incorporates such 'rules of international law as may be applicable' and requires the observance of 'best international standard'.[31] Similarly, by virtue of the Sysmin Agreement of 2005,[32] Sierra Rutile incurs further obligations under the World Bank Guidelines relating to EIA, involuntary resettlement, natural habitats, dam safety and pollution prevention.[33] Both agreements are also subject to EIA requirements under the Environmental Protection Act 2000 (EPA).[34]

The foregoing analysis of all three pieces of legislation indicates some elements of justice in some measure. For instance, in ensuring the process of justice, they formalise rights and obligations in the protection of mining communities. They introduce elements of distributive justice in the setting up of trust funds for agricultural and community development, and corrective justice in fines, imprisonment and compensation to respond to the environmental wrongs of companies. The adoption of general and specific international environmental guidelines and standards in the SRA

---

[27] Minerals Act ss. 23(b)(I)–(IV) and 107.   [28] *Ibid.*, ss. 95 (1)–(6) and 31 (1)(b).
[29] SRA, clause 10; KPML, clause 6:3:1 and clause 11.   [30] SRA, clause 10; KPML, clause 11.
[31] KPML, clauses 6:3:1 and 11:3; clause 11:1 and 2 (see also Schedule 8, para. 1); clause 21.
[32] Loan Agreement between SRL and the Government of Sierra Leone dated 2 August 2004 (Sysmin). Under this agreement, the EC will provide a grant of €25 million to the Government of Sierra Leone for lending to SRL for the latter's rutile and ilmenite mining and processing operations.
[33] Sysmin Agreement, s. 6.04.   [34] EPA, Act No. 14 of 2000, ss. 18–20.

and the KPML could influence the broad objectives of justice in mining operations. For example, the Multilateral Investment Guarantee Agency (MIGA) of the World Bank group withheld its facilities from KHL upon allegations that it failed to adhere to international environmental standards relating to EIA.[35]

However, the various acts, in particular respects, fall short of ensuring justice to the people. First, they entail no clearly defined role for the public in the mining decision-making process and in access to justice – administrative or judicial. There is no residual remedy before the courts in order to claim compensation or have environmental obligations enforced. Moreover, the sanctions for violating regulations, especially the stipulated quantum of fines in the Minerals Act, are inadequate and derisory. This provision is yet to be tested in a court of law, but, in my view, if it were to be enforced, it is unlikely to act as a deterrent on TNEs. In fact, the SRA lacks sanctions for breach of its pollution prohibition clauses, while the KPML maintains daring stabilisation clauses that limit the adoption of evolving standards and technology.[36] On a more general note, one could have difficulty ascertaining the correct legal situation of environmental obligations in formal rules due to inconsistencies, especially where laws regulating similar concerns create different obligations.

3 Institutional aspects: judiciary and administration

At another level of formalism, institutional aspects are relevant for ensuring the process of justice to the mining communities. The role of the judiciary is very important in ensuring rights and obligations in legal provisions and providing a formal redress forum for victims. Provisions in the Minerals Act, the SRA and the KPML discussed above provide for some form of judicial redress in cases of breach. These provisions unequivocally create a role for the country's judiciary in environmental decision-making and enforcement.

However, Sierra Leone's judiciary has a dismal record in the enforcement of environmental law against mining companies and officials. Moreover, there has been no attempt by the judiciary to fill gaps in the substantive content of the law by applying internationally recognised principles.[37] Thus, there is nothing in the Sierra Leone judiciary which resembles the Indian judiciary, which has adopted an explicit gap-filling technique by applying broad principles of environmental law to secure justice for communities affected by corporate development activities. For instance, in the *Dehradun Quarries* case, the Indian Supreme Court stopped mining operations, noting that any 'hardship' caused to the developers is a price that has to be paid for protecting and safeguarding the right of the people to live in a healthy environment.[38] Sierra Leone's judiciary could emulate this practice even in its application of common

---

[35] See note 57 below.   [36] KPML, clause 11:4:1.   [37] Advocated by Carnwarth 2004 at 317–18.
[38] *Rural Litigation and Entitlement Kendra* v. *State of Uttar Pradesh* (1985) 2 SCC 43; see also *Vellore Citizens Welfare Forum* v. *Union of India* (1996) 5 SCC 647.

law principles.[39] Environmental justice goals will be further enhanced by the development of generous standing rules allowing for public interest litigation at minimal cost to litigants. Other extra-judicial processes, such as the institution of the ombudsman and local inquiries, could also be utilised.

At the departmental level, there are a large number of problems making enforcement of the legislation difficult. These include state-centric albeit uncoordinated bureaucratic processes, corruption, ill-defined responsibilities between departments and lack of technical capacity on the part of regulatory bodies. A similar critique has been levied against the institutional framework of the Nigerian mining industry.[40] In a sense, these shortcomings are an unfortunate consequence of the operation of a lucrative activity in developing countries with weak institutional structures. In the case of Sierra Leone, there is no mechanism in place for addressing complaints made by persons affected by mining operations. Any available *ad hoc* meetings, arranged by mining officials in order to resolve disputes, would be viewed with suspicion, largely because there is usually collusion between government officials and the operating companies. The Environmental Board which has a mandate to investigate environmentally harmful practices and EIA is criticised for its structural and functional incapacity to effectively regulate development activities including mining.[41] In light of the foregoing shortcomings, if one is to assess Sierra Leone's environmental justice record against the standards of desirable social institutions, significant shortcomings become apparent, especially in procedural terms, as a system that affords justice to its mining communities.

4 Distributive justice: equity and fairness

A second category is commonly termed 'distributive justice'. These are normative principles designed to guide the allocation of the benefits and burdens of an economic activity and it can be transposed through formal or informal channels. It concerns the allocation of 'benefits and goods'.[42] It is also driven by the notions of equity and fairness. Equity allows for distribution and access to goods, the 'allocation of natural resources' and 'responsibility and liability for pollution'.[43] Fairness is understood as requiring that individuals get what they are *due as a matter of right* and not necessarily how much they get in relation to each other. This extends to considerations of fairness in the formulation, application and interpretation of laws aimed at regulating the adverse effects of development activities, and is determined either by the process or procedure for distribution or by a fair outcome.[44] Policy-makers and developers should, as corollaries to justice, always consider the social effects of their development

---

[39] Enforcements under tortuous common law principles of private nuisance and *Rylands* v. *Fletcher* (1868) LR 3 HL 330 is still the approach.

[40] Usman 2001 at 241–3.   [41] EPA, s. 4(e), (f) and (d).   [42] Almond 1995 at 12.

[43] Brown Weiss 1995 at 17.

[44] See Valentyne (note 23 above); International Law Association 2002 at 392; Almond 1995 at 12.

policies and the activities of TNEs, and ensure that communities are not deprived of
the benefits of mining proceeds and are protected as a matter of right from corporate
environmental burdens. This distributive component of justice is extremely important
in the environmental justice debate, and therefore the extent of application in Sierra
Leone's corporate mining is given extended treatment.

In terms of distributive justice, considerations such as benefit-sharing, equity and
fairness in the allocation of natural and financial resources due to mining communities, these are to some extent formalised in the Minerals Act, the SRA and the KPML
through requirements to set up compensation funds, environmental trust funds, agriculture and development funds and even insurance schemes. The respective funds for
agriculture and community development are in operation but do not appear to have
a well-structured mechanism for distribution of the proceeds. This has prevented the
even distribution of benefits amongst inhabitants of particular mining communities,
creating further scope for social discord.[45]

It has been suggested that local communities receive very little direct benefit from
mining revenues earned by central government.[46] Equally disturbing is the fact that
there is no legal or policy requirement holding officials accountable for such injustices.
These rights have yet to be directly and specifically secured through legislation with
provisions for individuals and communities to force official action to implement the
legislation, if distributive justice is to have any meaningful application within the
specific context of Sierra Leone's mining communities.

5 Participatory rights as justice

Participatory justice refers to a number of interrelated procedural aspects. This
includes the right of the public to have access to environmental information, participate in environmental decision-making, or gain access to a form of redress for
environmental wrongs, commonly described as 'access to justice'. This infers three
adjudication possibilities which could be administrative or judicial: to challenge the
refusal of access to information; to seek prevention of, damages for or compensation for environmentally harmful activities; and to enforce environmental laws
directly.[47] Participatory justice also borrows from other spheres of general environmental decision-making, such as planning, conservation of shared natural resources,
allocation and distribution issues, representing a broader developmental perspective
of sustainable development, which now interprets in the concept of 'good governance'
or an evolving 'environmental human rights'.[48] Agenda 21 extends participatory rights

[45] Report of Workshop on Policy Support Planning for Mining Sector held on 28–29 January 2004, Ministry
of Mines, Freetown.
[46] *Ibid.*, paras. 5ff.   [47] Pring and Noé 2002 at 44.   [48] International Law Association 2002 at 834–5.

to 'groups' and 'organisations', thus opening the door for NGOs to seek justice for disadvantaged communities.[49]

A very prominent policy and regulatory tool through which participatory justice is sought is EIA, a strategy adopted by over 70 per cent of the world's nations, including Sierra Leone.[50] EIA involves a systematic assessment of the potential environmental impact of a proposed project and its alternatives, in order to propose appropriate measures to mitigate negative environmental impacts and optimise positive effects, and assist the decision-making process by impressing the need for consultation and public participation.[51] It is in the context of the legal obligations of the SRA and the KPML to conduct EIA that the extent of community participation as a justice process is analysed below.

In the case of the SRA, the official position is that the company has a proven record of compliance with legal EIA requirements in accordance with government laws and regulations and the policies and guidelines of international lending institutions.[52] On another view, the company failed to effect actual and constructive dialogue with local people, but, that notwithstanding, did obtain an EIA licence upon publication of an assessment report. Company consultants did undertake a 'fast track' assessment project, which allegedly involved 'public consultation disclosure'. Yet the report claims to have relied heavily on the 'recall by SRL site personnel' in some respects and on independent profiling of site conditions.[53] Both methods hardly suggest community involvement at any stage. The procedure was, however, 'valid' enough to secure grants and loans from SRL's international financiers including the European Development Fund (EDF). The EDF does mandate the conduct of EIA, including requirements that public participation and consultation of stakeholders be integrated into this process within the local institutional framework. The Dutch Directorate-General for International Cooperation (DGIS) did request an evaluation of the environmental aspects of the project proposal of the reopening of the Sierra Rutile Mine, and the Netherlands Commission on EIA offered to comment on the EIA report when requested by the European Union. It is not clear whether any such request or review was conducted as was done for the Limestone Open Pit Mine at Obajana, Nigeria.[54]

---

[49] Agenda 21, UN Doc. A/CONF.151/26 (vols. I–III), reprinted in Quarrie 1992 at Chapter 23:2.

[50] 'Rio Declaration on Environment and Development: Application and Implementation', Report of the Secretary General, UN Commission on Sustainable Development, 5th Session, UN Doc. E/CN.17/1997/8 (1997).

[51] See Environmental Mainstreaming in EC Development Cooperation, available at www.environment-integration.org/EN/D123_EIA.htm.

[52] Kamara, Mansaray and Wright in 2003.

[53] See J. Sisay (Director of Operations, Sierra Rutile Ltd, Freetown), *Executive Summary to Sierra Rutile Environmental and Social Impact Assessment Report*, Vol. 1, October 2001, prepared by Knight Piésold Consultants, available at the Ministry of Mineral Resources, Freetown, Sierra Leone.

[54] See Advice No. 0315, 18 September 2003; and Advice No. 0501, 10 January 2005, available at www.eia.nl/ncea/products/secretariat.htm

In respect of KHL, community participation was allegedly solicited by consultants acting on its behalf.[55] Contrary claims suggest that the local communities never made an input on the EIA and were unrepresented and completely ignorant of any agreement made between the company and the government.[56] KHL is reported to have carried out blasting operations without adequate resettlement action plans.[57] Yet the company's consultants maintain that the affected people were squatters on KHL lease areas, who had deliberately trespassed thereon in order to acquire new homes through the process of relocation. Overall, the participatory dimension of justice needs to be improved on through clearly defined legal rights for mining communities with provisions to access justice including state-funded class actions to compel corporate adherence to their obligations.

6 Corporate accountability

Making TNEs accountable for the social and environmental externalities of their activities and policies has, since the WSSD, received wide support. The strategy to ensure this has been termed variously as corporate accountability, corporate responsibility (CR) or corporate social responsibility (CSR). Each of these dimensions in relation to the behaviour of TNEs are susceptible to being portrayed as an ethical or moral commitment to behave responsibly; as a legal corporate regulation; or as a risk-management instrument geared towards addressing the concept of environmental justice understood here as what TNEs morally owe to victims of corporate *abuses*, where this is a matter of respecting each person's rights. According to the European Coalition for Corporate Justice (ECCJ), measures are necessary to ensure all corporations abide by national and internationally agreed standards for human rights, labour rights and environmental rights.[58]

Thus corporate accountability can ensure justice through transparent regulations, international initiatives, public–private partnerships and effective municipal legal systems.[59] On the one hand, the strategy speaks to the responsibilities of states to regulate and adjudicate corporate activities through administrative sanctions and judicial punitive measures based on corporate liability or responsibility for violation of legal obligations, such as undertaking EIA. On the other hand, it concerns voluntary responsibility identified as individual company initiatives or industry activity potentially covering all actions not required by legislation undertaken as a moral

---

[55] Cemmats Consultants, 'Notification of the Development of a Diamond Mine in Koidu, Sierra Leone, by Branch Energy', Freetown, 2003.

[56] A. Kamara, 'Human Rights, Mining and the People of Kono', available at www.minesandcommunities.org.

[57] See Bank Information Center, 'Civil Society Groups in Sierra Leone Voice Concerns About Proposed MIGA Project', available at www.bicusa.org.

[58] Olivier de Schutter, 'Towards Corporate Accountability for Human and Environmental Rights Abuses', ECCJ Discussion Paper No 1, available at www.corporate-accountability.org/eng/28/04/2007.

[59] Johannesburg Principles, note 20 above.

duty to redress wrongs or avoid them.[60] To what extent is this paradigm of corporate accountability applicable to SRL's and KHL's activities in Sierra Leone?

The scope of accountability of SRL and KHL is thus defined by their legal obligations as well as by possible voluntary initiatives undertaken (such as any industry guidelines), which in particular instances may include international best practice in development planning. In relation to compliance with the formal obligations, corporate accountability is mixed. On the one hand, general evidence suggests that both companies are meeting their responsibilities relating to payments of licences, fees and contributions to funds even though, as already mentioned, the distribution mechanism is inadequate. SRL is noted to have violated international resettlement and environmental guidelines before.[61] Even today, local people seriously affected by mining operations have obtained no redress or compensation.

If legislation and administrative control has failed to provide justice, could this be achieved through voluntary measures undertaken by the corporations concerned? As a voluntary initiative, SRL maintains aquaculture fishing facilities to improve resource allocation. KHL participates in the kimberley process certification scheme that currently reflects international best practice in the diamond-mining industry. KHL may have also shown good practice to some extent when, during a confrontation with the local inhabitants over its mining lease area, it undertook dialogue and voluntarily agreed to construct additional homes, and to include community participation in the planning, layout and design of the dwellings yet to be built.[62]

Overall, the extent to which SRL and KHL adopt international best practice in their operations before and after the scrutiny of EIA is not clear. Companies are accused of conducting EIA not so much out of compliance with legal requirements, but largely through a desire to obtain environmental certificates in compliance with other international demands.[63] Once this is obtained, they are known to take advantage of the weak inconsistent rules and collude with officials against the interests of the communities affected by mining operations. These conditions truly impede the processes of justice. It would therefore help the course of justice if international lending institutions placed equal emphasis on company violations of statutory prohibitions as they place on documentation of environmental and social impacts. By doing so, they would enhance company compliance with national legal requirements. This would provide the basis upon which environmental justice could be truly localised and corporate accountability effectively monitored and measured.

---

[60] For more analysis, see Mullerat 2004 at 236; and Walker and Howard 2002.

[61] See Friends of the Earth (USA), *Review for Sierra Rutile Limited*, 20 July 1997; and 'Sierra Leone: Another Round of Mining Difficulties?', available at http://www.wbcsd.ch/plugins/DocSearch/.

[62] L. Lartigue, 'USAID's PDA Mediates Community Dispute in Kono' March 30, 2004 available at www.usaid.gov/sl/sl_new/news/2004/040401_khblasting/index.htm (visited 29 July 2008).

[63] A. Sellu, Director of Environment, Ministry of Lands, Housing, Country Planning and the Environment, Youyi Building, Freetown, Sierra Leone. Interviewed by author in December 2004.

7 Cooperative aspects of justice

The notion of cooperative justice appeals largely to ethical and moral issues but also has a firm root in the norms and underlying principles of the United Nations Charter, which seek to achieve international cooperation in solving international problems of an economic, social, cultural or humanitarian character, and in promoting and encouraging respect for human rights and for fundamental freedoms for all.[64] The imperative of economic, social, political and legal cooperation represents a global response to the need for justice in the sense of addressing the disproportionate wealth and power struggle between *rich North* and *poor South* nations of an environmentally interconnected and interdependent global heritage.[65]

Efforts in this regard are directed through international institutions' commitment of development aid, technical assistance and specific privileges for developing countries on the one hand, and the formulation of policies, guidelines and best practices that will attract investment and enhance development objectives on the other.[66] Cooperative justice will thus require the transnational application of law beyond national prescriptions and conditions against persons or entities that perpetuate environmental wrongs or violate internationally recognised environmental and human rights norms. It essentially also advocates transnational enforcements to secure justice for environmental victims.[67] It also acts as a constraint on the attempts by TNEs to evade accountability by taking advantage of inadequate national institutions and laws.[68]

Corporate activities in Sierra Leone are dominated by international influences in various ways. This includes aid and technical assistance given by international institutions. Many financial institutions also act as lenders and guarantors of projects undertaken by TNEs. Many of these agreements take place on the international level and are enforced through the medium of bilateral investment agreements as well as by diplomatic interventions. Although corporations are, technically speaking, not subject to international law, they are increasingly forced to submit to the jurisdiction of arbitral forums by way of compulsory arbitration clauses contained in investment agreements. The pressures of the global trading system and competition policies force company adherence to international industry standards. Lastly, the presence of NGOs

---

[64] UN Charter, preamble, para. 3, and Art. 1(3).

[65] Declaration of International Law Concerning Friendly Relations and Cooperation Among States in accordance with the United Nations Charter, UNGA Res. 2625 of 24 October 1970.

[66] Examples include OECD Declaration and Decisions on International Investment and Multinational Enterprises (Paris: OECD, 1992); the Doha Development Agenda and Monterrey Consensus on Development Financing.

[67] Ingleson, Urzúa and Holden 2006 at 61–3. See also 'ILC Draft Principles on Environmental Liability', (2005) 17 *Journal of Environmental Law* 155; Lugano Convention on Jurisdiction and the Enforcement of Judgments in Civil and Commercial Matters (88/592/EEC), [1988] OJ L319/9; Alien Tort Claims Act, 28 USC § 1350 (2004); ILA, 'Transnational Enforcement of Environmental Law' (Second Report) (2004) (ILA/TEEL) Berlin Conference (2004), available at www.ila-hq.org.

[68] See Ebbesson in Chapter 14 of this volume.

as non-state actors on the international arena is the predominant influence shaping environmental justice objectives.

Where international institutions finance or guarantee corporate projects, these institutions will impose their own environmental policies and standards on companies as conditions upon which they would finance or guarantee such projects. For instance, under the Sysmin agreement, the European Union, in its financing of SRL, insisted upon the observance of the World Bank guidelines, which until now were omitted from the company's guidelines.[69] The intention is to ensure that mining operations are carried out in accordance with sound practice, and with minimal impact on communities. However, they are nevertheless of a finite duration. In most cases, compliance with environmental and social obligations underpinning them will only last for the duration of the loan rather than until the completion of the project.[70] Thus, since the loan to SRL was technically made in favour of the government of Sierra Leone, that country's already weak regulatory and enforcement mechanism will have to be relied on.

The effect of international donor relations in Sierra Leone goes beyond imposing international standards in mining agreements. Other influences are apparent in mining legislation and policy reform. Donors, particularly UNAMSIL, the UK government's Department for International Development (DFID), USAID and the World Bank have supported the government of Sierra Leone in the development of the Core Mineral Policy (CMP) which improves on earlier ones by its unique inclusion of corporate social responsibility, and details measures by which government aims to institute and enforce them. USAID technical assistance and policy dialogue, for the first time, made it possible for local diamond mining communities to receive direct financial benefits in proportion to the legal mining taking place within their chiefdoms.[71] The World Bank funded a review of all aspects of the mining industry, with special emphasis on the legal framework, mineral laws and regulations.[72] This practice has most recently also been implemented in the Democratic Republic of Congo, which is expected to review three of its biggest mining contracts after the World Bank questioned the transparency of the contracts.[73] Such reviews improve transparency and help to uncover obstacles to effective application of the justice mechanisms in various forms. For instance, the Sierra Leone EC Cooperation mid-term reviews highlighted problems of impunity and abuse of power in both the customary and the formal

---

[69] Sysmin Agreement (note 32 above), s. 6.04. For applicable World Bank Guidelines see s. 1.01.
[70] *Ibid.*, s. 6.05 and Exhibit A (B).
[71] Julie Koenen-Grant, Mark Renzi and Laura Lartigue, 'Sierra Leone Peace Diamonds', available at www.usaid.gov/sl/(last visited June 2007).
[72] Wright 2002 at 1.
[73] 'Congo to Review Three Top Mining Contracts After World Bank Scrutiny', available at www.marketwatch.com/news/.

judicial sectors.[74] The reviews were conducted to ensure equal access by the general population to a competent and fair system for the administration of justice.

Also, KHL was able to obtain a political risk guarantee from MIGA, the chief insurance agency of the World Bank Group. MIGA later withheld its insurance facility from the company, after allegations were made of breach of community participation and resettlement requirements provided for under domestic law. It was this threat by MIGA to withhold approval that triggered official attention and consideration of concerns of the local community which until then had largely been ignored.[75] The efforts of NGOs and the civil society coalition in influencing the MIGA decision and their vigilance in several other respects in the campaign for justice for mining communities should also be mentioned. These groups represent the wave of environmental justice movement in Sierra Leone, although, unlike developments in South Africa and the United States, this movement has not been driven by concerns about 'civil rights', racial prejudice, migration or marginalisation of poor communities.

It is clear that international influences play a significant role in enhancing the effectiveness of judicial processes for the purpose of enforcing environmental rights and obligations. There is in general a preference for arbitration such as under the ICSID regime. However, the operation of these arbitral frameworks is largely influenced by concerns over investment protection rather than social justice. It is suggested that there is still a distinct role for transnational enforcement especially by courts in developed countries where companies are incorporated or have their registered offices. Cases have been litigated in recent years with respect to access to justice for overseas victims of TNEs. One such case, *Shalke Willem Lubbe et al* v. *Cape* plc, concerned South African asbestos victims claiming in England.[76] In another case, *Wiwa* v. *Royal Dutch Petroleum Co*, claims were brought in the US for human rights violations by Shell in the Ogoni region of Nigeria.[77] These legal trends could enhance the cause of the environmental justice in a fundamental way.[78] This is important considering the largely multinational and transnational nature of most of the companies holding various mineral rights in developing countries, including Sierra Leone.

While international influences can facilitate domestic measures promoting environmental justice, such as through coercion and leverage, representatives of international institutions including diplomatic missions are not unknown for their manipulation of local processes. This is often done in favour of companies which share their interest

---

[74] 9th EDF Mid-Term Review, 2004, available at www.delsle.cec.eu.int/en/pr/ar-2003/Annual-Report-2003.doc, p. 10.

[75] An agreement was signed in September 2004 between 112 property owners in the 'blast zones' and KHL representatives, in which KHL had agreed to pay for the relocation of their houses. See Lartigue, note 62 above.

[76] See Judgment of House of Lords delivered on 20 July 2000; R. Meeran, 'Access to Courts for Corporate Accountability: Recent Developments' available at www.minesandcommunities.org/company.

[77] See 226 F 3d 88 (2nd Cir. 2000). See generally Belgore 2003.

[78] See also Ebbesson's analysis on the 'triangular constellation' of transboundary environmental justice in Chapter 14 of this volume.

whether by nationality or as stakeholders. In one case, the DFID policy advisor to the department of mineral resources had recommended that the current Sierra Leonean Director General in the mines department be replaced by a British national. As it turned out, this same advisor moved to become Director of KHL when that recommendation could not be implemented.[79] Such conflicts of interest are not uncommon in an industry that is dominated by wealth and power struggle.

8 Conclusion

Environmental justice in Sierra Leone's corporate mining is neither indicative of concerns with issues of racial or ethnic discrimination nor is it evidence of project location biases against local communities. Minerals come with the territory; a fact that deprives political, administrative or other agency machinery of location manipulations. The real concern for environmental justice in the country is how to protect the rights of communities from the adverse effects of mining, corporate power and influences, in tandem with corrupt officials and weak institutions. The approaches to justice in environmental law identified herein can serve this purpose. It has been applied in the country in some measure, both in the context of formal and informal guarantees of protection; and in the practical appreciation of its principles of distributive justice. International efforts in directing cooperative justice are evident and probably more reliable in the current assessment, though not the most effective. Corporations are learning the hard way of the importance of accountability to local institutions. Progress in developing a coherent framework of accountability is likely to be influenced in the main by developments in the US and UK, which increasingly advocate the transnational application of laws and enforcement mechanisms in the pursuit of cooperative justice. To their credit, but also in part as a result of pressure from NGOs and civil society, mining communities are increasingly becoming aware of the various environmental justice mechanisms as a process. Yet environmental justice will remain elusive under the current institutional structures no matter how compliant or motivated TNEs become.

Bibliography

Almond, B., 1995. 'Rights and Justice in the Environmental Debate', in D. Cooper and J. Palmer (eds.), *Just Environments*, London: Routledge.

Belgore, Y., 2003. 'Forum Non Conveniens in England and USA for Litigation Against Oil Multinationals'. 1 *Oil Gas and Energy Law Intelligence*. Issue 1.

Brown Weiss, E., 1995. 'Environmental Equity – The Imperative for the 21st Century', in W. Lang (ed.), *Sustainable Development and International Law*. London, Dordrecht and Boston: Graham & Trotman and Martinus Nijhoff.

---

[79] An official of the Department of Mines, who wished to remain anonymous.

Bullard, R., 1996. 'Environmental Justice Challenges at Home and Abroad', in N. Low (ed.), *Global Ethics and Environment*. London: Routledge.

Carnwarth, R., 2004. 'Judicial Protection of the Environment at Home and Abroad'. 16 *Journal of Environmental Law* 317.

Cleeve, E. A., 1997. *Multinational Enterprises in Development: The Mining Industry of Sierra Leone:* Aldershot: Ashgate Publishing Group.

Dobson, B., 2002. 'Searching for a Common Agenda', in D. A. McDonald, (ed.), *Environmental Justice in South Africa*. Athens, OH: Ohio University Press.

Goldman, B., 2006. 'What Is the Future of Environmental Justice'. 26 *Antipode* 122.

Ingleson, A., Urzúa, A., and Holden, W., 2006. 'Mine Operator Liability for the Spill of an Independent Contractor in Peru'. 24 *Journal of Energy and Natural Resource Law* 53.

International Law Association, 2002. *Report of the 70th Conference (New Delhi)*. London: International Law Association.

Kamara, U. B., Mansaray, M. B., and Wright, L., 2003. *Mining Annual Review 2003: Sierra Leone*.

Low, N., and Gleeson, B., 1998. 'Situating Justice in the Environment: The Case of BHP at the Ok Tedi Copper Mine'. 30 *Antipode* 201.

McDonald, D. A., 2002. 'What Is Environmental Justice', in D. A. McDonald (ed.), *Environmental Justice in South Africa*. Athens, OH: Ohio University Press.

Monsma, D., 2006. 'Environmental Rights, Governance and the Environment: Integrating Environmental Justice Principles in Corporate Social Responsibility'. 33 *Ecology Law Quarterly* 443.

Muchlinski, P. T., 2003. *Multinational Enterprises and the Law*. Oxford: Blackwell.

Mullerat, R., 2004. 'The Still Vague and Imprecise Notion of Corporate Social Responsibility'. 32 *International Business Lawyer* No. 5.

Popescu, M., and Gandy, H., 2004. 'Whose Environmental Justice?'. 19 *Journal of Environmental Law and Litigation* 141.

Pring, G., and Noé, S. Y., 2002. 'The Emerging International Law of Public Participation Affecting Global Mining, Energy and Resource Development', in D. M. Zillman, A. Lucas and G. Pring (eds.), *Human Rights in Natural Resources Development*. Oxford: Oxford University Press.

Quarrie, J. (ed.), 1992. *Earth Summit '92*. London: Regency Press Corp.

Schlosberg, D., 2004. 'Reconceiving Environmental Justice: Global Movements and Political Theories'. 13 *Environmental Politics* No. 3.

Schwartz, P., 2006. *Sustainable Development and Mining in Sierra Leone*. Belvedere: Pneuma Springs Publishing.

Stallworthy, M., 2006. 'Sustainability Development, Coastal Erosion and Climate Change: An Environmental Justice Analysis'. 18 *Journal of Environmental Law* No. 3.

Usman, N. L., 2001. 'Environmental Regulation in the Nigerian Mining Industry'. 19 *Journal of Energy and Natural Resources Law* 241.

Walker, J., and Howard, S., 2002. *Finding the Way Forward: How Could Voluntary Action Move Mining Towards Sustainable Development*. London: Environmental Resource Management (ERM), International Institute for Environmental Development (IIED) and World Council on Sustainable Business Development (WCSBD).

Wright, L., 2002. 'Sierra Leone', in *Mining Annual Review*. London: Mining Journal Ltd.

23

Environmental justice and international trade law

NICOLAS DE SADELEER

1 Introduction

The aim of this chapter is to answer the question whether environmental justice could influence the trade–environment debate. At the outset, one needs to define the concept of environmental justice. Environmental injustice in this context occurs whenever some individual or group bears disproportionate environmental risks, or has unequal access to environmental goods.[1] The issue of environmental (in)justice usually arises with respect to the localisation of hazardous plants close to poor urban communities or minorities. Given that they have fewer resources to defend their interests than richer communities, these poor neighbourhoods have less ability to challenge administrative decisions entailing environmental risks imposed on them. Understood in this sense, environmental (in)justice is largely an American concept, that has never really gained a strong foothold in Europe. Moreover, this topic is related more to polluting installations and access to natural resources than to free trade.

Thanks to the entry into force of the 1994 Marrakesh Agreement, free trade liberalisation in goods and services has been gaining momentum. The WTO provides not only the principal forum for negotiations on multilateral trading issues, its rules underpin to some extent the development of international as well as municipal environmental law. In this context, free trade has been sparking off heated debates also with respect to fairness as to the access to natural resources.

First, free trade has been criticised for widening the economic gaps between nations. Indeed, not every nation is taking advantage of the increase in trading in goods. Obviously, marked differences in terms of economic development can be observed across the world. The increase in production, and as a result in trade, has been concentrated in a number of countries. By way of illustration, if Asia represents 50 per cent of the world's economic exchange, Africa contributes only 1 per cent.[2] As a result, disparities in income between rich and poor countries have widened.

Furthermore, free trade has been criticised as a significant factor compounding the environmental crisis. For instance, the liberalisation of trade could unleash a

---

[1] Shrader-Frechette 2002 at 3.   [2] Castri 1996 at 71.

flow of economic investments, which could generate an uncontrollable process of environmental degradation across the globe. The situation is aggravated by the resulting overexploitation of natural resources for trading purposes, which may accelerate environmental changes, and these changes may in turn impinge negatively upon regional or local economic development. By way of example, the economic impacts of over-harvesting natural resources, such as timber or fish, can compound the vulnerability of these resources, on which indigenous populations depend for their livelihoods.

This chapter does not focus on these deeply contested issues. Rather, it takes a fresh look at this debate from a legal perspective, by comparing the developments and considerations in international law with those of the European Union (EU) (formally speaking, the European Community, EC). In this respect, account must be taken of the fact that we have been experiencing in these last decades two parallel developments without precedent in the history of mankind. On the one hand, the emergence of ecological crises of global scope (climate change, loss of biodiversity, ozone depletion) leading to the enactment of a flurry of international agreements. On the other hand, a progressive liberalisation of world trade, embodied at the international level by the conclusion of the Uruguay Round in 1994, leading to the establishment in 1995 of the World Trade Organization (WTO), and at the European level by the functioning of the internal market. Underlying these parallel developments is a clash of legal rules on several fronts that go well beyond the disputes of the past. The doctrine of free trade, based on the premise that products should be able to circulate freely without hindrance from technical obstacles erected by states, is diametrically opposed to national or regional regulations in the areas of public health or environmental protection. Indeed, the need to open up markets directly conflicts with the need to promote legitimate environmental objectives; until now, efforts to reconcile these two goals have been rather unsuccessful.

Although the academic literature on the relationship between trade and environment is rife with controversies, issues of environmental justice have not gathered momentum so far. In most cases, the genuinely environmental considerations are usually taken into consideration in this debate (conservation of protected species, waste management, clean air) irrespective of the groups at risk. That said, products such as waste or pesticides could nonetheless have a significant effect on the environment of poor people or minorities. Depending on their composition, their production method and how they are used, they can become a source of pollution, or they can entail specific hazards. Given that they have less access to education, populations of poorer countries could more easily become vulnerable to these products. Moreover, cheap products can entail greater hazards for consumers unable to purchase better quality products.

In an attempt to manage these conflicts and facilitate commercial exchanges, international organisations have sought to harmonise national rules (positive harmonisation) by agreeing on common standards. Nevertheless, positive harmonisation is difficult to achieve at the international level, and even at the EC level. When no common ground can be found between states that do not share the same goals, free trade is encouraged by a principle of mutual recognition that allows goods lawfully produced and marketed in one state to be commercialised in another state (negative harmonisation), and by placing the burden of proof on the states which impose stricter standards in order to achieve a higher level of protection than those applied in the producer country.

Ideally, free trade presupposes that states share a concept of product safety on the one hand and of human health and the environment on the other hand. In real life, however, goals for the protection of human health, the environment, consumers, as well as some specific social groups vary appreciably from one state to another.

2 International environmental trade measures driven by justice considerations

Although the United Nations Conference on Environment and Development[3] has expressed some scepticism towards the use of trade measures enacted with the aim of fostering the effectiveness of international environmental agreements, this did not preclude the enactment of further trade restriction regimes. In this connection, a few examples will suffice. The Montreal Protocol on Substances that Deplete the Ozone Layer adopts trade controls that are more restrictive as to non-parties than parties. CITES allows the enactment of punitive trade restrictions on non-complying parties. In so doing, parties to these agreements enact legal regimes that could hinder trading rights stemming from other international agreements, and in particular those laid down in the WTO agreements. Nonetheless, it should be stressed that, among the hundreds of environmental treaties, only a small number of MEAs allow their parties to restrict the trade in specific goods as a means for increasing their effectiveness. For instance, restrictions on trade with other parties as well as non-parties may be set out with a view to protecting the populations of poorer countries unable to protect themselves against particular risks. Conversely, the vast majority of international agreements concluded with a view to protecting the environment, such as the 1971 Ramsar Convention on Wetlands of International Importance,[4] or the 1991 Helsinki Convention on Environmental Impact Assessment in a Transboundary Context,[5] do not regulate trading activities. Since most international environmental agreements purport to protect the global commons and not to regulate trade, and since only few WTO litigations so far concerned the validity of international environmental agreements, one could take the view that the trade–environment debate is nothing but a purely academic exercise, at least as far as conformity of MEAs with WTO rules

---

[3] 1992 United Nations Declaration on Environment and Development, 31 *International Legal Materials* (ILM) (1992) 876.

[4] 1971 Convention on Wetlands of International Importance Especially as Waterfowl Habitat, 11 ILM (1972) 963, amended in 1982, 22 ILM (1983) 698.

[5] 1991 Convention on Environmental Impact Assessment in a Transboundary Context, 30 ILM (1991) 800.

are concerned. That said, an assessment as to whether the few international agreements allowing their parties to curtail trading rights were driven by environmental justice considerations or were underpinned by a more technocratic approach gives a rather nuanced answer.

Since waste disposal has featured prominently in the environmental justice movement (waste facilities are often located in minority and poor communities), the international regulation of trading in hazardous wastes appears to be a good case in point. Public awareness of potential threats from inadequate waste disposal as well as the rising costs of complying with waste regulations fostered the emergence of an international trade in hazardous wastes.[6] For a long while, the dumping of wastes on less developed or poorer countries in Africa or in Latin America was left unchecked. The discrepancy in costs has been clearly considered the result of lower environmental standards in the countries importing waste.[7]

However, in the course of the 1980s, this trade in waste began to be commonly associated with egregious cases of waste dumping by undertakings from OECD countries on poorer countries. Indeed, a spate of scandals sparked off a protracted debate as to the responsibility of industrialised countries. The concerns about the ecological and human damage attributable to this practice resulted in the negotiations, under the auspices of UNEP, of an international agreement of global application. The outcome of the negotiations, the 1989 Basel Convention on the Transboundary Movement of Hazardous Wastes (Basel Convention)[8] had the initial purpose of regulating trade in hazardous wastes from developed to less developed countries.[9] The Convention is the product of a particular set of circumstances that occurred in the 1980s, and its *ratio legis* must be understood in light of the contentious process between developing countries, advocating a ban on transboundary movements of wastes, and developed countries, arguing for regulation of these movements.

However, the call for a ban was not endorsed. Aiming at promoting the protection of human health and of the environment, the Convention was intended to minimise the generation of wastes and to control their transboundary movements instead of banning them. In other words, the Convention was based on notification rather than prohibition. To achieve these objectives, trade-related environmental measures (TREMs) were laid down. For instance, waste exports are prohibited to countries that have banned such imports.[10] Likewise, the Convention requires that states of export ban shipments of hazardous wastes if there are reasons to believe that these will not be managed in an environmentally sound manner in the country of import.[11] In addition, exports and imports of hazardous and other wastes by parties to the Convention to and from non-parties are banned.[12]

---

[6] Kummer 1999 at 6–7.   [7] *Ibid.* at 7.
[8] 1989 Basel Convention on the Transboundary Movement of Hazardous Wastes, 28 ILM (1989) 657.
[9] O'Neill 2000 at 37.   [10] Basel Convention, note 8 above, Art. 4(1)(e).
[11] *Ibid.*, Art. 4(2)(e).   [12] *Ibid.* Art. 4(5).

Following the publicity given to cases of illegal waste dumping, many African countries, with the support of non-governmental organisations (NGOs) such as Greenpeace, have begun again to advocate a global ban on hazardous wastes with the objective of protecting the poorer countries from the toxic imperialism of industrialised countries. In response to the frustration of the African countries, work on an African convention on hazardous wastes began, under the auspices of the Organization of African Unity, shortly after the adoption of the Basel Convention. This resulted in the adoption in 1991 of the Bamako Convention on the Ban of the Import into Africa and the Control of Transboundary Movement of Hazardous Wastes within Africa (Bamako Convention).[13] Likewise, several decisions of the Conference of the Parties (COP) of the Basel Convention were enacted, in 1992 and 1994, in order to ban the export of hazardous wastes from OECD to non-OECD countries.[14] Finally, in 1995, it was proposed at the instigation of the Nordic countries that the ban enshrined in the 1994 COP decision should be formally incorporated by way of a new provision into the Basel Convention.[15] However, this amendment to the Convention has not yet entered into force.

Needless to say, a ban on waste movements from developed to developing countries mirrors a strong public perception that industrialised nations should keep their own wastes and not dispose of them in poorer countries. To some extent, both the Bamako Convention and the Basel Convention reflect the aim of fostering the disposal of hazardous wastes in an environmentally sound manner (principle of prevention) as close as possible to the place where they have been generated (proximity principle), and to minimise the production of wastes (principle of rectification of environmental harm at source).[16] Since the entry into force of the 1989 Basel Convention, the worst forms of waste dumping in developing countries have ceased. Despite its relative success, vigorous debate has ensued as to the extent to which the provisions of the Basel Convention are compatible with WTO regimes.[17] So far, this controversy rumbles on unresolved. Different solutions to solve this conundrum were set forth and discussed in Geneva. These solutions range from amending GATT Article XX to endorsing a collective interpretation of that provision with the aim of validating existing MEAs.[18]

The 1998 Rotterdam Convention on the Prior Informed Consent Procedure for Certain Hazardous Chemicals and Pesticides in International Trade (Rotterdam Convention) is also illustrative of the evolving regimes of trade in hazardous wastes.[19] This Convention contains several lists of chemicals, classified as especially hazardous, which are subject to a procedure known as the 'Prior Informed Consent procedure'

---

[13] Kummer 1999 at 99–102.   [14] Krueger 1999 at 31–2.   [15] Kummer 1999 at xxviii–xxxvi.

[16] 1991 Convention on the Ban of Import into Africa and the Control of Transboundary Movement and Management of Hazardous Wastes Within Africa, 30 ILM (1991) 775; Basel Convention, note 8 above, Art. 4A.

[17] Calster 2000.   [18] Birnie and Boyle 2000 at 706; Calster 2000.

[19] 1998 Rotterdam Convention on the Prior Informed Consent Procedure for Certain Hazardous Chemicals and Pesticides in International Trade, 38 ILM (1999) 1.

('PIC procedure'). The chemicals subject to the PIC procedure can be exported only if the *prior consent of the country of destination* has been given. In this respect, the Rotterdam Convention enables importing countries to oppose the import of hazardous chemicals on the ground that they could harm vulnerable groups of people. Some pesticides producers have been contending with this procedure on the ground that it could be inconsistent with WTO obligations.

Whether or not they were driven by environmental justice considerations, both the Basel and the Rotterdam Conventions have been criticised for abridging trading rights stemming from the WTO legal regime. In this respect, one should bear in mind that, despite the aim of the WTO, set out in the preamble, i.e. 'an optimal use of the world's resources in accordance with the objective of sustainable development', the fundamental principles of the GATT remain unaltered; environmental concerns are still considered an irritating obstacle in the trading community. Indeed, Principle 12 of the Rio Declaration on Environment and Development, by stating that '[t]rade policy measures for environmental purposes should not constitute a means of arbitrary or unjustifiable discrimination or a disguised restriction on international trade', in its own way also recognises the primacy of free trade over environmental interests. Furthermore, Principle 12 clearly discourages unilateral action to deal with environmental challenges outside the jurisdictions of importing countries; transboundary or global issues should be based, as far as possible, on international consensus.

3 EU environmental trade measures and justice considerations

3.1 EU internal market: negative harmonisation

In the European context, considerable tension exists between protection of the environment and the operation of the internal market as regards conditions relating to placing products on the market. Since products are intended to circulate and to be the subject of physical movement for the purpose of trade, national environmental requirements may impede ease of access to the market of the member state, taking the measure in question. This tension between trade and environmental justice has different permutations depending on whether the measures in question are also the subject-matter of European harmonising legislation.

It is equally important to stress that the Treaty Establishing the European Community (EC Treaty) at Articles 28 and 29 prohibits quantitative restrictions on imports and exports as well as all measures having equivalent effect, which affects trade between member states. Any trade measures taken by member states, which is likely to restrict intra-Community trade – directly or indirectly, actually or potentially – is to be considered a measure with effects equivalent to a quantitative restriction. However, this is not an absolute prohibition. At present, two types of measures with potential barriers to trade are permitted, subject to very specific conditions.

The first is based on the exception set out in the EC Treaty, Article 30, which permits restrictions to intra-Community trade, provided that they could be based on the following reasons: public morality; public policy; public security; the protection of the health and life of humans, animals or plants; the protection of national treasures possessing artistic, historic or archaeological value; or the protection of industrial or commercial property. Moreover, they are subject to the condition that they do not constitute a means of arbitrary discrimination or a disguised restriction on trade between member states.

The second possibility arose from the extensive interpretation of the EC Treaty by the European Court of Justice (ECJ), in what is know as the *Cassis de Dijon* case.[20] In this case, the ECJ was led to rule on restrictions of a quantitative character which had been drawn up at national level in order to meet objectives other than those mentioned in the EC Treaty, among them protection of the environment. In doing so, and drawing from the *Cassis de Dijon* case, the ECJ has acknowledged the status of environmental protection as a 'legitimate objective of general interest', which could form the basis for a possible barrier to trade.

In reviewing the validity of national measures akin to technical restrictions, the ECJ has so far paid scant heed to the issue of environmental justice.[21] Its considerations have then generally focused on the extent to which the national measures are proportionate in meeting the critera for trade restrictions allowed by the EC Treaty or as interpreted by the ECJ in the *Cassis de Dijon* case. However, environmental considerations involve deeper environmental justice aspects only in a few ECJ cases, relating to the rights of local communities affected by pollution arising.

The judgment of the ECJ in the *Wallonia Waste* case provides a fine example of integration of local environmental considerations in the field of trade law. The case arose from a challenge by the European Commission to the Walloon ban on waste import. This ban was justified by Belgium on the ground that huge quantities of foreign wastes were imported illegally into Wallonia. As a result, several communities living close to contaminated landfills were likely to be affected by leaks of hazardous wastes dumped illegally. The ECJ took the view that 'waste is matter of special kind. Accumulation of waste, even before it becomes a health hazard, constitutes a danger to the environment, regard being paid in particular to the limited capacity for each region or locality for waste reception.' In addition, the ECJ stressed 'the real danger to the environment having regard to *the limited capacity of that region*'.[22] As a result, the ECJ reached the conclusion that the ban on import of foreign wastes was justified by imperative requirements of environmental protection.[23] It is worth noting that the Court was aware that Belgium was subject to an 'abnormal large scale inflow of waste

---

[20] Case 120/78, *Rewe-Zentral AG* v. *Bundesmonopolverwaltung für Branntwein* [1979] ECR 649.
[21] French 2000 at 21–2; Temmink 2000 at 291.
[22] Case C-2/90, *Commission* v. *Belgium* [1992] ECR I-4431, para. 30.   [23] *Ibid.*, para. 32.

from other regions', that 'there was a real danger to the environment',[24] and that several landfills were severely polluted because foreign hazardous industrial waste had been dumped illegally at the time when the case was being adjudicated. As a result, local NGOs ignited at that time a heated political debate on waste management practices in Wallonia.

Another issue with some bearing on environmental justice is aircraft-related noise and its impact on neighbouring populations. With a view to protecting the health of these populations, several member states have enacted acoustic thresholds. In so doing, national authorities can jeopardise the free movement of aircraft. In the *Aher-Waggon* case, the ECJ took the view that German legislation, which laid down acoustical technical standards for certain aircraft, was proportional to the environmental objective sought, for the measures adopted were necessary in order to reduce nuisance caused by noise. In particular, the ECJ stressed that 'such a barrier may ... be justified by considerations of public health and environmental protection'. In that respect, the Court highlighted that the German authorities 'attached special importance to ensuring that *its population is protected from excessive noise emissions*'.[25]

Greater use of public infrastructures by freight carriers can also hinder the quality of life of communities living near to motorways. In this respect, the Brenner motorway, linking Innsbruck in Austria to Verona in Italy, has been at the centre of a spate of lawsuits, some of which have been adjudicated by the ECJ in light of the principle of free movement of goods. The Brenner motorway is one of the very few which cross the Alps, and it is predominantly used by lorries over 12 tonnes. As Switzerland had for decades contemplated a policy restricting road traffic in favour of rail traffic, the traffic along the Brenner motorway has increased significantly. Given the residents' complaints about the pollution stemming from the increase of traffic, the Austrian authorities adopted different measures with a view to affording better protection to the local communities living along the motorway.[26]

In particular, Austria increased the tolls paid by the users of the motorway. Whereas the tolls for full journeys were considerably increased, the tolls for short journeys were hardly increased. In so doing, Austria was confronted with the provisions of a European directive on the application of taxes on certain vehicles used for the carriage of goods by road as well as of tolls and charges for the use of certain infrastructures.[27] This directive acknowledges the right to maintain or introduce tolls, provided that they do not discriminate between hauliers, but the European Commission was of the opinion that the Austrian tolls were discriminating against goods vehicles over 12 tonnes from other member states. The ECJ accepted this argument and held against

---

[24] *Ibid.*, para. 31.
[25] Case C-389/96, *Aher-Waggon* [1988] ECR I-4473, para. 19 (emphasis added).
[26] Krämer 2002 at 100.
[27] Directive 93/89/EEC on the Application by Member States of Taxes on Certain Vehicles Used for the Carriage of Goods by Road and Tolls and User Charges for the Use of Certain Infrastructures, [1993] OJ L279/32.

Austria for treating non-Austrian hauliers less favourably.[28] It held that the tariff differences cannot be justified on grounds relating to environmental protection or by considerations based on national transport policy.[29] The Austrian government argued that the environmental problems did not stem from Austrian vehicles which partially used the motorway, but from the influx of foreign hauliers. However, the Court rejected that argument, and stressed that the directive at issue did not provide for invoking environmental considerations in order to justify tariff arrangements, which give rise to indirect discrimination.[30] Austria could have avoided these adverse findings by applying similar fees for both short and full journeys, but that was impossible at the time for local economic reasons.

Likewise, the freedom of expression, in the form of a right to protest, is also relevant from an environmental justice point of view, as it may jeopardise free trade of goods. In this respect, *Schmidberger* is a good case in point.[31] The case arose out of a challenge to a permission implicitly granted by the Austrian authorities to an environmental group to organise a demonstration on the Brenner motorway, the effect of which was to completely close that motorway to traffic for almost 30 hours without interruption. As a result, heavy goods vehicles that should have used the Brenner motorway were immobilised. The demonstrators were intent upon persuading the competent authorities to reinforce measures to reduce that traffic and the pollution resulting therefrom, in the highly sensitive region of the Alps. Given that the motorway was the sole transit route for vehicles between Germany and Italy, the operator of several vehicles brought a claim for damages for the alleged breach of Community law, on the grounds that the Austrian authorities should have banned the demonstration. In particular, the claimant argued that the failure on the part of the Austrian authorities to ban the demonstration and to intervene to prevent that trunk route from being closed amounted to a restriction of the free movement of goods.

Relying on provisions in the EC Treaty which allow national courts to seek a preliminary ruling from the ECJ (Article 234 EC), the Austrian court (Oberlandsgericht Inssbruck) adjudicating claims filed by an economic operator whose lorries were blocked, asked for clarification, whether, and if so to what extent, there was a breach of Community law giving rise to liability on the part of Austria. Since the Austrian authorities did not ban the demonstration, which resulted in the complete closure of a major transit route such as the Brenner motorway for almost 30 hours, the ECJ held that the omission to ban the demonstration 'must be regarded as constituting a measure of equivalent effect to a quantitative restriction which is, in principle, incompatible with the Community law'.[32] According to the ECJ, the protection of the environment and public health, especially in that region, may, under certain conditions, constitute a legitimate objective in the public interest capable of justifying a restriction of the fundamental freedoms guaranteed by the EC Treaty, including the

---

[28] Case C-205/98, *Commission v. Austria* [2000] ECR I-7367, para. 79.   [29] *Ibid.*, para. 90.
[30] *Ibid.*, para. 95.   [31] Case C-112/02, *Schmidberger* [2003] ECR I-5659.   [32] *Ibid.*, para. 64.

free movement of goods. However, the liability was to be inferred from the fact that the national authorities did not prevent an obstacle to traffic from being placed on the Brenner motorway.

In this respect, the Austrian authorities were inspired by considerations linked to respect of the fundamental rights of the demonstrators to freedom of expression and freedom of assembly, which are enshrined in and guaranteed by the European Convention on Human Rights (ECHR) and the Austrian Constitution.[33] As a result, the ECJ took the view that 'since both the Community and its Member States are required to respect fundamental rights, the protection of those rights is a legitimate interest which, in principle, justifies a restriction of the obligations imposed by Community law, even under a fundamental freedom guaranteed by the Treaty such as the free movement of goods'.[34] Nonetheless, the ECJ did not take the view that a fundamental right should prevail over free trade. On the Contrary, the court was adamant to reconcile the freedom of expression and freedom of assembly, guaranteed by Articles 10 and 11 of the ECHR, and the free movement of goods, and this for two reasons.

First, whilst the free movement of goods constitutes one of the fundamental principles in the scheme of the Treaty, it may, in certain circumstances, be subject to restrictions for the reasons laid down in Article 30 of the EC Treaty or for overriding requirements relating to the public interest, in accordance with the *Cassis de Dijon* case law. Secondly, 'whilst the fundamental rights at issue in the main proceedings are expressly recognised by the ECHR and constitute the fundamental pillars of a democratic society, it nevertheless follows . . . that freedom of expression and freedom of assembly are also subject to certain limitations justified by objectives in the public interest, in so far as those derogations are in accordance with the law'.[35]

Unlike other fundamental rights enshrined in the ECHR, such as the right to life or the prohibition of torture and inhuman or degrading treatment or punishment, which admits of no restriction, neither the freedom of expression nor the freedom of assembly guaranteed by the ECHR appears to be absolute, but must be viewed in relation to its social purpose.[36] As a result, the ECJ concluded that 'the exercise of those rights may be restricted, provided that the restrictions in fact correspond to objectives of general interest and do not, taking account of the aim of the restrictions, constitute disproportionate and unacceptable interference, impairing the very substance of the rights guaranteed'.[37]

As regards the proportionality of the measure, the ECJ took into account that the decision not to ban the demonstration was taken following a detailed examination of the facts, that information as to the date of the closure of the Brenner motorway had been announced in advance in Austria, Germany and Italy, and that the demonstration did not result in substantial traffic jams or other incidents. Given the wide discretion which must be accorded to the national authorities in striking a balance between the opposing freedoms, they 'were reasonably entitled to consider that the legitimate aim

[33] *Ibid.*, para. 69.   [34] *Ibid.*, para. 74.   [35] *Ibid.*, para. 79.   [36] *Ibid.*, para. 80.   [37] *Ibid.*

of that demonstration could not be achieved . . . by measures less restrictive of intra-Community trade'.[38] As a consequence, the protesters' right to freedom of expression and freedom of assembly, the restriction was not in breach of Community law.

Needless to say, the cases commented in this section mirror justice considerations rather imperfectly. The ECJ would probably have reached the same conclusion if the national restrictions were justified by air or water protection considerations, irrespective of the potential impacts on the neighbourhood. Furthermore, one should point out that nothing is said in these judgments as to the vulnerability of the populations likely to be disturbed by the noise of aircraft or traffic.

3.2 EU internal market: positive harmonisation

Most European product standards set at national level are derived from EU law. The general objective behind these standards has been to create a common market through harmonised technical norms. On occasion, the content of these standards also stems from international environmental obligations. The advantage of such a harmonisation at the European or, more rarely, at international level, is undeniable for producers and distributors since it allows the setting, on the scale of a large territory, of environmental standards which then govern the marketing of products and their free circulation within that area. Purely national norms by the member states, on the other hand, may require that the product be conceived or adapted specifically in order to gain access to a particular national market. These measures are likely to restrict intra-Community trade, directly or indirectly, actually or potentially.

Article 95 of the EC Treaty provides the basis for hundreds of directives laying down health, consumer or worker safety and even environmental standards. In order not to favour trade to the detriment of other values recognised by the EC Treaty, Article 95, dealing with the proper functioning of the internal market, provides certain guarantees. It states that measures proposed at the European level concerning health, safety, environment and consumer protection are to take as a base a high level of protection, taking account in particular of any new development based on scientific facts. However, there is no mention that greater protection should be given to groups at risk in light of environmental justice commitments.[39]

The question, therefore, is whether there is a space left in the EU internal market for *national* measures driven by environmental justice considerations. We shall explore the means by which environmental justice considerations could come to the forefront in this debate.

Article 95 of the EC Treaty includes two derogation mechanisms allowing member states to attain a higher level of protection than the one achieved at EU level. The requirements laid down by Article 95 vary depending on whether the intention is to introduce new national provisions,[40] or to maintain provisions existing prior to the

---

[38] *Ibid.*, para. 93.   [39] De Sadeleer 2003 at 889–915.   [40] EC Treaty, Art. 95(5).

instrument of Community law.[41] In both cases, those requirements must be strictly construed, given that they lead to a level of protection which the EC directive or regulation does not in principle authorise.

A new measure must satisfy several conditions, among which is the requirement that the measure is necessary to deal with a problem specific to the member state in question. Indeed, the intention of the framers of the EC Treaty was clearly to avoid the enactment of measures of general character. In other words, the member state seeking the exemption from the European Commission has to demonstrate that the existence and the extent of the risk justifies the enactment of a national measure more stringent than the one laid down at the EC level. In so doing, the member state could give emphasis to specific demographic, geographic or epidemiological circumstances should render the problem particular. In this respect, issues of environmental justice could arise. Indeed, the population density, the degree of industrialisation, the vulnerability of some social categories could exacerbate the impacts of specific risks. By way of illustration, in the case concerning the Danish ban on pentachlorophenol, the European Commission held that it was demonstrated that the Danish population ran a *higher allergy risk* than other populations as the result of genetic predisposition, eating habits and natural environment.[42]

On the other hand, if the measure is already in existence in national law, the requirements for its maintenance are less strict. The state must then notify the Commission about the reasons for the maintenance of the national measures on grounds of major needs referred to in Article 30 of the EC Treaty (which include protection of health and public security) or relating to the protection of the environment or the working environment. However, in contrast to the preceding case, the risk must not be specific to the member state. Accordingly, whenever the European Commission has been adjudicating the member states' requests to maintain higher protection standards, it did not take into account the vulnerability of local populations.

3.3 Health regulation

As regards the protection of health and trade-restrictive measures, the European judiciary – i.e. the Court of Justice and the Court of First Instance – has stressed that the probability of the occurrence of the harm must be determined through a risk assessment procedure, in which experts examine both hazard and exposure – generally by mathematical modelling – in order to calculate an acceptable or tolerable level of contamination or exposure.[43] Once the risk assessment procedure has been completed, a *risk management* decision must be made by politicians, taking into account both legislative requirements and the economic, political and normative dimensions of

---

[41] *Ibid.*, Art. 95(4).
[42] European Commission Decision 97/783/EC on the prohibition of pentachlorophenol; [1996] OJ L68/32.
[43] De Sadeleer 2007.

the problem. Risk management, in contrast to risk assessment, is the public policy process of deciding how safe is safe enough. In this respect, environmental justice considerations could be taken into account. At least, nothing prevents the national legislator from placing greater emphasis upon the social groups at risk (elderly people, babies).

Indeed, it is settled case law that it is for the institution concerned to determine the level of protection, which it considers appropriate for society, depending upon the circumstances of the particular case.[44] Moreover, in the absence of harmonisation and insofar as uncertainties continue to exist in the current state of scientific research, it is for the member states to decide on the desirable level of protection of human health and life.[45] This means that the risk management decision rests with each member state, which has discretion in determining the level of risk it considers appropriate. Accordingly, the member state may invoke the precautionary principle with the objective of thwarting the occurrence of uncertain risks.[46] However, the precautionary measure must be based upon a scientific approach, although national experts are not required to prove extensively the existence or the extent of the risk. So far, the use of precautionary measures in EC food law has been embedded within a scientific context paying little heed to sociological issues that could encompass environmental justice considerations.

That said, the margin of appreciation reserved to the member states specifically allows them to set a very high level of protection where there is scientific (including technical) uncertainty. This approach is encapsulated in the *Melkunie* case, where the ECJ found that zero tolerance towards the admissibility of pathogenic microorganisms in food waste was admissible, falling under the protection of human health under Article 30 of the EC Treaty.[47] More recently, in the *Walter Hahn* case, the ECJ accepted that a member state could opt for a tolerance level equivalent to zero regarding the presence of listeriosis in fish, finding that, 'as long as the provisional results of those scientific discussions have not been translated into Community law, Member States have the right, by way of precaution, to set more stringent microbiological standards in order to protect human health and *in particular the health of susceptible groups*'.[48]

With respect to genetically modified organisms (GMOs), the EU legislator has given greater emphasis to societal factors in regulating the risks stemming from this technology. Indeed, 'societal, economic, traditional, ethical and environmental factors as well as the feasibility of controls' might appear as factors legitimising the regulation

[44] Case T-13/99, *Pfizer Animal Health SA* v. *Council* [2002] ECR II-3305, paras. 151 and 153.
[45] Case C-174/82, *Sandoz* [1983] ECR 2445, para. 16; Case C-42/90, *Bellon* [1990] ECRI-4863, para. 11; Case C-400/96, *Harpegnies* [1998] ECR I-5121, para. 33; and Case C-192/01, *Commission* v. *Denmark* [2003] ECR I-9693, para. 42. See also Case E-4/4, *Pedicel*, EFTA Court, judgment of 25 January 2005.
[46] Case C-286/02, *Bellio F.lli Srl* v. *Prefetura di Treviso* [2004] ECR I-3465, para. 58.
[47] Case 97/83, *Melkunie* [1984] ECR 2367, para. 15.
[48] Case C-121/00, *Walter Hahn* [2002] ECR I-9193, para. 31.

of a specific risk.[49] By the same token, the EC regulation on genetically modified food and feed provides that, as risk assessments cannot provide all the information on which a risk management decision should be based, 'other legitimate factors relevant to the matter under consideration' may be taken into account.[50] Nevertheless, the various regulatory measures enacted in the field of GMOs are based upon general health concerns and not justice considerations.

4 Conclusions

When considering the nature of trade-related environmental measures, one is drawn to the conclusion that so far broader health and environmental factors, rather than justice considerations as a discrete concept, have had a key role in shaping these instruments. That said, only a few international agreements, in particular in the field of waste shipments, came in direct response to a set of concerns about the impacts of dumping wastes on poor countries. By the same token, the growing awareness at the EU level of the need to offer better environmental protection has led the ECJ to pay attention in several cases to concerns of local communities. However, these cases are so far the exception rather than the rule. Therefore, the central finding of this chapter is that the concept of environmental justice does not occupy centre stage in discussions about trade and environment.[51]

Bibliography

Birnie, P., and Boyle, A., 2000. *International Law and the Environment*. 2nd edn, Oxford: Oxford University Press.

Calster, G. V., 2000. *International and EU Trade: The Environmental Challenge*. London: Cameron & May.

Castri, F., 1996. The Interactive Chain of Globalizations: From the Economic to the Ecologic One', in J. Theys (ed.), *L'Environnement au XXIe Siècle*. Paris: Germes.

De Sadeleer, N., 2003. 'Safeguard Clauses under Article 95 of the EC Treaty'. 40 *Common Market Law Review* 889.

 2007. 'The Precautionary Principle in EC Health and Environmental Law: Sword or Shield for the Nordic Countries?', in N. de Sadeleer (ed.), *Implementing Precaution. Approaches from Nordic Countries, the EU and the USA*. London: Earthscan.

French, D., 2000. 'The Changing Nature of Environmental Protection: Recent Developments Regarding Trade and the Environment in the EU and the WTO'. 47 *Netherlands International Law Review* 1.

Krämer, L., 2002. *EU Casebook on Environmental Law*. Oxford: Hart.

---

[49] Regulation EC (No.) 178/2002 Laying Down the General Principles and Requirements of Food Law, Establishing the European Food Safety Authority and Laying Down Procedures in Matters of Food Safety, [2002] OJ L31/1, recital 19, and Art. 3(12).

[50] Regulation EC (No.) 1829/2003 on Genetically Modified Food and Feed, [2003] OJ L268/1, Art. 6(6).

[51] See also Krämer in Chapter 10 of this volume.

Krueger, J., 1999. *International Trade and the Basel Convention*. London: Earthscan.

Kummer, K., 1995. *International Management of Hazardous Wastes*. Oxford: Oxford University Press.

   1999. *International Management of Hazardous Wastes: The Basel Convention and Related Legal Rules*. Oxford: Oxford University Press.

O'Neill, K., 2000. *Waste Trading Among Rich Nations*. Cambridge, MA: MIT Press.

Shrader-Frechette, K., 2002. *Environmental Justice*. Oxford: Oxford University Press.

Temmink, H., 2000. 'From Danish Bottles to Danish Bees: The Dynamics of Free Movement of Goods and Environmental Protection – A Case Law Analysis'. 1 *Yearbook of European Environmental Law* 291.

INDEX